The Years of O'Casey, 1921–1926

The Years of O'Casey, 1921–1926

A Documentary History

Robert Hogan and Richard Burnham

Newark: University of Delaware Press

•

COLIN SMYTHE
Gerrards Cross, Buckinghamshire

1992

Associated University Presses
440 Forsgate Drive
Cranbury, NJ 08512

Associated University Presses
P.O. Box 39, Clarkson Pstl. Stn.
Mississauga, Ontario,
L5J 3X9 Canada

The paper used in this publication meets the requirements of the American National Standard for Permanence of Paper for Printed Library Materials Z39.48-1984.

Library of Congress Cataloging-in-Publication Data

Hogan, Robert Goode, 1930–
The years of O'Casey, 1921–1926: a documentary history/Robert Hogan, Richard Burnham.
p. cm.
Includes bibliographical references and index.
ISBN 0-87413-421-8 (alk. paper)
1. English drama—Irish authors—History and criticism. 2. English drama—20th century—History and criticism. 3. Theater—Ireland—History—20th century. 4. O'Casey, Sean, 1880–1964. 5. Ireland in literature. I. Burnham, Richard. II. Title.
PR8789.H66 1992
792'.0415'09042—dc20 90-50841
CIP

First published in Great Britain in 1992 by Colin Smythe Limited, Gerrards Cross, Buckinghamshire, as the sixth volume of The Modern Irish Drama Series.

A catalogue record for this book may be obtained from the British Library.

ISBN 0-85105-428-5

PRINTED IN THE UNITED STATES OF AMERICA

To the Memory of Liam Miller
and the Dolmen Press

I wonder what will happen to this country. The genius for pulling down is at work as he always is when we look like getting something done. I think we have among us some of the most mischievous and perverse people under the sun.

—Frank J. Fay, 17 March 1922

Is there anybody goin', Mrs. Clitheroe, with a titther o' sense?

—Mollser in *The Plough and the Stars*

Contents

Acknowledgments

The *Irish Independent* for quotations from the *Freeman's Journal*, the *Irish Daily Independent*, the *Weekly Freeman's Journal*, the *Evening Herald*.

The *Irish Times* for quotations from the *Dublin Evening Mail* and the *Irish Times*.

Michael and Jennifer Johnston for quotations from the unpublished autobiography of Shelah Richards.

Gerald MacDermott for quotations from Joseph Holloway.

Michael Yeats for quotations from published and unpublished work by W. B. Yeats.

Colin Smythe, Limited, for quotations from Lady Gregory.

The Macmillan Company of New York for three letters of Sean O'Casey printed in vol. 1 of David Krause's edition of O'Casey's *Letters*.

Proscenium Press for quotations from *What Is the Stars*? by Robert James, and for quotations from *Players and the Painted Stage*, the autobiography of Ria Mooney, edited by Val Mulkerns.

The National Library of Ireland for quotations from manuscript collections.

The Berg Collection, the New York Public Library.

Introduction

Salve

This volume is something of a sequel to, or perhaps climax of, five other documentary histories that were published from 1975 to 1984 by Dublin's Dolmen Press under the general title of *The Modern Irish Drama*. Whatever the merit of the present volume, "climax of" may be the more appropriate term, for the dramatic years of 1921 to early 1926 are ones of climactic interest and of more than simply Irish importance.

They are of climactic interest because both the country and the country's major theater attained a position, however uneasy and precarious, of stability. De Valera and the Republicans came into the Dail; by a state subsidy, the Abbey was formally recognised as the Irish National Theatre.

They are of more than simply Irish importance because the very Irish masterpieces of Sean O'Casey made an impact upon world drama nearly as profound as that of Luigi Pirandello or of Eugene O'Neill.

As this is a documentary history, we have told the story primarily through the words of the writers, actors, producers, critics, and members of the audience who themselves lived and created the story. We have done this because a historian sixty years after the events can only through a literary *tour de force* catch the reality and the excitement that he himself has not experienced at first hand.

In the first three volumes of *The Modern Irish Drama*, James Kilroy and Robert Hogan kept more to a presentation than an assessment of facts. However, a number of readers and reviewers expressed a desire for more authorial judgment and critical guidance; and on reflection it appeared that their point had considerable justice. To the intelligent common reader, 2,500 pages of facts about often unfamiliar or unknown plays and productions must have seemed daunting indeed. Therefore, in the last two volumes of *The Modern Irish Drama* and in this present volume, we have occasionally merged the voice of the critic with that of the historian. We have especially allowed ourselves critical summations at crucial moments, such as a major production, a final production, or a death. We have particularly done so about writers of some importance, such as Edward Martyn, William Boyle, or T. C. Murray; and we hope that such occasional signposts will help and inform the reader's journey. On the other hand, we have refrained from adding to the considerable critical commentary on such a well-known play as *The Plough and the*

Stars. Whatever value such a work as this may have, it would seem more valuably to lie in accreting a mountain of facts than in contributing to the more copious cairns of criticism. Which is not to say we do not hope our mountain may move minds.

The theater of these years was more than usually influenced by the state of the country. We have, then, rather more than has been our custom, given space to the disruptive political events of the times. However, we have done so from the particular vantage point of the theater and its workers. It is to us a source of some surprise and of much admiration that the theater so vigorously reacted to and so quickly assimilated the political events of the day.

These 1,800 days really break down into two periods. The first comprises the violence of the Tan War, the exhaustion that led to the Anglo-Irish Treaty, and the bitterness occasioned by the treaty that led to the culminating ferocity of the Civil War. The second is politically and theatrically a time of consolidation and assimilation. The two early plays of O'Casey, *The Shadow of a Gunman* and *Juno and the Paycock*, might well be seen as symptoms of this process of healing. Indeed, not only as symptoms, but even as aids to the healing.

However, the wound in the body politic was deep and not to be so quickly or so easily healed. From our vantage point as theatrical historians, such matters as *The Plough* row and O'Casey's departure from Ireland inevitably seem symptoms also—later, more lasting symptoms of divisions that still fester in the state today.

Robert Hogan
Richard Burnham

Vale

The publication of this volume marks the completed execution of an idea conceived in 1967. The idea was to document as fully as possible the rise and development of the drama in Ireland in what are generally thought to be its greatest years, from the inception of the Irish Literary Theatre in 1899 to the departure of O'Casey in 1926. When the project was conceived by Liam Miller, James Kilroy, and myself, a few figures such as Synge, Yeats, and O'Casey had received much critical attention, and so also had one theater, the Abbey. It was our feeling that these few much-discussed topics were but the tip of the iceberg, and that there were other significant writers, other significant companies, and other significant incidents than the *Playboy* and *Plough* riots. And also that there were great players whose artistry had never received proper due.

Whatever the success or failure of this endeavour, I think that initial notion, that there was more to talk about, has been borne out. And I also ruefully note that talking about the Irish theater in some semblance of its totality has taken almost as much time as the actual living and writing and playing originally took the participants.

A second matter for ruefulness is some feeling of failure in scanting certain topics—among them, the professional fit-up companies that toured the provincial towns, and the growth of amateur drama throughout the country. Yet to have treated such matters in detail would have vastly extended our labors and prohibitively extended our already excessive number of pages.

In any event, I hope that the principal features of the whole landscape have been charted more fully and in juster proportion than they had been. Or, to change the metaphor, I hope that my colleagues and I have recorded the major matters about the difficult infancy, the troubled adolescence, and the turbulent coming-of-age of the modern Irish drama.

It would be highly tempting to extend these investigations into the young manhood and the coming of middle-age—the period of, say, from 1926 to about 1960, when Beckett, Behan, the new Abbey, Leonard, and Keane, and Friel brought about a change in the theater that could be seen to parallel a similar deep change in Ireland itself. But even these middle years, still so uninvestigated and undervalued, are ones of much interest and great merit. They saw the development of one major playwright, Denis Johnston, and of one major company, the Gate Theatre of Edwards and Mac Liammóir, which opened the theatrical window on the world that Edward Martyn had so persistently tried to unlatch. They saw two superb plays by Paul Vincent Carroll, the artistic maturation of George Shiels, and the emerging talents of Teresa Deevy, Louis D'Alton, and, perhaps most importantly, M. J. Molloy. And they saw a new generation of players that included such talents as Shelah Richards, Cyril Cusack, Walter Macken, and Siobhan McKenna. But the overwhelming attraction to the historian is that many of the participants of these years are yet alive, and that their memories and impressions might be gleaned at first hand.

At this point, though, the temptation of those years is one to be firmly and perhaps finally rejected. The sword, as Byron said, outwears its sheath; the sword, I know, becomes battered; and the sword, I suspect, becomes dull.

There only remains to record—to my collaborators, our publishers, and the innumerable people who have helped in innumerable ways—my deeply felt if quite inexpressible thanks.

Robert Hogan
Summer, 1983

• • •

Postscript, 1989—This volume was announced for publication several years ago, but was delayed for several reasons, particularly the ill health of the publisher. Then when the publisher, Liam Miller, died, his firm, the Dolmen Press, died with him; and for some years the text of this book was lost.

This explanation is really meant as a prelude to the following remarks.

In modern Ireland, there have been three preeminent literary presses—the Cuala Press of Miss Yeats, the Maunsel and Company of George Roberts, and the Dolmen Press of Liam Miller. If the collapse of the Dolmen left something of a bitter taste, that fact of its excellence might well be borne in mind. Also, if few publishers have ever given their writers such moments of frustration as did Liam Miller, few publishers have ever given their writers such opportunities. Also, the impetus that the Dolmen gave to Irish writing, particularly to poetry, is incalculable; and the standards that the Dolmen set for fine printing are a lasting conscience; and several fine, flourishing young Irish presses of today owe much to the Dolmen's quarter century of activity. It was a marvellous press.

The Years of O'Casey, 1921–1926

1
1921

On 1 January 1921, these were the headlines of the notable news stories on one page of the *Irish Times*:

> Man Shot Dead in Co. Tipperary
> Man Found Shot Near Athlone
> Man Shot Dead in County Limerick
> The Shooting on Aran Island
> Two Attacks on Police[1]

On 2 January, Lady Gregory described the Irish situation to her friend John Quinn in New York:

> . . . fiercer methods of the last war are accountable for the Black and Tans, whose methods are beyond anything I can put on paper. In the Aran Islands the police had been taken away to other places because the people were and remained so quiet. The late expedition there has been described to me by an *English* friend who has business connections there, and has had letters, as simply "an expedition for plunder." The people were terrorized by indiscriminate firing, one wounded to death and left in agony; the invaders got drunk and stole everything they could get their hands on, even the wedding rings of the women. Another Englishman, who joined the R.I.C. says, "he don't go to took for revolvers or criminals but for loot. They ought not to be allowed out without a keeper." Yes, I will put on paper what I was told by our own doctor. He came to beg me to get people over from England to investigate and find what was going on. He said a man (gave me his name) had come to him the day before and said he and his son had been held by those brutes against a wall, while in his presence others of them attempted to violate (and the doctor is certain they succeeded) his daughters. . . . I wrote to Bernard Shaw begging him to come over, but he did not think it advisable. Yeats is too settled in England.[2]

On 21 February, Maud Gonne also wrote to John Quinn about events in Ireland during the early weeks of 1921:

> Dublin is a terrible place just now. Hardly a night passes that one is not woke up to the sound of firing. Often there are people killed, but often it is only the crown forces firing to keep up their courage. One night last week there was such a terrible fusilade just outside our house, that we all got up thinking something terrible was happening. That morning, when curfew regulations permitted us to go out, we only found the bodies of a cat and dog riddled with bullets.[3]

There were, however, individuals like St. John Ervine who believed that both the British and the Irish were at fault and that each side was responsible for innumerable atrocities:

> I am very unhappy about Ireland these days. The crimes committed by both sides are horrible and it is difficult to retain one's hold on sanity when one observes how easily men destroy life in the name of decent ideals. I seem to be at one moment execrated by Sinn Feiners and praised by Orangemen because I condemn murder by the former, and at the next execrated by the Orangemen and praised by Sinn Feiners because I condemn murder by Black-and-Tans. I believe intensely in Irishmen and long deeply to see Ireland a united nation, but I disbelieve with equal intensity in Sinn Feiners and Orangemen, and I loathe the smugness and self-satisfaction of both of them. I can see no good coming to Ireland out of this horrible hate.[4]

To take but two more dates at random, we find on 1 April these headlines on but one page of the *Irish Times*:

Fierce Attack on Barrack
A Running Fight
Ambush in Dublin
The Amiens Street Bombing
Murder Near Bandon
Murder in Leitrim
Seizures in Dublin
Express Train Under Fire
Woman Murdered in Dublin
Mail Car Robbed
Civilians Arrested in Dublin
The Shooting at Ballybaunes
Foulkes Mills Barracks Attacked
Attacks on the Police, etc.
Blood-Stained Motor Cars
The Ballybay Shooting
Lawlessness in Co. Cork
Alleged Raid for Arms, etc.[5]

And on 11 June:

Ambushes in Dublin
Murder in Belfast
Police Lorries Bombed
Bombs in Mount and Dorset Streets
A Blackrock Outrage
Forty-Two Arrests in Dublin
Cork Man Shot Dead
Several Ambushes
Monaghan "Round Up"
West Donegal Isolated
Court House Burned[6]

Nevertheless, hope for peace was in the air, and on 8 July Lady Gregory wrote to John Quinn:

> Oh John, this very day on which I am writing is the day of the second meeting of the Sinn Feiners and Southern Unionists in Dublin! I stop to say a little prayer now and again. Did you see that there were crowds outside the Mansion House saying the Rosary at the first meeting? Just a few hours of this day may make the difference between peace, a lasting peace, reconciliation, responsibility on our own shoulders, construction work for all, the opportunity of using every faculty to the utmost—and on the other hand a continuance of battle, murder, and sudden death, murder of both sides—ill will, bitterness, unrest—I have been so hopeful all through, even last month when things looked very black. . . . Now, when there is justification for hope, I am terrified, shaking, I feel just now that if a telegram should come saying it was to be war, it would kill me like a bullet![7]

On 11 July, however, a truce came into effect, but that truce brought little lessening of tension. There were weeks of negotiation in London; and, when news of a peace treaty reached Lady Gregory in December, she wrote to John Quinn:

> These last weeks have been terribly anxious, one knew so little of what was going on, and then there was always the damper of the truce being broken . . . . So when yesterday, Tuesday, I had a wire from Dublin saying "Agreement reached in London," and when today's paper told what a good one it seems, all anxiety was turned to joy; it seems a new world to live in.[8]

That new world was still to be a world of tensions and terrors, of bullets and bombs; and it was in such a milieu that the business of the stage attempted, as best it could, to carry on.

• • •

In 1920 a curfew had been imposed upon Dublin, and no one other than a member of the Crown forces was allowed to be on the streets between midnight and 5:00 a.m. By early 1921, the curfew had been moved up to 10:00 p.m.; and the *Evening Telegraph* wrote, "the effect of the present curfew hour on the theatres and cinema houses is practically to cut out one performance in most cases, and that at the period when, under the former regulations, most of the patrons attended." The Gaiety now opened its doors at 6:30 and ended its performance by 9:00. The Empire and the Queens raised their curtains at 7:00 and also ended at 9:00, which meant only one house per evening. The Theatre Royal still ran two houses nightly, but advanced the curtain times to 5:30 and 7:20.

The times were really too troubled and the streets too dangerous for theaters to prosper. Indeed, it was sometimes even dangerous to be off the streets and inside a theater. For instance, on the evening of 12 January, there was an attempted assasination at the Empire. As the *Evening Telegraph* reported the next day:

> On inquiry at Mercers Hospital this morning it was learned that Mr. Wm. P. Kennedy (38), 129 Island Bridge, Dublin, who was shot in the Empire Theatre last night, was progressing favourably. His condition is stated to be not serious. The injured man, who is said to be an ex-serviceman employed as a clerk by Island Bridge Barracks, was accompanied by his wife at the time. Conflicting accounts were present last night, but it is known he was fired at in the theatre by several men and wounded in the chest. The bullet glanced off his ribs, but not inflicting a fatal injury. According to one account, Kennedy left his wife behind him and went into the bar during the intermission. On his return he remained in the passage beside the stalls watching the performance. A man approached him, followed by two others, who asked him to accompany them outside. One assailant drew a revolver and fired. Kennedy rushed into the booking office, and kept the door closed with his foot, loudly shouting for help. One of the bystanders heard him cry, "They want to assassinate me!" . . . The occurrence created a panic in the building, and many sensation stories were afterwards afloat in the city.[9]

From the first week in February, a warning was issued by Major General Boyd, who was commanding the Dublin district, that more stringent curfew restrictions would have to be imposed on the city if attacks on the military and police in Dublin did not cease. The *Evening Telegraph* mentioned numerous hardships that would result from an earlier curfew:

> On Saturday night motor lorries containing crown forces are reported to have been attacked in several parts of Dublin, and this has caused considerable speculation as to what action, if any, the authorities may take. *The Evening Telegraph* understands that the military authorities are considering the question of making curfew an hour earlier—nine o'clock instead of ten. So far, however, nothing definite has been decided. It is scarcely necessary to point out the serious injury that will be caused to the Irish capital should such an extension of the curfew hours take place. Theatre and other places of amusement will be faced with the prospect of closing down or continuing under ruinous conditions, and railway and other services also will be seriously interfered with. The interference with the social life of the city will be very grave. Thousands of Dublin workers will have only three hours liberty between the cessation of work and the coming of curfew.[10]

The hysteria of the times may be also indicated by the following news story, "Invasion of the Abbey," which appeared in the *Irish Independent* of 23 February:

> A party of armed men raided the Abbey Theatre, Dublin, on Monday night in search of a photographer alleged to be attached to the staff of the *Daily Sketch*, who was questioned regarding pictures which had appeared in that paper, and whose camera was removed. The incident occurred during a rehearsal of the late Terence J. MacSwiney's play, *The Revolutionist*, which commenced at about 6 o'clock.
>
> Half an hour later the building was surrounded by men armed with revolvers. Some entered the stalls, where a number of people were witnessing the perform-

ance, and crossed to where a group of Press photographers were waiting to take a flashlight picture.

Inquiries were made for the *Daily Sketch* representative, and raiders were informed that he was at the back of the stage. The men then took up positions about the theatre, and shortly after the photographer . . . was located and questioned.

He explained that he was not the *Daily Sketch* photographer, but was working for a number of papers, including American and Australian journals, and agencies all over the world. He was not molested in any way, and the raiders appeared to be satisfied with his answers, stating that they had nothing against him personally but against some faked photographs which they thought were his work.

They then took his camera, intimating that if his statements were found to be correct it would be returned to him. The party then withdrew, and the rehearsal was proceeded with.

Mr. Lennox Robinson, manager, seen by an *Irish Independent* representative yesterday, declined to say anything about the raid, beyond characterising it as a "ridiculous incident."[11]

The 10:00 p.m. curfew created difficulties, and the announcement on 4 March of its extension to 9:00 p.m. caused additional consternation in the theatrical world. As the *Freeman's Journal* said:

Since the inauguration on of the 10 o'clock curfew the theatres have been hard hit, and in some cases have been run at a loss, but hoping for an amelioration of conditions and out of consideration for the employes and directors they have kept business going. Yesterday's announcement proved a veritable thunderbolt, and it stated that nothing now remains for the different managements but to close down. In some cases this course has already been practically decided on, and the hardships that will ensue to the employes who are thrown out of employment cannot be underestimated. Mr. Charles Hyland, manager of the Gaiety Theatre, interviewed last night by our representative on the subject of new drastic restrictions, said the effect would be, in his opinion, simply disastrous. The existing curtailment even has considerably hampered the convenience to the public. This was especially so, of course, with reference to those who live in the suburbs or outlying districts. It involved an alteration in the hours of commencing performances, which was most unsuitable to the majority of the patrons of the Gaiety. For years the Gaiety did not start their performances until 8 o'clock p.m., and it was something in the nature of an unheard of demand to expect the public to come now to the theatre in time for representations commencing at such an early hour as 5.30, as must be the case so long as this order prevails. It would also mean, so far as matinees are concerned, that they would have to start a half-hour earlier.

Mr. Hamilton, of the Theatre Royal, stated that beyond the alteration of the hours of the show, which, after tonight, will be limited to one performance each evening, nothing definite has been decided on. In the course of an interview with our representative, Mr. C. Jones, the popular manager of the Tivoli, said that there was nothing for it but to close down. "Since the 10 o'clock curfew came into operation," he said, "we have been running the show at a dead loss; hardly drawing enough to pay the artists. As artists have already been engaged to appear next week we will carry on with one house each night, commencing at 6 o'clock. After that you can safely assume that the theatre will close down. Only a fortnight age I had a consultation with the principals of the theatre in London, and the advisability of closing down was considered."

On inquiry at the Empire Theatre it was learned that after Saturday night next the theatre would close down. All engagements for next week would, it was stated, be cancelled by wire, and the staff had already received notice. The manager of La Scala told our representative that he greatly feared they would have to close down. They have been losing heavily since the introduction of the 10 o'clock curfew.[12]

On 10, 11, and 12 March and also on 17, 18, and 19 March, the Abbey continued giving evening performances; but to comply with the nine o'clock curfew, the performances had to begin at 6:15. On 20 March, however, the curfew was moved forward to eight o'clock. This was too much, and Lady Gregory wrote:

A meeting with Robinson and Harris in the office and we decided we must close. Even at 9 o'c. curfew we can't carry on but at a big loss, and now from today it is to be at 8. Robinson will try to get the Players into a tour with *The Whiteheaded Boy*. Failing that I don't know what we can do for them. It will be very sad.[13]

The Empire had already closed on 7 March, and the Tivoli and the Queen's on 14 March. Now on 21 March, the Abbey and the Gaiety closed, and only the Royal remained open. For the week of 21 March, performances at the Royal commenced at 5:30, and for the week of 28 March performances were from three in the afternoon until seven in the early evening.

It should always be borne in mind that theater, even an art theater like the Abbey, is a business. Even when the Abbey managed to keep its doors open, playing under the curfew restrictions was just disastrous business. Except for a profitable two weeks of Terence MacSwiney's *The Revolutionist*, the Abbey houses in the first months of 1921 were very small; and even before the theater closed, its financial position was difficult.

However, schemes were afoot to retrieve the situation. Some of the notable Abbey alumni were playing in London in Robinson's successful *Whiteheaded Boy* at the Ambassadors' Theatre; and even before the Abbey closed, Sara Allgood began organizing a matinee benefit at the Ambassadors' for the Abbey. On 12 March, she wrote to Yeats:

Thanks so much for your letter. I called on G. B. Shaw yesterday and he promised to write a paragraph and send it to all the papers. The matinee has been postponed till April 6th which we all think is a better day than 23rd [March] (Spy Wednesday) and will give us more time to work up people. I think the whole object of the matinee is to keep the Abbey open. At present I believe the players are managing to exist on one third of their salary but it's the poor Abbey that can't pay other expenses and I imagine that when the players draw their one third there's hardly anything left to go on with. Captain Harwood has most generously given us the use of the theatre free. The orchestra has graciously promised to play for us and even the old stagedoor keeper offered me his 5/- (his pay for the afternoon). So if we manage to keep down expenses we ought to be able to give a fairly good sum to the Abbey. We think it would be rather a good thing to send a small circular out, which I enclose a rough draft of—and circularize all the Irish Clubs, etc. as well as our many personal friends. Thank you for your letter and if you can make any suggestions to help us, I'll be most grateful.[14]

Sara Allgood's proposed draft circular read as follows:

We old players of the Abbey Theatre are giving a matinee for its benefit in the Ambassadors' Theatre on April 6th and ask for your help. The Abbey Theatre, the oldest repertory theatre, has been in continued existence since its opening in 1904. During the war when we were unable to play outside Ireland we were able to play and pay our way, but the "curfew" regulations in Dublin of the last twelve months have been the cause of a loss of over 800 pounds—which must seriously hamper a theater with so small a capital. We therefore ask our friends to help us to make up at least a part of this loss.[15]

On 3 April, St. John Ervine in the *Observer* eloquently pleaded also for the survival of the theatre:

In the confusion of war and politics noble things are sooner disregarded than base things, and it may very well be that, without the support of valiant persons, noble things may perish. At all events, the noble things are slower to be received back to the regard of the multitude after times of trouble than are vulgar things. In happens that in the confusions of the Irish problem a fine and courageous enterprise is threatened with extinction. The Abbey Theatre in Dublin, the oldest and seemingly the most vital of the repertory theatres in these island, has been compelled through the curfew regulations to close its doors, and is thus prevented from earning its support. A theatre ceases to be an asset when its doors are shut, but it does not cease to be a liability. The directors of the Abbey, Lady Gregory and Mr. W. B. Yeats, though they can not receive one farthing through performances for the maintenance of the theatre, are, nevertheless, obliged to find money for the rent and upkeep of it. I appeal to those who read these columns—lovers of good drama and good acting—to come to the rescue of this gallant enterprise and save it from ruin.

The Abbey Theater, in face of many difficulties and grave discouragement, has done a notable work for drama. It provided a stage for a man of strange genius, John Millington Synge, and it gave many young dramatists an opportunity to test their skill in the most profitable fashion—through public performances of their works. There is little exaggeration in saying that if the Abbey Theatre had not existed Synge's plays would not have been written, or that if the Abbey is compelled to keep its doors permanently closed, or is obliged to suffer the fate of similar theatres in England and go over to the movies, another man of equal genius with Synge may be diverted from the theatre, not to his loss, indeed, since genius like youth will find a way, but to the grave disprofit of the theater. Not only did the Abbey bring Synge to the theater, and many other dramatists, of whom Mr. Lennox Robinson, the author of *The White-headed Boy*, is the most distinguished, but it also provided a training school for a very capable group of actors and actresses. No one who has seen the performance of Miss Sara Allgood, Miss Maire O'Neill, Mr. Arthur Sinclair, and Mr. Sydney Morgan in Mr. Robinson's play can fail to realise how immensely valuable to those gifted players was the training they received in the Abbey Theatre. Their teamwork alone caused students of acting to exclaim with astonishment. One of the most remarkable actors in America today, Mr. Dudley Digges, is an old Abbey actor. Both as a training house for dramatists and actors, therefore, the Abbey has done great service to the drama, and it would be a most lamentable thing if it were to die now, not because its functions are fulfilled, but because of political factors which are, please goodness, of a transient character. How little will it profit any of us if the political problem is solved and material advantage gained for all concerned in it, when, in the meantime, one of the sources of spiritual and mental growth in Ireland is destroyed?

Mr. H. M. Harwood and Mr. James Bernard Fagan have kindly lent the Ambassadors Theatre for a matinee performance on Wednesday, April 6, when three favourite plays from the Abbey repertory will be acted by former members of the Abbey Company, including those named above. The plays are *Cathleen ni Houlihan* by Mr. Yeats; *The Shadow of the Glen* by J. M. Synge; and *Spreading the News* by Lady Gregory.[16]

According to the *Evening Herald*, the benefit was a considerable artistic and financial success, and the *Evening Telegraph* added that at the close of the performance Robinson thanked everyone involved for their generosity, and said that the Abbey

was threatened with extinction, not from lack of players or theatre-goers, but owing to the conditions of life in Dublin. . . . £1000, which no London theatre manager would miss, would be sufficient to save the Abbey, and he had already received cheques from a number of friends in London.[17]

In Dublin, there was a relaxation of the curfew, and so the Abbey played for four weeks in April, commencing at 7:15. But the night of 30 April was announced as the last performance of the season.

Meanwhile, another scheme to pay off the Abbey's debt was a series of afternoon lectures in London. To announce the lectures, Robinson wrote a circular, "The Abbey Theatre Fund":

The Abbey Theatre is the fruit of seed sowed more than twenty years ago by Mr. W. B. Yeats and others when they founded in 1898 the Irish Literary Theatre. It owed much in its early days to the genius of the brothers Fay and to the generosity of Miss Horniman, who acquired the lease of the Abbey Theatre, rebuilt it, and from 1904 to 1910 assisted the company of players by an annual subsidy. To this Theatre we owe the discovery of the dramatic gifts of Synge, Lady Gregory, Padraic Colum, T. C. Murray, St. John Ervine and many other playwrights; to it we owe the evolution of a school of natural acting and the art of Sara Allgood, Maire O'Neill, Arthur Sinclair, Fred O'Donovan and J. M. Kerrigan; its players have appeared in all the English-speaking countries of the world, and its plays have gone into the repertory of every art theatre in Europe. It has created a distinctive Irish drama and a distinctive school of Irish acting, and has inspired imitators all through Ireland. Belfast has its own "Ulster Literary Theatre," and Cork its "Munster Players," and there is not a town of any size in Ireland now without its local company of amateur players.[18]

Then, after rehearsing the theatre's current problems, Robinson added:

If the Abbey Theatre were dying of inanition, of a lack of players or playwrights, it were better it should die at once; but no one who knows its work of recent years

> doubts its vigour. We are confident of the future if we are helped now through these dark days. If the Abbey Theatre dies the whole art of the theatre will have suffered a loss, and we confidently appeal to all friends of the theatre for help.[19]

Robinson then went on to say that four lectures were to be presented in London in May at the residence of J. B. Fagan. On 5 May Yeats would speak on the Irish theater; on 12 May, Lady Gregory on making a play; on 19 May, St. John Ervine on the theater in America; and on 26 May, Bernard Shaw would give a lecture and reading called "The Spur of the Moment."

Lady Gregory's reaction to Robinson's circular was one of considerable irritation. As she wrote in her journal on 1 April:

> Afternoon post bought circulars from Robinson. I have made spills of them; quite useless and untrue about the foundation of the Theatre. Miss Horniman made the *building*, not the Theatre, and we bought it from her when she stopped her help. The Theatre—the Irish National Theatre—was in existence before her—we did not "take it over" from her. An afternoon working in the garden, and at "Sir Henry Layard," calmed me down.[20]

In Dublin, there was a good deal of press comment about the Abbey's plight, but no one summed the matter up better than did Frank J. Hugh O'Donnell in the *Irish Independent* of 11 April:

> When the Abbey is gone the Mirror of Ireland is broken, and not for a long time can we again see our sins and our virtues, our follies and our wisdom, our satire and our invective, reflected so truthfully and so fearlessly as we have seen from the stage of this cloistered room by the Liffey side.[21]

In the 23 April issue of the *Freeman's Journal*, Robinson was asked about the future of the Abbey, and replied that he expected the theater would get the necessary support from Irish, English, and American friends. He thought that it was difficult to ask the Irish people for anything because of the existing want and distress; nevertheless, "the largest subscription received as yet came from a Dublin man." He mentioned that there would be another benefit matinee in London for the theatre, and hoped "that before the end of the summer we will start with a clean sheet." He then answered some recent criticism that the Abbey did not give sufficient opportunity to young dramatists:

> We are getting comparatively few new plays sent in. That is probably simply owing to the state of the country. They have not got the time or the opportunity to write, so we are getting comparatively few new plays. . . . We at the Abbey have got a very large repertory of what might now be called classical plays—Synge's, Yeats', Lady Gregory's and other plays. These we feel we have got to play to a certain extent every year, simply because the young people coming up to Dublin and being educated, and others, ought to have the chance of seeing these classical plays.
>
> It is not like the old days when we had to give a chance to almost everything that came along. What it really means is that we have not a great deal of room for work which is not very good, and which is just beginner work. One would like to give a

chance to young dramatists to see their work on stage, and lead them probably to do something better. But these are the circumstances. I always felt that it was time for some new movement to try plays in an inexpensive way and give young playwrights their chance on that line.[22]

On 6 May, the *Irish Times* gave an account of W. B. Yeats's London lecture:

The Abbey Theatre in Dublin, said Mr. Yeats, fulfilled, more than any theatre he knew, the possible definition of a people's theatre, where the actors were chosen from the general mass of the people, the plays written by people chosen from the general mass. In the same way they drew their plays from all classes. They were mainly realistic descriptions of the actual life of the people. Very often plays were sent to him to judge. If he thought by the handwriting that the play was by a person of University education he regarded it with some prejudice, because the author would be writing about a life he did not know, and would not have the same vivid sense of character as the man whose handwriting suggested the National schools.

The Abbey Theatre was not the kind of theatre Lady Gregory, Mr. Synge, and myself set out to found, Mr. Yeats continued. We were in love with the poetical theatre and did not at all want a theatre of realism. We were not alone in that. Every young Nationalist wanted a poetical theatre, because we were in the midst of the great Gaelic movement, which was thinking about old poems, songs and fables. It was the only possible kind of theatre to think of, and, in setting out to create a poetical theatre we seemed to be representing the deepest instinct of the people. But when we got to work we found that the old poetical world was dead. It belonged to the time of religion, when a man hated his own sins, and wanted to have the human soul revealed to him. But another age has come, in which we do not hate our own sins, but hate the sins of our neighbours. That is the world of political partisanship and economic strife in which we live. The great need is not the revelation of our neighbour, as seen by just men, and sometimes as seen in his own eyes. Very gradually we discover that this was our duty, or rather our necessity, and we were wise enough to accept our necessity as our duty.

They had been at work only a short time when Lady Gregory wrote her first little comedy. It was called *Twenty-five.* There occurred in the play the character of an emigrant who had returned with £100, and the actors refused to play the piece because they said that the fact that an emigrant would come back with £100 would encourage emigration. (Laughter.) A little later Lady Gregory wrote *The Rising of the Moon*, which was now recognized as almost a ritual of Nationalism. There occurred in the play the character of a policeman who allowed a Fenian to escape after an appeal to his patriotism. For two years the company refused to attempt the play, because they said that a policeman was incapable of a patriotic act. (Laughter.) It was a question of art or morals, said Mr. Yeats, and when there is a clash between art and morals art always has to give in, and morals required that the policeman should be represented as black as possible. (Laughter.) When the play was produced there came a difference from the other side. A leading Dublin newspaper declared that it was an insult to His Majesty's forces, and from that day we have been denied the privilege of having the cast-off clothes of the police. With the growing crisis in Ireland it is becoming a greater deprivation. If we do not have Home Rule after the present crisis is over we cannot go on, because there are so many police in our plays. (Laughter.) The object of the realistic drama was to show man as he appeared in the eyes of a just man, and in his own eyes. In the Middle Ages man had a prolonged fight with his own violence and passion. The reply to the passion and violence was the creation of artistic beauty over the whole world. There was another fight now—it was the fight with social bitterness and passion and all kinds of partisanship. The reply to that was truth to fact—the great realistic literature. The Abbey Theatre had won its fight, and could produce anything it liked. But for some time to come the great bulk of their plays would be plays of social realism. In the period after the terrible crisis through which Ireland was going, the work of the Abbey Theatre would be more necessary than ever in the past, because it could do a great deal to soften the terrible bitterness that would remain over—to explain party to party and section to section.[23]

In paraphrase, the lecture seems interesting and provocative, but Lady Gregory wrote in her journal:

Yeats' lecture not very good. He didn't get fire. However the audience liked it and an American lady said, "I never had any idea that Mr. Yeats could be so amusing!" He was probably less amusing when, he having asked for questions, suggested his saying something about the fight with the Castle over *Blanco Posnet*, and on hearing my voice he exclaimed, "I had been for a long time wondering where some bright beams of intelligence were coming from among the audience, and now I see it was from Lady Gregory!!" (No applause!)[24]

A week after Yeats's lecture, Lady Gregory spoke about making a play, and at the close *The Gaol Gate* was performed by Sara Allgood, Maire O'Neill, and Sydney Morgan. According to the *Freeman's Journal*, Lady Gregory said:

One must, before writing, choose the fable and stick to it. Many good plays had to be rejected by the Abbey Theatre because of irrelevancies. A playwright must keep to essentials, and remember that the play must ascend to a climax. Living speech was very necessary—literary speech would not do. The Irish, their ordinary living speech, had the art common to the Hebrew poets of repeating in the second part of a sentence an idea embodied in the first. This sometimes leads to an embellishment of the truth. Tragedies were much easier to write than comedies.[25]

At the end of her talk, Lady Gregory said that she was not, as Bernard Shaw had remarked, "the fairy god-mother of the theatre" because this was far too poetic and romantic a description of her. Rather, said Lady Gregory, she was the charwoman of the theater and only took credit for her industry.[26] A brief newspaper account, of course, can capture only a certain amount of truth. It can never, like Lady Gregory's journal, reflect the turmoil and indecision that she felt while she prepared for her lecture:

My lecture, after the long misery of thinking of it—And to think, and go over it without interruption, I had in those last days to wake myself up at 7 o'c. and work at it before breakfast—perhaps too much, for my nervousness grew and when I got to the platform I was actually trembling so that I had to lay my hand on Robinson's chair to steady it. . . .

We have made: Lectures £175.4.8 (but expenses of lectures, about £30, will come out of this). Matinee, £84.11.7. W.B.Y. reading, £39[27]; Donations, £172.13.4. In all £471.9.7. But I think anyhow we shall be able to pay our £500 debt to the Bank.[28]

The third lecture was given by St. John Ervine before a large audience, but was the one lecture that Lady Gregory did not enjoy. As she wrote John Quinn, "I think we gave our audiences good value (except Ervine whose lecture was poor)."[29] A brief account of Ervine's talk appeared in the *Irish Times*:

> Mr. John Galsworthy, who presided, said that they of England had rung the curfew which threatened the existence of the gallant little playhouse. Would it not be a crime, he asked, to ring the curtain down? While they had guineas in their pockets let them help to keep the curtain of the Abbey Theatre up.
>
> Mr. St. John Ervine, in the course of his address, comparing the American with the English theatregoer, said that the former was perfectly willing to gain experience, whereas the latter was not. The American was able to look at a tragic play without having his feelings harrowed. Instancing scenes in some of the Shakespearian plays, he said the English race was so weak that it could not look on such things without qualms. In America again they had got to a point at which they could contemplate gloomy plays and tragedies without being scared out of their wits—that meant that there was going to be a revival of romance on the American stage. It was possible there might be a revival of romance on the English stage when they recovered from the wounds of the late war, but it was absolutely certain, in his judgement, that they were going to have it in America.[30]

The final lecture was given by Shaw and presided over by John Drinkwater who said that "it was a patriotic duty to support the Abbey Theatre, for in doing so they would be supporting the national spirit."[31] Shaw's amusing lecture was restated at some length by the *Irish Times*:

> Taking for his subject "On the Spur of the Moment," Mr. Shaw said that he was an Irishman, and as he stood looking at the distinguished audience, hurrying to the rescue of the Abbey Theatre, his mind went back to a series of desperate enterprises in support of English theatres. They had the same object—to try and get the drama out of the commercial rut. He could remember one manager who had made a tremendous effort in that direction, sitting swinging his legs, and wearing the only pair of boots the pawnbroker had refused to accept. (Laughter.) Curiously enough, he was an Irishman, but he concealed the fact. (Laughter.) Wondering why it was that Ireland had a big fascination, Mr. Shaw suggested that, perhaps, some of those present who had not burned Cork, might feel it would mitigate the thing if they kept the Abbey Theatre going. He did not particularly want the Abbey Theatre. It was a horrible place, founded out of a Mechanics' Institute and a morgue. (Laughter.) It was very inconvenient; there were horrible draughts, and the stage was nothing like what they would call a stage.
>
> He felt the despair of his country when he thought that the Abbey Theatre was within a stone's throw of the most beautiful building in the kingdom. He did not know who had done it, but in Ireland they had managed to burn the Customs House, but not the theatre. The insurance would have got them out of their difficulty. (Laughter.) Referring to the good works done by the Abbey Theatre, he mentioned that it discovered Lady Gregory, and that was a wonderful thing. Speaking of himself, Mr. Shaw said that he was now what was called a back number. People called him even a classic. (Laughter.) One knew what that meant. Mr Shaw then referred to his latest play *Back to Methusaleh*. It was not, he said, in response

to a demand for a play in the theatre. It was really a response to his friend's (Mr. Wells') desire for a new Bible. It was not yet published. He had passed the proofs. Would they like to hear some of it? (Cries of "Yes," and applause.) It took three nights and two matinees to perform. (Laughter.) It began where the Bible began. There were some gentlemen of the press present. He wanted to remind them it was copyright. If they took notes and published it in their papers their editors would be murdered. (Laughter.) The play was called: "In the Beginning." Although it began in the Garden of Eden, it ended 30,000 years hence—so it had a pretty large scope. (Laughter.) "As no one reads the Bible now, I want to explain that Adam did not live 1,000 years," he said.[32]

Back to Methusaleh was much appreciated by Lady Gregory, as she indicated to John Quinn some three days after the lecture. "I spent my Whitsuntide with the Shaws very pleasantly. He read me his wonderful new play—wonderful to read—he calls it a 'new Bible,' but it won't be as popular as his others."[33] A month later, in another letter to Quinn recalling the same Whitsuntide, Lady Gregory added:

I think the forest part the finest, Adam and Eve. And the idea of the continuity of life, or the replacing of the present race by another, is well worked out, only I don't think his people quite know what to do with their extra years.[34]

Many individuals, often in a small and unassuming way, contributed to the Abbey Theatre Fund. One touching contribution came from the northern playwright George Shiels. In a letter to Robinson, he said:

I have seen by the papers recently, and with peculiar regret, that the Abbey Theatre is feeling the pinch of bad times. My first impulse was to contribute my mite, but being a stranger to you and your colleagues I hesitated to take the liberty.

I notice however that you have been working hard yourself and are still short of the desired amount, and I trust you will favour me by accepting the enclosed cheque for ten guineas. It is all I can spare at the moment, but later on if the deficit is not wiped out I shall give myself the pleasure of sending in ten more.

Being a hopeless invalid I am never likely to see the inside of the Abbey, but the literature it created has given me many a pleasant hour. I sincerely trust you will be able to carry on, for I am convinced in my very soul that the curtain is about to rise on a new Ireland, grander than anything of which her poets ever dreamt.[35]

On 10 June, another benefit in aid of the Abbey was staged. A distinguished audience (among whom were the Duchess of Sutherland, the Countess of Arran, Lady Randolph Churchill, Lady Lavery, Lady Leslie, Mrs. Asquith, Mr. and Mrs. Bernard Shaw, and Augustus John) attended London's Court Theatre to see a matinee of *The Rising of the Moon*, *The Workhouse Ward* and *Riders to the Sea*. In the casts were Sara Allgood, Maire O'Neill, Nora Desmond, Arthur Sinclair and Sydney J. Morgan. After the performance, J. B. Fagan, who had lent the theater, auctioned off a painting by Augustus John, which represented three of the Irish players and had been specially painted for the Abbey Fund. The painting sold for £50. In thanking all present, Robinson announced that the matinee had secured £182 toward the upkeep of the Abbey.[36]

Also on 10 June, Lady Ardilaun wrote to Lady Gregory offering £500 to help the theater.[37] When Lady Ardilaun's check arrived two days later, Lady Gregory wrote exultantly, "So the Abbey is safe for a long time, I hope for ever! Such a joy. Lecture misery and matinee fuss wasn't thrown away—we shouldn't have had this without it."[38]

On 24 June, Lloyd George invited de Valera to a conference, and de Valera insisted that the signing of a truce was a necessary preliminary. That truce came into effect on 11 July, and to most of the civilian population it brought, according to Dorothy Macardle, "a sudden return to normality, release from a prolonged and almost intolerable strain . . . the removal of Curfew, freedom to walk at night in the streets."[39]

The Abbey did not reopen, however, until Tuesday, 2 August. Then to a packed and enthusiastic audience, it offered a triple bill for the rest of the week of *The Rising of the Moon, Meadowsweet*, and *The Shewing Up of Blanco Posnet*. Monday, 8 August, was the beginning of Horse Show Week, and the Abbey played six evenings and a matinee, on some nights running *John Bull's Other Island*, and on others *Aristotle's Bellows* and *Bedmates*. Then, however, the theater closed again and did not reopen with its own programs until 4 October. The reason for the closing, as Robinson explained to the *Evening Telegraph*, was that

> "we are going to have acting classes to find new people, for, you see, a good many of our old ones are going away.
>
> "We don't quite know yet what we are going to do after that. All cannot be done in a day, of course. But I am confident that we shall be able to work up things, and that there is a great future before us if we have any sort of settlement this winter. Of course, last winter was so disturbed. . . . if next winter is like that, it may ruin our chances of opening altogether."
>
> When speaking of . . . classes, again turning to the reservoir of undeveloped dramatic talent in Dublin, Mr. Robinson became almost enthusiastic.
>
> "There are, after all," he said, "as good fish—or at any rate, nearly as good fish in the sea as were ever caught. Of course, we can't expect a Sara Allgood, for instance, quite at once—that happens about once in a generation. But I expect we shall work up a very good company."[40]

Joseph Power, the drama critic, wondered if closing the Abbey for six more weeks was really necessary:

> Why? Haven't they collected about £680 more or less to avoid just such a contingency? What are they going to do with all that money? Wait till the clouds roll by? And all their best actors and actresses are gone to America? Or England? Never more to return to work for small wages? In a company with part time actors?[41]

According to Power, there was much ill feeling about the theater once again closing. "People have been speaking to me about it for the past few weeks—people of some repute in theatrical and literary circles. One or two of them wanted to start a sort of campaign against the Abbey." Something, Power thought, must be done to revitalize the theater:

> The Abbey cannot drag on the way it was going before the recent close down. That £680 should make a solution to the problem easy. If the part-time actor system cannot be done away with altogether it should, at least, be no hindrance to first-class players getting salaries sufficient to keep them in their own country. The Abbey cannot afford to stand still. Still less can it afford to go backward. A number of plays in its repertory should be unhesitatingly scrapped. They were well enough in their day—some of them—but that day is long past.[42]

Less carping for once was Jacques, (the pseudonym of the drama critic J. J. Ryce), who was delighted by mid-July to see the beginning of some theatrical activity:

> All the metropolitan places of amusement are back to old conditions again—back, as the funny man in the music hall says, to pre-war from pray-for-me times. At the Royal on Monday night one sensed the "peace" atmosphere. The crowd—a light-hearted, genial crowd without a trace of boisterousness—enjoyed the excellent fare, but on any night during the last six months not all of the performers would have been so strenuously recalled.
>
> The same spirit of good cheer was present at the Gaiety Theatre all the week. The O'Mara Opera Company, despite the out-of-doors weather and the in-doors-at-curfew regulations, drew crowds of very flattering proportions. . . .
>
> From what one hears in the way of gossip, it is fair to speculate that, in the near future, things will buzz again in the theatrical business in Ireland. For the present there is a feeling of indecision. Next week the Gaiety will be vacant. It may not open again until August in time for the Horse Show. The Queens will continue at pictures. Arrangements are being made for reopening of the Tivoli. It has been decided to continue pictures at the Empire until August, when a special big-bill performance will be provided for the auspicious occasion.[43]

With peace came a plea from Joseph Power for the writing of new plays:

> It is doubtful if there was much playwrighting done during the past few years—there was plenty of material, of course, but for obvious reasons it was not the sort of thing that could be written about—from any point of view—while there was a possibility of the building playwright's house being raided and the manuscript confiscated as a seditious document. However, with the return of the piping times of peace it is to be hoped that the dramatists, new and old, will come out of their shells and give us something that at least will not make us sorry that anything woke them up.[44]

A couple of weeks later, Frank J. Hugh O'Donnell echoed Powers's plea and also speculated about the new kind of drama that would be written:

> I do agree with Mr. Martyn that psychological drama is and should be the particular metier of Irish playwrights, and that plays of incident and propaganda are mere spoilations of better work.
>
> And so it is I would make an appeal to young Irish writers who are considering entrance into the lists of drama, to study the drama of the mind and write of it. The

day for heroic grandiloquent stuff is past. The peasant play, with its romantic garb, and its more romantic language, is attenuated to a shadow. The grotesque comedies of a certain type built of beautifully-inverted sentences, are laughing at themselves. And so it is well to get down to serious work of a high standard.[45]

AE was also hopeful. As he wrote to John Quinn:

Literature and art suffer in the turmoil as you might expect. Only Yeats, who keeps out of it and who lives in England, can keep on at his work. We have all got caught in the vortex and drawn out of ourselves. But if a settlement comes I expect a great literary movement will spring up.[46]

Jack Yeats thought that "the work of artists over here will be strongly national in spirit in the future":

Has the Republican movement found direct expression in art yet? Scarcely at all. Only one painter, to my knowledge, has drawn on the incidents of the last few years. We have no Sinn Fein war artist. The conditions of the conflict made that almost impossible. . . . the drama, on the other hand, seems rather more disposed to make direct use of it. There has already been one play, *Sable and Gold*, which has no oblique reference by the way to "Black and Tan" dealing with the Cork revolution period. The Abbey is shortly to produce one centering about a lonely lighthouse at the time of the Casement gun-running.[47] And there are others.[48]

Yeats was not quite on the mark, for the great new dramatic artist would write plays that many of his countrymen would think strongly antinational.[49]

About the Abbey closing, Lady Gregory was as unhappy as Joseph Power, and on 1 September she recorded:

. . . sad because the Abbey isn't playing, through Robinson taking his holidays at the wrong times, and I can't leave the place just now to start the plays, and with Dail Eireann sitting we should be making well and doing a service.[50]

By the middle of the month, she was able to get to Dublin, and on 16 September she noted:

To the Abbey. I saw Dolan and tried to hurry up plays, but can't get one on till 4 October, *The Lord Mayor*. A heartbreak that all these good weeks have been missed and the theatre let to outsiders who have profited. I went to see Dolan's class, it was rehearsing *Spreading the News* with great spirit.[51]

However, on 4 October, the theater did finally reopen, and Lady Gregory wrote:

A splendid opening night at the Abbey, a full house (but a good deal of Press &c) £40 in all; great enthusiasm for *Lord Mayor*. . . . Robinson came in the middle, back from Spain, a great triumph having the successful performance to greet him![52]

Not everyone was as delighted with the reopening as Lady Gregory. T. C. Murray remarked, "It's good to have the Abbey once more opening its doors to its many friends," but "I have got a little tired of *The Lord Mayor*."[53] And Maire nic Shiubhlaigh wrote to Holloway:

> I see the Abbey has reopened with new players but not new plays. Crowded houses, etc. I haven't heard from them so you see it doesn't really matter as far as I am concerned. . . . I know how you feel about the Abbey, just as I do myself—the people that support the theatre deserve the very best of fare. It isn't fair to be practising on them with the school—it is very mean of them to say they cannot afford to engage competent artists—when it is the public's demand. Don't you think so?
>
> Maureen Delany is a great loss and so is McCormick and Peter Nolan—I was speaking to McC. when he was in Dublin with *Paddy* and he told me Mr. Robinson told him and Peter Nolan it would be best for them to find some other work. Well of course they had to live and McC. is gaining experience. I was sorry to see him go. However, such are the lines that the Abbey has always been run on.[54]

There is, perhaps, a mordant moral to be drawn from these remarks, and from those of Joseph Power: after the vast difficulties in saving the theater in 1921—after fighting the curfew, after not having money to pay the best actors, after having to raise money by benefits and lectures in London—the theater was finally able to open its doors again. And, if the first audience reaction was applause, the second was devastating criticism. Often a thankless task, theater.[55]

Still, some of the criticism was benevolent. For instance, on 7 November O'Donnell wrote in the *Gael* of a revival of Robinson's *The Dreamers*:

> Considering that the actors concerned in its production were mainly amateurs, the high standard achieved was surprising, particularly so in the drinking scene at the inn. The new company shows promise, and from last week's caste one must give the laurel chaplet (in halves) to P. J. Carolan for his portrayal of Robert Emmet and Miss Crowe for her delightful presentation of Sarah Curran. Incidentally I was very glad to see Peter Nolan back again on the Abbey boards. And I need not add that both himself and Michael Dolan were perfect in their parts.[56]

With the cessation of fighting, the rest of the theatrical year proceeded normally. Meanwhile, the Irish delegation, headed by Arthur Griffith and Michael Collins, was engaged in London in long and torturous peace talks with the English. On 6 December, a treaty was signed, and the initial attitude of most Irishmen was probably expressed by Holloway:

> Nobody is satisfied with the terms of the Peace Treaty, as it is only a makeshift and settles nothing. By it, Ireland is as far off as ever from the freedom she has longed through centuries for. It is generally accepted that it was signed to avoid the further assassination by the foreign savage brutes who hold a strangle hold on our beloved land, and not by the delegates' free will.[57]

However, the Dail debates over the treaty revealed that many regarded the terms as quite unacceptable, and 1922 was not to see the longed-for coming of peace to Ireland.

• • •

Despite the curfew and the general disruption in Dublin, the Abbey managed to keep its doors open for twenty-eight weeks of the year. To be sure, many of these were short weeks in which performances were only given on Thursday, Friday, and Saturday nights and on Saturday afternoons. Still, five new full-length plays were mounted, as well as a new one-act, a revision of Yeats' one-act *King's Threshold*, and two one-acts taken over from earlier productions by the Dublin Drama League.

The first new production was on 6 January, a one-act comedy entitled *Bedmates* by the Ulster playwright George Shiels. The *Irish Times*, which thought it "capital," described the plot like this:

> Two ragmen engage the one remaining bed in a common lodging house, directed by Molly Swan. Bertie Smith, racecourse tout, thimble-rigger, and self-confessed trickster, a Londoner to boot, would persuade the landlady to turn out the two ragmen, and let the room to him. No Irishman could "blarney" as does this Englishman. However, the ragmen return from a visit to a neighbouring public-house, and then it becomes a duel between the keen wits of an unscrupulous Englishman and the rich sense of humour of a Southern Irishman. The former makes a tool of a simple-minded Ulsterman by playing on his fears of "Romish plotters." It would not be fair to indicate the victor, but the audience was vastly amused and highly delighted. Mr. Barry Fitzgerald was the ideal Irish tramp, and Mr. Tony Quinn acted the simple Ulsterman to the life.[58]

Indeed, only Jacques in the *Evening Herald* faulted Shiels's play. He suggested that it lacked originality because, like D. C. Maher's political skit *Partition*, it attempted to treat the subject of the North and the South. But while Maher created action to keep pace with dialogue and made every word in the script apt, Shiels's play, according to Jacques, was "more pretentious and not at all entertaining," in part because its author failed to grasp the dramatic possibilities of the doss house landlady.[59] At the first night, Holloway was talking to the drama critic, J. H. Cox, who much enjoyed the play and thought "the Abbey company at its best—he never remembers a better all-round company there."[60] Shiels himself thought the piece his favorite skit because it provided "a tangible picture of English trickery."[61] The play, which has not been published, had no pretentions to be more than a satiric skit, and was in its day quite successful.

A much more ambitious piece—indeed, probably the major theatrical event in Dublin in 1921—was also political. This was Terence MacSwiney's *The Revolutionist*, which had been published as early as 1914 but had found no one willing to stage it. Indeed, the *Evening Telegraph* believed that if it had not been "for the heroic tragedy of which the author was the martyr it might never have been seen by a Dublin or Irish audience."[62] This seems to us a sound conclusion, for the play intrinsically is very faulty. However, in 1921 the recent death by hunger strike of the Lord Mayor of Cork was still much in people's minds. Still it was a brave, if not foolhardy, act for the Abbey to stage the play; and the directors felt a justified political and artistic trepidation. As Robinson wrote to Lady Gregory:

> I hope very much you will be able to come up for L. M.'s[63] play, you would be a great tower of strength in case anything happens. I spoke to a prominent S. F.[64] about the matter you wrote of and he said their people had as a matter of fact been keeping away from the Abbey lately and he would advise them to keep specifically away next week—at least very continuously—and the *words* at any rate will be up, and that's no joke for it's a very long play (we shall have to begin at 6.15). I can't tell what the performance will be like. McCormick probably not sympathetic enough as hero—. The Co. are more and more interested in the play which means well. I have cut it very much.[65]

The play opened on 24 February and attracted a large and interested audience. As Jacques said in the *Evening Herald*, "about 6 o'clock the old Abbey patrons—all loyal first-nighters—came crowding in. When the curtain rose at 6.15 the house held a comfortably packed audience in proportion of about two ladies for every man, and all obviously keen in anticipation."[66] In the audience was MacSwiney's widow, who had come up specially from Cork, and Lady Gregory in her journal wrote, "I told her with what pride we gave this play for the first time, that we felt we were laying a wreath upon the grave."[67] Despite the ten o'clock curfew, many other Irishmen felt the same way, and Lady Gregory noted later in the week:

> . . . so many people were standing in the pit that I sent for Robinson, and we brought all we could find places for the front. Last night all places full, many turned away at the door. We had already decided to play it again next week, and Robinson announced this from the stage. I feel so happy that we have been able to keep the Abbey going if only for this one week, the production of a national play of fine quality by one who has literally given his life to save the lives of others. . . . It is strange to see the changes in political thought now; the audience (in spite of Robinson's request in the programmes for no applause during acts) cheering the revolutionist who stands up against the priest's denunciation, denounces his meddling in return.[68]

Most reviews praised the play highly. The *Evening Telegraph* said:

> A more moving piece of stage work, a more attractive plot, a more subtle presentation of character, a more gripping love story, a more affecting and powerful climax to a play it would be difficult to conceive. The work with its fine literary tone, its profoundly reasoned evolution, its wealth of feeling and masterly structure, proves beyond question that MacSwiney had studied dramatic literature deeply and had dramatic talents of no ordinary calibre.[69]

The *Freeman's Journal* called it "powerful" and thought the author "had an instinct for the really dramatic situation."[70] Both the *Irish Times* and Jacques in the *Evening Herald* admired the many epigrams and aphorisms.[71] However, neither the *Times* nor Jacques was as uncritical as the *Evening Telegraph*. The *Times* noted that the "political passages are crude and its love scenes lacking in polish."[72] And Jacques faulted the play for containing "periods of overwrought sentiment" and possessing an "obvious weakness in technique—the going and coming of different characters through the same door, for instance—that escape the mind when reading the play in book form, but assault the eye when witnessed in stage presentation." He also thought the last two acts filled with "longdrawn-out emotion and agony" that led to a weak climax.[73] James Montgomery, who was to be the film censor of the Free State, told Holloway that he thought the play clever "but could be pruned a lot." To which Holloway replied, "All Cork dramatists are inclined to be talky! It's a way they have!"[74]

Basically, however, the play received a chorus of praise, a view that seems to us highly colored by the still vivid emotional reaction to the Lord Mayor's death on hunger strike in 1920. Even a casual perusal of the play reveals glaring flaws of verbosity, stilted dialogue, and wooden characterization. There is also a nearly total absence of movement or action, and the upshot is a dulling sense of verbosity and tedium. However, as in Padraic Pearse's *The Singer*, there is a distinct resemblance between the main character and the author; and so an admiring public response was, to our minds, considerably engendered by the public memory of the dead patriot.

The leading character, Hugh O'Neill, also bears a resemblance to Ibsen's Dr. Stockmann. Both characters possess a curious mixture of realism and idealism, and in O'Neill particularly the conflict between conviction and expediency is well developed. The play's theme derives well out of O'Neill's character, but one character of some interest is hardly enough to sustain a play if the plot is static and all of the other characters are wooden, one-dimensional stereotypes.

Considering, though, that the streets were full of Black and Tans, and that *The Revolutionist* was a political statement by a man whom most Irishmen would see as a political martyr, we must admit that the decision to stage the play was indeed brave. Now that those times have receded, there seems little possibility that the play could be revived or hold the boards on its own merits. Pearse's plays, which have their own deep flaws, have at least the virtue of being short and simple.

The early curfew continued to plague all of Dublin's theatres, but on 9 March Maureen Delany told a reporter that as long as the Abbey had "anything at all like an audience" players would continue to appear. She also said that the Abbey program was set for the next few weeks and that on St. Patrick's night Lady Gregory's new play, *Aristotle's Bellows*, was to be staged: "It is really very funny and we enjoy rehearsing it immensely."[75]

Most individuals who attended the opening night on 17 March also found the play a delight—in part, no doubt, because it was a relief from the horrors of the time. As Maud Gonne MacBride explained to Yeats:

> I went on St. Patrick's Day to our Lady Gregory's new play the Bellows of Aristotle—It is a most charming fantastic little play. It has that good humoured gaiety and fantasy and charm of the best of Lady Gregory's work and should prove a great favorite at the Abbey—After the terrible week we had lived through I didn't think I could have endured an ordinary comedy. I went to the Abbey that afternoon in the same dread, chiefly because I wanted to talk with the Chairman of the American Relief Delegation who has asked me to see him at the Abbey—but I was quite charmed and felt much better for it—I am desperately hard at work for the White Cross Committees and terribly anxious . . . as the raids and arrests of every day particularly of students is going on worse than ever—and the treatment they get after arrest is shocking.[76]

In August, Robinson took James Stephens to see the play and then reported to Lady Gregory: "I wish you could have heard his praise. . . . He was charmed with it."[77] Yeats, however, did not like the play that much and had written in January "a bad opinion of *Aristotle's Bellows*."[78]

The first-night reviewer for the *Evening Telegraph*, however, was effusive in his assessment and appended a concise plot summary:

> A crowded audience at the Abbey matinee yesterday warmly welcomed the first production of Lady Gregory's new play, *Aristotle's Bellows*. The plaudits and repeated calls which brought the author on the stage after the last curtain were well deserved, for *Aristotle's Bellows* is a sheer delight. It is called a wonder play in three acts, but is really a farcical comedy of a very whimsical and imaginative character.
>
> Conan, a sort of half crazy old peasant scholar in the west is wondering what Aristotle left in Ireland before his departure. He hears it was a bellows with extraordinary power and virtues. Anything on which it has blown has changed to the reverse: black being made white, deafness turned into good hearing, and so forth. But the bellows has only seven blasts and its owner must need husband its magic powers and employ each blast in some great and worthy work.
>
> Conan finds the bellows and determines to change the face of Ireland and, indeed, reconstitute society and save the world. He thinks of the bellows as Mr. Wilson thought of the League of Nations. He gets ready to leave Connacht for Dublin but loses his temper with his indolent step-sister and blows the bellows upon her. Instantly she becomes the soul of energy, and her activities are soon a nuisance rather than a blessing. Soon, unheedingly, a neighbour wastes another blast on Conan's stupid old mother, whose memory returns in a flash and trots in many disconcerting things. She in turn restores the hearing of the deaf serving man that she may plague him with her vivid recollections. A little later two neighbours exchange their natures, the one generous and kind, the other mean and hard as flint by virtue of the wonderful bellows.
>
> At this moment Conan enters and sees how all his blasts have been wasted—only one is left—in doing petty things, while the world is still unchanged. He regretfully sees that his friends and kinfolk are all changed for the worse, and allows them to break the spell. However, his step-sister uses the last blast on himself, and from being a sour old crotchet, he becomes a kindly old fellow enough, and is the only change for the better in all the bellows transformations.
>
> The acting was without a single flaw or blemish and the entire production a real

success. The honours of the afternoon were divided between Maureen Delany as the mother and Barry Fitzgerald as Conan, which brought out his powers as a genuine comedian more fully than any part we have seen him in since the king in *The Dragon*.[79]

The *Irish Times* found the play made "ingenious and refreshing use of the element of enchantment," and also thought that the production of such a "highly mirth-provoking play was, at such a period, most salutary."[80] Among the few dissenting voices was that of Dr. Larchet, the conductor of the Abbey orchestra, who "thought *Aristotle's Bellows* the limit and the way snatches of song were brought in very absurd." In fact, Larchet told Holloway that he believed "the old lady had reached her dotage stage!" Holloway himself thought the piece a great success, "whimsical" and "droll." When he congratulated Lady Gregory, she said, "it was wonderfully played and Miss Delany sang delightfully."[81] Jacques, however, agreed with Larchet and thought

the most wonderful thing about it being that anyone would have the patience and pertinacity to write three acts of it.

It must be said for Lady Gregory, however, that she did not write all of it. A lot of it is made up of Moore's melodies, Irish ballads, and come-all-ye's. Five of the characters in the first act burst forth into song without any provocation whatever. They conversed in snatches of melody and relays of ballad airs until one feared the performance was going to develop into a song recital of selections from the "Music Album of Irish Composers."

Some of the songsters were quite pleasant to listen to, notably Miss Gertrude Murphy, who, as Cetra, warbled to a pigeon in a basket cage, and Mr. M. J. Dolan, who aired his sorrows in verses of the traditional. In fact the only ones that did not express themselves in terms of musical composition were the two Greek cats. They elocuted in lusty-tonged brogue.[82]

O'Donnell, however, noted that Jacques had left after viewing only one act, and Holloway agreed, saying: "his notice in *Independent* (March 18) clearly showed he didn't sit it out. It was full of misstatements." Holloway even wrote Jacques to this effect and also added, "you evidently drowned your shamrock before entering the theatre."[83]

The Abbey offered no new production until 18 October, when one of the pieces on a triple bill was Nikolai Evreinov's Russian one-act, *A Merry Death*. However, this was really only a somewhat recast revival of a Drama League production that had been done in June.

On 29 October, T. C. Murray mentioned to Holloway:

I had a letter from McNulty during the week. He too has got his latest venture accepted. I'm glad it is a comedy—Dublin is aching for a laugh—and the title if broad promises well. He calls it *The Courting of Mary Doyle*. The courting takes three acts![84]

McNulty's play was first performed on 8 November. Holloway said that there was a good opening night house, but that the play "alas, only proved a go as you please farce with an utterly hopeless third act."[85] Joseph Power agreed that the play "after creaking awkwardly through three acts, ends in the most approved, melodramatic 'Bless you me children,' 'They live happy ever after' style."[86] O'Donnell in the *Independent* found it

> a disappointing play, even though laughter loud and long greeted many of its passages. It was unreal and nothing could be more incongruous than the setting of the last act. We had here comedy, tragedy, melodrama, love-making, a marriage party, domestic strife, contemplated suicide, and wedding breakfast speeches on the edge of a graveyard, where nothing but crosses and tombstones met the eye. The entrances were false and artificial, and the whole ensemble seemed to be a melange of incidents strung anyway together.[87]

In the *Gael*, O'Donnell attempted to untangle the plot:

> Mary Doyle was the rather buxom servant in the house of one Thomas Kiernan in a town called Lishinashogue. By some method or other rumour got it that she possessed money. The result was that a man came and flung his heart at her. He managed to survive under the top-heavy nomenclature of John William Rattigan, and mended people's boots as a help thereto.
>
> But one day in a fit of confidence he told Peter Carmody, his friend, and local butcher to boot, that he shortly would be the husband of a lady possessing £500. Now, Peter Carmody's chief aim in life was to get hold of a neighbour's farm, which was valued at £500, an amount that never seemed likely to come his way. Peter, the man "who never did anything wrong," sees his opportunity, locks his man in a room, courts Mary Doyle, marries her, and upon his wedding day finds out that in reality his lady love possesses but the modest sum of £25 to pay for her burial expenses when need be. And Peter Carmody seeing no other way out of the difficulty, says that "with the help of God I'll make the best of it."
>
> This is the main story of the play, but Mr. McNulty, being a specialist in the making of love scenes and laughs, by way of contrast brings a young bank official called Tisdall into the house of Thomas Kiernan to make love to his daughter. Their love-making scene seems quite credible and artistically perfect. Furthermore, he strengthens his play and gets all the characters happy at the finish. The author gets Thomas Kiernan to mix up his grocery and hardware accounts, and deputes the young bank clerk to clear the air upon the matter. And for convenience sake, when Mary Doyle faints into Peter Carmody's arms outside the church after the wedding, and Thomas Kiernan has fully decided to test the toughness of his throat with a razor, the young bank clerk comes along and, being a smart lad at figures, puts everything right. For which, as you may guess, he is rewarded with the hand and heart of Jessica Kiernan.[88]

From these events, O'Donnell concluded, only a farce emerged, and, "It was sadly lacking in the matter of stage craft, and nothing but its brilliant dialogue and pointed witticisms could have saved it."[89] An ecstatic review in the *Freeman's Journal* found the piece a "delightful and hilarious comedy," and concluded that it could not be called a farce "because all the incident is possible, much of it probable, and the characters—though all of them decidedly amusing 'types'—have been met by most of us in real life."[90] If the *Freeman* disagreed with O'Donnell about the genre of the play, Lady Gregory disagreed with him about the dialogue, which she thought "rather poor."[91] An assessment of *The Courting of Mary Doyle*, taken from the various accounts of its first production, would prove little other than that the audience laughed a lot. However, a perusal of the script shows a simple, innocuous, conventional comedy of little literary distinction, but of sufficient theatrical vitality to keep it popular for some years among amateur players and their undemanding audiences.

The critics were also at odds about the acting of the play. While Lady Gregory and O'Donnell both found it excellently acted, Holloway thought the acting at best patchy:

> Michael J. Dolan has a part that suited his humour to a nicety and he made the most of the little man. . . . Florence Marks played the role of Mary Doyle. . . . But I could see Maureen Delany [in the part]. . . . Miss Marks' Mary was demure. Miss Delany's could have been jolly. Tony Quinn . . . and Eileen Crowe played a pair of turtle doves; just in the right spirit of rapturous exaggeration and got through each episode. Barry Fitzgerald's Terence Kiernan was a weak echo of Jimmy O'Brien in *The Lord Mayor* and Annie Kirby was his nagging wife. . . . She has not as yet got the art of speaking her lines convincingly.[92]

A week later, on 15 November, Bernard Duffy's new one-act, *The Piper of Tavran*, was performed along with a revision of Yeats' *The King's Threshold*. Duffy's play remains unpublished, but the *Independent* summarized its plot:

> The Abbot of the Monastery of Urlaur was seriously disturbed because of the presence of an evil beast that came from the sea and harried his monks. They were powerless against it, and it caused them much trouble. When it first made its appearance, a strange Brother, saying he had come from England, came to them and sought their hospitality. It was accorded to him upon the strength of his word, but upon being called upon by the Bishop to kiss the crucifix he refused to do so, and admitted he was upon the side of Satan.
>
> They hunted him from the monastery, and he threatened revenge, but the Abbot hearing distant music, remembers a dream he had of a saviour, and sends word for the playing Piper of Tavran to visit him. The musician on his arrival tells them of a girl he once knew whom he saved from an evil life, and who eventually joined a convent, and at her death weird music was heard.
>
> The piper, being weary, falls asleep after his recital, but on the church bell being rung the beast and the pervert monk come along to attack the monastery. Then it is that the piper, still sleeping, plays the weird music that he heard at the death of the girl, and a thunderstorm suddenly breaking out in the heavens, the evil spirits are stricken dead. Upon his reawakening, the friars inform him of the wonder he has performed, but the piper disclaims all knowledge of the power, and goes again upon the high roads playing to the rambling winds.[93]

The play met a mixed reception. Joseph Power wrote:

> To the majority of the new players at the Abbey I take off my hat, and likewise bow. . . . I don't know where Mr. Lennox Robinson finds them, but there evidently is more star dust floating around that I suspected.
>
> Pity they haven't had better vehicles of expression so far. I do not take off my hat to the new plays. Instead I rather hope that they will take themselves off. *The Courting of Mary Doyle* is a desperate crudity and *The Piper of Tavran* is not much better. They are the sort of productions that make the men in the auditorium thank heaven afresh for the soothing grace of Dr. Larchet's orchestra.[94]

Power then went on to criticise the music and the costumes:

> And why in the name of all that's sacred to the stage didn't they have some better substitute for the pipes than a fiddle playing "Carlin dear cruitin na mbo" off stage? Why not have a real piper and then the music if thought necessary by sticking him away in a remote dressing room or out in the lane? Why ban the piper, "silver-tongued, clean and sweet in their crooning"?
>
> And before I leave the Abbey production I would like to know who was responsible for the manufacture of the habits worn by the monks in *The Piper of Tavran*. Anything more uncouth it won't be difficult to imagine. They all seemed to be what the clothiers call "outsize." There were good grounds for believing that Peter Nolan was the Bishop but there was no ocular evidence: his voice was heard emerging from the depths of the most voluminous cowl I ever saw.[95]

Holloway also faulted the production, noting that the "stage management was defective on occasion; for instance when the bell rang before its time."[96]

One of the few critics who touched on the play itself was O'Donnell who thought it "rather slight and thin in the matter of real drama," but allowed the characterization and dialogue some merit.[97]

Most critics commended the acting, and a new actor, P. Kirwan, was said by the *Irish Times* to present his part with "convincing simplicity and a quaintness that lent much charm to the part of a wandering minstrel who proves himself nearer to heaven than the friars."[98] The *Freeman's Journal* added that the Abbey "got a rare interpretation from P. Kirwan. He made the character one of simplicity and artless comedy, never stressing too much or too little anything."[99]

Yeats's the *King's Threshold* had been one of the theater's first productions, and it was appropriate for Frank J. Fay to return to the Abbey and recreate his role of Seanchan. Most critics were pleased with Fay's reading, but O'Donnell found his voice "was pitched slightly too low,"[100] and the *Freeman's Journal* said that Fay, like his fellow Abbey actors, "in the beginning . . . shared the common fault of indistinctness."[101]

In his reworking, Yeats altered the play apparently to make it relate more to current political events. In the original version, King Guaire climbed down to the hunger striker, Seanchan, and granted the poet's demands so that the play had a happy ending. In the revision, the poet's demands were not granted, and he died on the King's threshold. O'Donnell thought that this conclusion and some weakening of the poetry of the original indicated that Yeats had "climbed down from his chariot of art to the donkey cart of the common people." He thought that Yeats was now "playing to the gallery," and that the ending of the new version had obviously been inspired by the death of MacSwiney in Brixton prison.[102] But if Yeats were playing to the gallery, the gallery was not all that attentive; for, as Holloway wrote:

> I got seated in back row of balcony to hear and see *The King's Threshold* and were it not for the noise of the people tumbling in . . . during most of the piece I should have enjoyed it immensely. . . . Two men in trench coats near me struggled in their seats and chattered also . . . started smoking cigarettes. . . . there was a good deal of coughing and sighs—the audience unused to poetic drama thought it wearying and long drawn out. . . . In the stalls I am told that an old countryman, who stayed on, yawned out loudly at intervals.[103]

On 6 December, the Abbey presented a triple bill of one-acts, which included the theater's first production of Emile Mazaud's *A Perfect Day*. Like *A Merry Death*, this production was taken over from an earlier staging during the year by the Drama League.

On 13 December, however, the Abbey did produce a new three-act play, the year's second piece by George Shiels, *Insurance Money*. In early November, Robinson had sent the play to Lady Gregory with the remark that he thought it would offend Ulster. Lady Gregory noted in her journal: "I think it a very fine comedy and that as to offending Ulster it would do a good deal to make up for the Ulstermen wrecking the last convention."[104] The *Freeman's Journal* thought less highly of the piece:

> The new play is poor as a dramatic work and as a comedy; the acting last night was likewise of almost consistently poor quality. The first act showed no promise—a cunning young farmer, and a pair of strolling tinkers, half in greed and half in devilment, draw out between them a policy for the life of a decrepit old servant-man.
>
> In the second act things brisk up; the servant-man has died, and the farmer gets the insurance money—though he has to give the agent a five-pound silencer. Then the Kerry tinkers come back—the man shamming illness farcically that he and his young wife (people now are to die in pairs for insurance money!) may be insured.
>
> The third act is "happy," the farmer no longer greedy, the insurance agent no longer dishonest and sceptical; all defrauders more or less repentant—the weekly payments have been returned by the agent, and the young servant-girl (who has been left £200 by the dead servant-man because she nursed him in his last illness) promised in marriage to her master; and the tinkers, who have spent the "insured" under the farmer's roof, depart sentimentally with a baby child.
>
> The action of the play takes place in the Co. Antrim; but the attempt of the actors to imitate the Ulster accent was lamentable. And the dialogue of the play was not such as to be independent of details.
>
> Peter Nolan, as the farmer, was passable in a poor part. Gabriel J. Fallon was responsible for any good acting in the first act.

> Eileen O'Kelly as the servant-girl, often spoke indistinctly and never got a natural accent; Eileen Crowe, too, was a most unreal tinker's wife. Tony Quinn was fair as the insurance agent. Michael J. Dolan put some life and humour into his part as the tinker in the second act.[105]

The *Evening Herald*, although admitting the play was "very amusing in its way," did not find it "overburdened with much complexity of plot [or] marked by any great display of dramatic achievements."[106] O'Donnell in the *Gael* emphatically agreed:

> Mr. Shiels has not yet got the dramatic sense. He had a good plot in his play, but lost his grip of it in the last act. . . . he got sadly sentimental and the end seemed as if it would never arrive quickly enough. And at times he displayed lack of knowledge in the matter of stagecraft. Two or three times the boards were bare of a performer, all having disappeared out one door or another. . . . the action was of the anaemic variety. There was no push or animation about.[107]

Holloway found *Insurance Money* "a bright little character-play," but noted on the first night "a plentiful lack of Abbey first-nighters present. It was sad to see so fine a performance wasted on so small a house."[108] A few days later Holloway dropped in again for a couple of acts and noted even more empty seats:

> It was a record bad week at the Abbey! There were great queues outside both Royal and the Tivoli for several houses. . . . If there are not better houses after Christmas at the Abbey, I don't know how it can keep open![109]

Insurance Money remains unpublished, but even a cursory reading of the manuscript, in the National Library, suggests that Shiels lost control of his play. In the third act, farce gave way to moral platitudes; and the personality of Richard Moore, the farmer protagonist, altered almost beyond recognition. Without explanation or justification, he changed from rogue to hero. Shiels was to do much better.

• • •

The Theater Royal doggedly kept its doors open all year, and for two weeks in March was the only live theater playing in Dublin. Like the other Dublin houses, however, it was forced to advance the times of its performances. For some weeks, the first performance bagan as early as 5:30 and the second at 7:20. For the week of 14 March, it gave only one performance, which commenced at 6:25 and concluded by 8:00.

The theater's offerings were its usual variety staples—singers, acrobats, comic sketches, and trained animals, such as four apes billed as "Tarzan's Playmates," who roller-skated and rode bicycles. An item of some Irish interest was the film *Paying the Rent*, which John MacDonagh had directed and which featured Arthur Sinclair. This comedy played during the week of 1 March, and for the week of 6 December there was an anonymous sketch called *Room 67*, which featured Sara Allgood, Fred O'Donovan, Breffni O'Rourke, and Moira Breffni. The *Freeman's Journal* believed that *Room 67* was "absolutely devoid of a semblance of originality, humour or common sense."[110] The *Independent* thought that the piece was saved from vapidness and melodrama largely because of Sara Allgood's acting: "Miss Allgood plays the part of Stella Courtland with much interest. The part is a combination of crude melodrama and light comedy, and is excellently acted."[111] Power in the *Evening Telegraph* said that, after the play's first two minutes, one was

> in the midst of the rawest of raw melodrama, flavoured strongly with the "Eternal Triangle" spice.
>
> Once more we heard the good old tags, or something very like them:—
>
> "Villyun! You hev stole my wife!"
>
> "You lie! Cur-r-r-se you!"
>
> And there was the dinky little automatic in the hip pocket of the aggrieved husband, and the false accused wife throwing hysterical fits all over the stage and the false accused hero doing the strong, silent man act for all he was worth.
>
> And murmurs of pained surprise from the literati and their friends:—
>
> "Good heavens! To think of Sara Allgood—Sara Allgood of the earlier and better Abbey—descending to such stuff as this!"
>
> "Such a splendid actress; such a finished artist, to inflict this upon us."[112]

Nevertheless, Power admitted that there were good comic bits and that the sketch in retrospect did not seem entirely inane and that the acting was excellent.

The Gaiety was almost as successful as the Royal in keeping its doors open, and was only closed for three weeks in March and April. Like the Royal, the Gaiety had to advance the times of performance, and for the week of 14 March the comic opera *La Poupée* began at 5:45 and was over by 8:00.

The theater's offerings were the usual light comedies, musicals, and old standards from England, plus the usual Christmas pantomime, the visits from the Carl Rosa and O'Mara opera companies, from Charles Doran's Shakespearian company, and from the Rathmines and Rathgar musical society and the Dublin University Dramatic Society. The only items of Irish interest were the December visit of the Ulster Players and a two-week stand in September of the *Paddy the Next Best Thing* company, which featured Kathleen Drago and F. J. McCormick in the leading roles.

The *Paddy* company played to packed houses for two weeks, and Joseph Power believed that it was Drago and McCormick who drew the large audiences to an inferior play.[113] Another reason, however, may have been that the troubled times made Irish audiences hungry for anything professionally done and funny. The *Irish Times* noted "the happy, joyous audience filling every available inch of the Gaiety Theatre," and went on to say:

> The play is one which Dublin playgoers will appreciate after a dearth of really good plays. It has its faults, of course, notably in the third act, in which the dispensary scene is unnecessarily long and somewhat tiresome, but they are lost in the wealth of merit which the piece possesses. . . . Miss Kathleen Drago . . . in all the varying moods and caprices of Paddy . . . caught the right note, and conveyed it straight to the hearts of her audience. When *abandon* was needed, it was there; when restraint was necessary it was not lacking, though at times, perhaps, she was a little too boisterous. It was, however, a great triumph for the artist.[114]

The play is really only commercial stage Irishry, and Paddy is only another Wild Irish Girl like the *Peg O' My Heart* character, which Sara Allgood had once toured. Still, in serious times, it gave people a laugh.

During the run, Kathleen Drago was interviewed, and, among other things, lamented the Abbey's hard times and the exodus of Irish actors to England and America:

> It is a long time since Kathleen Drago played to a Dublin audience. And her return to her native city as Paddy in *Paddy the Next Best Thing* this week had all the thrill of a big adventure for her. . . . "I was frightened," she said, "I was terrified. Very glad, but wondering what all the people who knew me here before would think." Then she broke in with a lament (for Dublin's sake), over the loss the city has suffered in the departure of some of the best present time actors for America last Sunday. Miss Drago and the Irish players with her in *Paddy* were just able to see them off at Liverpool, where they had been playing last week before coming to Dublin. Fate was kind to old comrades to give that chance; but the parting was a little sad, after the way of all partings.
>
> "Scarcely ever did I feel so desolate in my life," said "Paddy," with the shadow of memories passing over her face. "I cried. I felt that I would never see them again. It was ridiculous, of course, but it seemed terrible to see them leaving Ireland.
>
> "Coming here in *Paddy*? . . . If you knew how nervous I was. It seemed strange to be coming back—I felt frozen with fright, because I think so much of everybody over here and their opinion—more than anybody's anywhere else. I felt a little bit lost, too, for somehow I expected to see Arthur Sinclair and our own old crowd.
>
> "The last time I was here in the Gaiety was in William Boyle's then new play *The O'Dempsy*—a sequel to *The Eloquent Dempsy*. . . .
>
> "Last night was fine. It was glorious to get such a reception. . . .
>
> "Audiences in England and in Ireland? Well, there are some places in England where you may put on the most subtle and local Irish play, and you may be sure of it going well. Say London, Manchester, and Liverpool. We get what you might call a Dublin audience—our Irish following. Of course, the London audience after all is cosmopolitan, and I suppose that explains a good deal. London audiences are very intelligent. And I'll tell you where they're nice too—Lancashire. . . . It's funny how they love to hear a brogue over in England—not making fun of it or anything—they just love it. . . .
>
> "It's sad about the Abbey crowd going away. I do consider there's a great opening for the Abbey, and I think it's a crying sin they don't collect and keep Irish talent here. It would get huge and lasting support.
>
> "Audiences like 'popular' plays, and they should be given them, and yet substantially good stuff. Candidly and truthfully, I'd love to be here permanently in Dublin in the Abbey. Do you know what I'd love to see? The Abbey Theatre getting on at

the top of its success, paying well (for that's important), with good plays, a variety of them, and good acting. And it could."[115]

The Tivoli was the hardest hit of the Dublin theaters, and basically remained closed from the week of 14 March until that of 29 August.

The Queen's fared a bit better, although except for a couple of films, it remained closed from 14 March until 16 May, and then from 30 May until 1 August. Its offerings, as usual, consisted of old English melodramas like *East Lynne* and *The Face at the Window*, and of the usual Irish *Sarsfields*, *Father Murphys*, *Wolfe Tones*, and *Kathleen Mavourneens*. These were usually produced by such familiar names as Ira Allen, P. J. Bourke and H. J. Condron. However, the personnel, whoever the producer, remained basically the same—actors like Roberto Lena, Charles L. Keogh, May Murnane, May Craig from the Abbey, and other familiar Queen's actors.

The Empire had a difficult year. For the week of 14 February it opened its doors at 6:45 and ended its performance at 9:00. Then from the week of 7 March to that of 18 April, it closed entirely. For the last two weeks of April and the first week of May, it showed films and a few variety acts, but then it closed from the week of 9 May to that of 1 August, when it presented its usual two houses at its normal hours of 7:00 and 9:00.

There was little of Irish interest at the Empire during the year, save the *Paying the Rent* film in February and a revival of *General John Regan* on 19 December. The one exception was the week of 12 December, in which a new four-act comedy was presented. This was John MacDonagh's *The Irish Jew*, and on 11 December the *Weekly Independent* printed an interview with MacDonagh about the play:

> "In the words of the showman," said Mr. MacDonagh, "I hope *The Irish Jew* will please all and offend none—espcially our Jewish friends. As a matter of fact, I anticipated a perceptible expansion of Jewish chests, because the Jew I drew is more Irish than at least some of the Irish themselves.
>
> "Shaw wrote somewhere that 'the Irishman is the only person who makes a joke against himself.' I would add that we are inclined to get annoyed when people take us seriously and laugh, because our national pride is so sensitive that, having caused the laughter, we suspect its character.
>
> "At last, however, we can now afford to laugh at our little weaknesses, for we have lost our reputation of being a comic people. In our natural revulsion of feeling against the stage Irishman we are inclined to fly to the other extreme; but we should, as ordinary mortals, put all types of our humanity under the microscope to be studied and observed for our enlightenment and entertainment.
>
> "In the near future there ought to be a big crop of national plays based on actual experiences during recent years. A great wealth of material is wanting treatment, which, if handled with ability and discernment, will surely drive the old melodramatic Irish drama into well-merited oblivion."[116]

In an interview with the *Evening Telegraph*, MacDonagh mentioned that the idea for the play had originated as early as 1914 when he was manager of the Irish Theatre. He also hoped that the play would succeed because for "too long have we accepted 'London Success' as the hallmark of the highest merit. . . . it should be our ambition to raise the level again instead of weakly accepting the indifferent dramatic fare offered with wearying monotony." Nevertheless, Irish standards of stage production needed to be improved:

> For obvious reasons, such as lack of proper facilities for rehearsals, inability to devote sufficient time for the study of interpretation, productions organised locally have sometimes naturally not been up to the standard, such as it is, of visiting companies. And the tradition has grown of dismissing them with a good natured "they're doing their best" style of criticism. I ask for no such concessions. Such criticism is harmful, inasmuch as it encourages careless methods, and many a victim of such good nature to-day swells the unemployed of the "profession."[117]

MacDonagh apparently took considerable pains with this production, and his well-rehearsed and talented cast included such players as Paul O'Farrell, Jimmy O'Dea, Harry O'Donovan, Frank J. Fay, Fay Sargent, Dick Smith, and Ralph Goggins. Of them, the *Evening Telegraph* remarked:

> The piece was played in masterly fashion. The whole cast was good . . . the completeness of the performance was surprising, and there is nothing but praise for everybody concerned.[118]

The *Irish Independent* praised the play, which it said "displays a whimsical imagination" and which was "clever and entertaining." The review then summarised the plot:

> It is local in its action, dealing with the Dublin Corporation and Mayoralty, and if, in addition to the amusement to be derived from the play, a deeper aim is sought, it will be carried out in the name of the party machine. The author begins by making a Jew Lord Mayor of Dublin, and the Jew starts off by being a bit farcical, but he improves with acquaintance, and his part develops into pretty good comedy, which was very much enjoyed. The Jewish Lord Mayor associates himself with the "Extremists," hangs a picture of Robert Emmet in the Mansion House, and commits to memory Emmet's speech from the dock in order to deliver it at the Mayoral banquet. He is pressed on the one hand by party intriguers using various popular cries, and on the other by the offer of a title, to follow different courses, but resists all influences and shows a strength of mind which the audience might not be inclined to suspect on its first experience of him.
>
> In the three earlier acts, the scenes of which are laid in the Mansion House, the Lord Mayor is busy in the combat against inducements and blandishments, and in the fourth act, representing a meeting of the Dublin Corporation, his victory over trickery is complete, though it might be remarked that the finale is a little beyond what might be expected from even the most extravagant humorous critic.[119]

The *Irish Times* was full of praise, and The *Evening Herald* stated that "the dialogue is brisk and amusing, the dramatic situations are arranged with an experienced hand . . . . for a first night there was a wonderful sense of completeness and finish."[120]

MacDonagh's play remains unpublished, and we have come across no copy of the manuscript, so it is impossible to say if the piece, like *The Eloquent Dempsy* and *The Lord Mayor*, has lost most of its vitality. However, MacDonagh was an interesting writer who as both actor and director had learned much about stagecraft, and his play remained popular enough to be revived for several seasons.

• • •

In their pamphlet, *The Dublin Drama League, 1919–1941*, Brenna Katz Clarke and Harold Ferrar list but two programs for the Drama League in 1921, in November and in December. Despite the Troubles, however, the Drama League managed to mount four programs. The first was on 23 February, when the league presented H. Wiers Jennsen's four-act play *The Witch* in a translation by John Masefield. As the *Times* reported:

> The Dublin Drama League did a good thing last evening, when its company presented at the Abbey Theatre a Scandinavian drama, *The Witch*, in which its author, H. Wiers-Jennsen, depicts a strange mixture of religion, human passion, and Godless love for the edification of its disciples. The action is supposed to take place in Bergen in 1874, in the house of the Palace Chaplain. The play was produced by Miss Elizabeth Young, who played the title role of Anne with her accustomed ability and power. . . .[121]

The League's second production was on 29 June when it mounted at the Abbey the double bill of Nikolai Evreinov's *A Merry Death* and Anatole France's *The Man Who Married a Dumb Wife*. The *Times* reported:

> The silence of the Abbey Theatre was interrupted last night, when the Drama League staged two plays—a harlequinade in one act, *A Merry Death*, by Nicholas Evreinov, and a comedy by Anatole France, *The Man Who Married a Dumb Wife*. The dual offering was well received, but in the applause given to the Russian play there was a big element of charity. The audience was reminded "that the work of Evreinov, though cynical, has an air of gaiety and light-heartedness that are missing in Tchekof and Andreyev." The performance disputed the statement. Evreinov intended Harlequin to live his last fleeting hours gaily, and to meet death with a heart still light. Mr. Sydney La Velle's intention may also have been good, but he was too uncertain of his work to maintain the spirit of the *role*. Mr. Michael J. Dolan had a great responsibility as Pierrot. His performance saved the author's cynicism from being misunderstood, and he kept the play alive. Miss Aida Browne was an effective Columbine, and Mr. T. Quinn personified Death.[122]

The *Evening Herald* added that:

> The transmission of [C. E.] Bechhofer's translation from the stage to the audience was very often in relays—from prompter to player and thence to us. It was a rather tedious and irritating process.[123]

After a long interval without music, the second piece came on, and the *Times* reported:

The comedy of *The Man Who Married a Dumb Wife* has for its theme the subject of an old mediaeval ballad. A judge bewails his existence with a wife who cannot talk. An advocate secures the remedial services of a notable doctor, who loosens the tongue to the wife. This irretrievable blunder unhinges the mind of the whole household. The production of this comedy was a happy contrast to the other. Mr. F. J. M'Cormick's playing of the judge was of first importance, for every word and gesture as he gave them was full of meaning. Miss Christine Hayden as the wife appeared, while dumb, to have all the attributes which induce craziness in men, and when she talked an auditor remarked, "If this play is ever produced in Dublin again I'll buy my wife a seat in the stalls."[124]

On 13 and 14 November, the Drama League presented a triple bill at the Abbey, consisting of Strindberg's *The Stronger*, Henry James's *The Saloon*, and Emile Mazaud's *A Perfect Day*. As the *Irish Times* reported:

The three plays were a very good choice on account of their variety. In *The Stronger* we had a good example of the greatest writer of the problem play—probably greater than Ibsen. It was a very difficult play to act, because only one of the characters—Madame X—speaks, and Mademoiselle Y, the cynical, unmarried actress has a very difficult task in making the audience see her point of view. Up to a certain point Miss Dorothy Casey did this very well, but as the play developed she did not vary sufficiently her expression and thus tended to sink into insignificance. Miss Elizabeth Young brought out well the dramatic point when she realises that Madame Y is her hated rival for the affections of her husband, but her diction tended to become a trifle monotonous and unreal. She is more suited to classical than to modern, naturalistic parts. The setting of the play suggested more a cottage parlour than a cafe.

. . . We can realise that Henry James never was a great success when writing for the stage, for such an effort is required if we wish to follow his tortuous masses of thought, that inevitable weariness seizes us. The actors in *The Saloon* seemed perpetually on the *qui vive* lest they might miss the real point of the glittering phrases. At first the dialogue with its repartees went rather slowly and dully, but Mr. Brereton Barry enlivened it. He dominated all the other players even too completely—he produced the effect of a Gulliver in Lilliput. He is always at his best in passionate, declamatory passages and last night he was specially good. . . .

. . . The Drama League must be congratulated for the excellent way this charming *Vieux Colombier* play [*A Perfect Day*] was produced. . . . The actors did not set themselves out to copy the Parisian style of comedy acting with its piquancy—they made it into a real Abbey Theatre play. Instead of the *Argot Parisien* we got the rich brogue, even though in Mr. Peter Nolan's case it was a trifle exaggerated.[125]

On 11 and 12 December, the Drama League presented Harold Chapin's four-act comedy, *The Marriage of Columbine*, and the *Times* briefly noted:

Many quaint characters are introduced into the piece, including a clown, a circus rider, a local newspaper owner and journalist—and Columbine. In the latter part Miss Eileen Crowe acts with much grace and confidence, while P. J. Carolan as Scaramouche, the clown, is equally effective, and all the other parts are well filled.[126]

Among other notable amateur offerings in Dublin was the production on 24 and 25 June of *As You Like It* by the Dublin Branch of the British Empire

Shakespeare Society. The outdoor performance in Lord Iveagh's gardens featured Elizabeth Young as Rosalind and Sir Valentine Grace as the wrestler.

There were also some semiprofessional productions at the Abbey during the summer. Most notably, Mary Sheridan's Company and Madame Kirkwood-Hackett's Company mounted such plays as *General John Regan*, *Eleanor's Enterprise*, and *You Never Can Tell*. In the casts were such experienced players as Elizabeth Young, Margot Brunton, Ralph Brereton Barry, Paul O'Farrell, Harry O'Donovan, Jimmy O'Dea, May Craig, Maurice Esmonde, and Sir Valentine Grace.

On 4 August, an outdoor performance was given of an original piece in Glendalough. As the *Irish Times* reported:

> Something like an old mystery play, and the country folk acting? Incredible! Nevertheless true, and the last scene was actually in dialect.
>
> If you had wandered down to Glendalough last week, you would have seen, not far from the ruins of the churches, a play called *The Joy of St. Anne* in full progress, on the rustic terrace of the Lake hotel, the host himself, Mr. J. Richardson, taking the mountain shepherd in real Arab clothing (costly clothing at that, lent for the occasion), and his sister, Peggy, in the dignified *role* of Hannah.
>
> A wide-awake photographer was on the spot. It is to be hoped that he secured some record of what is surely a sign of returning joy and spontaneous expression among the people of this wonderful country. Even the sheep-dog had his part, and came on in the last scene with his master, "as to the manner born."
>
> Picture a green arbour of rowan (quicken) trees, already in crimson berry, draped with sundry curtains (blue, gold, and green), properly rigged-up between uprights (new-cut fir-stems), and well hung for drawing. The small audience was typical of all ranks and interests; it showed a breathless attention to the proceedings. Old Siberian and French melodies were supplied by the kindness of Miss O'Duffey with her fine Cremona violin. There was also singing. The play in four scenes, was written and staged by Miss A. M. Buckton, whose (non-party) work in this line is well-known.[127]

• • •

Not until the first week in November was a new play performed in Belfast. On 2 November, a three-act comedy about County Down fishing life, *Loaves and Fishes* by Charles K. Ayre, was produced for the first time at the Grand Opera House by the Ulster Theatre. The *Northern Whig* summarized the plot:

> Two of the principal characters are Charlie Curran, a young fish "cadger" and small farmer, and James Sloan, the local baker. They are rivals for the hand of Nelly Doran, the daughter of a schoolmaster, who has a passion for mathematics, and literally exists by mathematical calculation. In order to decide which of the two aspirants shall become his son-in-law Mr. Doran arranges that whichever of the two most successfully applies mathematics to his business shall attain his heart's desire. The baker resorts to the deception of making cylindrical loaves, which, appear to

the simple villagers to be considerably larger than the former block loaf, while the "cadger" daily inserts a five pound note in one of the herrings he hawks. The consequence is that while half the village is lined up in a queue outside Sloan's bakery, the other half is fighting for herrings at Curran's fish cart, with the result that the local police have a busy time. Mr. Doran eventually decides that the baker is entitled to the prize because he had employed legitimate algebra in improving his business, whereas the fisherman had done so by means of a bogus miracle. A fitting climax comes when the daughter reminds her father that there is one mathematical problem he has left out of consideration—viz., that ninety-nine daughters out of every hundred chose their own husbands, and she promptly throws herself into the arms of Curran.[128]

The *Northern Whig* also noted that, although the audience liked the play, "the humour is of the broad and vulgar type, and if the situations are not always relevant to the plot they serve their purpose."[129] The *Belfast News Letter*, which thought that it was about time for the Ulster Theatre to produce a few new plays, admired the "vivid dialogue written in idiomatic language and richly seasoned with native wit and humour."[130] The *Irish News* agreed that the play's success stemmed largely from the dialogue, which was "particularly good and always amusing."[131] *The Irish News* did not think that the plot was "extraordinarily deep," but admired the acting, particularly of the author as Charlie Curran: "his confident bearing and rollicking style gave to the role a rich and attractive basis. One would imagine it possible of Mr. Ayre to carry the play through successfully on his own shoulders."[132]

Excellent acting was also the order of the day some three weeks later when Charles Doran's company appeared at the Grand Opera House in *The Taming of the Shrew*. In this production "Mr. Ralph Richardson, as a pedant, and Mr. Hilton Edwards, as the stuttering tailor, ably performed their parts."[133]

If Belfast only managed to see one new play performed in 1921, Cork city saw no new productions. In part, the political troubles forced both the Leeside and the Munster Players to remain idle. As J. O'Flynn (Maurice Lee) said in a July letter to Holloway, "Theatres in Cork are closed and have been for some months past and both Leeside and Munster players are resting."[134] When the Cork Opera House finally reopened during the first week of August, the *Cork Constitution* wrote:

That the Opera House was reopened was to Cork people a very real gratification, and made possible by a Cork man [William Macready], who, in coming to his native city with his company, showed the same pluck that has won for him in wider fields the great successes that he has achieved. Patrons of the Opera House are, to put it mildly, tired of picture shows, and while this class of entertainment was on, the opera-goers always felt a great want. Times then got so bad that even pictures failed to amuse or interest, and eight weeks ago, owing to the awful times in which people lived, the theatre closed down, finding it absolutely impossible to continue. The coming of the great truce three weeks ago brought good tidings with it; at any rate shootings ceased, and this, we need hardly say, made everyone, well, almost happy. Since then great changes have taken place amongst them. All places of amusement

> have opened, and Cork people are heartily glad that amongst the first of these is the Cork Opera House.[135]

William Macready and his company played at the Opera House throughout August and for three weeks in September. Although the year was 1921, Macready was an old and old-fashioned actor, and his plays were theatrical, lowbrow, nineteenth-century fare, such as *Trilby*, *The Manxman*, and *The Christian*. By December of 1921, however, Brinsley MacNamara could report:

> The Cork Operatic Society are becoming a regular feature at the Opera House. They gave a splendid presentation of *The Mikado* not long ago and we are soon to see them in *The Pirates of Penzance*. *The Whiteheaded Boy* too by my old friends the Leeside Players was a genuine treat. I am very glad to say that they were patronized as we were never patronized in the old days. "House full" was the order for the week. They have some very good new hands but of course the old boys and girls were the mainstay of the show. McCabe's "Gentleman from the Department" . . . (You remember *Miah*) suited him very well in the name part while Miss Egar made a very clever study of the aunt. Tim O'Connell of course is a past master in parts like "Dempsey." Indeed, Tim is fast becoming the idol of Cork audiences. Between his comedy parts in Gilbert-Sullivan opera and his playing with the Leesiders he has earned for himself a reputation seldom secured by amateurs. That reminds me. Last time he was speaking to me he said the Leeside were somewhat "tied up" for plays. He finds it hard to judge from rehearsals how plays will go before an audience, and of course playing only a week now and again he cannot afford to take any risks. He was asking me if I knew of any suitable plays.[136]

Unfortunately, however, the Leeside players' performance of *The Whiteheaded Boy* and of J. B. MacCarthy's *Wrecked* during the first week in December were the only plays they performed in 1921.

• • •

Because of the Troubles, and with the Abbey closed for so much of the year, many of the best Irish players were forced to seek work elsewhere. Indeed, in 1921 it seemed as if there were almost as many Irish players working outside of Ireland as in it.

J. B. Fagan's London production of *The Whiteheaded Boy* was still running for much of the year and employing such actors as Sara Allgood, Maire O'Neill, Arthur Sinclair, Peter Nolan, Arthur Shields, Fred O'Donovan, Breffni O'Rourke, and Fred Jeffs. Then in September the Irish Players opened *The Whiteheaded Boy* in New York with not only such Abbey alumni as Sinclair, O'Neill, Morgan, J. A. O'Rourke and Harry Hutchinson in the cast, but also with such recent recruits from the Abbey as Maureen Delany, Shields, Gertrude Murphy, and Christine Hayden.

Incidentally, in New York the play was described by Alexander Woolcott in the *Times* as "a thoroughly diverting comedy," and Sinclair was mentioned as playing his part of John Duffy "with infinite relish." However, Maire O'Neill as Aunt Ellen must have been extraordinarily broad, and Woolcott wrote:

> She . . . manages to be as comic as you could ask at times, but she does it by clowning away in flagrant fashion, grimacing and choking in a fashion for which the author, no doubt, would gladly slay her. It is a kind of farce work not often attempted here nowadays except in vaudeville.[137]

Not every player was entirely happy with the prospect of working in America. For instance, Joseph Power wrote:

> Miss Maureen Delany had an almost tart little chat with me, and gave her latest photo the other day. She is not in entirely good form at the idea of going to America, but kept good-humouredly reasoning out with herself why she should be. "Of course it's a big thing," she said. "Ah, well! Of course I am pleased with it, really; and I know that it's a big chance, and one to jump at for some reasons. And so I do; oh yes, really I do. But it's hard to leave Dublin. You know we're like a happy family here in the Abbey—I'll never, never be so happy anywhere again. We all knew one another, and got on wonderfully together.
>
> Then there's Mr. Robinson. Now that I'm going, I'd just like to tell you how we feel about him. He has been awfully good to us—nothing but kindness, and doing his utmost for us. In a way, all I can say to describe it is that as a manager here he acted as a perfect man and a perfect gentleman towards us. And that was another of the things that helped to make us so happy here in the Abbey. . . .
>
> But what about the tour? Now, really, I can't tell you—I'm all mixed up. Of course, I've only signed on a year. It will be a tremendous experience, London nothing to it. London? Oh, I've little to say about that. Somehow, we had not much in the way of experiences, just night after night of enthusiastic audiences, (most of them Irish), and always sure of a good reception. But yes, America is more of an adventure.[138]

Another Abbey actor who was glum about leaving the theater was F. J. McCormick, who signed a contract to tour with Kathleen Drago in *Paddy the Next Best Thing*. Since McCormick was to develop into such a major Irish actor, he is worth quoting at some length. On 9 November, he wrote to Holloway:

> Of course, since I came away from Dublin, after playing the Gaiety, I have been sort of keeping an idea of going back to the Abbey. All the time I never seemed to say to myself that I was going to finish their tour with *Paddy*. I was, as it were, going on from week to week, keeping the desire for the Abbey at arm's length, and half-conscious that I would be going back there soon—away from the artistic aridity of the show. Everything reminded me, by *sad contrast*, of the old place. . . . But now a sort of resentment has "got" me. I "feel" as if I weren't wanted back—that somehow or other Lady G. would not be in favour of giving me a contract if I asked for it. . . . I feel that there are too many good new people to choose from and that I'm not wanted to fill any of my old parts—when there are so many willing "neophytes." Perhaps I'm wrong—for in spite of the fact that I don't think it wise to give up 8 pounds a week while I'm in debt—yet—I do long, in an idealistic manner,

for the satisfying work of the Abbey again. Did Robinson go back and if not who is managing the place? Mick Dolan I suppose. If Robinson were back again I'd write to him as he told me to go back whenever I wished—as it was on his suggestion I came on this tour.[139]

McCormick did wire Robinson but received this disheartening reply:

My Dear Judge,
Your wire has just come and been phoned out to me from Dublin, for I am taking a day off. Much against my personal desires I think I am right to tell you to sign on for the further tour. Things are still very uncertain here, we may have war again though I don't think that is very likely, but anyhow we are only just managing to pay our way, make a little one week and lose a little the next. This means we can't pledge ourselves for the future and we are not giving anyone contracts—and even if we stretched a point in your favour and did offer you a contract I am sure we could not offer you enough money to make you accept it. So I think you had better stick to the fleshpots for a little longer. I am sorry for of course I miss you very much.[140]

About Robinson's letter, McCormick wrote to Holloway:

. . . well—had Robinson offered me 3.15.0 pounds . . . I would, I think, have gone back and taken it even without a contract. You see, Mr. Holloway, *so many* things contributed to bring about my great desire to go back again. Abbeyistis! (the microbe of the place is well in my blood)—Love for the theatre and the work with its variety and appeal—being at home with my people—being in dear old dirty—as well as a great girl pal of mine!—not exactly love but something akin to it—the being in the atmosphere of things artistic—the desire to be near my people if there was more "trouble" and so on and so on. . . . Another thing, there was, as I now believe—a certain vanity of being thought well of amongst Abbeyites—you know what I mean—the very human weakness of wanting to be where you are doing something worthwhile and getting recognition of your efforts.[141]

Into Holloway's receptive ear, McCormick poured much of his feelings about acting:

Everyone likes encouragement and your encouragement was always *stimulating* and had the supreme merit of coming from a *lover* of acting and from one who was *sincere*. . . . Being "on the Abbey" is only of value when something *worthy* is *done while on*! Oh! but you know the distinction I mean. Lord! it sickens me to think of those who plume themselves over the accident of being "on the Abbey" in the same foolish way as silly young noblemen plume themselves on being born to a dukedom. If all actors in the Abbey would only think of *the* standard—the standard of what *should* be—the standard of the *highest* art in acting—how much conceit of being "on the Abbey" it would do away with. If actors were conscious of the high criterion of what *should* be—there would be far less of the self-satisfaction which kills effort and far more of the active spirit—whose motto is "Better still and still better." . . . the Abbey . . . somehow seems to cling to the stupid notion that Art and Business are incompatible. For instance—those artistically austere posters which manage to get stuck up in places where no one can see them. I often think that the Abbey Bills (the majority of them) serve no purpose whatever—artistic or com-

> mercial—for they are generally put up where their advertising value is nil and where the people who read them are blind to artistic austerity and "simplicity." . . .
> I wonder will I ever play again in the old place? I wonder? I can hardly realize yet that I'm going to miss *so* much rather being cut off by circumstances and other things. The old place *does* dig deep into one's heart—it gets into the blood.[142]

Sara Allgood worked most of the year in and out of London. She was in *The Whiteheaded Boy* company, and we have seen how she organized two charity matinees for the Abbey. She also had plans to start a small Irish company based permanently at the Everyman Theatre in Hampstead. There was occasionally talk of her returning to play at the Abbey, but, unlike McCormick, Sara was unlikely to return for much reduction of salary. And finally, as Lady Gregory noted on 18 December:

> Sara Allgood can't come to the Abbey, has engaged herself to Everyman. Says it is because of the long delay in signing her contract, she can't wait. But she might have written to me. It is a blow.[143]

However, there were other actors who wanted to return. In her journal for 12 October, Lady Gregory had noted that J. M. Kerrigan had written her from New York, "saying he would like to come back and do work in and for Ireland."[144] And also from New York, Dudley Digges, who was playing in the revival of *John Ferguson* for the Theatre Guild, had written on 14 August to Holloway:

> On the proper outcome of the present political negotiations, which we in this country are following so eagerly, depends new events in the lives of many a Dubliner wandering the world. If peace and justice, and understanding replace the bloody business of war then what a glorious resurrection for our country, and our city, and how many thousands will flock back to the old place. I will be amongst the number, I am sure, for in the immediate growth of metropolitan life there will surely be a return to the glorious days of the theatre in Dublin; not that I mean that I could bring such glory into the theatre, but Dublin will resume its old position of a great theatrical centre, and there will be room and welcome, I hope, for her actors who have found success in other hands. I am sure that such thoughts must be in the minds of many an artist, many a musician, many a singer, and even many a businessman, as he watches from afar the proceedings going on between the two countries, and I know of one actor who hopes to yet do his best work in his native city.[145]

It is curious how often in 1921 the artists struck such a note of hope for the future. But Ireland was still too turbulent to offer haven for her theatrical wild geese.

Still, one glimmering of that hope was Sean O'Casey's early play, *The Crimson in the Tri-Colour*, which the Abbey rejected during the year. For Lady Gregory the piece was too controversial for the times; as she noted in her journal on 5 November: "I read and wrote a long note on an interesting play *The Crimson and [sic] the Tri-Colour*, the antagonism sure to break out between Labour and Sinn Fein and sent it to Robinson."[146] On 10 November, Lady Gregory wrote in her journal:

> Then Casey, the author of *The Crimson and the Tri-Colour*, came in, and I had a talk with him about his play, and when I said we could not in any case put it on now, as it might weaken the Sinn Fein position to show that Labour is ready to attack it, he said, "If that is so I would be the last to wish to put it on." And he is a strong Labour man, and is collecting names to sign a message to Larkin in Sing-Sing.[147]

Although no copy of the play has come to light, Lady Gregory's report on it read:

> *The Crimson and the Tri-Colour*—(a very good name)
>
> This is a puzzling play—extremely interesting—Mrs. Budrose is a jewel and her husband a good setting for her—I don't see any plot in it, unless the Labour unrest culminating in the turning off of the lights at the meeting may be considered one. It is the expression of ideas that makes it interesting (besides feeling that the writer has something in him) and no doubt the point of interest for Dublin audiences. But we could not put it on while the Revolution is still unaccomplished—it might hasten the Labour attacks on Sinn Fein, which ought to be kept back till the fight with England is over, and the new Government has had time to show what it can do.
>
> I think Eileen's rather disagreeable flirtation with O'Regan shd. be cut—their first entrance—or rather exit (or both) seems to be leading to something that doesn't come. In Act II a good deal of O'Regan and Nora shd. be cut.
>
> In Act III almost all the O'Malley and Eileen part shd. be cut. The end is I think good, the entrance of the Workmen, and Fagan and Tim Tracy.
>
> I feel that there is no personal interest worth developing, but that with as much as possible of those barren parts cut, we might find a possible play of ideas in it.
>
> I suggest that (with the author's leave) it shd. be worth typing the play at the theatre's expense—with or without those parts—For it is impossible to go through it again—or show it—or have a reading of it—while in handwriting.[148]

Three years later, in March of 1924, after the success of *Juno and the Paycock*, Lady Gregory spoke with O'Casey about *The Crimson in the Tri-Colour*, and said, "I was inclined to put it on because some of it was very good and I thought you might learn by seeing it on the stage, though some was very poor, but Mr. Yeats was very firm." O'Casey then remarked, "You were right not to put it on. I can't read it myself now. But I will tell you that was a bitter disappointment for I not only thought at the time it was the best thing I had written, but I thought that no one in the world had ever written anything so fine."[149]

• • •

Among the miscellaneous happenings of the year, Arthur Shields married in London early in April; Rosa Mulholland, Lady Gilbert, the prolific writer of popular fiction who had once written a play performed by the Theatre of Ireland, died in Blackrock on 21 April; and Barney Armstrong, the director of the Empire and the lessee of other theaters in Belfast, Derry, Galway, Kilkenny, and Edinburgh, died on 29 September.

In February, the rather silly trial of Lord Dunsany in the Kilmainham courthouse created a big stir. Dunsany was charged under the restoration of order in Ireland regulations with keeping firearms and ammunition not under effective military control at his residence, Dunsany Castle, County Meath. As well as being one of the country's more prolific and produced playwrights, Dunsany had served as captain of the reserve Royal Inniskilling Fusiliers and had been a lieutenant in the Coldstream Guards. Although he pleaded guilty, his counsel described the offence as a technical one and said that, in spite of the act of Parliament conferring a form of Home Rule on Ireland, Dunsany remained a Unionist. Like his father and uncle before him, Dunsany was also a keen sportsman and noted shot, but much of the ammunition found was old, antiquated stuff that had belonged to his father and uncle. Dunsany's counsel also mentioned that his client had served in His Majesty's army against the rebels of 1916 and on one occasion had narrowly escaped with his life.

> In conclusion, said counsel, as far as Sinn Feiners are concerned they had punished him enough, because they have put a bullet in his face that had to be extracted in an operation; and it is hardly fair that he should be punished by both sides.[150]

In the course of the case, Dunsany himself testified about his politics:

> . . . he had been a royalist always, and had worked for the cause of royalism with all his brain so far as he was capable, and also in action, though his experiences in the latter capacity were brief, as he was wounded and taken prisoner. He had been in action against Sinn Fein, and had worked for the cause that the Irish landlords represented. His castle was one of the castles of the Pale, and had stood to maintain the crown, and no one ever lived in it who was not loyal.[151]

On 30 May, Dunsany's play, *If*, opened at the Ambassadors' Theatre in London. There was nothing Irish about the piece, but despite a strong English cast that included Henry Ainley, Gladys Cooper, and Leslie Banks, the reception of the piece was decidedly mixed, and it did not run long.

As a sad and ironic coda to 1921, we must mention that at the time the Abbey was struggling to keep its doors open Miss Horniman, the Abbey's original benefactor, was forced to sell the Gaiety Theatre in Manchester. This was, as the *Manchester Guardian* said,

> the suspension of an enterprise notable in the modern history of the British theatre. One prefers to think of it as merely a suspension, though there is danger of a complete collapse, and no doubt this danger was present to the minds of a large number of Miss Horniman's friends who had gathered to see the last performance at the theatre, for the occasion was strongly tinged with melancholy. To more than one mind the analogy of a funeral occurred. Indeed, this sombre comparison rather oppressed Miss Horniman herself when she came to say good-bye from the stage to

> her friends in the front of the house. But she wrestled with it, and dismissed it finally with a characteristic jest. "It is a funeral," she said, "in which the protagonist—the corpse—is expected to get on its hind legs and speak."[152]

Some months earlier, in November of 1920, Miss Horniman had written Holloway that she would have to sell the Gaiety: "it is a pity—but good work has been done and nothing can undo that."[153] In an interview then with the *Guardian*, she elaborated:

> I am obliged to sell the Gaiety. It has been run of late years as a lodging-house theatre with what should have been great pecuniary success, but owing to part losses and financial difficulties arising out of the war my overdraft has become such that I have no device before me except to sell the Gaiety. . . . If anyone wishes to run the theatre or a theatre of which Manchester may boast he should find people to do it with enthusiasm, devotion and common sense. Any help I can give in my way to those who would be willing and able to carry on the torch is at the disposal of my successor. I have not thrown up the sponge. It has been snatched out of my hands by a financial difficulty. . . . It would be a pity if the reputation of the Gaiety should be allowed to die out and become a legend referred to in newspaper articles on theatrical matters. Good work has been done here in the past and nothing can undo that. If good work can be done here in the future it will be to the gain of the intelligent people to whom the drama is something better than highly decorated rubbish or even the delights of the movies.[154]

Miss Horniman went down with her colors flying.

2
1922

On 7 January, the Anglo-Irish Treaty was ratified by Dail Éireann. On 9 January, de Valera resigned as president of the Dail. On 10 January, Michael Collins nominated Arthur Griffith as president, and de Valera and his followers walked out.

The stage was set for a bloody civil war.

On 29 January, Lady Gregory wrote to John Quinn in America:

> As to Ireland, we have ups and downs. Robinson had sent me a telegram telling of the ratification of the Treaty after those wearisome debates, and it was brought here on the Sunday morning by a tiny little boy on a bicycle who called out, "This is the first message I was ever sent, and I brought the best message ever was brought!" He had shouted it along the roads and the people cheered, and he was so excited when he got inside the gates that he fell off his bicycle. There was as far as I can judge universal delight and satisfaction. Then after a day or two came de Valera's manifesto. I think this has led in this neighbourhood to resentment against him, but the papers tell of division in the south, and one must be anxious until after the elections, whenever they may take place. . . . . One must respect de Valera, his honesty and idealism, but—"He follows on forever when all your chase is done / He follows after shadows—the King of Ireland's son."
>
> . . . Dublin was full of excitements every day. One evening as I came to the Theatre the streets were crowded, all looking at some passing lorries. I asked what was going on. "It's the Tans going." And indeed they will leave a black name for ever—but the crowd behaved very well, didn't cheer or boo, just kept up a sort of burr of delight! . . . The Abbey has turned the corner also, and is getting good audiences, many of them returned prisoners.[1]

Nevertheless, turbulent and terrible times were ahead. January saw lots of hold-ups and bank robberies; and on 3 March Joanna Redmond's husband was killed in Stephen's Green while grappling with a bank robber. In February there were rail strikes and killings in Belfast. In fact, between 11 and 16 February, thirty-six people were shot dead in Belfast, and over one hundred were wounded. Irishmen became used to newspaper headlines like:

Belfast Like Raging Inferno—the *Evening Herald*, 6 March.
Conditions Growing Worse in Belfast / Seven Killed During Bloody Week-end—the *Evening Telegraph*, 13 March.
Sensational Shootings in Galway—ibid., 16 March.
More Bombs in Belfast To-Day—ibid., 22 March.

Appalling Tragedy in Athlone Last Night—ibid., 25 April.
Battle in Streets of Mullingar To-Day—ibid., 27 April.
Two Killed in Fight in Tyrone To-Day—ibid., 8 May.
Armed Men Hold Up Train Outside Dublin—ibid., 11 May.

On 15 May, Joseph Holloway, who lived on Northumberland Road near the Canal, wrote:

> During the night I heard a few shots from very near range, and was surprised to see on going down in the morning a big splintered yellowish-white patch of some eight by three inches on back of the door, and splinters all about the hall floor, and up the stairs nearly to the first landing, and as far as the stairs to the landing leading to the basement. A bullet lay on floor near hall archway, and one of the pictures (Willmore's Autumn)[2] on right hand partition wall in the hall was splintered and the paper and plaster [word illegible], and an indentation of some half inch was in the side of the frame of one of Jack B. Yeats' pictures. Strange all glass escaped. I gathered up the splinters and bullet and put them in a bit of paper to preserve them. It is more dangerous to be living so near to the Bush now than during 1916 and the reign of the Black and Tans.[3]

The *Evening Herald* of 21 May described shootings in Dublin, Belfast, Athlone, Roscommon, Dundrum, Kilkenny, and on the Louth-Armagh border. On 5 June, Yeats wrote to John Quinn about trouble in the West:

> There is great disorder, as the newspapers will have told you, and even a little of it reaches us, and reaches Coole, but so far nothing serious. There was what seemed a raid at Coole; men came and shouted at night and demanded to be let in, and then went away either because the moon came out or because they only meant to threaten. This last was seemingly the explanation. Two men who were being prosecuted for theft thought if they created alarm the case might be withdrawn. Lady Gregory asked me to come and stay there as her gamekeeper who was staying in the house for its protection, was terrified. I went, but I got the Free State garrison at Gort to send two young soldiers, very nice simple country lads, to sleep in the house for the first two or three days, and after that to patrol the woods. We are hoping for better order since the pact but in this locality it has not come. Lands have been seized at Lough Cutra and 50 state troopers are there now to protect it.[4]

And on 13 June, the *Evening Herald* carried this story about Darrell Figgis, the politician, novelist, journalist, and one-time playwright:

> Mr. Darrell Figgis, Independent candidate for Co. Dublin, was the victim of a serious outrage last night.
>
> He was attacked in his home by three men, who declared that they had instructions to mutilate him by cutting off his beard, and proceeded to carry out their threat.
>
> A representative of the *Evening Herald* was informed by Mr. Figgis that at 11.40 three men knocked at the door of Mr. Figgis's flat, and it was opened by Mrs. Figgis. The three men rushed past her and demanded to see Mr. Figgis, who came out from his study, and pushed him into the sitting-room. Mrs. Figgis, fearing that they intended to shoot him, pushed into the room and attempted to lock the door.

The three men at once wrestled with her and endeavoured to wrench the key from her, but without success.

They flung her away from the door and then took hold of Mr. Figgis and stated that they were under order, to mutilate him by removing his beard. They were each equipped with scissors for that purpose. Mr. Figgis asked them not to be guilty of acts that would be disgraceful to Ireland, and Mrs. Figgis asked them if they were aware that during the war she had nursed and provided for wounded men.

One of the men said they knew all this well, and they did not like the job that had been committed to them. Mr. Figgis then asked under whose orders they were acting. One of the men who appeared to act as spokesman stated that they were acting under army orders, but refused to say from where they had been received.

Mr. Figgis asked them if they realised what disgrace would be thrown on Ireland's name when this news got abroad. Upon this the three men drew aside into a corner of the room and had a consultation.

They seemed, Mr. Figgis said, to be labouring under stress of great emotion, and the youngest of the three was in tears.

They returned, and stated that they would have to carry out their orders or it would be the worse for them. They then pulled Mrs. Figgis away from her husband and seized Mr. Figgis and placed him in a chair.

One of the men held back his head, another seized his arms, while the third proceeded to cut his beard and moustache.

Resistance on his part was useless, and when Mr. Figgis made an effort to throw the men off they said if he did not at once cease they would cut away his hair as well. In fact, one of them made an attempt to do so, when Mrs. Figgis again intervened. The three men then rushed out of the room, ran downstairs and out of the house. . . . Mrs. Figgis is suffering severely from shock.[5]

On 17 June, polling day, the *Herald* printed a photograph of Figgis outside the polling booth, and he clearly had quite a bit of beard and moustache left. He also was returned to the Dail and, indeed, easily topped the poll with more than 15,000 votes.

On 14 June, bombs with time fuses were planted in two Belfast cinemas, and, although the spectators were safely evacuated, "The bombs exploded when the spectators had left, and the buildings, the Clonard and the Diamond, were gutted by fire."[6]

At the end of the month came the siege of the Four Courts. On 28 June, the *Evening Herald* reported:

At daybreak this morning an attack was launched by forces acting under G. H. Q., I. R. A., Beggar's Bush Barracks, on the Four Courts.

For some hours previously there had been great activity in the city on the part of the Dail forces, who were evidently concentrating on their objective. The streets were being patrolled, and all pedestrians held up and searched. A few desultory shots were heard.

At 4.10 o'clock a heavy outburst of firing and loud explosions, followed by a number of rifle shots in quick succession, proclaimed the opening of the siege. . . .

Simultaneous Attack

Simultaneously with the attack on the Four Courts rifle and machine-gun fire was directed against the Fowler Hall in Parnell square, which for many weeks has been occupied by forces acting under headquarters at the Four Courts.[7]

On 30 June, the headline in the *Herald* was "Tremendous Explosion—Four Courts in Flames." Most of the cinemas and theaters were closed, although at the De Luxe in Camden Street one could have seen May Murray as Cleo, the Parisian Dancer in *Peacock Alley*, or at the Princess in Rathmines, Will Rogers in *Cupid the Cowpuncher*. On 1 July, when the front page headline of the *Herald* was "Land Mine Exploded in Talbot Street," the "Music and Drama" column of the paper noted:

> The O'Mara Opera Company were unfortunate in having their engagement dated for this week at the Gaiety Theatre. Performances were given as usual up to Wednesday evening, the closing performance actually taking place to the accompaniment of rifle, machine-gun, and artillery fire. Everybody was, of course, anxious to get home as quickly as possible after the show, but it is a tribute to both performers and audience that everything was carried on as usual till the fall of the curtain. The Gaiety was the last theatre to close, as it was in a more sheltered position than any of the other houses in the central district.
>
> La Scala opened as usual on Wednesday afternoon, but an attack on a tender conveying members of the National Forces created such panic in the vicinity that the management decided to close after the first showing of the programme. Snipers were very active in the locality during the afternoon, which made it unwise for people to venture down O'Connell Street.[8]

The O'Mara Opera Company had planned during its engagement to give the first performances of G. Molyneux Palmer's opera, *Sruth na Maoile*, but, as a result of the fighting, the premiere was postponed.

Some of the tension of these days was captured by Holloway:

> 28 June. From early morning bombing, machine guns, rifle shots, and all sorts of war alarms rang out, and continued into the working day. . . . I am sure that the Irish race will never be cowed by amateur Cromwells (like Collins of the lying tongue); or Griffith (of the swelled head). I . . . found in the streets little knots of people eagerly talking on every side, and in O'Connell Street several lorry loads of armed soldiers in Green with armoured cars and all sorts of guns passed down the street. . . .
>
> 29 June. After Mass I went on to Eileen's. Crowds were about the streets and eagerly reading notices pasted up on pillar and post. Eileen told me of all the excitement of yesterday, and the terrific shooting that took place just before the burning of Fowler's Hall, and of the crowds of people who were about when the Fire Brigade came on the scene. I saw Johnson, the labour "spouter," colloguing with another man in Eason's porch. While in Eileen's heavy firing cleared the streets for quite awhile. I waited till it had died down and hastened to the Pillar for a tram. . . . All business was suspended at an early hour in the city, and the trains were stopped, and West-British soldiers in Green held up and searched the passengers in trams in and out of town. Lawrence and Fay were searched; the latter told me in a gentlemanly way, whatever way that may be. . . .
>
> 30 June. I just went to Mass and remained in all the rest of the day. Heard a terrific explosion at about 12.30. It shook the city. Afterwards learned by the *Evening Mail* that it was fired from a 60 pounder gun which was brought into action this morning. It shook buildings to their foundations, and plate glass windows were

shattered and chimney pots and slates fell. Prior to it the Four Courts was seen to be on fire in one place. The shell caused a lot of damage in the vicinity of the Four Courts. The gun was again fired at a quarter past two. At 3.30 P.M. an order to cease fire was given to all the troops about the Four Courts, and immediately afterwards the survivors of the prison were seen coming out of the building led by a priest, and being mustered on Ormond Quay. The building burned fiercely and was enveloped in smoke. Rifle shots continued to be fired all afternoon and into the night in various parts of the city. . . . There is none so brutal as the Irish when they turn against their own country. . . . The "Die Hards" ought to be proud of their jackal Collins, tonight!

1 July. . . . People walked about streets and stopped to read Proclamations posted on post and pillars, and outside Trinity a newsboy was selling "War News No. 5" for a penny a copy, telling events from the Republican side. . . . When the tram I was on came as far as Gray's statue, shots rang out near the pillar, and people dashed about on all sides out of range, and I caught a passing tram that had just left the Pillar. . . . Of course I didn't venture up to see Eileen under the circumstances. . . .

All places of amusement were closed owing to the continual sniping all over the heart of the city. . . . During the night shots rang out, and machine guns and cannon were also to be heard. . . .

2 July. No trams are running to-day, nor are any bikes, nor yokes of any kind passing. Only the solemn church bell calling the faithful to prayers, and the wind whistling through the chimneys. Rifle shots in the distance at intervals disturb the deathlike stillness of the morning. Then all is silence again. Dread is in the air! . . . John Burke came in and we went for a walk together by Lansdowne Road and on to Pigeon House Road and back by Beggar's Bush. . . . The sharp ping-ping of the rifles punctuated our journey all the way. . . .

4 July. I had a surprise this morning when I got up by the arrival of all the children, servants, and Dr. and Mrs. Gordon from the seat of war. It was made so hot for them in Cavendish Row that they had to leave, and luckily got a car to take them through O'Connell Street in the thick of things. They had passed a night of horror as all O'Connell Street was ablaze with gunfire, And C.Y.U.'s building went on fire and was gutted during the night.[6]

On 2 July, Lady Gregory had written to John Quinn:

This is a time of revolution, we heard yesterday of the taking of the Four Courts and there was the sound of firing in the night at Gort. . . . Yeats and Mrs. Yeats were to have gone to Dublin last Thursday, but this Dublin fighting began, and no trains are allowed into Dublin, but no doubt they will soon be alright. It is all very lamentable, Irishmen shooting Irishmen. And it is so useless. . . .[10]

However, on 6 July, the *Evening Herald* reported:

This morning there were unmistakeable signs than Dublin was returning to its normal aspect. Beyond shots from snipers, fired at lengthy intervals, there was little to upset the equilibrium.

Large crowds watched the fires, which are still burning in O'Connell street. In this area more than a score of four storey buildings are involved, and many of them are completely gutted.

One estimate places the damage to property during the week's fighting between £1,000,000 and £4,000,000; another at between £5,000,000 and £7,000,000.[11]

On 8 July, Joseph Campbell, the poet and the author of the Abbey play *Judgment*, was arrested by the government and interned. Also on 8 July, Robinson wrote from Dublin to Lady Gregory:

> We're through the worst now I hope, though if ambushes are started in earnest they will be worse than anything. A few stray shots came into the Abbey through the windows over the stage, probably these came from National troops who were on one of the roofs of Trinity trying to get snipers who were on Hopkins' roof. . . . Mrs. Martin's son was in the attack on the Four Courts and got through safely. She is indignant because the Republicans are now mostly back at their work, having put hundreds of poor people *out* of work. Mr. Harris had a wonderful escape, got into the middle of an ambush on the metal Bridge but was untouched.[12]

On the same day, 8 July, a handful of cinemas were open—La Scala, the Metropole, and the Corinthian. At the Corinthian, one could have seen not only Mary Pickford in *Poor Little Rich Girl*, but also a news film of the battle of the Four Courts. The legitimate theaters remained closed for the week of 10 July, and the Abbey had closed before the fighting for its summer vacation and would not reopen until Horse Show Week on 7 August. On 17 July, the O'Mara Opera Company resumed its engagement at the Gaiety, and the Tivoli and the Royal reopened.

On 25 July, Holloway noted that:

> The Compensation claims arising out of the fighting in Dublin are now approximately £4,000,000. An interesting claim lodged yesterday is that of J. M. Muldoon for the Ms. of a play entitled *The Playwright* which was in a locker in the Law Library at the Four Courts. The play was in 3 acts, and for its loss together with wig, gown, etc., he claims £40.[13]

About the same time there appeared in the *Herald* a notice about the fortunes of the McNally Opera Company:

> Amongst the towns visited during the past three weeks by the McNally Opera Company were Kiltimagh, Castlebar, Westport, Tubbercurry, and Sligo. These towns are in the "war zone," and yet curiously enough, good business is being done by the company. Only on a few occasions has it been found necessary to cancel advertised programmes owing to actual firing being in progress.[14]

Meanwhile, the headlines were as bad as ever:

> Fighting in Waterford and Limerick—the *Evening Herald*, 20 July.
> Heavy Fusillading in Dublin—ibid., 22 July.
> Ambush in Wexford—ibid., 25 July.
> Robbery by Armed Men in Dublin—ibid., 1 August.
> Cordon Tightening Around Kilmallock—the *Evening Telegraph*, 2 August.
> The Capture of Carrick-on-Suir—the *Evening Herald*, 4 August.
> Train Derailed at Raheny To-Day—ibid., 11 August.

On 12 August, Arthur Griffith died of overwork, and it is interesting to note that the Abbey was the only Dublin theater to close its doors that day as a mark of respect. It is particularly interesting because Griffith, who had been a strong supporter of the theater in its early days, had then broken strongly with it over the production of Synge's *Shadow of the Glen*, and for a while the effective ally became the combative antagonist. On 16 August, Robinson wrote to Lady Gregory, describing the funeral procession through Dublin:

> Griffith's funeral was very wonderful today. I wrote for a ticket to the Requiem mass but didn't get one so I gave up the idea of going as I had a lot of rehearsal to do, but about 12.30 I had a break in rehearsal and went out with Dolan and Miss Crowe on the chance of seeing something. We found it just beginning to pass Beresford Place and stood there and saw everything. It was splendidly done, so dignified and impressive, the coffin very simple, covered by the tricolour. The procession took nearly an hour and a half to pass, and the crowds of spectators was immense. It seemed a wonderful ending after all those years spent in the office of an obscure journal in a back street in Dublin. Collins marched boldly at the head of some troops with Dick Mulcahy beside him. Michael looked very well and very much the soldier though they say he is drinking hard, but then Dublin does say fool things all the time.[15]

On 19 October, Yeats wrote to John Quinn:

> I suppose the country is returning to order but the signs are faint. We have not seen a shot fired, or suffered any inconvenience since we reached Dublin, but most nights we hear shots or the louder sound of a bomb.[16]

But the country was not yet returning to order. On 23 August, Michael Collins was killed in County Cork.

On 28 August, St. John Ervine wrote to Dudley Digges in New York:

> I hardly dare write to you about Irish things. God has cursed us, Dudley, and we are a doomed and damned race, incapable of governing or being governed. Ask Whitford Kane what he thinks of that damned dago, De Valera, now? If I had been Michael Collins I'd have given the Irregulars a week in which to surrender. At the end of that time, each of them still unsurrendered would have been adjudged a criminal and shot on sight. The best I'd have done for De Valera and Childers would have been to deport them as undesirable aliens. But what's the use of writing about Ireland? It's a cursed country.[17]

Meanwhile, the headlines continued to be grisly:

Deadly Ambush in County Tipperary—the *Evening Telegraph*, 22 August.
Deadly Attack on Monaghan Barracks—ibid., 5 September.
Dublin's Night of Terror—ibid., 14 September.

And there was a postal strike that lasted from 10 to 28 September. And more headlines:

Appalling Tragedy in Clondalkin / Riddled with Bullets—the *Evening Herald*, 7 October.
Casualties in Kerry Ambush—ibid., 14 October.
Fatalities in Limerick and Tipperary—ibid., 27 October.
Pitched Battle in City Suburbs—ibid., 4 November.

On 26 October, Holloway was chatting to F. R. Higgins, the poet, at the first night of Colum's *Grasshopper:*

> F. R. Higgins told me he had a great adventure since he last saw me. He was under arrest for ten days at Tallaght and Wellington Barracks. The green soldiers surrounded his house one morning at 6 o'clock, and on giving his name they said it was him they wanted. They had had information he had been drilling (which he never had been), He took it as a joke at first, but as day followed day it became serious. His friends interested themselves on his behalf and at last he was free again. Hundreds were in gaol like him, who were not in the movement.[18]

On 13 November, Holloway was visiting his niece and her husband at 4 Cavendish Row; and, as they were seated around the study fire about six o'clock, "a terrific explosion was heard close by outside, and a perfect fusillade started round and about the Parnell monument, and one of the bullets came in through the Drawing Room window and spent itself in the wall."[19]

On 23 November, Holloway reported:

> A night of terror in the city. I was one of a thronged audience at the Gaiety to hear *Aida* sung. About 9.30 a bomb went off, followed by shots and then died down for awhile but when the great scene for the Princess in the last Act was being sung a terrible tornado of firing—machine guns, rifles, pistols, etc.—were to be heard coming from all sides, and just as the final scene was commencing I left with Mr. and Mrs. Caulfield and luckily got a car going in towards town. Shots seemed coming from all sides, but luckily none were near. I got a tram home at the Bank, and, as the shooting got very intense as the tram was going up Nassau Street all tried to get down on the floor as best they could; and a soldier who had a little drop taken consoled the affrighted ones with the remark, "Cheer up! We all will soon be dead!" and drew the curtains to shade himself from being seen from the outside as he sat in a corner.[20]

On 24 November, Erskine Childers, who had written the literate thriller, *The Riddle of the Sands*, was executed. On 6 December, the Irish Free State came officially into existence; and, on 11 December, Seanad Éireann met for the first time. Among the new senators were Yeats and Gogarty, and Lady Gregory wrote to Quinn:

> I am delighted Yeats is in the Senate. He was anxious for it, and it gives him his chance of using his powers of thought and speech for the direct service of the country. His stars are in the ascendent just now. He is lecturing in England so I didn't see him when I had to go to Dublin a week or two ago for Theatre business. Our financial manager, our Auditor who has grown into that position, died

suddenly, and I don't know how we shall get on without him.[21] Neither I nor Yeats shine on that side, and Robinson is worse, and our affairs want careful steering, for we have been playing at a loss of late; because of the unrest and danger of the streets at night, people stay at home and theatres languish.[22]

On 7 December, the *Herald's* headline read, "Two T. D.'s Shot in Dublin—Sean Hales Dead"; on 8 December, "Four More Executions This Morning"; on 15 December, "Garrisons Overpowered in Kilkenny"; on 19 December, "Seven More Executions This Morning."

• • •

Despite the terror and the trauma, Dublin was still a city in which people carried on their lives as normally as they could. They lived in it, they worked, they played, they walked its streets; and Holloway ran into them as they pursued their more-or-less normal days. Early in March he wrote:

In the tram home James Stephens got into the car. His upper lip possessed about a half a dozen clipped hairs under his nose. He had on a light sack-shaped overcoat and a soft felt hat.[23]

On 24 March, he was at the Abbey:

Yeats dreamed his way into the Stalls and out again, through the people, seeing no one. He walked nearsightedly, and wore glasses, with very heavy ribbons attached. Larchet told me the poet was pleased last night with the playing of *The Hour Glass*. Few others were.[24]

On 17 April:

A little down [Nassau] street Austin Clarke with a great stoop walked along, his chin buried in his great coat and a stick under his right arm and a soft felt hat on. You'd think he was an old man instead of a very young man, the expression of his face was so settled and set.[25]

Or, as Nichevo noted of Yeats in the *Irish Times* on 3 June:

Now and then, however, you may meet him coming along the Green, tall as ever, with a slight stoop, his hands held tightly behind his back, and his eyes peering at the clouds, through glasses which are attached to his coat lapel by a heavy black ribbon. His hair has lost its raven splendour, and he is not so gaunt of figure as he used to be. But when you get up to him, you see that he is the same dreamer as of old, with something of a strange sadness in his face, as if he were looking in vain for the fancies which used to dance before him. He still wears the flowing tie, and the wide sombrero of his poet days. But you could hardly imagine him now watching the curlews flighting from Lissadell or crooning peerless melodies beside a cottage fire.[26]

Or, as Holloway noted on 23 June:

> I saw Arthur Griffith saunter along jauntily in his usual ambling way. He wore a dark velour hat and a gray overcoat with velvet collar, and used a walking stick in his right hand. A set, determined expression—almost dogged—captured the lines of his face, and mask-like settled there.[27]

And on 8 August:

> I walked into town before dinner and saw Darrell Figgis in snuffcoloured suit, hat, and spats over brown boots. He walked with his left hand in his trousers pocket, the tail of his Norfolk jacket suiting the position of his hand. His beard was red and flourishing and his hair black and glossy.[28]

Or on 10 August, Holloway and McCormick met Padraig O'Conaire,

> who had on his leprechaun's hat and tweed suit and a sprig of heather in the lapel of his coat and the ring as well, and looked as if he was after a hard tear.[29]

Or on 20 October:

> I saw Jack Morrow reading a letter as he waited for the tram. He was smoking his big pipe. . . . He spoke of Edward Martyn and his being very ill, having had a stroke in his house in Galway.[30]

Or 11 November:

> Old Frank Dalton and his daughter stepped off a tramcar and dodged the cycles. He is a stooped old man with bowed legs and long white locks and alert clean-cut face.[31]

On 22 November, Holloway ran into James Stephens again in Greene's and asked if he were writing anything, and Stephens replied, "Every day a pebble or so is added to the cairn." And on 7 December, Holloway ran into Padraic Gregory, the poet, whom he described as:

> . . . a strange little body with an unusually big head—pearshaped, so that he has to wear an unusually large hat, a jerry one. He is hollow-cheeked, and his nose is large and drooping. The skin on his face seems to be stretched to the utmost to cover the space required by it.[32]

• • •

And, despite everything, people tried to go to the theater. However, it was sometimes dangerous, and the Abbey had many thin houses. On 7 February, Holloway noted, "The night was cold and windy, and the Abbey very poorly attended for the revival of *The Revolutionist*. It wears badly."[33] On 14 February, he wrote that "The Abbey was almost deserted" for *The Serf* and *Meadowsweet*,[34] and a couple of days later he added, "What is to become of the Abbey if such houses continue?"[35] And on 18 March, the revival of

Family Failing and *The Rising of the Moon* "played before a very small house."[36] On 17 March, John MacDonagh, after remarking that "The Empire was only a public house with a theatre attached," then added, "It was doing very badly."[37] On 6 May, Joseph A. Power wrote of "the apathy and indifference" of Dublin playgoers to the Abbey.[38] On 13 September, Thomas McGreevy wrote:

> We seem to have practically no theatre enthusiasts. A week or so ago I went down to the Abbey on a Saturday night to see Mr. Fitzmaurice's *The Country Dressmaker* and found myself one of fourteen people in the stalls! The pit was not full and the circle was nearly as empty as the stalls.[39]

Nevertheless, the Abbey gamely kept its doors open for 35 weeks of the year. It revived more than thirty plays from the repertoire, and it mounted ten new productions.

The first new production was the T. C. Murray three-act, *Aftermath*. A serious piece with leanings toward tragedy, the play is probably too much of its time and too phlegmatic for revival. However, it fits well into the Murray canon; for, like *Maurice Harte*, *The Serf*, and *Autumn Fire*, it treats an important and often ignored issue of Irish life—in this case, the unhappy marriage.

Initially at least, Murray was not too satisfied with the new work. On 5 October 1921, he sent the script off for comment to Frank J. Hugh O'Donnell,[40] remarking, "I've been hammering at the middle act and despair of ever welding it into anything like harmony with the other two acts—but must just let it take its chance."[41]

The play was first produced on Tuesday, 10 January, but Murray was not fully apprised of all of the details, for on 6 January he wrote to Holloway:

> I learned only a few hours in advance of your card the news of *Aftermath*. I heard with something of dismay (from Dolan) that Miss Marks was to play the strong woman part in the play! It's hard luck but as the old woman says in *Riders* "we must only be satisfied." Carolan should make a good Myles. I thought Miss Craig would be cast for a better part. She would have played Mary, the wife, particularly well. Miss Crowe plays Grace, the young girl. I don't care particularly somehow for Miss Crowe but I haven't seen her for sometime and I believe she has developed her art a little. It's a disappointment remembering the talent of the old days and the wonderful interpretation which they gave a man's work at the Abbey.
>
> By the way I made a slight change in the final curtain. I felt somehow that Mary should have made a better fight to keep her husband and so she follows him into the night, leaving the old woman alone on the stage. Her sense of desolation is so overpowering that she turns in reproach to God addressing Him as if He were a visible presence . . . "Almighty God, you're very hard on an old woman."
>
> What a great thing Allgood would make of this closing-line![42]

The press was almost uniformly appreciative. For instance, the *Evening Mail* wrote:

> Its theme is the frequent evils of country matchmaking as opposed to love-making, the aftermath when boy and girl love are ruled out, and sordid considerations of worldly wealth step in.
>
> It tells of a high-strung and poetical school-teacher whom a mother's pride and materialism force into a marriage, when he comes back from Dublin to Ardnagreena (in the South of Ireland) with a plain farming-class girl, after making him and the girl of his heart—"a wisp of a teacher from Cork"—break with each other, with the result that after six years of misery, he leaves his unloved wife for ever. His sweetheart, in the meantime, had married the local doctor, who wanted her.
>
> It is a play true to life, full of great philosophies, of realities as we see them every day, and brimful of that kindly, honest, and racy humour which makes country life at once a beauty and a laugh. There is nothing absurdly comic, no buffoonery, in all its generous vein—the joy of all its fun is that every bit is living real. It is rich with the atmosphere of the country—there are conversations about the "awful" life in Dublin and the prices of the "digs," the good neighbour making the presents of the milk and butter (and the news), the "tiffs" between the women, Mrs. M'Carthy complaining that her little girl was put out of the local choir, and . . . that her Barty was "beaten by the master," the great price of the white oats, the teacher making the will, and a thousand and one other little idiosyncracies which only those who have lived in the country can appreciate. And rising gently above it all is the frank materialism—the "nonsense of poetry and art." But more than anything else in the play stands revealed the proud and jealous mother—proud of her family possessions, which she regained after her son's marriage from the labourer's cottage, and jealous as only a mother can be jealous. The play might have been given a different ending, but we admit it would have been hard to devise. . . .
>
> The play was rapturously received, and the author had to appear in response to repeated calls.[43]

The *Evening Telegraph* called it "a fine play, with truth and realism of plot and characterisation, a dialogue on the whole well-knit and apt . . . and each act well balanced."[44] Even Jacques in the *Evening Herald* was complimentary:

> It was all exceedingly interesting. It was—except the incongruously melodramatic exit in the second act—refreshingly untheatrical. The annals of match-making were ransacked for argument in the mouth of the rival actors. These were, of course, not new. How could they be? There was so very little action in the little play that really one marvelled how the situations developed and the interest reigned. The dialogue was smooth, natural, and witty at times. It had nothing of the peasant cottage kitchen, nor yet of the drawing room gilt chair brand. . . .
>
> The various characters were well drawn. The mother (Miss Florence Marks), was intensely real, with an accent that flavoured of goat's milk and butter pats. It burred Co. Cork. Perhaps it was nervous tension that whisked her that once into over-acting. Miss Eileen Crowe was grace in name and grace in bearing. Her best movements were when faced by the irate mother of a young pupil.
>
> Mr. P. J. Carolan was very sincere, beautifully intoned, and quite heroic, but not a bit like the average country schoolmaster, even though he had been through Dublin. Then, oh Myles, how could you, a learned grammarian, ever say such a thing as: "Who ever said there was anything between Miss Sheridan and I?" . . .
>
> There was nothing hypnotic about Gabriel Fallon's Dr. Manning, and he rather let down the scene in the second act between himself and the girl who had been playing Deirdre to his heroic pose.[45]

In the *Gael*, O'Donnell waxed utterly ecstatic, repeating several times that the piece was a great play, "a greater tragedy than perhaps either that of *Maurice Harte* or *Birthright*. There is no doubt about it but Mr. Murray is our greatest living Irish dramatist."[46] A trifle more critically, O'Donnell tilted at a few minor points of the play and the production, including on opening night the unexpected onstage appearance of a passing dog:

> The play was tragic right through. Here and there in the dialogue are good flashes of humour which were thoroughly appreciated. The appearance of a woman of the village whose daughter had been ejected from the choir of school children, and who as a result came for revenge on the Schoolmistress, was very helpful in relieving the gloomy atmosphere. So, too, was the gentle old servant to Miss Sheridan. She talked scandal in delightful fashion and philosophical bon mots dropped from her lips profusely as dew on the grass.
>
> Once or twice the dialogue between the matchmaking mothers in the opening act seemed tiring, but by a brilliant turn of speech Mr. Murray revived interest now and again and saved difficult situations. The unexpected appearance of a big Black and Tan dog on the stage the night I was present caused some heart throbs in the audience, for he had no part in the play and just entered at a critical moment. However, he was an intelligent animal, for after having looked interestedly at the audience and having wagged his tail into all sorts of positions he made a timely and graceful exit. In fact if one could be sure that he would act so well every night he would just give the finishing touch to a very homely posture of the play and his services would mark a new opening for canine endeavour.
>
> The mathematical capacities of some of the actors seemed to be at fault the same night, for whereas Myles tells us in the first act his age is 26, we learn in the last act, six years later, that he is only thirty. And, too, in the final scene, when his wife is pleading with him, his hat accidentally fell from his hand and rolled on to the floor. But unmindful of that he walked straight from his wife's arms out into the night. It seems hardly likely that any man, no matter what state of excitement he was in, would leave his own house and face the world, hatless!
>
> P. J. Carolan, as Myles O'Regan, seemed a little too restrained to fully represent the Myles O'Regan of Mr. Murray's creation. Yet his acting in general was very good, and he seems about the only actor in the Abbey at the moment that shows a possibility of filling the place of F. J. McCormick. As Grace Sheridan, Eileen Crowe was convincing, though her voice fell so low at times that she could scarcely be heard. One could easily recognise the finished artiste in Miss May Craig for her interpretation of the small part given her was delightful and certainly got the piece going with a bang. Helena Moloney gave a perfect study of an old servant girl. In fact it was a perfect characterisation, one which taken completely from the play, would be acceptable to any audience. . . .
>
> There has been a decided improvement in the acting of the younger players this past few weeks, and if they continue progressing at the present rate some of the old "stars" will need to look to their feathers.[47]

On 19 January, Murray wrote to thank O'Donnell for his notice, and in passing defended P. J. Carolan's Myles:

> By the way, you were overthrifty in your praise of the players last week—particularly in the case of Carolan whose restraint was the characteristic which charmed me as few Abbey players have done. Our friend McCormick would have

made Myles a little stagey. The Myles of Carolan had a delicacy of restraint which made the character to my mind more convincing than any other treatment would have. But these terrible critics must of course be grousing![48]

W. J. Lawrence in the *Stage* moderately groused about the language of the hero,[49] and Holloway recorded Murray's reaction:

Murray told me he felt Lawrence's criticisms on his play *Aftermath* keenly and said to his wife he'd never write another on reading the *Stage* notice of it. . . . It made him examine his conscience and read carefully over the play again and eliminate any word or phrase he felt might not ring true. Bookish people like the schoolmaster often use words unconsciously that they read.[50]

On Tuesday, 31 January, the Abbey gave the first production of Robinson's three-act, *The Round Table*. This domestic comedy in its first two acts had much to recommend it, particularly in amusing character drawing; but nearly every commentator balked at the Strange Lady who may have been an emanation from the heroine's unconscious, or a ghost, or even real. Whatever she was, however, most critics felt that she was distinctly out of tone with the rest of the play.

The *Evening Telegraph*, which took the play a bit too seriously, wrote:

In his new three-act play, produced for the first time at the Abbey Theatre last night, Mr. Lennox Robinson has chosen an experimental theme, and one not too easily to be understood. And for the first and second acts, his treatment of it has been an excellent and able one. Only in the third act, perhaps in the effort to sustain the adjective of "comic" with which he has prefaced his stated tragedy, and yet to keep the grim grotesqueness of the tragedy apparent, does he fail to quite win through.

Mr. Robinson's central idea is that of the instinct of adventure which is in some women, as in some men—the adventuring of the soul among the wonders of people and things in the world during the mortal span of life. But the tragedy of these women is that they are more tethered, more physically timid than men. Yet, they have essayed the adventure, some of them—in old days the spirit that impelled them, misguided, made the tragic courtesans of history. Later it made them fare forth alone.

The first act of *The Round Table* finds Daisy Drennan, a Dublin suburban girl, living her life out in the management and care of helpless mother, sister and two brothers, and faced with the problem of either rearranging matters satisfactorily for them, and so freeing herself for her own wished-for marriage, or abandoning them for her lover, or settling down to the old routine and abandoning him. In the first act she prepares to fit the family into her scheme of things. In the second act she has almost done so, when by tapping at the window a strange woman from the outside world, a wandering woman whom the cold night has driven to seek a moment's warmth at this house, greatly disturbs the course of things for Daisy Drennan.

And in the third act the difficult "endings" come. Daisy has just seen her brother and her sister married. She and her lover, Christopher Pegum, are seeing them off on their honeymoon. The unmarried brother, a freaky soulful youngster, now a normal best man (rather tipsy) will later start on his own. Daisy's mother and an old lady who lives with the Drennans, and Christopher's mother and aunt, in spite of little differences, will probably live with Christopher and Daisy. Then on the railway station Daisy sees her "strange woman"—whom Christopher cannot see, who now rather weirdly appears to be a prophetic phantom of Daisy's unseen self, with unmoral soul of adventure having left husband and child and humdrum home to wander the world—and Daisy, awakened by the vision, abandons lover, family, all her old life, and starts with little save her naked courage for the dreamed adventure. This is the big thematic part of the act; the superficialities, though clever and at times amusing, do not blend well with the whole—hence the weakness. . . .

Mr. Robinson was "authored" by an audience as enthusiastic and appreciative as could be desired.[51]

In the *Evening Herald*, Jacques was a little more accurate:

If we had not already seen *The Suburban Groove*, by Mr. Casey, and an excellent clash of city romance versus rural practicality by the Munster Players we could have sat at *The Round Table* at the Abbey Theatre last night without nodding. But Mr. Lennox Robinson, to be entirely different from those who adduced mere mundane reasons for their choice in matrimony, invoked the aid of "faces"—visions, alter egos, inner selfs, spirits, occult influences, et cetera, and so forth—and gave us three acts of household hints, hymen, and hallucinations. And in this he was entering into competition with Pepper's Ghost and Maskelyne and Devant.

And yet, mind you, all these people who came and went on the Abbey stage last night were likeable people. They were quaint, humorous, human—all except the "possessed" persons, and they were what the author made them and no doubt never meant them to be, unconsciously funny. . . .

And the play was amusing. It has some of the most humorous lines penned by Mr. Robinson, far better than some of the laugh-getters in his *Whiteheaded Boy*. Last night laughter came in billows. . . .

The acting was as good as the play deserved. In fact, it could not be much better in all parts.[52]

On 2 February, Holloway spoke to Lawrence, who thought "the first act fine and the last act poor and full of anti-climaxes."[53] But perhaps the most critical commentator was O'Donnell in the *Gael*:

Taking the play on the whole, it was never satisfying. Undoubtedly the first and portions of the second and third acts contained most delightful humour, and Miss Helena Moloney and Peter Nolan got every laugh that could be got from their lines. But though people will tell you that you must forget that the lady was real—that is the mysterious lady—you cannot do it nor can you accept as truth the statement that the conversation you have actually heard is all a dream. This may look all right in story form on paper, but on stage it is a different thing, and I think Mr. Robinson, though having a decidedly splendid idea for a play, did not get it across in just the right way. The form of his play was unconventional too. In the first act you find nothing that is intimately relevant to the idea until the curtain is actually falling, and then you are left wondering.

The acting in general was splendid. There was no hesitation or awkwardness from start to finish. I shall not for a very long time forget the delightful touches Miss Helena Moloney added to Mr. Robinson's humour, or Peter Nolan's confused philosophy on Time which was one of the cleverest bits of the play. Eileen Crowe as Daisy Drennan did not please me very much, for she seemed too wooden and cold-blooded to personify the creation of the author. And I think her attitude had a depressing effect on P. J. Carolan, her lover, who did not seem quite in his usual form though he had a rather thankless part to play. But why did Michael J. Dolan, the local stamp adorer, wear horn glasses and assume a tragi-comic air? And what was he supposed to represent anyway? Tony Quinn, who had nothing to say, spoke volumes by his funniosities in the last act, and gave the scene a touch of humanity which it needed badly.[54]

In his long career, Robinson was probably most successful in realistic, mildly satiric comedy; and his *The Whiteheaded Boy*, *The Far-Off Hills*, *Drama at Inish*, and *Crabbed Youth and Age* form an impressive quartet of accomplishment. In some other plays, he essayed mild experiments in form or content; and, most usually, as in *The Round Table*, he then muddied his palette and obscured the realistic truth of his picture. About *The Round Table*, however, we should cite one major demurrer, the always interesting and usually sound Stephen Gwynn who wrote in *The Stage*, "It would be ten thousand pities if the play did not catch on, for it is incomparably more interesting than *The Whiteheaded Boy*."[55]

The theater continued playing each week, but there was no new production until 9 March, when the play was the Abbey's first attempt at Shaw's *The Man of Destiny*. Napoleon was played by P. J. Carolan, although Barry Fitzgerald might have seemed apter casting. Holloway reported in a postcard to McCormick that Carolan was "not a bad actor, but his style is too monotonous."[56] Robinson, the director, also allowed the comedy to be inappropriately lit:

. . . the lighting . . . I didn't think successful as the players had mostly to go through their parts as silhouettes. . . . The faces of the players should always be seen by an audience—almost a blackout gives no stage illusion of darkness; half-light sometimes does.[57]

If Holloway's above description is correct, one wonders what was in Robinson's mind. Not only must comedy be played on a well-lit stage, but only toward the end does it become dark outside. Through most of the piece "the sun is blazing serenely."

On Thursday, 6 April, two new one-acts appeared on a triple bill with *The King's Threshold*. The new short plays were Dorothy Macardle's historical piece, *Ann Kavanagh*, and M. M. Brennan's slum comedy, *The Young Man from Rathmines*. As Jacques reported in the *Evening Herald*:

We had more than the blend of the rainbow in the bill submitted to the congested audience at the Abbey Theatre last night. The three one-act plays provided us with a blend of the jeer, the tear, and the smile. *The King's Threshold*, by Mr. W. B. Yeats, is quite all right for those who have the time and desire to sit down and carefully and conscientiously read it. But even as a poetical play, propped up by special stage-carpentry, decorated by costumed maidens with modern manners, and ornamented by uniformed satellites of kingly days in ancient Ireland—even as such it can never hope to please the vulgus. The centre character, Seanchan (presented last night by Frank J. Fay), becomes really a bit of a bore. It is not the fault of the actor. It is hard to give life to a dying poet whose stock in trade consists of jeers, curses, and high-flown imagery.

There followed *Ann Kavanagh*. It is one of the greatest plays yet made for the Abbey stage by a woman. It is twenty minutes of lantern drama, pulsating in every minute. It is great in its brevity, in its strength, in its realism, in the might of its onward rush, in its forceful yet natural development, and in its terrible aftermath.

Dorothy Macardle is the author. Her newest work, applauded last night with a fervour that was discerning and sincere, marks a distinct advance in technique. She gives us a darkened room in Myles Kavanagh's house in Co. Wexford. On a night in '98 Myles, officer in the Insurgent Army, is roused from his sleep despite the protests of his loving young wife, to deal with a young spy who has been caught red-handed. During Myles' absence the fugitive spy seeks shelter in the Kavanagh house. Ann at first thinks he is a poor boy fleeing from the British Yeos. She mothers him and shelters him. Later she recognises him as her sister's bethrothed. She hides him in her bedroom, faces his pursuers, lies to them and to her husband, embroils her husband in ugly complications, enmeshes him in suspicion and—the fugitive is found!

In production it was perfect from the light through the window to the hush of discovery. You held your breath at the awful silence that throbbed with tragedy. You winced at the agonised shrieks and frenzied protests that her husband is innocent vented by Miss May Craig; you sided with P. J. Carolan in the bigness of his loyalty to his soft-hearted wife and the dignity of his suffering. . . .

The faults were equally divided between the authoress and her interpreters. Did Miss Macardle write "Hands up!" in the script? Was this challenge to surrender in vogue in '98? I fancy our hearing it last night was due to the exuberance of first-night players. More serious, to my mind, was the stripping of Myles by Moran of his command and passing it immediately on to Myles's brother Stephen. Immediately before this takes place Stephen, venting his rage and spleen, calls down the "curse of God" on Ann, blasting her as a trailor. And Moran rewards this man who so far forgets himself in the presence of a woman, a prisoner, his superiors, and his fellows—he rewards him with command! That one incident jarred me.

Last on the bill was a one-act piece by Mr. M. M. Brennan, which gave us a room in a Dominick St. (Dublin) tenement. It is entitled *The Young Man from Rathmines*, and had a fitting first presentation from last night's company. It is spiced with love and laughter, and is a happy leavening in the three-act programme. Hear Mrs. Sullivan begging with a stuffed nose that Mary, the tenement flapper, might read her "dem luvly love-letters you do be gettin' same as I yewst to be gettin' meself when himself was coortin' me." Hear her, too, describing the young man, George Jackson—who turned out to be an Indian half caste—as looking "like a whippet in the meddle of winter." The play is really a sketch, and depends for its laughs more on its dialogue (or what the players make of the dialogue) than on action. As a medium of tenement humour it is clever.[58]

A correspondent in O'Donnell's column in the *Gael* briefly admired Brennan's play, but took issue with the high praise given to Miss Macardle's:

It isn't often that an Abbey play receives such appreciative notices from the dramatic critics as *Ann Kavanagh*. In quarters where lack of sympathy, if not frank hostility, has been shown towards the work of the National Theatre, Miss Macardle's play was proclaimed a great thing—"the greatest thing ever done by a woman

> writer by the Abbey." That sentence is in a surge of expectation to *Ann Kavanagh*. Having now seen the play for ourselves, we cannot in conscience describe it as either of these things. Comparisons are often stupid, particularly when instituted between plays of so different a genre as this and the plays of other women writers; but surely there is no comparison even in degree between *Ann Kavanagh* and *The Rising of the Moon*?
>
> Not that *Ann Kavanagh* is not a good play. There is skillful draughtsmanship, the dialogue rings true, and its twenty minutes' action is swift and cumulative. But though things may happen in a single moment in our own lives which will be remembered for an eternity, the mimic life of the stage will never enter into the depths of our consciousness in the time occupied by Miss Macardle's little play. But we are grateful for the promise revealed in it, and hope it is an augury of bigger things.[59]

O'Donnell himself added:

> The play certainly has grip and grasp in it, but I thought occasionally it bordered near the melodramatic. I must add a special word of praise for the brilliant emotional acting of Miss May Craig. Her rendition of the part of the woman—who was a real woman, full of maternal solicitude for all men—will rank amongst her highest achievements.[60]

Holloway echoed O'Donnell's praise of that rather neglected Abbey actress, May Craig, and then gave a few details about M. M. Brennan:

> *The Young Man from Rathmines* is by M. M. Brennan (who writes short stories). Kirwan met him and tells me he often dreams his plots, and not long ago awoke in the middle of the night with a ghost story in his head and had to get up to write it out there and then. He writes on the spur when a plot comes in a flash to him. He is a young, everyday-looking man; he with two companions was pointed out to me in the fourth row of the stalls. . . . Mr. Brennan's sketch recalls James Stephens' *The Wooing of Julia Elizabeth* and tells of a young girl, a labourer's daughter, who has answered a matrimonial advertisement in the paper of a young man from Rathmines; and, when the piece opens, the family is expecting him to call for the first time and are all excitement.[61]

Of the two new plays, Brennan's was to prove the more popular, and it remained for years a favourite of the amateur societies. Several people other than Holloway were reminded of Stephens's *The Wooing of Julia Elizabeth*; but, while Stephens's undervalued play yet remains droll, Brennan's play has lost whatever charm it once seemed to possess. Its lines and characterizations appear unimaginative and lifeless, particularly when compared to the work of O'Casey; and its basic joke now seems but a vulgar testimony to parochialism and snobbery.

Dorothy Macardle's play is a craftsmanlike enough job of journeyman play carpentry; but O'Donnell's friend was right in charging that too many incidents are jumbled together in too short a space. If there is no reason to revive *Ann Kavanagh*, it nevertheless does raise one point of interest.

Dorothy Macardle at this time was a teacher of English and Drama at Alexandra College. She was also a fervent Republican, and her friends numbered Hanna Sheehy-Skeffington, Maud Gonne, and other ladies prominent in the 1926 protest against O'Casey's *Plough and the Stars*. It is interesting to note that in *Ann Kavanagh* the Republican author made the point that an allegiance to general humanity was more important than an allegiance to patriotism. As O'Casey's *The Plough and the Stars* makes the same point, the fact is not without its irony.

Dorothy Macardle's best and most substantial work was not to be her handful of plays or her ghostly novels, such as *The Uninvited*, but her lengthy, partisan history, *The Irish Republic*.

After its usual summer vacation, the Abbey opened its new season on 7 August for Horse Show Week, and on 29 August presented a new one-act, *The Moral Law* by R. J. Ray. The critic of the *Evening Telegraph*, probably Mary Frances McHugh,[62] clearly described the plot of this yet unpublished piece:

> Perhaps the time is not yet ripe for the writing of plays, whether of problem or incident, portraying Irish life during the "terror" in Ireland—the days of war against English power. Events recalled after too short an interval may loom too large and grotesque in the mind, the atmosphere be in memory too clouded by the writer's own emotion to allow of a balanced vision. However that may be, last night's new one-act play at the Abbey Theatre, *The Moral Law*, by R. J. Ray, was a disappointment, and this in the play itself, for acting and production were adequate.
>
> Briefly, the foundation is this—an old man, ex Head-Constable, R.I.C., watching at two o'clock in the morning for his son, a young man, to come home. That son has, of course, been out drilling; he is addicted to talk of Ireland's wrongs and guns and swords. He returns dishevelled and capless, is confronted by father, and getting somewhat of a rating, taunts the latter with his "policeman's mind." The son goes to bed. His mother then appears, and father and mother awaken each other's uneasiness—she by inquiring about an old double-barrelled gun.
>
> They are about to go to bed (after she has taken a peep at the son now asleep) when military knock, are admitted, and search the house—all in what those knowing anything of such raids will find a most unrealistic fashion, even to the detail of the officer not leaving a man posted in the sittingroom with the old man. Then a police sergeant comes in (he and his men have seen the "door left open"!); and the sergeant unnerves the father by telling of the District Inspector having been shot at one o'clock by an ambusher with a double-barrelled gun, and produces a cap which he believes to be the murderer's.
>
> The father completely compromises the son; the sergeant appears a queer mixture of friendliness and suspicion—not a real-life hesitation, but as if the author did not know what to do with his creation.
>
> Military officer, police sergeant, father, mother, and later the three latter and the son have then a good deal of confused talk and action. In the end the raiding parties leave, the mother retires, and after father and son have parried talk with challenge, evasion and denial, sought and not quite given, with much harking back to the leading motif of "the moral law," the curtain descends, leaving one half bored, half baffled, and wholly unconvinced.
>
> For our quarrel with the play is that, if a problem play, it does not tackle its

problem; if dramatic, it is without incident (a house-search and hearsay tragedy do not count); and that this unsatisfactory material is given to us largely through the medium of maundering soliloquy.[63]

Jacques in the *Evening Herald* thought that the play "leads us nowhere,"[64] and the critic of the *Evening Mail* thought it "a disappointment . . . frankly, a disappointment,"[65] but O'Donnell in the *Gael* made a slight case for the piece:

I have heard the play described as unconvincing. Perhaps that is true, but in the case of drama of this category, what way could you have it logically portrayed but in unconvincing fashion? Yet all the characters were true to themselves, as far as humanity goes. John Shannon, even though he had wonderful respect for the moral law, and a peculiar love of justice, proved at the end that he was but what we all are, a feeble and weak believer. He might strike you as being back-boneless, but he was psychologically true, and the only person who struck me as not being up to type was the police sergeant, who had sufficient evidence to hang a man and yet did nothing.

The play was not without defects. It was enveloped in soliloquies and studded through with them. Men who know more about drama than I do say soliloquies are necessary at times and forgiveable. That may be so, but to hear a person muttering something to himself on the stage strikes me as being unnatural, and I feel that his thoughts are not worth, or he would get somebody to inflict them on. Mr. Ray, too . . . played an ugly trick on the audience when he brought the sergeant back to intrude upon a very interesting dialogue between the morally-muddled father and the strongly-minded son. And all the sergeant needed was a match to light his pipe! The author should have left him smokeless rather than drag him into a scene where he had no business, and did not develop its interest in any way. It strikes me, too, that Mr. Ray wrote the play in a hurry, and did not get all that he should have got out of the idea.[66]

Holloway, too, was sympathetic, but also concluded:

Ray's play didn't quite come off. Somehow the casting seemed wrong, and there was too much talk, and much of it didn't ring true. The play didn't get the grip it ought to have done, and Dolan wasn't suitable at all as John Shannon, the ex-Head Constable of R.I.C.—he struck too subdued a note. . . . All whom I spoke to thought there was good stuff in the play badly applied. . . . As a dramatist, Ray usually just misses. The audience weren't a bit helpful or sympathetic; they laughed at the sight of both soldiers and police, as if their mere coming on the stage were funny. This levity spoiled the dramatic tension.[67]

With Robinson, Murray and J. Bernard MacCarthy, Ray had been hailed ten years earlier as one of a new school of Cork Realists. He was the least prolific and the least successful of the quartet. None of his plays was published, and none was completely successful on the stage. From contemporary accounts and from a truncated radio version of one of his pieces, we might conclude that he was a grimly serious writer whose sombre studies of the West Cork peasantry often verged into melodrama. Readers of previous volumes of this history will recall that W. B. Yeats took a helpful interest in his work, but the problem of basic play structuring seems to have been one that Ray never mastered. This was the last of his handful of Abbey plays.

On 4 September, the Abbey presented another triple bill of one-acts, and among them was the first production of *The Leprechaun in the Tenement*, another slum comedy by M. M. Brennan. The piece has not been published, but the *Evening Telegraph* liked it and described its plot:

> A new one-act was produced last night at the Abbey Theatre—*A Leprechaun in the Tenement*—by M. M. Brennan, author of *The Young Man from Rathmines*, and though it is not so uproariously mirth-producing, we would prefer it. For it is funny, in a more delicate manner. It is frankly fairy-tale, really and truly, about a leprechaun, and in the unfolding . . . there is a quaint, pretty-cum-humorous touch nearly worthy, say, of James Stephens.
>
> Mrs. Reilly (of the tenement) and daughter are discussing love, men, and disillusions of marriage. (Alice Kate can't get a young man.) A comedy widow comes in to show her new dress, and just then it is torn by the dog of Mickey Reilly, grown-up idiot son of the tenement. Mickey's only friend is the dog, and Mickey puts fear into the widow Murphy when she offers a retaliatory kick. Mr. Reilly, labourer, on the exit of the widow, arrives home from Liffey fishing with a leprechaun—a real one. Mrs. Reilly, who has been brandishing an iron, joins Alice Kate in ecstasy over the "lovely little man with the tears on his cheeks.
>
> Mr. Reilly's tale of the leprechaun, whom he found weeping over the loss of his magic hat, is exquisite. "An' would you believe it, an old weasel insulted him something awful when he saw the defenceless state he was in." Alice Kate wishes for Widow Murphy's hat and dress. She finds them in her bedroom, but the delayed fulfilment of the wish makes Mrs. Reilly at first rate Mad for bringing home a poor worn-out "old-age pensioner of a leprechaun." Yet marital sparring is abated by the leprechaun's powers.
>
> The family are to move to Merrion square. But poor Mickey doesn't like that, and goes sadly out of the room telling his dog he doesn't want to leave the tenement. Then . . . Mrs. Murphy comes with a tale of woe of her vanished dress and sees it on Alice Kate. In the consequent semi-row Mickey comes and takes the leprechaun's basket out unnoticed.
>
> End—the dog has eaten the leprechaun (for Mickey won't leave his beloved tenement); and the widow's big row has yet to come off.[68]

Jacques was less kind:

> The farce talks itself to rags and ends up in tatters of bunkum and buffoonery. The audience laughed at such sayings as:
>
> "Did me da go down on his knees when he asked yous to marry him?" "He did not then, 'cos I was sittin' on his knees at the time."
>
> "Me first husband was that stingy he should have married a black woman, who would want only a bead necklace to dress herself."
>
> Apart from, and in addition to, the questionable taste of putting on the stage a poor, senseless imbecile for people to laugh at, the tenementy little play is very backroom and top storey. Misses Sheila Murray, Eileen Crowe and May Craig, with Messrs. Barry Fitzgerald and Tony Quinn, made the best of the material at hand, but all subsided badly just before the curtain.[69]

As far as we can judge, the piece was broad stage stuff better suited for the variety program of the Tivoli or the Empire. What is clear, though, is that the production continued the Abbey's difficulty with dogs onstage. Holloway wrote on 13 September:

> In speaking to Tony Quinn and May Craig about the change from fishing basket to sack after the first night of *A Leprechaun in the Tenement*, they told me they couldn't get the dog into the basket on the first night, and therefore decided on a sack instead.[70]

On 26 September, the *Evening Telegraph* printed a genial interview with Robinson, in which he defended *The Moral Law*, and talked about plans for the new season:

> Mr. Lennox Robinson declared that set "plans" could not be in such a theatre. But the possible programme of the theatre does not promise badly; it contains indeed some big "first nights" so far as imaginative hope can prophecy.
>
> "If we made cut and dried plans," said Mr. Robinson, "the next post—when Mr. Walsh sends us a next post—might contain half a dozen masterpieces demanding instant production and all our schemes would be thrown into confusion. No, all one can do at the beginning of a season is to determine to produce certain new plays, the scripts of which are already on one's desk, to determine further to revive certain old plays which have dropped out of our repertory and for the rest to trust to God and the Irish dramatists.
>
> "Count it to us for righteousness that we have already produced *The Moral Law* and *The Leprechaun in the Tenement*. I wonder why you didn't like *The Moral Law* as much as I did. I think it undoubtedly Mr. Ray's best play. You wanted something definite to happen, someone to be shot or arrested, or at any rate the young man indubitably proved to have shot or not to have shot the District Inspector. But doesn't the whole dramatic value of the play depend on that doubt being unresolved? Come and see it next time we put it on, and perhaps you will agree with me. . . .
>
> "But to turn to the future. We are now rehearsing a three-act comedy by George Shiels, the author of *Bedmates* and *Insurance Money*. It is called *Paul Twyning*, and it is quite the best thing he has done, and I hope it will be very popular. It is certain to be if the audience enjoy it as much as we are enjoying it in rehearsal. Paul himself is a lovable rascal, and all the other characters have something of the wild vivid quality that Mr. Fitzmaurice gets into his people. . . . No, I shall not tell you the plot, but it is all about those two old things—love and money. And I'm interested in watching Mr. Shiels gradually finding his stage legs. He is really a story writer who gets little opportunity of going to the theatre, and has never managed to see one of his plays on the stage. *Insurance Money*, for instance, is full of charming things but it is never dramatic, is it? But I'd rather see it than half a dozen Grand Guignol plays compact with thrills. . . . Yes, *Bedmates* was great fun. My one quarrel with the Treaty is that it has made *Bedmates* ancient history. We have almost a case against the Government for compensation. But, perhaps, Mr. Shiels will rewrite it, since we're not all in the one bed yet."
>
> . . . after *Paul Twyning* the Abbey company is to rehearse a new play, *The Grasshopper*, by Padraic Colum.
>
> "It's a long play," said Mr. Robinson; "four acts, a beautiful, moving thing. It won't be easy to do; it will take a lot of work; there's a delicate, tender passion in it that will need very careful treatment. And after *The Grasshopper*, for contrast, we'll

give you a wild, match-making one act comedy by George Fitzmaurice, and then—well, wait till I get the next post.

"But even if no post comes before Christmas we shall be busy enough, for I want to revive *The Countess Cathleen*, and that richest of all Lady Gregory's one act comedies *The Full Moon*, and Mr. Brinsley MacNamara's fine play, *The Land for the People*. And Padraic Colum has written a new last act for *The Fiddler's House*, which is a good reason for reviving that beautiful play, and I'd like to find time for a new Shaw play—new to the Abbey, I mean—And, if only to see Mr. Fitzgerald play Tony Lumpkin, what about *She Stoops to Conquer*?

"No, we have nothing else from Mr. Brennan, nothing since *The Leprechaun in the Tenement*. I think it and *The Young Man from Rathmines* are the only plays he has written. I have never met a young author with a better sense of the stage; he seems perfectly at home on it. If he has got ideas he will make his fortune in the theatre."

Mr. Robinson owes it to us to produce new work and realises the fact, but he is a little evasive.

"If I produce all these plays won't I have done enough for drama this season?" he asked. "Yes, I confess that I'm trying to write a one act comedy and finding it very difficult. . . . No, it's not about Ireland. I said it was a comedy!"[71]

On 3 October, the Abbey produced for the first time George Shiels' new three-act comedy, *Paul Twyning*. However, few of the reviewers thought that "comedy" was the proper description. The *Evening Telegraph* recounted the plot:

Last night we went to the Abbey Theatre to see a new three-act comedy by George Shiels, author of *Bedmates* and *Insurance Money*, a three-act comedy, part farce and part fantasy; and we found *Paul Twyning* a better play than either of its predecessors in several points. It's a rather highly-coloured comedy, properly speaking; but it has good action throughout, some excellent characterisation, and plenty of humour.

Paul Twyning, tramp-plasterer, is a rogue, and a glorious one. He is played by that very rogueish comedian, Barry Fitzgerald, and the fun is kept rippling. And Daisy Mullen, returned American, is a greater character in her way; Christine Hayden in the part gives some of the best acting we have known to her credit. . . .

James Deegan, farmer and magistrate (Gabriel J. Fallon) is given to us as a concentrated tyrant, aged and of intelligence, a quality sadly lacking in his elderly and much-bullied son, Dan (Michael Dolan). Dan, in the beginning of the play, egged on by Paul Twyning, whose hobby is matchmaking, proposes to and is accepted by pink-cheeked, pig-tailed Rose McGothigan, whose father (Eric Gorman) is the life enemy of James Deegan—both elders fond of law and desirous to use it one against the other. James, however, tasks Dan over Rose, and Dan in a scare denies all "for the love of God, amen, father!" He wishes Dan, moreover, to marry Daisy Mullen, who appears agreeable. In a screamingly funny tete-a-tete Daisy "makes up" to Dan, who flees before her advances loudly lamenting, the drift of his refrain being—"I'm a decent boy, that's all; don't crowd me, don't crowd me, keep a civil distance."

Congratulations ensue; Paul Twyning, arch-rogue as he is, giving everyone away to everyone else. But in the end James Deegan himself has "asked" Daisy Mullen.

The second act of the play, and the best, shows James Deegan's other son, Patrick, a publican in the near town; the action takes place in his house. Dan Deegan and Paul Twyning have come in to consult with Patrick (well acted and remarkably well made-up facially and otherwise by P. J. Carolan). May Craig and Tony Quinn suitably fill the parts of Patrick's wife and young son. Paul Twyning, after James Deegan and Daisy have come on the scene, gives a glorious display of mellow songfulness and demagogue's wit, telling keen truths to the old generation of farmers who "have not smiled since they got a cheque-book." There is plot and counterplot, now of breach of promise cases—Dan and Rose, James Deegan and Daisy; things not having turned out as expected with Daisy, largely because Paul happened to find some papers in her purse. Daisy is not what she seemed. In this act Peter Nolan comes on as the Attorney, Mr. O'Hagan.

But old Deegan is outwitted finally by all. Paul has split on everyone to their disaster—though Patrick and his wife, and Rose and Dan prosper—reserving a certain discretion in the end for his own advantage. For Daisy and Paul, the two bright wits, join at last in a trip to America.

The play lends itself to some fine character-acting. . . .

Almost enthusiastic reception was given to the piece.[72]

O'Donnell, now writing in the *Evening Herald*, did not attempt to describe the convoluted plot, finding it

much too difficult to write down in a few lines. It reminds me of strawberry shoots running wild in some quiet garden. Mr. Shiels apparently started off with a definite idea in his mind, but it got lost very often, and was only rescued by inartistic means towards the end of the third act.

It would not be fair to judge this play seriously, or even from the standpoint of an ordinary Abbey Comedy. It is farce, pure and simple, hilarious and melodramatic, and it undoubtedly will prove itself to be a good commercial proposition for the Abbey Theatre.

As a piece of dramatic writing it was full of weakness. There were soliloquies, impossible soliloquies of individuals addressing an audience of newly-plastered walls, topical references to Turks and the Four Courts, and a variety of curses and blessings that lent a sense of ridicule to the whole idea. In fact, the audience began to take the piece in such a hearty manner that a gentleman in the pit shouted "Hear, hear," after a speech in the third act!

You will laugh if you go to see *Paul Twyning*. It is the most gloriously farcical phantasy that has come our way for some time. Mr. Shiels can turn a sentence well, and his shafts of wit will strike you as they struck many an auditor last night, causing laughter long and uproarious. Apart from everything else, Barry Fitzgerald doing a musical turn in the second act will make recompense for your other disappointments. But don't go expecting to see comedy. Get your imagination worked up to a high pitch, and see in the world in general a highly fantastic and bizarre element, and then you will enjoy your visit. You will even see a boxing match a la mode Carpentier and Sengalese Siki!

The acting was exceedingly good. The make-up of the characters was even better. Never before was such an extraordinary collection of human beings on the Abbey stage together. At first they seemed strange and remote, but as the play wore on we accepted them for what they were, and the audience at the play's finish showed their appreciation in no half-hearted manner.[73]

Jacques in the *Independent* did not think the piece a comedy either:

The mistake at the outset was to describe *Paul Twyning* as comedy and to play it as melodramatic farce. There was door-opening, door-shutting, interrupted conversations, malapropisms, drink, dope, robbery and double dealing. . . .

It had a promising first act with Dan Deegan out-laughing every other character on the stage. It fell down in the second act, and was not saved by the fall-down of Paul Twyning, the tramp plasterer from Dublin, whose frothy ballad singing and Omar Khayyam rhapsodies were about the best things in an arid period. The dullness was as much due to misfits in caste as to the author's treatment of subject.[74]

However, Jacques did particularly admire the acting of Dolan:

If the work should fill a popular place in the repertoire of the Abbey it will be entirely to one player—Mr. Michael J. Dolan. In the character of Dan Deegan he has given us a study that ranks with the richest samples of humour presented in the home of the National Theatre Society. From his slattern trouser-ends gaping over his untied boots, via his baggy pants and awry waistband to his wild and wooly pate, he looked and was the last word in grotesque futility in the guise of a human being.[75]

Holloway called it a "farcical comedy," and thought it "started right merrily with an amazing first act and fell off considerably in Act 2 and almost got lost in a too complicated third act."[76] But even if the new play were merely undistinguished fun, it was greeted on its first performance by a distinguished audience. Among the crowd, Holloway noted Captain Bryan Cooper, Elizabeth Young, T. C. Murray, Lennox Robinson, Dermot O'Brien, Thomas McGreevy, Brinsley MacNamara, Frank J. Hugh O'Donnell, Darrell Figgis, Paul Farrell, P. S. O'Hegarty, Mary Frances McHugh, W. J. Lawrence, Jack B. Yeats and W. B. Yeats.[77]

On 23 October, the Abbey presented Colum's *Grasshopper*, which had had its premiere in New York in 1917, when it was directed by Ben Iden Payne and produced by, of all people, David Belasco.[78] The piece was not quite original, but based on a translation Colum's friend E. Washburn Freund had made of a German play by Count Keyserling. However, what Colum did was to Irish the translation thoroughly, and his adaptation was virtually a new creation, and his last strong work for the stage.

Nevertheless, the Abbey production was not entirely successful. For instance, M.H.J.B. wrote in the *Evening Herald*:

The Abbey Theatre was full last night when the curtain rose on a play called *The Grasshopper*, written by Padraic Colum and E. Washburn Freund, and founded on a play of Keyserling. The story is one that is ascribed to Irish life of a century ago, though the most casual observer of last night's performance of it could not fail to see that it has not the remotest claim to reality.

Michael Dempsey is the bad lot of the parish. He has many crimes on his conscience, but none seems to trouble him much. His "bychild," "Grasshopper," has been received in her home by his lawful wife, thus earning the love of the girl. Dempsey's wife falls ill, and the play opens in a dingy cottage with a deathbed scene, which has an atmosphere of horror not usual outside Grand Guignol. The dying woman's mother works upon the imagination of the "Grasshopper," telling her the egregious story of a woman who saves the life of her child by entering into a compact with the Blessed Virgin to give her own life.

"Grasshopper" sees a way to save the woman she calls her mother, and consequently goes before a statue of the Blessed Virgin and makes a contract to sacrifice her own life.

But the thought that her sister's lover, Matt O'Connor, may, after a temporary estrangement from his fiancée, fall in love with her and so admit her to enjoy some of the life ordinary girls enjoy, makes her waver until she discovers that Matt cares nothing for her.

Then she is willing to fulfil her contract. And here the utter unreality of the play reaches its climax. "Grasshopper" forces the miracle of the Blessed Virgin's contract and commits suicide by taking the deadly medicine which she has given in small quantities to her "mother."

There are many parts of the play which make it inconceivable as a portrayal of Irish life. For example, we can hardly imagine a priest enumerating the crimes of one of his parishioners by the deathbed of his family and neighbours. Neither can we imagine even the most ignorant peasant sacrificing to ignominious suicide the life of a child simply because her unhappy mother could not face the disgrace of that child's birth.

Then there is the cheap and unreasoning introduction of the Blessed Virgin to provide a miracle by demanding a suicide. From a Catholic viewpoint the theme of the play is wrong, and more a betrayal than a portrayal of Irish peasant life.

There is a notable absence of that style we usually associate with the name of Padraic Colum.

Many times during the play there are banal sentences put into the mouths of the characters, which result in the breakdown of tragic moments. Nothing can be more harmful than that tragedy should grow grotesque—when laughter usurps the place of tears. Last night's audience laughed at tragedy at its height, and they did it because of the incongruous dialogue. The whole piece is one of fearsome tragedy, and as such should be put to the highest tests—tests to which, however, *The Grasshopper* cannot submit.

Of the acting of the piece it must be said that in the title role Miss Eileen Crowe was a revelation. Not in its heyday did the Abbey produce such a promising actress. Miss Crowe was mistress of her power from beginning to end. She entered into the spirit of her heavy role with the ease and grace of an experienced tragedienne—the audience gave her full credit. It was the largest and indeed the only well-drawn character in the play. Christine Hayden, as the superstitious, calculating, self-sufficient contract maker, was really convincing, while of the male parts Matt O'Connor's was admirably handled by Maurice Esmonde.[79]

In a later notice, a *Herald* writer found faults in both theme and production:

Did the professional "keeners" at any time in Ireland's history for the past century begin their atrocious whining before the death of the sick person? Mr. Robinson evidently thinks so in *The Grasshopper*. Is it believable that a pack of romping girls would come to the windows of a dying woman's room and quiz an outcast girl about their tomboyish pranks with the boys?[80]

The *Evening Telegraph* liked the play more, but also found flaws:

The play is to all intents and purposes an Irish play, with genuine dramatic poetry in the working of the theme. There is that in the theme itself—but that, we presume, belongs entirely to the original German.

And there is the virtue that in this play there is a wealth of moving incident and revelation of character—as, for instance, some seven progressive points in the first act to three in the usual Irish play. For our young writers have, we fear, the fault of taking a faint idea and flogging it down to a generally feeble death. . . .

The play is beautiful. Parts of it evade the conventional technicalities of construction; but there is material for beauty and a swift and sufficiently moving tragedy.

A fault, perhaps, is that false note in Act II, when Maeve and her "half-gentleman" come and exchange shallow, flippant compliments beside the holy well in the manner of a like couple of to-day. Such a scene was necessary, perhaps, to explain Matt's jealousy and give flesh to his rival, but it imparts an awkwardness to the stage devices, and, moreover, jars, as we have said, in the working out of the tragedy, which is sombre, poetic, and a romance which does not need that we should look inside the works. . . .

The staging was good, but the costuming sometimes struck one as farcical, even with the vaguest idea of how such people should be dressed in Ireland a hundred years ago. Miss Hayden's gown, for instance, might with advantage be relegated to comedy.

A large audience thoroughly appreciated the play, though occasional members persistently and irritatingly laughed in the wrong places.[81]

Jacques in the *Independent* found little to admire:

We got keening women, doddering old grannies, giggling girls bare-footed and Dublin-accented, drinking swaggerers, a rancid woman-beater, a raucous hag, and—the thing that made a portion of the house stand up—a bout of fisticuffs. . . .

The play was beyond the players. At times the dialogue filled one with dejection. . . .

There were twenty-one characters in the cast. Their services have been employed to better purposes.[82]

The *Irish Times* gave part of its notice to an increasingly necessary criticism of the Abbey audience:

It is the sort of play that audiences, other than those composed of seasoned Abbey playgoers, would regard as "uncomfortable" but even Abbey audiences are not what they used to be and the ill-timed laughter of a section of the audience last night was a frequent annoyance. They seized upon the bits of dialogue spiced with humour, with the greediness of babbled children, who thought that they were at least about to get the sort of fare which they were expecting.

The part of Sheila, the friendless, unnamed girl, whose disgraced mother had ended her troubles in the waters of the lake, is one of the most difficult in the Abbey repertory, and the most exacting in which Miss Crowe has yet appeared. It is a psychological study on which the authors have concentrated to the dwarfing of all other characters.

. . . It is a part that tempts to over-acting, but Miss Crowe was finely restrained throughout. Her study of the poor, pitiful, little "grasshopper" was one of the best things seen on the Abbey stage for a considerable time.[83]

Holloway did not find Eileen Crowe convincing:

Her method lacks variety, and her voice has little variety of tone. Her acting was therefore inclined to be monotonous.[84]

He did find the play, save for the second act, generally gripping, and with much of the strange weirdness of poetic plays of *The Countess Cathleen* type.[85] But, for the most part, neither he nor his friends liked the play:

> MacNamara . . . was greatly struck by Act One of *The Grasshopper*. Murray, Caulfield, and I thought it too long drawn out. And as to the second act, he found it hopelessly crude and undramatic; and, when Caulfield queried in what period was the play, I answered, "In the Queen's Theatre period!" . . . Acts 3 and 4 got back to the uncanny atmosphere created in Act One. The play is an unpleasant one, and its foreign origin always discounted its Irish setting. After Act 2, Murray said, "It is always best to write a play oneself." On hearing which I made the awful remark, "I bet it was no freund of the author who helped him with that act."[86]

Grasshopper was an ambitious production, perhaps a bit beyond the resources of the Abbey. It was long, four acts; and its cast was large, twenty or so characters. Most of the characters, except the simple heroine, were not greatly developed, but that role was as finely theatrical a one as any the Abbey was to see until Brigid in Carroll's *Shadow and Substance*. The play has not been published, but a perusal of the manuscript finds few weaknesses in it until the rather botched conclusion. Without really being fine enough to revive, it would be interesting to publish, for it shows the realistic strengths of Padraic Colum in their last dramatic embodiment.

On 14 November, the Abbey presented a double bill of Brinsley MacNamara's three-act *The Land for the People* and Robinson's new one-act, *Crabbed Youth and Age*. MacNamara's play had been first produced in 1920 and was now apparently somewhat revised. However, no one greatly liked the play in 1920, and no one greatly liked it in 1922. Still, it received much more attention from reviewers than did Robinson's play. For instance, the *Evening Telegraph* at the end of its review of the MacNamara piece merely remarked:

> This was followed by what the programme perhaps fittingly terms a little comedy. The title, *Crabbed Youth and Age*, almost suggests the plot, if indeed that word applies at all. The whole thing is really little more than a farcical sketch. . . .
>
> This simple idea is worked up with commendable humour, and considering the extremely slight and flimsy materials it is but fair to say that the audience enjoyed the skit, and I laughed and applauded to their heart's content.[87]

Robinson's Mrs. Swan is said to be somewhat based on the character of Sarah Purser, and his little piece drolly shows the exasperated frustration of Mrs. Swan's daughters when their beaux are much more dazzled by their mother than by them. Although unpretentious, this realistic little comedy is effective in characterization, charming in situation, and quite in Robinson's most successful vein.

• • •

At the end of the year, Bertha Buggy essayed a description of Abbey audiences:

> The stalls are usually only half-full (our new rich are not patrons of the Arts). But here and there are a few elderly white-haired ladies with keen intelligent faces and the almost inevitable piece of black lace at their throats, and here are a few young men wearing side-whiskers; at the back of the stalls are some tweed-clad, happy-looking, middle-aged women; a few flappers with sleek bobbed hair, eating chocolate; a few Trinity or National boys; and then—the gentlemen with red beards.
>
> I do not know why there is always a red beard in the stalls—but there always is—I counted as many as four one night. . . .
>
> The inhabitants of the Abbey stalls behave very much the same as the inhabitants of any other stalls during the intervals, except that there is more visiting done. The wearer of side-whiskers goes over and bends deferentially over to the little old lady with white hair; the tweed-clad ladies and one of the red-beards exchange criticisms of the play. There is an all-one-family air about the whole thing.
>
> The pit types are easily recognisable, too. Intelligent-looking thin young men, who usually come in twos and threes; plump middle-aged couples, who come early, study the programme, and discuss the actors. . . .
>
> Young girls in tweeds form a large part of a pit audience. They also come in twos and threes, and have eager intelligent faces, and a good many of them wear the Fainne.
>
> Then there are always a few young men up from the country, who are obviously strangers, and who drift into the Abbey because of a vague idea that it is Irish. . . .
>
> At the very back of the pit, sitting with their backs against the green curtain, are nearly always to be found about five or six workingmen—plain, simple workingmen. . . .
>
> Every audience has its quota of people who mentally (and often actually) rustle paper bags, and it is, after all, a matter for thanksgiving that their presence in the Abbey Theatre is only rendered so conspicuous because of the sharp contrast they present to the rest of the audience.[88]

Part of the entre-act interest at the Abbey was the occasional vague appearance of W. B. Yeats, but the tall and gangly Lennox Robinson was just as scenic. As a writer in the *Herald* noted:

> To be sure, Mr. Robinson is not to be seen in the stalls as frequently as of old, and in a way that is to be regretted. We of the pit liked to see him emerge from the small door on the left, gaze round the house with a bewildered air (never suspecting him of counting the house) until he saw one of his many friends in the stalls. To see him shake hands with someone three rows away or indeed hold a conversation was looked upon as the expected, so tall he seemed down there in the front rows.[89]

One growing characteristic of Abbey audiences was noted by several critics during the year—"their brainless, bovine laughter" at the most incongruous moments. For instance, at a production of *Birthright* on 22 September, Holloway noted:

> The audience was an extraordinary one; it giggled at everything, till at last I had to call out to one persistent loud giggler in the pit who guffawed even when the

> brothers fight—"Put that Idiot out!"—which stopped his giggles. Two men in the Stalls next Murray laughed persistently in the wrong places. . . . If it were badly acted, it would be another thing Murray said to me, "But it isn't." He couldn't understand the mentality of the gigglers at all.[90]

The tendency of audiences to snatch the opportunity of laughing at anything is a perennial problem. In serious plays, the reason might simply be a nervous reaction. Another reason might be the expectation that an audience has of being entertained at the theater. And another reason is doubtless that the theater is a particularly public, rather than a private experience. A reader, alone in his armchair, may vastly enjoy *The Importance of Being Earnest*, yet scarcely ever laugh out loud. The same person in a theater seat, watching a good production of even some much stupider play—say, *Charley's Aunt*—will probably find himself participating frequently in the joint public reaction of laughing out loud. The reason is not that *Charley's Aunt* is funnier than *The Importance of Being Earnest*, but that the reactions to a staged play are so different from those to a printed book that they almost seem differences of kind rather than degree.

Also, the longer that actors play a role, the deader their interpretation and, hence, the greater the temptation to make their effects bigger. Consequently, one often finds actors in a comedy pushing lines, and giving them an exaggerated theatricality that will cause a broader response than the lines are worth. Hence, the mugging and gagging that some Abbey actors indulged in.

Readers of volume 2 of this history may recall that W. G. Fay got laughs in the original production of *Kathleen ni Houlihan*, and then in later performances deliberately underplayed those lines so as not to hurt the cumulative tone of the play. Later actors, such as Sinclair and Sara Allgood, who had strong stage personalities, would often take incredible liberties with a script, unless they were firmly controlled by a stronger directorial hand than Lennox Robinson usually had. In the history of the Abbey, the tendency to push rather than to restrain was usually stronger and was probably most pronounced during the exile to the Queen's in the 1950s and 1960s. Then, particularly in long runs of broad plays like John McCann's, the company got very broad, and established a tone that encouraged the audience's bad habits. Hence, a popular comedian like Harry Brogan might enter in a serious role and be greeted with an outburst of laughter.

An audience is hard to control. When Lennox Robinson once in a programme note exhorted Abbey audiences not to clap during an act, they simply ignored his stricture. When Bernard Shaw in a programme note exhorted an audience not to hold up a play by laughter, they ignored even him.

There were certainly fine, controlled productions and fine individual performances at the Abbey during these years, but there was also great variation in quality. Critics frequently complain, for instance, of the necessity for the prompter. And even actors like Allgood and Fitzgerald often had their lines most imperfectly memorized. There is some excuse at least for actors such as Fitzgerald and Fallon who were full-time civil servants and could only rehearse during lunch hours or after work and before an evening's performance. There is also some excuse because the Abbey changed its program each week.

However, other matters were less excusable, and many of them were the faults of Robinson and Dolan who at this time directed most of the plays. For instance, a critic in the *Herald* had these strictures to make about the first staging of *Aftermath* in January:

> There are two particular matters to which our young friends of the company of the Abbey must give attention. They are accents and make-up. In Mr. Murray's play last week the schoolmaster of the ree-raw village in Co. Cork had an accent more associated with an Oxford youth than with a hard-working farming lad who never went farther than Dublin, where he became a scholar, and next a teacher, with a love for Russian literature and female prettiness. This week the Co. Down cobbler's wife [Eileen O'Kelly playing in Ervine's *The Island of Saints and Scholars*] who would consign "Papishes" to perdition had an accent that was never anything in particular. It wouldn't remain natural Dublin, with a cold in the head, but strove desperately to be Northern Counties. Her son Johnny battled manfully to give a hammer-on-an-anvil clip to his words and sometimes got it. His make-up! He is supposed to be coming home from the grimy shipyards after a series of fights, in which he gets his forehead opened. But, bless your soul, he had sweet, polished, clean-shaven cheeks and sleek hair that would rouse the envy of Claude in *The Suburban Groove*.
>
> These matters arise from pure indifference. They, like the bursts of blather and the bad exits and the clean polished shoes after coming in from the dirty lane outside, are all symptoms of, and are themselves, bad art. The present company of players can do good work, excellent work. They have already given us warrant of good service, and let us hope it will not be slipshod. The younger members might deign to learn something from such experienced players as Barry Fitzgerald (whose facial expression in *The Lord Mayor* was art from wrinkle to hair tuft), Peter Nolan (a master of restraint), and Eric Gorman (who can talk with a smoking pipe in his mouth so that every word is heard at the back of the house).[91]

In February, a critic remarked upon a notably amateurish bit of blocking in Robinson's first production of his own *Round Table*:

> And as we're on the matter of production and stage management, is one allowed to ask who was responsible for the "grouping" of the crowd in the last act—the railway waiting-room? In they came, the advance guards of the ladies' battalions of the Drennans and the Pegums, and lined up across the footlights, comedy chorus fashion, eyes front, facing out.[92]

Revivals, especially of frequently done plays, were often gone through too listlessly or too broadly, as if they had been but skimpily rehearsed. For instance, in October, Holloway reported:

> *The Serf* was, on the whole, listlessly and indifferently played, few in the cast suiting

their parts, and some being hopelessly misplaced, such as Eric Gorman as Jack Sheridan, Christine Hayden as Margaret Drennan and Clement Kenny as Father Owen (the latter was very weak and amateurish; it was his first appearance with the Abbey Company). They let down the play badly, and with Fallon as a not too effective Father Harold the piece almost collapsed at times.[93]

Or, on 7 February, he wrote of *The Revolutionist*:

The night was cold and windy and the Abbey very poorly attended for the revival of *The Revolutionist*. It wears badly. Michael J. Dolan is wrongly cast for "Hugh O'Neill," as he lacks enthusiasm and grip for the part. There is no sincerity in his playing of it; therefore, the play became tame and listless, and the cold night and small audience made it a cold dead thing indeed.[94]

Or, on 16 February, Holloway thought *The Serf*

too tamely and listlessly enacted on the whole, both Dolan and Eileen Crowe underplaying their parts, and the former pitching his voice in such an undertone as almost not to be heard. Natural acting is one thing; listless gabbing quite another! The present Abbey Company are often inclined to forget to "appear" natural and become merely listless repeaters of words.[95]

Except when the revival was a comedy. Then, as in the January revival of *The Country Dressmaker*, the playing could become much too broad:

Barry Fitzgerald overacted Edward Normyle and Tony Quinn made a hopelessly ineffective Pats Connor, and Kathleen Fortune a self-conscious Min, and overacted to excess. Eileen O'Kelly as Mary Ann and the rest of the Clohesy family were very crudely enacted.[96]

A particular offender was Dossie Wright who had been with the theater from the early days. Mainly he was used to run lights, but occasionally he played small parts. Valentine Vousden told Holloway:

He [Vousden] doesn't think U. Wright can act at all and wonders how he ever gets on the stage. . . . I told him that, "Will Fay worked at electric engineering, and Wright worked with him, and when the Abbey opened Wright found himself on the stage with Will Fay!" Wright, while on, grins like a looney and usually thinks himself vastly funny by gagging. And in the last act of *The Round Table* to-day, where he says he can't see the booking offices," added, "I'll tell you what I did see—McGilligan's daughter, Maryann!"

Dorothy Lynd is also a very ineffective actress as a rule; she minces her words too much, and then her North of Ireland accent scarcely suits Co. Cork plays.[97]

And discipline was, as in many periods of the Abbey's history, a problem. On 17 December, Holloway wrote:

I was speaking to Dolan re the over-acting of Quinn in *Meadowsweet*, and he told

> me that Quinn and Miss Crowe had gotten swelled heads and would take instructions from no one, especially from such as he who is friendly with them off the stage.[98]

The lack of discipline may be seen even in the performances of an actor on different nights in the same part—not to mention the widely different quality of performances in different parts. Sara Allgood is a good case in point. Used to being the Abbey's leading lady and used also to directing her own occasional companies, she was almost undirectable. As she remarked to T. H. Nally, "She thought Robinson an indifferent producer; she had to put him right on many points."[99] For his part, Robinson had most mixed feelings about Sara's occasional returns to the Abbey. As he wrote of her to Lady Gregory sometime in August:

> She has been very amiable since she came and giving very fine performances except in *Shadow of the Glen* in which she is downright bad. I saw it tonight and hated her, but her performance in *Building Fund* is simply marvellous.[100]

In some pieces, such as *Kathleen ni Houlihan*, Sally's playing still "inspired something akin to reverence."[101] Or, as Holloway wrote of her in the part, "The house rose to her at the end of the play, and seldom has such enthusiastic applause been heard for years at the Abbey."[102] In other roles, however, her years of playing to popular audiences in commercial theaters seem to have had a coarsening influence on her style. When Holloway saw her on 22 August as Aunt Ellen in *The Whiteheaded Boy*, he wrote:

> I regret to say that in conception and make-up she was too grotesquely farcical and not infrequently distinctly vulgar . . . and then in order to try to make the part a more farcical and low comedy study, she gagged quite a lot. Aunt Ellen is a delightful character study, but Miss Allgood treated her as if she were simply and solely food for laughter.[103]

Frank Fay, Sally's old colleague from the early days, had been also brought back to the Abbey for occasional roles; but Fay balked at Sally's suggestions for new business in *The Building Fund*. She "suggested his wearing a big white and black band round his hat in the last act. She saw such a band worn in London, and it got a big laugh."[104]

But the strongest indication of how far Sara Allgood had strayed from the traditions of the early days was Holloway's description of her Aunt Ellen on 26 August:

> It [*The Whiteheaded Boy*] was most naturally enacted by the entire cast save Sara Allgood who was just in the humour for gagging and foolery. When she tripped up in Act One in a hole in the carpet, she murmured, "I enjoyed the trip very much!" And again when Denis uses bad language over his treatment by the family in Act One, "There's language that's Trinity for you!" And when Hannah leaves to spread

> the news of Denis' trip, she exclaims after her, "Mind the cars!" Nearly every other minute she dropped in a gag of her own into the text. The company enjoyed the gags and the audience in many cases also.[105]

When Frank Fay was asked back to the Abbey in 1922 to play some of his old roles, he was sometimes still quite fine. For instance, the *Evening Mail* wrote:

> Frank Fay's acting made *The Building Fund* a pleasurable play, indeed, at the Abbey Theatre last night. There was a delicate touch about his performance that was felt rather than seen or heard.
>
> . . . The cunning, witty, miserly bachelor-farmer of 45 was to be pictured in the cut of his long frieze coat, in his soft, flat black hat, in his cute, sparkling eyes and the young-old expression of his face.[106]

As the Wise Man in *The Hour Glass*, however, he was apparently erratic from night to night. On one night, Holloway could write of him:

> Frank Fay as the Wise Man was tiresomely slow and precise in his delivery—hacking his sentences into a series of disjointed words and failing to rise to the drama of the climax. There was something artificial and stilted in his movements as well as speech that left me cold and completely unsatisfied.[107]

But then, only two nights later, Holloway could remark that Fay was "really fine."[108] Certainly, he had become a more mannered actor over the years, and John MacDonagh, who directed him in *The Casey Millions* and *Wicklow Gold* films, "told Nally privately that he found it very hard to get Fay to act naturally before the camera."[109] And Leo Keogh thought:

> There is too much of the ego about Frank Fay; he is all business and no art. The regular stage spoiled the natural charm of his delivery long ago.[110]

The most notable of the current actors were, of course, Fitzgerald, Crowe, and McCormick. Their talents had already been proven, but they were still learning their trade. Fitzgerald was already a consummate comedian, and had sometimes distinguished himself in straight character parts. For instance, of his Johnston Cooney in *The Land for the People*, Holloway wrote:

> Both in make-up and in the thorough realisation of the part, it was quite impossible to conceive anything finer, and it is no exaggeration to say that a better piece of character-acting, quiet, natural, and unexaggerated, has never been seen on the Abbey stage.[111]

However, his Eloquent Dempsy was not up to Sinclair's, and his articulation left, as it always did, much to be desired.

Eileen Crowe had proved her power in many young leading roles, but many writers still found her "amateurish in movements and gesture,"[112] and thought her musical voice monotonous—a fault which if anything, was to increase over the years.

The most versatile of this talented trio was McCormick, who spent much of the year still unhappily touring in *Paddy the Next Best Thing*. In August, however, McCormick briefly returned to the Abbey to play Maurice Harte, and Holloway reported:

> Murray didn't like McCormick as Maurice Harte as well as O'Donovan in the part, and I said he failed somewhat on being too conscientious in his realism of his neurotic conception of the character. I liked his playing in Act One. It was the crouching, shrivelled-up figure of the witless young student in the final episode that didn't carry the heart-twisting pathos that O'Donovan was able to give Maurice.[113]

"Conscientious" is probably the operative word about McCormick. During this visit to Dublin, he had the following conversation with Holloway:

> Speaking of Robinson, he said, "He was too fond of favouritism amongst the players and rarely ever gives an encouraging word." Robinson said to him on yesterday, "I'd like you to stay over. You seem to have improved so much in your playing of Maurice Harte." Mac remembered the first part of Freddy O'Donovan he was cast for after Freddy left the Abbey. It was that of the Coiner. He remembered it was with fear and trembling that he made up for the part and came down to rehearse it in character for the first time with the others running through it in ordinary clothes. The empty theatre with only Robinson in it seemed ghostly to him, and his heart sank as the little piece dragged its (to him on that occasion) endless length along; and when it had ended Robinson told him he was very bad, and he knew he had failed and his heart sank almost into his boots, and he almost broke down and cried on entering his dressing room, and he had it in his mind to throw up the part. But always being of a very determined nature, he resolved to stick to the part and do his best with it, and when the evening came he played it for all he was worth and scored. Ever since he has never refused any part, though it was hard at first to play in most of those made popular by O'Donovan, and people were always telling him he ought to do this and that as O'Donovan did. But he lent a deaf ear to them all and studied each part carefully for himself till he had won out on his own.[114]

• • •

The always precarious finances of the theater had become during the Tan War even more precarious, and so the ink was hardly dry on the treaty when the directors began discussing turning the theater over, in some fashion, to the new government. On 10 January, Lady Gregory had tea with Robinson and recorded in her journal:

> He had lunched with Desmond Fitzgerald and had spoken about turning over the Abbey to a National Government, said we had thought of doing so in Redmond's time, and had heard they were now going to establish one. Fitzgerald said there was no idea of taking the Gaiety or doing anything on a large scale, that he hadn't heard of any definite plan and that of course the Abbey is the National Theatre of Ireland. So we need not be in a hurry but just go on with our work.[115]

On 24 April, Robinson wrote to Yeats about the matter:

> I spoke to you when I last saw you about trying to get governmental assistance for the Abbey. I think we need it for these reasons (a) to make the Theatre's position financially secure, (b) to enable us to engage a permanent Company.
>
> I need say nothing about (a), you and Lady Gregory realise the anxiety of the present position as fully as I do. About (b) I must just say that to continue as we have for the last year using as our players men and women who have other employments and who, therefore, can only give us odd hours after their work (or their lunch hour) and who only rehearse when they are tired or hungry, is to make really good work almost impossible. It is heartbreaking for the producer to work under such conditions, it does not give the players or the play half a chance. I think it is wonderful that we have done as good work as we have during the last twelve months when we had only two men permanently with us (now we have only *one* and a couple of girls who happen to be idle and can give us their mornings) but I do feel strongly that an effort should be made to put things on a more business-like footing. It is the Government's disgrace if they refuse us help, not ours in asking for it.
>
> I believe we shall have a very poor chance of receiving such help unless we offer in return to do all we can to create and foster a Gaelic Theatre. For that purpose my budget includes a Gaelic-speaking man who has some knowledge of the stage and can produce Gaelic plays and, perhaps, teach Gaelic to those players who have scanty knowledge of it. Some of the players engaged should, of course, be Gaelic speakers. It is difficult to say how many performances of Gaelic plays should be given—the repertoire is so small—and I don't think we should guarantee any special number but aim at about one Gaelic play to four English, and the Gaelic plays should be performed separately, not mixed with the English. We should also promise to give special performances on occasion when asked to do so by the Government and should accept suggestions from them as to the plays given on such occasions. I should not suggest that they have any representation on the Directorate or Management.
>
> The expenses and receipts in my budget are calculated on our playing for 40 weeks in the year, during the remaining 12 weeks the permanent players and permanent staff would receive half salaries. We should be able to tour during part of these 12 weeks and make money but I have thought it better not to calculate definitely on that. The house receipts are calculated on our takings during the season 1919–1920 which was a fair average season, we had no "star" players but a good all-round company and a good many new plays. I think that next season—especially if we had been officially "recognised" as the Irish National Theatre—we should do quite as well and probably much better but we must be prepared to get small audiences for the Gaelic plays.
>
> I think that we should ask for at least £1,000 a year, but in addition for the first year we should try to get an extra £500 for furnishing and repairs. New carpets are badly wanted (the one down the stairs to the stalls so worn that it had to be taken up altogether), many of the seats need repairing, scenery wants repapering and repairing, lighting could be improved.[16]

After this sensible and realistic assessment, Robinson then appended a tentative yearly budget for the theater:

> EXPENDITURE
>
> *Actors.* A Company of 12 permanent players under contract for a season of 40 weeks and 12 weeks at half-salaries, the players' salaries to vary from £3 a week to

£7. Also an average of 6 extra players each week, not under contract, at £2 per week.

2 players @ £7 = £	644. 0. 0.	
4 players @ £5 = £	920. 0. 0.	
6 players @ £3 = £	828. 0. 0.	
6 extra @ £2 = £	480. 0. 0.	
		£2,972. 0. 0.

Manager & Producer. @ £5 per week, 40 weeks, 12 weeks ½ salary:	230. 0. 0.
Gaelic Producer & Teacher. @ £4 per week, 40 weeks, 12 weeks ½ salary:	184. 0. 0.
Secretary. @ £3 per week, 52 weeks full pay	156. 0. 0.
Publicity Man. @ £1 per week, 40 weeks only	40. 0. 0.
Permanent Staff. all for 40 weeks, 12 weeks ½ salary	

Carpenter	£184. 0. 0.	
Property Man	138. 0. 0.	
Chars	164. 9. 0.	
Wardrobe Mistress	69. 0. 0.	
Box Office	86. 5. 0.	
Messenger	26. 0. 0.	
		667. 14. 0.

Night Staff. all for 40 weeks only.

Front of house	£ 520. 6. 8	
Stage	351. 6. 8.	
Orchestra	700. 0. 0.	
		1,571. 13. 4

Advertising, 40 weeks	665. 0. 0.
Authors' Fees	340.
Lighting & Heating	330.[117]

With the addition of a few miscellaneous items, such as Bill Posting, the total came, in round numbers, to £8,000, to run the theater for a year. At the same time, Robinson appended a tentative, somewhat optimistic estimate of a year's receipts:

RECEIPTS

House receipts, 40 weeks	£6,785. 6. 8
Profit on 5 weeks lets[x]	85. 0. 0
36 Sunday lets	144. 0. 0
15 afternoon lets	90. 0. 0
Rents receivable	110. 17. 0
Advertisements in programme	98. 0. 0
Profit on Cafe	40. 0. 0
	£7,353. 4. 0

[x]It is calculated that at least 5 out of the 12 weeks the Company would not be playing might be let.[118]

On 20 October, Lady Gregory noted that Robinson sent for her approval a formal statement to be presented to the government. She remarked:

> The paper was too much a S.O.S. and did not give an idea of the value of the property we propose to present to the Nation. And the figures were nearly all wrong, and though I didn't mind Yeats being given credit for "Collecting money in 1916 that helped to keep the theatre going" (the £200 through his lectures) I thought the sum, over £2000, I had raised in 1911 to enable us to buy and continue the theatre should be mentioned also.[119]

A draft of Robinson's statement, with a few corrections in Yeats's hand, is in the National Library of Ireland, and reads:

THE ABBEY THEATRE

A Statement made by its Directors to the Irish Provisional Government.

1. The following statement is made with the object of bringing before the notice of the Government the present precarious position of the Abbey Theatre and the reasons why it should receive help from the Government.

PAST HISTORY

2. It is unnecessary to relate at any length the history of the Abbey Theatre. It began as the Irish Literary Theatre in 1899, became the Irish National Theatre Society, Ltd. in 1903 and, aided by Miss Horniman, opened in the Abbey Theatre in December 1904. In 1911 the Theatre building was taken over from Miss Horniman and it is now entirely controlled by the Directors—Lady Gregory and Mr. W. B. Yeats—who are unpaid. The Patent of the Theatre is granted to Lady Gregory and the work of the Theatre is restricted by the Patent to the production of Irish plays, plays by Irish authors and translations of foreign masterpieces. Since its inception it has inspired the writing of several hundreds of plays by Irish authors, and has always carried on its work as a repertory Theatre, that is to say it changes its programme each week and does not put on plays for a "run." It has never earned enough money by its performances in Dublin to enable it to pay its way but before the European War it was able, by visits to England and America, to keep solvent and to give its players a fair remuneration for their work. The war put an end to touring abroad but in 1916 some money was collected in England by Mr. Yeats and in the spring of 1921, after a disastrous winter when curfew had ruined nearly every Dublin theatre a sum of £700 was raised in England by lectures given by Lady Gregory, W. B. Yeats, Bernard Shaw etc., and by subscriptions. This money was just to pay existing debts and the Theatre's position was then clear.

THE PRESENT

3. Since the Truce to Aug. 31st, 1922 the Theatre has incurred a loss of £683. As there is no accumulation of Cash Capital and the only assets are the Theatre premises and contents the Directors feel that they cannot continue playing and run the risk of bankruptcy. The position during the last year has been so uncertain that they have been afraid to engage a permanent company of players and have had to depend on men and women who have other employments and who have only been able to work at the Theatre after their other work was over, or during their lunch hour. Under such conditions it has been very difficult to keep up the high standard of acting and production which have been associated with this Theatre; the Directors believe that, by a great effort, the standard *was* kept up, but it is not

possible indefinitely to continue under these circumstances. It has also been impossible during the last few years to spend money to keep up the fabric of the Theatre both on the stage and in the house, and at the present moment money is urgently needed for carpeting, repairing of scenery, lighting etc. The Directors feel that they can no longer appeal to England for help; their appeal must now be made to their own Government.

A NATIONAL THEATER

4. It was always the Directors' intention to hand the Abbey Theater over to the Irish Government as soon as that Government was established. The Directors believe that they are correct in stating that every Government except that of England and its Colonies, the United States of America, and Venezuela possesses its subsidised State Theater. The Comédie Française is one of the glories of France, the famous Moscow Arts Theatre is subsidised by the Soviet Government. Germany possesses hundreds of national Municipal Theatres. These countries believe that a theater which is not dependent for its existence on the caprice of the public can play a great part in the education of the nation. The Abbey Theatre may be considered by the Irish Government to be too small and too humble to be the Theatre of the Irish Nation. It may contemplate building a State Theatre or taking over one of the large Dublin Theaters for this purpose but the cost of such an undertaking would be very considerable, the Irish playgoers have become to a great extent denationalised and the support given by the public would be likely to be small.

A GAELIC THEATER

5. The Directors know that the Government desire to build on a Gaelic civilisation. They therefore intend, if the Government will assist them, to engage a Gaelic-speaking producer of plays and to form a company of Gaelic players. The number of plays in Gaelic is not considerable but if it were known that a Theatre and a company of Gaelic players were in existence the beat possible impetus would be given to Gaelic writers to write for the stage. The Gaelic plays would not be mixed with the English ones but every five or six weeks the Theatre would be given over for a week of Gaelic drama. It is not possible to go into exact details in advance; much would depend on the number and the quality of the Gaelic plays submitted for production, but the Directors would undertake to give every facility to the creation of a Gaelic Theatre. If the Government intend to make a great National Theatre the Abbey Theatre might eventually be turned into the Gaelic Theatre.

6. In the meantime the Abbey Theatre is in danger of being forced to close its doors. For eighteen years the Directors have carried on its work. They carried it on in spite of the European war (which killed every repertory theater in England save one), and in spite of the English war in Ireland. Ungrudgingly and without pay they have given their services to the creation of the Irish drama, they have created the Irish Theater—a mass of plays, dramatists that have brought honour to Ireland all over the world, a type of acting that has largely become the model of all modern acting, players of genius. They think that the time has come when the responsibility of the Theater should be borne by the State.

WHAT IS ASKED FOR

7. For the present, and as a temporary measure to save the Abbey from closing, they suggest:

(a) That the Government should make the Theater a grant of £2,000 pounds, £500 to be spent on necessary repairs and renewals and £1,500 on carrying on the Theater for a period of 12 months.
(b) That the Theater should be publicly recognised by the Government as being the National Theater of Ireland.
In return the Directors would undertake to do everything in their power to foster the growth of a Gaelic Theater; would give special performances on such occasions as the Government might require, would engage a permanent company of Players for a year and would accept any reasonable method of supervision by the Government that the Government might desire.

A YEAR HENCE

8. At the end of the twelve months the position would be reconsidered. The Government will then be in a better position to judge whether the time has come to form a National Theater on an ambitious scale, or whether the Abbey Theater should continue to be the National Theater. Some opinion too can be formed then as to the importance the Gaelic Theater is likely to assume.

Below is given an estimate of the probable expenditure and receipts. The door receipts are calculated on the season 1919–1920, allowance being made for the fact that the Gaelic plays would be likely at first to draw small audiences. It should be noted that the *net* door receipts are given, the Government tax being deducted first. This tax amounted last year to £933. The tax is about 25% of the receipts so that if, as is calculated, £6,000 was taken the government would receive £1,200; therefore the subsidy would in reality be only £800.[120]

• • •

Little or nothing of Irish interest appeared during the year at the Royal, the Gaiety, the Empire or the Tivoli. Typical of the Royal's fare was the engagement for the week of 6 March of "Winston's Water Lions and Diving Nymphs," who disported themselves in a six thousand gallon tank of water; or on 17 April of Long Tack Sam, "the Master Mind of Chinese Necromancers"; or on 24 April of Fujiwara, "the Japanese McCormack."

The Empire and the Tivoli were lower-brow and cheaper in their variety programs. The Empire, however, did present two revivals of MacDonagh's popular *The Irish Jew*, and on 20 March the first production of his shorter and slighter *The Pride of Petravore*, which Jacques adequately summed up in the *Evening Herald*:

"Tell me, Flannery," roared the Major, "have you got an alibi?"
"A wha', major?" croaked Flannery, confused and gasping.
Major Darling, R.M., gave an imitation of a Punjab gourd in a fit of apoplexy, and yelped again, "An alibi, damn you! Have you got one?"
"Oh, no, yer worship," replied Flannery; "shure I'm not married at all."
Loud, rolling, explosive laughter.
The scene was the courthouse in Petravore; the reason of the scene was the production at the Empire Theater of a new playlet by Mr. John MacDonagh, entitled *The Pride of Petravore*, and the laughter boomed over the auditorium.

The author describes his new work as a sketch. It is rather long for such a description. It stretches out into a one-act play. The Major Darling, R.M., on the occasion was Mr. Charles L. Keogh, and in make-up to wearables, from riding-boot to eyeglass, as well as in equipment of vocabulary, from damn to flow of language, he looked as popular imagination expects an R.M. should look in a stage picture of Irish court-life in pre–Free State days. But in attention to careful detail of make-up he could give no points to Mr. Patrick Hayden in his presentation of the country car-man, Paddy Flannery. Nothing was astray. The dirty, hob-nailed boots, the slopping trousers, the soled and heeled face, the slobbery voice, and the steam-escape accent, particularly in jocularity—it was unique and original.

If the playlet was a sketch at all, it was a sketch of character studies. Mr. James O'Dea adorned the jaws of "P. J. Mullarkey, J. P., U. D. C.," with side-whiskers and sang his ballad with the gusto of a "native." Mr. Dick Smith had nothing to do with "Samuel Lock, J. P.," except frame his face in a black beard and preach law and order, with a blue uniform as its symbol. Mr. Harry O'Donovan was a long-winded R.I.C. sergeant, who could assume refreshing familiarity when speaking of the country bench J. P. There was little for Mr. Ralph Goggin except to call for order in court, being petty sessions clerk; and Mrs. Fae Sargent came to court as the defendant, Mrs. Ellen O'Brien, in high heels and high dudgeon and variable accent, as perhaps might be expected in the circumstances, she being "the Pride of Petravore," renowned in ballad of fair and cross-road.

The court-house scene, the story of which it is unnecessary to unfold, was made because the Pride of Petravore was being prosecuted for a breach of the licensing laws, to wit, et cetera. Mr. John MacDonagh also wrote *The Irish Jew*, and, no doubt, soon again he will give us something as good.[121]

A sterner but juster view was that of O'Donnell in the *Gael*:

I find it hard to forgive John MacDonagh for producting *The Pride of Petravore* at the Empire Theater last week. It is of that particular class of poor fun, neither farce nor comedy, with a constant "It's meself-do-be-thinking" atmosphere, which leaves one cold and indignant. . . . I am sorry that a man who has done such fine work for real, legitimate drama should write down to the level of cheap, musical, half-crosstalk. I do not say that the sketch is not good in its way, or that it failed to bring laughter loud and long. Certainly, on Thursday night, when I was present, I saw one lady laugh so much that I thought she would faint. As a music hall sketch it is all right . . . not quite so banal as others . . . but what I complain of is that one of our leading playwrights should turn out such poor-class goods. . . . The best part of James O'Dea's performance as "P. J.," the gallant, oily-tongued local magistrate, was his singing of a verse from "The Pride of Petravore." Somehow or other I felt the rest of the time that he was over-acting his part, and I never got as near to enjoying him as I did when he made his Corporation speech in *The Irish Jew*. It is the first time I have seen Mr. O'Dea in a peasant part, and I hope it will be my last, for his genius—and I consider him the most amusing of all our Irish entertainers—lies in entirely different parts, such as some of those he has done in plays produced by the Dublin Drama League.[122]

In his Hardwicke Street days, under the wing of Edward Martyn, John MacDonagh showed more than serious promise as director, actor, and writer. In his Drama League days, Jimmy O'Dea played Chekhov, Shaw, and Brieux with considerable credit. Left to their own devices, however, they drifted into broad comedy and yet broader revues. MacDonagh wound up his days in Radio Éireann, and O'Dea became Ireland's premiere pantomime dame well into the 1960s. Both could have been much more.

On 20 February at the Empire, *Gassed* appeared on the bill, and on 22 May *Tactics*. The Dublin Jewish Dramatic Society rented the theater on Sunday, 2 April, to do *Special Pleading*, *Spreading the News*, and Sholem Aleichem's *Dear Doktor*. The Dublin Opera Company opened a two-week stand on 24 April, with such staples as *The Bohemian Girl*, *Maritana* and *Il Trovatore*. At the end of the year, however, the *Evening Mail* noted that

> the Empire Theater has been acquired by a syndicate, of which Mr. I. I. Bradlaw is one of the most prominent members.
>
> It is intended by the new proprietors to change the name of the concern to the Star Theater, and it may be possible that it may be opened early in the New Year.
>
> "So far as is possible," said Mr. Bradlaw, in an interview this afternoon, "we shall run Irish companies. . . ."[123]

About the only items of Irish interest at the Tivoli during the year were two Chris Silvester one-act farces, *All in the Play* on 7 August and *Tickle 'Em* on 9 October.

The Gaiety as usual depended on British touring companies in new musicals and light comedies. However, Fred Terry made yet another appearance in his sixteenth year of touring *The Scarlet Pimpernel*; also W. W. Kelly's Company appeared again in the long-lived *A Royal Divorce*, and even *The Belle of New York* appeared once again. Two touring companies with some stage-Irish interest also reappeared: J. Hartley Manners' *Peg o' My Heart* in the week of 3 April and Gertrude Page's *Paddy the Next Best Thing*, with Kathleen Drago and F. J. McCormick, in the week of 4 September.[124] The Carl Rosa Opera Company appeared for a week, and the O'Mara Opera Company for several weeks in February and also in July. On its second appearance, the O'Mara Company advertised the premiere of Molyneux Palmer's new Irish opera, *Sruth na Maoile*, but had to postpone it because of the fighting in Dublin. (On 28 July, incidentally, the government arrested four men in the theater.) The Rathmines and Rathgar Musical Society gave a week of *Ruddigore* in May and a week of *The Mikado* in December. The Dublin University Dramatic Society gave Milne's *Mr. Pim Passes By* and Monckton Hoffe's *The Little Damozel* for the week of 6 March. And for the week of 11 December, the Ulster Theater presented three programs of old and new work: *Loaves and Fishes* and *The Mist That Does Be On the Bog*, the still popular *Drone* and *Thompson in Tir na' nOge*, and *The Throwbacks* and *Turncoats*. The new piece was *The Throwbacks*, which the company had first played on 4 September during a week's visit to Liverpool.

In an article of 2 May, John W. Coulter, who was to write some interesting Irish plays and some interesting Canadian ones, made these trenchant criticisms of the Ulster group:

What has been said above regarding the dangers of a too rigid adherence to stereotyped dramatic forms applies with equal force to the policy of the Ulster Theater. Mr. R. Mayne, in his play, *The Drone*, an indubitable masterpiece of folk comedy, set a catching fashion. And now, apart from the exigencies of commercial production, it is become by far the most dangerous limitation of the art of the Northern playwrights that it, too, has placed an almost exclusive emphasis upon the folk element. It is as though the folk who speak in dialect were the only class of persons in the community whose struggles and foibles are capable of being dramatically exploited.

The later Ulster plays have mostly been of the frankly farcical kind, in which a loose and highly improbable sequence of circumstances is invented for no better purpose, apparently, than that of airing the very broad humour, droll *nuances* of inflection, and quaint confusions and anachronisms which characterise the speech of the Ulster peasant. That vein is now a little overworked. . . . Local colour is apt to become very much local and very little colour. Besides, from the point of view of dramatic art, there is something inferior in the appeal these grotesque exaggerations make to the risible propensities of an Ulster audience. Perhaps it is that the laughter which they draw is, in the last analysis, the patronising laughter of superior folk but lately grown secure in their superiority.

But that, after all, is a moral stricture. There is a damaging aesthetic one. It is that farce is but caricature in terms of the drama, and farce, like caricature, can never be the staple of any worthy national art. It is has a legitimate place, it is merely that of the buffoon at the artistic feast.

The Ulster Players and playwrights have accomplished much good work in the face of many difficulties. That meagre tribute is willingly paid. But candid criticism is bound to add that the later playwrights have fallen away from the first standard; they have begun to remember their public in the creative moment when the artist must think only of his art. . . .[125]

This seems one of the soundest analyses of the faults of the Ulster Theatre in these years.

On 23 August, during an intermission at the Abbey, Holloway had a cup of tea with Rutherford Mayne, and reported:

Mayne had just come up from Ballinasloe where he has been stationed for years, to rehearse up North for Liverpool Week. They will play one play by Lynn Doyle . . . that has not yet been shown in Dublin. He has been playing in *The Enthusiast* since 1904. The company are practically the same all down the years. He accounts for this to their loyalty to each other in never refusing any character in this or that play, no matter how small. They all getting their chances in turn. On reading *Loaves and Fishes*, he didn't see much of a play in it, and even less in rehearsal, but when it came before the public it brightened up into a big success. Usually a play that rehearses well acts well.[126]

On 12 December, the *Evening Mail* criticised some of the Ulster acting:

Messrs. Ayre, Kennedy, and Mayne spoke out loud, and can be heard without straining all over the theatre. . . . Terrible offenders in this respect were Gerald MacNamara and Fred Mecredy, as the fishermen in Act 2. It seemed to those striving to catch their lines that their voices could not get beyond their beards.

> . . . the efforts of the players to put on what they call a "Rathmines accent" is quite distressing. Between the natural Ulster, Connemara and Dublin imitated, they produced a mongrel we were never sure of, and it grated.[127]

On 13 December, Holloway caught the matinee of MacNamara's *Mist That Does Be On the Bog* and of Lynn Doyle's *Loaves and Fishes*. He thought that MacNamara's satire of the Synge type of peasant play had "become stale," but that Charles K. Ayre was excellent as Michael Quinn and also "quiet and natural" as Charlie Curran in *Loaves and Fishes*. Also in that latter play:

> Rutherford Mayne, as the Sergeant worried over trifles, was quaintly droll in an easy natural way. Gerald MacNamara's old drunken fisherman was a perfect little character study. . . . The Ulster Players play with ease and a great sense of character. Their style is ambling and their method realistic.[128]

On 15 December, the *Irish Times* reviewed Doyle's *Turncoats* and MacNamara's *Throwbacks*:

> It is a pity that the Ulster Players should have waited until towards the end of their season to give us their best all-round programme—both as regards plays and acting. There is probably better individual acting in *The Drone* and more brilliant "spots" in *Thompson in Tir na' nOge* than in either of last night's plays, but the general level is by no means so high.
>
> Mr. Lynn Doyle's play, *Turncoats*, came first. It is an amusing comedy of a widower and his son, and a widow and her daughter. The son and the daughter are matched, but the son is scarcely a tempestuous lover, and he is discarded by Minnie Ross in favour of his father: the boy then pairs with Minnie's mother, but new wine and old bottles do not go well together. So matters are duly righted. Mr. Doyle's comedy, which is new to Dublin, was well acted by Miss Crimmins, Miss M'Quillan, Mr. Hayward, and Mr. Ayre.
>
> Mr. Gerald MacNamara improves by geometical progression. For all I know he may have written *The Throwbacks* before either *The Mist . . . or Thompson*. . . . I hope not. For *The Throwbacks* is as much better than *Thompson* as *Thompson* is than *The Mist That Does Be On the Bog*, and represents an advance in technique and in stage craft. There is fine comedy and real poetry of idea in this play. It never descends into cheapness of any kind; it never jars.[129]

On 18 December, Mayne humorously summed up the Ulster Theater at the weekly luncheon of the Dublin Rotary Club:

> In the absence of Mr. Harry Morrow, who, the chairman announced had been called away to Belfast, Mr. Rutherford Mayne addressed the gathering.
>
> In a humorous speech, he said that, according to Professor Einstein's theory of relativity, nobody remained in the same place at the same time. They were always rotating. He could, therefore, to some extent, claim to be a Rotarian.
>
> Referring to the work of the Ulster Players, the speaker said that the Dublin people had always given them a good reception since 1907, when they first appeared in Dublin. They were very small fry in Ulster until they came to Dublin, and their present position was largely due to the Dublin Press, because it was the pressmen of that city who had placed the stamp of their approval on their plays in such a way that they changed their reputation, even in Ulster. . . .

"In Ulster we have no highbrows," concluded Mr. Mayne, "except of course in the Queen's University, and from what I know of the Queen's University they don't shake hands with us, but that's neither here nor there." (Laughter.)[130]

• • •

In 1922, Dublin's Queen's Theater was inhabited almost entirely by Irish companies—amateur groups like the Ballykinlar Players; the usual professional companies of J. H. Mackey, Ira Allen, P. J. Bourke, and H. J. Condron; and from September the Queen's Repertory Company, a stock company based at the theater and directed by the veteran actor, Frank Dalton.

The plays were mostly the familiar ones. Among the Irish pieces were *The Colleen Bawn*, *Arrah na Pogue*, *Kathleen Mavourneen*, *The Boys of Wexford*, and *Willy Reilly and his Dear Colleen Bawn*. The English plays still included such popular "classics" of the nineteenth century as *East Lynne* and *Lady Audley's Secret*, but a Hall Caine or an H. J. Byron (to get a little highbrow about it) could still hardly vie with that king of melodrama, Arthur Shirley, whose *The Stepmother* and *The Grip of Iron*; *or*, *The Stranglers of Paris* proved as crowd-pleasing as ever.

A special interest attached to the Ballykinlar Players, which was an all-male company whose members had begun to produce plays while they were Republican prisoners at the Ballykinlar Internment Camp. For the week of 6 February, they presented McNulty's *The Lord Mayor* to a packed house twice a night. Holloway reported that "Kit Mulkerns overplayed the part of Jimmy O'Brien, the Lord Mayor, but got the laughs all right."[131] One of the company's members, Fred Allan, wrote to Holloway about the performance:

> I'm glad you thought well of our Ballykinlar Players, for to tell the truth I didn't think their performance last week anything like so good as they were in the camp.
>
> They played (in the camp) in a quiet easy natural way that was very telling, but last week some were nervous and others playing to the Gallery—and the Queen's Gallery at that. . . .
>
> I'd like to have your opinion of *The Rising Generation*. . . . Bernard MacCarthy told us when he sent on the Ms. to us, that he'd hawked it about everywhere but couldn't get it produced, yet it went remarkably well in the Camp though it's a bit thin in places. It's been tightened up here and there for the two-shows-a-night arrangement.[132]

The first public performance of *The Rising Generation* took place at the Queen's on 20 February.[133] Holloway "found it interesting from start to finish,"[134] but there is nothing really memorable about the piece. The *Evening Herald* reported:

> The clever author adopted a rather commonplace theme in constructing a play round the intrigues in a Southern town to have a contract for public lighting adopted by the local municipal body. There is a good deal of comedy acting which makes the play amusing, and it is, generally speaking, cleverly presented.[135]

On 4 September, the theater's new stock company, under Frank Dalton, produced *A Living Wage*, and followed it in later weeks with old-fashioned pieces like *Orphans of the Storm*, *A Woman's Devotion*, an Irish-American Western called *True Irish Hearts*, *The Face at the Window*, *The Queen of the Redskins*, *The King of Crime*, and some Boucicault and Whitbread. Hardly an innovative season, but the Queen's was a traditional theater, even to still using a musical accompaniment to herald the entrance or exit of a leading character. On 9 September, the *Evening Herald* printed an interview with Frank Dalton:

"You would like to know my record?" began the old actor. "Well, I may say I have zig-zagged most through my business than any actor I know of. Graduating at the old Theatre Royal, under John Harris and stage direction of C. W. Granby, I was in the best possible school of its time for an all-round actor.

"From thence I joined the first stock company at the Gaiety, playing with such men as Charles Mathews, J. L. Toole, Lal. Brough, George Belmore, and also Ada Cavendish. Then, thinking my wings sufficiently developed I took to the road—joined Charles Dillon (the most accomplished actor I've ever seen), playing "Horatio," "Young Lorenzo," etc. From Dillon I joined another tragedian, T. C. King, and was afterwards associated in the Shakespearian line with Barry Sullivan, Charles Calvert, Irving, Lorraine, and others.

"*The Shaughraun* boom gave Irish actors a vogue. I played with Boucicault's company at York, was seen by Hubert O'Grady, and engaged by him; I dropped the 'Young Lorenzo's' and started the 'Harvey Duffs,' in which I rather unfortunately scored too well, and so became identified with such parts which at an age of specialism meant I could get little else.

"Irish characters served my turn for years, during which I was engaged for America by Hubert O'Grady, playing 'Rooney,' a character bailiff in his play *The Eviction*. The tour finished suddenly when, with great good fortune, I met a dear friend, Frank Clements, of whose heart I had won the key—a Shakespearian. Frank introduced me to a Colonel Sims, manager of the Brooklyn Theater, and lo I plunged from 'Rooney' the bailiff into a round of French comedies and society plays, with Rose Eytinge, an American actress of the highest class, with whom I toured two hundred leading American cities.

"Homesick, I returned—started all over again. Toured with Charlie Sullivan, and occasionally with others; toured as a German with W. H. Sharpe; played leading Scotch parts in stock at Glasgow; English dialect and negroes in stock for three seasons at the Comedy Theatre, Manchester; and toured as 'Harvey Duff' in Hardacre's *Shaughraun*, with Teddy Mathews as *Conn*; played all Jimmy O'Brien's parts in the Whitbread plays. Then, a few years ago, again toured in Shakespearian work with Estella Stead, editress of *Review of Reviews*; on tour as 'Ghost' (*Hamlet*), 'Capulet Baptista' (*Taming of the Shrew*), etc.; have, at times, played thirty London theatres, and every first-class theatre in England, Ireland, Scotland, the Channel Islands, Jersey and Guernsey, also the Isle of Man, Beare Island, and Valentia—so there—."[136]

In the Queen's company from time to time were Dalton, Valentine Vousden, Charles L. Keogh, M. P. Flanagan, Gilbert Elvin, Leo Strong, D. J. Davis, J. Stapleton, Louis Dalton, P. J. Bourke, Gertie Lena, Dallas

Yorke, and Babs Dalton. And by constant theatergoers, their work, even in broad melodrama, was received with interest and often admiration. For instance, here are Holloway and F. J. McCormick on the subject:

> I saw *Orphans of the Storm* at the Queen's first house. Again two or three babies on top cried away much of the dialogue. The old melodrama was well staged and dressed. Old Frank Dalton as producer knew his business thoroughly and enacted the role of Pierre the Cripple convincingly and artistically. It was wonderful how he made each scene real in which he appeared. Doubly so when his great age was taken into condideration. . . . I went to the Abbey where I heard Peter Judge (F. J. McCormick) was enquiring for me. He had just been to the Queen's and was delighted by old Dalton's acting as Pierre. . . . All the old actors he sees could give most of the younger players points and a beating.[137]

Or here are Holloway and Valentine Vousden:

> I called in at the Abbey before going on to Sutton to Mrs. P. J. M'Call's and had a few words with Lady Gregory and a chat with Valentine Vousden. . . . We spoke of Frank Dalton and the new company at the Queen's. He thinks Dalton a delightful old man. The new company have uphill work before them owing to the unsettled times that are in it. Dalton is hoping to produce better work there and get the company to act instead of shout the lines. . . . He agrees with me that the leading lady, Dallas Yorke, has talent as well as promise. She gets her effects without undue emphasis. Vousden dislikes babies crying during a peformance, and a noisy gallery disturbs him greatly.[138]

Nevertheless, Vousden also thought that Dallas Yorke and many others in the company still could not refrain "from overacting or playing to the gods."[139]

And Dalton, despite his vitality, was far from a young man. His age was sometimes apparent in both his acting and his producing. For instance, when Holloway remarked to Vousden:

> "I noticed many of the players at the Queen's are beginning to mimic old Dalton's voice tones and to speak with the indistinctness of missing teeth." Vousden said that, "Sometimes even on the stage Dalton's words are hard to follow. But to act is meat and drink and life to the old actor." The rehearsals with Dalton as producer "are strange sometimes; sometimes the old man goes into dreamland, as he sits at the table, and then suddenly awakens from his daydreams and asks, "Where are we?" Vousden says the old band at the Queen's is the bane of his life. "Why doesn't somebody write about it? It would destroy any performance, and when it wheezes out its discordant 'slow music' the torture to the ear is acute."[140]

On 28 October, Holloway saw Vousden get in "a strong bit of natural acting into his Bob Bredon, the sea-captain" in Shirley's *The Stepmother*, and saw Dalton play Luke Trexel, the tramp, "with consummate art but some indistinctness of enunciation owing to the loss of his teeth." Later in the day he discussed the production with Frank Fay:

I said, "I go often of late to see Vousden play there," and he said, "Frank Dalton's the attraction for me. There are many Vousdens to be had, but few, if any, Frank Daltons. The dear old man is full of the best traditions of the stage, and his acting is always a lesson in the art of acting."[141]

Among the deaths of the year was that of the old Queen's favorite, James O'Brien, on 4 August in London. O'Brien had been retired for about twenty years, but Synge appears to have seen and admired him in Boucicault at the end of his career. Of O'Brien, the *Evening Herald* wrote:

Mr. Shamus O'Brien (James Fitzpatrick) or "Jimmy O'Brien," the darling of the old Queen's Royal Theater, and the creator of all the original Irish comedy parts in the historic dramas written by the late Mr. J. W. Whitbread, has passed quietly away in London, and it is only late in the day when Dublin receives the news, per Mr. Tom Bailey, who has often appeared in the same plays with the late Mr. O'Brien.

James O'Brien's family hailed from Castlewellan, Co. Down, and he early adopted the stage as a profession, while some of his brothers took to the sea and became captains.

Jimmy met his future wife, Miss Kitty O'Brien, when she was still Miss Kitty O'Keefe, at Limerick, and during a boating trip on the Shannon (another couple being with them), the skiff overturned and all four were thrown in the water. James O'Brien rescued his future wife and swam ashore with her, the other lady also being safely brought to land. On hundreds of subsequent occasions on the stage, Jimmy (or Myles) has dived to the rescue of Kitty (Eily) in the cave scene of *The Colleen Bawn*.

James O'Brien had been a member of the Drury Lane companies of the late Sir Augustus Harris, and appeared in *Youth* and other big productions at "The Lane," London. He was twice concerned with management—on the first occasion with the O'Brien and Gibson Company, and later with the O'Brien and Ireland Company, which toured Ireland up to some years ago.

The most genial and generous soul on and off the stage, James O'Brien's "final exit" will be sincerely regretted by all who knew him, and by those who had the pleasure of witnessing his portrayals of rollicking Irish boys.[142]

And Holloway added in his Journal:

I read with deep regret of the death of Jimmy O'Brien, the Irish comedian, who played at the Queen's in all Whitbread's plays in the long ago, and was always an unctuous, good-humoured, genial Irish comedian. His real name was James Fitzpatrick. . . . The last time I saw him alive was seven years ago he dropped into the Abbey to sample modern Irish plays and modern Irish acting! One night at the Queen's I saw him play when news of his son's death came during the play's progress, and he bravely went through his part, and made those in front laugh as usual while sorrow lay heavy in his heart. The life of the player has many tragedies like that. O'Brien and Frank Breen as hero and villain were a pair dear to the heart of popular audiences twenty golden years ago.[143]

Readers of previous volumes of this history will be well aware of the artistic gulf that existed between the Abbey and the Queen's. The plays and the playwrights, as well as the actors and the audiences, were culturally worlds apart. The Seanchans, the Deirdres, and the Christys were a far cry from the upright heroes and roguish bosthoons and black-avised villains of the Burnswick Street house. A few of the artists from the Queen's, like F. J. McCormick or May Craig, would cross the river to play in the Abbey, but for the most part Queen's actors stayed Queen's actors. If we have somewhat neglected these artists and their theater, the reason is not cultural snobbery, but that their work was little reported in the press, and there is little solid testimony about them, their lives, their work, and their theater.

One of the best of the popular actors was Breffni O'Rourke, or O'Rorke; and on 13 April Holloway was strolling past the Queen's and came upon him:

> . . . he told me he had come up from the country to play in *The Memory of the Dead*, which he doesn't think much of as a play. Such plays fall very flat in the country now that so much exciting drama of a similar kind has taken place before their eyes all through the country for some years past. He was speaking to Monty lately, and he remarked that the three best Irish dramas were written by Boucicault, and he agreed with him. *The Colleen Bawn* was full of poetry. He had been reading Emily Soldene's [*My Theatrical and Musical*] *Recollections* lately, and . . . she had often played with him, and that Boucicault himself engaged her for *Babil and Bijou*—Miss Vesey was Soldene's daughter. His father told him all about John Brougham who was the original "O'Grady." Brougham wrote *My Dear Land*, and O'Rourke's grandfather wrote the music to it. His father was trying to remember the words and airs for him, but couldn't very well recall them. His grandfather also wrote songs for Lewis Reeves. He was connected to the old Royal as was his father before him. "I come of an old theatrical stock," he said with pride, and I said, "You uphold the name and its fame well."
>
> Mrs. Hackett wrote wanting him to play in *The Ideal Husband* and other good stuff which he regretted not being able to accept as he had to return after next week to the country again to play in *The Grip of Iron* and *The Face at the Window*, two very similar plays in which he plays the detective parts in both. *The Face at the Window* is the better play of the two, and the detective part is a fine one with a disguise in each scene. He makes up all his disguises with crepe hair and spirit gum so that they could be pulled off quite easily.[144]

On 30 September, Ira Allen published an article in *The Evening Telegraph* about what life was like in the popular theater:

> "Curse you, let me go. You won't? Then, curse you, take that!"
>
> How often have I used the above stereotyped words during my theatrical career! Melodrama has been my fate, though some of my "charitable" friends say my real forte is the "legit" (wonderful word—I fancy I hear gongs and the rustling of silk.)
>
> Being unable to afford a hobby, however, I adhere to the good old rough and ready, get-it-over, let it rip, red fire melodrama. It has its following, its admirers—they love it. What matters, that though the hero's innocence be proven at the end of Act One, you'll always find him in prison in Act Two? What matters if the villain be killed in Act Two so long as he comes on in Act Three? Inconsistencies can always be explained away in a few words—the cruder the play the better it is liked—but the acting and characterisation in melodrama must be good, and the actor must know

how to handle his part to suit his audience, for melodrama acting is an art in itself, as many a wanderer from the "legitimate" ranks has found it so.

One night in the gallery of the Theater Royal I was enjoying a performance of *The Merchant of Venice*, and when that old "daddy" of us all, Sir Henry Irving, was in the middle of one of his most beautiful passages, a gentleman by my side rose up, and saying to his friend, "Will ye for ——— sake, come on to the Queen's?" But I am digressing. For myself, I "nearly really" killed on one or two occasions during my theatrical career.

One of my first parts was the bold, bad villain (I've always had a failing for villains' parts—my friends say they suit me) in a play with the explanatory title: *Bitter Cold; or, The Murder in the Snow*. Now in this wonderful play, the old man of the piece has returned from India with undeniable proofs that "I am not my father's son." Therefore he stands between me and my inheritance and he must die. But how? Ah, the hero's pistol—how does it come to be lying in the snow? He must have dropped it—his name is on the handle. Enough, fate has placed this weapon in my hands—now, old man, will you give up those papers and so prevent me having your blood upon my soul? Never (big speech from old man). You won't? Then, curse you, I'll take them—big struggle—snow falls—Christmas Bells heard off—we break apart. I raise the revolver saying, "You will have it, then curse you, take that." I pull the trigger—"click" (No shot). I pull again, same result. The old man is waiting to be shot—he must be killed. Oh, lucky inspiration—I hit him on the head with the butt-end of the revolver. He falls down. He has no choice in the matter, for in my excitement I have hit hard.

Enter the hero. I accuse him before the world of the murder of the poor old man, when that individual comes to life, and raising himself up holding the back of his head, exclaims: "You lie. I was shot by you."

The following semi-tragic mishap, which happened in my youthful amateur days, may appear ludicrous, as it is my endeavour to treat it from a humorous point, but I can assure you that I have never passed through such mental agony as I did during the long minute the "dead man refused to come to life." Everybody looked "don't let him escape" at me. I could visualise policemen, prison, judge and jury, the scaffold and all the horrors of a "conscientious murderer." But the dead man spoke at last; "his blood was on his own head," or rather all over his face, but I was saved. Let me explain.

How it came about was my tampering with firearms, of which, at the time, I had very little knowledge. The firearm in question took the form of an old-fashioned muzzle-loading pistol which I bought for a few shillings in an old curio shop. Such weapons, through age and rust, are often as great a source of danger to the person pulling the trigger, as any target at which they are aimed. I brought the pistol home, cleaned and oiled it, sought the necessary, if somewhat doubtful information as to loading, and learned that you filled the muzzle with gunpowder, ramming it "home" with a paper wad; that you placed an ignition cap on the touch-hole pivot, and that you pulled the trigger.

Right. I set to work. I procured a box of caps and a large sporting gun cartridge, from which I extracted the powder and proceeded to load my pistol. Now the question was the exact quantity of powder necessary to give a good report—but I took no risks. I filled it, as the old saying has it, "up to the muzzle" (one-third of this quantity would have been sufficient). The powder in, I rammed "home" the paper wad with the aid of a hammer, and placed the cap in position. It was done. Unconsciously I held in my hand a pistol, or a bomb, for if it went off the right way it was a pistol, and if it went off the wrong way it would have certainly demonstrated the destructive capability of a Mills bomb, but I am glad to say it eventually took the form for which it was originally intended.

Now the drama in which I intended to use my pistol was called *Disinherited; or,*

Tracked to Doom, and was billed to take place in one of our local Temperance Halls for a charitable object. I, as usual, was "the villain of the piece," and in the baronial chamber I had to stab to the heart the usual old man. Now this is where I was going to spring a surprise on the old man and the rest of the amateur company by using my muzzle-loader. I succeeded only too well.

The stage was small; the lights were low, for murders in melodrama invariably happen in the dark. One of the advantages is that you can always work your "spot-focus" on the comedian who has been secreted during the murder without raising a hand of interference, but merrily comes forward to denounce the murderer.

I enter through the French window to "creepy" music and I creep to the safe. I force it open. It is wonderful how quickly you can do these things on the stage. I am rifling the contents—£10,000, if I remember aright, and the plans of the old man's invention—when I am discovered in the act by the old man in question, who, seizing me by the throat, exclaims, "Ah, villain, now do I know the real thief!"

"Curse you, let me go," I cried, fumbling in my pocket for my muzzle-loader; but the old man would not let me go. He had been rehearsed to hold on to me till I stabbed him. I could not shoot him in that position, and he was unaware of my intention to shoot him. I was going to shoot him, I was dying to shoot him, and I did shoot him; but that's to come.

With a superhuman effort I threw him from me; he staggered back. I drew my muzzle-loader and raised it. He rushed into the line of fire. BANG!! What a report. The old man fell—it was a splendid fall, so lifelike—but the effect of the shot took all my attention.

The stage shook, plaster fell from the ceiling, nearly all the lights were extinguished, and the scene was wreathed in smoke.

No matter, I had to "carry on." The spellbound audience was stricken dumb, and most of the actors sought safety in their dressing-rooms.

"Ha, ha!" I cried, triumphantly. "Curse you—you made me do it!" and kneeling down to still further rob my victim, I gazed upon his face. Horror of horrors!—What did I see? What had I done? His face was all—ugh—it was wet, and the colour was red! Oh, shade of Eugene Aram, aid me—what am I to do? Between the author's lines I whispered, "Are you hurt, Shaun?" No answer.

I must continue and get the curtain down. If the audience get to know I really killed him—for such I believed him to be—there will be a panic, or something worse. I carry on. The hero enters. I accuse him of the crime—what a ghastly joke on my part! I am accused in turn by the comedian, and the curtain descends in an icy stillness, for the musicians were vainly endeavouring to scoop the dust out of their eyes.

The curtain down, lights were procured. The "dead man" was shaken. They called him by name—"Shaun, Shaun, are you hurt?" But Shaun was in no hurry to answer to his name, or perhaps he was "enjoying" the situation. It was then all eyes were turned upon your humble, the bold, bad villain, but now "meek as the mildest of milk," tremblingly standing apart with the still smoking muzzle-loader in my shaking hand. Torrents of abuse were about to descend upon my head, when the "dead" man spoke, saying, "Is the curtain down?" Poor Shaun! We helped him to his feet, we washed his bloodstained face; but what a changed man he was! The blazing gun-powder had caught him full in the face, and had transformed him into a nigger—and he danced like one for he was in great pain. We brought him to the nearest chemist, who exclaimed after gazing on his darkened countenance: "My God! man, you've been shot!" "No," says Shaun: "it's a black draught Allen has given me."[145]

• • •

There was also in Dublin during the year some interesting—what one might call semiprofessional—activity. In May, Madame Kirkwood-Hackett rented the Abbey and presented two plays, both billed as new to Dublin. The first, which opened on 1 May, was Shaw's *Captain Brassbound's Conversion*, in which Barry Fitzgerald distinguished himself as the Cockney sailor. The second was "Anthony Wharton's" old London success, *Irene Wycherley*, of which *The Evening Mail* remarked:

> Mr. James O'Dea appeared in the new role of kindly Sir Peter, in which he was an entire success, and his portrayal of the final pathetic scene, the heartbroken father, was immensely good. Pol O'Fearghail, as the brutal, drunken husband, could hardly be surpassed. . . .
>
> It is hard to understand why the prompter should insist on annoying the audience by his (apparently quite unnecessary) presence, audibly and physically.[146]

However, there were few paying patrons, and so on the last night of *Irene Wycherley* Harry O'Donovan, Madame Kirkwood-Hackett's manager, announced that the repertory season would be curtailed.[147] Luckily, though, Madame Kirkwood-Hackett received an infusion of money from a local physician, Dr. W. M. Crofton, and so for the week of 22 May she was able to produce his new play, *The Tangle*. The piece was pretty generally slated. For instance, the *Evening Mail* reported:

> No doubt Dr. W. M. Crofton's solution of *The Tangle* makes excellent reading in the book by Mr. White, the American novelist. As a psychic play, by the doctor himself, it appeared a very ridiculous affair, indeed, when produced at the Abbey Theatre last night.
>
> Dr. Crofton told us, after the cheering and boohing had died away, that he had met Mr. White, who was on a visit here, and who told him that he was writing a novel, and had reached the stage when he had got his characters into a marriage tangle. So Dr. Crofton provided a solution for getting them out of it. Mr. White must be very grateful, for he went back and finished his book on the lines of the solution, and the doctor himself wrote this whole new play.
>
> The tangle is an elderly professor of bacteriology, with a good wife and children, in love with his laboratory assistant. And the solution works out some way like this: the professor's wife leaves him; a friend, Dr. Donovan, cures by suggestion, the assistant of her very platonic love; the wife comes back without a hard thought in her heart for either husband or rival; and, finally, in order to get Marjorie Jackson (the professor's assistant) to marry himself, Dr. Donovan gets his former wife to speak to her, while he has her hypnotised, or spiritualised, or coued—at least he puts her under some spell when lying on a sofa. And the dead wife comes forward and places her twelve months' old baby—by the way, we weren't told what the baby was fed on—in Marjorie's arms.
>
> There is nothing, indeed, objectionable in the play, except its utter nonsense. Of course there is a lot of silly dialogue about the physical side of love, and things like that, but it was all received with good-natured laughter.
>
> The players certainly deserve the sympathy of the audience, particularly Mr. Harry O'Donovan, who, in the second act, had to wade through the rigmarole of love-making. He was entirely unlike a passionate professor, and the lines he had to

speak—well, doctors and professors may make love like that, but plain people never.[148]

Holloway thought the play "very crudely constructed and the dialogue strangely unnatural at times,"[149] and Brinsley MacNamara thought it "the worst yet."[150] However, Holloway and Lawrence ran into John MacDonagh who had some kinder things to say:

He had heard it was dreadful from the players and he went to laugh at the burlesque of the whole thing. He became interested instead and was quite impressed by Captain Bryan Cooper's playing, especially in Act 2. Harry O'Donovan was out of the picture altogether; his accent and appearance were against him in the part. Dr. Crofton selected him for the part and even wrote it up for him. . . . When the piece had such a good reception on Monday, the author said, "I mustn't allow myself to get a swelled-head." I said . . . that he must be a very innocent, simple sort of man to say such a thing, and MacDonagh replied, "He's just that." Lawrence said that he liked the idea of the play so well and most of the playing that he didn't like to write any hard things about it, "and so didn't write anything at all." He said to MacDonagh, "If you looked over the script, you could smooth out crudenesses and turn it into a rattling good play!"[151]

There were also several performances by the Dublin Drama League. On 29 and 30 January, the League presented a triple bill at the Abbey—Chekhov's *The Bear*, Oscar Wilde's *The Florentine Tragedy*, and Arthur Schnitzler's *The Festival of Bacchus*. J. H. Cox remarked in the *Evening Herald*:

"Pretty strong fare for a quiet Sunday evening"—that was one's feeling last night at the Abbey Theater. The audience seemed greatly taken with the experiment, so the courage—or audacity—of the Dublin Drama League was vindicated.[152]

However, on the tram home from the theater, Holloway heard a different opinion:

Two ladies in evening dress came in shortly after me, and sat down next to me, on saying, "Oh, what a night, and what a show!" And the other replying, "Deadly!"[153]

Holloway himself thought that in *The Bear*, Katherine McCormack

filled the role of the widow excellently while Paul Farrell was a peppery, middle-aged landowner. . . . James O'Dea as an old footman gave a perfect little character study of the part. . . . Farrell's study of the landowner would be improved by less movement and less hesitation between speeches. . . . The heart of the evening was the fine setting and excellent playing of Oscar Wilde's one-act play, *A Florentine Tragedy*, produced excellently by Dorothy Macardle. . . .

Years ago I saw Mrs. Patrick Campbell play Bianca in this play at the Dublin Gaiety. Miss Young is thought by some to have formed her style of acting on that actress. She played to-night with great intensity, and Barry as her lover played with fervour and glow. I was deeply interested in the piece. Alas and alack that there was such a lamentable falling off in the last piece. . . . The producer, Thomas McGreevy, had nothing to be proud of. This is the youth of whom one of the Reddin boys told me had queried, "Who is Murray? I never heard of him."[154]

Holloway also noticed several directorial gaffes in the Schnitzler play:

. . .non payment for drinks, customers coming on and leaving the drinks they called for untouched, the Doctor going off with the lady and leaving his hat and coat on the rack after him.[155]

The League gave occasional "At-Homes" for members only, and one occurred at the Abbey on 6 March. As O'Donnell noted in the *Gael*, it

afforded us an opportunity of judging the powers of Mr. Lennox Robinson as the creator of burlesque.

The idea of this hotch pot play was that all the actors who have appeared in the various League productions during the past season would come in at intervals and by doing certain portions of such plays cause a semblance of reality to the whole. The dialogue was well worked out, and sentences from Strindberg, St. John Hankin, Andreeyef, Tchechoff and others ran into their various grooves so efficiently that one, unless he had previously seen the plays, would think that this venture was exceedingly clever and amusing.

Before the party broke up we had a taste of George Bernard Shaw who told us how "Augustus Does his Bit."[156]

On 19 and 20 March, at the Abbey, the Drama League presented Eugene O'Neill's two-act *Diff'rent* and Harold Chapin's one-act *Augustus in Search of a Father*. Before the performance, Holloway was chatting with Dolan and Brinsley MacNamara:

. . .and in the course of our chat Mac mentioned the fact that he and Dolan met old James O'Neill, the actor, with his young son, Eugene, when they were in New York years ago. The old man was a fine actor and a grand old man in every way you'd take him. The old man is dead, and his son Eugene has become a noted dramatist. Dolan likes *Diff'rent* and thinks it strong stuff.[157]

Holloway, however, thought the first act of *Diff'rent* "talky and unconvincing" and "indifferently played save in a few instances."[158] He also noted that Chapin's piece "was played in a blackout save for the light from lamps on the stage."[159]

On 16 October, according to the *Evening Telegraph*, the Drama League opened its fourth season with an "At Home" at the Arts Club. The program was described as "attractive and varied," but we have not discovered what it consisted of.

On 5 and 6 November, at the Abbey, the Drama League presented St. John Hankin's translation of Brieux's *Three Daughters of M. Dupont*.

The *Herald* thought it was the League's "most finished production" since Hankin's *The Cassilis Engagement*, and remarked also that:

> The acting, too, was far, very far, above the average. James O'Dea has made great progress since first he appeared at the now extinct Irish Theater.[160]

Holloway disagreed about both the production and Jimmy O'Dea:

> I left the Abbey at five minutes to 11 o'clock as the third act of *The Three Daughters of M. Dupont* had just concluded. . . . I wonder what time the play was over! The fourth act had yet to be played. I found the play, as far as I witnessed it, somewhat tedious, Act One particularly so—and also found fault with the jerkiness and uneven acting of the players. For instance, James O'Dea as M. Dupont was all explosiveness and bluster and self-assertiveness; and Christine Hayden as Mme. Mairout was aggressively loud and blustery also, while other of the characters were almost tamely limned and didn't fit in with the boisterousness. . . . Mr. O'Dea as an entertainer thinks when he acts he must dominate the stage instead of becoming part and parcel of the dramatic picture.[161]

On 3 and 4 December, at the Abbey, the Drama League offered a double bill of Browning's *The Blot on the 'Scutcheon* and Chekhov's *The Jubilee*. Browning's piece had been cut by Robinson, but O'Donnell still found it undramatic: "No amount of highly wrought phrases or sentimental tongue-twisting can justify its claim to being a play."[162] Holloway too thought it talky and undramatic, but admired the playing of Eileen Crowe and Dolan. The audience was very sparse.[163]

Toward the end of the year, ambitious plans were announced for the formation of a new theater, to be called the Everyman, at the Rotunda. On 2 December, the *Evening Herald* noted:

> The Everyman Theater, Rotunda Buildings, will shortly open its doors to the Dublin public. A repertory company has been engaged and placed under the direction of that well-known actor Frank Fay. It was intended to launch the new enterprise with a series of new plays prior to Christmas. These plans miscarried owing to the sudden and serious illness of the manager, Mr. C. Stewart MacQuaile. The repertory season has been deferred until after the run of the pantomime, *Jack the Giant-Killer*, or *Seaghan agus an Sthochtha*, which will now herald the opening performances. . . . Mr. MacQuaile is anxious to foster the production of plays in Gaelic, and in this connection has secured the co-operation of Mr. Gerald O'Loughlin, who has performed so much good work in this sphere, not only in Ireland, but in Continental cities.[164]

On Christmas Day there was an inaugural celebration for the new theater:

> On Sunday night the Everyman Theater, Dublin, was formally and privately opened by Mr. Frank J. Fay, actor and producer, before a gathering of well-known

authors, journalists, musical producers, and the friends, artistes, and directors of the theater.

Mr. Fay said he felt honoured in acceding to the request of the management by opening this enterprise, and commended the moral courage of the directors in their undertaking, particularly under the present abnormal conditions. Although he regarded it as a little theater, he believed that it would meet with the success that their efforts deserved, and he hoped that it would do useful work as a theater and become established as a social institution of Dublin life.

Mr. Arthur Gaynor, Secretary, in proposing a vote of thanks to Mr. Fay, said he regarded the association of Mr. Fay with their initial ceremony as an augury for the success in view of his splendid pioneer work for the Abbey. They hoped in the Everyman to establish something in the nature of a People's Theater where they would endeavour to cater for the taste of every class in the Dublin community. He referred to the Irish nationality of the directors, musicians and players, and of the forthcoming production of two new Irish comedies, followed by a new Irish musical production. It had been the intention to introduce a Gaelic scene into the pantomime, but difficulties had arisen, despite which they were determined to have the unique distinction of having the mother tongue spoken for the first time in a pantomime, and the later stages of the present production would see that desirable object achieved.[165]

According to Fay, who was to direct the plays in English, "The carpenter of the Queen's had erected a stage, and the scene painters of the Gaiety painted the scenery. The hall holds 800."[166]

On St. Stephen's Day, the theater opened with the pantomime of *Jack the Giant-Killer*, which prominently featured Noel Purcell in one of his first roles. The *Herald* welcomed the theater by remarking:

To those who have not yet had the pleasure of visiting the "Everyman" Theater a simple word of advice—Go there, see the transformation which has been effected in the historic "room," enjoy your comfortable tip-up and plush armchair.[167]

But, despite the fanfare, the new theater was not to last long.

Earlier in the year, "F. Jay," who had once had a play on at the Abbey, wrote to the Press to inquire, "Have the dramatic societies gone out of business? Is the Dramatic Union asleep or dead?"[168] Arthur Gaynor, the Secretary of the Irish Dramatic Union, wrote back explaining:

I desire to point out that in consequence of the internment of myself and several of my colleagues on the executive of the I. D. U. from November, 1920, to December, 1921, the work of the Union fell into abeyance during that period, and consequently it could scarcely be fairly placed in either of the above-mentioned categories.

At the latter date, being then midway through the dramatic season proper, and inasmuch as there was a general lull in matters theatrical, particularly in the amateur sphere, the time did not seem propitious for the re-establishment of the Union on its former basis.

However, I am summoning a meeting of the executive at an early date to review our present position and to consider the re-organisation of the I. D. U.[169]

Frank J. Hugh O'Donnell wrote in to remark that

> the times we are passing through must be taken into account, and it is difficult for anybody to sit down and write with the country in its present state.
>
> I have spoken to Mr. Gaynor on a few occasions as to the advisability of resurrecting the Irish Dramatic Union, but I think the time has not yet arrived for doing so, and I do not think there is any possibility of it being successful until next winter arrives.[170]

Gaynor did make an attempt to revive the Irish Dramatic Union, but not much happened, unless the Everyman be taken as an outgrowth of his efforts, for it did plan to stage plays by Jay, Martin J. McHugh, and others.

In his letter above, O'Donnell wrote as Secretary of the Irish Playwrights' Association which, he assured his readers, was "as much alive as ever." In June, Holloway described a meeting of that group:

> I attended a meeting of I. P. A. at O'Donnell's office, No. 4 Abbey Street, where T. K. Moylan, T. C. Murray and Frank Hugh O'Donnell and myself were in attendance. I was in the chair. . . . Mr. Bernard Duffy couldn't attend but wrote stating that he'd like the new Government to look after the copyright laws for playwrights as well as authors. Some member said Darrell Figgis was the man to apply to to see that such steps would be taken. . . . George Shiels, Lady Gregory, Harry Morrow ("Gerald MacNamara") have become members of I. P. A. lately. £5. 0. 0 was voted to Miss Bushell for looking after the interest of the Association at the Abbey. O'Donnell showed us a copy of *The Dawn Mist* printed by the *Gael* at a cost of 6d. a copy—sale price 1/6. McNulty wanted to have his comedy, *The Courting of Mary Doyle*, published in Dublin, but couldn't get it done under £30 a thousand by any of our publishers. . . . Moylan is writing a play ending with a wedding and ceidlidh. The country players want dance and song introduced into the plays they produce. "Quite so," said Murray. "A clergyman once said to me that I missed a great opportunity in not introducing the dance to which Hugh goes off to [in *BIRTHRIGHT*]; it would have been a capital second act, and given all a chance to sing and dance." They also in the country dearly love a scrap on the stage; horseplay appeals to them. . . . Moylan says *Paid in His Own Coin* and *Lawsy Me* continue to be popular all over the country. We all parted at the corner of Abbey Street about 4 o'clock. As I went to the meeting I saw a string of three armoured cars pass through O'Connell Street manned by khaki-clad soldiers.[171]

• • •

As the public's fascination with films increased, so also did the clamor for film censorship. In November, the Irish Vigilance Association, having conferred with the Priests' Social Guild, sent to the Public Health Committee the following list of matters deemed censorable:

> Films to be condemned are those containing the following:
> 1. Scenes suggestive of conjugal infidelity.
> 2. Scenes depicting or suggestive of illicit love.
> 3. Passionate or prolonged embracing, or kissing scenes.

4. Scenes portraying or advocating the doctrine of free love.
5. Scenes showing prostitution and procuration, or disorderly houses, or referring to illegal operations.
6. Scenes showing attempted criminal assaults on women or children.
7. Seductions of girls and attempts thereat.
8. Indelicate sexual relations, bedroom, bathroom, and mixed bathing scenes of suggestive character.
9. Nude figures, impropriety of dress, and needless exhibition of women in their night dresses or underclothing, or improper exhibition of female underclothing.
10. Indecorous dancing, suggestive gestures.
11. Stories or scenes introducing the unfortunate class, or demi-monde.
12. Stories which accept divorce as lawful.
13. Stories or incidents disrespectful to any religious belief, or to religion in general.
14. Stories holding up the sacrifice of women's virtue, suicide, or any other crime as laudable.
15. Stories or scenes objectionable under any of the above heads, even though in the end virtue triumphs.[172]

Comment seems superfluous, but we might note that the considerable ferment about film censorship had somewhat replaced the uproars of previous years about stage censorship. The reason is basically that by 1922 many more people were getting their drama in the cinemas than in the theaters. And, as the film was attracting a bigger audience than was the theater, it was also attracting a broader and a more lowbrow audience. The makeup of the Irish cinema audience might also be suggested by the following remark made at the January meeting of the Dublin Municipal Council:

> Mr. M. J. Moran said that he was a fairly frequent attendant at the pictures, and he had to admit that he had never come away from them without a feeling that there was something unclean in them. There were shown pictures of American and English life which were unsuited to this country (hear, hear), and might have the effect of corrupting the morals of young people.[173]

In such an atmosphere, the voice of common sense was infrequently raised, but a columnist of the *Evening Herald* did remark:

> In connection with the actual censorship of films an interesting case has been mentioned to me, where a censor took serious exception to the ladies' dresses in the ballroom scene of a certain picture. It was pointed out to that censor that the same kind of dresses were frequently to be seen at big charitable dances in Dublin.[174]

And after the Medical Officer of Health of the Dublin Corporation had officially appointed thirteen honorary censors, "Visitor" wrote a letter to *The Evening Telegraph* noting that

> the only complaints I have heard from average, normal people is that the censorship if anything seems to be a trifle too drastic, and that interesting films which do not apparently contaminate other cities might also be shown in Dublin without very disastrous results.[175]

Nevertheless, on 6 February, the Public Health Committee of the Dublin Corporation forbade the exhibition of films in Dublin without the approval of the censors. "That," remarked the *Evening Telegraph*, "is a step in the right direction."[176]

On 21 January, the *Evening Herald* reported a trade showing of *Father O'Flynn*, a film said to be based on Alfred Perceval Graves's ballad. The film had been shot in Killarney, and, "It was a unique production in the sense that it is a synchronetic singing picture at which Miss Marie Santoi, of musical comedy fame, and Mr. Tom Power, the well-known baritone, accompanied the screening."[177] Late in February, the film had its first public showing at the Phibsborough Picture House.

For the week of 30 January, La Scala showed P. J. Bourke's film, *Ireland a Nation*, which had been immediately withdrawn after its initial Irish showing in 1917 because the British Military authorites thought it inflammatory. Said to be based on Father Kavanagh's book, *The Insurrection of '98*, the film was described as

> a complete record of the country's fight for freedom in the days of Robert Emmet, Grattan, John Philpot Curran, Daniel O'Connell, and other Irish patriots.
>
> The film was produced by Walter M'Namara in Ireland on the actual spots hallowed by the history of the country. . . .
>
> Appearing in the cast . . . is Mr. Ralph Goggin, the well-known Dublin baritone, who plays the part of "D'Esterre," who fights the duel with Dan O'Connell. Mr. Goggin has also played in the successful Irish comedy film, *Paying the Rent*, and productions of the Barker and London Film Company. He also made a hit in Mr. John MacDonagh's recent comedy, *The Irish Jew*, in the character of Claffey at the Empire Theater, Dublin.[178]

The only print we have seen of this film was somewhat incomplete and most unsatisfactory, and it was difficult to come to any fair judgment. Most of the time was taken up with the Emmet story, and there was a good deal of rather baffling dashing about and broad romantic action and acting. For instance, in his trial scene, Emmet turned melodramatically to Sarah Curran and melodramatically mouthed the words, "I love you!" Some exteriors offered interesting shots of Glendalough, but most probably *Ireland a Nation* in its original print was a broad, simplistic, Queen's Theater version of Irish history. And apparently the reviewers of the day agreed. Jacques, after comparing the film to Whitbread-like melodramas, wrote:

> Of course, it was rather surprising in the *Ireland a Nation* picture to see Robert Emmet depicted in the trial scene standing a few feet from the judge, and at the counsel's table (and "kissing the Book" the same as a witness would) and not in the dock. In fact I saw no dock. It was intriguing, too, to see Sarah Curran sitting in court during the trial and see her walk over to Emmet and embrace him after sentence had been pronounced. . . .
>
> There are other abnormalities which might be claimed by the American producers as at least palliated, if not justified by "dramatic licence" or the exigencies of production, but really the scene showing Anne Devlin leaving Ireland on a ship for

Australia makes us feel the point of the statement that novels state facts about fictitious people, while cinema pictures state fiction about real people. . . .
Perhaps some day we may get a filmed play or photo drama by an Irish film-producing company in sympathy with the subject that will do for this country what *The Birth of a Nation* has done for America.[179]

Indeed, a reviewer who thought the film "wonderful" and "a very interesting, instructive and fascinating lesson in Irish history from the closing years of the eighteenth century to the middle of the nineteenth," also remarked:

There is, perhaps, an element of melodrama present which is sometimes unavoidable. Film actors, no doubt, like other actors and poets, have a certain licence, but there is a good deal of unnecessary if not extravagant action and gesticulation displayed in some of the incidents.[180]

One cinema owner in Limerick, after booking the film, refused to show it because of unfavourable press comments and because the film was inaccurate.[181]

On 10 June, the *Evening Herald* announced the formation of a new Irish film company:

During the past few days a new Irish enterprise has been launched upon its career. Irish Photoplays, Ltd., after months of careful preparation and planning, has embarked on the actual work of producing films in Ireland, and the first scenes of the first production have been taken this week.
All the capital of the new company is Irish and the board of directors is composed of leading business men and members of the cinema trade in the country. There is Mr. C. E. McConnell, an Irishman whose name is known throughout the advertising world. Mr. McConnell . . . will have the benefit of the advice and assistance of Maron Hartley, partner in the well-known firm of McConnell-Hartley, pioneers of film advertising. . . .
While the productions will be truly Irish of the Irish, they will be entirely free from any suggestion of the stage Irishman, or anything that might offend the most susceptible Irish spectator. . . .
The promoters intend to work from an entirely new angle, and, whilst there will be genuine humour in plenty, and of the most laughter-provoking kind, the clowning which has come to be known as Slapstick will find no place in their productions. In short, the humourous films to be produced by this company will go far to satisfy the demands of the great cinema public that was grown weary to death of the feeble fatuousness which is served up at present as the humour of the silver screen. So confident are the directors of the world-wide appeal of their productions that they are completing a scheme for marketing their films to the best possible advantage in America and the British colonies.
They have secured an expert camera-man in the person of Mr. Alfred M. Moise. Mr. Moise, who is of French extraction, comes to the company from the United States, where his name bulks largely in trade circles. He has filmed some of the big American stars, such as Norma Talmadge. . . . As producer the company have secured the services of Mr. John MacDonagh, author of *The Irish Jew*. He it was who produced *Paying the Rent*.
The first production of the new company will be another comedy by Mr.

MacDonagh, entitled *The Casey Millions*. It will be followed as quickly as possible by other comedies, and it is hoped to have two ready for screening during Tailteann Week. The comedies will deal with various phases of modern Irish life, and the locations will be selected so that the whole country will be represented in the series.

The principal actors include Fred Jeffs and Chris Sylvester, Jimmy O'Dea, Harry O'Donovan and Barrett M'Donnell, whilst on the ladies' side is Miss Nan Fitzgerald. Miss Kathleen Drago has also joined the company.[182]

The first film was shot, partly in Swords and partly in the Pine Forest, during the last two or three weeks of June; and the *Evening Herald* gave this résumé of its plot:

The story of *Casey's Millions* is one long laugh from beginning to end. The principal characters concerned are two broken actors whose stars have long since waned, and we find them tramping an Irish road with nothing much in their possession save a skull which formerly played its part in their production of *Hamlet*. The skull is destined to play an even more important part in their exciting career, for when by accident they learn that Luke Casey, of Lock-jaw, Kentucky, U.S.A. has died and left his millions to a Casey in Caseytown, they set about finding that Casey at once.

Being badly in need of cash, they set up a bureau to register all the prospective claimants to the Casey millions, and for the small sum of ten-and-sixpence per head photograph the would-be millionaires who line up in queues outside their bureau. Our ex-actors blandly inform the claimants that the precious skull they carry is none other than that of the famous Casey himself, and by comparison in phrenology they will arrive at the true claimant.

However, Irish villages are full of nice sweet girls, and our actor friends are only human, so there is a little tangle in which the father and the country suitor and our actor friends are all mixed up. The laughable situations which result are side-splitting, and cinema audiences will have a task to see the film between their tears and laughter. Actors and cinema men are not usually provoked to mirth by the comedy that they have laboured on, but the makers of *Casey's Millions* could not restrain themselves when they saw it screened for the first time.[183]

A trade showing of the new film was given on 25 July at the Grafton Street Picture House before a large, invited audience; and the response was overwhelmingly enthusiastic. O'Donnell in the *Gael* was particularly effusive and thought the film rivaled the California product.[184] Holloway thought it a big success in every way. "At last we have an Irish film that can compare with the best American film comedies, such as those of Sydney Drew and his wife."[185] The *Evening Telegraph* quite agreed:

This is far and away the best Irish-made film, yes; real comedy and restraint, yes; interest from start to finish. The photography leaves nothing to be desired. Mr. Moise, responsible for it, has reason to feel elated. The sub-titles are excellent humour. Acting is superior in proportion . . . though, maybe, James O'Dea overdid the hapless youth a little, and was too weirdly resplendent at the end; and Chris Sylvester's grimaces—though some *were* worth making—were too many and queer.[186]

The *Evening Herald* was a bit more specific:

> The film was amusing and the sub-titles were very good. That comparison of a woman's conversation being "like a telegraph wire—length without depth"—was an example of the humour which permeates all the work of John MacDonagh. . . . Considering that for several this was their first appearance in film-acting, the acting was very natural and spontaneous. Miss Kathleen Drago, although she had only a small part to play, was extremely good. Miss Joan Fitzgerald was inclined to over-act; otherwise her interpretation of the country servant-girl was amusing. Miss Nan Fitzgerald looked pretty, but dressed rather too fashionably for an innkeeper's daughter in such a remote, sleepy village. This could be also said of the crowd of women supers.
>
> Mr. James O'Dea was a distinct success, and should be a valuable asset to the film world when he has more experience before the camera. All the men were good. Mr. Fred Jeffs looking so genial a host that his smile alone should have brought customers to his "Grand Hotel."
>
> The photography was clever and clear, and showed that in Mr. Moise the company have secured a first-rate man.[187]

By early August, Irish Photoplays had finished shooting its second film, *Wicklow Gold*, and had already secured the locations for its third, a five-reel comedy-drama about horse racing. *Wicklow Gold* was also written and produced by John MacDonagh, and the *Evening Herald* thus described its plot:

> The story in brief is the age-old story of human nature; love and money in conflict. The miserly farmer does not want his son to marry the widow's daughter, as the widow's land is not larger nor rich enough to satisfy an aspiring pater familias. Love braves many difficulties, and some of the boys in the neighbourhood strike on the happy idea of getting some fake experts from Dublin to come to the district and discover gold on the widow's land. This [word illegible] father, who straightway hurries the marriage he formerly disapproved of.
>
> After the new couple have settled down, and the father-in-law has arranged matters, he sets about gathering in the gold which appears so profuse in the widow's lands. After many months of labour he finds himself baffled, and finally calls in some real experts, who laugh at his story.
>
> There is quite a lot of trouble after this, but the miser gets a change of heart on the arrival of a new addition to the family, which he considers is worth more gold than all he had hoped to find by digging up the soil.
>
> The film is replete with humorous situations, and the characters act the parts splendidly. The scenic effects are very fine, and the photography is excellent.
>
> . . . Negotiations are still in progress for the sale outright of the film in America.[188]

Obviously, these films were little different in kind from the two-reelers that J. M. Kerrigan had directed for the Irish Film Company a few years earlier. They were longer and probably better done, but they were still simple, broad, crowd-pleasing entertainments that owed something to the Abbey Theater comedies. But, as MacDonagh remarked somewhat lyrically of *Wicklow Gold*:

"It will come as a welcome relief . . . for it exhibits no spectacles of colossal magnitude and no alluring vampires insinuating themselves into the affections of unsuspecting millionaires. There are no bloody thrills, but a simple story, simply and beautifully told. The story runs as clearly and smoothly as a stream trickling down the Wicklow Hills, whereon the scenes are laid. The photography is perfect, the plot interesting and sustained to the final fade-out, and the acting natural and unforced."

Wicklow Gold will be, like its predecessor, *The Casey Millions*, in four reels, though there is much natural pathos here and there in the picture which *The Casey Millions* does not contain. Mr. MacDonagh describes it as the story of a miserly father, whose match-making plans for his unworldly son are all upset by the good-natured intervention of the local doctor. The scenes are carefully chosen to present the Wicklow hills in all their glory, and the characters typify the charm of rustic life, the simple devotion of lovers and the matter-of-fact plans of the farming class to marry their children to the best possible advantage, while throughout the entire film are delightful characterisations and incidents of life in Ireland which will pull at the heart-strings of people the world over.

In the end the miser discovers the real Wicklow Gold in the shape of a grandson, and delightfully fondles the infant while pretending in the inimitable Irish way to be incapable of such "weakness."

Chris Silvester, the well-known Irish artiste, who has taken part in the three productions of Irish Photo Plays, acts the part of the miser with an artistry that makes one love that character in spite of his avariciousness, and shows beneath the crust of miserliness a heart responsive to tiny hands and the first efforts of articulation.

Mr. MacDonagh's belief in the merits of the film will undoubtedly be shared by all who see it at the trade show, which will be held in Dublin very shortly. . . .

Indications from other countries give promise of a splendid reception for every production of Irish Photo Plays, Ltd.[189]

Wicklow Gold was given a trade showing at La Scala about the middle of October.

For the week of 18 September, the Metropole Cinema gave the first Irish showing of *General John Regan*, which Harold Shaw had produced for the Stoll Film Company. This film was based on George A. Birmingham's play which, as readers of Volume 4 of this history will remember, had caused a violent riot when performed in Westport in 1914. Birmingham's play is a genial, rather broad farce, but in 1914 it was considered a libelous attack on the Irish character. In 1922, several correspondents wrote to the press discussing the film in just about the same terms. For instance:

I availed myself of the earliest opportunity of seeing the production in the Cinema, and was horrified to think that such a travesty of Irish character and Irish life should be shown in the heart of Ireland. It is, indeed, nauseating for any self-respecting Irishman to see in the city of Dublin a film of Irish life in which the principal characters were pigs; the main scenery dirt; the chief characteristics of the people, quarrelling, fighting, ignorance, drunkenness, sloth and lying intrigue, with the representative of the Catholic Church an acquiescent buffoon. Imagine this film being advertised in a foreign country as being "eminently successful in Dublin," and you can readily realise why we are sometimes slandered. "The dirty, ignorant Irish."[190]

Of course, the knockabout Irish comics of the Variety stage were usually as violently moronic as the Three Stooges were to be; and quarrelling, fighting, ignorance, drunkenness, sloth, and lying intrigue abounded in the Queen's Theater Irish dramas; and, indeed, even in Lady Gregory's most popular plays, the Irish countryman was often portrayed as a credulous lout. So, if a moral is to be drawn about *General John Regan*, it continues to elude us.

On 8 December, *My Wild Irish Rose*, an American adaptation of *The Shaughraun*, was given a trade exhibition at the Corinthian Cinema.

• • •

Belfast, as we have noted above, suffered through a violent and disruptive year. At year's end, the press reported, "Of 500 inquests in Belfast in 1922, 344 were in respect of assassination, bombings and shootings; and murder verdicts were returned in the majority of cases."[191] Yet, despite an eleven o'clock curfew from late May to late September, and despite the frequent fighting that closed the theaters, there was a good deal of theatrical activity. Most of it was by English traveling companies visiting the Grand Opera House, and by English variety artists visiting the Royal Hippodrome. However, the Ulster Theater appeared at the Opera House both for the week of 3 April and of 16 October. The company also appeared for the week 4 September at the Playhouse in Liverpool and, as has been noted, for the week of 11 December at the Gaiety in Dublin. The only piece new to Belfast was Gerald MacNamara's *The Throwbacks*, which the company had first played in Liverpool on 8 September. We have noted above the Dublin response to the piece; in Belfast the *News-Letter* wrote of it:

> Mr. Gerald MacNamara is a playwright who has the gift of seeing the humorous side of things, and in *The Throwbacks* he provides a riot of fun. His humour is largely due to his genius for caricature, using that word in its best sense, as implying a discreet and good-natured exaggeration of characteristic traits of the persons whom he portrays. He makes his characters amusing, rather than ridiculous, and the result is that, although we are compelled to laugh at them very often, there are times when we also laugh with them. *The Throwbacks* is good, broad comedy.[192]

In Cork, the theaters were also closed for a number of weeks, although interesting touring companies—among them the MacDona Players, the Birmingham Repertory Company, and William Macready's Company in various nineteenth century pieces—appeared at the Opera House. There was some local activity, but little that was new. For the week of 6 February, the Munster Players at the Opera House revived *Sable and Gold* with *The Workhouse Ward*. On 2 and 3 March, the Queenstown Dramatic Society, directed by Mrs. Creagh-Barry, did an *Arms and the Man* at the Coliseum in Queenstown, and then repeated it later in the month for a couple of matinees at the Palace in Cork. For the week of 29 May, the Leeside Players did *The*

Whiteheaded Boy at the Opera House and preceded it by a new "Screaming Farce" by a local dramatist. As the *Cork Constitution* described it:

> The Leeside Players won a great success in the two plays which they performed last evening at the Opera House. . . . *A Cure for Nerves*, which was put on first, is a really splendid farce, full of amusing situations, and is from the pen of the well-known local playwright, "Fheir Maighe." . . . *The Cure for Nerves* is a great laughter-maker, and deals with a patient whose nerves are bad, and who is advised to go to the hospital. He does so, but his treatment in hospital by both nurses, doctor, and porter is so bad that he had to clear out.[193]

Nothing else noteworthy was produced, although on 17 July there did appear in *The Cork Examiner* this advertisement from Irish Photoplays:

> Irish Photo-Plays, Ltd., the new Irish Film Producing Company, who are at present engaged in producing the second of a series of six Comedy-Dramas, are open to consider a limited number of short humorous stories or Plays, pourtraying Irish Life, the scenes of which must be laid in Ireland. They need not be written in scenario form. A good price will be paid for any stories or plays accepted.[194]

T. C. Murray told Holloway that J. Bernard MacCarthy submitted a piece to the film company, but was turned down.[195] In any event, MacCarthy did publish in the *Independent* for 17 November an article entitled "How to Write a Film Play." The piece says little about films, but it does indicate some of MacCarthy's playwriting criteria:

> The faults of the novice in play-writing may be placed under three headings, faults of construction, of characterisation, and of dialogue; and of these the second is the most fatal. A writer can learn construction and how to write natural dialogue, but no amount of teaching will help him to depict character.
>
> One meets dozens of plays in MS., which show no sense of construction; they are composed of disconnected incidents strung together, and the most trivial ones elevated to an importance out of all proportion to their value.
>
> The architect views the house he is designing as a whole, and does not make the scullery bigger than the diningroom or introduce a room or staircase just because he thinks it would look pretty and help to fill up the drawing. The playwright should proceed on the same principle, for there must be architectural unity and utility in his planning. A very celebrated English scholar once wrote a drama in which a card game took three solid hours to play! You may have some nice poetical phrases or clever pieces of business in your mind, but if they don't fit into your work naturally you had better leave them out. And pay particular attention to your "curtains"; each should be the ending of one situation, and, at the same time, should arouse anticipation for the next Act.
>
> Dialogue has basic pitfalls for the eloquent writer. He pours it out in an easy flow, one character, though labouring under strong emotion, waiting until another has finished his argument. Now, in real life, our experience is that speech is brisk and staccato, with numerous interruptions, half sentences, and speakers breaking in impatiently. And don't make all your characters speak alike. We all have our characteristic mannerisms of speech, pet words and phrases and our special views which, often unnoticed by ourselves, we keep pressing on others, and without which

we could hardly be recognised. Make the speech of each character so characteristic that, were the names of the speakers erased, the reader could tell who was speaking.
And this carefulness in depicting speech will help your drawing of character. If you have a "good man" in the play, it is not sufficient for some friend of his to remark on the virtue of the character; you must show him being good and show him consistent. It is useless to enlarge on his amiability if he comes on and hits the heroine with a poker.
Similarly your "bad man" must act up to his reputation. Don't exhibit him sending presents to his mother, or weeping tears over the death of a favourite dog.
Nor must the heavy father, who has sternly forbidden the marriage of the hero and heroine for two acts and more, suddenly decide at the last moment, and for no apparent reason, to let the wedding bells go ding-dong. He may hear that the hero has been left £100,000 or that he is the son of an old flame of his, but there must be some convincing reason for his change of attitude.
However, the novice must remember that unless he has the root of the matter in himself—and many gifted writers are totally devoid of the dramatic instinct, which is the rarest of gifts—he cannot be taught to write a play. The most that can be done is to draw his attention to points of technique that, in the enthusiasm of youth, he may be inclined to overlook.[196]

And to this might be added some points from MacCarthy's article of 15 December, "The Literature of Simple Things":

Many persons interested in Anglo-Irish literature and sympathetic to its writers declare it is too insular, too parochial in its outlook, that it should deal with wider places and universal problems. Now, against whatever facets of our lives—customs, mentality, spirit of nationality—the charge of narrow-mindedness can be levelled, it is the very last accusation that can be brought against our literature, for literature, above all things, gains from insularity. Not that, of course, our Irish writer must refuse to learn from foreign literature; this he must study to develop his judgment and style; but if he wishes to write works of permanent value he must dig the common soil of his own country and turn the good brown earth of it open to the sun and air.
. . . A good writer will make a description of a village pump more interesting and readable than an indifferent author's description of Milan Cathedral. Thus in the same manner a skilled playwright can hold us breathless with a simple theme on the stage, whereas a melodrama writer's cramming of a railway accident, three suicides, a bank robber, and six murders into a single act of a play leaves us yawning with boredom. . . .
If any Irish author, holding the outposts of his craft against heavy odds in some isolated district, feels stunted and thinks that his art demands bigger territory, he needs reminding that the material about him is inexhaustible. The simple primitive things—birth, growth, maturity, decay, the four seasons of man and of nature—link him with the farthest ends of the earth. Should he interpret only an old man sitting on a lonely hill or a bereaved wife watching the sea that covers her hopes, and do it faithfully, he is writing for all time and all the world.[197]

• • •

During the year another Cork writer, T. C. Murray, discussed one more significant issue for the Irish dramatist—religion. Although Murray often discussed touchy issues in his plays, he was also a deeply Catholic writer. The unhappy marriage of *The Shadow of the Glen* considerably affronted the Holloways, but the unhappy marriage of *Aftermath* was considered a powerful and effective treatment of an important issue. In a speech to a meeting of the Catholic Truth Conference at the Mansion House on 12 October, Murray developed a liberal Catholic's viewpoint about the theater:

In his paper on "Catholics and the Theatre," Mr. T. C. Murray first alluded to a passage in Mr. Ernest Boyd's volume of literary studies in which it was stated that contrary to what obtained elsewhere Catholicism in Ireland was puritanical and inartistic, and the task of fostering thought and education had naturally fallen to Protestantism. The language revival alone served to show the illogical character of this claim, so far as education was concerned. Was it true, however, that to Irish Protestantism Ireland owed all that was significant in her art? What had Catholicism done for literature and art? Had it produced verse so rare and excellent as that of Yeats? Had it given drama as enduring as that of Synge? Had it evolved a literary personality so distinguished as that of George Russell? Were not James Stephens and Lady Gregory and Lennox Robinson the product of Irish Protestantism? Was there any fallacy underlying Mr. Boyd's argument? Or must Catholics merely sing dumb? To him the fallacy seemed obvious.

The above writers were not what they were because of their Protestantism, but in spite of it. Mr. Yeats reached his highest moments only when his mind was absorbed in Catholic thought and action. Synge's finest play, *Riders to the Sea*, reflected with truth the profound religious consciousness of the Irish peasant. A mind alien in faith to the people he describes betrays itself in almost every page of *The Well of the Saints*, *The Tinker's Wedding* and *The Playboy of the Western World*. These plays possess indeed a certain strange beauty—but it is beauty of speech only—the note of human life which he touches is absolutely false to the racial genius of the West, and jars accordingly.

Of the other writers who go to form this unquestionably brilliant company the same may be urged with as good reason—that is to say, their art gains in value in direct ratio to their power of apprehending and interpreting the Catholic mind. In Catholic Ireland there was the raw material of superb dramatic art. There were few countries, indeed, where a writer had such a wealth of the essentials on which to exercise his imagination. That was not to imply that he should be consciously Catholic or merely religious. Let him write of his people, as he knows them, as he sees them—portraying their faults no less than their virtues—the meanness as well as the largeness of their character—their strength and their tenderness—their intense love and more intense hate—let him, in a word, write sincerely and their Catholicity must reveal itself in every circumstance as a flower reveals itself even in the darkness by its perfume. It is impossible, indeed, for the Catholic playwright knowing his own people to think of them apart from their religion. The Irishman's Catholicity is as organic a part of his spiritual entity as are the heart and the brains of his physical organization.

The truth of this is borne in upon us in a study of almost any one of the plays written by Catholic authors for the National Theatre. No matter what the theme, the circumstances, the scene or the action, the atmosphere of Catholicity is ever there—subtly felt perhaps rather than visible to the senses. We get it in *Thomas Muskerry*, in *The Land*, and in all the plays of Padraic Colum; we have it in *The Building Fund* of William Boyle, and in *The Bribe* and other plays of Seumas O'Kelly. In the work of Daniel Corkery this Catholic note becomes more articulate, particularly in *The Yellow Bittern*, his best play. Speaking of one of his [Murray's] plays, the theme of *Maurice Harte* was so purely and intimately Catholic in its nature that it was necessary to touch on it. The play is a study of a young student who realises that he has no vocation. It may be considered that a theme like this should from its very nature be outside the domain of drama—such a view, indeed, has been expressed to me more than once—but to limit the dramatist's range, to fetter his imagination, to narrow his field of vision, is surely to do a great disservice to art without any corresponding service to religion—always assuming, of course, that the subject is treated with reverence and sincerity.

It is always worth remembering that art is life interpreted through the imagination—not life as registered by a camera.

One of the things he failed to understand was the storm raised by Catholic students in the theater on the production of Yeats's poetical play, *The Countess Cathleen*. A verse play is not a treatise or a tract. The poet is a child at play, as Francis Thompson says of Shelley. To apply the foot rule of reason and strict orthodoxy to the actions of the beings he evokes from his imagination is to misunderstand him woefully. One might as well object that Hans Christian Anderson or Grimm or *The Midsummer Night's Dream* is not orthodox. It is a tale told for its beauty alone, and to read into it any other purpose is but wilfully to misinterpret the dramatist's intention.

We must, in a word, said Mr. Murray, face the truth. The warp and woof of human life are wove not of good or evil, but of both.

To be insincere in the theatre is to fail. All real drama, like life itself, must be a fusion of the nobler and baser elements in man's nature.

The attitude of the Church to the theatre in Ireland is not easy to define. It might, perhaps, be described as a negative one. She does not condemn, except in extreme circumstances; neither does she approve. He pleaded for a fuller interest—a return in some degree to that which characterised her in earlier times. In its beginnings the drama was purely a religious art. If there were a Catholic Stage Society, the introduction of mystery plays—many of them very beautiful—would, doubtless, be one of its aims. Would it not be well, he asked, if the Church, for her children's sake, manifested that more direct interest in the theatre for which he pleaded? No art makes such a universal appeal as the drama. There was no use in urging that the stage had too often a questionable influence on morals. No one can deny it. But what human art is there that cannot ennoble no less than it can debase? Was it not for the Church, while sternly condemning what is deliberately bad or irreligious in the art of the theatre, to foster what is good?

The Catholic Church had been the nurse of so many arts. She looked askance at the art whose influence on the minds of her children was most direct and vital. For the painter in all ages she has shown almost a loving solicitude. Yet a picture gallery, stored with treasures of centuries, is perhaps in its aloofness the saddest building in any city. The masters had no voice to charm from the street one of the many passersby absorbed in themselves or in the noisy happenings of the hour.

Turn to the crowded theatres, the music halls, the cinemas, and translate its meaning. Is it not that our common humanity finds within those walls something which ministers to some real want inherent in our nature? Is it wise, then, to ignore an instrument so potent for good or evil as the stage?

That duty became all the more obvious at a time when the trend of the stage all over Europe is toward decadence. On the other hand, the Irish National Theatre had preserved on the whole a singularly healthy tone, far above any standard which obtains elsewhere. This is directly due to the fact that it derives its inspiration from the life and thought of the most Catholic nation in the world to-day. Its future should therefore be a matter of concern to all of us from a Catholic as well as a National point of view. It is battling as most good causes have to battle against odds.

One hears from time to time much talk of our Celtic sensibility to what is fine and beautiful. It was well to have a proper conceit of themselves. But no comment was necessary other than the queue at the doors of the Theatres. Ask those Irish Catholic people why they are there, and if they are truthful they will tell you that the production they are so patiently waiting to see has had a run of heaven knows how many hundred nights in some London theatre. The thinking Englishman might well smile. The thinking Irishman might well despair were it not for the hope that springs from that little theatre battling for life in Abbey street.

And let us remember, added Mr. Murray, that we Catholics, for all our puritanism, have had no small part in the kindling, as well as in the nursing, of that life. Edward Martyn was one of its sponsers. At a later period they had Thomas MacDonagh, R. J. Ray, George Fitzmaurice, Brinsley MacNamara, W. F. Casey, John Guinan, D. L. Kelleher, Edward McNulty, Bernard MacCarthy, Martin McHugh, and Con O'Leary. Later still J. P. Dalton, Frank O'Donnell, Miss Macardle, George Shiels, and the list was far from being complete. This brilliant little company of artists, too, had been always composed without exception of devoted Catholics.

Much speculation was to be heard these days as to its future, and more than one heard to prophesy "All's over." He thought it was far from being over. All periods of great creative activity were followed by seasons of comparative sterility. He had a profound belief in its future, and saw in its twenty years' achievement only a preparation for the greater and more significant drama of to-morrow. And he was not without reason for the faith in him. A deeper sense of nationhood than they had felt for a century is ours to-day. That it has led to such woeful happenings only shows its intensity. The new drama will reflect this heightened spiritual consciousness. With a return to honourable peace, the wounds of these unhappy days healed, and the nation marching onward as one man, I imagine a great Catholic artist emerging and giving our stage a glory such as Shakespeare gave to England.[198]

In March, in the *Gael*, Brinsley MacNamara inveighed against publishing and dramatic taste:

Some of the very worst plays that the Irish Literary Movement has produced have been published and some of the very best . . . have remained unpublished, or if they have achieved printed form have remained comparatively unknown and unplayed across the Irish countryside. The result has been disastrous for Irish drama—scarcely ever a new play at the Abbey Theatre, and empty houses for even the most popular of the old ones. Those who might come to write plays if they were given a consistent course of good models to inspire or at least excite them are given *ad nauseam The Lord Mayor* or *The Eloquent Dempsy*. Countless fearsome imitations of these two outworn plays have been written in consequence, until in the end one is forced to the conclusion that *The Lord Mayor* in particular is all that the Irish Literary Movement has produced in the way of a play—all that any writer should try to emulate if he hopes to get a production either in Dublin or in the provinces.

Those responsible for the production of plays in Ireland have been attracted by bad plays which read well, and, on the strength of mere facility in this respect (rather more that of the newspaper and the novel), have accepted them as good plays. This, however, is not a mistake so purely ignorant as it may appear at first sight. It is an attitude not at all uncommon among men of letters who take little interest in the theatre, and who are accustomed to consider the drama from the literary point of view. They also think of a play as something intended only to be read and to be judged solely in the study, and not also on the stage. Fine writing, any more than merely obvious writing, does not make a fine play; and it is because most of the finer poets took this view persistently in the nineteenth century that the English drama was then so sterile.

But no support for the view can be found in the practice or in the precepts of the great Greek dramatists or of the great dramatists of the modern languages. The great dramatists always seem to have felt that plays do not live by style alone, but by substance, by invention and by construction, by imagination and by veracity. A good play must be well written, no doubt, but before it is written it must be well conceived and well developed; it must have a theme; it must have a story which reveals itself in a sequence of situations; and this plot must be peopled with human beings who look like human beings, who talk like human beings, and who act like human beings. . . .

The Directors of the Abbey Theatre, in concentrating altogether upon plays of Irish life by Irish authors made a mistake which has resulted in the end in stultification of all their aims and almost complete obliteration of the force, both Literary and National, which at one time the theatre bade fair to be. If they had varied their seasons' programmes with the best work of modern Europeans or put their actors into Shakespeare and the English classical plays now and again the effect upon the writing of Irish plays must certainly have been excellent. . . . Another excellent thought would seem to have occurred later only, unfortunately, to be pursued in turn but a very little way. This was the sending of a second company through the provincial towns to give varied selections from the repertoire in places where only the lowest kind of English melodramas or the most benighted of the "Stage-Irishman" farces had been seen ever before. . . .

It would be altogether more probable for a person to write a good play without having ever seen any of the plays of prevalent production in the Irish provinces at all. Any natural ability he might have would be spoiled by having his mind forced into stilted and unnatural forms by the productions he had seen.

A remarkable instance of the probability of such a play is *The Dawn Mist*, by Frank Hugh O'Donnell, which is shortly to make its re-appearance in published form. This little dramatic work was executed at a time when Mr. O'Donnell had not yet seen the stage production of a play of any kind. Viewed in this light it is quite a remarkable achievement. In book form it has already exhausted several large editions. It was banned by the late British Government in Ireland and it has been produced all over the countryside. Before now its propagandist value may have been one reason of its great popularity. But now it can be viewed in quite a different light—as a model, or at *least* an example, for the young playwright, to whom any real dramatic culture or equipment has been denied in spite of all our boasted literary revival.[199]

• • •

By 1922 there seemed to be almost as many Irish actors working outside of Ireland as there were at home. Arthur Sinclair and Maire O'Neill were playing *The Whiteheaded Boy* in America and later in Australia. In their company were Christine Hayden and Arthur Shields. Sara Allgood returned to the Abbey for a few weeks, but mainly she was in management in England, and her company did such plays as *Mixed Marriage* and *Hyacinth Halvey* in London, Liverpool, and elsewhere. Appearing with her were Fred O'Donovan and Parker K. Lynch, the Cork actor who had become a permanent member of the Liverpool Repertory Company. W. G. Fay had been producing plays at the Nottingham Repertory for a couple of years, and A. Patrick Wilson was producing for the Scottish National Players. Dudley Digges and J. M. Kerrigan were both working in New York, and for much of the year Kathleen Drago and F. J. McCormick were touring in England in *Paddy the Next Best Thing*.

Among the people who stayed at home, Edward Martyn was not in good health, but in January he was still getting about, and Holloway reported:

> I was also speaking to old M'Gough and Edward Martyn. The latter told me the way Countess Plunkett shilly-shallied about Hardwicke Street Theatre for months and then refused to let him have it without assigning any cause. He afterwards heard that she objected to O'Duffy's play that he intended producing, as she thought one of the characters reflected on her son Joseph [probably a reference to O'Duffy's unproduced play *Bricriu's Feast*], O'Duffy having already written about him in his book *The Wasted Island*. Martyn told me he had read the book but saw no character he could recognise as Joseph Plunkett as he knew him. . . . He saw *The Irish Jew* and thought it the best thing John MacDonagh ever wrote, but the production of the Council Chamber scene didn't please him—there should have been some of the public present. When he suggested that to the dramatist, his answer was that "supers" cost 5/— a night a head, and so he cut the public out of the scene. It was different with crowds at Hardwicke Street—there they cost the management nothing! Martyn objected to music during the intervals; they never had it abroad. He would never have it in any theatre run by him. I said, Continental theatres are different; there the audience went out between the acts "en block"—a bell ringing them to their seats again. Few leave their seats in Dublin theatres; therefore something must be provided for them to while away the tedious intervals. "But they never listen to the music!" was Martyn's reply.[200]

On 3 February, John Butler Yeats died in New York. He was ever a partisan of his son's theater, and readers of volume 3 of this history will remember how he rose at the debate over *The Playboy* to cry, "This is still the island of Saints—plaster Saints!"

Also in February, the amazing James Lynchehaun appeared again, this time in Athlone. Readers of volume 3 of this history will also recall that in 1907 the Lynchehaun case was often brought forward as an argument for the basic plausibility of Synge's rendering of the character of the Western peasant in *The Playboy*.[201]

In August, W. J. Lawrence received a Civil List pension for his services to dramatic scholarship, and O'Donnell remarked to Holloway:

> "He must be thought a lot of as a writer on Elizabethan Drama," and I said, "He was one of the greatest and most informing of all on that and other subjects on dramatic matters. He has this pull over most other writers in that he takes a practical as well as an historic interest in all things connected with the stage, past and present and to come. Ireland is very neglectful of his genius. . . . It was to such men as Sir Sidney Lee, William Archer, and Ernest Lee he owes the recognition he justly deserves."[202]

Also in August, Christine Hayden and Eric Gorman, both of the Abbey Theatre, were married.

On 25 December, Joseph MacDonagh died at the Mater Hospital Nursing Home of appendicitis. He had been moved to the Mater from Mountjoy. He was the brother of John and Thomas MacDonagh, and had acted at the Hardwicke Street Theatre. Holloway thought him "a clever character actor, with a strong dash of humour and sarcasm in his composition."[203]

On 28 December, Mrs. Max Green died. She was the daughter of John Redmond, and under her maiden name of Joanna Redmond had written some patriotic one-acts.[204]

Alice Milligan had not been active in the theater for a decade or so, but during the year she did contribute a couple of more pieces of information about the first play to be acted in Irish. In an interview in the *Gael* in September appeared the statement:

> In 1898 she assisted in rehearsing and staging at Letterkenny Aonach the first play to be acted in Irish. It had been written in English for the Most Rev. Dr. O'Donnell by Father O'Growney, and translated into Irish by "Padraic," the well-known Donegal poet.[205]

And on 21 October in the *Independent*, she herself wrote:

> The late Father Eugene O'Growney wrote a pageant play, dealing with Tir-Conail's history, for the Letterkenny Aonach in 1898, and it was stage-managed by the Rev. President of St. Eunan's Seminary. On the same occasion a second historical drama was produced in another hall having been rehearsed under the guidance of the Rev. Mother of the Loreto Convent, who also designed the decorations and costumes in superb style.[206]

And, finally, as a harbinger of things to come, there is the sentence that Lady Gregory wrote in her journal for 13 April:

> Read two plays *Kathleen's Seamless Coat*; and *the Drapier Letters*, an imaginative piece, I think powerful.[207]

Lady Gregory's editor properly notes that *The Drapier Letters* was a one-act by Arthur Power, which was produced at the Abbey on 22 August 1927, but "*Kathleen's Seamless Coat* was not performed at the Abbey."[208] It may, however, in some form have been. On 29 March, Sean O'Casey published a short, allegorical story in *Poblacht Na h-Éireann* that was called "The Seamless Coat of Kathleen," and which seems to fore-shadow his one-act political allegory called *Kathleen Listens In*, which the Abbey produced on 1 October 1923. The coincidence of the title strongly suggests that here is another lost O'Casey one-act, and perhaps also that the "Kathleen" play of 1923 was an outgrowth of it. In any case, O'Casey was knocking at the door.

3
1923

In January the Irish Republican Army became increasingly active, encouraged, at the beginning of the month, by the capture of three posts with much war material in Cork city. Ambushing, sniping, attacks on Government patrols and barracks, were carried out in Dublin and in the Midlands, as well as in the South and West. Railway workers were forbidden by the I.R.A. to assist the Government forces and much railway property was wrecked. . . .

The execution of Republican prisoners proceeded, during January, in every quarter of the Free State, North, South, East and West.[1]

So wrote Dorothy Macardle in her voluminous, if very partial account, *The Irish Republic*. Readers of the *Evening Herald* saw headlines like these:

Sligo Station Burned—Two Passenger Trains Destroyed. 11 January.
Three Executions in Dundalk To-day. 13 January.
Ambushes in Tipperary, Cork, Clare and Mayo—4 Dead. 18 January.
Eleven Executions This Morning. 20 January.
Mail Train Wrecked on Midland Railway. 22 January.
Barracks Burned in Co. Dublin and Co. Galway. 26 January.
Two Co. Limerick Ambushes. 29 January.
Orgy of Destruction in City, Suburbs and Townships. 30 January.

What Miss Macardle does not report is that during this period a favorite tactic of the I.R.A. was to burn the Big Houses of anyone connected with the government. To cite only instances with some theatrical or artistic relevance, we might note first a story in the *Irish Times* for 1 February:

All that remained of Sir Horace Plunkett's fine residence, Kilteragh, Foxrock, after Tuesday morning's [30 January] mine explosion was destroyed by fire before daybreak yesterday . . . .

It is estimated that the frescoes and various paintings by "A. E.," Jack Yeats, Hone, and 18th century Irish artists, which have perished in the fire, were worth £10,000.[2]

Sir Horace, who was in Madison, Wisconsin, remarked with a rather saintly stoicism, "While the house is a very fine one, the occurrence is not so regrettable as would have been the wrecking of some poor man's one-room dwelling."[3] On the same day, the *Irish Times* reported, "The latest information about the fire at the Earl of Mayo's house, Palmerston, Naas, on Monday night [29 January], is to the effect that of the valuable paintings, only three, by Sir Joshua Reynolds, were saved"[4] Also on the same day, the *Times* reported:

> Temple Hill, the residence of Captain Stephen Gwynn, at Kimmage road, Terenure, Dublin, was badly damaged by a powerful land mine yesterday afternoon. . . .
>
> The residence was a substantial one, but is now virtually a wreck; with the exception of two rooms in the left wing. The drawingroom and study seemed to escape much of the force of the concussion, and, as far as could be ascertained, the damage done to them was slight.
>
> The furniture, pictures, fittings, etc., in the remaining portion of the house are almost entirely ruined. . . .
>
> At the time of the explosion Captain and Mrs. Gwynn were in the city.[5]

On 2 February, the *Irish Times* reported that:

> "Rockfield," Artane, the residence of Mr. J. J. Reddin, father of Mr. Kenneth S. Reddin, District Justice, was burned last night by armed men, who told the occupants that the burning was a reprisal for the shooting of a man named Fisher.
>
> The house, which stood on its own grounds on the Malahide road, about a quarter of a mile from the tramway, was a fine two-storeyed building. It was occupied by Mr. Reddin, senior, and his three sons, Kenneth, Norman and Kerry. . . .
>
> At about 9:30 o'clock the lodge-keeper at Rockfield, Christopher Gough, was sitting in the lodge at the entrance gates, close to the road, when a knock came to the door. Almost immediately afterwards a young man with a revolver in his hand, put in his head, and warned the lodge keeper and his family "not to stir outside for half-an-hour." The armed man then closed the door, and was heard moving rapidly up the avenue.
>
> Almost at the same time several other armed men went to the halldoor of the family residence. In response to their knock Dr. Kerry Reddin came out into the hall and asked who was there.
>
> "Republican military," was the answer.
>
> "What do you want?" asked Dr. Reddin.
>
> He had barely spoken when there was a crashing of glass, and nine or ten men came in through the broken windows of the ground floor. They were armed with Colts and Parabellums. Nearly all of them carried tins of petrol, which they had taken from the garage attached to the house.
>
> The raiders then sprinkled petrol about the rooms; the furniture was piled in heaps about the house and set on fire.
>
> Soon the rooms were burning fiercely. The flames were issuing from the windows when the raiders left, making away through the fields at the rear of the house.
>
> Shortly after 10 o'clock the Dublin Fire Brigade received a summons to Rockfield, and the Tara street section, under Lieutenant Power, arrived about twenty minutes later. By that time the entire building was in flames. The nearest water supply was at the lodge gates, and to convey it to the house a very long line of hose was required.
>
> The fire had already taken a fatal grip on the premises, and the firemen confined

their efforts to preventing it from spreading to the out-offices and the conservatory, which adjoins the house.

An *Irish Times* representative was at Rockfield in time to see the blazing roof collapse. While yet a good distance away one could hear the crackle of burning wood and see the volumes of smoke belch from the front and back of the house.

Dr. Reddin watched the blazing pile from the avenue. "That's all that remains of it," he said bitterly to our representative. Pointing to a motor car which stood beside him he explained that it was the only thing which had been saved.

Complete editions of the works of Pearse, MacDonagh, and other leaders of the 1916 rebellion perished in the flames, and many of their manuscripts which the family prized very much. In addition, a valuable collection of pictures was destroyed. It included works by Yeats, Sir Joshua Reynolds, Slater, and Crampton Walker.

. . . Rockfield, it is stated, had been largely used by Patrick Pearse and his colleagues before 1916.[6]

And on 6 February, the *Times* reported:

Moore Hall, which was destroyed by incendiaries last week, was the property of Mr. George Moore, the distinguished novelist, brother of Colonel Maurice Moore. It was built in 1795 by George Moore, the grandfather of the present owner.

John Moore, son of the builder of the house, joined the French at Killala in 1798, but died in prison in 1799, before he could be tried by courtmartial.

George Henry Moore, father of Colonel Moore, and grandson of the builder of the house, was an Irish leader from 1857 till his death in 1870. In 1867 he was a Fenian head centre.

It is understood that after the arrest of Mr. Kilroy, leader of the anti-Treaty forces in Mayo, a message was sent seeking Colonel Moore to intervene in order to save Mr. Kilroy's life, and promising that if this was done no more attacks would be made in County Mayo. Colonel Moore is said to have taken the necessary steps in the matter, yet Moore Hall was burned last week.

The information at hand is that nothing was saved in the house; pictures, family portraits for over 200 years, all the furniture, books, papers, etc., have been destroyed.

The library, 40 ft. long by 20 ft. wide, was full of books of great historical interest. They were collected mainly by George Moore, grandfather of Colonel Moore, a well-known writer and historian.[7]

"Peace," wrote Lady Gregory on 4 January, " seems far away."[8]

In the middle of January[9], three gunman abducted Oliver Gogarty, now a Free State Senator, from his home in Ely Place. Apparently he was going to be shot, but managed to elude his captors by diving into the icy Liffey and swimming across the river to safety.

On 14 January, W. T. Cosgrave's house in Templeogue was burned. On 3 February, the *Herald's* headline was "Senator's Residence Burned in Kerry." On 12 February, the *Herald's* headline was "Father of Dail Minister Shot Dead."[11] And on 19 February, Gogarty's house in Connemara, Renvyle, was burned down. And on 20 February, the *Herald*'s headline was "Senator's Residence Gutted in Co. Waterford." The Free State took more precautions, and guards were assigned to prominent politicians, among them W. B. Yeats, who lived at 82, Merrion Square.

Meanwhile, the awful headlines continued:

> Daring Attacks in the City To-day. 21 February.
> Train Smash in West—City Raids, Arrests and Discoveries. 3 March.
> Trains Derailed and on Fire. 6 March.
> Government Offices Blown Up by Land Mine. 7 March.
> Raids, Arrests and Encounters. 8 March.
> Seven Executions This Morning. 13 March.
> Shootings, Burnings and Explosions. 19 March.[12]

Theaters did not escape the turmoil of the war. On 20 February, Lady Gregory recorded:

> Perrin came in here, says a rifle bullet came through the cafe window at the Abbey yesterday afternoon, troops pursuing a man who had thrown a bomb in O'Connell Street.[13]

Earlier, on 30 January, a *Times* story reported a new form of pressure from the Republicans upon the theaters:

> Following the notices purporting to come from the I.R.A. received by the managers of the Cork theatres and cinemas, directing them to close on days when any executions are announced, Major-General Reynolds, G.O.C., Cork, has issued an order in the following terms:—
>
> "Unless directed by me, there shall be no cessation of public services, or closing of places of public amusement, such as theatres, picture houses, etc., in Cork. Anybody disobeying this order will be arrested and charged with aiding the irregular forces, who are at present opposing the Government selected by the Irish people."[14]

And on 25 March, Lady Gregory wrote of a similar Republican attempt upon the Dublin theatres:

> A couple of days ago I had a letter from L. R. [Lennox Robinson]. He enclosed a typed order from the "Government of the Republic of Ireland" signed by Padraig O'Ruitleis, "Minister for Home Affairs", saying that because of the acceptance of the Free State, and the executions, and imprisonments "It is hereby decreed that the present be observed as a time of National mourning, that all sports and amusements be suspended, that all Theatres, &c be closed. . . ."
>
> Robinson wrote that he had not taken it very seriously and heard later that there was a meeting of Theatrical Managers at 1 o'clock . . . and at quarter to seven "rang up Mr. Armstrong of the Empire Theatre and found to my astonishment they were closing and that all the Theatres and picture houses were doing the same thing. So then I got in touch with Yeats and Government and went over to Merrion Square. The Government were debating their action and promised to let me know what they wanted done. I waited on and on, 'phoning Perrin not to open till I heard, till finally at 8.15 not having heard from Government I 'phoned the Abbey again and found that the Army had arrived and made us open. . . . It was a good performance and a

fair audience, well guarded by military at all entrances to the Theatre. During the show we took the portraits in the vestibule out of their frames and they are in safe keeping. After the performance the military left and the C.I.D. came but didn't stay all night. This morning I spent in Desmond Fitzgerald's office, all the other managers waited on O'Higgins who gave them great abuse I believe, and an order was issued to us all commanding us to open tonight. Fitzgerald has arranged that we are to be specially well guarded as we opened last night, and W. B. being a Senator makes us a good target, we'll have a guard all tomorrow. It seems queer that my stormiest moments in the Theatre have always been over the question 'To open or not to open'. It must be written in the stars somewhere. The Government knew nothing of the matter till my 'phone call to them last night. The Company have been splendid."[15]

In April, Maud Gonne MacBride and her daughter Iseult were arrested by the Free State government and imprisoned in Kilmainham. Maud Gonne went on hunger strike and was released on 24 April.

When Lady Gregory went to see Sean O'Casey's *The Shadow of a Gunman* in mid-April, there was still an armed guard on the theater, and she wrote:

> In Casey's play there were harmless explosions representing bombs thrown by the Black and Tans. And real ones were not far off for on Friday Perrin told me that a land mine had been put that morning by armed men who held up the caretaker, in the picture house "Olympia" close to the Abbey. But the fuse had burned out without exploding it.[16]

Despite the constant violence and disruption, the war was winding down. As Dorothy Macardle wrote:

> In that part of the country where the fighting had been most violent, there was a widespread desire for peace. The civil population no longer gave the Volunteers the help and sympathy which had sustained them throughout the earlier fight. The men were being continually approached by priests and laymen, moving on their own initiative or commissioned by the Free State Government, who engaged them in discussions on the advisability of ending the war.[17]

"This time," as Maire and Conor Cruise O'Brien put it, "the guerilla fish had run out of water. They abandoned their resistance on 24 May 1923."[18] It was the end of the Civil War, if not the end of its effects.

• • •

In January, St. John Ervine, who was never of the critical school of sunny optimism, reviewed some recent Irish plays, and was moved to proclaim the end of the Irish Renaissance of Letters:

> The Irish drama has fallen into a decline. . . . Whatever influence has been exercised over the minds of young Irish dramatists was exercised, not by Mr. Moore nor by Mr. Yeats, nor by "A. E.," but by John Millington Synge; and since it was

the influence of a sick and bitter man, it has served chiefly to destroy the renaissance rather than to strengthen it.

In each of the volumes now to be surveyed there are traces of Synge, especially in Lady Gregory's plays. Mr. T. C. Murray, for example, in the first act of his play, *Aftermath* . . . , makes one of his characters use this speech:

> . . . And look at the fine mornings with the frost on the ferns and the briars. And another time, maybe, the flood racing through the glen. And there's the thought of Spring leaping out of the dark some day and startling the hills into laughter.

That speech remarkably echoes the Tramp's speech in *The Shadow of the Glen*, when he says to Nora Burke:

> We'll be going now, I'm telling you, and the time you'll be feeling the cold, and the frost, and the great rain, and the sun again, and the south wind blowing in the glens, you'll not be sitting up on a wet ditch, the way you're after sitting in this place, making yourself old with looking on each day, and it passing you by . . . .

. . . Lady Gregory's work (*The Image and Other Plays* . . .) is so obviously derived from Synge that there is no need to argue about it. Her plays, like his, are about still life. The people are either looking back to a romantic past or forward to a romantic future, and dodging the sordid present. . . . It is interesting to observe how seldom an Irish dramatist can stay the course. Mr. Murray's strength gives out after two acts. His best plays, *Birthright* and *Maurice Harte*, have really been one-act plays, divided into two scenes. Lady Gregory seems totally unable to handle the two or three-act form. Her strength lies in the one-act play dealing with a single incident. Lord Dunsany, who has more sense of the theatre than either Lady Gregory or Mr. Murray, cannot control three acts with anything like the ability with which he can control one. . . . Mr. Murray's play, *Aftermath*, deals with two themes, which have evidently pressed upon his mind for the greater part of his life. All of his plays in greater or lesser degree are concerned with one or both of these subjects: the arranged and loveless Irish marriage, and the Irish peasant's hunger for the possession of land. A marriage in the country parts of Ireland is conducted on something of the principle on which a man buys a fat pig. I remember being told by a peasant farmer in Mayo before the war that his son had seen his wife for the first time at the altarsteps on the day of their marriage. All the arrangements for the marriage had been made by the parents of the bride and bridegroom, and were made on strictly commercial lines. Mr. Murray resents this method of marriage, but he regards the land-hunger of the peasant with greater resentment, for he sees it as something which saps the mind and the spirit of his countrymen. It would do Mr. Chesterton and Mr. Belloc good to have a long conversation with Mr. Murray. He could, I think, disillusion them about the bright paradise of theirs in which every peasant is a proprietor. Mr. Murray, however, has hardly written his play with the force with which he wrote *Birthright.* He is more intent on his argument than he is on his people, and since the three principals are either uninteresting as individuals or unable to hold our sympathy for more than a little time, his play has less effect on us than it ought to have.

When one turns from these three dramatists and remembers that the successors to them and to Mr. Lennox Robinson are now producing stories and plays which are full of nauseous piety and patriotism, one sees that the collapse of the Irish Dramatic Renaissance is complete. I am told by those who are competent to know that young Irish men and women are now producing work of incredible puerility. Well, well, Mr. Yeats has been made a senator, and Mr. "A. E." addresses pitiable open letters to gunmen, and the Irish Literary Renaissance is dead.[19]

In April 1923 the corpse gave one twitch of remarkable vigour, with the production of O'Casey's *Shadow of a Gunman*; but still Ervine's diagnosis had considerable point. In March it was spelled out more specifically by Claude Ashe in the *Sunday Independent*:

All the dramatic critics whose business is with the English stage are in a state almost of despair. They deplore the type of performance that is given in the great majority of theatres, and they are amazed that playgoers do not demand something better. They can do nothing except bewail the decadence of the drama, and look around eagerly for the smallest sign that might give hope of better things. Now, it is clear that we in Ireland must be affected by the state of the English theatre. We are only a small fraction of the world's English-speaking population, and as long as English remains the current language of our country we shall necessarily be dependent to a large extent for our plays as well as our books or writers from the other side of the channel or the ocean. Furthermore, we do not get the best of English plays. I do not know how theatrical touring managers classify Dublin—whether it is an A, B, or C city—but certain it is that we fare very badly in the general type of play that comes from the other side.

What about our own part in the world of the theatre? We have, of course, the Abbey as one regular, solid fact, and we have also occasional performances in various other theatres. We have all a very kindly feeling towards the Abbey, but it is due, we must confess, more to what it has done in the past than what it is doing at present. As the centre of a movement the Abbey seems dead. It is now doing little more than marking time and living on its laurels. We have much to be thankful for in possessing a theatre where we can see plays by Irish authors acted by Irish players working with a sincerity that we see nowhere else, but we are, nevertheless, sadly aware of the difference between the present and the days of ten or fifteen years ago, when every frequenter of the Abbey felt himself a participator in a vital, enthusiastic movement.

The intermittent production of new Irish plays in other Dublin theatres is something to be thankful for also. It shows that there are live dramatists among us still who can be modern and at the same time Irish as well, who can give us comedies that we enjoy, and who on the whole sound a note of hope. But it is an individual note. . . . I am sure that there are many in Ireland who are discontented with the state of the Irish stage, and feel that they would do something for it if they had a chance, who have ideas that they know are worthwhile, but who see no opportunity of carrying them into effect.

Could not a few of them give each other sufficient encouragement to attempt a new venture? The prospects of success are in reality considerable, especially if they give the Irish play-going public an opportunity of seeing at last something of the newer methods of production. We are probably one of the most backward countries in Europe in this matter. The use of a new stagecraft which depends for its effects on lighting rather than on elaborate scenery has found its way into every big country, and into small countries as well—Poland, Czecho-Slovakia, Holland and the rest—but here we have made no advance since the first introduction of electric light on the stage.

Many years ago the Dublin art students had a flourishing dramatic society (William Pearse and Thomas King Moylan were notable members) but art and drama seem to have had no union since then. Can we hope that an alliance of the arts will produce the next Irish theatre movement? It is a work for young people endowed with enthusiasm, energy and patience, but the ground seems ready prepared. . . . As it is we need fresh ideas and new men if the Irish theatre is to be anything but a backwash of London's second-best.[20]

• • •

Despite such critical gloom, and despite the disruptions of civil war, the Abbey stayed open for thirty-four weeks in 1923 and produced fifty plays. Some of the older work was rather roughly handled. Robinson's *Patriots*, for instance, was found by Jacques to be "taken from its musty pigeon-hole . . . old, stale, 'die-for-Ireland' flapdoodle . . . out-of-date stuff."[21] However, there were ten new productions of plays by J. Bernard MacCarthy, George Fitzmaurice, Sean O'Casey, Fand O'Grady, Brinsley MacNamara, George Shiels, Lady Gregory, Ibsen, and Goldsmith.

The Abbey's first new play of the year was MacCarthy's one-act, *The Long Road to Garranbraher*, which was first produced on 9 January, on a triple bill with *The Pot of Broth* and *The Man of Destiny*. The new play was not a success, but there was disagreement about whether the playwright or the actors were to blame. Or even, as W. J. Lawrence put it in the *Stage*, whether the policy of the management was to blame:

> If it be true, as Mr. St. John Ervine (himself a graduate of the Abbey) has recently been telling us, that "the collapse of the Irish Dramatic Renaissance is complete," then the misfortune is due to ill-laying of the foundations. For the past score of years the Abbey Theatre has been distinctively a theatre of snippets.[22] Its directorate has pursued the mistaken policy of fostering the single-act play to the detriment of more solid fare, and has vitiated taste by habituating the Dublin public to snippety programmes. Atrophied from disuse, the art of dramatic construction, as practised by a long line of distinguished Irishmen reaching from Lording Barry to Dion Boucicault, will be soon lost to a country that once had its secret. The mistake has been to encourage writers like Mr. J. Bernard McCarthy, who have demonstrated their capacity for sustained flights to waste their powers on trivial gliding. It is apt, as in the present instance, to lead to a halting between two opinions. In *The Long Road to Garranbraher* Mr. McCarthy has endeavoured to get all the details of a complex and really interesting plot within the narrow confines of the single-act form, but so tight has been the squeeze that the picture has burst the frame. The long arm of coincidence is much too apparent in the comings and goings of the minor characters, if characters is the word for ill-articulated puppets that clumsily respond to the author's pulling of the strings.[23]

The *Irish Times* succinctly summarized the plot:

> *The Long Road to Garranbraher* is an unhappy little scene. Old Peter Hanley, a retired sea captain, is forced to leave his beloved seaside cottage, and is about to go inland to live with his son-in-law. The son-in-law is arranging the sale of furniture with a neighbouring dealer when in comes his son, a young seafaring man, recently saved from a wreck. Dan, the son, explains that owing to his good work for the ship the owners have made him a present of £200, and that he will pay the debts, and so enable the parents to stay by the sea. The truth turns out to be that the ship was

scuttled (with the loss of two lives), and Dan's £200 is "hush money." Broken with grief, the old man goes off "the long road" with his son-in-law.

The idea of the play is good, and so is the little dramatic incident; but it needs a little pulling together. It was obvious that Dan's money was tainted, without the entrance of a shipmate to prove it; his story was not convincing enough. There is a little too much talk about the "old home"; and there is an unnecessary neighbour who comes in at the end to mourn the loss of one of the drowned men.

Mr. Dolan made another good study of an old man as Peter Hanley; Mr. McCormick acted well, but looked too much the picture post-card seaman, as Dan. Mr. Quinn was quite clever as the son-in-law, and Mr. Carolan, the tell-tale shipmate, was good, too. Miss Hayden was clever in her little comedy part of the dealer. Miss O'Kelly and Miss Craig wept well—that was most of their parts.[24]

In the *Irish Independent*, Jacques admired the writing and faulted the technique:

Mr. McCarthy knows his sea coast and his sea coast cottages. He almost breaks into poetry when he speaks of Roche's Point twinkling its lighthouse eyes in greeting to ships that pass in the darkness of the night and the greyness of dawn. There is grandeur in the mariner's rugged recital of the victories over storms and the battles with the elements. The spray of sea salt comes across the footlights. But technique is faulty, and the little piece wobbles towards the end, when it should be steadiest and readiest for the dramatic climax. There was an irritating delay before we came to that long road. The play was saved by the acting of Michael J. Dolan, the white-haired mariner, and Eileen O'Kelly as his wife. Others might have been more satisfying.[25]

The *Evening Herald* criticised the play but admired the acting:

His sailor men were not sailor men, and the story in which he wrapped portions of their lives was too artificial and unfinished to make great drama.

The play was not lacking in dramatic moments, for he had them when the old man refused, because of happy associations, to sell the picture of his ship, and when Seumas Doran accused Dan of villainy on the high seas. They were true enough, but they were happy interludes sandwiched by anaemic conversations and sentimental sobs.

Mr. McCarthy owes a great deal to the actors and actresses who strove, ineffectually perhaps, to infuse blood into his characters. Michael J. Dolan, as Captain Peter Hanley, gave again a delightfully quiet and subtle study of an old man. At his first exit his voice did not seem sufficiently modulated to round off the speech he was giving. . . . P. J. Carolan is to be praised for his "make-up," and as Seumas Doran the sailor in *The Long Road*, and a tramp in Mr. Yeats's play he again scored on this account.

Miss Eileen O'Kelly as Jude, the faithful wife of Capt. Hanley, was inclined to speak her lines a little low in tone, but one could easily forgive her for all the crying and sobbing she had to do at the play's end.[26]

A theatrical history must necessarily rely heavily on contemporary newspaper accounts of plays. However, such accounts—as theater people have long complained—are not always accurate or knowledgable. Theater people usually complain of reviews that are too unfairly critical, but it seems to us that many Irish reviews are too blandly uncritical. In this instance, however, there is an effective antidote to the newspaper praise of the acting. On 9 January, Holloway had a revealing conversation with F. J. McCormick about the acting and the directing of the play:

> The actors as a whole did little to make J. Bernard MacCarthy's one-act play, *The Long Road to Garranbraher*, a first night success. . . . Michael J. Dolan as old Captain Peter Hanley was somewhat tame in the part which at times suggested his old man in *Spring*. Eileen O'Kelly as his wife was crude and amateurish, and McCormick failed to make a live character of Dan. . . . Quinn's son-in-law, Marcus Coyle, was hard and unsympathetic. . . . As Jacques passed out after it, he whispered to me, ". . . badly acted." . . . Murray thought the author had compressed too much into an act. None of them thought favourably of the piece. . . . I went down to the Abbey and had a chat with McCormick . . . before the show and spoke about . . . careless playing of MacCarthy's play last night and told Mac to put more "go." . . . He told me that they all felt dissatisfied with the play from the time it was first read to them, and he dislikes his part and was careless how he filled it. I said . . . for the first night audience that they felt that the players were self-conscious and lacked sincerity in their work. That shouldn't be; they should always try to make the most of every play they have to act. They certainly let MacCarthy's play down badly last night. I advised him to put more "body" into his part tonight. . . . He told me one can't rehearse at the Abbey, and owing to the absence of Robinson at his father's funeral last week the play had to produce itself, and as nobody took the slightest interest in their work it was bound to produce disaster.[27]

A perusal of the printed play does not make one disagree with the contemporary critical disparagement of it, but a better initial production could certainly have glossed over some of its weaknesses.

For the first five weeks of the years, the company played its usual six performances, from Tuesday through Saturday, with a matinee on the last day. For the next six weeks, however, only four performances were given—on Thursday, Friday, and Saturday nights and a Saturday matinee. During this time, the Abbey offered a steady stream of revivals each week, including one of Colum's old *Fiddler's House* on 22 February, but there was no new play until George Fitzmaurice's one-act *'Twixt the Giltinans and the Carmodys* on Thursday, 8 March.

Despite its broadness, the new piece was not greatly liked. One of the better reviews was that of the *Irish Times*:

> Even had Mr. Fitzmaurice's play little of dramatic merit or values, it would—from the mere fact of its being a bright comedy—have been something of a relief after Mr. Ray's gloomy play. But Mr. Fitzmaurice's work has plenty of merit; anybody who has seen *The Country Dressmaker* must be aware that he knows very well how to write good comedy. His dialogue is really amusing, and his situations are ridiculously funny. In this play, however, Mr. Fitzmaurice has not ventured very far beyond his situation, and his dialogue; it is not unlike an extra act of *The Country Dressmaker*—with Julia Shea left out.[28]

Jacques in the *Evening Herald* was, despite the audience's laughter, much more dismissive:

> "Oh, God bless me! Mind the child." That was one of the last things heard last night from the stage of the Abbey Theatre. Just previous to that we heard Michael Clancy (whose hair was red and whose rage was ruddy) cry aloud " 'Tis blood I want and 'tis blood I'll have."
>
> And forthwith he seized a four-pronged implement used for scattering manure, and he scattered the Giltinans and the Carmodys, who a few minutes previously had been striving to scatter each other.
>
> This was all reminiscent of the "rough-house" scene in *The Playboy*, following a lot that was reminiscent of *The Country Dressmaker*. . . .
>
> Because the audience screamed at the show of back-lane fisticuffs is not to say that the piece has comedy merits. It is the easiest thing possible to raise a laugh in the Abbey Theatre these times. Last night Miss Maureen Delany's slick hair and way of talking, and Miss Christine Hayden's squat bonnet and way of walking—these were ever provocative of mirth.
>
> Other members of the company gave their aid to a piece that is written around the plots of Mike Clancy, a matchmaker, to bring off a deal between the respective rivals for the fortune and farm of a first-class imitation of a harmless imbecile returned from Chicago. Mike plays one family against the other in this very much " 'twixt" production— 'twixt flummery and foolery.[29]

Holloway, Murray, and Lawrence were not greatly impressed either. As Holloway wrote:

> The company played it with great farcical spirit but could make nothing out of it but poor talking stuff . . . echoing *The Country Dressmaker* at every turn. Dolan as Michael Clancy the matchmaker was a frisky Luke Quilter in a new suit; while Bileen Twoney was merely a slightly camouflaged Edmund Normyle and nothing more or less. . . . May Craig gave a clever character study of Old Jane. . . . Fitzmaurice's new piece is a farcical interlude. . . . Murray and others thought it too loaded with queer talk, and Lawrence couldn't get the why and wherefore that Bileen had to be married by a given hour; the whole quite escaped his observations. He thought poorly of the piece, but wasn't likely to say so in his notice in *The Stage*.[30]

Lawrence wrote in the *Stage*:

> Mr. George Fitzmaurice, one of the early Abbey dramatists, whose *The Country Dressmaker*, though dating back to 1907, still enjoys a considerable popularity, has at last broken a long silence. We are doubtful whether it was worth his while. After an interval of years one looks for something fresher and more material than a mere ringing of the changes upon the matchmaking theme discussed in the play just mentioned. Moreover, the embroideries of the Lady Gregory school, to which Mr. Fitzmaurice claims allegiance, have become out-moded. Wiser in their outlook, the younger Abbey playwrights have decided to look after the drama of their works and let the literature look after itself, knowing that the greater always includes the less. To consider how a play will read and not to trouble how it will act is to ride for a fall. Mr. Fitzmaurice has a sense of humour and some qualities of character-drawing, but

> he shares Lady Gregory's painful lack of restraint. In setting about once more to exploit the rich and fruity West Kerry idiom, his play develops into a pyrotechnic display of rapidly whirling words. Never, perhaps, save in *The Magic Glasses* and *The Image* was there heard such a flood of purposeless loquacity. Words drift about like leaves in the autumn wind until the path becomes obscured by a carpeting of verbiage.[31]

A Kerry friend of Holloway was a bit more understanding about the dialogue:

> I was speaking . . . with an old friend . . . who used to be interested in elocution. . . . He didn't think Fitzmaurice's new comedy anything as good as *The Country Dressmaker*. He comes from Fitzmaurice's part of West Kerry and knew Fitz there some forty years ago. He was the son of the Rector. He echoes the speech of the people correctly; their speech is a free translation of the Gaelic, often very poetic in quality.[32]

Fitzmaurice was one of the most personally eccentric and artistically individual of all of the early Abbey writers. His only popular success, however, was *The Country Dressmaker*, which was one of the most frequently revived Abbey comedies up to the emergence of O'Casey. However, the *Dressmaker*, which was first produced in 1907, is a fairly conventional play and much more easily enjoyed than his brilliant, if perplexing, early one-acts. Even perceptive playgoers like Murray, Lawrence, and Holloway had difficulty in seeing what Fitzmaurice was about in his short early pieces, such as *The Pie Dish* of 1908 and *The Magic Glasses* of 1913. And the richest of Fitzmaurice's early short pieces, *The Dandy Dolls*, although published in 1914, remained unproduced until 1945. It is true that *'Twixt the Giltinans and the Carmodys* looks back to the conventionality of *The Country Dressmaker*, rather than to the individuality of *The Dandy Dolls*, and also it is certainly in no way to be compared to the brilliant later fantasies such as *The Enchanted Land* and *The Waves of the Sea*. But it is a charming and droll piece with racy dialogue and quirky characterization, and might have been much better received.

Save for the *Dressmaker*, Fitzmaurice had little luck as a play-wright. Indeed, he even purposely squelched some of his chances.[33] However, it may not be too farfetched to surmise that disappointment about the reaction to some of his plays, and about the failure of some of his best work even to reach the stage, played a part in his seeming indifference about his own work. There is a bit of evidence to suggest that his indifference may have been something of a pose, but it was a pose that he kept up ever more inflexibly till the end of his life. It was a pose that was already adopted by 1923. As Holloway reported:

> I came across George Fitzmaurice who hadn't yet seen his play or even a rehearsal of it (Mr. Perrin told me it is about a year and a half since Fitzmaurice brought us the play. . . . Fitzmaurice is one of those fellows whom one never gets to know, he added. He had written to him several times to tell him of his play being in rehearsal

> but Fitzmaurice never took any heed!) . . . Fitzmaurice can't sit out plays but likes operas and unusual pieces. . . . I left him going up the stairs to the balcony to see his own play for the first time. "Go in to see your own," . . . I said to him. "I have seen it twice already."
>
> "I pity you!" was his remark on hearing that.
>
> He was greatly amused by an argument outside in the street. "Real drama is being enacted out there," he said.[34]

In any event, *'Twixt the Giltinans and ther Carmodys* was the last new Fitzmaurice play to be staged by the Abbey during the playwright's lifetime, and it was probably the last new work that he submitted to the theater.

On Thursday, 22 March, the Abbey mounted its first production of Ibsen's *A Doll's House.* This was largely a showcase for Eileen Crowe, and the *Irish Times* reported:

> Many people have been in the habit of maintaining that the Abbey Company can only act really well in "pleasant plays." Their productions of Shaw and other non-pleasant plays have done much to dispel this myth; this production should blow it away altogether. From the acting of Miss Crowe as Nora, to that of the smallest of the three children, there was none that was weak. Miss Crowe played with genuine feeling, and thoroughly deserved all the applause that she got. . . . Mr. Robinson should be congratulated on his production.[35]

On 29 March, Yeats, who was no great Ibsen enthusiast, wrote to Lady Gregory:

> I thought the Abbey performance of *The Doll's House* astonishing—one of the best Ibsen performances I have ever seen. I told Miss Crowe that she had the makings of a great actress. . . . A Nora who is really young and plays young transforms the play.[36]

When the play was revived some months later, certain members of the irrepressible Abbey audience could not forebear laughing at occasional moments, but Pierrot in the *Dublin Magazine* wrote scathingly of them and glowingly of the acting:

> The crowd that turned up, the night I was there, to see the Ibsen play obviously and most pleasantly appreciate the fact that in the Abbey Theatre one is more likely to get an even cast than in, perhaps, any theatre either here or in Great Britain. Arthur Shields as Nils Krogstad exactly answered to the conception a reader at home would draw from a study of the book, and so the others; if the utter fatuity of Torvald at the close of the play bordered on the incredible it is to Ibsen the fault must be imputed. But the deportment of a by no means negligible fraction of the audience taught me trenchantly what a cussedly *sui generis* entity the Abbey actors have to play to. Every cultured person in Dublin knows what a masterpiece of interpretation Eileen Crowe gives in the part of Nora Helmer, what a poignant and charming, poignant because charming indeed, eclaircissement of the feminine heart brought for the first time shock up against the sordidness of social make-believe. She had the whole audience, as you knew by its almost tangible silence, keyed up to

every element of tragedy in the play. . . . and yet will it be believed that that fraction I have referred to laughed at the tarantella, at the cynical commentary made by Dr. Rank on his father's sowing of wild oats, and at the foolish "forgiveness" extended by Torvald to his wife at the end?

There is a distinct element of humour in these incidents, but that an audience soaked in the atmosphere of that doll's house could laught at them! Well, all that one can say is that it reveals new soul-strata for the investigation of the surveyor of modern psychiatry.[37]

The theater then closed for Holy Week, and re-opened on Monday, 2 April, for an unusual six days' run of Goldsmith's *She Stoops to Conquer*. Although quite out of the Abbey's usual vein, the production featured Barry Fitzgerald as a most attractive Tony Lumpkin. At a revival some months later, Pierrot praised some of the other actors and criticised some of the staging:

Goldsmith's was done in the traditional manner, and one could find a common ground of comparison between its rendition and that of eminent English companies now and years ago. In many details the Abbey production suffered by the comparison: the tavern scene was unconvincingly staged; so was the scene of the chaise breakdown; the attempt at a little realism of *decor* in previous scenes prepared you for something better than a screen, particularly a screen so well lit up: a stage as bare, *all through*, of appliances as a classical Japanese stage is quite all right, but it is not all right in patches. And that inimitable actor, Arthur Shields, made an even greater than usual number of false starts, or what sounded like them, in many of his lines. Again, however, the acting of M. J. Dolan [as Hardcastle], of Eileen Crowe [as Miss Hardcastle], and of Maureen Delany [as Mrs. Hardcastle] lifted the thing far and away above any production we had seen before. Hastings' discussion of the fashionable age with Maureen Delany gave her an opportunity for one of those bits of delicate detail that are the very quintessence of high comedy, which *She Stoops to Conquer* assuredly is not.

The chairs for Kate Hardcastle and young Marlow were, of course, placed at the extreme edge of the stage at each side outside the curtain, and Eileen Crowe's deliciously serious and maidenly demure completion of her suitor's stammered openings got, therefore, a perfect *mise*. And well the setting suited the study. Both Arthur Shields and Eileen Crowe materialised the very spirit of the comedy, and we do not know higher praise.[38]

About this production, Yeats remarked:

The Abbey's Goldsmith performance was almost as good of its kind as their Ibsen. It seems to me we've a different kind of human nature, probably without the old folk genius but with great variety of capacity and certainly nearer than the old company to the normal stage types.[39]

The theatrical event of the year was, of course, the first production of Sean O'Casey's two-act tragi-comedy, *The Shadow of a Gunman*, on April 12. On Tuesday, two days before the opening, Holloway was in Webb's Bookstore on the quays, and reported:

One of the assistants in the shop referred to the play, *The Shadow of a Gunman* by Sean O'Casey. "I know the writer well. He was telling me of its acceptance about a month ago. He had previously sent in plays which were rejected. He had always been fond of playwriting, and even made one about a lame alderman in the Corporation, called Cahill, which caused amusement for those who knew him. O'Casey is not too young. If his first-acted play is a success, he may do big things."[40]

Lady Gregory came up to town on 11 April for a meeting of the Carnegie Trust, and saw the first nights of the play. As she recorded in her Journal:

At the Abbey I found an armed guard; there has been one ever since the theatres were threatened if they kept open. And in the green room I found one of them giving finishing touches to the costume of Tony Quinn, who is a Black and Tan in the play, and showing him how to hold his revolver. *The Shadow of a Gunman* was an immense success, beautifully acted, all the political points taken up with delight by a big audience. Sean O'Casey the author only saw it from the side wings the first night but had to appear to make his bow. I brought him into the stalls the other two nights and have had some talk with him. Last night there was an immense audience the largest I think since the first night of *Blanco Posnet.* Many, to my grief, had to be turned away from the door. Two seats had been kept for Yeats and me, but I put Casey in one of them and sat in the orchestra for the first act, and put Yeats in the orchestra for the second. I had brought Casey round to the door before the play to share my joy in seeing the crowd surging in. . . .

. . . He says he sent us a play four years ago *Frost and Flowers* and it was returned, but marked "Not far from being a good play."[41] He has sent others, and says how grateful he was to me because when we had to refuse the Labour one *The Crimson in the Tri-Colour* I had said "I believe there is something in you" and "your strong point is characterisation." And I had wanted to pull that play together and put it on to give him experience, but Yeats was down on it. Perrin says he has offered him a pass sometimes when he happened to come in, but he refused and said "No one ought to come into the Abbey Theatre without paying for it." He said "All the thought in Ireland for years past has come through the Abbey. You have no idea what an education it has been to the country." That, and the fine audience on this our last week, put me in great spirits.[42]

O'Casey's play received really enthusiastic reviews. For instance, O'Donnell in the *Evening Herald* wrote:

It was indeed a welcome and wholesome sign to sit last night in the Abbey Theatre and listen to an audience squirming with laughter and revelling boisterously in the satire, which Mr. Sean O'Casey has put into his two-act play. Not for a very long time has such a good play come our way. It was brilliant, truthful, decisive. And, too, it came as a revelation, for Mr. O'Casey has in the matter of dramatic construction, broken completely away from the conventional. Of plot he had little, that that little only really interesting towards the play's end. But his characterisation was excellent and convincing. His characters were as perfect, and his photographs, for one really felt his men and women were but photographs, was nothing less than the work of genius. It is difficult to say anything about work such as this, so original, so brilliant, so true, and so finished in all its details. Out of small materials he pieced together the most genuine comedy that I think I have ever seen. . . .

The play being of itself so flawless, I should like very much to have something

> critically destructive to say of the acting or the production. But here again one is baffled, for its quality was of the very highest order. F. J. McCormick, as Seumas Shiels, has done one of the greatest pieces of character acting that has ever been done upon the Abbey stage. Each gesture, each bewildered look, each inflection of his voice served to get out every atom of satire and wit that was compounded in his philosophy. . . . it was indeed an amazing performance. . . .
>
> Michael J. Dolan, as Tommy Owens, got that adenoidal addition to his voice that one always instinctively associates with a certain accent, and his gestures and familiar methods of address, were representative of a certain type of "man about town". . . .
>
> But in general the acting was so good that one would never wish to see any other but the same cast in this play again.[43]

Even the criticisms of technique were minor. As Prior wrote in the *Irish Times*:

> If Mr. O'Casey will remove the small element of real tragedy from the end of his play (the audience is told that a girl has been shot), which does not really add to its merit, and if he will find a better title for it and call it a satire instead of a tragedy, there is no reason why it should not live for a very long time. There is really good work in the play, and the dialogue is very well done. From his bed, in which he lies for more than two-thirds of the time, Seumas Shields ("Jimmy" to the Auxiliary!) fires off shot after shot of scornful denunciation of war and war-mongers. His stock seems to be quite inexhaustible; and, though miserably frightened at every sign of physical danger, he is irrepressible.
>
> The plot of the play does not seem to matter very greatly. . . .
>
> Mr. McCormick played Seumas Shields. It is one of the best pieces of acting I have seen him do; it is certainly the best since he returned to Dublin. His accent was admirably flat and his make up, one was glad to notice, was good. He gave the impression of a real understanding of a part superficially easy but difficult to get the most out of.[44]

And even a year later, in P. S. O'Hegarty's account in the *Irish Statesman*, the approbation still swamped the criticism:

> Until quite recently Mr. O'Casey's *Guman* had eluded me, through being on only when I happened to be unable to go to see it, but a couple of weeks ago I did manage to get in. After seeing it my main thought was that it seemed hardly worth anybody's while attempting to record recent Irish history in sober prose, seeing that it was being done brilliantly by the artists. And not alone brilliantly, but in true historical perspective, for Mr. O'Casey records things as they were, but records them with that air of detachment and disillusionment which the historian aims at; he is usually wise after the event, and so is Mr. O'Casey. If he had written his play three years ago it would have been full of noble heroes and bloody ruffians, whereas now it is full of human beings, the only unnatural and unbelievable characters in it being those of the gunman hero and . . . of the Auxiliary ruffian. The gunman is a real shadow, while the Auxiliary, in many respects a true portrait, is spoiled by the cheap touch of his sudden exit from the stage when informed that there is whiskey on the premises.
>
> There is little or no dramatic idea in Mr. O'Casey's play but there is good character drawing and tremendous power of observation. It is a gramophone record

> of the Dublin accent and the Dublin tenement and the Dublin poor, all illumined by the Terror and sharpened and defined by it. It is not the whole terror, I agree, because it does not give, and does not attempt to give, the heroic side of it, the way life felt to the men on the run and to those who helped them. But it does give what life looked like to the common people of Dublin, between the devil of the Auxiliary's pistol and incendiary bomb and the deep sea of the Irish Volunteer's home-made bomb. That is why it draws the crowd. It tells everybody what they thought while the two armies shot up each other and made their life hideous for people who wanted to go about their business or live a normal human life. It gets back at the heroes. It is a play of disillusion for people who have been disillusioned, and can take their disillusionment without bitterness.[45]

O'Hegarty's closing remark brings up one little-discussed point. *The Shadow of a Gunman* was as bitterly critical of the era as was, three years later, *The Plough and the Stars*; but the earlier play was almost totally admired while the later one had the highly vocal condemnation of, at least, a significant minority. The reasons for this shift in opinion were, possibly, two.

First, the *Gunman* contains a much higher proportion of comedy and satire than does *The Plough*. The seriousness of the *Gunman* is confined to a few moments in the last act; by the last act of *The Plough*, comedy has almost disappeared. As the reaction of Shaw's audiences proved, if one is made to laugh, one may ignore the seriousness of what one is laughing about.

Second, when the *Gunman* was produced, a widely unpopular Civil War was still raging; and a people sick to death of violence were disposed to be critical of the practical patriotism of the gun. But when *The Plough* was produced, the country had basically been at peace for a couple of years; and the violence of ten years earlier was remote enough to have acquired a patina of glamour.

In any event, the original double bill of *Sovereign Love* and *The Shadow of a Gunman* played only for three nights and a matinee at the very end of the Abbey season. The *Gunman*, however, had drawn such crowds that, when the theater reopened for Horse Show Week on 6 August, it was repeated, paired this time with *Crabbed Youth and Age*.

The theater was now opening on Monday and playing six evening performances and a Saturday matinee; and the next new production was on 3 September when the one-act comedy, *Apartments*, was produced with a revival of O'Kelly's *The Bribe*.

Apartments was by "Fand O'Grady," which was the pseudonym of Kathleen Cruise O'Brien. Mrs. O'Brien was the daughter of David Sheehy, for many years a Nationalist member of Parliament. Her sister Mary married Thomas Kettle, her sister Hanna married Francis Skeffington, and she married Cruise O'Brien the journalist, and is the model for Miss Ivors in James Joyce's story "The Dead." Mrs. O'Brien's son, Conor Cruise O'Brien, is the notable politician, journalist, and man-of-letters who has himself written several interesting plays.

Of *Apartments*, *The Evening Herald* wrote:

> Boarding-house life has helped to better the stage with much that passed for playwriting; it has also helped to better the theatre with a little that proved to be genuine entertainment. *Apartments*, the new piece by Fand O'Grady (about whom rumour tells us nothing), may yet be burnished up into rollicking farce, and as such may be classed as genuine goods. As comedy it falls flat.
>
> Mrs. McCarthy (played by Miss Sara Allgood) runs a boardinghouse, and living in it are her husband, two bob-haired children, and their maiden aunt, and in addition a male teacher, a female teacher, a student, and a young married couple. Off the premises she helps to run a pawn-broker, a book-seller, a grocer, and sundry others in trade in the neighbourhood. She does this by pledging the lodgers' property on the principle of pawning Peter's to pay for Paul's. In the way, as the learned spouse of the landlady testified with a flow of words and crossings of Latin, a crisis was precipitated at irregular intervals. We saw last night one such crisis. The climax came with the temporary journey to Uncle's of the bride's dressing case.
>
> Of course, *Apartments* is a thing of laughter. It rarely ceased crackling through the play. But it is a one-woman piece. Miss Allgood was the one-woman, and soon she had used up every motion, gesture and expression to convey alarm, distress and subterfuge. Easily the finest figure in the piece was that of Mike MacCarthy, in which Michael J. Dolan gave an admirable presentation of a character that might have stepped out of Dickens. The repetition of situation almost to duplication in the action was the weak point of the piece. The author can do better.[46]

Prior in the *Irish Times* was a bit gentler, finding: "This amusing little one-act play . . . has very real merit, though it shows in places signs of unpractised work. Miss O'Grady should certainly continue to write comedy. Her dialogue is excellent, and her situations are extremely funny."[47] A perusal of the play suggests that the original critical response to the play was just enough. It is a pleasant, adequate, unpretentious piece, which might be interesting to read, but not really to revive on the stage.

The Abbey's next new piece was an O'Casey one-act, *Cathleen Listens In*, which was first produced on 1 October on a triple bill with *The Man of Destiny* and *Riders to the Sea.*

"Listening In" was a term that referred to listening to early radio broadcasts from England. In the 1980s, after twenty or thirty years of television, it may be difficult to remember what an exciting novelty radio was in the early 1920s. Even a few years later, in the late 1920s, Clifford Chatterley was still addicted to his wireless; and in an American boyhood in the 1930s, it was still exciting to construct one's own home-made crystal set.

O'Casey's play, then, was utterly topical. We have noted in the previous chapter that it may have grown out of a previously published sketch, which then grew into a play. In *Sean O'Casey, a Bibliography*, Ronald Ayling and Michael J. Durkan write that the 1923 play "is almost certainly a reworking of 'The Seamless Coat of Cathleen' which O'Casey submitted to the Abbey on April 10, 1922 as, in his words, 'an allegorical play in one act dealing with the present situation in Ireland from my point of view.' That version was rejected by the Abbey later in April 1922."[48]

The play is really a dramatic equivalant of a newspaper political cartoon, a satiric if unsubtle genre; and so it is surprising to find an unperceptive review in the *Irish Times*:

> *Cathleen Listens In* is a political skit which, with all its somewhat abstruse allusions, is a little difficult to follow. The main idea, however, Cathleen badgered by the representatives of the different political parties, is simple enough. There is in this play, as in Mr. O'Casey's former play, plenty of humour in the dialogue. He knows, by instinct, perhaps, how to make a play "go," how to provide all the trappings which mean so much. The construction, however, could be improved; the comedy tails off, and Mr. O'Casey should not be so mystifying. If one were able to read the play before seeing it, no doubt it would become quite comprehensible; but at first sight there seem to be several characters in it whose presence has no particular point.[49]

Other reviewers were less dense. For instance, O'Donnell in the *Evening Herald*:

> There was subtle inspiration in the idea of presenting to us last night at the Abbey Theatre Mr. Sean O'Casey's new play, *Cathleen Listens In*, considering the fact that about the same time Mr. Cosgrave was introducing Ireland to the Imperial Conference. Right about there the subtlety ended, for Mr. O'Casey's play is not a play at all, but a quip, a whimsicality, a safety valve for some funny opinions he holds on present-day Ireland.
>
> His new work will neither add to, nor detract from, the reputation he gained over his first play, *The Shadow of a Gunman*, but it is in itself clear proof that Mr. O'Casey, while having a good sense of the essentials of stage atmosphere, has very little dramatic technique, and that his work is inclined to be of the jester, ephemeral, type rather than that of real comedy or tragedy. Perhaps it is that Mr. O'Casey has not yet found himself and just cannot quite decide upon which is the better way of saying that which he has got to say, but producing topical tit-bits such as this play of Cathleen, the daughter of Mr. Meehawl O'Houlihan, will rather spoil the possibilities of his doing serious and better work and gives his plays a quality of facetiousness which is deceptive.
>
> The great fault of his twenty-minute sermon last night was that his tongue was in his cheek too often when he was writing the play, and the effect of such an action was quite too apparent to last night's audience. His words sought to be satiric, but because of the very blatancy they became hurts and broadsides and lost most of their effectiveness in their nudity of appeal. His similes were always of the crystal variety that a blind man could not but visualise their meaning. For example, satirising an extreme Gaelic Leaguer, he says, "Knock the house down and build it around the Hill of Tara," and telling of a Republican he says, "One minute he says he's a Roman and the next minute he's a Dane." And again, when Mr. Meehawl Houlihan is lamenting the loss of some window glass, he says: "They broke my windows because they said I sold the family cow." God help that cow!
>
> What is really wrong with Mr. O'Casey's play is that the majority of the plain people long ago have come to the same conclusions on the qualities of our political parties as he has, and consequently there was no necessity, either from an artistic or a natural point of view, for him to tell us such everyday facts from the stage.
>
> The cast was huge and effective, and as leaders in Mr. O'Casey's symphony, F. J. McCormick, Maureen Delany, Barry Fitzgerald, M. J. Dolan, and Gabriel Fallon deserve wreaths of congratulations.

> In J. M. Synge's *Riders to the Sea*, Miss Sara Allgood again demonstrated the beauty of her voice, and such a performance as hers in this poignant tragedy of the sea is worthy of its place in the annals of great acting.[50]

In the *Irish Statesman*, Susan L. Mitchell wrote:

> The new play at the Abbey Theatre, *Cathleen Listens In*, calls itself a phantasy, and is not, we imagine, taking itself very seriously as a play; but, it invites some serious consideration as an allegory, or perhaps we might say a rough-and-tumble morality play. In spite of the distraction of mind caused by the commotion of the acting, necessary, we admit, to the idea, the audience emerges from the tumult and the shouting a little breathless, but quite coherent. We have no fault to find with the obviousness of the play; there is comfort to the playgoer, often bewildered by subtleties, to find himself quite clear as to the idea the playwright had in mind; it puts him in good humour with himself, and satisfaction in the audience reacts on the players, establishing their morale, giving them confidence. In *Cathleen Listens In* this is an important point as the slight breathlessness in the witty dialogue when the stage is full hints at a team that is new at pulling together. This will, of course, disappear after a few performances. It is unnecessary to explain a play where the daughter is Cathleen, the daughter of Houlihan, and the characters are a Free Stater, a Republican, a business man, a farmer, a labourer. The mordant idea of the play is found in the spectral Gaelic League, under the figure of a feeble old man in Kilts—who receives solemn homage from the actors, whenever he appears, but is voted a nuisance and a lunatic when his back is turned. The climax of the comedy is reached when at the height of the shouting of the claimants for Cathleen's suffrages the Boundary question stalks by outside the gate playing on a big drum the appropriate air. Casey is not Shaw, but he has a lively mind and no bitterness, and though a guffaw so near tragedy as we are just now may offend the taste of some, others will find it salutary.[51]

O'Casey thought so poorly of his two early one-acts, *Cathleen Listens* In and *Nannie's Night Out*, that he did not allow them to reach print until late in his life, and then only reluctantly. Of the two, he quite preferred *Cathleen*. This preference was, we think, a mistake in judgment, but the reason was that *Cathleen* seemed to him to prefigure his later work in *The Silver Tassie* and other plays. In that opinion, O'Casey was undoubtedly correct. Also there is no reason to stage a revival of *Cathleen*, for its mild interest as theater or as literature would not outweigh its lost topicality.

The next new play at the Abbey was Brinsley MacNamara's three-act, *The Glorious Uncertainty*, which was first produced on 27 November. This was a comedy about horse-racing, which in English drama is a kind of subgenre with antecedents stretching back at least to Boucicault's *Formosa* and *The Jilt*, to *Ben Hur*, to Drury Lane spectaculars like *The Whip* and to many, many others. In Irish drama, there were precedents in at least *The Playboy* and *Shanwalla*, but MacNamara's play has many authentic native touches of its own. It does, however, remain merely an entertainment; and, although it achieved some popularity, its initial reception was not unjust. It offered some good opportunities for acting, particularly by Fitzgerald and Fallon, but its intelligent author had still not entirely mastered plot construction. As Jacques wrote in the *Herald*:

Just at the close of the second act of the new play at the Abbey Theatre, Dublin, last night one of the conspirators hoarsely remarked that: "Things do be gettin' more complicated—darker and darker." True words for him they were. There had been eighty-five minutes of congested complications, and the last act added more and more. At the finish I saw Miss Eileen Crowe in the arms of Mr. Arthur Shields and as, beyond doubt, that was what the author meant should happen, I presume the complications were cleared up to the general satisfaction. Though I do confess I have a fellow-feeling with Mr. Barry Fitzgerald, the gentleman in the cast who made the soulful remark about darker and darker complications.

It was not all the fault of Mr. Brinsley MacNamara. . . . He had material by the ream. He knew his Ballymacoyle, the village near the railway station. He knew the types that frequent Cunneen's hotel bar, that swallow half ones with one eye on the clock and the other on the street to spot the evening paper from Dublin with the latest racing news. He knew his "has-been" stable hand with the leather gaiters, the cocked cap, the apologetic whip and the wisp of straw stuck in the mouth. He knew his subject and his characters all right, but his characters didn't always know what he wanted them to say.

That was pretty obvious. They suffered from lack of gallops. More tries-out were needed on the private training ground of rehearsal before public performance on the stage of the Abbey. This unfitness did not apply to all, though one at least expected that experienced players would not mix up the names of the characters when speaking of them. We heard "Sam" for "Gabriel."

The play was about the Ballymacoyle Grand National, an annual event decided at the local flapper meeting. The hotel-keeper, his crony, Sam Price, his daughter, Susie; the broken-down jockey aforementioned, and a visitor from England, all become entangled in a conspiracy to "Square" the race. And let it be said they succeeded beyond telling. They not only squared, but queered it. It only needed the entry of the "Dark Horse" to make complications as dark as the Abbey itself before curtain-rise.

Mr. MacNamara was at pains to give us a sincere racy comedy with a colour, atmosphere, and topicality. He never changed his scene. The start was too slow. The pace increased at the second act, but the course was befogged at times. Action was needed, but this stimulus was absent.

From the dialogue we picked such sparks as "There are times when a woman has no right to do wrong." There were two great chances to lift *The Glorious Uncertainty* past the winning-post. One was handed to Sam in *his* version of the race, the other to Sylvester Seery in *his* description. Both, no doubt, will sound better at a second hearing. Neither Sam nor Seery got much help from their stage friends.

Miss Allgood was the mother, and Miss Crowe the daughter in the play. The author was very heartily called.[52]

The *Freeman's Journal* treated the piece more gently:

A good name sometimes covers a multitude of sins, and in this instance the faults were few and far between, and it is quite delightful to be able to say that the little play worked out with most commendable credit to itself and to all concerned.

Simple and indeed commonplace in some of its aspects, the author has, in his utilisation of the universal spirit of sporting and the betting craze, linked up with his episodes a touch of real dramatic seriousness as well as humour. . . .

Suffice it, however, to say that, with a certain amount of essential curtailment in dialogue and a concentration of some incidents at present too prolonged, the play is particularly good. Nay, in its more farcical phases, it is supremely excellent, and is a skit on the ways and methods of those who at publichouses and elsewhere "spot" winners and regulate prices it is quite clever. . . .

> In Mr. Barry Fitzgerald we had yet again one of those remarkable studies in which he has won so much distinction. His "Sam Price" is a picture full of interest, humorous and conveying as it does in every touch the master hand of an artist.[53]

But Susan L. Mitchell in the *Irish Statesman* was distinctly more curt:

> *The Glorious Uncertainty* . . . was received with rapture by an audience who seemed to revel in the racing talk. It played successfully, not on its own merits, which are poor, but on those of the Abbey actors, who are so clever that if they are not given a good play they make one. In fact, I can imagine Brinsley MacNamara, or another, just throwing down a few suggestions to this brilliant group of actors—in this play a warned-off jockey, an Irish village racecourse, a love interest, and an Englishman—and saying, like the Dublin cabman, "I lave it to yourselves," and lo! a play is played. . . . In *The Glorious Uncertainty*, the actors are everything; everything about them tells, accent, expression, and I was particularly pleased with the old lad whose name I can't recall who stumbled into Cunneen's bar and watched the race from the window of the snug. I do not know why he appeared at all in the play, but he was successful. . . . Mr. Brinsley MacNamara has a talent for holding up a mirror to the meanest humours of the Irish countryside; about his talent as a dramatist I am keeping an open mind. We are slowly becoming self-conscious here in Ireland and our writers and dramatists are helping us to a depressing if salutory self-realisation. Miss Allgood's inimitable talent enchanted me anew in *A Glorious Uncertainty*, when as the shrewd wife she rushes to get the money representing her daughter Susie's fortune out of her husband's thriftless pockets. She is pushed back by the wily Sam Price with the words: "Now Mrs. Cunneen, this is man's work"—an incantation never known to fail with a genuine woman. In an instant there envelops her like a mantle the traditional exterior docility of all wifehood in the face of the incalculable male, but not before we have caught a glimpse of the subhuman intelligence of all womanhood apprehending the absolute humbug of masculinity.[54]

After *The Glorious Uncertainty*, Brinsley MacNamara enjoyed considerable popularity as a playwright; but with one or two exceptions—particularly *The Master* of 1928 and *Margaret Gillan* of 1933—his plays were merely comic entertainments. His strongest work was done in fiction, and of his realistic depictions of the Irish Midlands Michael McDonnell wrote:

> . . . no Irish novelist ever so painstakingly delineated a rural Irish mentality. His novels and stories describe a people whose only traditions were the traditions of orthodoxy, greed, and ignorance—and always the antagonist is the Church and its clergy.[55]

MacNamara's first and best-known novel, *The Valley of the Squinting Windows*, had been published in 1918, but it made the news in 1923, in the culmination of one of Ireland's more celebrated literary court cases. The book had originally so angered the people of MacNamara's native Delvin in County Westmeath, that it had been publicly burnt. MacNamara's father, James Weldon, was the local schoolmaster; and he found his school being boycotted, and so brought a suit for £4,000 against the parish priest and seven parishioners for conspiring to arrange the boycott. In December, he lost the suit.

On 26 December, the Abbey produced another short political allegory, George Shiels's *First Aid.* The play has not been published, but the accounts of it suggest that it was a more dramatised, characterised story than was O'Casey's *Cathleen Listens In.* The *Irish Times* reported:

> *First Aid*, a one-act play be George Shiels, had a successful first production at the Abbey Theatre, Dublin, last night. Although the audience laughed pretty continuously, the subject of their merriment is a bitter, almost gruesome presentation of a modern Irish outlook on life, which, judging from all that one had heard and read during the past couple of years, is no mere stage exaggeration.
>
> Drogheda Moore, a ragman, and Tommy Moody, a Belfast dealer in dogs, arrive in the yard of old Nora, whose home, lying in the "centre of the whirlpool of chaos," had been looted and robbed frequently during the "war." They find that the old woman has fallen into the draw-well and is holding on for her life to a snag.
>
> For help to get her out Moody runs for assistance to the neighbours, Shawn Egan and Padraig Harte, between whom there is an old feud. Both, however, are united in their detestation of the black Orangeman from the North, and pay no heed to the dying cries of the old woman, while Eileen Harte, in the intervals of strangling Moody for his birthplace, suggests praying for the release of old Nora. Then the young men, Shawn and Padraig, remembering their own enmity, draw guns on each other.
>
> The cries from the well grow fainter, and the ragman announces that the old woman, being able to hold on no longer, is dead. Thoughts of the position in which they may find themselves at the inquest make the young men, when too late, think of setting about a rescue, to which they had been so far indifferent. Eventually the Belfast man is lowered down the well and gets the old woman up apparently dead. Praying over the body is followed by attempts at resuscitation, which in the end succeed. Finally, Shawn and Padraig throw their guns down the well. Moody, who is the hero of the play, follows suit, and the curtain falls on a stageful of friends.
>
> For natural and affecting acting the play is one of the best that the Abbey people have produced for a long time. Miss Eileen Crowe's Nora is a piece of work that will add immensely to her reputation. Mr. M. J. Dolan as Moody very wisely does not attempt the Belfast accent. . . . Miss Delany followed what would seem to be the Abbey custom of keeping the hands whenever possible driven vigorously into the pockets of a jumper.[56]

Susan L. Mitchell in the *Irish Statesman* made some comparisons of *First Aid* and *Cathleen Listens In*:

> It resembles Mr. Casey's *Cathleen Listens In* in that the subject is an Ireland tormented by those of her own blood who profess to love her. Mr. Casey's play has more subtleties than Mr. Shiels', but I think the latter plays better. I confess I enjoy a play that appeals to sentiment, and one can not draw any fine distinction between the sentiment appealed to in, say, *Kathleen Ni Houlihan*, or *The Gaol Gate*, and that appealed to in Mr. Casey's and Mr. Sheils' plays, though the dramatic quality of the plays differs. We are not conscious of being preached to in the earlier plays, but there is a distinct pulpit flavour in the later. I do not think I resent the preaching in *First Aid*, though I can understand some of those who "sat under" Mr. Shiels last week might be a little restive, for his satire got home uncomfortably now and then. Ireland is represented as an old woman, Nora, who has fallen down the well in her dilapidated yard, and her neighbours from the four quarters of Ireland who come to rescue her waste so much time settling their own differences that the woman is

> submerged before aid reaches her, and is with difficulty restored to life after her tardy rescue by penitent and reconciled neighbours. . . . The interesting thing about the performance is the affection the Ulsterman evokes in the audience. Dublin has really keen affection for Ulster, and we wonder if the Abbey players, representing Black-and-Tan victims, would excite the same friendly emotion in Belfast as does the presentation of an Ulsterman, with all his convictions boiling hot, on the Dublin stage. . . . our hearts went out to the Ulsterman, and all our eyes were wet when he, last of all, flung his gun into the well. Call it sentimentality—we are all sentimentalists.[57]

The account in the *Independent* and the *Herald* recorded that "the clever play evoked hearty laughter and prolonged applause."[58] The theater, as early as *Kathleen Ni Houlihan* of 1902, had occasionally presented symbolic or allegorical plays about politics—among them, O'Riordan's *The Piper* and Shiels's *Bedmates*—but it is doubtful if any of these pieces retains sufficient merit to warrant a revival.

On the last day of the year, another somewhat similar piece appeared at the Abbey. As the *Independent* reported:

> Sara Allgood excels in dramatic recitation, and in Lady Gregory's striking poem, "The Old Woman Remembers," spoken by Miss Allgood in the Abbey last night, she gave a specimen of her power in that respect. As an old woman sitting, first by the fireside, and then at a table, she gave the recital, and, although the opportunity for adding effect by declamatory gestures was practically absent, her clear voice recalled with passionate emotion various phases of the struggles for Irish freedom dealt with in the poem.[59]

In the *Dublin Magazine*, Pierrot found the piece much more dramatic:

> Undramatic only in so far as it is a monologue, Lady Gregory's poem, *The Old Woman Remembers*, spoken in the silvery voice of Sara Allgood, moved a packed audience profoundly. An old woman, beads in hand, seated at the fire in her cottage, "remembers" the heroes of Ireland, Art MacMurrough Kavanagh, Shane, Hugh, Owen Roe, all of them down to the days we went through ourselves, and as she mentions each name she lights a candle. As I have implied, it is essentially dramatic rather than lyric. What most strikes one is the originality of its general conception and the characteristically easy simplicity and naturalness of its treatment.[60]

• • •

On 30 October, Yeats wrote to Lady Gregory:

> Lennox told me a little while ago that he wishes to cease to be manager of the Abbey. He says that if we agree about Dolan he will help to prepare the plays for the tours and help while they are in London. He suggests that we make him a Director. He could then meet once a fortnight, say, to get reports from Dolan, look after accounts and so on. I myself wish for this arrangement.[61]

A month later, the *Irish Times* printed an announcement about the change and an interview with Robinson:

We learn that Mr. Lennox Robinson, manager of the Abbey Theatre, Dublin, will resign from his post on December 1st, when he will become a co-director of the theatre with Lady Gregory and Mr. W. B. Yeats. His successor will be Mr. Michael J. Dolan, the well-known Dublin actor, whose work at the Abbey Theatre has gained him a wide reputation. Mr. Robinson's work for the theatre in Ireland is second only to that of Synge, Mr. Yeats, and Lady Gregory. His play, *The Whiteheaded Boy*, had a great success not only in London, where it was produced at the Ambassador's Theatre, but also in Australia and the United States of America. Interviewed yesterday by an Irish Times representative, Mr. Robinson said:—

"I came back to the theatre—I had been here before as manager from 1910–14—early in 1918. I came back when Mr. Fred O'Donovan left, taking a number of the principal players with him. The theatre was at one of those moments of crisis which are bound to recur in a "stock" theatre, the moment when a number of players decide to try their fortunes elsewhere, and as a consequence, the hard task is laid upon the theatre of building up a new company.

"Unlike the ordinary theatres, the Abbey Theatre cannot choose its players from the advertisement columns of the *Era* and the *Stage*. All the players' training, from the very beginning, needs to be in their own theatre, but by dramatic classes from which we draw promising new material, by the assistance of such of the old players who had remained behind, by devotion and hard work, we have gradually created the company that is playing in the Abbey Theatre now.

"I was with the theatre in the old prosperous days before the war, when its artistic reputation was world-wide, but I say without hesitation that the Abbey company to-day is as good as it ever was—indeed I dare to say it is better.

"I give up the managership of the company with deep regret, my association with the players leaves nothing but happy memories, but the manager and producer in such a theatre needs to have only one subject in his mind, only one aim before him—the theatre.

"I have too long been able only to give the theatre a part of my attention, and for its sake it is better I should retire. In Mr. Michael Dolan the directors have found a man who has long been associated with the Abbey, a man whose beautiful art is well known to all lovers of acting in Dublin, who will be able—as I have not been able—to put in long hours of hard work in the theatre. I believe the traditions of the Abbey Theatre are safe in his hands.

"Our theatre seems indestructible. It survived the European War, which extinguished every repertory theatre in England save one, it survived the Anglo-Irish war and its curfew, it survived the civil war last winter. But the struggle to survive has been a difficult one; we could not have lived without help from Irish and English friends, and I am convinced that a theatre such as ours—if it is to develop itself to the full extent of its powers—needs to be assured of its income.

"Sooner or later the choice will have to be made between an Abbey Theatre subsidised out of the public funds or no Abbey Theatre. I am fairly certain on which side the choice would fall, but, whatever be the fate of the theatre, I am proud of having been associated with in through fair weather and foul, and I am very proud of being allowed now to direct the theatre with those two people who have done so much for art in Ireland—Lady Gregory and Mr. W. B. Yeats."[62]

On 30 November, Dolan wrote to Lady Gregory:

> Permit me to offer you my deepest gratitude for the honour you have conferred upon me, in having chosen me to act as manager to carry on the good work of the National Theatre.
> I fully realise the importance of that work and need hardly assure you that the welfare of the theatre shall be my constant aim.
> Whether my term of office be long or short, I hope to be able to repay by constant endeavours, the confidence that you, Lady Gregory, and your co-Directors now repose in me.
> I shall feel justified if I can hear you say—well done, thou good and faithful servant.[63]

In a letter to Holloway on the same day, Dolan added:

> A thousand thanks for your letter and the kind wishes expressed therein. It gives me great heart for the work ahead to feel that the appointment of myself to manager of the theatre has given satisfaction to the people who really matter in the theatrical world.
> I would it had created the same good feeling within the camp, but even here I'm glad to say the heartburnings caused by the appointment are not numerous. . . .
> It will take time, patience and hard work plus the non-interference of the envious to bring about the improvements conducive to the well-being of a theatre and its patrons. I can assure you that is the goal I shall strive hard to attain—to make the Abbey a real national theatre.[64]

The problem of getting the government to admit that the Abbey was a real national theatre—in particular, by granting the theatre a subsidy—was still very much alive in the minds of the Directors. On 17 February, Lady Gregory "had a satisfactory talk" with Robinson about the matter:

> I said that although I had agreed to his and Yeats' proposal of asking for a grant from Government for the theatre because they were two against me, I do not think it worth losing our independence for £1,300 a year (we who used to turn over £7000 or £8000!). That I very much prefer my old idea and intention of giving the whole theatre over as a gift to the Nation whenever we had a Home Rule Government. That we want a new impulse in it, new energy; and that now Harris is gone who used to keep me up in finance knowledge, I don't feel that any one of us is capable of dealing with that side.
> He said he had been talking to Johnson, the Labour Member, about the grant and had found him very sympathetic and encouraging. I said that encouraged me. That we must if we went on have a business man or men among the directors and that it would be much better to give it over altogether and if Johnson will make a people's theatre of it, that is what I always wanted and would be glad to see done. To my surprise Robinson quite agreed with me, and will ask Johnson to see me.[65]

On the next day she talked with Thomas Johnson at the Abbey and found him quite sympathetic:

> He was interested when I told him of our wish and old promise to hand over the Abbey as a gift to the nation. However he doesn't think the Government could take it just now, perhaps after the elections. I told him we must put a business man in as Director at once, and he said it would be a good thing to have him chosen by the Government, and I said I would see McNeill about it.[66]

Later in the day she did see Eoin McNeill, who was the Free State Minister of Education, and she learned:

As to the Abbey he is anxious we should have the subsidy, it is to come on in the next Budget debate. He is asking for it as an aid to an educational work, our teaching of acting and dramatic writing. He is by no means sure we shall get it, but thinks even a discussion on the Abbey will do it good, get more interest aroused in it. I told him of our desire to give it over. He was rather startled, said he didn't want to manage a theatre and was sure the Government didn't, anyhow for some time to come. I told him of the necessity of a business Director, and he thought it wise it should be someone acceptable to the Government, but not appointed by them.[67]

On 14 April, Lady Gregory and Yeats again saw McNeill:

He thinks the Government will refuse to take the Theatre over. But they must give us a subsidy for now Harris is gone and I have been so much away we have overdrawn so heavily at the Bank that it will cash no more cheques. I had to speak plainly to Yeats and said I would not go on unless there is a business man put in to watch and control the expenditure.[68]

On 4 June, when Lady Gregory was in a Nursing Home in Leeson Street, recovering from an operation, she remarked that Yeats and Robinson had been in to see her, and said that the theatre's creditors were pressing for payment. "I urge," she wrote, "going to the Government at once for a subsidy."[69] On 9 June, Lady Gregory moved in for a few days with the Yeatses at 82 Merrion Square; and on 15 June she noted, "Robinson came in. Abbey valuation not ready, but I signed our letter to the Government asking for help."[70] This must be the letter which Lennox Robinson and Hugh Hunt date 27 June 1924:[71]

Dear President Cosgrave,

We have carried on our work at the Abbey Theatre for nearly twenty years and we may claim to have created a school of Irish dramatists and a school of Irish acting that has brought honour to our country. We have carried on our work in spite of the European War—which killed every repertory theatre in England save one—and in spite of the English war in Ireland. We do not claim to have done so unaided, at certain times we have had to appeal for help to friends in Ireland and England but always in times of stress we have said to our friends and to each other, "We must hold the Theatre together that we may offer it to the Irish Nation when Ireland achieves her independence." That, for many years, has been our determination. We believe that a Theatre which does not depend for its existence on the caprice of the public can play a great part in the education of a nation, can be—like the Comedie Francaise—one of the nation's glories, and we are aware that all civilised governments except those of English-speaking nations and Venezuela—possess their State Theatre.

In that belief we now offer the Abbey Theatre, its entire contents, scenery and wardrobe and the property it owns to the Irish Nation.

We do not pretend that our gift is of great value counted as money. Like others in Ireland we, who were once rich, are now poor; nevertheless that value of the property is not inconsiderable and there is some value in a tradition of fine work finely done.

We offer the Theatre without conditions or restrictions. We resign our Directorship. It is for the Irish Government, should they accept our offer, to determine the method of carrying on our work—whether they will ask us to go on for a little longer or whether they will at once accept entire control. By tradition and accomplishment our Theatre has become the National Theatre of Ireland, it should no longer be in the possession of private individuals, it should belong to the State. Having created it and fostered it through twenty years we believe we can now confidently trust it to the Irish Nation.

Augusta Gregory
W. B. Yeats[72]

Another reason for suspecting that this letter was sent in 1923 rather than in 1924 is that it was signed by the Directors of the theatre; but by July 1924 there was a third Director of the theatre, Robinson.

In any event, this letter or a similar one proposing to turn the theater over to the Government was apparently sent, and on 13 July, Robinson wrote to apprise Lady Gregory of progress:

Just a line to give you news of our struggle with the government. I told you how we had seen Blythe last week and found him friendly, Desmond Fitzgerald has been away so I made a point of seeing him on Tuesday—the day after he got home. He knew nothing of the application but went and asked Cosgrave (the Dail was sitting) about it. Cosgrave said the thing had gone to Education for report to be made there upon it. Saw Blythe and Fitzgerald together then, very friendly and said that a good report from Education would be of great value and might get the matter through Finance where the real opposition would be. So we tried on Wednesday to get hold of O'Neill (MacNeill's chief executive officer). . . . He had bad news—that the application had come to them with a note from Cosgrave against giving assistance. O'Neill is enthusiastically for helping us from the educational point of view and so is MacNeill but the latter will never take a strong line about anything and wouldn't dream of fighting Cosgrave. O'Neill advised personal influence to be brought on Cosgrave, and said that that had got Trinity its big grant, and that a letter from the Duke of Devonshire had turned the scale and made Cosgrave ride roughshod over Finance which was entirely opposed to helping T.C.D. So then we saw two Trinity members—Alton and Thrift, both promised to see President, Alton advocated an immediate campaign in Press and W. B. was for this. I thought President might get huffed at feeling his hand forced from outside and Fitzgerald agreed with this; it will be easier to work up an outcry *after* help has been refused. I have written to Plunkett asking him to write to President, and Gogarty and W. B. are to see him. I shall try and think of other personal pressure that can be brought to bear.

My plan of campaign is (and W. B. agrees) bring personal pressure to bear on President now and try and get an answer within the next ten days. If the answer is "no" at once publicly announce the fact, your letter published, etc., Johnson to ask question in Dail, question in Senate. Announce that we play during August the four last weeks of the Abbey unless the Government acts. Playing will help our case and we are sure to make money during Horse Show. I believe it will be easy to work up a lot of feeling in favour of Government assistance, if not of their taking over altogether. They will probably compromise by giving us money to carry on for a year or so.[73]

In *Ireland's Abbey Theatre*, Robinson quotes a statement, apparently written some years later, by Ernest Blythe who was in 1923 the Free State Minister of Finance:

> With reference to the point about the origin of the Government subsidy, President Cosgrave took no interest in the Abbey. In fact as far as I can remember it was his boast that he had never been to a performance in it in his life. He knew, however, that I had always had an interest in the Abbey and when the letter signed by Lady Gregory and Yeats arrived, he referred it to me and I received a deputation which came to Government Buildings. I may say that, personally, I thought the offer to give the Theatre to the Government was more tactical than serious [It was a perfectly serious offer. L. R.], and that in fact it was only an emphatic way of asking for a subvention, but in any case I should not for a moment have thought that the Government should accept an offer of the Theatre. I had visions of questions being asked in the Dail as to why particular lines were allowed to remain in a certain play, as to why the work of one dramatist had been accepted while the work of a more moral and patriotic dramatist had been rejected! As to why a particular actress had been given a part which could have been much more competently played by Miss So-and-so, etc. etc.
>
> I thought, however, that there should be no difficulty in giving a small annual grant to the Theatre to make it possible to carry on in changed circumstances. I rang Desmond Fitzgerald on the point and he agreed. Consequently, when I met the deputation I practically promised that a grant would be given. I mentioned the matter at the next meeting of the Government and no objection was raised.[74]

However, on 16 July, Lady Gregory noted in her Journal:

> Robinson writes about our offer of the Theatre to Government and Cosgrave's objection to do anything to help us, probably from economy. I think it may be necessary, this swing of the pendulum towards unimaginative construction after the recklessness of idealism run wild. The Republicans would have supported a theatre, though they might probably have wrecked it by putting their own people in.[75]

If, as it appears, we are correct, and Lady Greogry's and Yeats's letter to the government was really dated June 1923, then it would seem that Blythe, many years after the event, telescoped the ease and swiftness with which a grant was given. In fact, there seems to have been much more than a year yet of maneuvers and counter maneuvers. For instance, on 20 August, Lady Gregory recorded that Yeats said:

> Brennan of the Education Department told him when he asked if the Abbey's taxes could be remitted for a year that it was impossible without starving some other branch of education, that in the next two or three years there must either be the most drastic economy or a paper currency of our own. I said, and Yeats agreed, that if we cannot carry on the Abbey we should let it for a few years to a Film Company and save the money to open again. But I am not without hope that if the London tour comes off we may make money enough to carry on for a while, and perhaps pay our way. For we never could have paid it but for tours, English and American, and

> the English tours were only cut off by the war, the other by Robinson's catastrophe of running to wrong places on our last tour.[76]

On 16 October, Yeats wrote to lady Gregory about the stalled progress of the matter:

> Robinson called today having been asked by Desmond Fitzgerald for statement from government about nationalization of Abbey. . . . I believe the matter is pressing and you will I suppose hear from him. . . . I still have a number of copies of the pamphlet. . . . or will the pamphlet be wanted at all? Probably I may find out from Fitzgerald—there is just a chance of my seeing him or George and I am to hear the Dail debate some day this week. . . . I think they really mean to keep the Abbey.[77]

But there would be months more of such backing and filing.

• • •

Elsewhere in Dublin, the Tivoli was completely and the Royal mainly given over to Variety. However, the Royal did give occasional concerts during the year with such artists as Kreisler, Melchior, Backhaus, and Clara Butt. The Empire was closed until 5 February, when it was reopened by I. I. Bradley and Robert Morrison under its present name, the Olympia. As well as revues, the Olympia did present some traveling musical comedies, a traveling opera company, a couple of films, and an Italian circus. The only items of Irish interest, however, were the usual repertoire of Arthur Sinclair and his company, which appeared for two weeks in April.

The Repertory Company at the Queen's, which had been formed in 1922 under Frank Dalton, did not reassemble in 1923, but the offerings of the Queen's remained basically the same. Ira Allen and P. J. Bourke would still put on Irish pieces like *Father Murphy* and *Kathleen Mavourneen*, and May Craig would appear during the Abbey summer vacation in older English pieces like *East Lynne* and *Lady Audley's Secret.* However, the theater for about twenty weeks in the last half of the year was occupied by the Cork-born provincial tragedian William Macready who specialized in broad, sentimental, nineteenth-century melodrama, such as *The Two Orphans*, *Sweet Nell of Old Drury*, *East Lynne*, *The Face at the Window*, *The Grip of Iron*, and even a recent version of *Uncle Tom's Cabin.* Occasionally he would veer into the spectacular drama, but we have been unable to discover how he handled the sensational scenes in, say, *The Octoroon*, which he presented for the week of 26 August with himself as Salem Scudder and Vousden in Boucicault's old role of Wahnotee. The only new piece he produced, *Her Great Revenge* by St. Aubyn Miller in the week of 8 August, was apparently not Irish.

The Gaiety's year was also typical, with traveling comedies and musicals presented by the usual English entrepreneurs such as Robert Courtneidge,

George Edwardes, and Alfred Butt. Among the more notable actors to appear were Stella Patrick Campbell, Frank Forbes-Robertson, Gladys Cooper, Seymour Hicks, and Sybil Thorndike. Miss Thorndike and her company appeared in a mixed bill that included Ervine's *Jane Clegg*, Gilbert Murray's translation of *Medea*, a scene from *Henry VIII* and, surprisingly, a farce-comedy called *Advertising April* by Herbert Farjeon and Horace Horsnell. Thurston Hall, who will be mainly remembered as the blustery, deep-voiced politician of innumerable Hollywood B movies of the 1930s, appeared with his own company in *The Broken Wing*, which featured "the Sensational Aeroplane Crash."

The new plays were not much above the level of Robert Hitchens's *The Garden of Allah*, Edward Sheldon's *Romance*, the Rinehart-Hopwood *The Bat*, or, at the very best, Galsworthy's *Loyalties*. Old warhorses like *The Private Secretary* and *A Royal Divorce* (now in its thirty-second year of touring) were put through their paces also once again. The Doran Shakespeare Company, with Earl Grey in the cast, appeared for a couple of weeks, as did the O'Mara Opera Company and the Carl Rosa Opera Company.

Among local groups, the Rathmines and Rathgar Musical Society did two weeks of Gilbert and Sullivan, and the Dublin University Dramatic Society put on its usual week of English light comedies. Of distinctly Irish interest, however, was Oireachtas Week at the Gaiety. Several plays in Irish were presented, among them *Bean an Milliunai* by Gerald O'Loughlin, *Cluiche Cartai* by Piaras Beasley, and *Cambeal na Ceille Meire* by O Foghludha; but the chief interest was an Irish opera which was first produced on 25 July. As the *Times* reported:

> Last night at the Gaiety Theatre *Sruth na Moile*, an Irish opera, composed by Mr. G. M. Palmer, with the Irish words by the Rev. Thomas O'Kelly, was produced for the first time before a large audience.
>
> The story of this opera is that of the fate of the Children of Lir. The Children of Lir are turned into swans by their stepmother, and they are forced to spend a long period in this guise, undergoing great hardships. They are, however, befriended by a young farmer, Aebhric, and his lover, Caitlin. At the close of the opera Lir's children are changed back into their own forms, die, and ascend to heaven.
>
> Mr. Palmer's music is both graceful and dignified. The lack of action all through the first act is against him; one feels that he was able to make more out of the second half of the opera. His settings of some of the old Irish airs were altogether charming. The story is told in a simple and straightforward manner.[78]

And, as usual, the Ulster Players appeared at the Gaiety for a week in late November.

The new enterprise at the Everyman collapsed early in the year. The pantomime of *Jack the Giant-Killer* ran for the first two weeks of January, and on 13 January there was an announcement that the theater would do *The Trifler*, a one-act by Martin J. McHugh, and *Sir Oliver Oliphant*, a two-act by

R. J. Purcell, which featured the real-life eccentric Endymion as a character.[79] These productions did not occur; instead, the theater was hired by such groups as Jack J. Walshe's All Irish Company or Tom J. Powell's Company in such oldfashioned stuff as *Uncle Tom's Cabin*, *The Shaughraun*, *The Rosary*, and *The Tears of an Irish Mother*.

After the second week of April, the theater remained empty until the fall. Then, on 13 September, Harry O'Donovan announced that he and his brother would reopen the house with the new name of the National Theatre. The National Theatre opened on 24 September and for three weeks played a mixture of old-fashioned short plays and variety. The last week featured two Victor O'D. Power plays, a one-act farce called *The Boys of Kilkenny* and a longer piece called *The Lost Heir.* We have discovered no accounts of these productions, and do not know if these were the first productions.

The theater at the Rotunda opened its doors only once again during the year, for the week of 3 December when the film *For the Cause of Old Ireland* was shown. At the year's end, it was announced that Ira Allen would take over the theater.

Occasional entertainments, both professional and amateur, were seen in Dublin in the year. For instance, during the summer vacation, the Abbey was rented by the Dublin Drama League for A. A. Filmer's Company to produce Shaw's *Misalliance* and Pirandello's *Six Characters in Search of an Author.* For the week of 23 April, Mary Sheridan produced *General John Regan* with Ralph Brereton Barry, Sir Valentine Grace, Frank Fay, and others. For the week of 14 May, some of the Abbey players staged the first performance of St. John Ervine's *Mary, Mary, Quite Contrary*. This was a light comedy in the vein of Somerset Maugham and had nothing Irish about it. O'Donnell in the *Evening Herald* treated the new piece quite roughly:

> Mr. St. John Ervine is a man of repute. He stands high as a critic, novelist, and dramatist. Every Sunday he interests thousands of readers of *The Observer* by his acute and emphatic pronouncements on modern dramatic productions, and some few years ago his *Mrs. Martin's Man* caused a furore amongst the popular novelists of the day. Followers of the drama speak of him with admiration when they remember his three great plays, *John Ferguson*, *Jane Clegg*, and *Mixed Marriage*. . . .
>
> All of which leads me up to say that *Mary, Mary, Quite Contrary*, produced by the Abbey Players at the Abbey Theatre last night is far, very far below Mr. Ervine's standard. . . .
>
> As a technician Mr. Ervine can hardly be beaten. He has seen hundreds and hundreds of plays, and he ought to know his job. His dialogue is flippant, impulsive, natural, but his wit in this play, if one could call it wit, is anaemic, feeble, sometimes banal. If Mr. Ervine had made his chief denominator more human, if his Mary Westlake had not been so grotesque, perhaps he would have succeeded in interesting us. . . .
>
> I agree Mr. Ervine was satiric. He wrote with his tongue in his cheek, but I am afraid it would take a very astute member of the plain people to realise that it was his tongue and not a marble was there.[80]

The *Times* reported that the audience was large, the reception flattering, and that the players "made the most of their somewhat limited opportunities."[81] The piece fared better in September when Mrs. Fiske produced it at the Belasco in New York.[82]

For the week of 4 June, amateurs rented the Abbey for charity performances of another English play, Ernest Cecil's *A Matter of Fact.* O'Donnell saw nothing in the play to interest an audience for five minutes, except the acting of Elizabeth Young:

> From the moment of her entrance to the final curtain you felt the presence of a great personality upon the stage, and that all the display of emotion, the voice inflections, the actions and attitudes stressed the fact that Miss Young is still as great a tragic actress as modern Ireland has produced. Because of her undoubtedly fine qualities I regretted seeing such splendid emotion as hers being wasted upon what was but a High Society melodrama.[83]

On 17 and 20 June, Madame Itzkoritch and the Jewish Players from the Pavilion Theatre, London, appeared at the Abbey in a Yiddish operatic play, *Das Pintele Yid.* And on 26, 27, and 28 June, the group did Zloterski's "masterpiece," *The White Slaves*, a four-act drama with music. Both productions were arranged by the quite active Dublin Jewish Dramatic Society.[84]

Beginning on 9 July, the Grizelda Hervey[85] and Earl Grey Comedy Company did three weeks at the Abbey, and presented a couple of Milne plays, Robertson's old favorite *David Garrick*, and Sheridan's *The Rivals.* The company included Cecil Parker and Ralph Richardson and a few locals, such as Frank Fay. Apparently the pieces were underrehearsed, for as Sir Lucius O'Trigger Richardson was chiefly admired for requiring the prompter less than did his colleagues.[86]

At the Father Mathew Hall earlier in the year, on 25 February, amateurs presented the first production of John Stephenson's version of Kickham's novel *Sally Kavanagh.* For the week of 2 April at the Father Mathew Hall, a *Joan of Arc* was presented by Deaf Mutes of St. Joseph's, Cabra, and billed as "The most fascinating Play in Town." For the week of 9 April, there was a dramatic art competition at the hall, in which the Celtic Players were billed to do *Family Failing*, the Father Mathew Dramatic Society was to repeat *Sally Kavanagh*, the Third Order Dramatic Society from Wexford was to do Canon Sheehan's *My New Curate*, the Inchicore Mystery Players were to do *White Dove of Erin*, the Kincora Players *Sable and Gold*, the Miss Burkes's Dramatic Troupe was to do *The Admirable Crichton*, and Dalkey's St. Lawrence Dramatic Society *The Fenian.*

The affair was adjudicated by Lennox Robinson, and at the prize-giving he offered the following advice:

> Gesture was important, and a player should never use it except when it meant something, and when it meant something should use it for all it was worth.

Players should learn to be perfectly still, and to listen intelligently. It was the greatest help if the players listened to what was being said by another.

There was a great deal of very unnatural speaking. The players seemed to speak a great deal of the time with their lips, and not with their minds.

The wrong word was nearly always stressed. There was a good deal of speaking which was very sing-song; and there was a great deal of speaking which was really indistinguishable from where he was sitting. It was necessary to take lessons, not in elocution, but in voice production.

Good artistes like Sara Allgood did not get beautiful speaking without hard work and simple exercises. They had to have the vocal chords and the voices trained. They wanted to get speed. They had to practice a speech like that of Mrs. Fallon in *Spreading the News*—the long jumbling speech of an excited woman—see how fast they could go, keeping their voice clear all the time. And then they wanted to get passages of plays in which there was beautiful, moving, slow speech. . . .

The great thing was to try to make every part in the play a character part. . . .

They saw in the cinema wonderful and beautiful gesture, wonderful stillness, and wonderful acting when the actors had no words to help them. . . .

In choosing a play he suggested that players should choose one that was distinguished by the truth and the interest of its subject, or a play that was distinguished by its witty dialogue—a play that had been played often before and that had proved itself a success on the stage. . . .

As regards the scenery, the stage was getting away more and more from realistic scenery. When they came to deal with scenes which they could not get in reality on the stage let them see what they could do with light and shade. Let them see what they were doing in theatres in other parts of the world, particularly in Germany and America. . . .

His advice to intending playwrights was that before they wrote a play let them be sure that they had got something to say that had not been said a hundred times before, and let them be sure that they could say it in a way peculiar to themselves. Let them try to get into a dramatic company and act themselves. Before they wrote a word of dialogue let them write the scenario ten times over. . . .

He appealed to the actors and to the producers all through the country to realise that the art of the stage was an art as definite as painting or music, and that they could not take a play and play ducks and geese with it any more than they could take a sonata of Beethoven and cut it into pieces.

They had got to approach a play with a certain reverence, with a certain feeling that the author had really meant something in writing the play, and that the actors had to bring their art to bear upon the art of the author.[87]

The first production of the Dublin Drama League was St. John Hankin's *The Return of the Prodigal*, at the Abbey on 11 and 12 February. Of it, the *Irish Times* wrote:

Mr. Brereton Barry was good as the prodigal Eustace; only he and Mrs. White (as Lady Farrington) caught the true atmosphere of the play. Mr. O'Dea "Clowned" the part of Dr. Glaisher—but he "clowned" it so nicely that many thought it the best acting of the night. Mrs. Hackett was "safe," without being brilliant.

The production needs a little tightening up, and some of the players need to know their lines better.[88]

On 16 April, as we have noted above, the League presented A. A. Filmer's company from England in Shaw's *Misalliance* and, later in the week, Pirandello's *Six Characters in Search of an Author.* Of *Misalliance*, Jacques characteristically snorted:

> Sitting through two hours of *Misalliance* one wondered whose idea it was to close a theatre that had been re-opened by public subscription to the regular Abbey Company of Irish players and hand it over to a company of players from across the Channel. There is nothing in this hotchpotch of "Intellectualism" that the repertory company of the Abbey could not do quite as well as it could be done by any other combination. While the Abbey remains closed the Abbey players are unemployed. My protest is that the people's theatre, kept open by the money of the people publicly appealed for by the directors of the Abbey, could be better used in the public interest with productions of plays from the Abbey repertoire than in squandering it upon such samples of futility as *Misalliance.*[89]

On 21 and 22 October, at the Abbey, the Drama League presented Helen and Harley Granville-Barker's translation of the Spanish play, *The Kingdom of God*, by Gregorio Martinez-Sierra. Produced by Arthur Shields, this piece had a very large cast, in which Eileen Crowe's Sister Gracia was most prominent. O'Donnell found the paly

> deeply religious, written with delicate restraint, and containing within itself all the ingredients of exuberant comedy and heart-wrung tragedy. . . .
>
> The greater glory of the acting belongs to Miss Eileen Crowe. As Sister Gracia she gave a perfect interpretation of the mental oscillations of a young religeuse. Each time latterly I have seen her play she plays with more confidence and freedom than hitherto, and I feel that in Miss Crowe a worthy successor has been found to the very fine actresses of the Abbey Theatre.[90]

This review drew forth a critical letter from Laurence Elyan:

> When will our dramatic critics become critical?
>
> Reading the various reports by the critics of the leading Dublin papers on the play produced last night by the Dublin Drama League one would be left with the impression that the acting at the Abbey left nothing to be desired. The praise lavished in stock phrases on the whole of the forty players is a source of exasperation to anyone who takes an interest in the drama of Dublin.
>
> It was, therefore, a pleasure to read "F. J. H. O'D." in your columns. Your critic is extremely careful in avoiding to eulogise those who certainly do not deserve any praise. But it is a pity that he did not go further and point out a few very obvious defects in the performance.
>
> Eileen Crowe's study of Sister Gracia, in the first and second acts, was certainly splendid. But was it so in the last act? Did the audience feel that she was a woman of seventy?
>
> Then there was the extraordinary diversity of accents adopted by the players, ranging from the foreign accent of Gracia's father to the deep Dublin brogue of some of the others. One or two of the character studies were absolutely colourless, and your critic did well in not including them in the list of those whom he commended.
>
> "F. J. H. O'D's" return to your columns will be welcomed by all lovers of the

> drama in Dublin. Let us hope he will give a lead to the other critics in telling the truth at the risk of being invidious.[91]

To the question of "When will our dramatic critics become critical?" there was a forceful, if eccentric response, by James Murray:

> This is a question which Dublin people interested in the drama have been asking ever since the Abbey Theatre was founded. . . .
>
> There is not much variety in our dramatic critiques. The note is usually either the fulsome flattery or the insolent savagery of sheer ignorance.
>
> In my opinion no dramatic critiques in the Dublin Press show any discernment whatever, save those which appear occasionally overthe initials "H. R. W."[92] This critic, of whom I know nothing except his critiques, writes as an expert on musical subjects; on dramatic subjects he shows commonsense.
>
> "F. J. H. O'D" is much better as a playwright than as a critic of other people's plays. It is a pity the Abbey Theatre seems determined to produce no more new plays of merit. In *The Shadow of a Gunman*, a play which is beneath criticism, it has touched the lowest depths of degradation. One fears that the artistic conscience of the Abbey is seared. Time was when, revelling in artistic luxuriance, it sinned gravely and repeatedly against the nation and was, for Art's sake, forgiven. Now, stark and sterile, it blasphemes both.[93]

On 9 and 10 December, at the Abbey, the Drama League presented Henri Lenormand's *Time Is a Dream* in a translation by Thomas McGreevy, and Gilbert Cannan's short piece, *Everybody's Husband.* The evening, according to O'Donnell, was not a success:

> The real trouble with this play of M. Lenormand's is that it is inconclusive, and that he has been beating his wings upon empty spaces.
>
> Unfortunately, he was not helped a great deal by the acting. For the first four scenes, I could only hear occasional sentences drop from the lips of Miss Eileen Crowe, Miss Edith Dodd, and Miss Lini Saurin. They were entirely too impassive to be impressive, and the play got under way to a peculiar declamatory drawl that carried right through and became boring at the finish.
>
> [In Cannan] the acting . . . was not of a high level either. . . . The prompter, too, deserves my acknowledgments.
>
> And once again Dr. Larchet's orchestra proved consolatory to a brain-fogged audience.[94]

In *The Dublin Magazine*, on the other hand, Pierrot was quite bedazzled by the Lenormand, and thought that "it was an event of considerable importance in the Dublin theatre." He also remarked "the incomparable and fascinatingly subtle interpretation of Eileen Crowe," as well as "the masterly dramatic technique" of the author who "tracks the footprints of a mind through an ontological morass." One's faith in Pierrot is somewhat redeemed when he disposes of Cannan's play as one which "would, by its incredible dullness and drivelling stupidity, have bored a second-class scullery-maid had she come across it ten years ago in a threepenny novelette."[95] But, once more on the other hand, the clever Susan L. Mitchell thought *Everybody's Husband* "a delightfully-conceived trifle."[96]

On Monday, 12 November, the Gaelic Players rented the Abbey to produce *An Dutchas* by Maire Ni Chinneide, *Vaigneas an Ghleanna*, which was Fiachra Eilgeach's translation of *In the Shadow of the Glen*, and Piaras Beasley's *Fear an Sceilin Ghrinn*. Lady Gregory, who was at part of the performance, remarked:

> 11.30. Just back from the Gaelic plays, the first performance at the Abbey a great success, stalls full, pit full, gallery rather weak, but 115 season tickets sold during the evening, and they will take the Abbey for seven Mondays instead of four. *Shadow of the Glen*, the only one I saw through, went very well, the girl charming. It is sad Synge could not have seen it in its Gaelic speech.
>
> I was introduced to General Beaslai, whose play was to come on next. I was sorry Craoibhin was not there to see this latest success, for the first Gaelic play ever given in Dublin was his *Casad-an-tSugain*.[97]

On 17 December, the Gaelic Players again rented the Abbey and did translations of Chekhov's *The Proposal*, of Synge's *Riders to the Sea*, and a short version of Molière's *The Doctor in Spite of Himself*.

In December, about seventy schoolchildren from Dalkey and Killiney did some performances of a Nativity Play by Katharine Tynan Hinkson in the Dalkey Town Hall.

During the year the Dublin Vigilance Association again aired its opinions about the state of the theatre:

> The inspection of theatres and music halls has given cause for the latest conflict between the Irish Vigilance Association and the Public Health Committee of the Dublin Corporation.
>
> Hitherto the Public Health Committee have appointed four inspectors of theatres and music halls, and the work has been carried out voluntarily, without a penny cost to the ratepayers, by the Vigilante Association inspectors. . . .
>
> The work with which the Vigilante Association has concerned itself consists in lodging objections against immoral "turns," suggestive jokes, or the like, and much good has been effected as a result. The volunteer workers are men of the world, with no namby-pamby ideas of propriety.
>
> In a letter to the Public Health Committee they call attention to the fact that there are now seven theatres and music halls in the city. "These," they point out, "have to be visited by an inspector on each Monday evening."[98]

And the rest of the letter took issue with the desire of the Public Health Committee to have only three inspectors. Nevertheless, the inspection of the theatres was less institutionalised than that of the cinemas. In *Films & Ireland: A Chronicle*, Kevin Rockett reports that the censorship of films in 1923 became even tighter:

> The Free State Government received almost unanimous support for a national

film censorship from the local authorities. The Minister for Justice, Kevin O'Higgins, received a deputation of Catholic and Protestant Church representatives demanding legislation for a national film censorship. Two months later O'Higgins introduced the legislation into the Dail by stating that he had met a "thoroughly representative delegation," (Dail May 3). The Censorship of Films Act provided for a film Censor who shall not grant a certificate if he is of the opinion that a film is "indecent, obscene or blasphemous" or "would be subversive of public morality." There is no censorship of political films.

The first censor to be appointed, James Montgomery, was an employee of Boland's Bakery, Dublin. He stated that he knew little about film but took the Ten Commandments as his code. The first Censorship of Films Appeal Board included poet/playwright W. B. Yeats, writer Oliver St. John Gogarty, member of the Public Health Committee, Senator Mrs. Wyse-Power, Senator O'Farrell, who became chairman, 1929–64, Professor Magennis T. D. (Chairman 1924–29): "people, especially the rising generation, require to be protected from an environment that is certainly not conducive for good morals, and they require to be saved from themselves." (Dail, May 10).[99]

After shooting three films in 1922, nothing was heard of Irish Photoplays, and about the only films of Irish interest were both stage-Irish and produced in America. Mae Marsh was the lead in *Paddy the Next Best Thing* shown at the Metropole in the week of 13 August, and Laurette Taylor repeated her stage role in *Peg O' My Heart* shown at the Metropole in the week of 3 December.

Dublin's La Scala, which was almost entirely a movie house, could seat 2,500 people; and on 17 March the theater interrupted its films to present a boxing match for the light heavyweight championship of the world. The match went twenty rounds, and Mike McTigue of County Clare won on points from Battling Siki.

On 27 April, the Grand Central Cinema in Lower O'Connell Street was partially destroyed by a mine explosion,[100] but the other most violent incident in a city theater had no political motivation. This occurred on 27 March when a drunken army lieutenant, after an argument over a bag of tomatoes, shot a man dead in the parterre bar of the Theatre Royal. The lieutenant was sentenced to eighteen months' imprisonment.[101]

For the last two weeks in June, practically all theaters and cinemas in Dublin were closed as a result of a strike, and a statement from the managers indicates the generally depressed condition of the theater in 1923.

About twelve months ago the employers carried on negotiations with delegates from the Transport Workers' Union and came to an arrangement with them for a reduction of wages. When the proposals were submitted to the workers they were turned down, and a strike was then inevitable but for the fact that the Government intervened and pressed the employers to carry on owing to the disturbed state of the country. . . .

"The industry for some time past has been conducted under very trying conditions, and the majority of the houses of entertainment have been carrying on at a loss. Owing to the enormous increase which has taken place on the standing charges, rates, and other outgoings, and bearing in mind the heavy import duty recently imposed on films, a reduction in the working expenses is imperative if the industry is to be continued at all.

"In addition to this, it is now proposed to impose a further burden on the cinemas by the Censorship Bill, which is at present under consideration by the Dail. As the Bill stands at present, the entire cost of this censorship is to be met by the exhibitors."[102]

The depressed artistic state of the theater was bewailed by Edward McNulty. In a letter of 5 May, he pointed out, that, despite political independence, the Irish stage had again become dependent upon the English stage:

It is natural to expect that national art should synchronise with the awakening of national consciousness. But the superstition of the "latest London success" still dominates the slave minds of the threatrical public; and every peripatetic English production is hailed with a fulsome adulation which is a disgrace to Irish journalism. Our principal theatres are mobilised in the interest of British companies whose wares are frequently "adapted" from Paris.

Thus, with only two distinctive Irish theatres in Dublin—the Abbey and the Queen's—Irish actors are practically ostracised in their own metropolis; and the ambitious provincial amateur, raising his eyes towards the capitol that should be the Mecca of his heart's desire, sees it enveloped in a London fog. It is time that Irish culture should be assured of its natural right to unfettered development in the land of its birth.[103]

In a reply, Harry O'Donovan seems to us utterly correct:

Irish artistes have proved themselves worthy to take a place with the best cross-Channel talent; but they have only proved it as individuals. Local talent has never been well enough organised to enable it to submit to the theatres a sound, working proposition which would guarantee a supply of the best material, efficiently presented.

The matter will have to be approached in a clear-headed way. Abusing the theatre proprietors (even though they deserve it) will not get us very far. The theatre is ruled by its box-office, and, until we can show the threatre proprietors that the box-office will suffer by our exclusion or benefit by our inclusion, they will not listen to us.[104]

Over the years, there have been some consummate Irish actors, some brilliant Irish playwrights, and some extraordinary Irish productions. But these have always been exceptional. The rule of the good usual Irish acting, writing, and production—whether in the theater, in films, in radio, or in television—is only that "it is good for Dublin."

• • •

For Easter Week, the Ulster Theatre journeyed to Derry, and while there gave the first production of Gerald MacNamara's heroic farce, *Fee Faw Fum.*

During the week of 16 April, they appeared at the Grand Opera House in Belfast in nine plays from their repertoire, including on 20 April *Fee Faw Fum*. A reviewer in the *Belfast News-Letter* described the piece as "one of the most laughable that has ever been submitted by the company, and the large audience expressed their appreciation whole-heartedly."[105]

The play was next done on 27 and 30 November when the company was appearing at the Gaiety in Dublin. The *Irish Times* critic, who also liked the play, gave a good summary of the plot:

> The story is based upon an amusing legend, which is popularly attached to one of the ancient Irish heroes. Conn Ligg, an Ulster giant, is resting on the laurels won for him by his earlier feats. It is twenty years since he has had a fight, but he still retains his Roman trainer, Scrapius, whose job appears to be the turning away of likely rivals for Conn's fame. Olaf, a young and weedy Scandinavian pretender to glory seeks vengeance on Conn for his father's death at the latter's hands twenty years before. He is frightened away, however, by Conn's "Fee-Faw-Fum," growled through a megaphone from the interior of his castle. How Nab MacNab, the trainer of a Scots giant, is frightened away by Brigid—i.e., Mrs. Conn, with her stratagem of dressing Conn up to represent a young son of himself, and her grown-up daughter as an infant of four years old, gives plenty of food for laughter. The play is well constructed and worked out. There is a laugh in every phase.
>
> Scrapius, the Roman trainer, played by Mr. Walter Kennedy, was, perhaps, the most convincing and the best performance. He played the part of the optimistic pessimist to perfection. Mr Rutherford Mayne made an exceedingly humorous ogre, very respectful and obedient to his wife, very human and bombastic, when repeating his Coueistic saga: "I am Conn of the iron heart, and the fiery blood. I am the wind . . . etc." Mr. J. R. Mageean, who played MacNab, the emissary of the Scots giant bent on discovering the dimensions of his Ulster opponent, Conn, made a very plausible and natural Highland liar, singing the immensity of his master's feats. . . . The author of the play had a small part as Dubh, the Druid, but his acting was clever and satisfying, and his part was a distinct success.[106]

J. G. S. in the *Irish Statesman* added:

> . . . the play has the vintage quality of the inimitable *Thompson*. . . . Few dramatists would have had the courage to compound such a mixture, and perhaps nobody but Mr. MacNamara could have seasoned it with such irresistible fun and unending laughter. Dramatically *Fee Faw Fum* might be tightened and its pace speeded up by dropping the second Olaf scene, which, though it contains some good things, does not add much to the action.[107]

Fee Few Fum was not the theater's only foray in 1923 into prehistory. On 28 November, at a matinee at the Gaiety, the Ulster Players gave the first production of Rutherford Mayne's one-act play of the Bronze Age, entitled *Phantoms*. Nobody liked it. As the *Irish Times* reported:

> The Ulster Players produced *Phantoms*, by Rutherford Mayne, for the first time at the matinee at the Gaiety Theatre yesterday. It is a short play in one act, lasting

for thirty minutes, and is of a distinctly "highbrow" order. It seems to preach that if there were no armourers there would be no armed, and, therefore, "peace in the valley"; but if one is to judge from the remarks in the auditorium, the moral was rather lost—at least, on the afternoon audience.

The old and repulsive wife of a maker of weapons supplies arms to an outlaw and then to a tribal chief. While the inevitable fighting and burning are taking place in the valley, she gloats with horrible realism over bloodshed. The leaders of the respective fighters escape, and in turn call upon the old hag, who supplies them with weapons treated with a poison which she brews while she croons—"It is good to see the young die when one is old." Presumably, they kill one another.

The maker of weapons has a purely materialistic mind. He glories only in the profits to be made out of other people's hatreds, and nurses a private desire to take the daughter of the outlaw who has sought the protection of his bondsman. To further this end he scratches his wife with a thorn that has been steeped in the poison. In her dying moments she stabs him, and the young people plight their troth over the corpses.

The acting of Miss Josephine Mayne as Hag U and of Mr. J. R. Mageean as Gnu, the weapon-maker, was particularly fine. Mr. Richard Hayward as their bondsman was too refined in speech and bearing for a part which it would have been very difficult to have made convincing under any circumstances, while Miss Jean Woods invested the part of the outlaw's daughter with a culture and timidity which it was difficult to associate with the Bronze Age. . . .

It was a relief to hear *The Throwbacks*, which . . . dispelled the horrors of the preceding piece and sent the audience away highly delighted with the Ulster Players.[108]

In the *Independent*, Jacques asked:

What was it? A diatribe in allegory against militarism, armaments, incendiarism, poison ivy, drink, politics, or what? Nothing in the little play showed us how the thing, whatever it was, was to be put out of commission. Perhaps Mr. Mayne himself is the pursuer of phantoms.

It seemed Yeatsy without the poetry; trifling, but not at all thrilling. The audience, small in size, was generous in applause.[109]

And Holloway:

It failed to be impressive and it failed to thrill, and I pitied the poor players having to appear in such crudeness on such a raw afternoon. . . . Josephine Mayne scarcely made the old hag in any way creepy nor did J. R. Mageean make his old man—Gnu—convincingly bloodthirsty either. Charles K. Ayre's Seeki shouted a lot about vengeance and Rutherford Mayne was big voiced and unimpressive also. The lovers Danon and Deeva—Richard Hayward and Jean Woods—had little to do but enfold each other in their arms. The little piece fell perfectly flat and must be recorded a dead failure. The company with their Northern dialect seemed thoroughly out of the depth in it.[110]

For the week of 10 December, the Ulster Theatre played *Phantoms* and five other pieces at the Grand Opera House in Belfast. The reviewer for the *News-Letter* thought that the characters were well-drawn and that the players now "acted them with conspicuous ability; but the construction of the play is rather weak in parts, and the story becomes somewhat vague at times."[111] The play was published in December in the *Dublin Magazine*, and a perusal suggests that it is indeed a flat and distinctly minor work.

During the visit of the Ulster Theatre to Dublin, Gerald MacNamara spoke to the weekly luncheon of the Rotary Club. His speech was humorous, but he discussed a script called *William John Jameson*, which was one of several quirky closet dramas he published in the *Dublin Magazine*:

> Taking for his subject, "Play Production Made Easy," Mr. Morrow delivered an entertaining address which was much enjoyed. Authors, he said, were divided into two classes—living and dead—plays by dead authors being the easiest to produce. No self-respecing producer allowed an author to attend rehearsals of his own plays. Authors should be read, not seen. Owing to the prevalence of free libraries, playwriting had become simplicity itself.
>
> The first thing was to select a catching title—something easily produced, such as *The Drone* or *Loaves and Fishes*. Then select a plot from some old book if you thought no one had ever read it. If it was a folk play the author took a day in the country, with a note-book, and jotted down a few names of characters whom he made talk to each other. . . . When the play was then complete, it was chopped into acts and scenes.
>
> To illustrate his point, Mr. Morrow took as example a play which he himself was now engaged in writing, entitled *William John Jameson*, a tragedy in four acts, which he proceeded to describe in homely terms which kept his audience highly diverted. Then came the actual production of the play. Here the young producer must go through a course of training in all matters of stage craft. Methods of getting behind the stage were various, but the young producer would find that it cost more money behind the scenes than in front. A chocolate box behind would cost more than a Royal box in front, not to mention pearls and diamonds and furs in season, as well as keeping the stage hands wet in case of fire. When behind the scenes the embryo producer must make himself au fait with all the technical terms, such as long lines, short lines, and hard lines. Having dilated on the weaknesses of actors who were no longer youthful, he said as for supers, on the stage they were as frozen meat, and their training was, strictly speaking, a ringmaster's job. Every producer should have a perfect knowledge of the history of his profession, said Mr. Morrow, who proceeded to startle his audience with an entirely original account of the evolution of the drama. During the reign of Queen Elizabeth a great number of playwrights sprang up. They jostled each other in the streets of London, and it was then in a fit of jealousy that Shakespeare wrote the memorable lines, "All the world's a stage." After the Restoration, the drama got a new lease of life, but was characterised by folly and licentiousness. And this type of play would still be "running" had it not been stopped by William the Third at the Battle of the Boyne. No really great plays had been written except *Uncle Tom's Cabin*, *A Royal Divorce*, and *A Face at the Window*.
>
> A vote of thanks was passed after brief speeches expressing the club's keen appreciation of a refreshing experience in the lecture line.[112]

The year in the North saw many of the English touring companies that had visited Dublin also visiting Belfast's Grand Opera House. The visit of the Carl Rosa Opera Company, however, produced something of an Irish event, the first production of Hubert Bath's one-act opera, *Bubbles*. This piece was based on Lady Gregory's *Spreading the News*, and the Carl Rosa company had originally intended to give the premiere on 31 October at the Gaiety in Dublin, but was prevented by a dock strike, which kept the orchestral parts from reaching the city in time. Of the new opera, the *News-Letter* wrote:

> The music throughout is delightful, the overture especially being distinguished by melodic beauty, while the harmonies are richly woven, with the loveliest of tone-colouring and quaint effects. There is not much solo work, but what there is of it reaches a high standard. The ensembles are most effective, working up to some splendid climaxes.[113]

Frank Hugh O'Donnell journeyed up from Dublin to see the new piece, and was considerably more critical:

> The production of a new opera, *Bubbles*, founded upon Lady Gregory's play, *Spreading the News*, created a great deal of interest, and the people of Belfast packed out the Opera House last night in an endeavour to see it.
>
> The libretto is by Carlos Linate, who has also written the libretto of a version of Dr. W. B. Yeats' delightful phantasy, *The Land of Heart's Desire*, and the composer is Mr. Hubert Bath, the very well-known conductor of the Carl Rosa Opera Co.
>
> As an opera I must admit that *Spreading the News* is a disappointment. Or rather perhaps I should have said it is a mistake. All our old friends are there. Bartley Fallon and Mrs. Fallon, deaf Mrs. Tarpey, and obstreporous Mrs. Tully, the magistrate who civilised the Andaman islands, and the ever straitlaced policeman. All were there but only in spirit. The kindly humour, the Kiltartan quaintness of speech, the charming comedy of their complicated mentalities, all melted away into something nearing banality when they had to sing their troubles rather than talk them.
>
> Anyone will understand what I mean when I tell them that instead of Bartley Fallon's usual gem of philosophical brevity, "It's what I'm always saying if there's trouble coming to anyone in this world it's on myself 'twould fall," we had "The devil to my soul is everything gone wrong with me?" . . . It sounds so crude!
>
> There were many obvious defects in production. All the men smoked "dhudheens," and looked the stage-Paddy type, "Red" Jack Smith appeared in the full glory of his own black hair, and Miss Olive Gilbert by playing the part of Mrs. Tully as a cheap comedienne would have done it burlesqued the little opera to a humorless conclusion.
>
> It is only fair, however, to say that Mr. Bath has got a quaint strain of jig and reel melody running right through his music that gives the piece an atmosphere of at least being Irish (though the music is not derivatively Irish) and "different." His idea of making a sort of Greek chorus out of deaf Mrs. Tarpey was in itself a touch of genius, and her caoining droll of "Only twopence a piece for the oranges" at the beginning and finish of the opera gives it a roundness of completion that balances for a number of other faults. Unfortunately, Mr. Bath made a fatal error when he got the pivot sentence of the theme, "He is running down the village after Jack Smith with a hayfork," drowned beneath a crescendo of wind, wood, and drum. For an auditor not knowing the original play thoroughly, it would have robbed him of any continuity of idea.
>
> The cast, with the exception of Miss Gilbert, acted and sang their parts in quite a natural and acceptable manner, but in an especial way I must single out Mr.

Appleton Moore for his quiet and effective delineation of Bartley Fallon and Miss Gladys Parr for her extraordinary make-up as Mrs. Tarpey.

At the opera's conclusion Mr. Bath received quite an ovation.

I hear now that next season the Carl Rosa Opera Co. may produce Mr. Yeats' *Land of Heart's Desire*, and this, indeed, I am glad to hear, for I feel that it is a type of play that will lend itself ever so much better to the embroidery of music than did the tragi-comedy of a mislaid hay fork that we saw to-night. As an acting play *Spreading the News* stands apart in its class, but why present it as an opera? It did not quite fit into new clothes, though the designing of Mr. Bath came near to being perfect.[114]

There was considerable amateur activity during the year by such groups as the Bangor Dramatic Society, the Bangor Amateur Operatic Society, the Queen's Island Operatic and Dramatic Society, and the Players Dramatic Club, which had been organized in 1920 to give "musical and dramatic entertainments in the hospitals and kindred institutions in and around Belfast."[115] The Queen's Island group even preceded their *Pirates of Penzance* with an original one-act called *The Inheritance* by one of their members, Archie Inglis. Of it, the *News-Letter* wrote:

The plot is novel and cleverly conceived, and the acting was of a much higher standard than is generally attained by amateurs. The story tells of how the relatives of an eccentric old man (who saved his gold for his adopted daughter) attempted to get hold of his money, but were foiled through an unexpected development.[116]

In Belfast, the year also saw the formation of the Northern Drama League. As the Ulster Literary Theatre was originally formed in emulation of the Irish Literary Theatre, so the Northern Drama League sought to do in Belfast what the Dublin Drama League was doing in Dublin—that is, "to promote amateur performances of good plays which are not likely to be produced in the theatres of the city."[117] The main difference was that the Dublin Drama League was able to draw some of its players from the city's pool of professional actors, and the Belfast group of necessity had to use amateurs, for there were really no professionals.

The first, poorly attended production was in the Great Hall of Queen's University on 8, 9, and 10 November, when the play was Ibsen's *An Enemy of the People*. One observer reported:

Certainly, Thursday night's performance was a most interesting one, really good on the whole, and where it was weak, the amazing vitality of the play itself more than made up for that weakness. . . . But, undoubtedly, the feature of the evening was the acting of Miss Mary Crothers. . . . she *was* Mrs. Stockmann. And this with hardly a gesture, hardly a raising of the voice. Even when she was silent we had but to watch her face to know what was passing in her mind. I doubt if, in essentials, there has ever been given a better rendering of the part either by professional or amateur.[118]

On 6 December, under the auspices of the Northern Drama League, the Queen's University Dramatic Society did a *Shadowy Waters* with George Buchanan and a *Deirdre of the Sorrows* with Olga Fielden as Lavarcham. The second real production, however, occurred on 20, 21, and 22 December, again at the Great Hall of Queens, when S. M. Bullock produced Gilbert Murray's translation of Euripides' *The Trojan Women*. In intention, if not in accomplishment, the new group had made a bold beginning.

• • •

In July, Dudley Digges was home from America, and got a rather new impression of Yeats. As he wrote to Padraic Colum:

> We were at the United Arts Club with Senator and Mrs. Yeats and Lennox Robinson. Senatorial responsibilities seem to have humanized the Great One or is it the effect of domesticity? He even descended once or twice to my level of understanding and was quite charming—and then a few consul generals called to take him away to the burdens of state.[119]

Yeats was particularly genial also in a lecture on the Abbey, which he delivered on 16 November at the Ritz Cafe in Grafton Street. Of Lady Gregory, he remarked, "Any of her compact speeches, analysed sentence by sentence, was a masterpiece." He also said "that we should see very shortly a transformation in Irish dramatic genius—a psychological movement." And in the forefront of this movement would be Lennox Robinson, some of whose works "were masterpieces in technique and imagination."[120] Yeats's geniality was undoubtedly helped by some news he had just received.

On 15 November, Holloway read in the paper that Yeats had been awarded the Nobel Prize for literature, and he immediately wrote off a letter of congratulation, as "one of the oldest and earliest admirers of your work."[121] Lawrence, whose feelings about Yeats had sometimes risen to the level of virulence, wrote to Holloway:

> As for Yeats's windfall—variously announced in the papers as anything from one to eight thousand pounds, I only wish it had come his way a score of years ago. In that case the history of the Abbey would be written differently and Yeats, out of a mistaken sense of gratitude to an old benefactor, would have been saved from the painful necessity to damn his own judgement by denominating in public certain imbecile farces masterpieces. You will surmise from this that I still believe Lady Gregory the bete noir of the Irish Dramatic Movement.[122]

And the bête noire herself wrote to John Quinn in America:

> Well, there are still things to make one happy. I was of course very glad and proud that Yeats got the Nobel prize. I was in Dublin when it was rumoured, but only had

a telegram from him announcing it the day after I left. Yes, they will invest the money. . . . I am selfishly pleased, also, because in the years he came here my friends and family in the neighbourhood never realized that he had genius, and knew or thought he was a revolutionist, and lamented my folly and obstinacy in having him and other writers in the house instead of the ordinary "country house parties." Now such of them who remain are much impressed by the sudden descent of prosperity on him, and then respect for me has increased![123]

Early in the year Lady Gregory published *Three Wonder Plays*, containing *The Dragon*, *The Jester*, *and Aristotle's Bellows*. In the *Irish Statesman*, AE wrote:

The latest and in some ways the most delightful and original inventions of Lady Gregory are her Wonder Plays. . . . In these plays, the unflagging invention, the humour, vitality and good spirits which we are accustomed to in Lady Gregory's plays are at their highest. . . . Lady Gregory's fantasy has a wisdom underneath it which gives it real value beyond the humour. . . . the reader of Lady Gregory's Wonder Plays will always find some wisdom remains with them after the whirling words of the abundant dialogue. . . . A wise and wonderful book.[124]

One may quarrel with a certain garrulity and dullness in Lady Gregory's later plays, but her adventurous spirit even in quite old age certainly compels respect and admiration. For instance, sometime in October, she wrote to John Quinn that she had tried her hand at yet another dramatic genre:

I was a good deal alone this summer, and I have written what Yeats had often urged me to do, a Passion Play. It is not likely ever to be acted in regular theatres, it would not be permitted in England, and it may never be acted at all. But the great subject took hold of me. It is written with reverence of the chief figure, and no words given him but his own. It is really a study of his enemies, of the rabble and of the various interests that brought Him to his death. I was in Dublin for a few days last month, and read it to Yeats and Lennox Robinson. They both praised it very highly, Yeats thought it "the best thing I had ever done," and that it "showed great intellectual powers." . . . Robinson wants to put it on at the Abbey, but I will have it printed first, that any objections may be made beforehand. In case of such I would not put it on.[125]

The most important theatrical figure to die in the year was Sarah Bernhardt, on 26 March, but in Dublin some important figures from the early days of the dramatic movement also died. On 6 March, William Boyle died in London in his seventieth year, and Holloway wrote:

It was only last week that his comedy *Family Failing* was revived successfully at the Abbey. I spent some time shortly after the 1916 Rising with him and family at his house at Dromiskin, Co. Louth, built on the spot of the house he was born in, in April, 1853. Then he was happy in his retirement and pottered about the fields and garden, or fished in the river nearby, ever and always with a big pipe in his mouth. Unfortunately he held a different opinion from mine over the War and the Rising, and, as he couldn't brook opposition or silence on matters that moved him strongly,

> he grew cold to me and never replied to any greetings or good wishes I afterwards continued to send him. It takes two to make a quarrel, and I had none with him. May the Lord have mercy on his soul, amen.
>
> Boyle lost touch with the people of Louth, and when he became a magistrate he grew more and more unpopular, till some years ago he fled his new home in which he hoped, when having it built, to end his days, and returned to England.[126]

Readers of Holloway's journals or of previous volumes of this history will have gathered that Boyle generally felt that he had been illtreated by the Abbey Theatre, and that his work was much less highly regarded by Yeats, Synge, and Lady Gregory than was their own. His opinion was not at all without foundation, and it impelled him into a general disgruntlement, rising at times to a vitriolic irascibility, about the Abbey. The most dramatic embodiment of his feelings was when he withdrew his plays from the Abbey repertoire in 1907 in protest, nominally, over the staging of Synge's *The Playboy*. However, Boyle at the time had not read *The Playboy*, and his gesture seems more a sour protest against the theater than against Synge's play.

Nevertheless, Boyle's *The Building Fund* was a terse, hard, minor but Molièrian comedy, which quite deserved its twenty years of popularity and which is his one revivable and lasting contribution to the Irish drama. Some of his later plays, particularly *The Eloquent Dempsy*, were vastly popular and could always be counted on to bring in customers in the leanest early days. However, *Dempsy*, *The Mineral Workers*, *Family Failing*, and *Nic* were mainly broader, ever more crowd-pleasing entertainments, and none of them achieved the hard strength of observation of *The Building Fund*.

Incidentally, one indication that the day of Boyle's plays was past was that in 1923 the Abbey finally began to misspell his eloquent politician's name as the more usual "Dempsey."

On 10 September, Wilfrid Scawen Blunt died. He had been a close friend of Lady Gregory and left her his Douai Bible. His verse play, *Fand*, had been presented by the Abbey in 1907.

On 5 December, Edward Martyn died at Tulira Castle. When Lady Gregory heard the news, she wrote in her journal:

> Though he had been too ill to see of late and I had not been able to go and see him before that because of the broken bridge and my difficulty about rough roads, I feel a loneliness now he is gone. He was from the beginning of my life here at Coole a good neighbour. . . . And then, when Yeats' summers, and the theatre project began, he was constantly here, walking over and staying to dine. It was George Moore who broke that work together, putting his own name to the *Bending of the Bough*, rewritten by him and Yeats but on Edward's foundation. And Edward had been weak about the *Countess Cathleen*, and took a wrong turning I think in withdrawing his support from our Theatre.[127]

On 20 December, the *Evening Herald* reported the circumstances of Martyn's burial:

> Yesterday the funeral of Mr. Edward Martyn took places in Glasnevin cemetery in strict accordance with the terms of his will.
>
> By that instrument he directed that his body, like those of many of the friendless poor, should be placed at the service of the Cecilia St. School of Surgery, and , when it had served its purpose there, should be interred in the common grave which holds the unclaimed workhouse dead.
>
> His remains were conveyed to Glasnevin in the Workhouse mortuary van with bodies for which the public authorities were providing interment. His coffin differed in no respect from those supplied by the Union.
>
> No pomp or religious rites accompanied him to his resting place, no concourse of mourners followed him to his lowly tomb.
>
> A Mass celebrated in the cemetery chapel for him and the nameless six who were to share his grave; the "Benedictas" sung when he was lowered into the earth, by the choir he had endowed—this was the only ceremonial.
>
> Born to wealth and high station, the inheritor of an ancient name, he fulfilled becomingly in life the social duties of his position. But the poverty of spirit which gives entrance into the Kingdom of Heaven was an abiding characteristic of his religion. . . .
>
> There will be those who will regard his choice as whimsical, but judged by the Gospel standard it was not unworthy of the last Martyn of Tulyra.[128]

W. B. Yeats, Lady Gregory, George Moore, and Edward Martyn were the founders of the Irish Literary Theatre in 1899 and, therefore, really the founders of the modern Irish drama. Of this quartet, Martyn was far and away the least talented. None of his plays—not even *The Heather Field*—has proved of lasting value; and there is no point in, and small danger of, the revival of any one of them. Yet even the poorest of them had a touch of something remarkable—not talent, for Martyn was one of the least talented dramatists ever to have books written about him. And it was not that he was, as has sometimes been said, historically important as a follower of Ibsen, the social dramatist; for Martyn's Ibsenism had its real affinities with Ibsen's symbolism and mysticism in such late plays as *The Lady from the Sea*, *John Gabriel Borkman*, and *When We Dead Awaken*. And it was not that he could write dialogue, save perhaps in one act of *The Dream Physician* where a joyful malice triumphed over a hopeless ineptitude. It was, perhaps, in Martyn's awkward, dogged, ineffectual individuality.

He was, as William J. Feeney remarks, "a loser in everything he attempted."[129] Yet some of his losses did ultimately bear fruit. His plays were portentous, ambitious, and awful; yet the modern Irish drama is a major glory of modern dramatic literature. His attempts at creating a theatre, chiefly in the Theatre of Ireland and the Irish Theatre in Hardwicke Street, were amateurish failures; yet the Gate and the Pike and the Globe came out of them. He may have reneged on the principles and policies of Sinn Fein; yet a sort of nation, as independent as any poverty-stricken and debt-ridden country can be, came out of it. He may—in fact, he did—utterly fail as a writer; yet as "Dear Edward" he became one of Ireland's great literary creations. What more can fidelity and idealism and doggedness attain?

But perhaps the last word on Edward Martyn should be that of John MacDonagh who had worked with him in the Hardwicke Street theater:

Ireland can ill afford at any time, and particularly just now, when the voice of intellect is so faint among us, the loss of a man of such fine character and noble ideals as Edward Martyn.

It was my privilege for some years to spend hours each day with him, discussing plans, principally for The Irish Theatre, which he founded in 1914 with Thomas MacDonagh and Joseph Plunkett, and in which I acted as Manager and Producer. These hours will remain long with me in happy memory. One would be dull, indeed, who did not catch some spark from that mind, stored with culture and experience, and it would be a nature bereft of sympathy that did not expand in that kindly and genial presence.

Living such a detached life his visitors were very rare; he showed a childlike pleasure in having someone to talk to. "I thought you weren't coming," he would say. "Sit down and let us talk," and so the hours passed pleasantly. Pipe after pipe, he would smoke in his long "Churchwarden," and midnight often found me still there, held by the magnetism of his words.

During our season of plays he never would come on the first night, fearing, I think, lest his presence might un-nerve the actors, but he used to send his valet to report how the night went off.

Next morning I generally found him very excited to hear the full account, his first question being "Did they know their words?"

At rehearsals he sat long hours in our cold and draughty hall, interfering little, but glad when any problem of interpretation came up, so that he felt he was being useful.

On such occasions he was a pathetic figure, sitting hunched up, near the radiator, but we all knew the keen enjoyment he experienced as he saw the play taking shape, and his interest was always reflected in greater efforts by the actors.

The tragedies of late years saddened him beyond expression; one after another he saw his friends and associates pass away, and the hopes and ideals of his life pushed back into unfulfilment.

After Easter Week, 1916, he wrote me to Knutsford Prison: "I am glad of the prospect of seeing you soon again. Alas, for your poor brother, and the others! It was an awful shock for me, such great talents and high ideals, only the jobbers and placehunters left. Everything is in ruins in Ireland. I am trying to carry on the Theatre, but what can I do without your brother?

"Father Condon showed me his last letter to his family, it made me awfully sad. Those executions were abominable. I passed a horrible time during the rebellion, thinking of you all, and listening to that never-ending shooting. I think it is even sadder now when one reflects on all our losses. I am much the same since I saw you. I fear mine is a bad case."

His charm and grace of manner were not of this age, that courtly dignity belonged to the statelier periods, in which he lived spiritually. His dramatic dialogue showed this lack of contact with the world we live in, and once, referring to some criticism of *The Heather Field*, I had the hardihood to suggest this explanation, with which he agreed without regret.

He had a pleasant and joyous sense of humour, little suspected, I fancy, by those who only knew the Edward Martyn, founder of the Palestrina Choir, or the portly figure, who could sit stiffly through three solid hours of intellectual drama.

The main ambition of his life, exemplified by his many activities, national, literary, artistic, and musical, was to rescue Ireland from the blighting effects of

English culture and ideas, too often encouraged and perpetuated by our own inept acquiescence. To this end he devoted his life and money, and to-day there are signs, however shadowy and indistinct, that he did not labour in vain.

Often, during the few brief years of the "Irish Theatre" I looked on Mr. Martyn as a pilot, guiding us surely and skillfully forward. Some, often, were disheartened and dejected by the persistent indifference and misunderstanding of the public, but his unfailing encouragement, and clear vision, soon set our course again, and bended our backs to the work.

Many times he repeated to me: "We mustn't mind what they say, if we stick together we will achieve something."

In 1918 [actually in 1920] we were forced to suspend operations; difficulties, arising from the political situation, made the carrying on of the Theatre practically impossible, and added to this, was the increasing feebleness of the "Captain of the Ship."

About the last time I saw him out of doors was when he came to see the second night of my play, *The Irish Jew*, in December, 1921. He took great interest in its success, for he considered me one of his pupils, which, in fact, I was, for I had read and re-read the script to him, benefitting much from his extraordinary grip of dramatic construction, and unerring knack of putting his finger on the weak spots.

On the day of his death I intended writing to him at Tilira, with reference to a contribution for this Magazine, in hopes that his health would allow him to dictate a letter. On my way to the office I saw the newspaper poster announcing the death of a notable Irishman. I got the paper and read the sad news.

It is not now the time to attempt any estimate of Edward Martyn's achievements, but he has left a lasting memory in the minds of his friends, and he has given to his country an example of purest patriotism which may well stand beside the best.[130]

• • •

But, if something is taken away, something is often given. If 1923 took away Edward Martyn, it gave to Ireland a personality as interesting and a dramatist incomparably better.

This was, of course, Sean O'Casey. In previous years of this history, O'Casey and his writings have been tangentially mentioned. However, the man in his middle forties who appeared in 1923 as a dramatist of international stature had served a long apprenticeship; and from his early sentimental verse and journalistic polemics, few could have predicted the major writer of 1923.

By 1923, O'Casey had already opened, and closed, a great many doors. A product of the tenements, a manual laborer, a literary pamphleteer, a strident espouser and a disillusioned debunker of many causes—what kind of man was this unusual new Abbey dramatist? The ever-inquisitive Holloway immediately set out to discover the answer:

Saturday, April 14. . . . The author is a thin-faced, sharp-profiled man, with streaky hair, and wore a trench coat and a soft felt hat. He followed his play closely and laughed often, and I was told he was quiet-mannered almost to shyness, and very interesting in his views. . . .

Friday, April 27. . . . Sean O'Casey came in, and he and Dolan sat down on the oak seat in the vestibule and chatter over a Ms. of a play he had brought. I afterwards joined them and made myself known to O'Casey.

On the Run was the name he first called his play. He had the subject in his mind for two years, and took three to write it. He felt like a "spectator" at his own play. "The characters seemed strangers to me, but I enjoyed them." He didn't know Yeats when he sat beside him in the seat vacated by Lady Gregory. No author likes to be told his faults, and when Yeats wrote a letter of criticism about one of his plays—he had sent in several before one was accepted—he was so annoyed, he threw the letter aside and put away the Ms. for months, and, when he reread it, he found Yeats had been right and he wrong. He knows now that the Directors were wise in refusing his earlier plays, and thanks them and Robinson for their kindly criticism. He thought the Abbey Company played the piece excellently. . . .

There are no critics in Dublin—good criticism could not be dashed off. . . . Speaking of poets, O'Casey said he liked Byron very much, especially his humour as exhibited in *Don Juan*, etc. It was this humour that detracted from him as a poet. Shelley had none whatever, and his poetry is always taken seriously. Shelley was a poet who preached human fellowship, and John Kells Ingram who wrote when he was very young, at the wish of O'Connell, the fine ballad, "The Memory of the Dead," followed his doctrine and was the kindliest old soul O'Casey ever knew.

He hopes one day to write a play called *The Orange Lily* in which he will depict the feelings of a good type of Orangeman who wished well of Ireland, leading up to Easter Week, 1916. It would not be political; it would be more a character study. He was strong on character and weak on construction and could write dialogue with ease. He knew an Orangeman who could stand for his model. O'Casey was once an Orangeman himself and a member of The Purple Lodge, and getting on well till his love for processions and bands got him in disfavour with the members of his Lodge, and he left the body and joined a Gaelic League class and became a Nationalist which he remains.

It was in this way it happened. He always liked to go out to see the annual Parnell Procession to Glasnevin, and usually went up near the cemetery to see it without being seen by his sort. He had a Protestant friend in the Foresters, and one year he was looking on at the procession passing when his friend marched along with a green sash across his shoulder, and O'Casey being in the front row of the sightseers, his friend pulled him into the space beside him to make up a fourth, and he walked along till they came to the Brian Boru pub, and the Forester being a thirsty soul said he was off for a drink, and as O'Casey was a teetotaler at the time, the other said, "Here's the sash," as he took it off and threw it across O'Casey's shoulder. O'Casey, thus decked out, marched on to the cemetery with the procession, and when it was over he took off the green sash and concealed it under his coat. The Lodge called him to account for his marching in a rebel procession to a papist's churchyard and summoned him before them, and he being always of a pugnacious disposition read up about Parnell and defended him and his own action instead of apologising, and he got three years' expulsion from the Lodge and was stripped of all his Masonic trappings. On leaving the hall after the sentence, he told them all they might "go to Hell," and went out and joined the Gaelic League, learned Irish, and became a Nationalist there and then.

(I heard from Kavanagh afterwards that all his people save his mother disowned him after that, but she lived with him on Gardiner Street till she died. The Orangeman in O'Casey's play of *The Shadow of a Guman* lived in rooms in the same house, as well as others of the characters introduced.)

O'Casey thinks Father O'Leary by far the best Irish writer of all. Douglas Hyde is a good translator, but a very misleading Irish writer. Paddy O'Conaire is out by himself as a writer; in Gaelic he has imagination and power as a writer, and is not afraid of Zola-like realism at times. His writings when translated become but poor stuff. O'Casey thinks Yeats has humour.

"Well, if he has, he shows very little of it," chipped in Dolan.

"*The Countess Cathleen* has glimpses of humour here and there. Humour is not, as a rule, of service to a poet." O'Casey saw *Blight* and liked it. . . .

Dolan spoke of Terence MacSwiney's play as but poor stuff. I said I thought it effective when McCormick played the role of the hero, and Dolan said, "Mac made one fatal mistake in the part; he occasionally played for applause, and thus became self-conscious."

On hearing this, O'Casey said, "Sure, we all play for applause in life, from Jim Larkin down."

O'Casey had never read MacSwiney's "Thoughts on Freedom." "Freedom is a word with many meanings to many people, who all are right in their way. Such books, therefore, don't interest me." . . .

O'Casey in profile and build at first glance very much resembles Mr. Millington, who once was Secretary at the Abbey. He has strong bird-like eyes, and a sharp thin face. He speaks interestingly and well.

Saturday, July 21. In the evening I had a chat with Dolan, who showed me a letter he just had from O'Casey about his re-written play *The Crimson in the Tricolour*, which he had forwarded on to Robinson. As originally written, Dolan found it impossible. The first scene was outside a convent with people spouting socialism for no earthly reason. Dolan suggested if he wanted his characters to spout such stuff, the bar of a pub would be the most likely setting. O'Casey has acted on his suggestions and made one of his scenes take place in a pub. The play originally seemed written to get off a lot of good things he had to say, without any sense of characterisation or construction. Dolan told him to take *The Whiteheaded Boy* as an example of how a play is built up in interest from the rise of the curtain. "Always keep the interest on the move," was his advice. O'Casey takes kindly to advice.

Tuesday, August 7. After *The Shadow of a Gunman*, I walked home with Dudley Digges and saw him into a tram at Lansdowne Road. He went down to meet Sean O'Casey at the Abbey, and had a chat with him about his play, as to the advisability of turning it into a one-actor piece for the States. O'Casey said, "You'll have to do so yourself as I am too lazy to do so."

Friday, August 17. . . . I was speaking to Sean O'Casey who doesn't like Murray's plays because they take too much out of him. Both *Birthright* and *Maurice Harte* distressed him very much in witnessing. He likes his plays with brightness intermingled with sadness. The comedy of life appeals to him most. He once read *Tess* by Thomas Hardy and stayed awake crying all night after it. It had a surprising effect on him though he is not a sentimental fellow in reality; Murray's play has the same effect. O'Casey loves Shaw's work because in the very kernel of tragedy he can introduce something to make one laugh its sting away. Murray never does this; his tragedy is ever unrelieved.

Monday, September 10. . . . Sean O'Casey was behind me, and I joined him after Yeats's play and had a chat with him between whiles. He told me he had been raided several times lately. Last week he was awakened out of his sleep with hands pulling the sheet off him, and a light full in his eyes, and three revolvers pointed out. He was hauled out of bed and roughly handled, as they queried his name, etc. He knew of a young fellow, a member of the I.R.A., who was on the run, being taken in the middle of the night by C.I.D. men and brought out towards Finglas and brutally beaten with the butt end of their revolvers, and then told to run for his life while they fired revolver shots after him, taking bits off his ears, etc., and catching up on him again renewed their beating. Next day O'Casey saw the chap and could hardly recognise him, so battered and bruised was he. Such brutality demoralises a country. Flogging demoralises, but does not correct. . . .

O'Casey thinks Casey has put a lot of human nature into his plays. The opening of *The Suburban Groove* is a little slow, but the love of "Dick" for "Una" becomes almost tragic at the end of Act II. Truly the Abbey dramatists try to put nature on the stage, and the players do all they know to interpret it.[131]

4
1924

The most publicized cultural event of the year was the Tailteann Games which took place in Dublin in August. The games were a mini-Hibernian version of the Olympic Games and featured not only athletic but also various intellectual contests—among them chess matches and competitions for the best poem,[1] the best book, and the best play.

The play competition was adjudicated by J. B. Fagan and Lennox Robinson, and this was their judgment:

> We are grateful for the honour Aonach Tailteann conferred on us when they asked us to adjudicate in the Dramatic Section, but, indeed, our task has been a difficult one, for it is no easy matter to compare one-act with three-act plays, historical plays with farces, verse plays with prose plays. But almost without hesitation we quickly agreed on the play which merited the first prize, and award it to Mr. Kenneth Sarr for his one-act tragedy—*The Passing*. It is a little work of remarkable quality, and one of the judges is not afraid to call it "a little masterpiece." Mr. Sarr submitted another one-act play, not as good, but also possessing high qualities, and his future is one we shall watch with interest.
>
> The second prize was less easy to award, and we hesitated for some time between a play of startling strangeness by Lord Dunsany, called *Lord Adrian*, and a play by Mr. T. C. Murray called *Autumn Fire*. But, weighing things carefully, it seemed to us that Lord Dunsany's play wasted time in its earlier acts, and that the attention of the audience was likely to be dissipated over people and incidents which later on would be found to have little to do with the real subject of the play; Mr. Murray's construction, on the other hand, was almost faultless—the play's chief failing, perhaps, is its tendency to be a little verbose—but the play marches on without a deviation, it never changes its mind as to what it wants to interest you in, and we finally decided that it better deserved the prize than *Lord Adrian*. But we want to put on record our high appreciation of Lord Dunsany's play. We place it third.
>
> There were other plays sent in for competition which we could not award prizes to, but which we desire to commend.
>
> We mention them now—not necessarily in order of merit.
>
> We praise Mr. Bernard McCarthy for his three-act comedy, *The Rising Generation*, and Mr. Brennan and the late Mr. Seumas O'Kelly for their one-act comedies, *The Young Man from Rathmines* and *Meadowsweet*; we praise Mr. Nally for his grim play, *The Spancel of Death*—his treatment falls a little short of his great subject—and Mr. F. Jay for his fine historical play. *The House of Lynch*. Indeed, few of the plays submitted were entirely devoid of merit or without some interest.[2]

Some of these plays, such as *Meadowsweet* and *The Young Man from Rathmines*, had been earlier produced; some, such as *The Spancel of Death* and *The House of Lynch*, were hardly to be heard of again; and some, such as *The Passing* and *Autumn Fire*, were to contribute to the remarkable Abbey Theatre season of 1924.

The Tailteann Games promoted musical drama also, and one of the side-events of the week was a series of Irish operas staged at the Theatre Royal, the most interesting of which was a new work, *Shaun the Post* by Harold R. White and R. J. Hughes.

No doubt the games were basically a public relations stunt, but, despite the heavy air of Irish self-congratulation, they were quite successful. However, they certainly also represented a desire of the new Irish Free State to indicate to the world that a condition of stability had been established, and that Ireland was now capable of taking its place among the nations of the world. And finally, although a bit portentous and pompous and chauvinistic, the games did invest the arts with a certain priority; and it is, perhaps, a pity that they were not to be continued.

• • •

In 1924, Yeats, Lady Gregory, and Robinson continued their efforts to place the affairs of the Abbey Theatre on a stable basis, by securing from some place a grant or subsidy. Without going into the very involved politicking of the matter, we may note that much effort was directed toward securing a grant of £5000 from the Carnegie United Kingdom Trust. The Carnegie Trust had, of course, contributed vast funds to the founding of public libraries, and the Trust's Irish Advisory Board had among its members AE, Lady Gregory, and Richard Irvine Best, as well as Lennox Robinson acting as secretary. However, the minutes of 19 November show that the trustees refused the recommendation of the Irish Advisory Board that £5000 be granted to the Abbey, and so the way was now open for the theater to apply directly to the Free State government.

Among the people unconnected with the Abbey, Ralph Brereton-Barry made one of the most thoughtful and prophetic analyses about the future of the theatre in Ireland. In the course of a long article in the *Irish Statesman*, he wrote:

> At the present time, the development of Irish drama is confined within the four walls of the Abbey Theatre. In the enthusiasm of the Directors and in the devotion and ability of a small band of ill-paid players all our hopes must rest. These qualities have been, in the past, so generously displayed that there may be a tendency to place undue reliance upon them in the future. Again, the courageous ingenuity of the Abbey scenic artist may serve to blind us to the limited resources at his disposal. Particularly during the past year, the fortunate discovery of a dramatic genius has

made us forgetful of the defects of a theatre which housed Juno and her Paycock. The truth remains that the Abbey Theatre is a small, draughty, erstwhile morgue, with scenic resources which would break the heart of any ordinary stage-manager, with financial resources inadequate to reward any competent actor or actress. The danger of such a situation is obvious. Actors and actresses, however patriotic and however devoted to their art, must live. Irresistibly, they are drawn to the market where the talents they have to sell command the highest figure. Such a market is to be found in America and, in a lesser degree, in England. These desertions from the Abbey are usually undertaken reluctantly, since no actor with any faith in his calling would willingly leave the Irish theatre to figure in those grotesque travesties of his country, which are so popular among the English and Americans. If the present glaring disproportion of salary were, to some extent, removed, the artistic faith of the players could be relied on to do the rest. . . . This, then, is the first argument in favour of State aid. It would keep our theatrical wild geese at home.[3]

After arguing that one of the duties of a National Theatre, which was ill done at present, was to present classical Irish comedies by such writers as Congreve, Sheridan, Goldsmith, Wilde, and Shaw, Brereton-Barry went on to say:

The second duty of a National Theatre, the production of contemporary work, is, at present, the main function of the Abbey Theatre. This, on the whole, it does well. All the gold in the coffers of the most prosperous state could scarcely have improved the production of the O'Casey plays. But, here again, the theatre is at present necessarily limited in its scope. O'Casey chose as his subject a phase of Dublin life which could be faithfully represented at the Abbey; if he had happened to direct his attention to "higher" social circles than those in which Juno and the Paycock moved, he would have found just as abundant a field for his qualities of irony and pity, but it is unlikely that his play would have been staged at the Abbey Theatre. In a National Theatre, freed from box-office pre-occupations, our actors and actresses could be so trained, the scope of the scenery so extended, that a new Irish drama might reflect every aspect of our National life.[4]

Brereton-Barry then made two warnings. First:

If the price of State aid be to submit to Government restrictions, Government censorships, Government direction, it is a price that should not be paid. The experiences of England have demonstrated the absurdity of a Government censorship, giving power to those who, when judging a work of art, do not ask whether it is good or bad, beautiful or tawdry, true or a lie, but lose themselves in questions of morality and expediency, condemning beautiful things for reasons so irrelevant as to be almost intangible. . . . Perhaps the chief danger to be apprehended from our present rulers would be an over-insistence on one phase of theatrical progress—the development of a Gaelic drama—to the exclusion of all others.[5]

And second:

. . . a system which attempts to press genius into a certain mould, has its victories, the more dreadful because they are necessarily unrecorded. To anyone unacquainted with the work of the theatre, such an objection to a national theatre may seem fanciful and absurd; it is none the less real to those who know the conservatism of the stage against which, even in its unorganised form, every innovator has a hard struggle. At the present time—Mr. Yeats tells us—the actors of the Abbey Theatre must learn to walk as if they were in the habit of wearing the heavy boots of the countryman. This is a right and proper piece of technique for them to acquire, founded on the nature of many of the Abbey plays. Centuries hence, nimble-footed genius may be driven from our national theatre for refusing to submit to a meaningless formality, established by ancient custom and resting on a misunderstood text. Any school of acting that grows up in this country should be a school, where the pupils may often teach and the masters are always learning.[6]

None of these dangers—governmental pressure, emphasis on a basically Irish-speaking theatre, and the formulising of acting and writing—would the Abbey Theatre in the years ahead avoid.

Other dangers had already arrived. One commentator, possibly Brinsley MacNamara, voiced in the *Irish Statesman* a complaint that was to be increasingly heard:

That the psychology of the audiences at the Abbey Theatre has changed in some curious way, is very evident to anyone who attends the theatre from time to time. It is possible to go to humorous plays like *The Workhouse Ward* or *The Country Dressmaker* and be only mildly irritated by the loud bursts of laughter which interrupt the performances. But any discerning member of an Abbey audience is driven to murderous inclinations by the repeated bellows of stupid and prolonged mirth which punctuate plays like *The Shadow of a Gunman* and *Juno and the Paycock*. The habit of laughter seems to have seized the Abbey audiences, and even in the most poignant moments of Mr. O'Casey's plays, a meaningless titter will set your nerves on edge. A visit to the late performance of *The Gunman* sent one away with a very unfavourable impression of the increase of bovine merriment which spoiled every scene of the play. This brainless laughter sprang up continuously, and was so irritating that it became difficult to sit out the performance, despite the excellent acting and the great interest of the play.

. . . It is plain that something will have to be done at once, since our reputation as a sane and critical people (what is left of it) is rapidly vanishing in the eyes of strangers who visit Dublin and spend an evening at the Abbey Theatre.

A fair sprinkling of Americans are present nowadays at most performances at the Abbey, and it is very seldom that one does not hear them making pointed remarks about the indiscriminate and long drawn-out laughter which pervades even the most serious moments of the plays. It frequently happens that the more responsible members of the audience show their strong disapproval of the idiotic titterings, and cries of "Hush! Hush!" are often raised in all parts of the house.

It is a significant fact that the Abbey actors now speak on through the mirth, and no longer "wait for laughs," as is customary in theatres not cursed by such devastating merriment.[7]

Readers of a previous volume of this history may remember that Lennox Robinson actually once inserted a note in the programme in which he tried to dissuade excessive laughter. However, the actors themselves were not always guiltless, and sometimes attempted to get laughs by gagging or mugging. Even Sara Allgood would occasionally fall into these faults, and Maureen

Delany, despite her considerable talents, had a tendency that grew through the years to play broadly. Indeed, by 1937, George Jean Nathan was compelled to write:

> . . . the Abbey company is obviously unable to control its fundamentally talented but personally over-cocky actress, Maureen Delany, and to prevent her from indulging in an outrageous overplaying, winking, snorting, and mugging that wreck any serious play she is in.[8]

The tendency to provoke and to indulge in broad laughs, no matter how incongruous they might be, was to grow and grow, and not really to be significantly curbed until the Abbey opened its new theatre in 1966.

In a lecture given to the Oxford University Irish Society on 15 February, Lennox Robinson raised another point about the Abbey audience: who now constituted it?

> In reply to a question, Mr. Robinson was compelled to give the lamentable answer, that the patrons of the theatre consisted almost entirely of visitors to the city, and also that members of neither university seemed to take any interest.[9]

In the 1970s and early 1980s, it has become a common sight for bus-loads of tourists, many American, to be delivered to the Abbey a few minutes before curtain time. And criticisms have been voiced that such a high foreign proportion of the audience would not only have a deleterious effect upon the mass audience response to a performance, but would also help to determine the summer repertoire which would be composed of the best-known names, such as Synge, O'Casey, Behan, Friel, and Leonard. There is no simple answer to this question, and certainly no merely chauvinistic answer. Even though a theatre has a government subsidy, it must still sell tickets and fill seats—but one doubts that the answer, at least for a national theater, should be entirely economic either. At any rate, R. J. P. Mortished made some refutation of Robinson's charge, defined some continuing problems, and suggested some solutions:

> If Mr. Robinson gave such an answer, I submit that he was guilty of astonishing misapprehension and ingratitude. It is true that many members of the audience in the Abbey are visitors to the City, but most of them are brought there by Dublin residents who are faithful friends of the theatre. It may even be true—though I doubt it—that the majority of the occupants of the stalls are strangers. But I am very certain that the great majority of the occupants of the pit, who form the bulk of the house, are good Dublin folk, some of them with little money to spare, who attend the theatre with faithful regularity. . . .
>
> Having protested against the explanation of what is wrong with the Abbey attributed to Mr. Robinson, I should like to venture some suggestions for improvement. I agree that Dublin as a city ought to be able to support the Abbey by municipal help of some sort, but in a time which has seen a reduction of teachers' salaries, the complete neglect of secondary education, the closing down of the

College of Science, the cheese paring of old age pensions, and a general cutting out of all expenditure that does not give an immediate return of a kind comprehensible by a petty shopkeeper, it does not seem likely that the corporation will give any assistance, or that, if it wished to do so, the Ministry of Local Government would allow it.

I suggest, therefore, that any development must come from within the Abbey itself. Could not an effort be made now to remove the restriction which prevents the theatre from putting on plays by English authors? It is intolerable that one cannot see a Masefield and Galsworthy play simply because the Gaiety will not put one on and the Abbey may not. Even if this cannot be done, could not foreign-Continental plays be produced much more frequently? The fidelity of even the Abbey audience can be tried by too frequent a repetition of *The Rising of the Moon* or *The Shadow of a Gunman*. . . .

If stage plays are not sufficiently profitable, I suggest that they might be alternated with screen plays. . . . With the ordinary cinema, one has to endure reels of rubbish for the sake of the mere chance of a good play. . . . Occasional film weeks at the Abbey might help to refill a depleted treasury, and give the actors and audience a rest from too frequent repetitition of the ordinary plays. . . .

Finally, may I utter a prayer that some substitute be found for the atrocious gong? Its abrupt, cracked boom is so doleful that I am quite sure the audience on any night would gladly subscribe to a collection to pay for a substitute, if the management cannot afford to provide a mellow gong, an electric bell or even a bicycle bell or tin tray and wooden spoon.[10]

A writer in the Trinity College magazine, *T. C. D.*, supported Robinson's charge about the nature of the audience, and also supported the quality of the playing:

What strikes one most about the Abbey Theatre audience is the absence of Trinity men and women, and indeed the sparsity of the audience altogether. Nevertheless it is gratifying to note that the largest proportion of those present is drawn from among the most cultured residents and visitors of Dublin. We mention visitors especially because of the notable fact that the Irish theatre is better understood in any part of the world than in its native capital. That it is so poorly patronised must be because so many people have never paid it a first visit, for, those who once see the excellence of the acting and productions are sure to appreciate them. In the Abbey Theatre one is struck by the "evenness" of the cast, as compared to other theatres, where success depends entirely on some "star" or "super." The characters invariably answer to one's conception of the part they play, there is no deficiency or exaggeration of "make-up," and the simplicity and charm of every action cannot but please. The almost uncanny silence of the audience goes to show their appreciation of the fine acting.[11]

"Uncanny silence" or "bovine laughter"? Or both? It is difficult at this late date, we as historians have discovered, to establish truth, or even sometimes to define a fact; and perhaps all the conscientious historian can do is finally to cite contradictory evidence. So, as we have above cited some criticism of Abbey acting, perhaps we should cite Seumas O'Sullivan's estimation of what was, in the eyes of many intelligent observers, the finest company of Abbey players ever:

It is the best company by far the Abbey has ever had. Barry Fitzgerald, Arthur Shields, F. J. McCormick, M. J. Dolan, are four such actors as have never been brought together in our time on any stage. Of course, there have been individual actors, perhaps, better than they, but when they appeared they usually stood head and shoulders over a heavily disappointing company. . . . The Abbey Players that have gone had no one that could give us anything nearly approaching the exquisite delicacy of M. J. Dolan, the restrained yet ringing personality of Arthur Shields, the tragic power and versatility of F. J. McCormick, the rich comedy combined with interpretive insight of Barry Fitzgerald. The Abbey Players that have gone had one supreme artist amongst them, Sara Allgood, and she is still with us, but supported now by a troupe that supplements and completes her genius.[12] It is for this reason I am glad that Mr. Hubert Griffith, the dramatic critic of the *Observer*, invited over here by Mr. Lennox Robinson to see *Juno and the Paycock*, has been so enthusiastic in praise of the company. He saw with stranger's eyes. The acting of the Abbey Players, he says, "was the nearest thing to perfect I have ever seen in a theatre." I have been saying that for the past few months. . . . We, Dubliners, are so aesthetically constituted that we require a stranger, a foreigner, to tell us how good we are, what good things we have amongst us, before we feel quite comfortable when we dole out praise to one of our own.[13]

Praise, however, was amply due in 1924. The Abbey produced only four new full-length Irish plays in the year, but one was O'Casey's *Juno and the Paycock*, and another was Murray's strong *Autumn Fire*. In addition, Shiels and Lady Gregory contributed two long pieces that occasioned considerable interest; and there were four short pieces by Robinson, O'Casey, and Kenneth Sarr. Of the short pieces, O'Casey's *Nannie's Night Out* and Sarr's *The Passing* had some piquant similarities of theme and situation, and seem to the present writers two of the underrated one-acts of the modern Irish drama. With two plays by the Spaniard, G. Martinez Sierra, the Abbey mounted ten new productions in 1924; and, all in all, the year must be considered one of the most distinguished in the theatre's long history.

In October 1923, the Drama League had introduced the work of Gregorio Martinez Sierra to Dublin. Much of his work had a quiet, delicate and distinctly Roman Catholic atmosphere, and so was certainly appealing to middle-class Irish audiences. On 12 February, the Abbey staged his *The Two Shepherds*, which proved a pleasant, if not exciting evening. Frank J. Hugh O'Donnell's reaction was typical:

After seeing *The Two Shepherds* by Senor Martinez Sierra at the Abbey Theatre last night, I have finally decided never again to read a play immediately prior to its production. This work of his is so delicate, so fine, in its imagery, so subdued in motif that its atmosphere is entirely too elusive for stage representation. Somehow its intense moments when reading seem commonplace behind the footlights, and its extraordinary technique and subtle symbolism lose a great deal of their quality. . . .

Not that I can say anything against the acting—for this I can have nothing but the highest praise. The portrayal of Don Antonio by Mr. Michael J. Dolan was a triumph of subdued interpretation. You felt with him all the sincerity of his conviction, the tragedy of his suspension, the quiet suffering of too refined an intellect. So, too, could you feel the tragedy of Doña Paquita, his sister (tuned in delightful harmony by Miss Sara Allgood). . . .

With the exceation, perhaps, of the beginning of the second act, there was not a wrong note struck, and even then I do not blame the actors completely for the disharmony that stole in. It was a production which in its completeness was as satisfying as one could expect, and yet gave the impression that there was not sufficient body in it. And the fault lies in the play itself, not being, perhaps, as successful an acting as a reading piece.

Still, acting of this quality may not come our way again for a long time. It is different. It made you query and wonder. You realise that it has extraordinary qualities, that it has the atmosphere of indefiniteness, of swift beauty, of fragile conception. . . .

Of the play I will say that it is worthy of being the product of the creator of *The Kingdom of God* and *The Romantic Young Lady*. It has the greatness of one who, in his conceptions is always and above all a faithful Catholic and a true Christian.[14]

The Two Shepherds was a little short for a full evening and was played with *The Rising of the Moon*. A week later, on 19 February, *The Rising of the Moon* was replaced by Robinson's new one-act, *Never the Time and the Place*. Of it, the *Irish Times* remarked:

In this, Mr. Robinson measures his paces with other writers for the Abbey, who have made humorous use of lower-class life in Dublin. The scene is laid in the room of a "fortune-teller" somewhere in the centre part of Dublin. The "fortune-teller" is nothing more than a garrulous old match-maker, and a great deal of fun is extracted from her handling of her clients, and her own cynical chuckling over their gullibility. The dialogue is real Dublin talk, which always sounds so amusing when pieced together in a way in which Mr. Robinson shows himself as adept as those authors whose pieces in the same *genre* he has produced from time to time. . . .[15]

Nevertheless, the new piece was hardly another *Crabbed Youth and Age*, Robinson's little gem of 1922; and O'Donnell in the *Evening Herald* was quite dismissive:

It is a trifle, capricious, pleasant, perhaps I should say clever, because clever is a word that responds delightfully to varying inflections. But, withal, this play is dissatisfying, not that it is not "a little comedy"—vide programme—but that it was written by Mr. Lennox Robinson, who ranks among the distinguished of our dramatists. To such as he is, one looks for something new, something progressive, some new phase of construction. But his bag of tricks are old, though they are well disguised by crisp dialogue and excellent acting. He has got the defunct idea that a policeman on the stage is really funny, and that comicality, presented in police-like movements and police-like utterances, go to make good comedy.

To the majority of us to-day the policeman has lost all aspects of the comic. . . . The sketch, despite its ending in soliloquy, would probably be worth a good deal on the variety stage.[16]

On 3 March occurred one of the great theatrical events of the year—and, indeed, of any year on the Irish stage—the first production of O'Casey's masterly *Juno and the Paycock*. Even the caustic and critical Jacques was moved to say:

> There is much padding through the three acts. But making allowance for the author's thirst for dialogue with a dig in it, this play stands as one of the greatest things done by the Abbey players. It is more—it is a triumph of production. . . .
> This new play is a distinct advance and a courageous one. It provides entertainment for the many. Better still, it stimulates thought and exercises the intelligence.[17]

The *Times* noted that the Abbey was packed for the first night, and described the play like this:

> The title is nothing, and the story of the play is little more. It is called a tragedy, but it simply bursts its sides with comedy. Had it been described as a comedy, its tragedy would be no less terrible. Such was life in Dublin in the year of civil "war." Mr. O'Casey lived among the people he portrays, and he makes his audience live among them, too.
> There was not a weak spot in the acting. It probably attained the most level standard of good work that has been witnessed on the Abbey stage of late.[18]

Holloway, of course, was at the first night and was talking to D. C. Maher, the author of *Partition*, who said:

> "It is powerful and gripping and all that, but too damned gruesome; it gets you, but it is not pleasant."[19]

However, Holloway himself thought:

> The last act is intensely tragic and heart-rendingly real to those who passed through the terrible period of 1922. . . . The tremendous tragedy of Act III swept all before it, and made the doings on the stage real and thrilling in their intensity. The acting all round was of the highest quality, not one in the long cast being misplaced or for a moment out of the picture. . . . Sara Allgood as "Juno Boyle," with all the worries of trying to keep everything together was excellent, and in Act III she had great moments of heart-rending sorrow. . . .
> In Act III some in the pit were inclined at first to laugh at the tragedy that had entered into the "Boyle" family, but they soon lost their mirth and were gripped by the awful actuality of the incidents enacted so realistically and unassumingly before them. As I left the theatre, cries of "Author, Author!" were filling the air, and I suppose O'Casey had to bow his acknowledgment. He sat with a friend in the second row of the stalls with his cap on all the while, I noticed. He is a strange, odd fish, but a genius in his way.[20]

The theater was closed on Ash Wednesday, but the play became immediately popular. When Holloway attended the Saturday matinee, he heard

> that crowds were turned away last night, and that booking was complete for to-night. . . . James Stephens had to be accommodated with a chair last night, by the wish of Dolan. Lady Gregory was up and was astonished at the house.[21]

James Stephens, incidentally, wrote to thank Dolan for squeezing him into the theatre, and remarked:

I think everyone—the author, the actors, and the producer—is to be congratulated on that remarkable performance. It was the best acting I have ever seen at the Abbey, and I think better than could be shown anywhere in the world. It makes me young again to see such team work. My heartiest thanks to you and congratulations to you all.[22]

The play was continued for a second week, which was unusual in those days. On 28 April it was brought back for another two weeks, and has been so frequently revived ever since, that in 1963 Ernest Blythe noted that it was the second most frequently performed play ever done at the Abbey.

Although the reviews were generally glowing, they were not entirely free from censure. For instance, W. J. Lawrence wrote in the *Irish Statesman*:

I doff my hat to Mr. Sean O'Casey. He is the realisation of one of my longest cherished hopes. For many years past, practically ever since the opening of the Abbey, I have scanned the horizon anxiously for the looming of that new native dramatist whose powers would enable him to inflame the popular imagination. Synge, for all his transcendency, could not accomplish it: there was something in his chill austerity that repelled the man in the street. All sorts and conditions of writers have since been called to the task, but Mr. O'Casey alone has been chosen. His name has only been a few months before the public, and already it is one to conjure with. The spectacle of the Abbey crammed to the doors on the first week in Lent is eloquent of the fascinations of his curiously composite dramaturgy. He has been the means of showing us (unless, indeed, his unparalleled success is the mere swing of the pendulum) that what the great public hungers after is not poetic or historical drama, not even peasant drama, but the drama of palpitating city life. Democracy has at last become articulate on both sides of the curtain.

Years ago when the Abbey was in its crudely experimental stage, Senator Yeats, in one of those delightful little impromptus with which he used to favour us between the acts, expressed the opinion that the prevailing dramatic moulds had become outworn, and that we in Ireland would have to break them and fashion moulds nearer to the heart's desire. If he is as strong a believer now as he was then in the necessity to go back to first principles, he, as chief director of the Abbey, should be proud of the vogue of Mr. O'Casey's plays. For Mr. O'Casey is at once iconoclast and neo-Elizabethan. One cannot place his plays in any recognized category. Nothing in Polonius's breathless, jaw-breaking list applies; and he flouts all the precepts of Aristotle. He lures us into the theatre under the pretext of affording us hearty laughter, which, sooth to say, he most profusely provokes, and he sends us away with tears in our eyes and with the impression of direst tragedy lying heavy on our hearts. None but a neo-Elizabethan could accomplish this, since the secret of juxtaposing and harmonising the comic with the tragic, and thereby throwing the elements of terror and pathos into greater relief, has been lost to the English speaking stage for over a couple of centuries. Moreover, one-half of the fascination of Mr. O'Casey's work lies in its red-hot throbbing contemporaneity, and that too was a prime trait of Elizabethan drama. There are moments in his plays, such as the search of the Black-and-Tans in *The Shadow of a Gunman* and the haling to death of the crippled informer, Johnny Boyle, in *Juno and the Paycock*, so vivid in the light of recent experience that they transcend all theatricality and thrill me to the marrow like matters of personal suffering.

Mr. O'Casey will undoubtedly go far if he can only restrain his keen sense of the theatre and trust more fully to his powers of observation. At present he is apt to play a trifle too much to his audience. Wit he has in abundance, but occasionally his snappy dialogue degenerates into a sort of sublimated music-hall crosstalk. Truth to life is sacrificed for the sake of a cheap laugh. This is much to be deprecated, seeing that he has a Dickens-like eye for quaint characterisation, and has the capacity to make us see what he himself has so well observed. It is probably because of this excessive playing to the likings of his audience that we can not wholly believe in the existence of his "Captain" Jack Boyle in his last new play, despite the delights of his perennial Dogberryisms, as delivered with telling effect by Mr. Barry Fitzgerald. Though a lineal descendant of old Eccles in *Caste*, this hypocritical shirker is none the less a true type, and, if the machinery now and again creaks, it is not because of any falsity in the fundamental conception of the character, but in its extrinsicalities. With an exponent less dowered with the "ars celare artem" than Mr. Fitzgerald, the defects would have been more obvious, but Mr. Fitzgerald succeeded in infusing so much vitality into the heartless old wastrel as to make his perennial "nice derangement of epitaphs" plausible. But, for the matter of that, the acting in *Juno and the Paycock* was of a high, all-round standard of excellence. This may be largely attributed to the fact that since Mr. Michael J. Dolan's accension to managerial control there have been none of those flagrant examples of miscasting which formerly imperilled the success of many a new play. As for the rest, Miss Allgood rose to such fine heights of pathos in the harrowing last act that we would fain ask that the play should end with her agonised prayer to the virgin. This is the natural climax, a climax of rich nobility, leaving the echo in our hearts of the wish for peace on earth and good-will towards men. The drunken epilogue which follows is artistically indefensible, and cannot be characterised otherwise than a painful mistake. In a word, Mr. Sean O'Casey has something yet to learn; but, despite its blemishes, *Juno and the Paycock*, running as it does over the entire gamut of the emotions, is distinctly a play to be seen.[23]

Most modern playgoers and critics would disagree (as, indeed, did the author) with Lawrence about the final scene of *Juno*, and it is now generally felt that in context the final drunken antics of Boyle and Joxer are no longer broad fun but searing irony. Indeed, many of the original viewers felt the jolting shock of the final scene, which the traditional Lawrence had missed. For instance, Gabriel Fallon, who played Charlie Bentham in the original production, vividly described his initial reaction to the final act when he saw the dress rehearsal on the Sunday evening of 2 March:

As soon as I had finished my part of Bentham at the end of the second act I went down into the stalls and sat two seats behind the author. Here for the first time I had an opportunity of seeing something of the play from an objective point of view. I was stunned by the tragic quality of the third act which the magnificent playing of Sara Allgood made almost unbearable. But it was the blistering irony of the final scene which convinced me that this man sitting two seats in front of me was a dramatist of genius. . . .

The third act had been dominated by Allgood's tragic quality even though Barry Fitzgerald and F. J. McCormick were uproariously funny as Captain Boyle and Joxer. This was always so with Allgood in the part of Juno. She had the quality of pinning down preceding laughter to freezing point. When Juno returns from the doctor with Mary the author's simple directions are: "Mrs. Boyle enters; it is apparent from the serious look on her face that something has happened. She takes off her hat and coat without a word and puts them by. She then sits down near the fire, and there is a few moments pause." That is all. Yet Sara Allgood's entrance in this scene will never be forgotten by those who saw it. Not a word was spoken: she did not even sigh: her movements were few and simply confined to the author's directions. She seemed to have shrunken from the Juno we saw in Acts 1 and 2 as if reduced by the catalytic effect of her inner consciousness.

We watched the act move on, the furniture removers come and go, the ominous entry of the I.R.A. men, the dragging of Johnny to summary execution, the stilted scene between Jerry Devine and Mary Boyle, and then as with the ensnaring slow impetus of a ninth great wave Allgood's tragic genius rose to an unforgettable climax and drowned the stage in sorrow. Here surely was the very butt and sea-mark of tragedy! But suddenly the curtain rises again: are Fitzgerald and McCormick fooling, letting off steam after the strain of rehearsal? Nothing of the kind; for we in the stalls are suddenly made to freeze in our seats as a note beyond tragedy, a blistering flannel-mouthed irony sears its maudlin way across the stage and slowly drops an exhausted curtain on a world disintegrating in "chassis."

I sat there stunned. So, indeed, so far as I could see, did Robinson, Yeats and Lady Gregory. Then Yeats ventured an opinion. He said that the play, particularly in its final scene, reminded him of a Dostoievsky novel. Lady Gregory turned to him and said: "You know, Willie, you never read a novel by Dostoievsky." And promised to amend this deficiency by sending him a copy of *The Idiot.* I turned to O'Casey and found I could only say to him: "Magnificent, Sean, magnificent." Then we all quietly went home.[24]

Fallon's account was published in 1965, and, as some of his facts are demonstrably wrong, one might a bit distrust his memory. According to her journal entry for 2 March, Lady Gregory was not in Dublin, but in Coole Park where she had apparently been for the previous week.[25] Also, as far as is ascertainable from the various extracts published from her journals, Lady Gregory did not see the play until 8 March. And, as she mentioned in her journal entry for that date, neither did Yeats see it before then. As Lady Gregory wrote:

In the evening to the Abbey with W. B. Yeats, *Juno and the Paycock* (Sean O'Casey's)—a long queue at the door, the theatre crowded, many turned away, so it will be run on next week. A wonderful and terrible play of futility, of irony, humour, tragedy. When I went round to the Green-room I saw Casey and had a little talk with him. He is very happy. . . .

And he said, "I owe a great deal to you and Mr. Yeats and Mr. Robinson, but to you above all. You gave me encouragement. And it was you who said to me upstairs in the office—I could show you the very spot where you stood—"Mr. Casey, your gift is characterisation." And so I threw over my theories and worked at characters and this is the result."

Yeats hadn't seen the play before, and thought it very fine, reminding him of Tolstoi. He said when he talked of the imperfect first play, "Casey was bad in writing of the vices of the rich which he knows nothing about, but he thoroughly understands the vices of the poor."[26] But that full house, the packed pit and gallery, the fine play, the call of the Mother for the putting away of hatred, made me say to Yeats, "This is one of the evenings at the Abbey that makes me glad to have been born."[27]

And that remark of Lady Gregory can well serve as the last word on *Juno and the Paycock*.

The Abbey's next new piece was to be Lady Gregory's three-act passion play, *The Story Brought by Brigit.* On 25 March, Robinson wrote her that

> the company read the passion play yesterday. They were all justly impressed by it and think it will be liked. . . . The Christ is still unfilled. I want to speak about it to W. B. to-night. I suggest Keating the artist who looks rather Christ-like (has a beard) but I am not sure if his voice is good enough.[28] . . . I think your play better every time I read it. I saw George Shiels in Antrim. He had just been reading *The Old Woman Remembers* and said, "It's the greatest thing Lady Gregory has done." I wish you knew him, he is very nice and so gentle and patient though almost entirely confined to a little room. He said, "If you get a State Theatre make me doorman. I wouldn't want much salary."[29]

On 6 April, Lady Gregory journeyed to Dublin for the last rehearsal of *Brigit*, but learned that the production had been put off until Holy Week.

> I was vexed at first, but don't think my time was wasted as I decided on dresses from our own wardrobe, only four Roman soldiers' suits to be hired, and I saw rehearsals of the first and second acts. Both seemed to go well, but I had to make some slight alterations. And I heard of a Trinity College lad Lyle Donaghy who might fill the great part, and decided on him as he has a voice with some beauty in it and an impassive face that gives a sort of remote dignity.[30]

On Sunday, 13 April, Lady Gregory saw a couple of rehearsals of *Brigit*, and thought May Craig was inadequate as the Egyptian Nurse and Sara Allgood was spoiling the songs "by musical twists and turns, not her old simple style."[31] On Monday, 14 April, Lady Gregory rehearsed again, and hoped for the best.

The play opened on Tuesday night, 15 April, and Lady Gregory was well pleased:

> . . . a beautiful performance and received with reverence by the audience; no coughing or laughing, good applause at the end. I was near Jack Yeats, he liked it all through; the Christ especially pleased him, and the last Act. He came with me to the greenroom between second and third Acts. The players seemed content, W. B. Y. a little discontented, lack of the apron, which L. R. had put on, and the players had remonstrated against, they said because it made them miss their cues, but he says because it is shaky (which it certainly is) to walk on. The Craig screens made a fine background, and the yew branches I had brought from Coole were strewn. The actors made a beautiful picture in various groups. All but the soldiers' dress we had got out of the wardrobe, rummaging through layers from old plays. It seemed wonderful how smoothly all went and easily, and I felt well content and at peace. I had hidden from the audience but when I thought all had gone I found L. R. in the hall, he came holding out his hands and saying "Thank you, thank you" with real emotion, and said how beautiful he thought it. Then McGreevy spoke in the same way, he had been crying through the last Act.
>
> All liked the Christ, so young, fairhaired, with great dignity and speaking his few lines so well.[32]

On the following night, AE told Lady Gregory that he thought the play "most moving and beautiful," and Douglas Hyde told her, "I like it twenty times better than anything you have ever done."[33]

The Press was generally respectful, but considerably less enthusiastic. For instance, the *Irish Times* wrote:

> Lady Gregory has put the story of the Passion into Kiltartan, and under the title *The Story Brought by Brigit*, her new Passion Play was given its first production at the Abbey Theatre, Dublin, last night. The play, which is in three acts, was very carefully produced, and, with very simple scenery, the staging was often very beautiful, in conjunction with the costumes and the grouping of the players in striking *tableaux*.
>
> A note by Lady Gregory is printed in the programme. It says:—"Our tradition and that of Gaelic Scotland speak of St. Brigit as 'the foster-monther of Christ,' and I have been told by poor women of Slieve Echtge that she succoured both the Blessed Mother and Child when they were brought here by a Heavenly messenger for safety in Herod's time, and that she 'kept an account of every drip of blood He lost through His lifetime.' So it is not going very far from that tradition to suppose she may have been present at the end of his life, as at the beginning, and have told the story in her own way, as she had seen it in the body or in vision."
>
> In other words, Lady Gregory has found an excuse for giving a Kiltartan Irish flavour to the narration of the Passion story in dramatic form. Some people like that flavour; others do not. It is an essential element of Lady Gregory's version, and appreciation of this new Passion Play will vary with the taste for the manner of writing to which Lady Gregory adheres. Those with whom it agrees will probably find *The Story Brought by Brigit* a very moving and wonderful dramatic narration; and, indeed, there were moments in the production last night when no one could fail to be impressed.[34]

The *Independent* liked some of the acting and admired Eric Gorman's make-up as Judas Iscariot, but nevertheless added:

> There are considerable difficulties in making such a work convincing, and this was probably realised at times by last night's audience. Where an effort is made to treat a subject of the kind in a stage production, small things may grate on the ear, or seem to the eye a little at variance with pre-conceived ideas. It may, however, be said that the performance was followed with the deepest interest and attention, and in this respect the audience paid high tribute to the work of the authoress.[35]

Of course, in Ireland one could hardly hiss a Passion Play, and the subject seemed rather to cow the critics. For instance, Frank J. Hugh O'Donnell rather wafflingly wrote:

> It took one quite a considerable time to arrange one's mind to accept the idea of Jews talking in the idiom peculiar to the Gaeltacht districts, and even when the obstacle is overcome it took a further period to accept the treatment of so holy a theme in ordinary play form. But as progress is made you realise that this is a very human, very sympathetic, and very reverent conception. . . .
>
> The smallness of the Abbey stage did great injustice to the production. You felt it needed space, volume, larger mounting, a place in keeping with the immensity of

> the story. Everything seemed cramped and confined last night; the mob occasionally were pushed to the very footlights. Given a large theatre, a bigger and better mob, more detail and lighting, the play would be one that would live in the mind for ever.
>
> Despite the quality of its writing, the play gave no opportunities for great acting, and the acting was not up to its usual standard. The young man who played the part of Christ spoke his lines euphoniously, but his whole appearance had not in it the virility of personality which one associates with Our Lord.[36]

Perhaps the most critical notice was that farthest from home, in the *Manchester Guardian Weekly*:

> *The Story Brought by Brigit* does not seem to show her [Lady Gregory] at her very admirable best. Its machinery is Irish in particular, but . . . we feel, without any disrespect, that the theme is a little outside Lady Gregory's natural range. Her grasp of character is less profound than Synge's, but her contact with character is more immediate, less perplexed, often with great advantage to her comedy. Her poetic imagination, again, is far less fertile than Mr. Yeats's, but her poetic invention, on the other hand, is often far more ingenious than his, and consequently more responsive to her dramatic needs. Her dramatic purpose is far more superficial than theirs, but her dramatic touch is more assured. . . . A theme like that of the present play does demand ampler treatment than Lady Gregory gives it before it will yield new beauty. . . . But the inherent grandeur of the story is not here enriched, nor do its associations seem to affect us freshly in their new setting. Lady Gregory's hold upon her subject seems not to be very firm, so that her idiomatic speech, which is so effective when she is happy in her creation, becomes almost suspect as we read:
>
> Silas: Stop a minute.
>
> Judas (*Going on*): There is hurry on me.
>
> Or,
>
> First Woman: By treachery. The story is the breaking of my heart to me.
>
> The dramatist seems to be noting her speech from the outside, as she is noting her story, whereas she has so often shown us that in her more fortunate moods she can create speech and story together from within an organic whole.[37]

AE, however, writing in the *Irish Statesman*, noted that the Biblical words, no matter how beautiful, had tended "to lose their power of enchanting us through familiarity," and so defended Lady Gregory's Kiltartanizing. But he also made a couple of small, telling criticisms:

> The third act would gain, I think, if the women who keened changed the tune and made the second keening more intense than the first. As it was, the effect of the prolonged keening almost on one note was somewhat monotonous, and delayed the action without deepening the sense of tragedy. The alternative would be to shorten the keening. . . . I think also that the songs, which have a verbal beauty of their own, should be sung so that their words should be heard clearly. When the song is crooned so that the words are not audible there is an intelligent gap in the play for the listener, and no words should be written that are not intended to be heard.[38]

Perhaps the tersest summation of the rather ambivalant responses to Lady Gregory's Passion Play was O'Casey's. As Holloway reported:

At the end of *The Story Brought by Brigit*, I said to O'Casey who sat next to me, "It was very impressive!" And he replied, "It was almost too impressive for me!"[39]

The Abbey's next new play was George Shiels' three-act comedy *The Retrievers*, which was first produced on 12 May. On 8 February, Shiels had written to Lady Gregory about the play:

As I had heard nothing from the Abbey about my last play, your approval is almost too good to be true. I had this play finished some months since, but rewrote it again after reading Professor Baker's volume.[40] Your remarks on it give me new courage and tenacity. I just feel like one who has done a long day's work as well as he could do it and has got a good day's wages. The last act is, as you say, a bit mechanical, but it is so difficult to smooth out all the wrinkles and intricacy at the end.[41]

The Retrievers has not been published, but O'Donnell in the *Evening Herald* gave a detailed summary of its plot:

It was bound to come. Anyone who had the knowledge that Mr. George Shiels is one of our most successful writers of Wild West stories felt that sometime or another he would have to clothe his mind in dramatic form. Last night in *The Retrievers*, produced at the Abbey Theatre, he clicked the camera, and hey day! out came all his wild men and women, but dressed in Irish clothes. Irish accents, and, glory be, Irish wit.

I do not know of any writer to-day whose wit is so pungent, so satiric, so conducive to satisfied chuckling as Mr. Shiels'. He absolutely gleams and glitters and explodes with epigrams and loquacity. His people have the wisdom of philosophers and the roguery of hypocrites. They are human, endurable, provocative. And in this play he develops and expands them until they turn from burlesque into comedy, and finally, with the good nature of seventeenth century dramatists, he absolves their knavery and trickery and, full of plausible sentimentality, gives them a happy ending.

His plot is in itself complex in its productions, and in its facets. He gives us rogues and robbers, honest people and foolish Americans, "specials" and internees. He lumps them all into the kitchen of Sally Scullion, situate somewhere two hundred yards inside the Boundary, in the year 1922, and then begins to pull the strings. And he spits out invective and epigram until the game of thrust and parry becomes so fierce that you are inclined to forget that his people are what they are because of the glitter of what they say. And when John Dallas was robbed by somebody sometime before the play began, he said and he swore that he would have revenge, and, accordingly, disguised as a patriot who sang snatches of "Jackets Green," he set out to rob right and left and all round of him.

To make human nature balance Mr. Shiels obligingly got him to form an alliance with an unscrupulous "Special" named Mulgrew, whose atrocities went so far as to steal a cash box from under a corpse and to coolly carry away an eight-day clock on his back while it was still striking twelve! They were an outrageous couple whose names and whose actions terrorised the neighbourhood and despoiled households and cowsheds alike. But life being what it is and nobility being of world apportionment, to battle them came a quick-witted "Indian doctor" and an enigmatic lawyer.

The story of their victory is the story of the play. It was decisive, conclusive, and terrifyingly satisfying. It is interesting, full of action and good character-drawing but it is the telling of it that really matters. Mr. Shiels is a born story-teller, and *The Retrievers* is an achievement which shall be all the more appreciated as it matures.

The players last night made few errors, none in acting, some in the memorising of words and the inflections of accent. Miss Sara Allgood gave us Sally Scullion so finely drawn in its perceptions that the least over-stepping of it would lead to broad farce and blatancy. But every tremor of her hands, every expression of her half-witted delight and fear was so true that this doddering old woman became a great figure and a very human one. In swift comedy Mr. F. J. McCormick excels, and as Reub Snider, the American who loved Ireland before he saw it, he was excellent—excellent from the moment he appeared with the conventional umbrella and horn glasses until he became dreadfully drunk and disdainfully rhetorical.[42]

The other reviews were either mixed or critical. For instance. The *Irish Times* reported:

There was hardly a well-filled house at the Abbey Theatre last night to enjoy the first production of Mr. George Shiels' new comedy, *The Retrievers*, but the piece proved so heartily amusing, and went with such a rush of incident, that it may be expected to prove a popular success. Artistically, the play has the fault of hesitating between grim realism and farce. There were moments when the ugly conditions that have lasted too long in Ireland were borne in on us with shocking power; the man "on the run," the threatened tenant of disputed land, the sectarian rancour, terror and robbery, were represented, and the audience glimpsed something of what has happened in some strife-filled corners of our land; but the plot of the story was farcical, and several of the characters were frankly burlesque, so that realism dissovled in absurdity. None the less, the performance was one to enjoy, and to enjoy more than once. So packed were the three acts with action and vivid speech, that the play calls for a second seeing. . . .

The play was rich in smart dialogue, as when the gunman doctor said of a lawyer that he'd be on the Irish Woolsack yet, if he wasn't hanged; and when the Yankees were told of the state of Ireland, involved in "three sets of war," with everybody fighting for peace, but no two wanting the same kind of peace. There were passages of moving significance, as when the women could not listen to the old songs, and the singing of a country ballad in the robber's house was made to jar like blasphemy.

The acting was good, though only one actor spoke like an Ulsterman—Mr. Gabriel J. Fallon, as the "Special"—but Miss Allgood's playing had its usual distinction, makeng the rest commonplace in comparison. The obscurity of the plot—only half-way through the play did it become clear that all the pother rose from a dispute over a patch of land—hardly interfered with the rapt attention with which the house followed a Wild West farce in a border setting.[43]

Susan L. Mitchell in *The Irish Statesman* thought little of the plot or of the play:

It is less a play than a succession of amusing incidents and occasional witty dialogue. It is obviously intended to be political and to point a moral, but its construction is so poor that the moral is lost, and the audience waiting patiently through two acts for the point to become visible, at the third give themselves up to get what fun they can out of the show. There is fun and tragedy also, but in spite of the labours of Miss Allgood, who as Sally, the faithful servant, was perfect . . . and of Mr. Dolan, who very cleverly portrayed "The Walking Doctor." the play got no hold of this member of the audience.[44]

Holloway was equally critical of the plot:

> . . . the piece seemed very farfetched and unconvincing and almost incomprehensible for the first two acts. None of the characters seemed human beings, and many of them were overplayed. Sara Allgood has the strange part of an old half-witted woman—Sally Scullion—but her memory slipped her frequently in Act One, and she ceased to treat it seriously in the final act and consequently let the play down. . . . At times tonight one could easily imagine oneself in a lunatic asylum. On coming out O'Donnell asked to take me home by motor—MacNamara was in it. They both thought the comedy was very clever—too clever in fact and over the heads of the people, and I replied "that in action it was too complicated and unconvincing."[45]

When the piece was revived in November, Lady Gregory sat through part of the first act, and thought it "a thin play, but Sally wonderfully fine as the half-witted old servant."[46] The play was not often revived and never in recent years; and, without having discovered the manuscript, we might conclude that it was apparently not on a level with Shiels's better work. However, we might consider the remarkable tribute which the intelligent historian and editor P. S. O'Hegarty paid to the play. Although admitting it was "formless and undramatic," he added:

> . . . but what an exposure of anguish of mind, of fine thoughts and fine principles gone wrong and fouled until those to whom they are still clean cannot bear their mention. A queer play, a bewildering play, an unsteady and unstable play, which answers to no part of Ireland that ever was admitted. But is not the spiritual Ireland just like that now? Are we not going through anguish and disillusionment and doubt and materialism, fighting hard to recover stability, to see clearly into the future? We tore certain moral laws to pieces and they came back and rent us like seven toothed devils and tortured us, and we are like people recovering from a long madness, half conscious of some of the things we did in our madness and half afraid to be fully conscious of them. Mr. Shiels' play is not life in individual characters, but it is life in its totality, in its wildness, in its anguish, as we have been having it in Ireland, a true impression of our spiritual mood, rendered in a humourous grotesque instead of in the sardonic tragedy of Mr. O'Casey's method.[47]

There were no new pieces produced until after the Summer vacation. Then on 8 September, the theater produced what is undoubtedly T. C. Murray's finest, most lasting work, the three-act *Autumn Fire.* A draft of the play was finished in February, and, as was his custom, Murray asked several friends, such as Holloway and O'Donnell, over to hear him read it. As Murray wrote to O'Donnell:

> I'd like to have your views on it before sending it for production. I think it is fairly good stuff particularly in the third act. The other two amble along quietly enough, but there is sufficient in them to carry the argument through logically, and they have gleams of quiet comedy not unfrequently.[48]

Actually, Murray's description is a fair one of the final, published version of the play. In any event, he sent it along to the Abbey, and on 2 March Lady Gregory noted in her journal, "Last evening I read a three act of Murrays, rather heavy and machine made, but good enough to put on." Accordingly, the play was accepted, and put into rehearsal in late August. On 7 September, Murray wrote the following surprising note to John Burke:

> You have probably seen that *Autumn Fire* is to be produced on Monday evening next—you will hardly believe that it was merely be chance I learned the news through Joseph Holloway on Thursday. . . . That is a sample of the courtesy extended by the new management to the author. I saw Dolan this evening to arrange for . . . seeing the dress rehearsal. . . . What do you think if he didn't virtually shut me out. He pleaded that . . . they were to begin the dress rehearsal on Sunday noon, with the second act(!) and that he should much prefer that I should not be present. I was too annoyed to press the point. . . . I had looked forward for a long time to our seeing the show in rehearsal and I feel just rotten over everything. It appears to me that Dolan is a little nervy, having cast himself for a part for which everyone can see he is utterly unfitted. Owen Keegan is supposed to be a peasant Hercules and our friend falls a little short of that. That alone handicaps the play heavily but like the women in *Riders* we must only be satisfied.[49]

And to Holloway, Murray added that:

> He only knew of the production of *Spring* by seeing ad in the paper. The management had *Birthright* six months before its acceptance, and I told him that Dorothy Macardle told me they have a play of hers since the beginning of New Year and she has not yet heard from them. . . . Too many plays are turned down at the Abbey so that playwrights are disheartened and don't send in any and then the management cry out they have nothing to show their patrons.[50]

And on the first night, Holloway wrote:

> O'Casey, when I told him about Dolan's refusing Murray's request to be present at dress rehearsal, said, "Nothing would keep me out if I wanted to see a rehearsal of a play of mine!"[51]

There were a few cavils in the press, but by and large the reception of the play was overwhelmingly enthusiastic. Susan L. Mitchell, for instance, wrote in the *Irish Statesman*:

> Mr. T. C. Murray's latest play, *Autumn Fire*, performed at the Abbey Theatre this week, is a remarkable piece of work, and will, I think, deepen its effect on audiences as time goes on. It is stark, without trimming or extraneous matter of any kind, whether in incident, dialogue or character. The drama moves mainly between four persons. An elderly widower, Owen Keegan (played by Mr. M. J. Dolan), who feels no hint of age in himself, is attracted by and attracts the affection of a girl young enough to be his daughter. His son loves the same girl but she is unresponsive to his serious love, something light-hearted in the father appealing to her youth and gaiety, and she marries him. The dark figure in the drama is Keegan's daughter Ellen, who hates the marriage, distrusts the girl and believes that her father is

making himself ridiculous. Ellen is played as only Sara Allgood can play such a character, with a power elemental, ominous. The passions that move three of the protagonists gather in intensity as the play progresses, and in the last act Owen Keegan, the gay, confident husband, is caught in the net. Illness which came on him soon after his marriage did not break his spirit, but he was to be broken, and scarcely a more moving scene has been played on the Abbey stage than that where the young wife and her stepson, Michael, come face to face with their own hearts. . . . I have not seen Mr. Dolan in a part that brought out so fully his powers of subtle interpretation, as the tragedy shifts from Nancy and Michael bit by hit and is loaded on to him. The struggle between husband and father in him is given with complete understanding of the claims of both. I believe *Autumn Fire* will be one of the Abbey successes. It is big and vital and the actors will find in it more and more scope for their powers. The play disappoints me only in its ending. I am doubtful of it. It may mean that the optimism of Owen Keegan is not wholly shattered, and has found a new outlet, but this is not indicated, or it may mean nothing at all. In any case the lull after passion is too sudden for one act to contain it. The acting I would like to dwell on, but space forbids. It interested me mightily, and threw new light on the genius of the Abbey actors, on the subordinate characters as well as those who bore the brunt of the tragedy. In Miss Helen Cullen we welcome a confident and competent addition to their number.[52]

Jacques in the *Independent* had predictably some reservations:

In a sense, T. C. Murray's new play is a morality play. That is to say, the thing the author has to utter is told through the medium of the play itself—in the dramatic movement, in the situation arising out of the conflict of character and of will. Though the essential truth of the play is universal—the truth that it is dangerous for May to wed with September—and though the theme is vital, the general effect is not impressive. One serious fault is a lack of humour. And the tragic lugubriousness of some of the players with their variety of accents (not one of which intoned the sing-song of County Cork) did not help to relieve the sombre air of every scene.[53]

Nevertheless, even Jacques had high praise for Dolan's Owen Keegan:

It is not often that a single actor can redeem a play. It was so at the Abbey Theatre last night. Mr. Michael J. Dolan was the actor. He not only saved the play from being just ordinary. He actually made it feel like something extraordinary.[54]

And Holloway, although always a Murray partisan, was on this occasion distinctly bowled over:

Since I first saw Irving in the dream scene in *The Bells*, I have not been so thrilled by a scene as by Michael J. Dolan's playing of Owen Keegan in the final act of T. C. Murray's great play *Autumn Fire*. . . . The little theatre was crowded by a most attentive audience who were completely carried away by the superb playing of Dolan. . . . the agony of mind the old wreck of a man goes thro' in finding the mistake he had made was a wonderful if gruesome piece of acting that gripped one all the while. The stillness of the audience almost could be felt. Murray has written a very strong drama full of effective characterization, and, with the exception of Sara Allgood who hadn't her words sufficiently well off to give complete attention to her

> acting, the cast did remarkably well for a first night. The story of a father and son's love for pretty Nance Desmond—a part played with rare understanding by Eileen Crowe—interested from the first and never lost grip of the house. . . . Dolan's playing of old Owen Keegan . . . tonight marks the apex of the actor's career, and the word "great" can honestly and truly be applied to his art. . . . Murray came in with Bernard Duffy . . . and was all of a tremble during Act One. Sara Allgood's forgetfulness put his nerves on edge, and he moved restlessly in his seat when words failed her, and the prompter was heard. After Act One, he brightened up and went out after Act Two and came back talking to Andrew E. Malone (Byrne)—the highbrow critic of unacted drama—who told him he thought Miss Crowe too wooden. Murray didn't think so, though not a great admirer of her acting On the occasion he thought she had got into the skin of the character as he conceived it. Murray liked Dolan's make-up in Acts One and Two and thought his acting fine in Act Three. He forgot the Hercules of a man he conceived as Owen Keegan in witnessing Dolan's creation.[55]

Whatever Holloway's critical limitations, he was a sound critic of acting, and his opinion about Dolan's Owen Keegan has been borne out by everyone the present writers have spoken to who saw Dolan in the part. Indeed, Keegan was probably the highwater mark of Dolan's career, and the soundest testimony to his achievement is probably the judgment of his most talented colleague. As Holloway reported:

> McCormick told Murray that he thought Dolan's acting in the last scene of the first show was the best bit of acting he had ever seen at the Abbey. He could not attempt such a character with success.[56]

Murray's own final feelings on the first production he expressed in a letter to O'Donnell:

> Now that "the tumult and the shouting" of a first night has passed I feel that the play didn't get a fair chance. Dolan was magnificent particularly in the third act. It was a supremely good piece of work. Miss Crowe was quite excellent in the first two acts but less so in Act III. But Allgood was all bad all through! She spoiled the movement of the play whenever she appeared, and it is something of a miracle considering the way in which she tore the text to rags that the others were able to save the situation. Our friend Jacques—well, I'll not discuss that distinguished critic's notice.[57]

Murray has been little revived in recent years; and, despite his high seriousness and considerable craftsmanship, it seems little likely that he will be in the future. His other most popular plays, *Birthright* and *Maurice Harte*, were sound products of their own era, but do not really transcend it. In *Autumn Fire*, however, Murray did light on a theme so central and so traditional that it impelled masterpieces by Sophocles and Euripides. And the theme still worked for the almost exactly contemporaneous *Desire Under the Elms* by Eugene O'Neill and the *They Knew What They Wanted* by Sidney

Howard. It even made the reputation of a modern Irish play-wright, Eugene McCabe, when he used it as the basis of his *The King of the Castle* in 1964. Nevertheless, *Autumn Fire*, for all of its truth and thematic centrality and craftsmanship, now seems more a play for historians than for living playgoers. Part of the reason was suggested in a contemporary review in *The Voice of Labour*:

> The construction of the play is perfect, as is all of Mr. Murray's work for the "Abbey" stage. The momentum is gradual and painstaking. But there's the rub! Its dramatic effort is not unlike the leisured urbanity of the English novel. Had it a little of the terseness that characterises the modern short story it would have redeemed itself of insipidity and monotony. One feels the dramatist attempting the peak of fine moments; but his characters shirk the work and fail to "rise to the occasion."
>
> More notable was the absence of a few spells of sustained humour. There is, it is true, a golden five minutes in the second act, but the amateurish acting of Helen Cullen destroyed it. Somehow I always felt that Mr. Murray would, sooner or later, fail at rural drama and had hoped he would turn to some other facet of life. There is always the pit-fall of hack phraseology in drama such as he has written. If he should look somewhere else I feel he would succeed. He has the technique of drama at his fingers' ends and is talented with seeing life steadily and seeing it whole.[58]

Two qualifications might be added to this analysis. Murray's leisureliness in constructing his foundation might be forgiven, for he makes his audience strongly conscious of form, of pattern, of being inexorably led somewhere. However, in tragedy the erection of a form leads to the explosive destruction of what is formed; it does in *Oedipus Rex*, in *Medea*, even in *Desire under the Elms*. But in *Autumn Fire*, there was hardly a sin and so there is hardly an explosion—there is only a bleak and polite crumbling.

The point of *The Voice of Labour* about Murray's humourlessness might be more tellingly stated if more broadly phrased: what Murray lacks is any richness of style whatsoever. To open the text at any point is to find only terse, flat statement.[59] Here, for instance, is the beginning of Act One:

> ELLEN (*looking up and then rising*): O, is that you, Nance? Welcome home again.
> NANCE (*shaking hands*): Thanks, Ellen.
> ELLEN: A wonder now you didn't call to see us long ago? 'Tisn't a great way from the cottage up here.
> NANCE: Why, I'm home hardly a week, Ellen. I scarcely stirred out except to go to Mass o' Sunday.
> ELLEN: O, it's no matter. You're—looking nicely.
> NANCE: I'm delighted to be home again.
> ELLEN: You were tired o' the town?[60]

And on and on. However, to be fairer, one might consult the emotional last page and a half of the script—but one will still find only one-liners. Or here is Owen's last speech to Nance, which does indeed have some structural strength, but which collapses into under-statement, flatness, and banality:

OWEN (*very quietly, after a long pause*): No, Nance, I'll not blame you. . . . There's only myself to blame. Myself. I see it now—I see it. . . . "Fool," they all said, "he'll rue the day." I laughed at that. . . . "A couple o' years and she'll be dancing a jig with some fine young fellow on the grass of his grave." I laughed at that too. "Liars, every one o' them," I said. "Mad jealous they are because she's so high above their own bits o' women." And now. . . God, 'twas a pity . . . a pity- . . . Lave me to myself.[61]

Or to given an example that combines both the charges against Murray's emotional reticence and his stylistic flatness:

I—I only hinted-like to Uncle Morgan and you.
And—and Michael gone? (*Alarmed.*) You're—you're not well.
I—I don't like to be leaving you by yourself.[62]

Or this similar exchange at a crucial dramatic moment:

OWEN: Why did you turn from me?
(*Nance is silent.*)
OWEN: Why did you turn from me?
(*She gives no answer.*)
OWEN: I ask you again, why did you turn from me?
Nance (*timidly*): I—I didn't, Owen.
OWEN: More lies.
NANCE: I—I don't know myself. I cared for you nearly the same.
OWEN: Aye.[63]

It is this emotional reticence, which substitutes structure for power and which utterly understates emotion, that is Murray's final undoing. However, what seriousness and honesty and craft could accomplish, Murray did accomplish; and, when totting him up, it is necessary to define his limitations by the accomplishments of the greatest Irish plays.

On 29 September, the Abbey gave the first production of a new comedy in one act by O'Casey. On 7 June, O'Casey had begun a visit to Coole Park, and had mentioned to Lady Gregory that he was

writing a new short play, *Penelope's Lovers*, founded on the existence of a widow in the milkshop where he buys his eggs, who has three elderly admirers always hanging about, and who was once held up and robbed by a gunman.[64]

On 22 July, he was still calling the piece *Penelope's Lovers*, but apparently then submitted it to the Abbey under the title of *Irish Nannie Passes*. This shift of title would seem to mark a shift of emphasis from the comic part of the play dealing with Polly Pender and her decrepit swains, to the dramatic part dealing with the young spunker, Irish Nannie, who has just been released from Mountjoy. On 3 September, Lady Gregory wrote to O'Casey:

> I have just had the real pleasure of reading "Irish Nannie"—a fine and witty piece of ironical comedy—I look forward to seeing it on the stage. L. Robinson says he saved Nannie's life—and I applaud him—I should not easily have forgiven her death—Perhaps she may come into another play one day.[65]

In the original ending of the play, O'Casey had Nannie die onstage; in the revised and originally produced ending, she is carried back to Mountjoy after a fight with the police. Like the Polly Pender character, Nannie was taken from real life, and makes an appearance in O'Casey's autobiography, *Drums under the Window*, under the name of Mild Millie. Part of O'Casey's dissatisfaction with the play was probably that he felt the one-act form did not give sufficient scope for the development of the Nannie character, and he may have planned to use her in a longer, aborted piece called *The Red Lily.* Certainly, something of her character reappears, however, in the young whore of *Within the Gates.*

On Saturday, 27 September, Lady Gregory saw a rehearsal of the new piece, and thought it

> very ironical and amusing, but too short to be of much use, and I couldn't quite enjoy poor Sally rolling about "drunk and disorderly." I hope he will make a big play again, perhaps his Labour one.[66]

The play opened on Monday, 29 September,[67] and was played after Shaw's *Arms and the Man*. Holloway reported:

> I left to catch the eleven tram home, and O'Casey's play was in progress. . . . From the bit I saw, it seems very rambling, go-as-you-please dialogue, with little form or story, save the love episodes of three old codgers for the hand of "Mrs. Polly Pender," who keeps a dairy. "Nannie" of the title comes and goes through the piece, in an excited mad way, singing snatches of songs or shouting out wild words. . . . Sara Allgood was fantastic but unconvincing as "Nannie" as far as I saw. Fitzgerald, Dolan, and Fallon differentiated the roles of the old lovers of "Polly" effectively, and Maureen Delany made a popular "Polly." The little piece seemed weighted down with talk. . . . Certainly O'Casey has caught and noted down many Dublin expressions and embodied them in his plays. It is only when you hear them on the stage they ring familiar to the ear. O'Casey hasn't lost his power of strong character drawing, and his power of observation is as keen as ever. I shall be surprised if *Nannie's Night Out* proves as magnetic as either his *Guman* or *Juno.*[68]

The *Irish Times* gave the new piece quite a good review:

> The announcement of a new play by the author of the *Gunman* and *Juno and the Paycock* filled the Abbey Theatre, Dublin, in every part last night. Mr. O'Casey's new work is a one-act comedy of Dublin tenement life, or, rather, it is to be hoped, what was tenement life in the city. As a stage production *Nannie's Night Out* is not to be compared with the plays named above, but in some respects it surpasses the best in either.

"Nannie" is a poor unfortunate of the street, "out again, fresh as a daisy, and lookin' for trouble." Mad with methylated spirits, singing a wild song, smashing windows, beating the police, and finally striking terror into the "hold up" man, she is a type that Dublin used to know. Miss Sara Allgood makes a wonderful study of the outcast. She is seen in a new mood, and many, before the week is over, may consider it her best. She sends "across the footlights" the dread and the curiosity of the street when Nannie is "on the loose."

Apart from this fine character acting, the play is centred in the funny ways of the three "oul' fellas," each anxious to marry Polly Pender, who owns the Laburnum Dairy at the corner. These parts are well played by Messrs. Barry Fitzgerald, M. J. Dolan and Gabriel J. Fallon, and Mr. F. J. McCormick gives an excellent portrayal of an insistent street singer. An instant success is the couple of seconds' appearance of Miss Eileen Crowe as a customer who tricks Polly out of a shilling doll.

In spite of its comedy, the tragedy of tenement life dominates the little play, as it asserts itself in all of Mr. O'Casey's work. Nannie, herself, is a full expression of that tragedy, enforced again with the appearance of her little boy, half starved and half naked, but knowing all about the day's "runners." "God knows," says Polly, "it would be better for them to do something for poor things like him instead of tachin' them Irish," and the house applauded in decided approval of her comment. *Nannie's Night Out* excites thought—and pity—as well as laughter.[69]

In the *Stage*, W. J. Lawrence gave a thoughtful "mixed notice":

It takes a clever man to break all the chief rules of the theatrical game with impunity, and Mr. Sean O'Casey, a workingman dramatist, is undoubtedly a clever man. His two long tragi-comedies. *The Shadow of a Gunman* and *Juno and the Paycock*, have so inflamed the popular imagination that he has become the god of the Abbey audiences' idolatry. Confining himself almost wholly to studies of Dublin low-life deeps, he has hitherto "made good," despite his flouting of the conventions by a remarkable truth of characterisation, aided and abetted by a certain perky wit and an intense topicality. But the one-act form is ill-adapted to his leisurely methods of attack, and in *Nannie's Night Out* he falls between two stools. He makes attempt to combine an old-fashioned farce with episodic slices from slum life, with the result that the one element makes mocks and mows at the other. Even the very character whose painful idiosyncracy gives the title to the little play is extrinsic to the story, as it were an unmeaning refrain to the ballad. . . . Equally episodic and equally true to sordid actuality is Nannie's child, Robert, a waif of the streets, who earns his living by selling newspapers and giving tips. Added to this, there is a third character of the sort in a cynical, sharp-tongued ballad-singer. The misfortune is, however, that in giving atmosphere to the farce these delicate etchings only serve to reveal the machine-made nature of the thin theme discussed. Three old men, all laying absurd pretensions to the preservation of the vigour of youth, are suitors for the widow Pender's hand, and by their intense personal rivalry effectively nullify each other's chances. To tell a story of so little plausibility with tints of an intense actuality is only to accentuate its artificiality. Mr. O'Casey stands at the parting of the ways. He must elect to be either iconoclast or conventionalist: he cannot be both.

To say that to some extent the acting pleasurably obscured the weakness of the play is to say that the Abbey Players were on the top of their form. Miss Sara Allgood shirked none of the issues in her portrayal of Irish Nannie, and gave a vivid exposition of the horrors of that common Dublin vice, methylated-spirit drinking. In sharp contrast was the wholesome buxomness of Miss Maureen Delany as the much-besieged widow, a character excellently adapted to the broad methods of the actress who may be styled the Mrs. John Wood of the Irish stage. Mr. Barry

Fitzgerald . . . requires to be warned against a growing disposition to talk in his boots. Occasional inaudibility in so small a theatre as the Abbey is a grave offence. Remarkably effective as was Mr. F. J. McCormick's depiction of the grumbling ballad-singer, it was really nothing more than a repetition of the characteristics of his excellently conceived Joxer, in *Juno and the Paycock*. One can have too much of a good thing, and some distinction should have been made, especially as Mr. McCormick is lacking neither in versatility nor technical resource.[70]

The most ecstatic notice, however, was that of AE in the *Irish Statesman*:

Sean O'Casey is nothing if he is not immersed in his humanity. He is full of tragical humour. I feel all the time as I watched *Juno and the Paycock* or this new play that while he is laughing he is grieving. He is suffering because the humanity about him is cast into rich moulds. It is a heart-rending laughter. When that wild Nannie comes in drunk on methylated spirits, I laughed but I felt truly I ought to be sobbing. All through that drunken speech there shone out a submerged spirit. We felt that in other circumstances Nannie might be an enchanting creature, dazzling us with pure poetry and courage. I do not think Sean O'Casey writes these plays that we may laugh at them, but that we may know what genius is obscured and perverted by circumstance in these terrible underworlds he knows so well.[71]

And there is a good deal more of this in an even gushier vein. In *Inishfallen Fare Thee Well*, O'Casey tersely disposes of both the play and of AE's opinion:

. . . a one-act work called *Nannie's Night Out*, a play no one liked, except A.E., otherwise known as George Russell, who thought it O'Casey's best work; an opinion that didn't bother Sean, for he knew A.E. knew nothing about the drama, and felt it a little less.[72]

Still, AE and the *Irish Times* were hardly the only critics to admire the play. For instance, on 18 October, Bertha Buggy wrote, also in the *Irish Statesman*:

If I go to a tragedy or an ordinary "straight" drama I likewise adjust my mentality to the prompting of the play-bill. But at a play of Mr. O'Casey's I am a thing without anchor—to be tossed from one side to the other at his strange behests.

Take his latest play—*Nannie's Night Out*—a rocking, roaring comedy—Dublin accents; queer "characters": window-smashing; burlesque love-making. Our sides ache; we laugh; we roar; we gasp—and then—a sudden feeling of discomfort, a queer, stupid feeling as if we wanted to cry. . . . He brings us to his plays and then he heaves life at us, with its sharp corners and its untidy jumble of laughter and tears. . . . And the worst of it is, that if we go on allowing him to make us laugh and cry together in this hysterical manner, we may end by insisting that he is a genius.[73]

But O'Casey's own opinion of the play remained low from the first. In a letter to Lady Gregory, written sometime in October, he remarked:

Nannie's Night Out went well; Mr. Perrin tells me the "houses" were remarkably good: I don't like the play very much myself.[74]

And on 4 October, Holloway recorded:

> At the Abbey in the evening, the theatre was thronged, and motors lined up each side in the street. I was speaking to Carolan and Sean O'Casey in the tea room before the performance, and O'Casey told us that the "doll incident" occurred to him when in a shop. The real "Mrs. Polly" was at the performance on Monday and one of the "oul fellas." The man who goes about the city with the fur cap was the model for "Oul Jimmie"; he often presented the real "Mrs. Polly" with jewellery, but begged it back on seeing other candidates in the field for her hand. O'Casey doesn't much care for the farce himself, now that he sees it on the stage. . . . The sentiment of "it is better to feed half-starved little boys before teaching them Irish" was hissed last night, and won rounds of applause at the matinee.[75]

At any rate, despite the mingled hissing and applause given to the critical line about children learning Irish in the schools. *Nannie's Night Out* seems to have been received with considerably more approval than O'Casey's earlier one-act, *Kathleen Listens In.* However, the playwright himself was basically responsible for squelching this play and for keeping it for many years out of his canon. The reason, if we may speculate, was that he had grown in critical power, that he was well aware of the accomplishment of *Juno*, and that he was full of his plans for the even larger and more powerful play of *The Plough and the Stars*. In such company, *Nannie* must have seemed a regression indeed, and the form of a one-act play must have seemed a waste for such a vibrant character.

In consequence, both *Nannie* and *Kathleen* just disappeared, and, when in later years O'Casey was occasionally queried about them, his answer was that he had no copies and that both had been destroyed in the Abbey fire.[76] It is our opinion that the writer did himself a considerable injustice, and one of the present writers has elsewhere remarked:

> *Nannie* is of the same family as O'Casey's three great early dramas—the two-act *Shadow of a Gunman*, the three-act *Juno and the Paycock*, and the four-act *Plough and the Stars*. The one-act *Nannie* is the least of these plays, but it is cut from the same cloth. And, to this reader, within its narrower scope, it has the same excellences. . . . Nannie is one of the most demanding and exhausting and flamboyant parts that O'Casey has every written for an actress. To my mind, she must surely take her place next to Juno Boyle and the Bessie Burgess of O'Casey's most brilliant early plays. Directing the play merely confirmed for me the conclusion I had reached after reading the manuscript and preparing it for the printer: *Nannie's Night Out* is one of the superb one-act plays of the modern stage, and it must take a place next to the great one-acts of O'Casey's colleagues—Strindberg, Synge, and Shaw.[77]

And, although the writer of those remarks was a theatrically naive young person, he sees no reason after the passage of some thirty years to renege greatly on the statement. In any event, it can be said that Nannie, like Juno and Joxer, and like Fluther and Bessie, was ripped directly from reality. For, as Lady Gregory tellingly remarked:

> As I left the theatre with Perrin the street was rather crowded and we saw a girl being brought along by two policemen, one on each side. Her hair was flying and she looked young and defiant, was singing—the very song "Nannie" sings in Casey's *Nannie's Night Out*—"Mother of mine." A tragic sight, the reality of what had been put on the stage.[78]

On 3 November, the Abbey gave its first production of Martinez Sierra's *The Kingdom of God.* This play, with its very long cast, had first been introduced in a Drama League production in October 1923, when it was directed by Arthur Shields. The Abbey revival was directed by Dolan but included a number of the original cast in their same roles, most notably Eileen Crowe, who was again admired for her Sister Gracia.

In December, the Abbey produced two one-acts by Kenneth Sarr, which was the pen name of the barrister and novelist, Kenneth Reddin. The first play, *The Passing*, had taken the first prize in the Tailteann Games drama competition, winning out—unfairly in the view of the present writers—over T. C. Murray's *Autumn Fire.* Nevertheless, this "Tragedy in Vignette," which was only twelve minutes in the playing, does have distinct points of interest. It is, for instance, vaguely reminiscent of Fitzmaurice's *One Evening Gleam*; and it could almost be a sombre sequel to *Nannie's Night Out*, and Sarr's Nan or Nannie could be O'Casey's Nannie twenty years on. Of the new piece, the *Independent* wrote:

> With commendable brevity last night at the Abbey Theatre Mr. Kenneth Sarr reesented a subject that one contemplates with a shudder—viz., *The Passing*, a Dublin tragedy.
>
> In the tenement attic an unfortunate is dying, while her idiot son at the window gibbers and laughs over the night vices of the city. Before breathing her last she gets him to fling her guilty savings into the river, that he may ' 'starve and be clean." The tone is melodramatic (if that be any fault), and the spectacle of the woman dying without the presence even of a neighbour seems needlessly pessimistic. The audience was pleased with the dark little tragedy, which owed something to the realistic acting of Mr. Dolan and Miss Allgood.[79]

The *Irish Times* added a moral demurrer:

> The language is appropriate to the theme. The author in his work has attempted to show a repellent phase of life, and the more faithful he remains to his subject the most distasteful it necessarily must be.[80]

This view was held by some members of the audience. A solicitor remarked to Holloway that *The Passing*

> should never have been staged at the Abbey. Its subject is not for the stage. My daughter often comes to the Abbey and I should not like her to see such scenes. . . . The splendid acting made it all the more gruesomely distasteful. Such things may be, but the stage is not the place to mirror them. . . . I am a man of the world and not a priest that says so.[81]

Although this attitude foreshadows the imminent difficulties over *The Plough and the Stars*, neither of those belligerent guardians of public morality, Holloway and Lawrence, was offended. As Holloway wrote:

> The atmosphere was captured from the rise of the curtain in Kenneth Reddin's little tragedy. *The Passing*, and Dolan and Sara Allgood . . . just hit off the right note, save that it was hard to follow what they said. It was surprising how the piece gripped despite the text for the most part not being heard. I sat by Lawrence who failed to hear many important lines and told him the gist of them—having read the piece lately. The setting was just right, and the seagulls' call splendidly realised. Lawrence thought it a masterpiece in miniature! . . . I was speaking to Kenneth Reddin (who by the way, got a call at the end), and he said to Lawrence that, "I approved of it when I read it a long time ago!" In talking to Tom Moran afterwards, he thought the piece was trying to out-O'Casey O'Casey, and was astonished when I told him it was written long before O'Casey's plays were staged.[82]

In any event, when *The Passing* did finally make it to the stage, its strong qualities were immediately recognised—the fine use of lighting, the offstage sounds, and particularly the characterization and broken dialogue of the idiot son, Jimmie. Susan L. Mitchell, who was especially impressed with the short play, wrote:

> Its intense grip of life during those few minutes amazes one. . . . The drama is heightened by the sense that comes through the idiot's talk of brilliant starlight and the glitter of the city lamps on ice-bound streets outside the dark room; and when we hear the raw, lonely whistle of the gulls that to our strained emotions wrought upon by the poor Jimmie's terrors, seem beings come up from some elemental underworld cognisant of a human dissolution. It is an uncommon gift in a playwright upon what seems a mere dramatic fragment to hang such tremendous issues, and to do this without a wasted word, for the passing shapes itself in phrases singularly austere and sparse.[83]

Sarr's next one-act, *Old Mag*, subtitled "A Christmas Play in One Act," was first staged at the Abbey on 22 December. In it, P. J. Carolan, as the wandering sailor son, received quite his best notices, but the coincidences of the plot were generally felt a little too contrived. Nevertheless, the *Irish Times* thought it "a gripping little piece,"[84] and the *Independent* described the slight plot:

> "Old Mag" is a hawker seeling her wares off a barrow on the quay at Waterford. It is Christmas Eve and she mourns the absence of Terry, her sailor-son, "lost four years ago in the 'says' of America." Sailors on the spree jazz to and fro across the stage, with their girls. And then comes the son—drunk! There is talking, some warm words by Terry, some drunken sailor talk and—recognition. Mother knows son through the aid of a body-belt, and they go home together.
>
> It is an interesting little play that will be enjoyed. There is a wonderful bit of acting by P. J. Carolan, as the son. He brings a realism into his every word and lurch and gesture that lifts the piece high off the average, and changes what might have been dullness to brilliance. Maureen Delany in the title role was good, but it is really a one-man play.[85]

Valentine Vousden, an actor whose opinions are worthy of respect, remarked to Holloway that "He didn't like *Old Mag*. It wasn't in any way convincing, and Carolan played his drunk too much for laughs. He thinks Dolan's superb acting in *The Passing* made that little piece plausible and gripping."[86] In the *Stage*, W. J. Lawrence wrote:

> Coming so soon after the produciton of Mr. Kenneth Sarr's powerful little prize drama, *The Passing*, this bustling playlet from the same pen, though not without its good points, is a retrogression and a disappointment. At the vital moment there is a painful lack of definition in the evolution of the scheme, turning what should have been otherwise a well-rounded, sentimental piece into a guessing competition. It is a grave mistake to map out certain lines on which an emotion may be expected to run its course, and ultimately to deny the audience honest outlet for that emotion.
>
> . . . In no slightest way does the hawker indicate that she has recognised her son. Very remarkable, indeed, and by no means satisfactory, is the way in which the play ends. Placing Terry's kit on top of her barrow, she pleads fatigue, and persuades her son to wheel the barrow home for her. And so the audience departs marvelling why Mag should have delayed giving expression to her joy and deprived them of an opportunity for giving vent to a happy and most humanising emotion.
>
> . . . We trust that in future Mr. Sarr will solve his own problems and set us no more riddles.[87]

The author himself remarked to Holloway that he "did not think *Old* Mag worked out satisfactory in rehearsal."[88] "Kenneth Sarr" was not primarily a man of letters, but served for 22 years as a District Justice and died in 1967. His best writing is probably to be found in his novels, *Somewhere to the Sea* and *Another Shore*; nevertheless, *The Passing* might well bear revival.

In his article, "A Drama of Disillusionment," P. S. O'Hegarty attempted to characterize recent dramatic writing:

> The dramatists keep pace with the nation. In the old untroubled days we were angry with them because they did not show us a life in Ireland like the life that came to us out of foreign plays. They only showed us what was in us. Now that strange and terrible things have come to us, they show them to us. And that is one of the necessities for a cure. We are finding ourselves out—the first step on the road to sanity and health. The new drama is a drama of disillusionment—but of great promise.[89]

The new Abbey repertoire of 1924 would not entirely support O'Hegarty's claim, but *Juno*, *Nannie*, *Old Mag*, and *The Retrievers* did provide cumulatively persuasive support.

• • •

The Dublin Drama League gave during the year, three new public productions and one private "At-Home." Publicly, at the Abbey, Paul Claudel's *The Hostage* in a translation by Bryan Cooper was seen on 17 and 18 February; Luigi Pirandello's *Henry IV* was seen on 27 and 28 April and then revived on 10 August; and Jacinto Benavente's *The Passion Flower* was given on 9 and

10 November, and then revived on 7 and 8 December. Privately, at Yeats' home in Merrion Square, there was a production of the poet's Noh play, *At the Hawk's Well*, in March.[90]

The first night of the Claudel play apparently had a large but unreceptive audience. As the *Irish Times* reported:

> *The Hostage* cannot hope to rank among the best of the League's productions. It is a gloomy series of conversations, with little or no action until the last act, and when it does then come it seems to be somewhat unreal. . . .[91]

The April production of *Henry IV*, however, proved to be both popular and a personal triumph for Lennox Robinson as an actor. Physically, Robinson was unfitted for many parts. He was very tall, very thin, and had in private life a high, reedy voice and a Yeatsianly abstracted manner. However, in the handful of parts he played for the Drama League, under the *nom de theatre* of "Paul Ruttledge,"[92] he was extraordinarily fine; and his Henry IV is often coupled with Rutherford Mayne's Emperor Jones as one of the remarkable pieces of acting on the modern Irish stage. As the *Independent* reported:

> Paul Ruttledge . . . was a splending success. He inspired his audience with a full realisation of the events . . . and thrilled in his characterisation at many points.[93]

Or, as Mary Frances McHugh more fully wrote:

> When Lennox Robinson took the leading part in the Dublin Drama League production of *Henry IV*, Luigi Pirandello's three-act tragedy, on Sunday and Monday evenings in the Abbey Theatre, one was left with a burning feeling that the importance of the event was not sufficiently commemorated. Everybody who knew of Dublin and the Drama League should have been there, and all who had any passion for the drama and literature; and there should have been also artists, to leave us by pen or brush a record of that gaunt, pitiful, marvellous figure which dominated the play. . . .
>
> This was no mere mimetic act. Paul Ruttledge (to give Mr. Robinson his programme name) was bone and sinew of the acted play. His work, like the written play itself, had the thousand shades, the words in many tones, which when not intellectually realised seem obscurity. . . . That pitiful haggard face, showing everything from horror to age-old wisdom; those gestures and crouchings and lordly ways, and humilities and defiances; the shrinking back at last among his affrighted attendants "for ever"—some of these things in the playing of "Paul Ruttledge" needed to be caught to permanency by a magic pencil.[94]

Holloway thought Robinson's performance "a triumph"[95] and the *Evening Herald* "the greatest piece of acting that Abbey patrons have ever seen."[96]

During the year, Robinson also launched out as a drama critic, replacing St. John Ervine as the weekly dramatic correspondent for the London Sunday paper, the *Observer*, for which it is reported that he received the much needed stipend of £500 a year. His articles were considerably less outspoken than Ervine's and rather more general (and, according to Holloway, O'Casey did not think much of them).[97] However, the following reflections might be intruded here as both interesting in themselves and for the light they shed on Robinson as director of plays:

> I have seen my work so altered and disfigured, so coarsened and vulgarised, that I have left the theatre miserable and ashamed and praying to God that no one of my friends was watching the play and holding me responsible for every word that was uttered. Yet on some other occasion one of these same players might in a moment of inspiration have capped my best line with one so superlatively better that it would have been conceited and churlish not to have acknowledged its wit with laughter and thanks. Have I not grown weary of being praised for the brilliance of a remark in an old play of mine, weary of conscientiously explaining that the praise belonged to the actor, and not to me? Have I not gratefully adopted gags, printed them as part of the authentic text, and carefully taught them to every successive player of the part?
>
> The truth, of course, is that there is good gagging and bad gagging and only the insufferably conceited author, the author who believes in his own verbal inspiration, who refuses to smile at the witty gag that is perfectly in the character of the part.

And also:

> We argued the point for an hour, my friend and I. He is a fine actor, and he maintained . . . that great acting is great because it is intelligent acting. I, on the other hand, who am hardly an actor at all, declared that great acting, indeed that almost all merely "good" acting, is instinctive. We both admit and agree, of course, that other qualities are necessary besides either instinct or intelligence, qualities of voice, of movement, of all that goes to make up what is called technique; we only argued as to what was the driving force behind that technique and whether at the supreme moment of creation that technique was used consciously or unconsciously.
>
> It is one of those questions which can never be answered definitely and conclusively. . . . If we are perfectly frank, shall we not have to declare that the very few great actors we have known were not people of outstanding intelligence. . . . There is a quality of mind which we have learned to look for in an actor, but it is not that of a startlingly keen intelligence. The quality, I expect, that I have come to recognise as typical, is something very hard to put into words, but it makes an impression of something lying very ready and open, a body and mind ready and willing to be taken hold of and used, and sympathetically open to influences and forces coming upon them from outside themselves. . . . The "typical" actor so often reminds me of the typical medium—wayward, sensitive, receptive, generous beings. Indeed, their professions are not unlike, for do they not each put themselves at the disposal of another's personality and speak with a changed voice words that have not sprung spontaneously out of their own consciousness, and act and move as they would never do did they remain in possession of their own personality? . . . The question remains whether the actor becomes the perfect medium by an act of intelligence or by the blind force of instinct. I shall be quite emphatic in saying that, on occasion, he becomes the medium by instinct and by nothing else.[98]

After French and Italian plays, the Drama League turned to a now somewhat ignored modern Spanish master, Jacinto Benavente; and the *Irish Times* reported:

The Passion Flower last night proved to be, as to stagecraft, a wonderful demonstration of Benavente's mastery; but the interplay of thought and motion was so indecisive that the effect was that of a very intense melodrama. It resembled the Irish peasant plays, and yet contrasted with them. There was a greater subtlety of passion, and a greater variety of colour, than is seen in the somewhat monotonous Abbey plays.[99]

The Yeats play was done at the end of March at Yeats's home in Merrion Square as a private At-Home for members of the Drama League. Brinsley MacNamara and Sean O'Casey were there. O'Casey, reported Holloway, "couldn't understand it, he candidly confessed. Mac enjoyed Yeats's speech about the 'Noh' plays of Japan on which his play was built."[100] The costumes, the masks and the music were by Edmund Dulac, as they had been in the original private production at Lady Cunard's house in London on 2 April 1916. The best account of the 1924 performance was O'Casey's years later in *Inishfallen Fare Thee Well*:

Yeats had read in a big book all about the Noh Plays, had spoken about them to others, and had seized on the idea that he could do in an hour what had taken a thousand years to create. And so with the folding and unfolding of a cloth, music from a zither and flute, and taps from a drum, Yeats's idea of a Noh Play blossomed for a brief moment, then the artificial petals faded and dropped lonely to the floor, because a Japanese spirit had failed to climb into the soul of a Kelt.

Passively funny was the sight of Mr. Robinson doing a musician, and Mick Dolan, the Abbey actor, acting Cuchullain, so serious, so solemn, his right hand, extended, holding a spear, saying so surlily-amiable, I am named Cuchullain; I am Sualtam's son. No; charming and amiable as it all was, it wasn't a Noh Play. Poet and all as he was, Yeats wasn't able to grasp a convention grown through a thousand years, and give it an Irish birth in an hour. Zither and flute and drum, with Dulac's masks, too full of detail for such an eyeless play, couldn't pour the imagination into the mind of those who listened and saw. The unfolding and folding of the fanciful cloth couldn't carry the stage to the dressing-room. No, the people's theatre can never be successfully turned into a poetical conventicle. A play poetical to be worthy of the theatre must be able to withstand the terror of Ta-Ra-Ra-Boom-Dee-Ay, as a blue sky, or an apple tree in bloom, withstands any ugliness around or beneath them.

There was a buzz of Beautiful when the cloth had been folded, and the musicians had taken their slow way from the room; and Sean wisting not what to say himself, added Very. There was grace and a slender charm in what had been done, not that he had a long time to look back at it; but it wasn't even the ghost of the theatre.[101]

• • •

The Gaelic Players, na hAisteoiri Ath Cliath, completed their first season with five Monday evening performances at the Abbey, given each month from January to May; and then began their second season with Monday night performances in November and December. The plays were mainly short and mainly comic. There were revivals of a piece or two by Douglas Hyde, there were translations from the English of Lady Gregory, Rutherford Mayne, and Daniel Corkery; and there were foreign translations from Chekhov, Schnitzler, and some lesser known writers. The original works by Piaras Béaslaí, Gearoid Ó Lochlainn and Tadgh Ó Scannail seem not to have outlived their day.

The performance of 11 February was among the more interesting of the year. As the *Irish Times* described it:

> There was again a well-filled house at the Abbey Theatre last night, when the Gaelic Players produced *O'Falvey Mor*, by Daniel Corkery (translation by Sean Toibin), and General Pierse Beasley's *Cluiche Cartai*. Several members of the Government were among the audience.
>
> Mr. Corkery's play offered the players an opportunity to exhibit the poetry of the Gaelic mind and speech, and the romance of Ireland's troubled history; for its author has quarried gold from the intellectual content of the old language. Unhappily, however, it was badly acted, except by the three chief characters. The other players hobbled uneasily about the stage when they should have allowed attention to be concentrated on the speakers. The action of the play takes place in a poor cottage in the 18th century, where Shaun O'Falvey, the poor cottier, spends his time poring over an ancient Gaelic book, striving to make out his genealogy and prove himself the O'Falvey. The shanachie of Iveragh—a romantic figure like the wandering Carolan—visits the cottage and resolves the old man's difficulties; and just as the storm outside breaks the dyke, which he has been too proud or too lazy to mend, and lets the flood sweep away the last poor remnants of his property, he learns that he is the descendant of those who once were lords of all that country, and they kneel to him, the beggared O'Falvey.
>
> On the programme Mr. Corkery quotes a passage from Lecky, describing the ejected proprietors of proud descent who lingered, impoverished and too haughty to retrieve their fortunes by manual labour, in the cottages, receiving sceret homage from their old tenants. The play is a fine dramatisation of Lecky's picture, and the old man, who Gearoid O'Loughlin acted with musical speech and dignity of bearing, was a true type of the dispossessed aristocrat living in dreams, and drunk with the futile words of the poets.
>
> General Beasley's play is a three-act comedy of middle-class life turning on a family's addiction to card playing. A shy young man cannot get the father's consent to his marriage with the daughter of the house owing to his inability to play cards: but so many quarrels spring from the family vice that at last the timid youth is the chosen suitor for the very reason which had banned him hitherto. This play is an old favourite, and was acted with greater success, the card playing scene in particular giving a lively piece of comic characterisation. There was scarcely a break in the stream of laughter. Maire Ni Oisin, as a servant girl with a taste for matchmaking, was the success of the evening.[102]

According to the *Irish Times*, the 10 March production had "a better filled house . . . than at any former performance by the Gaelic players."[103] On this occasion, three one-acts were presented: *Crua-Chas na mBaitsileiri* (*The Bachelor's Plight*), translated by Mrs. Una Dix from an unnamed German source; *An Bear*, Fiachra Eilgeach's translation of Chekhov's farce; and *Beirt na Bodhaire Breige*, a translation by Béaslaí of a piece called *The Two Deaf Men Who Heard.*

On 7 April, there was another triple bill: a revival of Hyde's *An Tinceir agus an tSidheog*; *Sinead*, a translation by Fiachra Eilgeach of a one-act tragedy by Donald Colquhoun called *Jean*: and *Eis-Eirghe Dhonncha*, which was An Seabhac's translation of MacManus' folk-farce, *The Resurrection of Dinny O'Dowd.*

On 5 May, the players again mounted a triple bill: Ó Lochlainn's *An Cheist Chinniunach*, a translation of Schnitzler's *The Fatal Question*; a revival of Hyde's *An Posadh*; and a new play, *Eirghe Anairde* (*Snobbery*) by Tadhg Ó Scannail. Of Ó Scannail's piece, the *Irish Times* wrote:

> It is a propagandist piece, inconsiderable as drama. Two bank clerks, ignorant of Irish, go courting a farmer's daughters, and are astonished to find themselves treated scornfully by the father's aged mother—an old woman who has no English, and bears the name of Cait Ni Dhuibhir, which, in the songs, is a symbolic title for Ireland.
>
> So ended a season which has been a pleasing surprise to all lovers of the Celtic idiom. We have seen plays translated from French, Russian, German, and English, some historical, and some modern of the moderns. Comedy, poetic, farce, melodrama and tragedy have all been represented, and it is clear that these players and their work have come to stay.[104]

The second season opened promisingly in November with three new Irish pieces, and the *Times* reported:

> There was an overflowing attendance at the Abbey Theatre last night when the Gaelic Dramatic League opened its second year's activities. The three plays produced went with even a better swing than at the best performances of last winter.
>
> The first play, *The Parliament of Women* [*Dail na mBan*], by "An Seabhac," was a breezy little comedy, the theme of which is indicated by the title. When the Woman of the House (Mrs. Fitzgerald) went out to Parliament and the Man of the House (Tadhg O Scannaill) kept at home, it only needed the appearance of a mischievous Yankee to set up domestic anarchy, from which "Cait" learnt her lesson, though the author made the men the bigger fools.
>
> The second piece *An Craipi Og* was a musical episode, in which the popular ballad of "The Croppy Boy" was acted to the melancholy music of the old air. Muiris Ó Cathain played the betrayed boy, and Gearoid Ó Lochlainn was finely impressive as the Yeoman Captain. The make-up was remarkably effective, and the piece was a little triumph of stage-craft.
>
> The last piece, in which most of the company had parts, was *His First Wife, A Chead Bhean*, by the well-known novelist, Mr. Padraic Ó Conaire, being a dramatisation of a short story in his book, *Seven Victories.* The theme was simply the escape of two rebels, who pretend to be a honeymooning couple, one of the lads dressing as a girl. It gave scope for some rattling broad comedy, but the actors, mostly Munster folk, seemed a little uncomfortable with the Western idiom, and there were some halting passages.
>
> As last year, the success of the performance rested very largely on Mr. Ó Scannaill's humorous acting.[105]

The final performance of the year was on 16 December, when the program consisted of three translations: a revival of *Díurse-Dáirsé* from Lady Gregory's *Spreading the News*, *Fe Brigh na Mionn* from Rutherford Mayne's

The Troth and *Heircileas* which was a translation by Gearoid Ó Lochlainn of Adolf Recek's Danish play *Hercules.*

• • •

Among the predictable offerings at the Queen's Theatre, Dublin, was a handful of new Irish pieces, but none of extraordinary interest. On 4 February, John MacDonagh's new revue, *Dublin To-Night*, opened, and this detailed account from the *Evening Herald* indicates that the work was much the same as all the other MacDonagh revues:

> The author of the *Irish Jew* has again given us something deliciously Irish in the way of a revue called *Dublin To-Night.* Two full houses saw its first production at the Queen's Theatre last night, and not one of those audiences had any doubt as to the possibilities in Dublin of making as good entertainment as any of the imports. . . .
>
> A very faithful glimpse of a queue outside a gallery door sets the piece in motion. The little boy selling oranges, the street singer (Fay Sargent), the mortar-board step dancer (Dick Smith), and the queue breaker (Jimmy O'Dea) are very real persons. Not less realistic and amusing the section of the gods with the appropriate commentaries and orange biting during a McCormack recital, in which one recognizes the fine voice of Joseph O'Neill.
>
> Harry O'Donovan's singing of "Duffy" with the Lennox troupe of dancers is a splendid revival to the thoroughgoing music hall light comedy song. There is a pretty Venetian scene when Joseph O'Neill, Florena Howley, and May Doyle sing charmingly from a gondola. The bar scene, with Jimmy O'Dea as the customer who pays, Dick Smith as the customer who does not pay, and Fay Sargent as the bar maid, caused a good deal of laughter on account of its vivid truth to life.
>
> In the dramatic sketch, "A Night in Dublin," the audience is thoroughly thrilled by the acting of a raid by an Auxiliary lorry load, reminiscent of the bad times. Those ghostly whistles and reverberating lorry outside add terror to the clever acting of Jack Dwan and his officer, Irvine Lynch (who, by the way, should be more familiar with his lines), Harry O'Donovan, and Ria Mooney, who, however, lacks the strength of voice to reach the dress circle, though possessing all the timidity and naivete of a girl in such a trying position.
>
> The scene behind the scenes of a concert platform is, perhaps, the most humorous part of *Dublin To-Night*. In it Jimmy O'Dea and Ralph Goggin, Harry O'Donovan, Fay Sargent, and Dick Smith make everything done a source of healthy laughter.
>
> Miss Maureen Ryan, the *Evening Herald* Prize Beauty, is the centre of a very artistic scene representing "The Ould Plaid Shawl," which is admirably sung by Mr. Irvine Lynch, and "Drink to me only with Thine Eyes," in which Mr. Joseph O'Neill puts all his gifts of interpretation and sympathy. The lighting effects of Miss Ryan's poses could be vastly improved by the casting of head lights to counter-act the intense limelight so destructive of distinctive and natural featuring. Miss Ryan's appearance was heartily greeted by the audience at both houses.[106]

The great strength of the MacDonagh revues was, of course, the work of Jimmy O'Dea. The great weaknesses were the frequent thinness of the material and the often casual haste of the staging—faults which have persisted in Dublin revues to our own day. On this occasion, Jacques took issue with the anonymous puff quoted above:

> Last week the suggestion was made by an eminent colleague after seeing *Dublin To-Night* on its first production that what the revue needed badly was a bad-tempered producer who would make the performers sweat at rehearsals. If merit in achievement is in direct proportion to bad temper by the master of rehearsal, the producer in this case must be in the same championship class as the traditional drill-sergeant. For merit in last night's nerformance . . . was plentiful. . . .
>
> The dramatic sketch about the visit of the Black-and-Tan raid was thrown down by bad lighting. The sketch is a little cameo of its kind. It should race along, tense, trite, nonstop. Get the thrill into it. . . .
>
> The stage speech of the "Has-Been" operatic singer in the second last scene is above the heads of the audience; too subtle altogether, and wholly lost in its sarcasm, however true to life. The lady with the adenoid voice and the two chisslers by the hand promised excellent fun in the concert scene. Why didn't the thing develop? Without Jimmy O'Dea this revue might conceivably fall flat. Someone to cross talk with him would make it positively fizz.[107]

On 25 February, the Irish Players, minus for once the commanding presence of Arthur Sinclair, staged a new full-leangth comedy by J. Bernard MacCarthy. On this occasion, the acting honours went to the veteran J. A. O'Rourke. The *Irish Times* reported:

> The Irish Players produced at the Queen's Theatre last night *The Down Express*, a new farcical comedy by Mr. J. Bernard MacCarthy. When the company gets into its stride the comedy will make people laugh, for there is a good foundation of fun-making in this work. It suffers from slow action, but, on the whole, the play tells naturally a laughable story, and tells it in some smart dialogue. With better acting it could be a real piece of pleasing characterisation. It all happens at Ballyconeen railway station, to which the eloping Patricia Maud, daughter of the gentleman farmer Tobin family, and Donal Oge O'Sullivan, the son of a wealthy horse-dealer, once stable boy, are supposed to have come on the start of their matrimonial journey. Mrs. Tobin and Peter O'Sullivan arrive to stop the pair, who escape the storm by hiding in the porter's room. The *deus ex machina* comes in a telephone measage that the Down Express has been wrecked, and "they lived happy ever after."
>
> The soul of the play as produced last night is J. A. O'Rourke, who as Thady, the station porter, carried out a fine comedy part naturally and consistently. At times Mr. Hutchinson, the station-master was very good; at others he was not. Patricia Maud (Nora Kane) and her selected (Felix Hughes) were colourless and insipid, and neither Kathleen Drago as Mrs. Tobin nor Sydney J. Morgan as Donal's father convinced that such people could ever behave in such a way under such circumstances. Those characters cleverly portrayed would give the comedy a good deal of the action it lacks. The cast was completed with Fred Jeffs as a railway shareholder.[108]

O'Donnell in the *Evening Herald* was more enthusiastic and gave special praise to Jeffs:

> Fred Jeffs, who was about five minutes on the stage, gave a perfect character sketch, and his accent proved so reminiscent to a Cork gentleman near me that he gave utterance to the war whoop, "Up Cork!"[109]

Jacques in the *Independent* was absolutely gushy. Both O'Donnell and Jacques hugely admired the wit of MacCarthy's dialogue, but in truth the lines are little more than stage wit. Lines like "Matrimony is a journey for which no one can issue a return ticket" may appear momentarily sparkling by the droll delivery of an experienced comedian, but have little life of their own. In sum, *The Down Express* was not so much an improvement on, as it was a variation on and an expansion of the situation in Martin J. McHugh's *A Minute's Wait*. And, in fact, the response of its audience was poor. As Holloway reported:

> There was only a scattered audience at the Queen's and the farce didn't seem much to their liking—melodrama being their pet form of amusement. . . . The audience was very dead—not even applauding at the end.[110]

If MacCarthy was a leading purveyor of broad comedy, and MacDonagh the leading purveyor of Irish revues, the leading local exponents of musical comedy were Tom Madden, the composer, and Edward McNulty, Shaw's boyhood friend. Their new piece, *Acushla*, opened at the Queen's on 28 April, and the *Evening Press* affirmatively but without great enthusiasm reported:

> *Acushla*, unlike most entertainments of its kind, has a plot which although simple gives scope for many amusing situations which the authors have not been slow to seize, while the music, which is entirely original, is quite the prettiest and most tuneful yet written by Tom Madden, whose popular melodies, "Because I love you so," "Bridget Donohue," the recent Queen's Pantomime hit, and "I want to go back to Tipperary," Mr. John MacDonagh's clever lyric, now being sung at the Olympia, are so well known to the public.
>
> The scene is laid in a hotel where there is a very free and easy atmosphere. The staff dance for the amusement of the guests. There is a carnival scene with a sprinkling of love-making. This scene is nicely staged, and the whole company made a satisfying display.[111]

So far as one is able to determine, the various Madden-McNulty productions seem to have had one or two catchy tunes, a generally thin book, and a somewhat amateurish staging.[112]

On 5 May, an original comedy called *Liz*, by Fred J. Cogley, was first done at the Queen's. The reviews would seem to indicate some similarity to *Peg O' My Heart*. As the *Evening Herald* reported:

> Mr. Fred J. Cogley, in his new play, *Liz*, which was produced for the first time in the Queen's Theater last night, does not seek to do more than provide a few

> incidents calculated to cause amusement, and in this respect a good deal is left to a few of the players to give effect to points in the dialogue and to enter the spirit of humorous situations. The production is meant to be farcical, and at times it is extremely so. The entire fun of the play turns on the quick change in the attitude of the Larissey family towards Liz, who is bustled and bullied as a poor servant girl, and then courted and made much of when a newspaper report mentions that she has become an heiress owing to the death of a relative in America. The audience laughed heartily at the spectacle of Martin Larissey, the father; David Larissey, the son; and Daniel O'Dowd, an old friend of the family, all seeking opportunities of proposing to the girl, and each giving her a ring, while she, unaware of the newspaper report, is in a state of bewilderment.
>
> The climax is reached when another quick change takes place on its becoming known that a mistake was made in the amount of the fortune, the actual sum which Liz is to receive being only about fifty pounds. There was much merriment on the part of the audience as the suitors endeavoured to get out of their matrimonial complications. . . . The author, who also played a part, was called before the curtain and applauded at the close.[113]

After this production, which did not generate much enthusiasm, nothing was ever heard of *Liz* again, and so one might plausibly assume that it was a conventional comedy with little original or individual about it.

On 1 September, the Queen's presented a play interesting mainly because it was one of the last tremors of the Whitbread tradition of patriotic melodrama. This was *Wolfe Tone*, written by the veteran actor Frank Dalton who was old enough to have acted with Boucicault in his last appearance in Dublin. This conventional anachronism was probably quite adequately summed up by the *Irish Times:*

> The play in general is rather awkward, and there is a tendency to be over-dramatic. The name part is taken by Noel Dalton, who, were it not for his monotonous delivery, would be quite good; his courage and demeanour are beyond reproach. . . . Valentine Vousden must be commended for his playing of the part of Sir George Hill, and the able manner in which he handles the role of Napoleon. May Fitzpatrick, who plays Madame Nuneil, a Frenchwoman, would be well advised to speak the part "straight" all through.[114]

The Olympia staged mainly revues from England, with names like *Hot Lips* and *A Little Bit of Fluff*. The Dublin Jewish Dramatic Society, however, did a Sunday production there on 9 March, and sponsored a couple of Sunday performances in April by a traveling company, the Vilna Troupe of Jewish Players. On 6 April, the Vilna Troupe did Max Mardau's *Dr. Kohn* and on 13 April S. Ansky's *The Dybik*.

The notable Irish production of the year at the Olympia was John MacDonagh's four-act comedy, *Brains*. In his work for Edward Martyn's Irish Theatre in Hardwicke Street, MacDonagh had been a very seriously intentioned playwright. After the collapse of the Hardwicke Street venture, however, he had gone into commercial work, scripting and directing comic films, producing his own broad comedy of *The Irish Jew*, and finally writing and producing several revues each year. Nevertheless, he was still not quite willing to give up the writing of plays, even though those plays had, for commercial reasons, to be broad comedies. According to the *Evening Herald*:

In producing *Brains* . . . Mr. John MacDonagh tells us he is trying to find out just what Dublin audiences want. "The directors of the theatre," he says, "gave me a free hand, and I could, and perhaps should, have produced one of my revues, which have been so well supported. Instead, I am putting on a 'legitimate' comedy, and, at least, can look my accusers in the eye next time they charge me with having gone over to 'bare-legs.' Millions have been lost trying to guage the public taste, and yet every season, in the producing centres of the world, the 'sure thing' of the experts flops badly, while the 'not a ghost of a chance' romps home.

"Within the past ten years a big change has taken place in the theatre, and we are told most of the blame rests with the 'Pictures.' There are no great plays and consequently no great actors, because the public are doped by swiftly-changing pictures specially prepared to please every intellect, i.e., the meanest. This doping paralyses the mental faculties, and so a play requiring the exercise of any intelligent interest on the part of the audience is doomed, on the principle that you can't get juice out of a squeezed lemon. Well, be that as it may, there is in Dublin, I hold, and hope, a chance for plays requiring grey-matter, both before and behind the footlights.

"In England this apathy is also attributed to post-war mental lassitude, and the thoughts of theatrical purveyors are turning back in despair to the grand manner of the old school, in hopes that the thundering voice, the rolling eye, and the majestic gesture may make the tired business man again sit up and take notice. 'I go to the theatre to be amused,' one hears repeatedly, and personally I applaud the sentiment, for I find that the standard must be raised to meet this demand, and not lowered, as is erroneously supposed.

"It is comforting for us to pretend that the standard of theatrical taste in Dublin is high, though sometimes our pride should be jarred somewhat by the quality of the goods presented for our amusement. Last year in London a theatrical manager informed me that a play produced, say, in Chortley-cum-Puddle would stand infinitely a better chance of consideration in London than one produced in Dublin. This is quite understandable from London's point of view, but why should Dublin share it? I am not pleading for any preferential tariff in favour of 'home produce.' I would have the home article stand every test of comparison with the foreign one in the matter of presentation and general efficiency. For my own productions I try to secure the best available artistes, and to instance this I have brought over Miss Drago specially for next week."[115]

The play opened at the Olympia on 2 June, and the *Independent* reported:

Mr. John MacDonagh's latest production, *Brains*, a four act comedy, was seen for the first time at the Olympia last night, the audiences at both houses being large and most appreciative.

The comedy is cleverly conceived and contains many highly humorous situations, but can hardly be placed on a plane with other work by the author. The Hon. Reginald Wye embarks on an aeroplane flight, comes to grief, and has his brain surgically treated, the brains of a music hall artiste being transferred into the noble noodle in order to preserve life. Reginald, under the care of am eminent scientist, returns to the bosom of his aristocratic family with the face of an aristocrat, but three-fourths the brains of a low comedian.

His language, demeanour, and general habits have so completely altered that his mother, Lady Amberdale, is grief-sricken, his father exasperated beyond measure, and despair almost takes possession of his fiancée, who, however, eventually works the cure. The invasion of the lordly home by Bessie Best, seeking for the brains of her dead lover, furnishes one of the brightest scenes in the play, and the humourous complications are added to by the arrival of her father, also a music hall artiste, who proceeds to establish a claim to the property of Reginald now that he possesses the brains, and speaks with the mannerisms of his now defunct stage colleague.

At last Reginald recovers his aristocratic reason, ignores his whilom friends, and becomes again the "Honourable." The acting, beyond a few slight blemishes incidental to a new production, was excellent. Jimmy O'Dea, as the Hon. Reginald Wye, maintained his high reputation, and Kathleen Drago displayed great ability as Bassie Best, the music hall actress. It would be difficult to excell the manner in which Mr. Jack Dwan impersonated the role of Lord Amberdale, and more than a passing word of praise must be bestowed on Mme. Kirkwood Hackett as Lady Amberdale. Mr Frank J. Fay characterised the butler, Shaw, with his usual capacity and was particularly clever in the love scene with Bessie.

Mr. Valentine Vousden submitted a genuine Rev. Canon Flagg, and praise must also be bestowed on Pol Ó Fearghail as the surgeon, F. J. McCormick as Horatio Best, and Mabel Home as Mabel Flagg.[116]

Holloway was at the first night and gave a less gentle view of some of the performances:

. . . a most ingenious idea is very cleverly worked out. . . . Valentine Vousden gave a character sketch of the Rev. Canon Flagg, perfect in every detail. Lawrence, whom I met after the show, said . . . , "he was the most perfect clergyman I have ever seen on the stage." . . . Jimmy O'Dea was gloriously comic. . . . In Act One he was inclined to play to the house, but afterwards he was ever and always splendidly in the part. . . . These two made big hits in their parts, and Kathleen Drago as Bessie Best touched off the music hall miss with sure artistry and effect, while as her old actor father F. J. McCormick suggested in his cockney study and make-up Joxer Daly too vividly for me to knowingly enjoy his study as anything but a reflection of the other role. Mme. Kirkwood Hackett was forgetful and too tame as Lady Amberdale. . . . However, the clever little piece was well cast, and after a few shows ought to be a thoroughly enjoyable comedy. As a first show it went remarkably well, and when taken a little brisker will be capital fun. . . . Jimmy O'Dea passing stopped for a word. I congratulated him . . . on his work in *Brains* and also Valentine Vousden and Kathleen Drago. He was pleased for Vousden's success as he suggested him to MacDonagh. He agreed with me that Farrell was too melodramatic . . . owing to not having his lines off pat. At the second house the gallery became restless and shouted for, "Jimmy, give us a song!" "Cut the talk and give us a dance." The Olympia is certainly not the place for a comedy.[117]

In chatting with W. J. Lawrence, MacDonagh remarked:

Fay and O'Farrell didn't hit it off as the former interfered with his business at the sideboard . . . as it was not so done at rehearsals. MacDonagh wanted to know of Lawrence could Fay ever act; he doesn't know how now; and Lawrence told him, "Years ago he could; before he came so painfully self-conscious and stilted in delivery."[118]

Fay's reaction to *Brains* was also reported by Holloway:

> Speaking of *Brains*, he was delighted with Valentine Vousden's acting of the clergyman; he could hardly keep from laughing on the stage at his natural by-play. Miss Drago was too nervous to do herself justice, and O'Dea had not enough of experience to make the two brains part plausible. MacDonagh will write a good play yet. He is delicate, and it affects his virility as a dramatist, Fay thinks.[119]

In any event, the reception of *Brains* was not enthusiastic enough to persuade MacDonagh to persevere in playwriting, and he turned again to the concocting of revues.

In 1924, nothing Irish appeared on the variety bills of the Tivoli; and, with the exception of Marie Kendall during the week of March 3, and some real ice and real ice skaters during the week of 28 April, nothing awfully unusual appeared either.

The National Theatre at the Rotunda had not been a successful venture. Ira Allen's Company played melodramas there for the first three weeks of January, and the "theatre" was only open for one other week during the year. This was the week of 21 April when the Maryboro' Players presented Allen's *Father Murphy*. The Maryboro' Players were a group of ex-political prisoners, like the Ballykinlar Players, and had originally presented Allen's play when they were interned.

After its Christmas panto, the Gaiety presented the Dublin University Dramatic Society for the week of 4 February in Anthony Hope's *Pilkington's Peerage* and in F. Anstey's *The Man from Blankley's*, which gave Joyce Chancellor an early role. The rest of the year was notable only for its usualness. The Rathmines and Rathgar Musical Society did a week of Gilbert and Sullivan. The O'Mara Opera Company, the Charles Doran Company and the MacDona Players appeared. There were new musical comedies like *Stop Flirting*, old musical comedies like *The Belle of New York*, and very old musical comedies like the recently revived London Success of *The Beggar's Opera*. Popular actors such as Fred Terry and Bromley Challoner appeared in their old standbys, *The Scarlet Pimpernel* and *When Knights Were Bold*. There were some newish plays with some claim to merit, such as A. A. Milne's *The Dover Road*; and there some some newish plays with no claim to merit, such as *The Cat and the Canary*, or a play based on George MacManus's newspaper cartoon strip *Bringing Up Father*, or a play based very distantly on Conan Doyle's Sherlock Holmes stories.[120] But there was nothing really of Irish interest until the Ulster Players made their annual visit in December.

The Theatre Royal pursued its usual policy of presenting revues, variety shows, and musical comedies from England and with a rather higher standard of talent than what might be seen at the Olympia or the Tivoli. However, in August during the Tailteann Games, the theatre presented a week of Irish opera. On 11 August, Sir Charles Stanford's *Shamus O'Brien* was revived, and *The Irish Times* reported:

> . . . it is not much short of thirty years since the first production of the opera. With a tour in the United States of America, added to its seasons in London, in Ireland, and in the English provinces, it must have been performed over a period that would leave its last performance at four or five and twenty years ago. In more recent years Sir Charles Stanford set his face against all proposals for revival of this particular work of his. His death a few months ago freed it, and Mr. Joseph O'Mara, who helped the opera to popularity, and enlarged his own reputation by his singing and acting in the part of Mike Murphy, was able to join the accomplishment of his own eager wish to bring the opera to light again with the celebration of the new Aonach Tailteann.
>
> *Shamus O'Brien* pleased the last generation of Irishmen by the homely flavour of its libretto, its melodies and its humour. The libretto belongs to the school of Dion Boucicault—that school which the Abbey Theater has taught us now to call "stage Irish," the school whose work reminds one of the picture postcards sold to English tourists, showing the Irishman of caricature, with shillelagh, squat nose, green knickerbockers, and pig complete. It made a hero of the rebel, a fool of the British soldier, a heroine of an Irish colleen, and a despised rascal of an informer. Its unrealities did not prevent it from appealing to one set of people, and they made it possible for the other set—even to stout "removables" and Castle stalwarts—to take it as caricature, and enjoy it as such. As comic opera of that kind, the libretto was good work; it contained plenty of fun, a good dramatic episode here and there, and many well-turned verses. The music was sounder and more worthy as art. Stanford's score, in its technique a model for many composers of its own time, and of the new generation, is remarkable, too, for its flavour of Ireland, with rhythms and melodies all in the spirit of our native music.[121]

At a matinee on 12 August, there was staged by Madame Rock a rather hybrid concoction by Major A. T. Lawlor. This was *The Vision Play of Queen Tailte*, a series of narrations spoken by professional actors and then followed by Madame Rock's pupils in illustrative "living tableaux" of mime, music, and dance. The *Irish Times* reported:

> The author is Major A. T. Lawlor, National Army, who has given in the play the results of his researches into the records of the past with the object of reconstructing and portraying the story of the Queen and the life of her times. The forms and most of the language used by him are drawn from Gaelic literature and tradition. A seanchuidhe or narrator (Miss Elizabeth Young) recites the story of the Queen to the accompanying chant of the cantora (Mr. M. J. Dolan and Mr. F. J. McCormick). After each of the six narrations there is shown an aisling, or vision, depicting in living tableau what the seanchuidhe has just described. Nothing is spoken during the aisling, which tells its story completely by rhythmical movements to the accompaniment of music.
>
> The aislingi, as a series of spectacles, of life and colour and movement, with appropriate scenery and stage accessories, are beautiful alike to the eye and to the imagination; and the lines are spoken with marked effect by Miss Young.
>
> It cannot be said that there was anything very brilliant in the portrayal of the characters in the aislingi. . . . The dances were all very pretty indeed.[122]

Molyneux Palmer's *Sruth na Maoile*, which had been first given in 1923 at the Gaiety, was revived on the evenings of 13 and 14 August, with Vincent O'Brien conducting and with many of the original cast repeating their parts.

On 15 and 16 August, Harold R. White's *Shaun the Post* was given its first production, and the *Irish Times* thought it

> the most important musical event that has occurred in Dublin in recent years. *Shaun the Post* is full Grand Opera, and in scope and size goes beyond any other musical work of an Irish composer, given first performance in Dublin. Not withstanding some defects in performance, a large audience at the Theatre Royal last night recognised the high quality of the work, and were impressed by its effect. The production was a great success for the composer, whose honours were shared by Mr. R. J. Hughes, the librettist, and Mr. Herbert Bailey, the producer. Mr. White, who conducted, was called with his colleagues and the principles to receive, at the close, the acclamation of the audience.
>
> For Mr. White's sake, it is necessary to see more about the defects in performance than would otherwise need mention. It is the composer whose case is under judgment on such an occasion. His is the heaviest toil beforehand, and his the work which may, perhaps, outlast the passing reputations of performers.
>
> In the first place, the performance was largely in the hands of principals who are not accustomed to the stage, and lack the ways of giving ease and natural flow to the action. That inexperience extends also to singing against a full orchestra in a complex score, and picking up a lead quickly from the fleeting instrumental passages. Again they were such local singers as were available, and had not always the type of voice required for the particular part.
>
> In the second place, the players—the theatre orchestra with a number of additional players—were faced with a score much more difficult than the music normally within their practice, and that they had to perform with less rehearsal than a work of this calibre ought to receive. The brass, the section in which the most prominent disfigurements occurred, had received the parts only a little while before the performance.
>
> These points need mention so that the members of the audience may know that the designed effects were not always realised last night, and that the opera is an even finer thing in its conception than what they heard last night.
>
> Yet, mention of these things must not be taken as indicating any considerable roughness. All the artistes gave of their best, rendering loyal service towards the success of a work of which they knew the merits. The result was a great success. The opera will have to be "cut," and Mr. White will know, as well as anybody, what other changes actual production has shown to be advisable. Very little, nevertheless, could be called ineffective in last night's performance, and the lasting impression is of an opera well designed as regards the "book," and a score full of beauty of melody and powerful dramatic expression—reminiscent here and there in theme and orchestral method of other composers, but on so lofty a plane that those reminiscences are connected with examples of the best in music, while the main body of the work shows an individual grasp of operatic resources that is wonderful in the composer who has had so little opportunity of hearing his own compositions "cried out" in performance.
>
> The opera of *Shaun the Post* is founded on Boucicault's drama, fairly familiar in Dublin, of *Arrah-na-Pogue*. . . .
>
> These scenes give the composer occasion for descriptive effects in the orchestra, while the incidents of the piece afford him opportunity in abundance for effective solos, love duets, concerted numbers and choruses.

> Mr. Joseph O'Mara had evidently taken a good deal of care with his preparation of the part of Shaun the Post, and did it full justice. In numbers such as his "Leprechaun" song, in the first act, in the meditations in prison (where he sings the "Londonderry Air" very beautifully set, and also used as a theme at other places in the opera), and in the love duets, Mr. O'Mara sang splendidly.[123]

The only other item of Irish interest during the year at the Royal was the appearance of Arthur Sinclair for the week of 27 October. The comedian had been touring America and returned in a short farce called *McFee M. P.* Frank J. Hugh O'Donnell thought that Sinclair was merely prostituting his talents;

> A few weeks ago Mr. Arthur Sinclair appeared in the Theatre Royal in a playlet entitled *McFee M. P.* Mr. Sinclair is a great actor, a comedian of excellent calibre, an artiste who knows all about his business. And yet Mr. Sinclair probably to amuse and appropriately cater for his patrons in the "halls" drags the old skeleton from the cupboard, and . . . gives us the stage Irishman all over again. The audience laughed and howled and applauded! Wasn't he one of themselves, this ridiculous, blustering playboy—this delightful enlargement of the man in the street? I do not find fault with satire or ridicule or a sense of the grotesque, but it makes me fairly sick to hear an audience howl because a man says "Bedad" and "Begorra" and "Begob.' . . . But get a gentleman into a swallow-tail coat and a billy-cock hat and let him repeat them between expectorations on the stage, and our Dublin audience will laugh till the dead complain of their boisterousness.[124]

The Censorship of Films Act came into operation on 16 January, and the first film censor was the Dublin wit, James Montgomery.[125] Fred Leroy Granville, an American film producer and the husband of the actress Peggy Hyland, came to Dublin with a film producing scheme

> for the purpose of making a picture which will represent Ireland of to-day as she really is, and not as she has been known hitherto on the American and English stage.
>
> "A big production," he says, "Irish actors, Irish customs, and the life of the people as it is lived to-day. . . .
>
> "The question of the story to be made is, of course, the most important thing. I want a story of to-day, and I invite Irish men and women to send me suggestions for a suitable play.
>
> "I don't want religion or politics, but a story of human heart interest, which will break away from the old tradition."[126]

Or, as he remarked in another interview, "We want a good, strong, heart-interest story with some punch, and we want a modern story, that is, not of the Kiltartan variety."[127]

On 15 February, the Stoll Film Company gave a private showing of *The Colleen Bawn*, which had been filmed in Ireland in the autumn of 1923. All the chief actors in this version of the Boucicault play were English, but "the excellence of the acting, picturesque and lovely scenes, and, most important of all, the beautiful, clear, soft photographic quality" were admired by the press.[128] The film opened at the Theatre De-luxe, Camden Street, on 17 March; and another foreign-made film, *My Wild Irish Rose*, opened on 21 April at the Mary Street Picture House. This was a version of Boucicault's *The Shaughraun* and featured Pat O'Malley as Conn. Also, a "Mystery Film Girl" appeared in and around Dublin early in the year, and with a small film crew shot short scenes at the zoo and elsewhere. These were supposed to be part of a film being shot all over the world, and it was not too long before she was making appearances at various Dublin cinemas with the bits of local film that had been shot.

• • •

Readers of previous volumes of this history will possible have noticed the reappearance of certain themes and topics, some of the most prominent being the immorality of the stage, the rowdiness of audiences, and the innumerable faults of the Abbey Theatre. In the 1920s, the most dramatic charge of stage immorality was probably the appearance of the prostitute in O'Casey's 1926 play, *The Plough and the Stars*. (Of course, anything even faintly approaching the nudity and near-nudity of various contemporary New York confections by Florenz Ziegfeld, Earl Carroll, or George White would have been anathema; and we have had to wait until the 1970s to view the delights or horrors of the naked human body on the Irish stage.) However, as noted above, the Censorship of Films Act did come into being in 1924, and there were also occasional noises made about a censorship for the stage.

The matter of rowdy audiences was still much alive in 1924 also. For instance, on 6 February, "Padraig" wrote to the *Evening Herald*:

> Would you allow me a small space on your valued paper to draw attention to an incident which occurred in the Gaiety Theatre on Friday night last?
>
> I happened to be sitting near a friend of mine who is bald. We were seated in the dress circle. A young lady in the upper circle persisted in dropping some hard white sweets on his head. Each time she hit the mark she drew back in her seat in convulsions of laughter while the poor gentleman looked up in bewilderment. The last thing she dropped was a lighted cigarette end. He could stand it no longer, and, rising from his chair in evident pain, he beat a hasty retreat.
>
> Surely something can be done to put a stop to this conduct.[129]

And on 13 March, there appeared another complaint about behaviour in the Gaiety:

> I seldom write to the Press, but feel compelled to send you this letter in regard to my experiences of this and last week when attending the admirable performances of Shakespeare by the Charles Doran Company at the Gaiety Theatre. It is nothing short of astonishing how much the Dublin public appear ready to endure in the way of vulgar rowdyism, without making any effective protest. On each of my visits bands of youths not only made the air hideous with shouts, cat-calls, feeble efforts to

sing songs, etc., during the waiting periods, but also constantly interrupted the plays themselves with loud calls, throwing of missiles on to the stage, into the orchestra, and on the heads of the audience in the parterre. . . . I am informed that much of the rowdyism is carried on by boys from various colleges, who are apparently allowed to attend these plays with no adequate supervision of masters.[130]

• • •

In the week of 25 February, a revue was presented at the Olympia, entitled *Aerial Flashes*, "a Wireless Whirl in Six Flashes"; and for the week of 3 March Harry Tate appeared at the Royal in a confection called *Broadcasting*, "a Wireless Wave of Laughter." The topical themes of these popular entertainments reflected, of course, the growing public fascination with the new toy, radio; and probably the most far-reaching cultural event of the year was the opening of the first broadcasting station in Ireland. On 24 October, the *Irish Times* reported:

The Belfast Station of the British Broadcasting Company will be officially declared open at a ceremony in the Ulster Hall, Belfast, to-night. The station has been transmitting since September 15 last, and the reception generally, not only in Ireland, but in Great Britain, has been very satisfactory.[131]

In September a young actor and stage director, Tyrone Guthrie, went to work for the BBC in Belfast; and years later he wrote this short account of his experiences:

I presume I had been appointed because I am Irish. Not a bad reason. But no one had given me any brief. I had not the faintest inkling of what I was supposed to do. About the policy of the BBC, its constitution, finances or function, I had not one clue. I only knew that politics, religion and advertisement were tabu, unmentionable.

When I arrived in Belfast, my colleagues seemed equally vague about the whole business. Our station producer was a charming, elderly gentleman of distinguished pedigree. He was mildly interested in dogs and woman, keenly interested in pheasant shooting. Belfast, broadcasting, science, art, literature and, especially, office routine he openly and cordially detested.

I was placed in charge of all programmes other than music: that is to say all talks, plays, poetry readings, debates—any programme which depended, apart from the bare announcement, on the spoken word.

At twenty-three years of age I found myself convening meetings of archbishops, bishops, moderators and ecclesiastical bigwigs of many creeds; the Vice-Chancellor of the University, the Director of Municipal Education and a covey of headmasters; mayors, deputy mayors and town clerks from all over the province; of the officers of local debating, philosophical and dramatic societies in order to break to them the glad news that radio, or broadcasting, as we called it then, had come to the North of Ireland; in order to seek their advice as to how this new medium could most wisely be used; and to induce them to elect some of their number to constitute a Broadcasting Advisory Committee.

I found myself hiring elderly and sometimes distinguished professors to talk about their subjects; hiring local comedians and introducing variety shows; hiring reciters and choosing their programmes; ensuring fair do's between the broadcast religious rites of Catholic and Protestant—a ticklish business in Belfast. It was all very interesting and would have been highly unsuitable, if anyone had taken it seriously. But this was early days. No one much was listening, and anyway all they heard was a faint word here and there in between the Morse code of ships' wireless officers exchanging betting tips and the howls and squeals of lost souls, which were called "atmospherics."

The technical aspect of radio still completely dominated not only the public imagination but also that of the BBC. An odd instance of the relative importance of the technical staff was the fact that all the office equipment, painting, decoration and upholstery were under the control of the Engineering Department. In consequence, our studio—as we absurdly called the noisome den where performances took place—was one of the ugliest-looking things ever conceived by the mind of man.

It had been—and no expense was spared—lined with curtains of a terrible shade, somewhere between the colour of a dandelion and a ginger pudding; upon them there was a "frieze"—a wide stripe arranged in what is called Greek key pattern, in a lurid violet; the floor was covered with a carpet which was meant to match the ginger pudding, but did not quite. The lighting was arranged on the new principle of reflection off the ceiling, then very fashionable and utterly impractical. The ceiling was dazzingly bright, but down in the depths of the room you could read only with difficulty.

The head engineer had installed a fabulously scientific system of ventilation. A series of gold levers could be pulled and gold arrows pointed to signs on gold dials, which purported to announce the temperature. The room was supposed to be filled with an especially invigorating ozone, which blew in through a golden grille. In fact, the temperature never changed. The room was perpetually cold, but at the same time stuffy.

Some of us were silly enough to think that there was also a very queer smell. The engineers laughed this idea to scorn, and pointed out that it was an aroma of ozone and infinitely healthy. Yet things were better when, from behind the golden grille the caretaker removed the carcasses of two dead rats.

Gradually it became evident that this new medium was going to exert a tremendous influence upon public opinion and the public imagination. It also appeared that overnight the reputation of actors and politicians, musicians and preachers could be made or ruined; also that there was "big money" to be made. At first many important public figures refused to broadcast on the ground that it was *infra dig*. None of them held out long.

But, as the power of broadcasting became more apparent, and not before it was time, the BBC began to put its house in order. Young men of twenty-three no longer convened its committees and improvised its policy. Regulations, like nettles in a hotbed, took root and flourished exceedingly. Things sobered up, but also dulled down. Gradually a routine of administration evolved. Memos were passed from wire basket to wire basket. Questions were asked and answered in triplicate, files bulged, secretaries multiplied. Gradually officials in the BBC became more and more like civil servants, concerned with administrative and not with creative work.

After two years in Belfast, I began to feel the time was coming for a change. Once more I began to look about. They had been for me two happy and formative years.[132]

The Ulster Players added three new pieces to their reportoire in 1924, and all were given first productions during the annual visit to the Gaiety in Dublin. On 8 December, *The Land of the Stranger* by Dolly Donn Byrne was first produced. The author was wife of the popular novelist Donn Byrne, and her play had been briefly seen on Broadway and was a blandly told story of how an Irish–American yearned to return to Ireland, and then was so disillusioned by the experience that he was happy to hasten back to America. The theme of the exile and his nostalgia for home has been a perennial one in Irish letters, even embodied in retellings of the stories of Oisin and Columbkille; and the main point of interest in Mrs. Byrne's play is that it refutes and deflates the usual nostalgia. Jacques probably caught the typical reaction of the Dublin audience:

> Although the bones rattle in the nice little play contributed by Dolly Byrne to the Ulster Players under the title *The Land of the Stranger*, the skeleton is never quite in evidence, and there are some genuine laughs which will probably grow as the land becomes less strange. . . .
>
> There are five scenes: three in a New York grocery store and two in a farmhouse in Co. Armagh. Through the three acts the author labours considerably to hammer out the one idea, and does so with a set of characters that are not particularly funny. The one idea is that it is the Irish people who emigrate to America who are the spouters, flagwavers, bands and banners demonstrationists and St. Patrick's Day processioners, and it is the Irish people who stay at home who are the hard workers, talk sense and substance, and achieve progress. The Irish girls in America are bleating little heifers, and the Irish boys are moony calves. Maureen O'Brien in a Brooklyn procession dresses like Kathleen Ni Houlihan at a fancy fair. Her sister Ellen in Armagh dresses like a golfer, and has installed a gas cooker, electric light, and an egg incubator in place of the insanitary hen. As evidence of progress, Ellen wears a green tam and green, orange and white jumper.
>
> The method of enforcing the argument is all in the manner of kindly comedy. Old Exile Pat McCann, with his son Dennis, come to Ireland to see the old folks and the old sod, the green hills of Erin, the mists that do be—well, anyhow, they come to Ireland. And they don't find pigs in the kitchen. Everything is up–to–date and new fangled. They can't find an Orangeman who curses the Pope, and in fact find their own Catholic relations on the best of terms with their protestant neighbours. Not a bit like the Ireland they helped to keep alive in America—a strange land entirely. So they slipped away while the slipping was good—at dead of night. This is a creditable play. It is a skit in the shirt sleeves of satire; quite wholesome and agreeable. The fault I had to find with it was that it at times was tedious. One tired of the variations upon one theme. One tired of the prompting and the gagging by actors who should have made themselves line-perfect.
>
> But Dolly Byrne said some good things and said them frequently. . . . At times the author is somewhat inclined to preach a sort of pessimistic optimism, but failed to let herself go. The result is a thing of rather frayed edges. . . .
>
> The audience were in the mood to donate laughter and applause, despite the rather lengthy intervals of waiting between changes of scenery.[133]

Susan L. Mitchell did not think the piece "a very taking play," but in Gerald MacNamara's "Exile Pat McCann" she saw "the art of a rarely accomplished actor."[134] W. J. Lawrence attended the opening night with Holloway and wrote:

> Mrs. Byrne's good–natured satire has much of the exhilaration and all of the surprises of one's first switchback ride. After a clumsy start it bumps along joyously, as often off the rails of reality as on, and only averting disaster by the steadying quality of its wit and humour. For, sooth to say, the play, in exploiting a bright new idea, sets it forth without much technical accomplishment. . . .
>
> Full as it is of well–diversified characterisation, *The Land of the Stranger* is essentially an actor's play, and the Ulster Players, with one or two exceptions, made the most of their opportunities. The burden of the piece falls largely on the shoulders of Exile Pat McCann's representative, and Mr. Gerald MacNamara, though somewhat unequal, was greatly helped by his curiously individual, half-jerky, half-explosive methods in striving to give illusion to a character operating on the outer edge of reality. . . . As Maureen O'Brien, Miss Jean Woods acted on the wrong lines, endowing this sweet, unaffected girl with a highly artificial, pretty method of talking, quite alien to the character, and, in the circumstances, distressing to listen to. Ever since the genesis of the Ulster Players there has been a convention that the ingenue of the company should act in this absurd way, and the sooner it is knocked on the head the better.[135]

And Holloway himself summed up the generally uninterested reaction to the piece:

> The piece is more a series of episodes than a play. . . . The piece interested but didn't excite unduly . . . and old Gerald MacNamara as Pat McCann was a delightful old soul.[136]

The exploitation, rather than the refutation of the exile's nostalgia, has continued up to our own time, the most notable recent examples being John Murphy's *The Country Boy*, which was presented at the Abbey in 1959 and remained popular through the 1960s, and Brian Friel's *Philadelphia, Here I Come*!, which was produced by the Gate in 1965, went on to a year's run on Broadway, and established its author's reputation as a leading Irish dramatist.

On 10 December, the Ulster Players offered a double bill of two new pieces, St. John Evine's *The Ship* and H. Richard Hayward's *Huge Love*. In September, Hayward, looking forward to the production of *The Ship*, had written an appreciation of Ervine in *The Ulster Review*. There, he attempted to pinpoint the outstanding characteristic of Ervine's writing:

> That characteristic I would unhesitatingly name—The Ulster Quality. The hard commonsense. The hatred of pose. The terrific sense of humour. The pride of race. The belief that an Ulster man has no business with a Chelsea accent.[137]

A more interesting and specific summation of Ervine was made by T. C. M. (undoubtedly T. C. Murray) in the *Independent*:

> One of the most forceful personalities in the Belfast of to-day. . . . An element of intense self-assertiveness is common to all his writings. . . . I do not think that Mr. Ervine is capable of writing a dull line. He can write foolish ones, but writes them in such a way that they entertain the reader more than the wisdom pretentiously uttered by less nimble spirits. Loving a fight he is contentiously provocative. . . . No

dramatic critic ever antagonised so many actors and playwrights, or evoked so many controversies. I believe that many of his utterances were not the expression of his reasoned opinions, but sprang solely from that spirit of impishness which delights in startling tame people by challenging their dearest convictions.

He has written at least three plays that will live. *Mixed Marriage*. . . . *Jane Clegg*. . . . The third of these plays is *The Ship*, which the Ulster Players are to give us for the first time to-night. I have read *The Ship*, and in some respects consider the play his finest achievement. The motive is the clash of conflicting ideals between father and son, and the argument is developed with extraordinary skill. There is a study of an old lady as beautiful in its tenderness and humanity as any I know in modern theatre.[138]

Our own feeling is that Murray is somewhat out in his judgment, that *John Ferguson* must be ranked among the very best of Ervine's plays, and that *The Ship* sails nowhere near excellence. With that low opinion of *The Ship*, all of the 1924 Dublin commentators were in agreement. The *Irish Times* wrote:

The Ship received several curtains at the close, but the tribute was to the players rather than to the play. The latter is constructed around a trite subject, the conflict of purpose between a successful business man and his only son, whose ideas of life are in direct antagonism to the father's. The play is cleverly put together, but its philosophy is little above the commonplace and the dialogue lacks the sparkle and the unexpected turns that we get in Shaw.[139]

H. R. W. in the *Independent* thought the good acting did much to make the play "a real live piece of drama," but found some fault with it:

The play is apparently intended as a commentary on the artificiality of life. As such it ought to have made an interesting comedy. But the author instead has preached us a sermon on the slavery of servitude, and is, therefore, often dull. Had Bernard Shaw treated the subject he would have rammed his point home with conviction, and yet would have maintained his comedy interest.

The character of the old lady, who ought to be attractive, becomes at times prosy and tedious.[140]

And Susan L. Mitchell wrote soundly in the *Irish Statesman*:

The Ship dramatises the eternal revolt of youth from the imposition on its plasticity of the will of a generation that has solidified its ideas in a different mould. Thurlow, the great ship-builder, has an only son who hates machines and resolves to leave the yards and become a farmer. The conflict of two equally stubborn wills makes the tragedy. An aged grandmother acts as a sort of omniscient Providence and is really the pivot on which the whole family revolves, the other members are the nonenities that Nature throws into families to balance her big individuals. Mr. Rutherford Mayne as the great shipbuilder was the outstanding figure in the play, a remarkably fine actor; I wish I saw him oftener. His power might well intimidate, but Mr. Hawyard, in his understanding presentation of Jack Thurlow, holds his own with admirable tenacity and a subtle appreciation of his part as one of a generation that had been toughened in a more tragic school. Mr. Mageean's study of the disillusioned soldier was clever and convincing. My only serious quarrel was with old Mrs. Thurlow's enunciation. Such a powerful character ought not, I think, to have spoken so slowly and haltingly. I have known old ladies of 80 to speak with the speed and volubility of 18. The age in her voice did not correspond to the youth of her language. But in the last scene no fault could be found with her.[141]

Brinsley MacNamara, W. J. Lawrence and Joseph Holloway were not greatly impressed either. As Holloway reported:

Outside the Gaiety I came across Brinsley MacNamara. . . . Mac had seen the plays before on Wednesday night. He thought *The Ship* a poor play and *Huge Love* a too drawn-out skit. Lawrence wasn't impressed with the first act of *The Ship* and the preachy chant-like monotony of delivery of Josephine Mayne as old Mrs. Thurlow irritated him quite. The Company were not at home in such a play; the homely Northern peasant stuff suits them all right, but they haven't body enough in their style for straight drama like this. Rutherford Mayne's big, noisy, deep voice as John Thurlow, the ship builder, drowned out the other voices. The dialogue was didactic and stilted, and the players made it more so by their long, drawn-out, hesitating method of speaking their words. I liked H. Richard Hayward's playing of the shipbuilder's son, Jack . . . and in Act Two, the most interesting act, J. R. Mageean gave a . . . character sketch of the role of Captain Cornelius, the best drawn character in the play. . . . The piece is long drawn out, and the scenes in the final act drag and scarcely grip.[142]

Hayward's *Huge Love* was a burlesque melodrama in four short acts or scenes, and it got a mixed response. The *Independent* called it.

a ramping satire on the melodrama, replete with its curses from the villain, its Gilbertian love-making, its heroics and its advertisement curtain. It is one of the most amusing "skits" which has been given by the Ulster Players.[143]

And Susan L. Mitchell thought it

really funny, a genuine extravaganza in which every absurdity of the stage was caricatured—a veritable apotheosis of melodrama. There is a delightful comic advertisement curtain that ought to make the raddled old sinner in the Gaiety Theater blush if it was not hardened beyond that possibility long ago.[144]

Holloway, however, thought that the play failed

quite despite J. R. Mageean's efforts, as the cigarette smoking villain . . . to import the proper spirit of burlesque into the hopelessly disjointed, long, drawn-out . . . joke. . . . The thing fizzled out badly . . . dismal.[145]

And, as the play has never been published, with this contradiction we must presumably let matters rest.[146]

The Northern Drama League opened its second season at the Rosemary Street Hall in Belfast on 28 November with a program of four one-acts: Helen

Simpson's *Pan in Pimlico,* Eugene O'Neill's *Ile,* Anton Tchekhov's *The Bear* and a new Northern play, Sam Bolton's comedy, *Miss Clegg's Legacy.* In writing of the program in the *Irish Statesman*, F. R. remarked that what most interested him was the reappearance after some years of James Hodgen:

> The North has produced some excellent actors (Mr. Storey, Mr. Gordon, Miss Crothers, who with Mr. Hodgen took part in Mr. Bolton's charming little comedy, were all good), but there is something about Mr. Hodgen that places him apart. I don't know what it is—whether it is his technique, or whether it is his personality that he somehow "gets across," but I do know that he achieves his effects by a kind of beauty that fills me, at any rate, with delight. Beauty may seem a strange word when we think of the kind of part he usually plays; nevertheless, I am convinced it is the right word. I have heard that he is not always easy to act with, that those pauses, hesitations, when one is waiting anxiously for one's cue, are a little nerve-racking; but to the audience, watching, as it were, the soul of the words dawning in the eyes, spreading gradually across the whole face, before the words themseves are actually spoken, they are a sheer heaven-sent joy. What do we care about cues when we are under the spell of an artist so certain, so natural; one who never strikes a false note, but keeps his whole part keyed to a kind of unity that produces the very illusion of life! We may pooh-pooh technique, finish, all the so dangerous qualities of the professional "star" but the fact remains that when we are in the presence of an actor like Mr. Hodgen we sink back in our chairs with a sigh of contentment. And it is precisely because his acting has this finish, beacause we know he will not want us to make allowances, because we can surrender ourselves completely to the charm of his performance, with its subtleties and hints and half-tones and reticences, that we feel so grateful.[147]

And of Bolton's play, F. R. remarked that it was "as fresh as primroses, in spite of the familiar turns of the plot."[148]

A writer in *The Ulster Review* speculated about "the aims and ideals of the Northern Drama League,"[149] but a writer in *T. P. and Cassell's Weekly* had probably already answered his points in an article called "Literary Life of Belfast":

> Not long ago you would have said without hesitation that Belfast was altogether a city of warehouses and shipyards, of cautious men. It is still a good ideal like that, but there are changes, and the possibility of great changes before long. We do not, as was our wont on puritanic grounds, fly with long faces from aesthetic enjoyment. There is evident among us now a desire to make our city more and more pleasant to live in.
>
> I suppose the recent founding of a Parliament in Northern Ireland induces certain responsibilites, among which, it may be, is the beginning of an individual culture. Who knows? It seems natural now when the long quarrelling and bloodshed are over, when we are on the threshold of a new epoch in our history, to turn with vigour to the arts of peace. Already one may perceive an unusual interest in literature, drama, music and painting.
>
> In time new writers will appear who will be inspired to sing songs peculiar to the province and will reach greater audiences that our gruff dialecticians have reached hitherto. To think of the literary life of Belfast, then, seems at first to think of

promise rather than of achievement, in a community with an awakening literary consciousness.

A symptom of the general trend towards art is the Northern Drama League, which started its first series of literary plays this winter. So far the members have performed works by Ibsen, Euripides, Yeats and Synge. The aim is to bring in the traits of local temperament so that, in the end, the actors may perform plays in a fashion of their own, with vivacious speech and perhaps a slight stolidity in movement.

Professor Meredith, one of the leaders of the movement, contends that there is too much mannerism and convention on the stage nowadays. With amateurs he finds it possible, by the skillful avoidance of professional tricks, to introduce a certain simplicity and freshness. Simplicity is also in his staging, often dubbed "Naive" by the older generation. Yet this unpretentious expression of his, as in *The Shadowy Waters*, is liked by the more discriminating.

The Ulster Theatre still carries on its seasoned work, reviving the old favourites by Lynn Doyle, Gerald MacNamara and Rutherford Mayne and our fondness for them seems almost imperishable. The themes are chiefly evolved in the setting of farm kitchens in County Down, and there is a lot of good-natured laughter. Indeed, so friendly is the give-and-take of their humour, even their political satire, that, be they in north or south, they are equally popular. . . .

Still, the stern unsympathetic atmosphere of Belfast has this, at least, to its credit. Only the fittest can survive its rudeness, and there is very little affectation about its literature.[150]

• • •

In London, the theatrical event of the year was the production of Shaw's *Saint Joan* at the New Theatre on 26 March.[151] With Sybil Thorndike as Joan, the play ran for 244 performances; and, despite some criticism of the beautiful and necessary epilogue, established itself immediately as one of the preeminent plays of the modern repertoire.

To turn from the major to the very minor, however, we might note that the Irish Literary Society in London occasionally staged evenings of plays, and on 4 April produced a triple bill at the Ashburton Club Theatre, which included the first production of a play by Bernard Duffy, entitled *The Spell*. As the *Independent* reported:

It is a one act comedy depicting the adventures in the Dublin Mountains of an umbrella-maker and his wife with the fairies. The dialogue throughout is very amusing.[152]

On 21 December, the Irish Literary Society at the Rehearsal Theatre, Bedford Street, Strand, presented three one-acts by Shan F. Bullock, the Ulster novelist. These were *The Turf Cutters*, *Country Wives*, and a new play called *The Stranger*, which, according to the *Independent*,

is an amusing comedy. The scene is laid in an Ulster farmhouse parlour, and depicts a discontented girl who, convinced that she does not love a local farmer to whom for all intents and purposes she is engaged, is finally convinced that her "ideal" man, whom she had met some years previously, is an ordinary, self-assured commercial traveller. Her illusion having been dispelled on her second meeting with her "ideal" matters with her recognised lover are amicably adjusted.[153]

• • •

The notable theatrical death of the year was that of the great Eleonora Duse, on Easter night, 21 April, in Pittsburgh. In Ireland, Nora Desmond died on 29 June, and Holloway wrote:

> I was shocked on opening the paper to read of Mrs. Jack Meade's (Nora Desmond's) death in a Dublin Nursing home on yesterday (Sunday) after a brief illness. It is only a couple of years ago since I spent an afternoon with her at Miss O'Brennan's. Strange in a conversation, she happened to say, "I wonder will I ever act again; it looks as I have been shelved." . . . In the old Abbey company, she played many parts, but none better than old Mrs. Grogan in *The Building Fund*. She toured a lot of late years with Arthur Sinclair and Co.[154]

In London, early in June, Ralph Silvester died, and the *Evening Herald* reported:

> Born in Dublin 74 years ago Mr. Silvester was a favourite with the audiences which patronised the old circus in Brunswick Street, the Queen's Theatre, the old Star Theatre, and the Mechanics' Hall, and was a contemporary of Whitbread, Dan Lowry, Pat Kinsella, and Kennedy Millar. Perhaps he was best known as "Silvester the Flying Man," and his association with variety, drama, and circus extended over a great many years.
>
> During his career he was the proprietor or lessee of hippodromes, theatres, or Town Halls in numerous towns, including Barrow-in Furness, Scarboro', Grimsby, Ashington, Carlisle, Whitehaven, and Falkirk. His last venture was in the cinema business.
>
> In his later days he confined his enterprises to Ireland, which are being continued by his two sons, Ralph and Chris, who are presently on tour here, and recently had an engagement at the Theatre Royal in the revue *Signals of 1924*.[155]

• • •

During the year, Joseph Holloway had many chats with Sean O'Casey, and those we have not had occasion to allude to previously we have gathered together here.[156]

> *Thursday, January 3.* At the Abbey I saw Sean O'Casey who said he handed in a new three–act play [*Juno*] last week. . . . He often loves to put in a character he has known into a play without the character having aught to do with the plot. He likes to read Chekhov's plays; Chekhov seems to let his characters speak as they please and get them into his play's scheme. O'Casey is not a racing man and, therefore, didn't much like *The Glorious Uncertainty*.

Tuesday, February 12. . . . I sat it [*The Two Shepherds*] out alongside Sean O'Casey and W. A. Henderson. The former told me his play has not yet been put into rehearsal though down for production on February 25 (Monday). He likes Dolan best of all the actors in the company, though McCormick acts many parts supremely well and is over-conscientious if anything. McCormick almost annoyed him asking him to explain what he meant "Seumas Shields's" part to be like, and when O'Casey had explained to him over and over again, Mac said he'd carry out his own conception of the part, and did, and was right. O'Casey thinks him really great in the character. He didn't like him in *A Doll's House*; it was beyond the company, he thought.

Tuesday, March 18. . . . I had a chat with Sean O'casey in the vestibule. He told me that when he started to write plays he thought he was a second Shaw sent to express his views through his characters, and was conceited enough to think that his opinions were the only ones that mattered. It was Lady Gregory who advised him to cut out all expression of self, and develop his peculiar aptness for character drawing. At first he didn't take kindly to her advice, but afterwards on consideration felt she was right.

He was so poor when he took to writing first that he hadn't the money to supply himself with paper to write his stuff on, and a pal supplied him with paper filched from his employer's store. His first two plays were written in his cramped handwriting, and yet the Abbey directors read his script and expressed sorrow at having to reject both plays, and gave him sound critical advice which he resented at first, but on second thought accepted, and was determined to profit by and did. He was determined to succeed. . . .

He has a small typewriter now. He intends to stick to playwriting; he thinks Robinson his too many irons in the fire to do himself juntice. O'Casey reads Robinson's *Observer* article each week, but doesn't think very much of it. He should concentrate more; only those who do reach the very top. This is the age of the specialist.

Friday, March 21. . . . I had a chat with lame Maguire. . . . Speaking of Sean O'Casey, he remembered him as being one of the first to join the Piper's Band and wear the kilt, and an ungainly figure he cut in it. He was more like a country lad than a Dubliner. He always walked with a near-sighted bend of the head. He was always strong and energetic, and when he played hurling he looked a guy in short knickers, and once in a match in the park—so it is said—he killed a sparrow, thinking he was swiping at the ball. He agreed with nobody and believed in nothing. He was strangely distant and silent always. He wrote for *The Irish Worker* and was secretary to the Citizen Army. The book he wrote about the Citizen Army wasn't thought much of by those connected with it. He was a shunter on the Northern Railway in those days. He was always sore-eyed and took an active part in the Gaelic movement. He was very energetic in all he undertook. Now he has struck oil as a playwright, he is determined to work hard to reach the top in that branch of literature. His friend out of Webb's joined us in the latter part of our conversation about O'Casey. It was he told the sparrow incident.

Friday, March 28. A bitterly sharp evening with an icy cutting wind about. I had a long chat with O'Casey in the vestibule of the Abbey. He thinks the Government is proving a set of woeful incompetents—egotistical and intolerant of criticism. They are going from bad to worse. They'll be nobody's friend shortly. He spoke of the hypocrisy over the shooting of the soldier at Cork. "The honour of Ireland is at stake over it, people say who don't know what honour is!"

He witnessed terrible deeds during recent years; a friend of his was riddled with bullets and mutilated in a horrible way by the Green and Tans, a young Tipperary lad. Nothing could be more brutal than the treatment he got. It is hard to think Irish people capable of such savagery. Savages would be decent in comparison to them. After the inquest his remains were brought to his digs, and O'Casey helped to carry in the coffin to his friend's upstairs. Another lad he knew was taken out and tied up by his hands—this feet dangling some distance from the ground, while they poured salts through a tin dish down his throat. The poor fellow was cut down alive, but he is a human wreck ever since—always shaking, though as brave as ever.

O'Casey believes the oath is the peace destroyer. Irishmen as a whole will never be got to take the oath of allegiance to the King. It is all folly to think otherwise. All oaths should be abolished, O'Casey thinks. Sean Connolly would never take one, yet he died fighting the first day of Easter Week, 1916. O'Casey believes in paying his way and doing without when he can't. "No amount of pledges or oaths will keep a person from breaking them if they have no principle to go by. The present day creed is to teach all to be dishonest. Hypocrisy is over all."

Tuesday, April 15. . . . O'Casey likes some of Lady Gregory's work, but lately read *Shanwalla* and some others of hers, including *The Wrens*, for which he didn't care. MacNamara likes *The Dragon* and *The Golden Apple*, and thinks she found herself in them.

. . . Speaking of Shaw's play *Saint Joan* breaking all records at the New Theatre. O'Casey remarked that Shaw could never be repaid sufficiently for his work—which is great. . . .

O'Casey, speaking of the English and Irish, said, "Although I write cynically about the Irish in my plays, I have a much greater opinion of their intellects than I have of the English. I understand English politics, but I never met an Englishman who understood the Irishman's outlook."

Wednesday, April 23. . . . At the Abbey I had a chat with Sean O'Casey in the vestibule during Act I of Shaw's play, and I showed him some drawings I had made on postcards, and he said, "You seem to me a wonder—a man who takes things easily, or seems to shirk them altogether, yet having a great memory, and very tolerant of other's views and holding very fixed and unshakeable views of your own on many things—very affable to all, and, in fact, a type all to yourself." He hoped I didn't mind him saying so, and I said, "Not at all. But you are wrong in thinking I take things easily, as I am ever and always busy when at home—reading, writing, drawing, etc. It is only when I am out I take it easily or seem idling time away, and yet all the time I am absorbing material to jot down when I return home. Architecture gave me up before I thought of giving it up. The War killed for the time domestic architecture, and my work ceased to exist in consequence. That was how it was. When it revives, I will probably be too old to resume again."

When I told him I wrote some 2000 pages a year on events and things, he added. "You are hard to understand." . . .

Speaking of a visit to Belfast. O'Casey said he went there with the intention of spending a week in that city, but on being there a few hours he wished for Dublin and returned to the railway station to find no passenger train starting for some hours, so he got on a luggage train that was just starting. He was working on the railway at the time and travelled free. Protestant and all as he was, Papish Dublin was the place for him.

Saturday, May 10. . . . O'Casey told me he came to the rescue of a lady in the vestibule who didn't seem to know her way about, never having been in the Abbey before, and he found out she was a cousin of his he hadn't seen for years. Her father was 89, and as bitter a Protestant as ever he knew, but a fine old fellow if you kept him off his pet subject, hatred of Roman Catholics. O'Casey escaped the narrow environment in which the old man was brought up, having always to work for his living and meeting all sorts of people, and he found all sorts, the good and the bad, in all walks of life and all religions, and his mind broadened to all humanity. . . .

When I mentioned to Sean O'Casey that Frank Fay was to speak on "Dramatic Art" tomorrow. Sunday (May 11) at the Father Mathew Hall, he said, "I don't hold with Fay's views on dramatic art at all, though I admire the enthusiasm with which he upholds such views. It's difference of opinion that keeps the world fresh for people to live in. If we were all of the one opinion, Earth would soon become Hell through monotony."

Tuesday, May 20. At Webb's I came across Sean O'Casey. . . . O'Casey is amused when he hears people say, who never were in a tenement, that his plays are photographic of the life he depicts. They not knowing anything at first hand of what they are talking. . . . He didn't care for Shiels's play, *The Retrievers*; it was but poor, ill-digested stuff. He was amused when I told him that MacNamara said to me that, "It was a wonderfully clever satirical comedy and far above the heads of the audience." He wondered if it were more subtle than Shaw's plays or Nietzsche's writings, and yet they were easily understood. O'Casey thought Sheils's *Bedmates* and *First Aid* good and understandable satires. But in *The Retrievers* things were too far-fetched and unconvincing. . . .

On his telling me he had purchased a volume of AE's collected poems, I mentioned that he would be writing his next play amongst the stars. Then he told me of the play with the title *The Plough Amongst the Stars* he had in his mind to write. He also got two volumes of Nietzsche at Webb's. . . . He regretted the loss of several books he lent, such as McGill's *The Rat Trap* a very realistic book. He thinks James Stephens' *The Charwoman's Daughter* a very pleasingly written story, but scarcely true to slum life.

Tuesday, June 3. . . . I met Sean O'Casey looking into Eason's, and he asked me what way I was going, and I said any way if he waited a moment till I got the papers. Then we strolled up and into St. Stephen's Green and saw the young swans and sat down near the bandstand and had a chat on all sorts of topics. I told him of the reception of the play *Juno* in Cork. He knew Liam O'Flaherty well years ago when he was a Socialist speaker. He thought his sketch, "The Hook," splendid. He liked Kelleher's "Glamour of Dublin," but not his articles or play in *The Dublin Magazine.*

We spoke of *The Gunman* and "Maguire" and Knocksedan with regard to the time that should elapse. I also referred to the pedlar's sleeping out Mass time, and yet the others acted as if it were a weekday and O'Casey said to me. "It was a weekday, but the pedlar went to Mass each day and was a daily communicant."

Fay wanted O'Casey's earlier plays that were refused by the Abbey, but he couldn't give them to him or anyone. He said he destroyed them, but he didn't. He hopes to use some of the dialogue later on. He thinks Fay's art of acting is dead. He is pompous and dictatorial now.

O'Casey told me of an evening he spent in one of the intellectual's houses, where the three or four present talked art at top speed. He was struck dumb and listened after awhile for scraps for future plays. Conversation should be free to roam at will here, there, and everywhere, and be natural and never conclusive. Everyone have their say, but none lay down the law.

On Saturday next, O'Casey goes to Coole on his vacation. He is not enamoured of the idea. He stays for a fortnight. O'Casey wrote an article for *The Irish Statesman's* "Literature and Life" column under the head of "Life and Literature" from the workman's standpoint. AE asked for more. He has notes for fifty articles by him, but is too lazy to write them. He thinks the *Statesman* an interesting paper. The new aristocracy is ignorant and selfish, and he told me of a farmer in a small way who purchased a castle recently vacated by its appropriate owner, who on leaving took the pictures from the frames as the transit of the latter would be exorbitant. O'Casey heard of the farmer writing to a firend to know where he'd get pictures at 2/6 or 5/– to fill the frames. That was the new Irish rich for you.

Friday, July 25. . . . I was speaking to Sean O'Casey in the vestibule. He spent most of the time when in Galway wandering about the woods of Coole. He found the country people much like anyone else, singing, "Yes, we have no bananas today!" He met one Irish-speaking peasant woman whom he had a delightful chat with. He read *Saint Joan* and thought the dialogue fine and chockful of raps at England. Shaw dearly loves such sallies.

O'Casey told me he has a one-act play nearly finished. He can write dialogue easily enough, having no difficulty in doing so, but construction does not come so easily with him. It is a very long one-act, and he has been cutting it down as much as he can.

Shiels ought to be made to come and see his own plays; he has the gift of drama, but his plots are as complicated as detective stories and get the spectators into black knots; in fact, they "dunno" where they are often. His dialogue is excellent and his character sketching strong and effective, but if he saw his pieces on the stage he could improve them much, He is sensitive in coming up to the Abbey, having only two stumps of legs. O'Casey likes his tramps in *Insurance Money*; they are very poetic, but, like all the tramps in modern Irish plays, are in no way like the real article. Shiels has the knack of writing exciting pot-boiling stories of the wild and wooly west cowboy type. It was in the States he lost his limbs. His American types in *The Retrievers* are composite ones, Mr. Kelly and others tell me. . . .

Thursday, July 31. . . . At the Abbey . . . I told Sean O'Casey that Colum was anxious to see him. He came in with me, and we sat out the balance of the programme together. He thought *Maurice Harte* a great play greatly acted, and *The Rising of the Moon* was also impressively played by Nolan and Dolan as the Sergeant and the Ballad Singer. . . .

O'Casey again spoke of *Ann Kavanagh* as real poor stuff. To him Miss Macardle as a dramatist is nil. He looks at strikes from the workman's point of view, and thinks all arbitration biased in favour of capital and the state. The workman has always to fight bitterly for his existence; all the world is against him.

Tuesday, August 19. . . . Sean O'Casey told me of all whom he met with in the old Sinn Fein days, he liked Mrs. de Valera the best. She was a very bright, unassuming, intelligent woman; he knew her as Miss O'Flanagan, and heard her lecture very agreeably in Sinn Fein halls. "It is such as she should represent Ireland in Parliament," he said. The Countess was always in hysterical terror. Marriage seems to have blotted out publicity from Mrs. de Valera's life, and more's the pity, O'Casey thinks.

He told me of a poor girl he knew and liked in the old days, and does so still, who married, and whose husband is now a general in the army, and she drives about in a motor and aftects a cockney accent which amuses Sean. He is friends with her still, as I said, and sometimes when she is passing in a motor and sees him, she stops to give him a lift. Lately on one of these occasions, she invited him "home to tea," and he happened to say, "Now?" by way of interrogation, and she interpreted it as "No." This was the last straw, and Sean asked her for God's sake drop the cockney accent and speak as she used to do in the old days. The new rich are all beggars on horseback riding to the Devil.

Saturday, August 23. . . . O'Casey, referring to the way some are flashing money about asked me had I ever been to the Labour Exchange? He had been there lately and tried to get to the hutch his docket was made out for, but the great crush of men in the queue almost made him faintish, and after about an hour and a half of it (and he still hours away from the hutch) he had to try to push his way out of the crowd. It is a terrible sight to see so many men out of work. Some are there from six in the morning though their cards state the hour to apply to the hutch, and if they arrive there before the time specified, "They are told to go to Hell!" He should like to show Yeats or Robinson such sights. Then they would be less ready to advocate the use of the lash.

Friday, October 10. Spoke to Sean O'Casey on the inclination of people to laugh at the tragic incidents in life. He told me of an incident he witnessed years ago in the street. A blind man came along and bumped into two men conversing on the kerb, and a little further on a blind man coming from the opposite direction collided with him; and he angrily exclaimed, "Is the town full of blind men today?" O'Casey said he laughed at the incident without considering the terrible tragedy that lay behind it.

5
1925

By 1925, the movies had far outstripped the theatre in popularity. For instance, the *Irish Times* reported:

> During the first eight months of this year the Free State's official censor viewed four million feet—or some 760 miles—of film, and eighty per cent of the films shown in these islands derive from Hollywood. In other words, a substantial and, perhaps, the most abiding part of the education of the three and a half million inhabitants of the Saorstat is conducted from the State of California. In the first place, as Horace and Tennyson have said, things seen are mightier than things heard: the "movies" are more striking and more attractive than school-books. In the next place, every Irish village has a picture-house to-day, which offers a couple of hours' daily excitement all the year round, for a few pence, to every school-child. These houses do not close for two summer months in order that the attendants may learn the Irish language. A census—if it were possible—of the total number of persons, young and old, who visit the picture-houses of the Saorstat in a single day would provide the serious citizen with much food for thought. What do our Irish children learn at the picture-houses? Occasionally they see a really instructive film which explains a process of industry or reveals the beauties of nature, but, in the main, they take the following impressions to bed with them:—that America is the grandest and most adventurous country in the world; that wealth, fine houses and luxurious motor cars represent the summum bonum; that the means by which such wealth is acquired need not be investigated too closely; that "quickness on the draw" is a most desirable accomplishment, and that, over and above all these things, sexual passion is the pervading interest of life. We think that this is a bad sort of education for Irish youth, but we can propose no remedy. The films cannot be banished, and apparently they cannot be reformed. The queerest feature of the whole business is the complacency towards it of the people whose ideal is a Gaelicised and isolated Ireland. They strain violently at the gnat of "Anglicisation," but swallow this camel of Americanisation without a murmur.[1]

The extent to which indigenous Irish virtues were being eroded or perverted by Hollywood is debatable, but the *Times* was correct in saying that it was difficult, if not impossible, to counteract the popularity of Hollywood. Ireland was a poor country, and movies were a cheap and accessible entertainment whose popularity remained unchallenged at least until about 1960 and the coming of television.

Nevertheless, there were two somewhat effective Irish antidotes to Hollywood. One was the increasingly rigorous film censorship. For instance,

Chaplin's *Woman of Paris* opened in New York in October 1923, but it was not until October 1925 that this hardly sexually explicit comedy was cut enough to satisfy the Irish censor and to be released in Dublin. A second antidote was that the values which Hollywood advertised were simply unrealisable for most Irish people. It was poverty that impeded change, and, when Hugh Leonard in his charming *Home Before Dark*, wrote about the films he saw as a boy, he was talking about a vision of life that may have seemed glamourously admirable, but that was as unattainable as the moon.

But the effect of the movies was, perhaps, not all bad. From the establishment of some stability with the Irish Free State, and for several decades afterwards, Ireland was a tight, uptight little island. The movies and, to some extent, radio offered a small window on the world, a small dream of escape from the dreariness and the poverty of both urban and rural existence.

And occasionally the dream touched lightly on reality. When, for instance, a film star came to Ireland, he was adulated and mobbed; and he responded with an appropriate gush. On June 15, the *Evening Herald* reported, "'Sure it's God's country it is,' said Colleen Moore, the famous Irish-American film star, after landing at Dun Laoghaire Pier with the first glimpse of the Irish coast in her mind."[2] And her visit only deepened her perceptive initial impression: "Ireland! Well, it's just great. I kissed the Blarney stone, saw wonderful Killarney, and visited the gorgeous vales of Wicklow. And the folk there! They gave us a great reception, and, well—I loved them."[3]

The dream also touched lightly—very lightly—on reality in the movies that were shot in or partly in Ireland. These films reflected mainly the glowing traditional views of popular nineteenth-century Irish fiction and drama—the broad comedy, the pulsating romance, the heroic patriotism. Consider the following press reaction to the trade showing of the Irish Photoplays film, *Cruiskeen Lawn*, at La Scala on 16 January:

> Anyone who has watched the progress of the film producing industry in this country during the past few years and compared *Cruiskeen Lawn* with its predecessors must admit that it is a tremendous advance upon those efforts of the past. All the best known people on the Irish stage have parts in the film, which has been made amidst beautiful scenery, and photographed with remarkable skill.
>
> The story is principally concerned with two young lovers, Nora Blake (Kathleen Armstrong) and Boyle Roche (Tom Moran), both of whose families are chronically poor. All that remains of the former glories of the Roche establishment is a dilapidated mansion and "Cruiskeen Lawn," an old racehorse, once famous throughout the country. To make matters worse Nora's father is heavily in debt to Samuel Silke (Jimmy O'Dea), a member of the "new rich," whose purse is considerably longer than his family tree, and Silke desires to wed Nora.
>
> Then we are introduced to Sheila and Darby, Boyle's faithful servants, who between them provide a considerable part of the amusement in the picture. From a most fascinating character called "Dublin Dan" (Barrett MacDonnell), disguised in full war paint as "Rolling Thunder," and describing himself as "a lineal descendant of "The Last of the Mohicans," Darby buys a bottle of physic guaranteed to cure his

aches and pains (he suffers from rheumatism), but the racehorse drinks it and is promptly rejuvenated.

When Boyle discovers the miracle, he hastens to arrange a bet with Silke of £10,000 to £500 that Cruiskeen would win the Calaghan cup. Old Blake, who saw all the Roches had a mad streak, agreed that if "Cruiskeen" did win the Cup, Boyle should marry his daughter. The secret of "Cruiskeen's" transformation was well kept, and, amidst scenes of wild excitement, the race was won. After the victory, Silke retires from the scene, and we see the establishment of "The Elixir of Life, Ltd.," a wealthy company which "converts 'Tishys' into Derby Winners."

The picture is undoubtedly great fun. . . . It is an Irish story, acted and directed in this country by native players.[4]

As this account makes clear, this film was an obvious attempt to attract a broad, lowbrow audience. The author and director of the three Irish Photoplays Films was John MacDonagh; and his film work was a far cry from his art theatre work with Edward Martyn in Hardwicke Street. It did, however, prepare him for his assault on the commercial stages with his series of revues at the Olympia.

In December, MacDonagh's *Wicklow Gold* opened in Dublin, and the *Irish Times* reviewed it:

In that humorous vein so characteristic of him, the author unfolds a very amusing tale of one Ned O'Toole, an old Wicklow farmer, who has a fixed idea that there is plenty of gold in the rivers of his native county. The opening scene is laid in Avoca on Fair Day, when Ned makes up his mind to "make a match" for his son, Larry. The latter is by way of being browbeaten, but withal finds stolen moments to make love to Kitty O'Byrne, the pretty daughter of a widow. Old Ned's choice, however, lies in other directions, and there are some very funny situations showing the old man trying to make a bargain in marrying off Larry to a "strong" farmer's daughter. By a clever trick old Ned is persuaded that there is a gold deposit in the river that runs through the Widow O'Byrne's land, and this situation is used as the lever to force his consent to the marriage of Larry and Kitty.

The story is cleverly conceived, and swings along from one humorous position to another. The parts have been very well allocated, and are creditably acted. Chris Sylvester is very effective in his study of old Ned O'Toole. He has a very long and intimate knowledge of the ways and customs of country folk in all parts of Ireland, and this has enabled him to bring an atmosphere into his acting. There were one or two little things that did not run too well—in some of the scenes his "make-up" was too youthful and somewhat at variance with the general idea. Another fault, or rather awkwardness, was the too lavish use of his arms. At times he threw them about too much and not at all naturally. It may help out a situation or help home a point on the stage, but on the screen it looked simply awkwardness. It was a fault more or less with all of the company, possibly excepting the Dr. McCarthy of Mr. Fred Jeffs, whose hands invariably were buried in his pockets when he was not writing certificates. . . .

The filming is very naturally done, without aids or artifices of any kind, most of the scenes being in the open air in familiar spots in county Wicklow; but, probably from lack of experience in "shooting" scenes, the impressions are too often of the "close-up" type. There was a sense of being a little bit too near, but, after all, that is a fault to be expected, and one which will be remedied with experience. The production was very creditable indeed.[5]

In 1924, a film was shot in Dublin, Enniskerry, and Powerscourt which was a good deal more serious in its conception than the Irish Photoplays films. Called *Land of her Fathers*, it was given a private showing at the Grafton Picture House early in October.[6] The *Evening Herald* reported:

> The producer, Mr. Winslow, explained that several alterations and improvements had yet to be done, and consequently allowance had to be made for the "raw" state.
>
> The photography was splendid, and proved that our climate is quite suitable for "movie-making." The particular beauty spots chosen were magnificent examples of Irish scenery. And the interior settings were the best yet presented by Irish cinema productions. The acting was very good, and there were few weak points, anywhere.
>
> The heroine's part was interpreted by Miss Phyllis O'Hara,[7] while Michael MacLiammoir, the well-known young artist, was surprisingly good as the patriotic hero.
>
> The popular playwright, Mr. Frank Hugh O'Donnell, gave a clever study of the kindly friend of the hero, while Tom Moran, no novice to the films, was exceedingly good as the "bad man."
>
> The Abbey Players, Mr. Dolan, Miss Crowe, Mr. F. J. McCormick, Mr. Barry Fitzgerald, and Miss Maureen Delany were each excellent; Miss Delany's droll humour "registering" as well on the screen as on the stage. It was a pity Mr. McCormick was not seen more, as the little acting he had to do could not have been better done. His introduction and sudden exit left us wanting more.
>
> Taken all round, the producers may well congratulate themselves on the success of their achievement. It is not the first "Made-in-Ireland," nor all Irish-cast film, but it is certainly the most ambitious yet attempted.
>
> Special attention must be made of the clever photography of Dublin, starting from the Kingsbridge Station, and carrying on through the various streets. . . .
>
> The story of this film has much in it that will make a universal appeal. There is a complete absence of any of the stage Irishism common to all previous attempts at motion picture-making. It is a splendid portrayal of modern Irish life and conditions of which no Irishman need be ashamed.
>
> We welcome the *Land of her Fathers* as the first successful enterprise in the motion picture industry in Ireland.[8]

John MacDonagh's "stock company," which he used in the Irish Photoplays productions and then later in his revues included actors like Jimmy O'Dea, Fay Sargent, and Fred Jeffs, who were basically music hall artistes; but the extraordinary cast of *Land of her Fathers* makes one whish that this film might be disinterred.

In 1925, an even more ambitious film, *Irish Destiny*, was being shot in Dublin by Eppels Films; and a highlight of this film was the burning of the Custom House during the Civil War.

One commercial film was partially shot in Ireland during the year, and this was *Irish Luck* with the American film idol Thomas Meighan. Meighan and his party arrived in Dun Laoghaire in early August, and the *Evening Herald* described their plans:

> The first scene of the picture would be made at the Phoenix Park races to-day, and they intended to make a first-class Irish film which, from the pictorial side, would

show Ireland at its best, and include about 1000 scenes in all. Over 100 scenes would be taken in Dublin, including Grafton St., Merrion Sq., College Green, Glendalough, Bray, Killiney, Dalkey, etc., following which the party would proceed to Killarney, Blarney Castle, Cobh, etc.[9]

After several weeks of shooting, Meighan returned to New York to film the interior scenes, and was interviewed about his experiences:

Just before a scene was taken the other day in the Astoria studio . . . Mr. Meighan said that while he was in Dublin there was no little difficulty in making some exterior scenes because of the tremendous throngs that surrounded the spot where he was acting. One morning in the Irish capital he was playing a scene near the O'Connell Bridge, and just as the photographer had started to grind a young man stepped in front of the camera. Mr. Meighan told him that he must get out of the line of the camera, whereat the Irishman insisted that he wanted to be in the picture, that it was "a free street and a Free State."

While speaking of Dublin, Mr. Meighan mentioned the Dublin cinemas.

"Once your eyes have become accustomed to the darkness in a Dublin picture theatre," said the actor, "the first thing that strikes you is the blue haze of cigarette smoke floating up from the seats all over the place. . . .

"Dublin exhibitors are about five years behind their American contemporaries in picture presentation.

"The Irish feel that if the picture is in focus, and accompanied by a six or seven piece orchestra, they owe no further obligation to their patrons. And the Dublin picture-goer expects nothing more.

"The Government tax cuts heavily into the Irish theatre's revenue, for one fifth of all the money taken in at the box office goes to the tax collector, and consequently admission prices are relatively high, averaging more than two shillings. Curiously enough the orchestra seats are the cheapest, while the first balcony is the highest in price. After the main title of the picture is thrown on the screen, a title in Gaelic appears, which informs the spectator that the production has passed the Free State Board of Censors. This board has been the cause of more than one American film being witheld from the public. It may be because the story is too suggestive or the picture may contain a theme which is offensive to Irish sensibilities. . . .

"There are five or six cinemas in Dublin, none of which is anything like as large as the principal ones on Broadway, nor are their appointments anything to compare with the New York theatres.

"In Belfast, however, there is a new theatre seating about 2,500 persons which compares favourably with the best on Broadway. . . ."

Mr. Meighan said that while he was in Ireland he saw John MacCormack, the singer, and several other Irish friends. He also met William Butler Yeats, the poet, and attended a performance of Bernard Shaw's *Man and Superman* at the Abbey Theatre.[10]

Film madness included public discussions about the feasibility of Ireland as a film centre, the announcement of new film companies and projects, a garden party in which one could be photographed wearing Tom Mix's hat, beauty contests, a school of film acting, and dangerous public stunts.[11] It also included some violent Irish criticism of this basically foreign medium: one Dublin lady was one or twice in court for hurling ink at the screen during a newsreel appearance of the Prince of Wales; and the republicans not only seized and burnt films they did not like, but even bombed Dublin's Masterpiece cinema for showing such a film.[12] Despite such forceful criticisms, and also despite the government passing a law to extend the censorship to the advertising outside the cinemas,[13] the popularity of the movies in Ireland was entrenched by 1925; and it would not be notably dissipated for more than thirty years.

• • •

The chief rival to the popularity of films was radio, and by 1925 "listening in" had become widespread. It was not only a novel, but also a cheap entertainment. As one commentator put it:

> It is already the cheapest form of entertainment, but now with the reductions that have taken place during the past few weeks in valves, batteries, and other wireless components, we are approaching even closer to the Valhalla of something for nothing.[14]

Even the theatre reflected the interest in radio: In March, the Abbey staged a revised version of O'Casey's one-act, *Cathleen Listens In*; and in May MacDonagh's revue, *Dublin Listening*, appeared at the Olympia. The potentialities of the new medium seemed limitless, and, according to one report, it might even cure cancer. However, it might also be the cause of pernicious new diseases. For instance:

> Radio wrinkles are the latest dread of American women who see their faces marred by folds and creases brought on by the strain of listening to wireless programmes. Beauty specialists affect to find that the faces of female radio fans acquire a strained expression from listening night after night to radio. Their brows become knitted, their lips firmly pressed together, and their whole expression hardened and less womanlike, say the beauty experts. The consequence is what is called the "radio face," of which the chief characteristics are wrinkles.[15]

Belfast had its own transmitting station and developed its own programs before Dublin did; and in January the comic monologuist, Cathal MacGarvey, traveled to Belfast for a broadcast, and then reported what the new medium was like:

> It was at the Belfast BBC Station last week that I had my first real experience. . . .
>
> The studio was as capacious as some of our concert halls, and in the luxuriousness of its furnishing it resembled the reception room of some great Oriental potentate.
>
> The ceiling, walls, and pillars were beautifully draped in a mauve and cream fabric of what material I don't know. It didn't look like silk, it had a look like that crinkly paper; but it wasn't paper, it was of a clothy nature, and I have no doubt it had something to do with the acoustics of the studio and the resonance of the music and speech. The carpet on the floor was fully five inches deep, and it gave you the

feeling that it would be a crime to speak above a whisper until you faced the starter. That was a wrong impression. It was permissable to talk as much as you like until the danger signal—the red light—was switched on, then you were up against it. . . .

They were all behind me when I took my stand as directed about five feet from the microphone, which, as well as I remember, is the name of the machine you are talking to. It's funny having an audience at your back. I had only one of an audience in front of me—a little chap whom I knew out of the station orchestra. I determined to tell the tale to him, for he's at all times a good audience for me.

But whist! steady! There goes the danger signal. Mr. Guthrie has made the dreaded announcement; the lever is pulled; up goes the barrier, and I jump off. By sheer good luck I get quickly into my stride and settle down comfortably to my work.

I haven't gone far when I hear at my back subdued tittering, then more tittering not so subdued, then bursts of unchecked, or not to be checked, laughter that, as I afterwards learned, was heard distinctly by the listeners-in.

This was very encouraging and spurred me to do, as the folk song says, "my whole endeavour." I did it, too, and I understand I was a howling success, though I didn't howl. I only talked; I gave a couple of humorous monologues, and told a number of witty stories.[16]

The bulk of early radio programming was musical, but occasional interludes, such as MacGarvey's comic monologues, looked forward to the development of an original radio drama.

In the Free State, according to one estimate, there were already ten thousand wireless sets, and by the end of the year a number of experimental broadcasts had been made from Dublin. On 14 December, the *Evening Herald* reported:

Experiments have been conducted at Dublin Broadcasting Station, Denmark St. (2RN), and the results were highly satisfactory.

A number of personal friends of Mr. S. Clandillon, Director, and Mr. V. O'Brien, Musical Director, gave their services free, and provided a really good concert. Inquiries showed the clarity of reception was satisfactory.

The Station last night relayed between 9 and 10 o'clock the London programme.[17]

And on 16 December:

A notable advance in the working of the Dublin Broadcasting Station was made last night when Mr. John Moody's orchestra and the Independent Choir, conducted by Mr. W. McGouran, were relayed by outside broadcast from the Scala Theatre. The experiment will be repeated to-night.[18]

But in the general chorus of praise, there was already some criticism, and one correspondent wrote:

On Saturday night the reception was, no doubt, clear, but the matter broadcasted was of the most trumpery description even for a test performance. Selections from *Maritana*, no matter by whom played, fill me with homicidal thoughts, and to hear an ultra-refined lady vocalist pronouncing the word "vale" as if it meant the flesh of a calf made me weep aloud.

It is stated that some difficulty has been experienced in finding the proper distance at which the announcer should stand. Failing the adoption of my suggestion of no place within a radius of ten statute miles, I think he should be taught that the name "Charles" is not pronounced as he thinks it ought to be, nor is the word "route" the same as that which is applied to the disastrous termination of a battle.

Cats-whisker[19]

Despite Cats-whisker's strictures, preparations proceeded for the Free State's broadcasting station to give its first official broadcast on 1 January 1926.

• • •

An Comhar, the Gaelic Dramatic League, occasioned much less interest than Irish films or an Irish radio station, but it mounted eight programs in 1925, usually on a Monday night at the Abbey Theatre. On 19 January, An Comhar staged again *An Dochtúir Bréige*, the adaptation of Molière's *Le Medecin Malgre Lui* by Fionan Lynch, and also the first production of *Fíoraon le Fiarán*, an adaptation of Tolstoy's *Falsely True* by Fiachra Eilgeach. The *Irish Times* thought that the Molière production was no improvement over its original production in 1924, and that "There was less colour and exuberance in last night's performances than is usual with the Gaelic plays . . ."[20] As usual, the voice of the prompter was much in evidence.

On 16 February, An Comhar presented a triple bill at the Abbey, which included the first production of the Oireachtas prize winner, *An Saoghal Eile* by Liam Gogan; the first production in Irish of Contance Powell-Anderson's *The Courting of the Widow Malone* under the title of *Au Suirghe leis an mBaintreach*; and a revival of Béaslaí's *Fear an Scéilín Grinn*, copies of which were now published and sold in the foyer. As the *Irish Times* reported:

Last night the Gaelic players had a crowded house at the Abbey Theatre—for the first time this season. They rewarded their large audience, for they offered a very interesting programme, and—taking criticism to heart, perhaps—they had prepared their parts thoroughly.

The first piece was Mr. Liam Gogan's one-act prize play, *The Other World*. A party of young men in dress attire are talking over their drinks at midnight, and they debate the question, Is there another world? An agnostic—played by Piaras Beasley—mocks at the idea of the supernatural, and at last, after much eerie talk, they all agree that the first of them to die will return and tell the rest. One of them has to leave the party to go home early. After some moments, when the talk has grown more eerie still, and the lights are low, this youth appears and repeats three times, "Tá saoghal eile ann"—"There is another world." The others try to seize him, but he has vanished, and a servant rushes in with the tidings that five minutes earlier, in an accident the youth was killed. It was a well-acted little piece of sensation, but the preliminary discussion should be shortened, and the staging should be toned down to suit the weird subject of conversation.

The second piece was in cheerful contrast, being a translation of Miss Constance Powell-Anderson's little comedy, *The Courting of the Widow Malone*. This is the sort of piece—the racy country comedy with a dash of poetry—which the Players do particularly well. The widow's two suitors gave good scope to Tadhg O Scanaill, the ever-comical, and to Gearoid O'Loughlin, who has versatile gifts. Maire Ni Oisin, as a roguish servant, was in one of her best parts, and her coaching of the shy suitor in a poetical proposal was pure delight.

The third piece was *The Man with the Funny Story*, by Mr. Beasley. The excellent stagecraft and neat dialogue of Mr. Beasley's plays were here a little strained by the length to which the simple central idea was drawn out. Tadhg O Scanaill played the man who was for ever trying to tell a certain funny story and forever being interrupted. He gave a rich study of the bore whom we have all met too often. Seumas Og—played by Muiris O'Kane—was sorely perplexed in his courting of the story-teller's daughter by his dilemma as to whether he should neglect the young lady or break off listening to her wearisome parent. It was excellent character comedy and sent the audience home in high good humour.[21]

On 9 March, two plays were done: *Eiséirighe Dhonncha*, which was a translation of Seumas MacManus' *The Resurrection of Dinny O'Dowd*; and *An Foghmar*, which was Rev. Thomas O'Kelly's three-act tragedy, *The Harvest*, revised by Gearoid O Lochlainn. The *Irish Times* reported:

There was an unusually sparse attendance at last night's Gaelic plays at the Abbey Theatre. The first curtain was over half an hour late in rising. The players should acquire more briskness, and reduce the tediously long intervals between scenes and plays if they wish to keep the audience in good humour.

The first play was *The Harvest*. . . . This is a three-act tragedy of the '98 Rebellion, and Dr. Larchet's orchestra contributed to the effectiveness of the production by playing '98 airs. The first act depicts a peasant's cottage in the West of Ireland, where a young man, about to be married, promises to join in the Rising if the French land. In the second act the French arrive. The drums are heard "off," and a French officer—half an Irishman—enters and talks in broken Irish. The lads depart with him, with their pikes and muskets, and the womenfolk are left stricken with foreboding. In the third act the last shots of the broken Rising are heard, and a wounded rebel enters, tells—in a fine piece of narrative acting—how the lad of the house fell, and then the dead youth is brought in, and the curtain falls.

This "historical drama" is one of the best things done by the native Gaelic playwrights, for it is a piece of pure, direct tragedy, like *Riders to the Sea*. Its chief fault lies in an unnecessary first act, and last night, though the acting was in some respects the best we have seen from the Gaelic Players, the forebodings of the women were overdone. The two women—the old mother (Maire Ni Chinnéide) and the girl bride (Brid Ni Eigeartaigh)—acted splendidly, but they should have shown more courage at the moment when they found their pleadings against the Rising wholly vain. The French captain (Tormad O Roideain) was a fine character sketch, with a flavour of humour. The leading part, done by Muiris O Catháin, was excellent. Mr. Beasley, as the old father, delivered some eloquent passages well.[22]

On 12 April, which was Easter Sunday, and again on 15 April, An Comhar presented a triple bill, which consisted of revivials of *An Craipi Og* and *Heircileas*, and apparently its first production of *An Bherdhlin Buadha*, which was a translation of François Coppée's *Le Luthier de Cremone*. Of these performances, however, we have discovered no reviews.

On 18 May, the group presented *An Bear*, a translation of Chekhov's one-act comedy, and also *An Sgaothaire* or *The Boaster* by Pierce Beasley, a three-act comedy, which was played for the first time. The *Irish Times* reported:

The Russian play was a feast of excellent Gaelic, thanks to the translator, Fiachra Eilgeach, but as it is largely a monologue, very Russian in its hectic quality, it is not among the most interesting of pieces. The audience was somewhat bored by the slow action, although the culmination, when the Russian noble who is dunning a widow for a debt, is offered pistols to fight a duel with her, and proposes marriage instead, evokes volleys of laughter. . . .

Mr. Beasley's new play is one of his best, and is marked by the skilled stagecraft which renders him the one really interesting Gaelic playwright. It is a jolly piece of youthful humour, racy and brisk in action.

The "boaster" is a university student—brightly played by Gearoid O Lochlainn—who, with his friend—acted by Muiris O Cathain—tries to impose on simple country maidens by representing himself and Muiris as foreign grandees. This is a familiar *motif* for light comedy, but if the play had freshness and charm, the good team work of the players must be thanked. Maire Ni Oisin, as the damsel who saw through all pretences, acted with her usual impish humour. Mr. Beasley himself took a part, acting a third student, who wins the leading lady. The third act, when the boaster finds himself defeated on all sides through his own overweening cleverness, and declares that he is off to America, is heartily satisfying.

We would like to see a more ambitious comedy from Mr. Beasley's pen. The actors now have reached a pitch of skill fitting them for something more subtle than old-fashioned amateur theatricals, and Mr. Beasley could give it.[23]

After their summer break, the Gaelic Players opened their fall season at the Abbey on 5 October with a double bill, the first production of Padraig O Broithe's one-act *Reidhteach na Ceiste* or *The Settling of the Question*, and a three-act comedy by Alphons O Labharada called *An tSnaidhm*. The *Irish Times* reported:

Last night's performance had two specially interesting features—the production of a new play by Mr. Patrick Brophy, one of the most popular of the players, and the first appearance in Dublin of Miss Mary Bastable, a player who already has won a considerable name in Cork. It is safe to say that Miss Bastable is a discovery for the Players—her acting is charming and finished, and she gives the Gaelic drama the touch which has lent distinction to the work of the Abbey Theatre in English.

Mr. Brophy's play, *The Settling of the Question*, was little more than a curtain raiser; but it showed skill of stagecraft and much promsie. It gave a novel turn to the familiar match-making theme. The girl is to be wedded, not to the lad of her choice, but to a man chosen by her mother. Her lover is killed in an accident, and his ghost appears, saving her, but at the cost of her life. Her death upon the stage was not dextrous: the shock could be heightened by a more dramatic presentation. Muiris O Catháin was the lover's ghost. Máire Ní Oisín played well, but the audiences would have been glad to see this talented player longer on the stage.

An tSnaidhm, by Alphons O Labhradha, was the piece of the evening. It gave three acts of hearty comedy, played with a finish that was lacking too often in last year's performances. A grumpy, wealthy old manufacturer (Michael Sugrue) is fooled by his clerk (Mr. O Cathain) into promising him his daughter. The young man plans business projects which entail the building of a factory on three fields, which are required from the Earl of the Plain (admirably played by Gearoid O Lochlainn)—but the Earl demands the girl's hand for the fields.

The comedy turns upon the girl's breezy management of the situation. The part was acted by Miss Bastable, who makes quite a Shavian heroine of the young lady. She pretends to accept the Earl, and then gives a dazzling account of the life she will lead among the *daoine uaisle*; she will show how money should be spent. The Earl begins to relent, and finally the young lady extorts the coveted fields from the Earl as the price, not of marrying him, but of releasing him from the engagement. Miss Bastable's vivacity, and her ease of acting, made of a somewhat unambitious comedy one of the Players' best successes. . . .

The men acted a great deal better than they did last year, but Tadhg O Scanaill was sadly missed.[24]

On 2 November, a double bill was presented, Beasley's *Cluiche Cartai* and the first production of *Na Dibheartaigh O Shean-Shasana* or *The Exiles of England* by Sean O Ciarghusa who usually wrote under the pseudonym of Marbhán. The play was laid in the year A.D. 2025, and the *Irish Times* reported:

"Marbhán" imagines that Ireland has become wholly Irish-speaking, even his Orangeman having no English. A group has assembled to form "the English League," which seeks to restore the English language in Ireland. One character, a Miss Birrell, knows English, and translates the names of the characters into that tongue, telling the Irish Jew, Deaglan Gabhnóir, that his name is Goldsmith. Some living folk of to-day seemed to be hit off in some of the characters, but the fun was good-humoured.

Nothing happens. It is a Shavian play, with the enjoyment wholly in the wit of the dialogue around the table; and in this respect it makes a large advance on the crude drama given us hither-to by many Gaelic playwrights. There was many a laugh, as when English was praised as the language of Shakespeare, Milton, and Shaw. A Belfast professor wrote to complain that he had only three English students. Dr. Douglas Hyde was adapted to justify the cause by turning his Irish propagandist dicta against himself. Plantagenet Gogarty, an Irish poet of past times, was involved as an exponent of the beauties of English. Finally, the meeting was broken up as seditious by green-badged police, and the English Hall, with its portraits of Queen Bess, Gladstone and King William, was dismantled. The satire pricked the Gaels of to-day no less than others.

A large company played in the piece, and it would be unfair, perhaps, to single out any for special praise; for, apart from some defects natural to players without long experience in a piece lacking action, the whole thing was admirably done.[25]

And finally on 11 December, the group presented *Athbarra*, a translation of T. C. Murray's *Aftermath* by Michael Sugrue. By this time, An Comhar felt itself fairly established, and on 17 November the *Irish Times* printed the following sanguine report:

The annual meeting of An Comhar (the Gaelic Dramatic Leauge) was held last night at 25 Parnell square, Dublin. Mr. Piaras Beaslai (President) in the chair. The Secretary, Mr. Leon O Broin, reported that 32 Gaelic plays had been produced, and that 40 more were contemplated or in course of preparation. It was decided that in view of the satisfactory progress of the Leagure, it would be possible now to extend its activities. Plans were laid for visits by the players to Cork, Galway, and other centres in which a considerable audience understanding Irish would be obtainable. It was decided also to hold matinees in Dublin for school children, and to give preformances in schools of plays suitable for young folk. Arrangements were made to publish plays which prove successful at the Abbey Theatre for the benefit of readers and of other companies of players.[26]

• • •

During the year, the Dublin Drama League gave five public productions of two nights each, on Sundays and Mondays, at the Abbey. These included Ernst Toller's *Masses and Man* and George Dunning Gribble's *The Scene That Was to Write Itself* on 4 and 5 January; Benavente's *The School for Princesses* on 1 and 2 February; Verhaeren's *The Cloister* on 15 and 16 March; Strindberg's *The Spook Sonata* and Schnitzler's *The Wedding Morning* on 19 and 20 April; and Strindberg's *The Dance of Death* on 29 and 30 November. In addition, the League gave an "At Home" for its members on 11 July, presenting Euripides' *Iphigenia in Tauris*. Although nothing of Irish interest was produced, the Strindberg and Toller plays impressed and influenced Sean O'Casey.

Among the odder semiprofessional productions of the Dublin year was one of Marlowe's *Doctor Faustus*, at the Abbey on 20 September. This was ambitiously mounted by Lyle Donaghy who also undertook the title role. Donaghy was to become a poet of minor note, but was at this time merely a university student. The cast he assembled was rather impressive and included Frank Fay as the chorus and John Stephenson as Mephistopheles, as well as Gabriel Fallon, Shelah Richards, and Madame Kirkwood Hackett, whose statuesque proportions were apparently effective for the role of Gluttony. One of the more tolerant remarks about this gently received production was that the producer and star should be congratulated for "a high degree of bravery."[27]

Of the commerical theatres in Dublin, the Royal, the Olympia, and the Tivoli adhered almost entirely to revue and variety, offering patrons such enticements as "Popgun the Wonder Horse that plays a musical instrument;" as well as Niobe the Aquatic Marvel who "Talks, Sings, Eats and performs other sensational feats under water;" and Sampson, the world's strongest man, who could drive nails through three inch thick wood with the palm of his hand.

However, each house presented some work of passing Irish interest. At the Royal, for the week of 25 May, Joe O'Gorman presented a revue called *Irish and Proud of It*,[28] and for the week of 10 August, Shaun Glenville and his wife, Dorothy Ward, headed the variety bill.

The Tivoli was closed for most of the year, from 15 March to December 21. When it was reopened, it had been bought by J. J. Farrell, the owner of several Irish cinemas; and it continued to operate on its old lines as a music hall. For a week in January, however, a part of the bill featured the Irish Players who, minus Arthur Sinclair, appeared in J. Bernard MacCarthy's *The Down Express*.

With Sinclair, the Irish Players appeared at the Olympia for two weeks in June with their usual repertoire. The Abbey Players, on vacation from their own theatre, appeared for the week of 6 July in McNulty's *The Courting of Mary Doyle*. Most of the new Irish work at the Olympia, however, was in the form of revue, and most of that was concocted by John MacDonagh and featured his usual troupe of comedians, singers and dancers, headed by the increasingly popular Jimmy O'Dea. For the week of 13 July, however, there was a new revue by Joseph Sweeney; this was called *The Girl from Rathmines* and appears to have been a pretty amateur effort. The *Evening Herald* remarked, "The artistes being local, and known to many present, imperfections of acting were generally overlooked. . . . The singing and dancing were applauded, and some humorous interludes afforded scope for laughter."[29] When the piece was revived at the Queen's for the week of 7 December, however, the paper added, "The revue had a better caste than it deserved. It is a pity to see such talent wasted on such a rapid piece of chatter."[30]

As usual, the Queen's ran its pantomime into February, and then for the next six months depended basically on variety programmes with English performers (although the Irish Players, minus Sinclair, did appear on the bill for the week of 9 February in *The Rising of the Moon*). During this seven months, one full-length imported play, *Derby Day*, was also produced, its main feature being three horses, which one reviewer described as "perhaps the best part of the cast." Late in August, however, and until the end of the year, such Irish producers as Ira Allen, P. J. Bourke, Andy Dunne, H. J. Condron, and Mrs. Kirkwood-Hackett presented the usual *Shaughrauns* and *Father Murphys* and an occasional English perennial such as *East Lynne* or *The Face at the Window*.

The Gaiety's offerings were a trifle more distinguished, or at least more professionally mounted, but basically consisted of such lightweight fare as operettas, musical comedies, comedies and farces. The only piece of Irish interest imported from abroad was Shaw's *Saint Joan*, presented for the first time in Ireland by Charle Mac Dona's rather second-class touring company, for the week of 22 June. The indigenously Irish offerings appeared in a week in December when the Ulster Theatre paid its usual visit in mainly its usual repertoire. The only variations were Lynn Doyle's *The Lilac Ribbon*, which was now seem for the first time in Dublin, and C. K. Ayre's *Missing Links*, which was given its premiere on the second night of the run, 15 December. Despite a jocular interview from Ayre in the press,[31] no one really much liked his play. The *Evening Herald* reported:

If one is permitted to pun upon a punning title I must confess that there was a missing link amongst the Ulster Players at the Gaiety Theatre last night. Their combination seemed broken and awry, and we only got occasional glimpses of the accustomed shuttle that spins banter and cross-word and subtle satire in their ever-welcome presentations.

Mr. Charles K. Ayre was not over kind in the furnishings he gave to the marionettes of his imagination or their circumstances that encompassed their lives in the fishing hamlet of Ardheel. He set out to write a satire on golf and Darwinism, but as other matters of dull routine obscured his vision, his wit lost sharpness in the progression of development. The central idea was good, was even excellent for a more crisp comedy, but the subject involved such wide expanses that the creation burst away from the creator's control.

The result was not over-satisfactory. Everybody talked anyhow and anywheres, and under any circumstances. Two fishermen fell into anecdotal dotage on the left side of the stage, two others discussed golf on the right. The diversion of objective lent to looseness of construction, and while one could glimmer an aura of the central idea and applaud its intention, one also could not be but regretful for the author's abandonment of his customary stagecraft. It was Mr. Ayre, the imaginative, wrote the *Missing Links*, but it was not the same Mr. Ayre who gave us that excellent pieced comedy, *Loaves and Fishes*.

The personation of a "haw-haw" lord by H. Richard Hayward was a cameo of delineation that stood apart by itself. He lit every moment of his presence, and by his complete sang-froid often times lifted the piece by its straps.

Miss Jean Woods is an actress who is capable, charming and natural, but fidgetty, and if she could but control her movements slightly, her performance would have been complete.

The author, Mr. Ayre, Miss Rose McQuillan, and Mr. J. R. Mageann made gallant efforts to set the combination right and lively.

Our two old friends, Gerald MacNamara and Walter Kennedy, made a bold effort at resuscitation in the third act, but they lapsed beneath the strain, and this moment of victory was short lived.[32]

• • •

In 1925, the Northern Drama League mounted five programs in the Central Hall in Rosemary Street, Belfast. On 23 January, the League produced *Everyman*, and to fill out the bill offered seven Elizabethan lyrics spoken by George Buchanan; late in February it produced Stanley Houghton's 1910 play, *The Younger Generation*; on 27 and 28 March there was Chekhov's *Uncle Vanya*; on 13 and 14 November, there was an ambitious production of Beaumont and Fletcher's *The Knight of the Burning Pestle*; and on 18 and 19 December there was the only Irish production of the year, Synge's *Playboy*.[33]

The style of acting of the League seems reminiscent of what Yeats and Frank Fay favoured in the early days of the Irish National Theatre Society. For instance:

In amateur acting, as we conceive it, the play is of the highest consideration. Therefore team work among the actors is essential. We wish to avoid the "star" system. The players will think out their technical requirements entirely in reference to the particular play which they are rehearsing, because nothing is more tedious to an audience than to see reiterated imitation of the tricks of well-known professionals. It is this habit of second-rate imitation, combined with an occasional desire to "show off," that has frequently degraded amateur acting, so that to suggest watching amateur theatricals is to suggest, for many, the worst possible form of mental and artistic torture.[34]

And further:

> Movement of gesture will always be simple enough to avoid self-consciousness. A slight natural clumsiness is preferable to anything obviously affected.
>
> By these means a certain individuality rewards a performance, making it often more delightful than a professional performance. It may not be so deft, but it is, at least, fresh and interesting. And, through the intelligence and sincerity of the players, a purer interpretation of dramatic work is given. The play being the highest consideration, all the actors will work together to translate the author's intention into terms of the stage instead of exploiting him for personal profit.[35]

Such a manifesto about acting would have been the last thing that a group of old stagers like those in the Ulster Theatre would have thought of producing; and, of course, in comparison to the usual Northern comedies and farces that the Ulster Theatre had been producing for years, the plays of the Northern Drama League would have seemed highbrow indeed. And actually, George Buchanan wrote an article to defend the Northern Drama League against being highbrow:

> . . . our aims are to interest and entertain through the medium of dramatic art, to produce those plays, good, amusing, beautiful, that are unlikely to be seen otherwise in the city, to give an outlet simultaneously for whatever acting ability may exist locally. . . .
>
> There are many good plays that are seldom produced. Some people have time to read them in books. Others have not. Those who read them talk with one another about the plays, and unfortunately talk too often with a pedantic critical jargon. Those who have not read them, hearing this talk, are bewildered and resentful, and make a mental note of objection against the plays. So, in nine cases out of ten, a play of this kind suffers because of the behaviour of its critics and praisers. And whereas the unreading public would be right in calling the critics "highbrow," it makes a mistake in labelling the plays "highbrow," and often deprives itself of enjoyment.
>
> . . . the Northern Drama League policy and "highbrowism" do not coincide.
>
> It may be that we have some "highbrows" among our critics and praisers; but the plays we produced are intended to be taken on their intrinsic merits as entertainment. No play, as I say, is in itself "highbrow." *It is the audience that is "highbrow"* (I suggest that ours is). And that is why we would sooner see a Dryden or a Moliere or an Elizabethan play hissed off the stage, if it were not liked, than a bored audience chattering platitudes about the great old dramatists. . . .
>
> If the audience expresses candid liking or disliking, and if no section of the community treats our work pretentiously, the Northern Drama League ought to fulfil a splendid purpose in adding variety and discrimination to the enjoyment of the people of the city.[36]

Buchanan's defense against being highbrow may strike the reader as being somewhat specious, but one sympathises with his motives, which were basically to avoid a kiss-of-death taint that would keep audiences away.

In January, the Queen's University Dramatic Society mounted a double bill of *The Countess Cathleen* and *O'Flaherty, V. C.*, and in mid-February a double bill of Chesterton's *Magic*[37] and Gordon Bottomley's *King Lear's Wife*. The audiences in the examination hall of the university were small, and K. T. Little in the *Ulster Review* was also driven to assert that the productions were not the least bit highbrow.[38]

Much more in the tradition of the Ulster Players was the Carrickfergus Players, whose productions early in January of D. M'Loughlin's *Andrew M'Ilfatrick, J. P.* and Sam R. Bolton's *Going West* needed no antihighbrow defense whatsoever. But even M'Loughlin's "rollicking Ulster comedy in three acts" and Bolton's "exceedingly tense one-act war drama" drew a "miserably poor audience."[39]

Drama, even serious drama, was obviously alive in Ulster; but its vitality was hardly vigorous.

• • •

Around the country, an old company was revived and a new one was born. The new one was called the Martin Doran Players and opened on 15 June in Wicklow town with *Romeo and Juliet*. The Martin Doran name would not be kept too long, but the company was to become the most ambitious and prestigious of the Irish fit-ups, as well as the crucible of the Dublin Gate Theatre. On the eve of this first production, the *Irish Times* wrote:

> An experimental season is being opened to-day at Wicklow by the Martin Doran Players, who intend to tour many of the towns of Ireland off the beaten track of London theatrical companies with a repertory consisting of a number of Shakespearean plays.
>
> The company, which has been formed by Mr. A. McMaster, who many years ago began his theatrical career with touring companies in Ireland under the name of Martin Doran, and is to-day one of the leading London actors. A number of Irish artists are in the cast, with Miss Idina Scott-Gatty, a niece of the well-known composer of the same name, as the leading lady.
>
> They open with *Romeo and Juliet* to-night; to-morrow they will give *Hamlet*, and by way of variety they will present *Trilby* on Wednesday night.
>
> The last three days of the week will be spent at Arklow, to be followed by three days each at Enniscorthy, Dungarvan and Waterford.
>
> Subsequently Mr. McMaster, who is unable to act personally owing to a barring clause in a London contract, hopes to present *Othello* and *The Merchant of Venice*, and to give a week's season at some of the bigger towns. He will present Shakespeare in a new way for Ireland, principally in the draperies, which have been designed and painted by the well-known Irish artist Michael Mac Liammóir, whose exhibitions and paintings have earned for him a big success on the Continent.

Considerable difficulty has had to be overcome with regard to the lighting, but by hiring a big lorry Mr. McMaster will be able to obtain the necessary power for the stage lighting, which is a feature of the productions.

The wardrobe has been designed and executed expressly for the tour by Andrew Storie, the Dundalk artist, who created all the costumes for Mr. C. B. Cochran's London and New York productions.

"I have," said Mr. McMaster to an *Irish Times* reporter, "made very extensive cuts in the Shakespeare plays, because I wanted to keep closer to the story. I believe audiences prefer melodrama, and, if I have deleted a number of the famous soliloquies, it has been purely with the desire of emphasising the story. The beauty of the lines will not be lost, because the dramatic element of the plays is emphasised.[40]

The old company that was revived was the Tawin Village Players. As Roisin Walsh summarized their early history:

Twenty-three years ago Dr. Seamus O'Beirne, when a medical student in Dublin, wrote a bilingual play called *An Dochtúir*, a farcical satire on the anomalous position of an English-speaking doctor in an Irish-speaking district. The best incidents in the play arise from the amusing action and dialogue of the Irish speakers. It was written for the people of the village. Many of the characters are drawn from living people, and on its first production some of the parts were filled by the people for whom they were written.

It was a huge success. The actors were the people of that remote village which even to this day has not achieved the distinction—or incurred the odium—of a police barracks. After acting the play to Galway audiences the company went to Dublin where they were welcomed uproariously in the Rotunda, night after night, for a whole week by ever increasing audiences.[41]

One of the early Tawin actors was Michael Conniffe, who acted for some years with the Abbey and then with Arthur Sinclair before retiring professionally in 1919, and readers of volume 4 of this history may recall his reminiscences of the early Tawin Players. However, Roisin Walsh continues:

That was the beginning. It created a tradition of play-writing and play-acting in the village of Tawin. It is reminiscent of Elizabethan times in England when the theatre was of the people, and expressed the vigorous national life.

The production of *An·Dochtúir* was an education to the people of Tawin. It was much more, accustomed as we are here to regard education as the equipping of young people for positions. It brought culture, that is, the great widening of outlook and deepening of spaciousness of mind that springs from a genuine interest in one of the arts, to every man, woman and child in Tawin.

Each actor knew not only his own part but the whole play from the rise to the fall of the curtain. Not only the actors but everyone else in Tawin knew the play by heart. It entered into and became a part of the lives of the people. For one whole Summer the people of Tawin had *An Dochtúir* with their meals, took it into their blood with every breath they drew.

The properties of the Tawin stage are few, severe enough to satisfy the yearnings of a Gordon Craig. . . .

The activities of the Tawin people have gone beyond mere acting. A couple of the members of the present company of 1925 have lately translated and produced *The Workhouse Ward*, by Lady Gregory. Some of the original company of twenty-three years ago retain their old parts. But, on the other hand, several of the present players, now grown men and women, were children when the play was first produced. It is, in its way, in the true Oberammergau tradition.

An interesting aspect of all this work is that the best part of *An Dochtúir* is in Irish, that *The Workhouse Ward (Teach na mBocht)* is wholly Irish, that they are produced by native Irish speakers and are played to Irish-speaking audiences in the most Gaelic part of Ireland, the district around Galway, particularly that lying to the west of Galway city. Already, this Winter, the Tawin players have appeared on six different platforms. The people flock eagerly to hear them.

The work of the Tawin people is a beginning. It may have far-reaching results if the good example spreads.[42]

Among the forgotten fracases of the Irish theater was the following incident, which occurred in Waterford on 26 August:

An unusual incident occurred last night at a Waterford cinema during a variety turn known as "Sawing Through a Woman."

The trick consists of placing a lady in a locked box, which is then sawn through transversely with a cross-cut saw. Before the lady is placed in the box she is tied with cords round the ankles, wrists, and neck. These cords are passed through holes in the box and held by four members of the audience while the operation is being performed. One member of the committee insisted on tying a slip knot around the neck of the unfortunate lady, though she resisted stoutly. Fearing that the lady would be strangled, the illusionist's assistant, after the box had been sawn through, hurriedly separated the two portions revealing the lady curled up in one end.

Immediately there followed a wild clamour amongst the audience, several members of which arose in their seats and hurled jibes and insults at the producers.

The lady, who was subsequently extricated from the box, appeared on the stage in a very distressed condition and, bursting into tears, disappeared in haste behind the wings.

Ordering a burst of orchestral music to deaden the tumult, the illusionist and his assistant feverishly bundled the properties off the stage and made a hurried exit.[43]

It is difficult for the judicious historian to discern what precisely was being protested against, but perhaps it was not that the woman remained unsawn and unthrottled.

Certainly, after some years of study about the habits of Irish audiences, the present writers find themselves confirmed only in confusion. When, for instance, a fire broke out in the circle of the Olympia on 25 November, "The majority of the people appeared to be more interested than alarmed, and the attendants had considerably difficulty in clearing the theatre."[44] In any event, the rambunctiousness of the Irish audience, particularly in the popular houses, might be suggested by the following typical letter of complaint to the press:

Sir—I wish to draw attention to the wanton and disgusting practice carried on during the performance by the patrons of the gallery of the Queen's Theatre by the throwing of orange peels and spitting on the occupants of the dress circle and parterre. Myself and friends who are constant patrons of the dress circle are frequently subjected to this disgusting annoyance. Complaints to the attendants seem to be of no avail. Perhaps the management will have this matter attended to.

L. Fallon[45]

Among the happier events of the year was the wedding of the Abbey actors Peter Judge ("F. J. McCormick") and Eileen Crowe; among the unhappier were the deaths of George Sigerson and Darrell Figgis. Dr. Sigerson died on 17 February. As translator, particularly of *Bards of the Gael and Gall*, and as president of the National Literary Society, which had early in the century given much support to the fledgling dramatic movement, he was an impressive and much respected figure. On 27 October, Darrell Figgis, the politician, journalist and man of letters, committed suicide in London. Figgis's literary production was prolific, wide-ranging and extraordinarily uneven. Readers of this history will recall the 1913 production by F. R. Benson of his *Queen Tara*. That excursion into drama, as well as Figgis' poetry, was unmemorable, but two of his novels, *Children of Earth* and *Return of the Hero*, are striking and even brilliant but lamentably ignored work.[46]

• • •

Nineteen twenty-five was quite a good year for Irish playwrights on the London stage. On 13 March, Arthur Sinclair and the Irish Players presented Lynn Doyle's *Love and Land*, under the new title of *Persevering Pat*, at the Little theatre. Although the *Evening News* thought the play refreshing and the *Times* considerably admired the "easy and abundant" flow of fluent dialogue, the *Times* also thought that four acts of little more than such dialogue were a bit much.[47]

Lennox Robinson's *The Round Table* appeared at the Q Theatre on 16 March. The cast was basically English, but the play was apparently directed by W. G. Fay. Of it, the *Times* wrote:

> Mr. Lennox Robinson calls it a "comic-tragedy"—a difficult form in the theatre. Wit must be there, and humour, too, that is not too sharp and not too broad; something very near to poetry must be there, and the steadiest of hands to hold the balance. Mr. Robinson's hand is perfectly steady. He lets us pass from nonsense to seriousness and back again without a self-conscious shudder. . . . In short, a bold and dangerous experiment that comes off.[48]

On 11 May, the play reappeared in a new production by Sybil Thorndike at Wyndham's. Miss Thorndike, fresh from her triumph in Shaw's *Saint Joan*, played Daisy Drennan; and Raymond Massey and Lewis Casson were in cast. On this occasion, the *Times* was a little less kind:

> Miss Thorndike gives to Daisy strength, seriousness, and gaiety. She lends significance to her part and beautifully preserves its proportion. It is not, however, a part that gives full scope to her powers, for when once she has seen her vision her essential development is ended, the secret is out, and what follows is in a sense a re-statement of what we already know. For the same reason there is, in the third act, some farcical uproar which cannot rank with the earlier passages of the play. But by this time the audience had been thoroughly amused and was too well occupied in remembering its pleasures to be very careful for minor disappointments.[49]

Edith Craig's production of Lady Gregory's *Mirandolina* appeared at the Everyman on 17 August. The London correspondent of the *Evening Herald* noted Ellen Terry and John Galsworthy in the audience but reported that

> the concensus of opinion of those who did notice the piece is that it was not a success.
>
> One writer, recording the play's failure, says, "*Mirandolina* is the kind of play that must be all sparkle, or it is nothing. The actors last night realised this, and did all they could to infuse sparkle into their acting, but somehow the production refused to come to life. Miss Ruth Brown, trying her very hardest to show us the charm of the little innkeeper, only succeeded in making us realise dimly what the part might become in the hands of Miss Athene Seyler."
>
> According to another paper: "Lady Gregory's adaptation is simple comedy, conspicuous more for its high spirits than any brilliance of dialogue. There is a certain charm about this dainty innkeeper who keeps her amorous clients at arm's length, conquers a woman hater for the pleasure of the thing, and casts him aside in favour of her serving man. That there was more in the original, and yet again more when Duse played it all over the world, many have testified."
>
> A third writer says Lady Gregory's *Mirandolina* is " a truncated version, with two of the visitors to the inn—namely, the actresses—dropped for purposes, one presumes, of speed and concentration. This narrowing of the canvas is a mistake," and adds that "Miss Edith Craig's production did not show as much resource as one expects from so skilled a theatrical directress."
>
> Yet another critic says Lady Gregory's adaptation is singularly devoid of real wit and humour "and any entertainment there was was solely dependent upon the situations, and as the story is of the slightest substance it was very thin entertainment indeed."[50]

On 12 October, *The Playboy* was revived for a limited, three-week engagement at the Royalty. The principal parts were taken by Maire O'Neill, Fred O'Donovan, Arthur Sinclair, Sara Allgood, Sydney J. Morgan, and J. A. O'Rourke. And, although these old-stagers were getting a little long in the tooth for the roles, the *Times* thought the production "a pleasant oasis in the midst of an arid desert."[51]

On 16 November, O'Casey's *Juno* opened at the Royalty in a production by J. B. Fagan and Denis Eadie, and the *Times* thought the piece

> A play of real artistic value . . . familiar, old-fashioned almost, in its formula, yet strange, and, we suppose we must say, characteristically Irish in its atmosphere of mingled humour and melancholy. Very delightful humour it is, racy, unctuous, a little *baroque*, and very moving in its pathos. As to the acting, these Irish players are

superb. Miss Sara Allgood and Miss Maire O'Neill and Mr. Arthur Sinclair—what an incomparable trio! Mr. Sydney Morgan bravely supports them. And so you leave your seat not with the feeling of placid comfort with which you settled into it, but with the sense of surprise which accompanies all true art—surprise at a strange blend of rollicking fun and grim tragedy. The tragedy will have given you a pang, but you cannot but have revelled in the fun.[52]

• • •

In 1925, the Abbey mounted only seven new productions: Dorothy Macardle's one-act, *The Old Man*; Frank J. Hugh O'Donnell's *Anti-Christ*; George Sheils's conventional comedy, *Professor Tim*; two works in rather a new manner by Lennox Robinson, *Portrait* and *The White Blackbird*; and the theater's first productions of Shaw's *Fanny's First Play* and of Chekhov's *The Proposal*. This was neither a prolific nor a distinguished season for new work; but, although there was no new O'Casey piece ready, there were quite a few new plays that the Abbey could have staged—and, indeed, subsequently did stage. The reason for not putting them on in 1925 was economic, as is quite clear from this letter of Yeats to Lady Gregory on 26 March:

We have been doing so badly at the Abbey that we have decided to close at end of April and put on *Fanny's First Play*—a certain draw— . . . and abandon everything experimental. We have therefore thought it best to put off your new Molière til the autumn. I insisted upon this as I saw it was not fair to you to put on new work with the sinking audiences. The same applies to your passion play. I am very sorry about this last but it would mean a loss and a loss on a play of yours could be a bad preparation for the Molière. If we get a rising audience next autumn I would like to see the passion play near Xmas if there is any suitable day. . . . I have taken it on myself with Lennox's consent of indefinitely postponing (as this will seem less hard than absolutely refusing) MacNamara's new play and Shiels' new play. . . . I saw a rehearsal of Lennox's play [*Portrait*] yesterday and find it plays better than it reads. . . . Did you read me in *Irish Statesman*—it has made rather a stir and think I was so excessively candid. I have terrified Russell who does not know how to get rid of the resultant controversy. . . . Shiel's play good if he takes the drunkenness out of it.[53]

The Abbey's first new production of the year was to be Dorothy Macardle's *The Old Man*. On 6 January, Robinson wrote rather unenthusiastically to Lady Gregory about the piece:

I've at last sent back Miss MacArdle's long play, saying we wouldn't do it but would do *The Old Man* instead. It's quite short and can't hurt us as the long dreary show would have done.[54]

The play was first produced on 24 February on a triple bill with *The Land of Heart's Desire* and *The Coiner*, and both the new play and the acting received a distinctly mixed reception. As Holloway wrote:

I arrived in time at Abbey for second scene in new piece, *The Old Man* by Dorothy Macardle which I saw from balcony. I couldn't rightly judge of its merits by what I saw. Quinn and Joyce Chancellor seemed miscast as grandson and granddaughter of the old man, Cornelius Sheridan. The latter was played by Barry Fitzgerald, and McNulty whom I saw go out said he played the part . . . without the slightest trace of comedy. The play he thought but poor stuff. . . . John Burke thought the play poor and the acting ditto. T. C. Murray . . . wasn't so condemnatory. . . . To Lawrence it was pure drama, nothing more or less. The piece had gripped him, he added. . . . I saw Mrs. Macardle (who got a call) leave with Madame Maud Gonne MacBride.[55]

Susan L. Mitchell in the *Irish Statesman* wrote somewhat of a mixed notice:

It plays well, and the audience took to it. The scene is laid in Dublin in 1848, at the moment of the arrest of John Mitchel under the Treason Felony Act. The Council of the confederation had forbidden a rising as premature, and this action effectually stopped any chance of rescuing Mitchel. A few men of the Young Ireland Clubs, led by the young hero of the play, Robert Emmet Sheridan, determine to die rather than seem to fail Mitchel; they plan a forlorn hope of rescue. When Robert Emmet Sheridan's grandfather, himself one of Emmet's men, discovers his grandson's intention, he goes secretly at night to the Council and tells them of it. Two members of the Council, Meagher and Scully, come to the Sheridan's house to forbid the young man's venture. The boy, though broken-hearted when he learns that it is his grandfather who has betrayed him, determines to go, and in trying to escape by the window is overtaken by Scully and killed. The moral—for a moral is everywhere intended—is that the young man's vision is a truer guide than the old man's dream. It may be so, the Abbey audience felt it so, but the last words of the play, natural perhaps in the mouth of the murdered boy's sister, "they did not go (to rescue Mitchel) because they were afraid," let down an audience wrought up to enthusiasm for the beauty of self-sacrifice. It was a false note and a bad curtain. It led off from the true theme of the play, and broke up unpleasantly the concentration of the audience upon it. Mr. Quinn's interpretation of his part pleased me very much.[56]

The *Irish Times* thought the play a success and "well constructed." And, after highly admiring the acting of Barry Fitzgerald, added:

Miss Joyce Chancellor plays quietly, but effectually the part of Robert's sister, who shares all her brother's patriotic enthusiasm. Mr. Tony Quinn was a good Robert, but virtually all his work is of the speech-making kind, and the book gives him but little chance to be convincing. If Barry Fitzgerald were not in the cast, the playing of F. J. McCormick and Tom Moran, as Meagher and Scully, would be applauded as something of the very best that the Abbey has yet seen.[57]

After remarking in the *Dublin Magazine* that, "This play seems to be political propaganda," Andrew E. Malone went on to give the piece a thorough panning:

It is reasonable to suppose that an allegorical parallel is to be drawn between the events portrayed and current politics; certainly that is the impression left upon the

> mind. The propagandist intention is very obtrusive, the characterisation is slight, and the whole atmosphere definitely melodramatic. Emotion is roused, but it is not satisfied, and that, it must be supposed, is the deliberate intention of the dramatist. Such an intention must defeat drama, and drama is not achieved. The play will not enhance the reputation of Miss Macardle. . . .
>
> Again the acting was indifferent. Tony Quinn as young Sheridan failed completely to grasp the significance of his part, and upon him the entire play rested. Barry Fitzgerald was excellent as the Old Man, and F. J. McCormick and Tom Moran were both good in the very small parts allotted to them.[58]

Although harsher than the other critics, Malone was sound enough. As patriotic drama, *The Old Man* possessed none of the broad crudities of the neo-Boucicaultian melodramatics of P. J. Bourke and Ira Allen. And certainly it was more dramatised than the patriotic didactics of Thomas MacDonagh or Terence MacSwiney, which did have some claim to literary merit. But that really is all that can be said; neither *The Old Man* nor *Ann Kavanagh* found a place in the permanent repertoire. And to this day, despite some admiration for occasional works like Brian Friel's *The Fall of the City*, works like *The Plough and the Stars*, which have been critical of patriotism, have been much better dramas than plays which lauded it.

The Abbey's second new piece, *Anti-Christ* by the prolific and indefatiguable Frank Hugh O'Donnell, was critical of patriotism, but of an international patriotism fostered by the allied governments during the Great War. In O'Donnell's disillusioned piece, catchcries such as "the war to end wars" seemed hollow indeed when applied to the reality of the post war world.

Anti-Christ, which was first performed on 17 March, was for Ireland new in its statement, ambitious in its scope, and provocative in its structure. This new tone of disillusionment, which may also be discerned in Robinson's 1925 plays, made Dorothy Macardle's conventional patriotics seem an outworn convention. Also, the cast list was very large, required considerable doubling of roles, and probably strained the resources of the theater more than any other play since A. Patrick Wilson's *The Slough*. The five scenes of the play seemed to many members of the audience to tell the story disjointedly. The first scene suggested that the play was the story of John Boles, the war veteran who initiates a political movement; and, when Boles disappeared from the later scenes, the audience felt cheated. However, O'Donnell was not telling Boles's story, but the story of the rise and fall of a protest, rather as Gerhart Hauptmann had done years previously in *The Weavers*. That generalized, rather than individualized story, when coupled with two bridging scenes of some newspaper sandwichmen and of a policeman and a newsboy, gave the play some affinity to the even more generalized Expressionistic plays of Toller, Kaiser, and others in Germany. In actuality, O'Donnell's bridging scenes were closer to a movie montage, such as photographed headlines or the rippling calendar, than to Expressionism.

All of these innovative qualities made the play something of a momentary conversation piece; and yet, even when it was realised what O'Donnell was attempting, few people thoroughly admired the play, and the reason was that O'Donnell had conceived better than he had wrought. The best notices were ones of tempered admiration. The *Evening Herald*, for instance, reported:

In *Anti-Christ* . . . Mr. Frank Hugh O'Donnell has given us a new idea in a new form.

That the form in its production last night was not entirely successful goes without saying, but the fault perhaps does not entirely lie upon the author.

In this play, where so much depends on the sustanance of a certain atmosphere, there should be a quick tempo, and the intervals could be curtailed somewhat by the many long intervals, and also by the disconnected film of its pictures. . . .

The whole atmosphere of the play is rather elusive, and the necessary analysis of the idea could be expanded into a volume of many pages. The development of material progress versus the recognition of natural beauty is strongly denounced, and in the last scene we are shown the idolatry of the new age exulting in contempt upon the heroism of the old.

The play in its entirety is vigorous and thought-provoking, though the repetition of ideas in some of its scenes was rather wearisome. The shorter scenes were so short as to nearly completely miss their point of the continuance of the idea, and perhaps when the actors become attuned to their parts the grooving will be more acceptable.

If Mr. O'Donnell did not entirely succeed in introducing to us something different from ordinary Abbe fare, not alone in form, but in idea, he at least has given us a commentary of modern existence which is undoubtedly correct and beneficial because of the sincerity of its appeal. . . .

It was not a play that lent itself to great acting, but Mr. Michael J. Dolan effectively conveyed his sincerity as the blind hero, Captain Boles. The cast was a huge one, and of the other actors and actresses one must play special tribute to Messrs. F. J. MacCormick, Tony Quinn, and Barry Fitzgerald, the latter for his extraordinary make-up as a sandwichman.

The audience clamoured for the author, who bowed his thanks. The play will probably cause discussion, and is well worth seeing.[59]

The *Irish Times* added that:

The play opens well and ends well. Between the opening and the close its dramatic merit is small. In spite of good acting by everyone in the cast, Scenes 2 to 5, inclusive, were tiresome, except for a powerful piece of characterisation by Tony Quinn, as a smashed-up corporal of the Irish Guards. Nothing could be finer than M. J. Dolan's playing of Boles in the first scene, when the hero of the play states the results of his introspection. Even the length of the speech cannot take away from the superiority of both the author's and the actor's work in this scene. The exposition of ideas, much the same in Scene 3, is, for the most part, wearisome.[60]

After summarizing the plot, Susan L. Mitchell analyzed its deficiencies:

This is the circumstance in which the play is set, but the idea is of a nature to go beyond the circumstance, and I think the dramatist has not made his machine strong enough to sling it. The scene of the sandwichmen bearing the advertisement "Anti-Christ is here" and their comments on it, the back-chat between a newsboy and a policeman in another scene are clever devices well carried out, but what I feel about the play is that the central idea is not brought out strongly enough. It is not made to bulk up so gigantically in the minds of those who accept it that revolution is the inevitable outcome. The dramatist's presentation of Boles' idea in the first scene may carry far enough to suggest a newspaper stunt, but neither there nor in its development in the third scene is it dynamic enough to lead to revolution. These two scenes could be developed, intensified. Boles' malefic vision should be so presented by the dramatist that we are not surprised he is overwhelmed by it, he should be knocked from his bearings as completely as was St. Paul by his Beatific Vision. If he has not had a genuine vision, interior or exterior, the motive is not strong enough to lead to scene five. Cabinets may be flustered, but they do not act without seeming danger.[61]

The worst notices were those by Jacques in the *Independent* and by Malone in the *Dublin Magazine*. Jacques's notice is hardly reasonable enough to reprint, but it did elicit a sympathetic and constructive letter from T. C. Murray to O'Donnell:

I hope you are not feeling sore after the abominable notice of friend Jacques? Console yourself by remembering that he described *Harvest* as "beneath criticism," pooh-poohed *The White-headed Boy*, and called *Spring* a "Maeterlinckian poem" to be read "sitting on a fence in the sunshine" but not acted. I thought he had some personal spleen in wording of myself, and I know that all his notices of Robinson were written in a spirit of vindictiveness, but I expected at least some sense of fair play in dealing with you. . . . At any rate his notice is not a reflection of the mind of the audience who are the only people who really matter in the end. . . . I felt myself that you should eliminate the newsboy policeman scene. It would tighten up the play considerably by reducing the number of scenes, and it serves no serious purpose. I should also make that curtain to the thrid scene—I think it was the third—not quite so unexpected. Most people thought that something had gone wrong. With these two changes I think your play would go with a bang, and produce the effect you intended. . . . It is a piece of ill luck, I have often thought, to have one's work sized up by critics on its first and always its worst performance.[62]

Andrew E. Malone's notice raised an argument that W. B. Yeats was also to use in rejecting O'Casey's *The Silver Tassie* in 1928:

Anti-Christ . . . is entirely a bad play. In justice to its author, Mr. F. J. H. O'Donnell, it must be said that he does not describe it as a play, he calls it "A Commentary." But it was staged as a play so it must be judged. The stage is not the place for commentaries; the newspaper is the appointed place for such. That is not to say that Mr. O'Donnell's theme is not proper to a play; it is. But is is not handled in terms of drama and most certainly it is not couched in terms of literature. . . . It might read well, but even that is doubtful, as there is not a distinguished line in the play. There are, indeed, many lines which disfigure the play. . . . *Anti-Christ* is journalism in its crudest form—a form that is not now often encountered except one reads the obscure little sheets, once called in Dublin the "Mosquito Press," published in the interests of lost causes in every country in the world.[63]

This comment, incidentally, drew forth another note of fraternal sympathy from Murray to O'Donnell:

> I can't think of Malone either with patience or charity just now. His attack is the expression of a very mean mind. Cut the fellow dead in future. If you don't, you have only white blood in your veins. Nothing . . . would justify his writing of your work in that way—and he professed I think to be a friend. It takes an Irishman to do thoroughly mean things.[64]

Of the considerable subsequent discussion about the play, there were two outstandingly thoughtful letters to the *Irish Statesman*. One by Maurice Donne charged that *Anti-Christ* was neither literature nor drama:

> Four of its six scenes are totally irrelevant. The remaining two, in which the author endeavours to portray the lot of the disabled ex-Service man, and merely succeeds in burlesquing it, could undoubtedly be dispensed with. It is so evident that the author of *Anti-Christ* could not have been in earnest. (There is not a single suggestion of sincerity in any one of its six scenes). It is hardly credible that the Literary Theatre which gave Synge, Robinson and O'Casey to an appreciative world, has placed its seal of approval on such a production as this. Unfortunately, *Anti-Christ* does not stand alone. It is only one of a number of recent productions that have succeeded in tarnishing the reputation of our National Theatre, and have helped to drag public taste to the low level at which it now stands.[65]

In the same issue, J. J. Hayes made a long and impressive defense of the play by arguing for a broader conception of drama than the conventional. He also defended the structure of the play and made a finely detailed analysis of the acting:

> *Anti-Christ* has no visible conflict, but that does not mean that there is no conflict. . . . The conflict may be and is, at times, elusive, but it exists. Its elusiveness is due partly to the looseness of Mr. O'Donnell's writing and partly to the failure of the players to come up to the requirements of some of the scenes—at least on the opening night. This latter particularly applies to the scene in the home of the Prime Minister, which is the culminating scene of the entire work. Here we have in substance the trial and condemnation, *in absentia*, of another Christ. It is here that the conflict becomes very emphasised. It may not be visible, but it *is* tangible. Hovering over the meeting is the influence of Captain Boles, whose liberty and life are summarily disposed of as mere specks of dust in the machinery of a system represented by a Machiavellian Chief of State, and his sycophantic Minister of Public Safety. . . .
>
> This scene, well written, was entirely marred in the playing. The cause of the meeting was forgotten, whereas the unseen presence of Boles should have been made felt. The scene gave evidence of insufficient rehearsing; the physical movements of the players were conventional, and never for a moment reflected the mental condition of the characters. This more or less applied to the whole production, and there were moments when one expected to hear the voice of the director supervising a rehearsal or of the prompter "throwing a line." The tempo was much too slow, and there was a strange misplacing of vehemence of tone. It was used where mild but firm tones would have been convincing, and when vehemence

> was called for it was absent. Most of the scenes lent themselves to "still" playing but there were occasions when the director could have imparted movement and life to the action. Lines were spoken, but they lacked the sincerity of feeling. This was particularly noticeable in the scene in Captain Boles' home when a crowd of men smarting under their grievances were as gentle of demeanour as a Sunday school class.[66]

Except for a small portion of its concluding scene, *Anti-Christ* has not been published; and a perusal of the manuscript in the National Library of Ireland indicates that there is no compelling reason, other than the historical, for it to reach print. It is a play unfortunately much more interestingly conceived than executed. Nevertheless, it had one significant reverberation. On 17 August, when the play was revived, Holloway had a few words with O'Casey in the foyer of the Abbey, and O'Casey remarked that he found the piece "compelling."[67] One of the present writers has argued that O'Casey was so impressed by the theme, the technique, and some of the specific situations (particularly the concluding dance), that the plan of *The Silver Tassie* took root in his mind.[68]

On 31 March, the Abbey gave the first production to Robinson's new two-act, *Portrait*, a play that without enormous success attempted to capture something of the attitude of the postwar generation. Although the first-night audience strongly applauded the rather bizarre ending—which was again a dance—the critics had many reservations. Probably the play's strongest supporter was Susan L. Mitchell in the *Irish Statesman*:

> There are only two scenes in Mr. Lennox Robinson's new play, but one received the impression from it that in those two scenes the whole comedy of life passed in review. Maggie, one of the daughters of an ordinary prosperous middle-class family, is engaged to a "nice boy" Peter. Her father and mother approve the match, and with the prospect of Peter's promotion in the office a speedy marriage is predicted. But Peter begins to be disappointing to Maggie; he is not a "pusher," he does not want to "get there." He does not know where "there" is; he questions life. Prosperous families like the Barnados do not question life; the parents have their sentimental side; they read their *David Copperfield* to the accompaniment of knitting jumpers; the daughters do not read Dickens or knit, but they foxtrot and make love, are independent, and do not want to lean, or are dependent and want something solid to lean against. Peter is not solid. Nobody could lean against him. He cannot even force his way into a crowded tram. Maggie feels herself drifting away to the strong, ruthless man, Tom Hughes. She is a decent girl; she does not want to drift; she wants Peter to hold her back; to be masterful, savage. Peter cannot assert himself. He cannot fight. He cannot fit into the pattern of life that Maggie has instinctively designed for herself out of the materials of her environment. When one thinks over it, the suicide in which the play culminates is an amazing development, but as the drama evolves under our eyes we are amazed at nothing. Everything is natural; in order. Peter finds no reassurance in himself; no answer to any of his questions. He steps back from the scene of life as he stepped back from the swarming tram. When the comedy of life drifts into tragedy we are overwhelmed, forgetting how precarious at all times is the movement of that piece. The extraordinary invention of Maggie's dance with the dying man, designed to

> prevent his mother seeing the tragedy, as, aroused by the shot, she peeps into the room, with its horrible accompaniment on the gramophone, "For to-night we'll merry, merry be," gives the play the crowning touch of the fantastic. I cannot understand why Maggie, as she leaves the room where the dead man is stretched on the floor, turns on the gramophone. But beyond this one I have no questions to ask. To me it seems that *Portrait* is the strongest of Mr. Lennox Robinson's plays. The very narrowness of his stage seems to deepen the emotion pressed into it, and how admirably it was played![69]

The *Irish Times* found the play "a complete contrast in conception and dialogue to the preconceived methods of the Abbey."[70] Frank Hugh O'Donnell in the *Evening Herald* saw "a decided leaning to the Futuristic School."[71] And Andrew E. Malone, after remarking that *Portrait* was the best of the "very mediocre" plays the theater had so far produced in the year, described it as

> an experiment which shows many traces of very close study of Pirandello and Susan Glaspell, and with close affinity with the newer school of drama which is comprehensively termed expressionist. The term expressionist is almost as wide as charity, and it covers nearly as many sins. The theories of Freud and the practices of D. W. Griffith have gone to its making, and the interest of the resultant play depends largely upon the proportions, and the way in which they are mixed. *Portrait* is too small and too thin a play by which to judge the method, but it does say that Mr. Robinson is not yet a master. It is a portrait of our time in two sittings, and, of course, a finished portrait could not be expected in such a hurry. A vaster canvas is necessary, and greater detail, before such a portrait can be judged. However, Mr. Robinson does succeed in sketching in black and white the main features, and the sketch suggests that its features are blurred and indistinct.[72]

Malone then criticized parts of the plot, particularly the ending:

> Brandon drunk with whiskey and emotion, snatches the gun and shoots himself. His corpse is used in Grand Guignol fashion in a dance to prevent his mother making the discovery of his suicide, and Maggie Barnado adds another Guignol touch when she says "Blood! And I said he had none!"
>
> From this outline the weaknesses of the play may be judged. There is no reason inherent in the play why Peter Brandon should shoot himself. If every rejected lover followed that example the streets would be littered with corpses. And why try to prevent his mother making a discovery that is inevitable within a few minutes? The cramped ending makes the use of Grand Guignol tricks necessary, but they spoil the play, making mockery of the obvious sincerity of its idea and plunging the whole into the crudest of melodrama.[73]

Reading the play today, one cannot but agree with Malone, although for some members of the first-night audience the intense acting of Sara Allgood as Maggie made the final scene work. It did not work for everybody, however, and some critiques of the acting passed over Sara completely. Certainly, she was curious casting for the Dublin version of a flapper. Maggie was an obvious Shelah Richards role, and Sara was distinctly, as Holloway remarked, "too matronly."[74] In fact, as production photos make clear, she was rather embarrassingly fat. However, Sara was a strong-mined woman and the company's premier actress, and Shelah Richards was at this time only the company's most promising ingenue.[75] And as Murray remarked about Sara, " . . . when all is said, she has more of the artist in her than any of those who appear on its [the Abbey's] stage."[76]

In any event, *Portrait*, despite its melodramatic conclusion, was recognised as a serious attempt to contrast Victorian morality with modern; and thus, like *Anti-Christ*, it sounded a distinctly new note for the Abbey. Not quite a successful note, however; for, as the *Manchester Guardian* remarked, "Perhaps it is old-fashioned, but Dublin still prefers *The Whiteheaded Boy* of Lennox Robinson to his essay in psychoanalysis."[77]

The Abbey's next new production was on 21 April, and it was Shaw's *Fanny's First Play*, which had originally been staged in London on 19 April 1911. Shaw's *jeu d'esprit* was, according to Yeats, "a great success; £57 in house Saturday night; £40 on Friday and we continue it this week."[78] The second week of the Shaw run was notable for the inclusion on the bill of a curtain raiser, the Abbey's first production of Chekhov's comic one-act, *The Proposal*.

The theatre then closed until Horse Show Week, which was always a profitable time at the box office. The reopening came on 3 August with *The Playboy* and Robinson's popular one-act, *Crabbed Youth and Age*; then the last half of the week presented another attractive double bill, *Arms and the Man* and *The Rising of the Moon*. In the following weeks, the Abbey played to good houses for *Man and Superman* and to crowded ones for *Juno and the Paycock*.

Then, on 14 September, there was the first production of George Shiels's new three-act comedy, *Professor Tim*. Some of Shiels correspondence with Lady Gregory indicates the help that the Abbey directors often gave to their playwrights. On 29 May, Shiels wrote:

> I am glad to have this play sent back for revision, for I see how it can be improved. Many thanks to you and Mr. Yeats for your kind and helpful advice regarding it. After reading your letter and Mr. Yeats' marginal notes I felt rather ashamed of myself.
>
> Whether I knew it or not, I have been writing down in spots to an imaginary audience of the meanest intelligence. The too frequent use of the bottle, of cheap slang, of swear-words, and of the name of God has been a peculiar weakness of mine. But of late I have seen my own faults in the work of others, notably in that of Eugene O'Neill, and I think it is all a ghastly mistake. Common sense tells me that these vulgar elements are a handicap instead of a help. But I hope it is not too late to mend. I know that in the pieces I have so far written the good qualities predominate; otherwise you would never have permitted them to appear at the Abbey.
>
> In future, without taking myself too seriously, I will make an earnest endeavour to eliminate all such matter. My own instinct is pretty true. I not only see but sense the rightness of every point made by Mr. Yeats.

> I am greatly taken with your suggestion to make the old "Professor" feign poverty and intemperance in order to test the "sincerity" of his friends. It will improve the piece out of all measure, and if it turns out a success you will know where I got the idea. Meanwhile I am sincerely grateful to you for your assistance.
>
> There is no chance of my being in Dublin this summer. So long closed by myself, I have developed a perfect dread of meeting strangers. But I have a great kindness for all my unseen friends at the Abbey.[79]

On 15 June, Shiels wrote:

> I have been working on my play *Professor Tim* with a pencil for the last 16 days and am now going to retype it. May I sent it back to you when finished? Your previous suggestions were of great assistance. I have used them to the extent of my ability and think the play will be greatly improved. There is no longer any sign of drink nor an unnecessary expletive from first to last. I have made the old "professor" an eccentric character instead of a toper, which gives considerable scope for his quaint humour.[80]

Everybody thoroughly enjoyed *Professor Tim*, but nobody thought it important. As Susan L. Mitchell wrote:

> Laughter could hardly have been out of place anywhere during its three Acts. Professor Tim is the Scally's distinguished uncle, long expected by them from abroad. Instead, however, of returning in a style to do his family credit, he disguises himself in drink and penury in order to test their quality. The play has a familiar Christmas story air and after a number of mystifications on the part of Uncle Tim that would not deceive a hen, all ends in general benevolence and a couple of weddings.
>
> *Professor Tim* is rather a series of rough-and-tumble incidents than a play, but the knockabout business is diverting though Uncle Tim was, perhaps, a little too drunk, but the acting all round would have put life into a turnip. One's intelligence not being needed in the play one was at liberty to concentrate on the actors, and their individual gifts in every case made themselves felt. . . . Mr. Barry Fitzgerald as the foolish son of the Kilroys imagined his part delightfully and unexpectedly. If the actors could not make a good play out of a poor one at least they put out all their strength to make the audience happy.[81]

The difficulty of the play was not that it was an unprepossessing farce, but a thin and highly conventional one, thus offering opportunity for the broadest kind of playing. As the *Manchester Guardian* soundly reported:

> Its plot was conspicuous by its lack of originality all through, and sometimes by its apparent absence. In truth, the three acts were reminiscent of scenes at a rather old-fashioned pantomime, wherein sentiment and "comic business" were skilfully blended. The play would make a fitting, and not at all incongruous, ending for a minstrel show on the sands of, say, Blackpool. All the favourite characters are there—the shrewish wife and meek husband, the uncle who appears as a penniless drunkard and turns out to be a high-minded millionaire, the impossibly manly hero and the incredibly foolish oaf who strives to filch the happiness of the heroine. Barry Fitzgerald, as the oaf, has full scope for his gifts as a comedian, and he made the

most of them. Sara Allgood, as the shrewish dame, was in a merry mood. The despairing voice of the prompter often rose above those of the players, who "gagged" remorselessly. At some of the impromptu thrusts it seemed as if even Sara Allgood could scarce forebear to laugh outright.[82]

Professor Tim and its playing could well stand as a herald of worse to come: thin scripts which actors, insufficiently controlled by their director, mugged and gagged.[83] But, although the audiences were vastly entertained by the goings-on, some Abbey-goers had further thoughts. On 16 September, Holloway wrote:

I saw Hayes chatting to John MacDonagh and the former joined me. . . . He asked me what I thought of *Professor Tim*, and I said it is a good night's entertainment! "That is just what it is and nothing more," he said. "The old-fashioned Irish stage type of play over again. Why did they accept it at the Abbey?"[84]

For years, *Professor Tim* was to be among the most popular pieces of the amateur companies around the country, and that really is the appropriate venue for it, a jovial entertainment in a village hall. It was also the type of play that was to solidify Shiels's reputation as a mere purveyor of popular entertainments. Fortunately for the Irish drama, he became much more than that, but even in 1925 he himself had no illusions about the play. As he wrote to Lady Gregory on 17 September:

Will you let me thank you again for those previous hints which you so kindly gave me about *Professor Tim*. Mr. Robinson and Mr. Dolan have both written to me in the most glowing terms about the first night's production, which they say was an unqualified success, but this, I am certain, could not have been written if the play had been done in its original shape. . . .

The play in itself is not much, but its aim was a modest one—namely, to give a night's simple entertainment.[85]

The Abbey's last new play of the year was Robinson's *The White Blackbird*, which was first produced on 12 October. The play had bothered George O'Brien, the economist who was the government's newly appointed representative on the Abbey Theatre board. In her journal for 25 September, Lady Gregory remarked that O'Brien was "in disgrace with Robinson having told him he had taken *The White Blackbird* to the Kingstown Club and consulted various people, 'legal men,' as to whether the end is improper! I have told Perrin plays sent to him to future must be marked private and confidential."[86] O'Brien's view is more fully reported by Holloway:

I went home with George O'Brien, the Director of the theatre appointed by the Directors to see that the grant is properly used. He has to read and approve of the theatre's new plays. . . . He thinks it is a fine play and likely to be very popular. . . . he saw the nasty words . . . and the suggestion of incest, [but] he didn't like to turn it down for fear it might be said that the government was interfering unduly with the liberty of the theatre! So let it pass—though in fear and trembling at what might be the result. He wouldn't like a row or for instance the Catholic Truth Society to march with banners up and down outside the theatre, or rows like the *Playboy* ones to occur inside . . . or that the play should cause anything that might interfere with the grant being continued now that the theatre is proving a success. I assured him that none of these things would occur. . . . That the days for rows at the Abbey were over. That the audience knew better than [to] make another *Playboy*. This very much relieved O'Brien's mind. . . . When the government asked him to look after their interest at the theatre [he] didn't like to refuse. It meant free admission for his mother and self. . . . He would be anxious to read what the papers had to say about the play—the acting was so good that it glossed over the dangerous incidents. Of course, Robinson having written it made its unsavory undercurrent appear worse—his blasphemous story . . . in *Tomorrow* still rankles in the mind of all.[87]

The most contradictory reports of the play were those of the *Evening Herald* and the *Irish Times*. The *Herald* reported:

In the Naynoes' garden was a white balckbird—it was not even white—a mottled grey—which hopped about all day long, always alone, never singing but ever busy. In the Naynoe household was William, the eldest son, whom his mother detested because he had his father's will proved in his favour when two years old. His stepfather regarded him as a stern young man, but just; his stepbrother and sister looked upon him as an ogre who prevented them having a good time. William interfered with their plans and settled their affairs to suit himself. The pathetic figure who is brought from Spain by his vindictive stepbrother to spoil his plans, considered him a man too good to love, and who to himself was a being with one purpose—the realisation of his father's dream of success in working the family's copper mine. . . .

The White Blackbird is a drama of repression. The author has a theory or a message, but he either is not prepared to give it to the world yet, or he does not wish to give it, but it is there, and its faint cries are heard throughout the play. According to William the aim of life is not happiness either in his young sisters' meaning of the term—a jolly time and marriage with a good man to make him unhappy; neither is it happiness in the scholastic sense of duty done in spite of difficulties, and, generally speaking, without regard for the feelings of others. Williams is selfish, but we have not time to tell whether his selfishness is a means to an end, or the end in itself—just self-glorification in being able to show the ghost of his father that the son could succeed where the father had failed, and which success was gained in the face of much more numerous and formidable obstacles.

Mr. Robinson has presented an interesting problem, and has presented it exceptionally well.[88]

However, the *Irish Times* wrote:

The overcrowded state of the Abbey Theatre last night showed the interest taken in the first production of a new play by Mr. Lennox Robinson entitled *The White Blackbird*. The audience saw a poor play splendidly produced and beautifully acted.[90]

It is written in three acts, and, as far as dramatic interest is concerned, could have finished at the end of the first. By that the people had got the whole story of the Naynoe family, and found it dull. Two more acts carried on the history, and although there was the usual first night call for the author, everyone must have been relieved to find that they had seen the last of a lot of impossible, colourless nonentities, to whose doings they had become completely indifferent.

There is a will and a law suit; a copper mine and a Swiss crevasse; a strong, silent man, whose strength is shown in bossing the members of a useless family; a courtesan from Spain, who loves one of them because he is a *galopin*, although there is nothing in the play except her word to make us suspect that he is more than a brainless fool, to say nothing of the utter scoundrel who will stop at nothing.

Some people will object to the creation of a situation in which an eighteen-year-old girl is placed with regard to her step-brother, but that is understandable if it were but a link in the working-out of a dramatic story. There is nothing dramatic in *The White Blackbird*. There is nothing smart in the dialogue, and the one attempt at comedy is clumsy.[89]

Although not a thoroughly successful play, *The White Blackbird* is a thoughtful and interesting one that might almost be seen as the opposite side of the coin of *The Whiteheaded Boy*. Both plays present family situations in which a son rules the roost. In the lighthearted comedy of *The Whiteheaded Boy*, the family members dote on the son; in the somber drama of *The White Blackbird*, the family members thoroughly dislike him. In *The Whiteheaded Boy*, a thoroughly conventional comedy gently joshed the foibles of family life; in *The White Blackbird* a thoroughly realistic drama took a sour look at family life under a modern microscope.[90]

In fact, the two plays seem symptomatic of the Abbey repertoire of 1925; half of the repertoire was conventional and traditional, and plays like *Professor Tim* and *The Old Man* looked back to the past. But the rest of the repertoire was untraditional in theme or unconventional in technique, and plays like *Portrait* and *Anti-Christ* reflected the modern world and the modern theatre. In sum, the Abbey in 1925 seemed hesitating at a crossroads, with the directors rather dissatisfied with the old work and yet delighted with the fat boxoffice receipts it brought in. In the letter of 27 April, partly quoted above, Yeats exulted in the boxoffice receipts of *Fanny's First Play*, but went on to say, "I want to weed out all weak plays and I think *Mixed Marriage* one of them and make this possibly by gradually substituting stronger work."[91] In her journal for 3 February, Lady Gregory wrote:

Yesterday, Monday, I went to the Abbey, I was dissatisfied with the plays arranged for the next weeks, poor revivals or revivals of poor plays. . . . I say if we have to lose money we must keep self respect and keep up good work, and I got L. R. to come there and we decided to drop *The Man Who Missed the Tide*, and *Young man from Rathmines*, and to hurry on *John Bull* for next week, and put *The Playboy* this month, and to put Casey's *Kathleen Listens In* on with *Heart's Desire* and Miss MacArdle's *Old Man* instead of *Rathmines Young Man*.[92]

Lady Gregory's deletions were sound enough, but her additions were hardly new. Of the three directors, Robinson, with his work for the Drama League and his fondness for Pirandello and Benavente, was the most aware of new developments in the theatre; and these new developments were apparent in his new work, mildly in technique and rather more strongly in theme. But Robinson was no violent experimenter and no strong personality.

When the issue was finally joined, it was fought out early in 1926 over O'Casey's *The Plough and the Stars*. The directors stoutly defended O'Casey and ultimately won the fight, but the O'Casey play was more modern in theme than in technique; and winning the fight took a lot of abrasive psychic energy out of the Abbey. Two years after *The Plough*, when a question of modernist technique arose over O'Casey's *The Silver Tassie*, the directors opted for the traditional; and the Abbey pattern wes set for years.

For the Abbey, the great event of 1925, a culmination of much backstage maneuvering, was the award by the Free State government of a grant of £850. The announcement was made by Yeats on 8 August:

> Speaking from the stage of the theatre on Saturday night, Mr. Yeats, on behalf of the directors, thanked the Government for what he described as "an act of intelligent generosity."
>
> "They have," he said, "given this theatre an endowment of £850, and we hope for the continuance of that endowment. We have become the first State-endowed theatre in any English-speaking country, but the example of our country will probably be followed. All nations except the English-speaking nations and, I believe, Venezuela, have considered that their theatres are a most important part of national education, and have endowed those theatres that they may not have to lower their quality through the struggle for existence."
>
> Mr. Yeats recalled the vicissitudes through which the theatre had passed, but said that now they had founded an art of drama and an art of acting which were in the first rank. The fame of the Abbey Theatre had gone everywhere. There was no European nation where its plays had not been performed, and he is constantly hearing of some new translation of some one or other of their dramatists.
>
> After the performance the directors and staff entertained to supper on the stage Mr. Ernest Blythe, the Free State Minister for Finance, who was accompanied by his wife. Mr. Blythe said the Abbey Theatre had done work of national importance. The Government recognised the value of that work, and he thought would continue to recognise it.[93]

According to Holloway, Yeats further said:

> Now we can assure you that this government subsidy and your continued support will enable us to keep a brilliant company and to offer in the future, as in the past, a means of expression to Irish dramatic intellect. Neither Lady Gregory nor Synge nor I ever thought of this theatre as an educational theatre in the ordinary sense of the word: we had nothing to teach but clarity of expression and that for the most part was taught not by us but by the opportunity of the stage, and the opportunity that you gave by your critical enthusiasm. The credit belongs to the dramatists, actors and audiences; they have been worthy of one another. We have, however, created in this little theatre an assembly where we can discuss our own problems and our

> own life and I think we have the right to claim that we have founded an art of drama and an art of acting which are in the first rank. . . . I think at this moment I may be permitted to boast of our work, for without doing so I cannot praise the government aright for this new maifestation of their courage and intelligence.[94]

One far-reaching result of the government subsidy was the appointing of a government representative to the Abbey board. For years, the theater had been directed by the major writers—first Yeats, Synge, and Lady Gregory; then for most of its history Yeats and Lady Gregory until Lennox Robinson was added to the directorate in 1923. George O'Brien, the economist, who was the first government representative on the Board, was also the first nonliterary man to be added; and that fact in the view of the present writers, was an ominous portent of a slow change for the worse.

At the end of 1925, however, there was little indication of storms ahead. Indeed, the theater had never seemed in a stronger position, artistically or financially; and on 27 December there was a celebration of its coming-of-age, its twenty-first year. An elaborate special programme was printed with portraits of Yeats, Synge, and Lady Gregory, and with an impressive list of 237 plays that group had presented since the beginnings of the Irish Literary Theatre in 1899. The *Irish Times* gave the following detailed account:

> The celebration last night of the twenty-first anniversary of the opening of the Abbey Theatre, Dublin, was an event of considerable importance in the life of the city. The theatre was filled to the doors, and many who arrived even before the opening hour could not be admitted. During the night the thanks of the public were given to the players, past and present.
>
> The audience in the stalls included many who are well known in the intellectural and artistic life of Dublin, while the pit and balcony held theatre-goers who for years have gone to the Abbey for love of drama and of fine acting. Lady Gregory got a great ovation when, in the course of the evening, she came on the stage to make a short speech.
>
> Three one-act plays were selected for the coming of age celebration, all old favourites, and all of the highest Abbey standard of dramatic writing and theatrical production. They were *The Hour Glass* (Yeats), *In the Shadow of the Glen* (Synge), and *Hyacinth Halvey* (Lady Gregory). In the first of those there appeared Mr. Frank Fay and Mr. Udolphus Wright, who were in the caste of the first play ever seen on the Abbey stage.
>
> The three pieces are dramatic productions in which the present company are completely at home, but the enthusiasm of the occasion seemed to have got to the other side of the foot lights, and the work there was never better. Mr. Fay's Wise Man in the *Hour Glass* is famous at the Abbey. Mr. Dolan's study of the Fool is among the greatest of his creations, and Miss Eileen Crowe's dignified acting of the Angel is now a Dublin story. The stage scene, so true to the dramatist's message, was designed by Mr. Gordon Craig.
>
> With Miss Crowe, Mr. Barry Fitzgerald, and Mr. Peter Nolan in the principal parts, Synge's masterpiece is to be seen at its best. The feature of *Hyacinth Halvey* was the acting of Miss Maureen Delany. Mr. Arthur Shields has a thorough grip of the part of Hyacinth. It is interesting to know that the back cloth used for this comedy is among the oldest of the Abbey property, and was designed by Mr. Jack B. Yeats, R. H. A.

For the occasion a handsomely turned out souvenir programme was issued. In it was the list of the 216[95] plays produced by the National Theatre Society, the Abbey's official title, a *facsimile* of the first programme, and some interesting pictures. On the cover was an enlarged reproduction of the Abbey "girl with the hound," which is known in every country in which the theatre is honoured. It has adorned the Abbey programmes from the beginning, and is the work of Miss Maunsell, a London artist, in whose portfolio the design was discovered accidentally by Mr. W. B. Yeats.[96]

The little Abbey orchestra, formed and conducted by Dr. John F. Larchet, played a popular part in the night's celebration. Their programme was:—Overture, "Oberon" (Weber); Irish airs (arranged Larchet); Prelude, "L' Apres-midi d'un Faune" (Debussy); Irish airs—(a) "The Wheelwright," (b) Reel (arranged Larchet).

At the conclusion of Synge's play the thanks of the audience were tendered to the players, past and present, in an agreeable little ceremony, at which Mr. Thomas Johnson, T. D., leader of the Irish Labour Party, was Chairman. With him were Mr. Ernest Blythe, T. D., Minister for Finance, and Mr. Gerald O Lochlain, of the Gaelic Drama League. At frequent intervals the appreciation expressed by the speakers was emphasised by round after round of applause from the house.

Mr. Johnson said that he took his appointment to the chair that evening as a compliment to those who frequent the pit. That celebration of the coming-of-age of the Abbey Theatre was unique; was, in fact, a performance that could not possibly be repeated.

Mr. Blythe proposed a vote of thanks to the Abbey players, past and present, who had done so much to create their Irish national theatre. It was hardly sufficiently realised that in the Abbey Theatre they had a most important national asset. It was no exaggeration to say that the work of the Abbey Theatre had shed lustre upon the name of Ireland—(applause)—and had aroused an interest in, and respect for, Ireland in places where, but for the Abbey, there would have been neither. It was not necessary for him to give praise to everyone to whom praise was due, but he had to mention, first: Miss Horniman. (Great applause.) It was through the generosity of that lady that the Abbey got its habitation and its name; it owed its twenty years' of existence to the tenacity and firm purpose of Lady Gregory and Dr. W. B. Yeats. (Applause.)

The theatre could never have been carried on but for the talented players who were available from the start. There had been established there a school of acting of which any country might be proud, and which had sent forth actors and actresses to win admiration in other lands. Those responsible for the foundation of the Abbey owed a great deal in the beginning to the brothers Fay. (Applause.) They and their associates were filled with the spirit of devotion to their art and to the objects ever present to the minds of the founders of the Abbey. But for that spirit existing from the beginning to the present day, it would not have been possible to get such magnificent combinations of players as they had seen in the Abbey without a break for the past twenty-one years. Owing to financial difficulties it had not been possible to remunerate the players at all proportionately to their work, but those splendid men and women kept on night after night for twenty-one years in a spirit of self-sacrifice for the establishment of a national theatre worthy of the name. He hoped that for the future it would be possible to recompense them with more suitable salaries. (Applause, and a Voice—Thanks to you.)

There was one group of Abbey players that he would have to refer to specially—the players who perform under the *bâton* of Dr. Larchet. (Loud applause.) The performances of the orchestra were in keeping with the high standard at once suggested by the name of the Abbey.

Mr. O'Lochlainn, speaking in Irish, seconded the vote of thanks.

Mr. Johnson, putting the vote to the house, said that it conveyed the almost unanimous feelings not of that audience, but of twenty-one full years of aduience—feelings of friendliness and at-homeliness. Older players always spoke of the old stock companies in terms of the greatest intimacy, entered into their lives, knew all about their trials and their difficulties. There was a great personal interest taken by the audiences in the players of the past. That relationship between the stage and the house was always marked at the Abbey. Those who attended fairly regularly, as he did, felt that they were personal friends with people on the stage, whom they had never met. It was that human relationship and the wholehearted work of the players that had made the Abbey the delight and the joy of Dublin. (Applause.)

Lady Gregory, who was affected by the wonderful enthusiasm with which the vote of thanks was received, said that, perhaps, she had a little claim to express the gratitude of the players, past and present, for had she not on two successive nights played an old woman for one of the company, who was unable to come to the theatre. She felt that night at if she were one of the players, and could speak in reply for them, and not in her capacity as director or producer, or, as Shaw once called her, the charwoman of the Abbey. (Applause.)

The appreciation expressed that night had gratified the players, including herself, who witnessed it, and would be heard of with keen pleasure by their old friends now absent. Frank Fay was there, but his brother was not, and it was very much due to William Fay that they had been able to begin at all. (Applause.) Then there was Arthur Sinclair and J. M. Kerrigan. Once when they played in London, one of the newspapers, having exhausted its terms of praise, came to "Oh, but Kerrigan!" (Applause.) There was Philip Donovan,[97] now playing in South Africa; Maire O'Neill and Sara Allgood. (Applause.) A week ago she had a letter from Mr. Augustine Birrell in appreciation of that most moving play, *Juno and the Paycock*. In it he wrote: 'Sara Allgood is doing everything that any actress ever has done." (Applause.) That was great praise, indeed.

Others that came to her mind were Eithne Magee—whose husband fell in love with her the first time he saw her when they played at Oxford; Miss Coppinger, now in Melbourne building up an Abbey Theatre there; Maire Nic Shiubhlaigh, Maire ni Gharbhaigh, Eileen O'Doherty, Miss Darragh, Cathleen Nesbitt, Emma Vernon, Seumas O'Sullivan, George Roberts, and many others who carried on the tradition. They, all the players, would never forget that night's appreciation of their work.

Actors knew how much they owed to the audience. They were encouraged by the spontaneous laugh and grateful for the moment of silence in tragedy. An audience could amuse itself elsewhere, the dramatist could turn to writing poems to the moon, but without his audience the player was lost. He could not play to a looking-glass. They of the Abbey had played to many great audiences in London and in America. They remembered their reception there with gratitude, but their feeling for their Dublin audiences was affection. The Abbey players loved everything in their old theatre. They loved Dr. Larchet and his little company; they loved the stalls and the balcony; but above all they loved the pit, "perhaps because we and they have had some little lovers quarrels together" (continued applause). She hoped that they would continue leaving a good name, a good tradition, or, to put it in the words often spoken from that stage, "and long-remembering harpers, will have matter for their song." (Applause.)[98]

6
Early 1926

> You have disgraced yourselves again. Is this to be an ever-recurring celebration of the arrival of Irish genius? Synge first and then O'Casey. The news of the happenings of the past few minutes will go from country to country. Dublin has once more rocked the cradle of genius. From such a scene in this theatre went forth the fame of Synge. Equally the fame of O'Casey is born here tonight. This is his apotheosis.[1]

These were the words that W. B. Yeats shouted from the stage of the Abbey Theatre on Thursday night, 11 February 1926. The occasion was the fourth performance of Sean O'Casey's masterpiece, *The Plough and the Stars.*

During the second act a terrific row broke out from a portion of the audience. Some people stormed the stage, some threw missiles, and some boohed, jeered, catcalled, hissed, and sang patriotic songs. Nothing had been seen like it since the 1907 row over J. M. Synge's *The Playboy of the Western World*, and truly it seemed that the clock had been turned back twenty years. For the protests against *The Plough* were basically the same as those against *The Playboy*. Nothing seemed to have changed, and nothing seemed to have been learned.

According to some people who were there, what Yeats said was almost entirely lost in the din; but the poet had the foresight to send the statement to the papers. Well that he did, for that statement has since been admired as the most intractable and indomitable description of what the Abbey Theatre at its best was—a belligerent and unyielding temple of dramatic art.

From the first, there were rumbles of trouble about O'Casey's new play. On 1 September 1925, Michael J. Dolan wrote to Lady Gregory about various theatre matters, and then turned to one matter that was particularly bothering him:

> Mr. Perrin had the new O'Casey play and a letter from Mr. Robinson telling him to have the parts typed at once. I take it from that letter that the piece is to be produced in its present form. Now Lady Gregory I respectfully beg of you to pause and think what it will mean. As you know we cannot afford to take risks especially at the present moment. The theatre is booming at the present and unfortunately there are too many people who are sorry that such is the case. We don't want to give them anything to grasp at. At any time I would think twice before having anything to do

with it. The language in it is—to use an Abbey phrase—beyond the beyonds. The song at the end of the second act sung by the "girl-of-the-streets" is unpardonable.

I consulted Mr. G. O'Brien about the whole play. He said he had written to you a general benediction about it, but agreed with me in that there is a huge difference between reading a play at home and hearing it from a stage. I don't want to protest too much, particularly as O'Casey and myself had a heated argument about the production of *Man and Superman*. I can assure you the latter has nothing to do with it. As a matter of fact, when and if it is read to the company, I feel there will be a real difficulty in getting them to play in it. You can rely on me not to try to influence them in any way. Let them judge and decide for themselves.[2]

Then on 5 September, George O'Brien, the government representative on the Abbey board, wrote to Yeats in the same vein:

Dear Mr. Yeats,

I have read O'Casey's new play and am convinced that it would be quite as successful as any of his others if produced. There are, however, certain particulars in which I think the play in its present form would seriously offend the audience, and I think that it must be amended in certain respects before it can be staged.

The love scene between Clitheroe and his wife in Act I does not read true, and I am inclined to think that it could be easily improved. But even if it is let stand as it is there are a couple of phrases which I think would annoy the audience. These are:

"You can; come on, put your leg against mine—there."

"Little rogue of th' white breast."

(Act I, p. 19)

My most serious objection is to Act II where, in my opinion, the introduction of the prostitute is quite unnecessary to the action. Of course the mere introduction of a prostitute as a character in the play is not in itself objectionable but I think that the character as presented by Mr. O'Casey is objectionable. The lady's professional side is unduly emphasised in her actions and conversation, and I think that the greater part of this scene should be re-written. In view of this general objection I shall not trouble you with the particular phrases in this act to which I take exception as they are very numerous, and I think could not possibly be allowed to stand. The song at the end is an example of what I mean.

My only other objections to the play are to particular phrases and modes of expression which could easily be omitted or altered without in any way interfering with the main structure of the play. I will go through these seriatim.

(1) The words "Jesus", "Jaysus" and "Christ" occur frequently (e.g. Act I, p. 12; Act III, p. 8; Act IV, pp. 15 and 18). These words used as expletives would certainly give offence.
(2) On Act I, p. 11 there is a speech "I'll leave you to th' day when th' all-pitiful, all-merciful, all-lovin' God'll be rievin' an' roastin' you; tearin' an' tormentin' you; burnin' an' blastin' you'.

There are similar phrases to be found on Act III, p. 10 (near the top) and Act IV, p. 3 (at the bottom). These speeches would offend the audience and must be altered.

(3) On Act II, p. 10 the speeches of Bessie Burgess and Mrs. Gogan contain objectionable expressions which could be considerable toned down with advantage.
(4) The vituperative vocabulary of some characters occasionally runs away with itself. As examples of what I mean I would refer to the last words of The Covey before his exit on Act I, p. 17, the last two speeches on Act II, p. 16, and the last speech on Act III, p. 13. I think that the numerous references to "lowsers" and "lice" should be changed.

(5) The word "bitch" occurs on Act I, p. 15, Act III, p. 4 and Act IV, p. 17. I think this should be altered.

I think you will agree with me that the play would be improved if the foregoing suggestions were accepted and hope that Mr. O'Casey can be prevailed on to take the same view. I do not think that any of these alterations will materially alter the main action of the play, which, while excellent in its conception and execution, could not possibly be produced in precisely its present form.

Yours sincerely,
George O'Brien[3]

To this letter, Yeats replied on 10 September from 82 Merrion Square:

Dear O'Brien,
We agree with you about Clitheroe and his wife, that love scene in the first act is most objectionable and, as you say, does not read true. What is wrong is that O'Casey is there writing about people whom he does not know, people he has only read about. We had both decided when we first read the play that he should be asked to try and modify these characters, bringing them within the range of his knowledge. When that is done the objectionable elements will lose their sentimentality and thereby their artistic offence. We decided that if he cannot do this that the dialogue would have to be greatly modified in rehearsal.
Now we come to the prostitute in Act 2; she is certainly as necessary to the general action and idea as are the drunkards and wastrels. O'Casey is contrasting the ideal dream with the normal grossness of life and of that she is an essential part. It is no use putting her in if she does not express herself vividly and in character, if her "professional" side is not emphasised. Almost certainly a phrase here and there must be altered in rehearsal but the scene as a whole is admirable, one of the finest O'Casey has written. To eliminate any part of it on grounds that have nothing to do with dramatic literature would be to deny all our traditions.
The other passages you mention are the kind of thing which are dealt with in rehearsal by the producer (in almost every one of O'Casey's plays the dialogue here and there has been a little modified and he has never objected to our modifications) but we are inclined to think that the use of the word "bitch" in Act 4 is necessary. It occurs when Bessie on receiving her mortal wound turns furiously on the woman whose delirium has brought it on her. The scene is magnificent and we are loth to alter a word of it.
If you do not feel that this letter entirely satisfies you we can have a Directors' meeting on the subject.[4]

This noble and perceptive letter drew the following answer from O'Brien on 13 September:

Dear Mr. Yeats and Lennox,
Thanks very much for your letter from which I am glad to learn that you do not think my criticism of the play unreasonable. I appreciate your willingness to secret my objections, and I take it that the offensive passages I mentioned will be changed. As regards Act 2, I am in a certain amount of difficulty. I quite see your point that "to eliminate any part of it on grounds that have nothing to do with dramatic literature would be to destroy all our traditions"!! I feel, however, that there are certain other considerations affecting the production to which it is, in a peculiar way, my duty to have regard. One of these is the possibility that the play might

offend any section of public opinion so seriously as to provoke an attack on the theatre of a kind that could endanger the continuance of the subsidy. Rightly or wrongly, I look on myself as the watchdog of the subsidy. Now, I think that the play, just as it stands, might easily provoke such an attack.

Your statement that "a phrase here and there must be altered in rehearsal" suggests that there may not be so very much difference of opinion between us. If you could let me know the phrases or passages in Act 2 which you think should be changed, I would consider the scene as altered very carefully, might perhaps suggest some other minor changes, and in this way we would most probably reach a compromise. I hope you will not be annoyed at my insistence in my objection, which is based altogether on my desire to be of service to the theatre. Not being a dramatic author or critic, I feel that the only assistance of nature I can render is by attemnting to prevent the outbreak of a movement of hostility that would make it difficult or impossible for the government to continue or to increase their subsidy.[5]

On 20 September, Lady Gregory wrote in her journal:

Yeats came on Friday evening, "important Abbey business," his telegram had said, and it is important. "Trouble with George O'Brien, the new Director," he said, and showed me the letters. He objects to *The Plough and the Stars*. I said at once, "Our position is clear. If we have to choose between the subsidy and our freedom, it is our freedom we choose. And we must tell him there was no condition attached to the subsidy, and though in connection with it another Director was suggested, I cannot be sure whether by me or Blythe, there was no word at all of his being a censor, but only to strengthen us on the financial side, none of us being good at money-matters or accounts." Yeats thinks we should have a meeting and make new rules, that a majority vote on plays should decide. Anyhow we wired to Robinson to call a Directors' meeting for Tuesday and I will go up with Yeats to-morrow.

Yeats says Casey said about the song that must be removed from his play, "Yes, it's a pity. It would offend thousands. But it ought to be there."[6]

On 24 September, there was a Directors' meeting about the matter, and Lady Gregory described it in her journal:

Dr. O'Brien making his objections to the play: I, chiefly spokesman (by request), telling him Blythe had made no condition whatever in giving the subsidy and certainly no hint of appointing a censor. I told him of our old fights about *Countess Cathleen* (with the Catholic Church), *Blanco Posnet* (with the Government), Lord Aberdeen's efforts to get passages left out of the play (as now played in England), and my refusal (though there was a real threat of closing the Theatre). Yeats also spoke in the same sense. O'Brien sat up in his chair reiterating at intervals, "That song is objectionable." (We had already decided that it must go, but left it as a bone for him to gnaw at.) "And that word bitch," etc. We told him cuts are usually made in rehearsal, by producers and players, but that we had at the beginning told Casey the Clitheroe parts must be rewritten, etc., and at last got O'Brien to confess, "I had mistaken my position" (of censor). But he wants to see a rehearsal a little later. I then proposed (already arranged) that now we are four Directors we had better bring a rule of majority voting or we might come to a deadlock, two and two; and we passed that resolution; the Chairman to have a casting vote. It was a long meeting: I wished some artist could have looked in, Yeats and I so animated, Lennox Robinson so amused, George O'Brien sitting upright repeating, "That song must be left out!"[7]

According to Ria Mooney, who played the prostitute, the song was left out of the original production; but many years later when she returned to the Abbey to produce plays, she gave Rosie back her song.[8]

Gabriel Fallon describes a meeting at O'Casey's "digs" in 422 North Circular Road, with Lennox Robinson, during which the play was cast:

> Sean insisted on my being present and so I went, though I wasn't feeling very happy about it since I knew that Lennox would prefer to be alone with Sean. I was already familiar with Sean's casting. He wanted P. J. Carolan to play the part of Clitheroe. Carolan was a forthright, upstanding figure of an actor with a fine commanding voice and presence. His Clitheroe, had he played the part, would have gone down in flames in the General Post Office without the slightest suggestion of nervous hysteria being a part of his character. Sean had written the part of The Covey for F. J. McCormick . . . He had already told McCormick about The Covey and the actor was understandably looking forward with some relish to the part.
>
> Sean had written the part of Bessie Burgess for Sara Allgood but since Sara was playing in London in *Juno* he was satisfied to accept Maureen Delany as a substitute. He wanted Eileen Crowe to play Mrs. Gogan, Shelah Richards to play Nora Clitheroe, Ria Mooney to play Rosie Redmond, and Kitty Curling (who had just joined the company) to play Mollser. He was particularly anxious that I should play Peter Flynn. Outside of this casting he didn't care who played what.[9] That evening Lennox was in his most skittishly quarrelsome mood. He wouldn't hear of Carolan playing Clitheroe. That part was simply crying out, he said, for F. J. McCormick. Sean protested, but it was no use. Lennox politely pointed out that it was he, and not O'Casey, who would have to direct the play. Who then would play The Covey, Sean asked. Lennox insisted that the part should be played by Michael J. Dolan. This infuriated Sean, but there was little he could do about it. . . . There is not a doubt, of course, that Lennox knew at the time that Dolan was O'Casey's greatest enemy. . . . When the casting had reached this point I could see that I was not likely to get Peter Flynn. Lennox gave the part to Eric Gorman who, incidentally, made an unforgettable characterisation of it. Having made these radical changes in O'Casey's plans for his play Lennox abruptly left.[10]

When the actors received their parts, more complaints were heard; and on 10 January 1926 O'Casey wrote to Robinson, actually offering to withdraw the play:

> Dear Mr. Robinson—
>
> I have carefully and (I hope) impartially re-read The Plough and the Stars, lingering thoughtfully over those passages that have irritated or shocked some of the members of the Caste, and I cannot admit into my mind any reason for either rejection or alteration.
>
> Miss Crowe's hesitation over part of the dialogue of Mrs Gogan seems to me to be inconsistent when I remember she was eager to play the central figure in "Nannie's Night Out", which was as low (God help us) and, possibly lower, than the part of Mrs. Gogan.
>
> Neither can I see any reason standing beside the objection to such words as Snotty, Bum, Bastard or Lowsey. To me it isnt timidity but cowardice that shades itself from them. Lowsey is in "Paul Twyning": is it to be allowed in that play and rejected in mine? Bastard in "The Devil's Disciple" is said with all the savagery of a callous bigot to a young child: is the word to flourish in that play and wither in mine? Snotty is simply an expression for sarcastic or jeering.

The play itself is (in my opinion) a deadly compromise with the actual; it has been further modified by the Directors but I draw the line at a Vigilance Committee of the Actors.

I am sorry, but I'm not Synge; not even, I'm afraid, a reincarnation. Besides, things have happened since Synge: the war has shaken some of the respectability out of the heart of man; we have had our own changes, and the U.S.S.R. has fixed a new star in the sky. Were corrections of this kind to be suffered the work would be one of fear, for everyone would start a canonical pruning, (As a matter of fact Miss Mooney has complained to me about the horror of her part) and impudent fear would dominate the place of quiet courage.

As I have said, these things have been deeply pondered, and under the circumstances, and to avoid further trouble, I prefer to withdraw the play altogether.

Sincerely Yours,
Sean O'Casey[11]

On 12 January, the *Irish Times* noted that rehearsals had started, however, and that the play would be produced in about a month. And further:

Mr. W. B. Yeats . . . said that it is a much finer play than *Juno and the Paycock*; more profound and more original, as much an advance on *Juno* as *Juno* is on the *Gunman*. "In this play we have O'Casey more entirely himself. He is no longer hampered by traditional plot elements. The writing is as original and as profound as a novel by Dostoievsky."[12]

On 15 January, Yeats wrote to Lady Gregory, describing the various problems that were arising during rehearsal:

We have had an aggravating comedy behind the scenes at the Abbey. On Monday Casey wrote to withdraw *Plough and the Stars* because Miss Crowe would not speak his lines and because her husband objected to something else. Lennox came to see me and we agreed that Miss Crowe was not to be told about Casey's letters, but given her choice of shirking this line or giving up the part. Casey was to be told of my advice by Saturday and that we were acting upon it. The essential thing was not to be pushed by Casey or anybody else. Miss Crowe took some hours to think it over—said she would consult her priest—and then refused. She suggested changing parts with Miss Craig. This we agreed to. Lennox went off to see Casey and was very nervous, as Casey's letters seemed to suggest that he might not reconsider his withdrawal. Lennox found Casey full of amiability, though he was rather shocked at our putting Miss Crowe out of the part and he offered to re-write it. This offer Lennox rightly refused and said that Miss Crowe must remain out of the part. We decided to let her husband leave out the word he objected to, as Miss Richards, who replies to him, means to use it—that line is "no I will not be called snotty!" "Snotty" is old English, according to Webster, for "A mean ugly person" and quite innocent.[13] We were anxious partly because we did not know what might be going on under the surface. All is all well now or both parties have been punished—Casey gets a less effective performance of a favourite part and Miss Crowe loses a part she was playing exceedingly well. The part is small and will hardly affect the success of the play. Even if it did we had no choice as Miss Mooney I gathered would have been the next to start objecting, and there might have been no end to it.[14]

The play opened on 8 February; and the expectations were high that this would be a memorable Abbey first night. The *Dublin Evening Mail* wrote:

> Practically all the seats had been booked last week, and still at the pit door there was a queue. In the front lobby before the play started there was a bubble of conversation and a feeling of interest that was quite exciting. Inside members of the audience were content to stand two and three deep along the walls. And at the final curtain no one in the stalls or pit moved; those on the balcony were standing; and amid the continual clapping and cries of "author" Mr. O'Casey himself appeared to receive an ovation.[15]

And Holloway wrote:

> There was electricity in the air before and behind the curtain at the Abbey to-night when Sean O'Casey's play *The Plough and the Stars* was first produced. The theatre was thronged with distinguished people, and before the doors opened the queue to the pit entrance extended past old Abbey Street—not a quarter of them got in. The play was followed with feverish interest, and the players being called and recalled at the end of the piece. Loud calls for "Author!" brought O'Casey on the stage, and he received an ovation.[16]

These two descriptions make it amply clear that the reception of the initial performance was overwhelmingly enthusiastic. Nevertheless, even then there were quiet and ominous murmurs of dissatisfaction. As Holloway went on to say:

> Monty[17] said after Act II, "I am glad I am off duty." Some of the incidents in Acts I and II had proved too much for the Censor in him. Mr. Reddin after Act III said, "The play leaves a bad taste in the mouth."[18] George O'Brien was happy after Act II when he saw it went without any opposition. . . . The dialogue at times seemed too long and wordy, kept back the action, and will have to be tightened up. . . . The second act carries realism to extremes. On the whole, it falls far short of *Juno and the Paycock*.
>
> F. R. Higgins, Liam O'Flaherty and others were in a group. Ernest Blythe and Mrs., the Lord Chief Justice and Mrs. Kennedy, Kevin O'Higgins, Yeats and party steered into the Greenroom after Act II. Robinson was about also. T. C. Murray . . . Andrew E. Malone . . . F. H. O'Donnell. Sean O'Casey contented himself with standing room on the balcony. . . . I wished O'Casey luck before the piece. The first-night audience stamped the play with their approval in no uncertain way. . . .
>
> The street outside the theatre was packed on either side with motor cars. In Abbey Street a policeman was stalking after four "Rosie Redmonds" who flew before him, and I am sure the dispersing audience found no interest in their flight, although they had applauded "Rosie" plying her trade in Act II of *The Plough and the Stars*. The fight between the two women in the pub scene was longly applauded, yet who is not disgusted with such an exhibition when one chances on it in real life?[19]

Gabriel Fallon remarks that when Yeats lead his party backstage after Act II, Holloway "was heard to voice his Republican sympathies in the clearly audible remark: 'There they go, the bloody murderers!' "[20]

Ria Mooney, the original Rosie Redmond, remembered this about the first night:

> At last the great night came, February 8th, 1926. Every thing was normal, no more excitement than actors usually experience when they are about to appear in a new play. When the show was over, I met Sean O'Casey as he crossed the stage. He stopped for a moment, and, unlike previous occasions, when his face would be screwed up while he gazed out of his better eye, there was a pale seriousness about our usually animated author, and his face was calm. "Thank you for saving my play," he said, and when I looked incredulously at him, he added, "I mean that." Then he walked away.
>
> Quite honestly (and you may find this hard to believe) I had reached twenty-three years of age without knowing precisely what was meant by a "prostitute." I had certainly learned what prostitutes looked like and how they dressed, by following the advice I had been given, but that was as far as my knowledge went. Without knowing exactly why, however, I felt very sorry for these young girls I had seen in the lane [behind the theatre]. So when the Covey sneers at Rosie, and says he is not "goin' to take any reprimandin' from a prostitute," I was so hurt that real tears came as I rushed at him, crying "Yer no man! I'm a woman anyway, an' I have me feelin's. . . . "
>
> I learnt a great deal about acting from this incident. When in later years I have given exactly the same performance technically, and (so far as even those members of the public who had seen it several times before could judge) the very same interpretation, it never again was really the same, because my total sympathy with the character had gone.
>
> Technique, without feeling and concentration, is like Faith without Good Works: it is dead. When I had felt sympathy for the character, the audience felt it too, and so Rosie received understanding of her plight, when she might have aroused antagonism. This was, I suppose, what Sean meant when he thanked me for "saving his play."[21]

Really all of the reviews finally admitted that the play was remarkable, but the *Irish Times* was perhaps the most nearly unqualified in its praise:

> The high-water mark of public interest in the work of the Abbey Theatre was reached last night, when Mr. Sean O'Casey's latest play, *The Plough and the Stars*, had its first production.
>
> Although it was well known that the house had been booked out many days ago, people who had not secured seats began to gather outside the theatre as early as four o'clock in the afternoon, in the hope that standing room at the back of the pit might be available. The first curtain went up with the packed theatre in a state of tense expectation, after each of the four acts there was a demonstration of approval, and when the end came the author received an ovation.
>
> *The Plough and the Stars* is a tragedy of Dublin tenement life of the period of the Rebellion of Easter Week, 1916. It has no plot in the ordinary theatrical meaning of the word. It has not got even the flimsy thread of a story on which *Juno and the Paycock* is worked out, and yet, with all the shortcomings of a first performance, with the audience as well as the players in a condition of high tension, the play progressed to its inexorable climax without the interest flagging for a second.
>
> Mr. O'Casey paints the people among whom he has lived until quite recently. While history is being made all around in scenes of death and destruction, these people live their lives as they have lived them all along—drab and shiftless, in

middle age or abounding in hope and expectation in youth; and we know that when the last curtain has fallen the round of existence will continue in the same tenement way. Mr. O'Casey's play is more than realism; it is naturalism—a faithful reproduction of what happened, with the truth of the picture apparent to the dullest imagination. Great events are outlined only in so far as they have had reactions on the lives of the men and women that Mr. O'Casey recreates.

The title of the play is derived from the flag adopted by James Connolly's "Citizen Army" of 1915 and 1916. The earthly implement of toil is idealised into the heavenly constellation. The author translates that idealisation into the misery that its pursuit involves. He hates human suffering, and in incident after incident, just as they would naturally happen in such surroundings, he makes the audience feel that it was not worth it: that one drop of the milk of human kindness is worth more than the deepest draughts of the red wine of idealism. Time and again that thought is forced home, now in the form of broad comedy, again in biting sarcasm, and finally in racking tragedy. . . .

It is a woman's play, a drama in which men must fight and women must weep. Poor little Mollser, the dying consumptive girl, speaks the curtain of the first act:—"Is there no one with a titther of sense?" That phrase may be described as the *motif* of *The Plough and the Stars*: the tragedy of the women. None of the men characters adds to the development of the play, except that they are part of the life that is pictured.

Miss Delany's Bessie is great acting at what is undoubtedly the most perfect stage personality that Mr. O'Casey has yet created. We do not except even the lovable "Juno." For acting to character, Miss Craig was the big success of the night. Her presentation of the thriftless, shiftless, careless, reckless charwoman deserved all the praise that it received. Miss Mooney, the young actress already noted for her vitality, had a part to play that was in no way inviting, but which she made an integral portion of the play. The introduction of Rosie Redmond, a street girl was a risky thing on the part of the author, but with Miss Mooney portraying her we felt again that Mr. O'Casey was giving us Dublin life as it was lived. Miss Crowe's lady from Rathmines, lost in tenement land in the upset of the times, was a cameo of theatrical beauty. Miss Curling made a completely successful *debut* as the consumptive girl.

Of the men, Mr. Fitzgerald plays a "Captain Boyle" part, conceived and carried through on the plane far above that of the genial old ruffian, so delightful in *Juno*. He is as irresistible when merely doing nothing as when carrying through the comedy that makes the first two acts stage-fun of the best. In Mr. Gorman and Mr. Dolan he has two splendid helpers. Even Mr. McCormick, with all his talent, cannot make a live man out of Jack Clitheroe, but Mr. Shields's acting of the wounded lieutenant is fine work. One of the many thrills that the audience expeienced came from Mr. Stephenson's declamation of the speech by the platform orator outside the window of the public house in the secnd act.

The play is remarkable for the sparkle of its dialogue, even when, as often happens, character after character has to speak long-drawn out sentences. When these miniature speeches have been trimmed a little, *The Plough and the Stars* will be a better work.[22]

Some of the other reviews were a bit more mixed. For instance, the *Evening Herald* volubly criticised and rather grudgingly admired:

Sean O'Casey has yet again reminded us of the "troublesome times" in his *Plough and the Stars*, produced at the Abbey last night. The hundreds present had already been made acquainted with a later phase of those times, and they came convinced that what was done so brilliantly for a later phase would be done for an earlier one. Whether they were disappointed or not, it was clear that *Juno and the Paycock* was not surpassed. The caption of James Connolly's banner of the Citizen Army gave the author his title. The author knew his Libety Hall, the tenements out of which came the denizens of the army, the publichouses where red catchcries were muttered in dribbles. He had seen the happenings of Easter Monday, 1916, its stampede of Lancers, its looting, its sniping, and its gun fodder. As a good journalist he tells of it all in the vernacular and gives us "comic-tragedy" rather than tragi-comedy.

There were very slender dividing lines between laughter and tears in this play. Just at one of the most tragic mments, when Bessie Burgess, the virago of the tenement, was shot protecting the mad Nora from the rifles, the audience tittered! The utterance of vulgar expletives by male and female characters caused many laughs. One wished to know did the author write these words for his players with this sorry motive. Must "strong" plays get across by means of unrefined words?

The author succeeded in making the impression that he has no reverence for the courage of those who risked their lives during that struggle for an ideal. He saw fear in all their eyes, and it was fear that urged them on. His male characters betrayed his theme.

This plotless play is a true picture of a series of incidents well known by many in Dublin. Its success has been achieved chiefly on account of its cast. Any role in the play could not be more competently filled.

Maureen Delany represented Bessie Burgess, a tough tenementer ready for a scrap with tongue and fists, but withal the owner of a feeling heart under her rough exterior. She embodied the spirit of the character with rare enthusiasm. Nora Clitheroe was splendidly portrayed by Shelah Richards. She was the centrepiece of all the tragedy in the play. Not till the last act did she show her best acting, and the act was the most powerful of all.

A most difficult role was admirably played by May Craig as Mrs. Gogan, the charwoman. It was a fine example of the author's descriptive powers and delineation of character.

Of the male characters in the play that of "Fluther" Good interpreted by Barry Fitzgerald was the most outstanding. He is as Falstaffian as he could be. He carried the continued interest in the first two acts, and perfected it in the following ones. Peter Flynn (Eric Gorman) and The Young Covey (Michael J. Dolan) were a perfect pair of naggers. The part of Jack Clitheroe, taken by Frank [*sic*] MacCormack [*sic*], was acted with a refined restraint and thorough understanding.

The audience did not hesitate to show their appreciation of the author and his work at the end of the performance.[23]

In the *Independent*, J. W. G. (probably James Winder Good) accurately analyzed and strongly admired tha play, but had also some reservations:

Not since *Blanco Posnet* has an Abbey first night aroused as much excitement as the production of *The Plough and the Stars*, and Mr. Shaw had the advantage that his play had been banned in England, and there was a sporting chance that Dublin Castle at the eleventh hour would enforce a censorship of its own.

For the rest of the week, the bookings have broken all Abbey records, a proof that one at least of our dramatic prophets does not lack honour in his own country.

Preliminary trumpetings about a new play, though they may be good business from the management's point of view, are not always fair to the author. I suspect a good many people went to the Abbey last night under the impression that *The*

Plough and the Stars was as far above *Juno and the Paycock* as that piece was on *Kathleen Listens In*.

While I have little doubt that this drama of Easter Week will prove to be the most popular of Mr. O'Casey's works, I do not think that artistically it marks an advance. This feeling may be partly due to the fact that we are all familiar by now with Mr. O'Casey's method. In *The Plough and the Stars* the method can still spring surprises, and the author gets effects with his material that no one else could equal; but, roughly speaking, the tragedy conforms too closely to one's preconceived idea of the sort of play that one who had mastered the technique of *Juno* would make out of a theme like the Easter Rising.

In some respects Mr. O'Casey has bettered his hand. No figure sticks out so incongruously as Davoren the supposed poet did in *The Gunman*, or Bentham, the freak theosophist in *Juno*, and Mr. O'Casey no longer hampers himself with such dead theatrical lumber as the legacy that is the fount and source of Captain Doyle's [*sic*] misfortunes. In *The Plough and the Stars* the characters seem to me part of their environment, and though the construction is of the loosest, the development, if not perhaps inevitable, is logical.

Mr. O'Casey does not deal in heroes or heroines. His real concern, as I see it, is with individuals as members of a group, and it is the skill with which he translates into dramatic form the interplay of emotions inside the group that makes him unique amongst Irish dramatists. We get this in comedy in the two opening Acts, which contain more laughs than anything the author has yet given us, though dramatically it would probably improve the play were they compressed into one.

Yet I should hate to see sacrificed Uncle Peter at the teatable arrayed in all the glory of his Forester's uniform with the Citizen Army mobilising in the street, or the heroic encounter, as a result of too many "balls of malt," between Bessie Burgess and Mrs. Gogan in the corner publichouse. And if the opening Acts were fused there are other episodes equally good which would have to go.

In this play, unlike *Juno*, the tragic note is sounded only in the last Act. But there is no mistake about the vigour with which Mr. O'Casey sounds it. He makes more vivid than any of our dramatists before him the brutal crash of war and bloodshed upon the lives of ordinary people.

There is no hint of polemics, no question of taking sides. It is not a question of whether Commandant Clitheroe, of the Citizen Army, is right, or Bessie Burgess, who chants "Rule Britannia" wrong. What the play drives home is the strength of the common ties that bind humanity, the impulse that nerves the virago Bessie to face a storm of bullets to bring aid to a sick woman, and raises drunken Fluther Good almost to heroic level.

I am convinced Mr. O'Casey would be even more effective if he did not heap up the corpses so lavishly. The last Act has Elizabethan precedents in its favour, but that is the best that can be said for it.

The acting was as good as I have seen at the Abbey. There was a fear that the absence of Miss Allgood would make a difference, but Miss Maureen Delany, in her part as Bessie Burgess, made one of the big hits of the play. She has never lacked forcefulness, but last night she combined it with restraint, and her tragic passages were finely handled. Miss May Craig painted an unforgettable portrait of the depressing Mrs. Grogan [*sic*], whose talk is all of graves and epitaphs; and Miss Ria Mooney, as Rosie Redmond, managed a difficult part admirably.

If the play has a heroine, it is Nora. Unfortunately, she is not an altogether convincing figure, though the fault rests with the dramatist, and not with Miss Shelah Richards, who was excellent in the first Act, and did make something of the last scene, though a mad woman in a nightgown is always too reminiscent of Hamlet burlesque.

One does not need to praise Mr. Barry Fitzgerald. It is sufficient to say that his Fluther Good is in his best style. He is splendidly partnered by Eric Gorman and Michael J. Dolan.[24]

The Dublin Evening Mail wrote:

Some of us had been forewarned that the play would contain "strong language." It was not as bad as we had been led to expect, and I could not condemn the "language" without condemning the play, of which it formed a necessary part. And judgment on the play is, as Fluther Good would remark, "vice versa." One wonders, however, how far realism will go.

Mr. O'Casey again selects a period in the troubles of the Irish capital as material for his play-writing: this time it is Easter Week, 1916. *The Plough and the Stars* may well rival in popularity *Juno and the Paycock*, but the latter, being the firstborn, will be retained in affection to the last. And when one knows the framework of *Juno* one has a good idea of what the author is likely to do with his material. This, then, is the life of the occupants of a tenement prior to and during Easter Week. It is as if the author had taken us by the hand and brought us down to this tenement at any of the stages he has pictured, and told us to watch what was going on, and showed us how the events that took place affected those lives. He seeks few artificial aids for his effects; he hides nothing; he exaggerates nothing. . . .

The humdrum, humorous, pathetic, miserable tenement life is here portrayed with undeniable power. Nothing redeeming about it except the humour and the bonds of human sympathy which are to be seen in a kindlier, if more tragic, mood in the second and third acts, which takes us to Easter Week.

In those acts we have the rich comedy and the deep tragedy intermixed. Commandant Clitheroe is killed; his wife has her own misfortunes; umbrellas and loads of other loot are brought to the tenement in fine fashion; there is alternative wrangling and friendship. On the stage is the coffin of Mollser, Mrs. Gogan's daughter, who has succumbed to consumption, while the Covey, old Peter, and Fluther play cards, all the while the cannons boom and there is the rattle of machine guns.

Mr. O'Casey's is a distinct dramatic achievement, woven from what anyone can realise might be in keeping with events. Without the aid of Easter Week, one knows he could paint the tenement life with the same truth to-morrow, and make it just as interesting. But Easter Week gave him an opportunity for indicating how futile are the hate and the bloodshed and the disturbing things, and that the real and lasting element through all time is the charity which shines through sordid lives.

The acting was on a high plane. Miss May Craig we have never seen in a greater role than that she has created of Mrs. Gogan. Barry Fitzgerald made a perfect success of Fluther; only see him when he is "on the water-cart," and Mrs. Gogan suggests the danger of neglected cold, with a hit of a possible "cure." Miss Shelah Richards worked excellently as Nora, the wife. Miss Maureen Delany almost equalled May Craig as Mrs. Burgess. Miss Ria Mooney played a difficult role with imminent [*sic*] success. . . . As Commandant Clitheroe Mr. F. J. McCormick found little for his ability, but that little required something beyond the ordinary to make the character a living reality.

In the dialogue there are two miniature speeches which sound unreal; the voice we heard at the meeting delivered, strange enough, a portion of Patrick Pearse's speech on the occasion of O'Donovan Rossa's funeral at Glasnevin. "Lead Kindly Light" is sung by Mrs. Burgess to the insane Mrs. Clitheroe. Poor Bessie, who has

> spent nights watching her, is shot at the window, and her corpse lies huddled up while the Tommies sing "Keep the Home Fires Burning."[25]

Despite some cavils and some surliness, these were generally admiring and sometimes quite perceptive reviews, much more affirmative and much more intelligent than most new Irish plays got.

In the 1920s, as well as now, most reviewers treated the director's part in a production quite skimpily and usually confined themselves to a simple sentence like, "So-and-so displayed a firm directorial hand" or "The direction fo So-and-so was sure and briskly paced." The reason is that in most instances it is impossible for even the perceptive reviewer to have any accurate idea of what the director did. Broad matters like blocking or pacing are obvious enough, but in particular matters—say, the reading of a line, the inclusion of a bit of business, or even the entire interpretation of a role—it is impossible to know, without having been at rehearsal, what the actor did and what the director did.

Many years after the first production of *The Plough*, one of the present writers asked O'Casey what he thought of Robinson's direction of the play; and O'Casey replied that, although he thought Robinson was sometimes a slack director, *The Plough* production was meticulous, painstaking, and excellent. Shelah Richards, who played Nora Clitheroe and who was often directed by Robinson, has made some interesting generalizations about Robinson's work:

> As a director, the word was all important to Lennox. He was utterly uninterested visually. Indeed, at rehearsals, half the time he would be sitting with an elbow on the arm of his seat and his hand over his eyes, listening—and, of course, his long legs twisted around themselves two or three times. I don't think he ever closely looked at what was going on. Sets just did not matter much to him, nor did the costumes, and I am sure that he never looked at the players' make-up. Of course, he would catch something like one actor standing in front of another, but the visual part of our shows was treated pretty casually. That is my chief criticism of Lennox as a director. Sad and a pity because vocally he was absolutely splendid.[26]

In *Sean O'Casey, The Man I Knew*, Gabriel Fallon, who played the small part of Captain Brennan, criticised Robinson's direction of *The Plough*: "Lennox Robinson had not over exerted himself so far as production was concerned."[27] And even: "When I had time to think things over I began to consider that, consciously or unconsciously, Lennox was out to damage O'Casey's play."[28] That last charge strikes us as much too strong, particularly as the admiring reviews cited above all indicate that the production was extremely successful. In any event, Robinson is briefly on record with his feelings about the play from the director's standpoint. On 1 February, he wrote to Lady Gregory:

I am busy putting the last touches to *The Plough and the Stars*—all the effects "off" have me heartbroken. In some ways I think it's the worst written of his plays, *Juno* was child's play compared to it. It will do all right because of good characters and good acting but he hasn't made it easy for players or producer.[29]

And after the first night, Robinson wrote again to Lady Gregory:

Casey's play went I think very well last night. It was a very excited first night audience, a bad audience to judge a play by and I'll be better able to judge in another night or two. I think my opinion of it is the same as when I read it—that it's a better play as a whole than *Juno*—nothing as bad as the bad young man in that play or the unnatural scene when the young man gives up the girl—but lacks a character strongly running through it and it is seriously hampered by long rambling speeches. Some I cut a bit but Casey doesn't like drastic cutting and the speeches are so much part of the style of the play—as much its style as Synge's but he hasn't got Synge's clarity of expression. Of course the tendency with the plays I write recently is to have very bare thin dialogue—close packed, no oratory—and so I expect I'm not quite fair to long-windedness—but other people have remarked it. It had a very perfect performance, everyone very good . . . and I heard of no one being shocked! The booking all through the week is extraordinarily heavy and I am sure the week will be a record. Are you coming up? We'll only do it for one week.[30]

On Tuesday night there was some very mild hissing during the second act, and Holloway reported:

Some four or five in the pit objected to the Volunteers bringing the flag into a pub in Act II. Kevin Barry's sister was one of the objectors. The pit door had to be shut to avoid a rush being made on it, and two policemen were on the scene. The audience relished the fight of the women in Act II and didn't object to the nasty incidents and phrases scattered here and there throughout the play. . . . Lord Chief Justice Kennedy frankly declared he thought it abominable. Kevin O'Higgins was silent until Monty thanked God he was off duty, and added, "This is a lovely Irish export." Then O'Higgins owned up he didn't like it. Meeting Dr. Oliver Gogarty, Monty said, "I hope you are not going to say you liked it?"

"I do," owned up Gogarty (whose reputation for filthy limericks is very widespread), "It will give the smug-minded something to think about."[31]

On Wednesday night, there was also a momentary, minor disturbance, which Holloway reported:

At the Abbey I saw Frank Hugh O'Donnell on the balcony during Act II. He joined Sean O'Casey and a lady in the vestibule. . . . O'Casey was besieged by young ladies on the balcony to sign his autograph in their programmes, and on a gentleman asking him to do so for him, O'Casey replied, "I only do so for young and pretty girls." . . .

A sort of moaning sound was to be heard to-night from the pit during the "Rosie Redmond" episode and when the Volunteers brought in the flags to the pub. (I noticed Arthur Shields unfurled his tricolour, as he came in, in a defiant manner. He usually is out for cheap notoriety, such as repeating dirty remarks in *The Playboy*, usually omitted in representation). . . .

The actors rattle through those interminable word-twisters in a gabbly, inflectionless manner. Miss Delany repeats much she has to say in a loud, monotonous, meaningless way, and Barry Fitzgerald fails to articulate clearly in his longer speeches. When he is silent he is usually drollish; witness his facial expression when asked to take the baby in Act II![32]

On Thursday night, the trouble erupted,[33] and, as *The Irish Times* wrote:

Mr. Sean O'Casey's new play, *The Plough and the Stars*, was the cause of scenes in the Abbey Theatre, Dublin, last night reminiscent of the days, close on twenty years ago, when a prolonged and organised, but unsuccessful, effort was made to prevent the showing of Synge's *Playboy of the Western World*.

The Plough and the Stars presents a picture of tenement life in Dublin before and during the Easter Week rebellion, 1916, and the four acts show the reactions of that event on the lives of the poorest in the city.

At the first performance on Monday night the play and its author had an enthusiastic reception. On Tuesday night there was a scene in the back pit, when six women sitting together tried by voice and foot to prevent the hearing of the concluding part of the second act, in which the happenings in a publichouse in tenement land are depicted. The interruption lasted only a minute or two. On Wednesday night one woman made a very feeble demonstration.

Last night the situation assumed a more serious aspect. From the start of the play there were minor incidents, such as stamping of feet, hissing and shouting. Those came mostly from the pit. When the curtain went up for the second act there began a pandemonium which continued until the curtain fell. It was carried on for the most part by women, who shouted, boohed and sang, occasionally varying their demonstration by a set speech.

The noise was intensified by counter-demonstrations of applause by the majority of the audience. The players carried on in dumb show, and in the second act hardly a word of the dialogue was heard. In their unflinching stubbornness the company followed the example of their predecessors of the *Playboy* days.

When the lights went up at the end of the second act everyone could see many women who are prominently identified with Republican demonstrations in the city. Shocking epithets were hurled at Miss Ria Mooney while she played Rosie Redmond in pantomime, but the wrath of the interrupters was for the most part directed against the political significance of the play, its brutal exposition of what took place in the homes of the rank and file of the Citizen Army, while the leaders were making speeches about freedom in the abstract.

After the start of the third act, notable for Mrs. Clitheroe's description of what she saw of the fighting in the streets, when, half demented, she sought her husband, about a dozen women made their way from the pit on either side of the theatre and attempted to scramble on to the stage. After a time they succeeded, and there ensued on the stage a regular fight between the players and the invaders.

One young man succeeded in getting on to the stage along with the women. He deliberately struck Miss Maureen Delany in the face, and then aimed a blow at Miss May Craig. In a moment Mr. Barry Fitzgerald ("Fluther Good") with one blow sent him sprawling to the wings.

The play, of course, was stopped, and the curtain was lowered. The women demonstrators were bundled off the stage by the male members of the company, and the attendants. In a high state of hysteria they were pushed out of the theatre altogether.[34]

It was difficult to see how it was done, but the stage appeared to be cleared in very quick time, and Senator W. B. Yeats, one of the directors of the theatre, came forward to address the audience.

During the few minutes that those incidents occupied, a number of people, probably thinking that the final curtain for the night had been rung down, left their seats in the stalls to go home. A number of women swarmed from the pit into the empty chairs and kept up a din while Dr. Yeats was speaking.

In a lull, here and there, he was heard to say that once again a minority in Dublin had tried to disgrace the reputation of the city.

"Is this," he shouted, "going to be a recurring celebration of Irish genius? Synge first, and then O'Casey! The news of the happenings of the last few minutes here will flash from country to country. Dublin has once more rocked the cradle of a reputation. From such a scene in this theatre went forth the fame of Synge. Equally the fame of O'Casey is born here to-night. This is his apotheosis."

Suddenly and unexpectedly the shrieks and turmoil from the pit and from the invaded stalls died down, almost before Dr. Yeats had finished. The explanation was found with the arrival of half-a-dozen men of the detective branch, who had heard un-officially that an attmept was on foot to wreck the theatre. They took up positions here and there, in the noisiest centres on the floor of the house, and the noise ceased almost entirely.

The next unexpected incident was the raising of the curtain and the continuance of the interrupted Act 3. This was hailed with a wild outburst of enthusiasm from the general body of the audience, in which the counter-demonstration was entirely drowned. The members of the company on at the time proceeded to take up the thread of the act as if nothing had happened. They finished the third act, finished the fourth act, and finished the play, and the audience left scarcely five minutes later than the usual time.

After the resumption of the play half-a-dozen women, who had taken possession of the front row of the stalls, kept up a fire of interruption, until they were forcibly ejected from the theatre by the uniformed policemen, who had been summoned. One of the women protested against her removal as an interference with personal liberty. Another woman, in a high *staccato* voice, made a speech from the balcony, until she was invited to go out, and took the advice.

From start to finish the whole thing was a woman's row, made and carried on by women. It is, perhaps, significant, under the circumstances, that Mr. O'Casey's play is directed mainly to show to the world the misery of the lives of the women population of the tenement rooms of Dublin.

The net result was that little damage was done, except perhaps to the face of the man that Barry Fitzgerald tackled on the stage. Two of the new footlight lamps were injured, and portion of the curtain was torn. The orchestra lost a few sheets of music (which were torn) and the cover of Mr. Fred Deane's double bass fiddle. There was no necessity for arrests as in the *Playboy* scenes.

The most remarkable incident of the whole evening happened after everyone had left and the doors of the theatre were closed. It took place in the green room, when the company of the players—men and women, some with the grease paint but half off their faces—gathered around Dr. Yeats to assure him of their determination to carry on.

Addressing them, he expressed his admiration of their conduct that evening. He said that they and their theatre had got an advertisement of the utmost value in the eyes of the whole world. Such an incident could not take place in the commercial theatre. That a small minority could be found in Dublin to try to stop the showing of Mr. O'Casey's play was a proof to him that Mr. O'Casey had in *The Plough and the Stars* cut very close to home.

An *Irish Times* reporter was informed that last night's display will not in any way interfere with the continuance of the play in its entirety. Furthermore, the directors will take into serious consideration the suggestion from many members of the audience that it should be put on again next week. The intention was to finish the initial run of *The Plough and the stars* to-morrow night, and to put on *Doctor Knock* from Tuesday of next week. The number of people who have been unable to book this week is sufficiently large to fill the house for another seven performances.

Simple but effective steps have been taken to ensure, first the safety from molestation of the theatre and all connected with it, and, secondly, the comfort of each succeeding audience. There can, we are assured, be no repetition of last night's attempt to prevent theatre-goers from seeing Mr. O'Casey's remarkable play.[35]

Ria Mooney remembered Thursday night like this:

After the curtain went up on Act II, I heard voices raised above a whisper in the house. The voices grew louder. Then lumps of coal were thrown at me, and pennies fell noisily beside me on the stage. There were shouts from members of the audience, urging me to "get off," which only made me more determined to stay on. I think it was not until that night that I ceased to be an amateur and became a professional actress in the truest sense of the word. Neither coal, pennies nor threats stopped us playing. When the curtain came down at the end of the act, we knew that we hadn't been heard because of the uproar among the public. A girl tried to set fire to the curtain, which act of hysteria must have prompted Seaghan Barlow not to set the stage for Act III, but to bring the curtain up on an empty stage.

The entire cast wandered on to see the excitement: to see Barry Fitzgerald having a boxing match with one of the men from the audience who tried to rush onto the stage: to hear F. J. McCormick disassociating himself and his wife from the play—which astonished me, and for which Sean never forgave him. I, who had been in the wings looking on, decided to join in the fun on the stage, but the sight of me seemed to increase the fury, so that Paddy Carolan advised me to stand at the side. Then Yeats came striding on stage, and there was silence while the grey-suited, grey-haired figure spoke to them.

"You have disgraced yourselves again. . . . "

At the time, however, the abuse and the missiles seemed to be directed at me. Even in the newspapers, the fuss was not, apparently, over the flag, or the Volunteers about to drink port on the stage—but about the prostitute, and the girl who played the part. My Aunt Kitty and her two friends were sitting in front that night, and saw a girl trying to get onto the stage to attack Yeats. My aunt told me that someone else I knew in the audience took off her shoe and aimed it at the would-be attacker, but hit Yeats instead. The poet did not flinch, but went on with his speech as though he had been merely brushed by a fly.[36] After he had left the stage, there was silence. The curtain was brought down, and the set put up for Act III.[37]

Shelah Richards remembered the night like this:

. . . everything went well enough until the second act when the prostitute, Rosie Redmond, well played by Ria Mooney, entered. Then there were disturbances and hisses and boohs, but we proceeded with Act III. Nora, whom I was playing, returns to the steps of the tenement house, having spent the night at the barricades, searching for her husband—a difficult scene for a teenage actress. O'Casey in this scene makes Nora step above the hilarious O'Casey comedy, to deliver a long speech of classic stature—the message of his tragi-comic masterpiece.

I suddenly noticed as I sat on the steps, relieved that the house was quiet for this difficult speech, several female figures climbing up from the auditorium onto the stage, and trying to set fire to the front-of-house curtains. With a scream, I dashed to the side of the stage, followed by the other players, and a hand-to-hand battle took place!

We somehow managed to get the ladies off the stage, up some steps, and out to a little landing that led to the Stage-door and to the front of the house. It was a pitched battle—fisticuffs, bum's rush, the lot!

When we came back to the stage, F. J. McCormick was speaking to the audience to tell them that we, the players, were not responsible for the lines we spoke and, consequently, could not be held responsible for what the author had written. We, the pro-O'Caseyites, felt that this was a betrayal. We were involved, and we were prepared to fight, literally, for Sean O'Casey and his play. So we pro-O'Caseyites brought the curtain down on McCormick.

In the meantime, the Directors were being 'phoned all over Dublin. The police had been sent for too, and were now in the front of the house trying to bring some semblance of order to the milling members of the audience. I had already been struck on the head by a shoe which I recognised as belonging to a friend of mine who was in the audience. When, some days later, I charged her with this act of disloyalty, she assured me it had not been meant for me, but for one of our attackers.

I slipped away from the stage to see how the ladies (very brilliant and well-known ladies who had been deeply involved in the 1916 Easter Week tragedy and the Civil War) were, and what they were up to.

When I reached the top of the stairs and opened the door to the little landing where we had incarcerated them, I found them happy, smiling-faced, listening to somebody hidden from me, who was talking to them soothingly and wittily. I had to look and see who had turned these wild ladies of ten minutes ago into sweetly-smiling, pretty female beings.

It was Sean O'Casey.

He was saying, "Now, my dear young ladies—." And charming them like a blackbird singing to them.

And they were all twittering, "Yes, yes, Mr. O'Casey. Yes, we see!"

I returned to the stage as the curtain was being taken up, and W. B. Yeats was advancing slowly to the footlights, with raised hand, looking like an ancient Roman Senator. The house at last was silent, and he started his speech, in splendid sonorous tones, with the words, noble and implacable, "You have disgraced yourselves again!"[38]

Holloway, of course, was there too, and he wrote:

The protest of Tuesday night having no effect on the management, a great protest was made to-night, and ended in almost the second act being played in dumb show, and pantomiming afterwards. People spoke from all parts of the house, and W. B. Yeats moved out from the stalls during the noise, and Kathleen O'Brennan, who came in afterwards, told me Yeats went round to *The Irish Times* office to try to have the report of the row doctored. On his return to the theatre, he tried to get a hearing on the stage, but not a word he spoke could be heard. Nulty was in great *Irish Times* form, foaming against those who objected to the play, and vowing he'd write up Dorothy Macardle, who was one of the protesters to the Volunteers' introduction into the pub on Tuesday last, and accuse her of doing so because of the failure of her play, *Ann Kavanagh*. I reminded him that that would be an untruth, as the play has always been well received and liked.

> . . . But, alas, to-night's protest has made a second *Playboy* of *The Plough and the Stars*, and Yeats was in his element at last. . . .
>
> After Act I was the first I heard that a storm was brewing from Dan Breen, who was speaking to Kavanagh and said, "Mrs. Pearse, Mrs. Tom Clarke, Mrs. Sheehy-Skeffington, and others were in the theatre to vindicate the manhood of 1916." . . .
>
> Few really like the play as it stands, and most who saw it are in sympathy with those who protested. Some of the players behaved with uncommon roughness to some ladies who got on the stage, and threw two of them into the stalls. One young man thrown from the stage got his side hurt by the piano. The chairs of the orchestra were thrown on the stage, and the music on the piano fluttered, and some four or five tried to pull down half of the drop curtain, and another caught hold of one side of the railing in the scene in Act III.
>
> The players headed by McCormick as spokesman lined up onstage, and Mac tried to make himself heard without avail. Then a man came on and begged the audience to give the actor a hearing, and they did, and Mac said he wished the actors should be treated distinct from the play, etc., and his speech met with applause. Then the play proceeded in fits and starts to the end, and the whole house in a state of excitement.
>
> Mrs. Fay protested to me that the play didn't get a hearing. Mrs. Sheehy-Skeffington from the back of the balcony during the din kept holding forth, and at the same time others were speaking in the pit; all were connected with Easter Week. A great big voice called, "O'Casey Out!" on "Rosie Redmond" appearing in Act II. Shouts of "Honor right" were heard.[39]

Later, Arthur Darley told Holloway that he and his wife

> saw Sean Barlow handle roughly and throw a woman off the stage into the stalls. Fitzgerald had a stand-up fight with a man on the stage and succeeded in knocking him over into the stalls. O'Casey was surrounded by a crowd of questioning women, and his answer to one of them was, "I want to make money!"—sums up his attitude toward art.[40]

A few days after the row, Lyle Donaghy was talking to Lady Gregory and told her that

> He had been at the Abbey the night of the riot, had seen the first attack on the stage, a woman climbing up on it, and then the ferocious face of Seaghan Barlow, almost petrified with astonishment at *his* stage being invaded, and who had then stepped forward and flung the invader off it. Donaghy had met Holloway in the hall, in a state of fury—"An abominable play!"
>
> D.: "I see nothing abominable in it."
> H.: "Then you have a dirty mind."
> D.: "No, I haven't."
> H.: "Well, you have a filthy mind. There are no streetwalkers in Dublin."
> D.: "I was accosted by one only last night."
> H.: "There were none in Dublin till the Tommies brought them over."[41]

The *Irish Independent* added more details. During the second act, its account ran,

The interrupters began to keep up a continuous shouting, and the players could not be heard, even in the front row of the stalls.

Then a man in the pit shouted: "Send out O'Casey—O'Casey, the coward!" There were cries of "Put them out," and similar exclamations from other members of the audience.

In the gallery, Mrs. Sheehy Skeffington, with whom were a number of young women and men, endeavoured to make a speech.

Amongst remarks that were heard from her were: "The Free State Government is subsidising the Abbey to malign Pearse and Connolly. We have not come here as rowdies. We came here to make a protest against the defamation of the men of Easter Week."

At the same time a young man in the pit began to address the crowd, but owing to the cheering and counter-cheering only fragments of his eloquence could be caught. He was heard to say:

"We fought in Easter Week, and we don't want any more of that play. It is a slander on the Citizen Army."

"We cannot allow any more of this play," he declared a moment later. A lady occupying a near seat in the stalls stood up and also endevoured to make a speech, but it was impossible to hear a complete sentence, so general was the noise, cheers and counter-cheers.

Amid the din of boohing and yelling, the players steadily continued the performance, but those of the audience who continued to watch them could not hear a word they said.

When "Rosie Redmond," a woman of the streets, appeared on the stage, there was another violent outburst. "Put that woman off the stage," was hoarsely shouted from various parts of the hall.

The uproar continued right to the end of the act, and when the curtain fell the lights went out, and there was something of a lull. A good number of the audience left at this period.

A man who seemed to be very excited was led away by some friends.

He was shouting at Mrs. Sheehy-Skeffington: "You are a disgrace to your sex."

The orchestra played a selection during this comparatively mild disturbance, and, in a momentary interval, when its strains were heard at the back of the hall, the cry of "Stop that music" was taken up.

When the third act—"the outside of a tenement house"—began, two young women from the pit climbed on to the stage. Between 15 and 20 other women rushed to the front of the stalls at the same time.

A melee took place on the stage between the actors and the two women, who invaded it. The women were thrown off the stage, but were apparently unhurt.

Then a young man mounted the stage, but the curtains were lowered. The intruder swung out of the curtains, and tried to pull them down.

Some of the actors engaged him in a fistic encounter.

The women underneath the curtains then tried to tear them down, and while they were so engaged their male companion was suddenly thrown down amongst the audience.

The pandemonium caused a number of the audience to become panic-stricken. They ran for the exit doors and left the theatre.

The curtain went up again, whereupon Mr. F. J. McCormack [*sic*], at the head of a group of the players, made several unsuccessful attempts to address the audience. He was greeted with cheers mingled with groans and hisses.

One of the young men who had been leading the interrupters appealed to the others to let Mr. McCormack speak. There was comparative calm for a few moments. Mr. McCormack appealed for fair play for the players and audience.

"Please differentiate between the players and the author," he said.

He did not get a good hearing, and again the uproar re-started.

A young man who figured prominently throughout, here ascended the stage and attempted to speak, but was shouted down and shoved off by the players, amidst cries of "Go on with the play."

During another brief lull, Mr. McCormick, again addressing the audience, said: "Everybody has a right to object. Please, do you think it is fair to come up and mob us. We play in all sorts of plays. We play in *Nan* [*sic*] *Kavanagh*, by Miss Macardle. Don't mob us. We have our rights as human beings and as players."

A voice—"Ask O'Casey to remove that scene and we will willingly look at the play. It is a disgrace in a Catholic country."

"I am only speaking for the players," Mr. McCormick reminded him. There were further shouts of "Carry on the play." "It is a scandal," cried another voice.

Another actor asked: "Are you going to listen to the remainder of the play?" This query was given a mixed reception, and the curtain was lowered.

Comparative quiet followed, but as soon as the curtain was raised again a young woman jumped on the stage, and got into grips with the two lady players who were opening the scene.

Simultaneously a couple of actors rushed on and pushed the intruder out. Just then a young man, who had dashed from the centre of the stalls and vaulted on to the platform, was attacked by a number of the players.

He retaliated, and after several blows were exchanged, he was administered a hardy punch on the jaw which hurled him bodily into the stalls.

During the next few minutes matters looked so ugly that several people hurried out of the theatre.

The footlights were again switched on, and all the players reappeared. Throughout the auditorium several altercations took place among individuals, but the general commotion had to a great extent died down.

For several minutes the players walked calmly up and down the stage, but the play was not resumed. Approaching 10 o'clock a number of members of the detective division arrived and took up positions in different parts of the building. Two or three went into the wings.

About the same time a number of Gardai in uniform entered. Senator W. B. Yeats then appeared on stage amidst loud cheers and boohs, hissing continuing all through his speech.

Although he made a great effort to make himself heard, his words were inaudible to a large section, who could merely see his lips moving, and his hand waving dramatically. . . .

As Senator Yeats retired, shouts of "We want the play," mingled with counter-cries of "Up, the Republic."

Over a dozen of the women interrupters accommodated themselves in a front row of seats, vacated during the disturbance, and began to sing "The Soldier's Song." A number of others at the rere of the stalls and in the gallery joined in the song.

Three or four Gardai in uniform approached the women at the front and forcibly ejected a number of them.

Comparative quiet was one of the sequels to this development. The play was proceeded with amidst faint attempts at interruptions from various parts of the house.

"We are now leaving the hall under police protection," declared Mrs. Sheehy Skeffington as she rose to leave the gallery, with a number of others, about 10.15.

She attempted to address the audience amid cheers and jeers. Above the din she was heard to exclaim: "I am one of the widows of Easter Week. It is no wonder," she proceeded, "that you do not remember the men of Easter Week, because none of you fought on either side.

"The play is going to London soon to be advertised there because it belies

Ireland. We have no quarrel with the players—we realise that they, at least, have to earn their bread; but I say that if they were men they would refuse to play in some of the parts. All you need do now is sing 'God Save the King.'" She then left.

Hissing, whistling, and singing still continued in pit and gallery, and two policemen in uniform were applauded by a section as they approached a noisy element in the centre of the pit.

At 10.30 a whistle, which was being freely and vigorously used alternately by two young girls, broke down under the strain.

Frantic efforts to repair the damage met with no success.

The play was proceeded with to its close, subjected at periods to interruptions, less violent than those described. While applause punctuated the performance, there was a renewal of hissing and boohing.

At a corner of the stalls a youth stood and blew a "pip squak" at intervals, and there was an occasional cry of "Get off the stage," countered by loud applause in approval of the acting.

There were no arrests as no disturbance took place in the street, and no formal complaint was lodged against the offenders inside the theatre.

The play will be reproduced to-night, but Senator Yeats was unable to say whether it would be presented next week until he had consulted the directors of the Abbey.

M. Collins (65 Parnell St., Dublin), writes to say he came away from a performance full of disappointment, and that apparently he was not the only one.[42]

Collins's note was printed in the *Evening Herald* for 11 February, and immediately evoked several other letters to the editor.[43] A more significant reaction was a long article on page one of the *Evening Herald* of 12 February. The piece was entitled "New Play Resented," and its anonymous author wondered if he could get his money back for Thursday night's performance because he had not been able to hear the play:

This was my chief grievance until I saw Senator Yeats rush on to the stage of the Abbey Theatre last night in a Sydney Carton attitude, correct pose, arms raised in studied movement, to make a characteristic speech, and having failed to get his voice overheard he hurled epithets at the audience which refused to listen. I also began to think. Evidently Senator Yeats has made up his mind that the plain people of Dublin have no right to think—but I made that mistake.

I looked around and saw one of the most excited crowds that ever assembled in the theatre. It was not an organised mob. The gallery and pit were the same as usual, supported by the people. I did not know that Mr. O'Casey's new play had caused any protest during the week. Indeed, the reports of the play, with the exception of the *Herald* critique, gave no indication that it contained anything objectionable. Therefore, when the second act was put on, and a group of women rushed the stage and tried to prevent the performance, I tried to understand what was the reason. When the din began and the stalls, as usual, quickly emptied, I tried to gather from all around why the people were so infuriated.

That the tactics adopted by the women interrupters were bad is certain. They have advertised a play that would have probably have given as much offence to the stalls as to the plain people, but Irish blood is hot and the feeling last night in the theatre was desperate.

Nevertheless, feeling does not run high without a reason, and it showed to those who are in doubt that people are not "half alive" when it comes to something fundamentally affecting the Irish race, and this, in spite of recent happenings, unfortunate to the reputation of our city, is the moral standard of the Irish people.

It would appear the second Act is the objectionable part in Mr. O'Casey's play. It is objectionable to a large section of the people. It is repulsive for several reasons, and such a play would not be permitted by the government of any other country—certainly not in America, France, Germany, or under Mussolini at the present time. So that Senator Yeats, who is as well as a leader of an Art movement, but also a politician and a representative of the people, ought to know this. There is an effort abroad to destroy Nationalism and supplant it by internationalism, and the desecration of the National flag of a country. I should imagine the play would come under the Treason Act. It is quite possible that during the world war national flags were carried into publichouses, and it is evident that Mr. O'Casey saw such an incident. But what are national censors for? There was an effort, too, last night to turn the incident into a political split, but this did not succeed. Free Staters and Republicans seemed to resent what they considered an attempt to desecrate the Easter Week rising and the memory of the dead.

I understand that the speech of Padraic Pearse is the one used by Mr. O'Casey in this play, and the world as well as Ireland knows the character of the leaders of the Easter Week Rising. It was a well-known fact that they were pioneers in the temperance movement. It is absurd to imagine or state the Volunteers were teetotallers, but what those who hold Easter Week sacred feel is that while the Abbey Theatre is quite willing to minimise the sacrifice of the men who went out and the sufferings of their relatives, no other nation would permit this insult to the nation which permeates the second act.

The women of Ireland are evidently beginning to resent the immortalisation of the underworld, and are beginning to realise that it is becoming a menace to the healthy outlook on life which the Irish people have preserved through all the bitterness of their social conditions. This evidently was the reason of the demand that the objectionable woman should not be permitted on the stage, or the language she uses be glorified, even in the interests of Art.

Mr. O'Casey is writing of things as he knows them; so could others. Has Senator Yeats had the courage to produce a play dealing with Easter Week—of the poets who threw aside the laurels, the visionaries and dreamers who forsook the flowered path of literary reward for their country? Yet Easter Week has inspired the idealists of the world! The magnificent gesture of the poets and artists who went to their death for love of their people, with no fanfare of trumpets, in Easter Week, was one of the greatest epics of history. Let us have both sides in the Abbey Theatre, and there will be some tolerance in Dublin. It is all very well to show courage in producing plays and talk tolerance when but one point of view is shown, and that the minority. Let us have both. . . . [44]

We have quoted this article at some length because it starts out in a reasonable tone and ends up stridently, and because it well sums up the usual reasons for protests against the play. That attitude was pushed a bit further in a leading article in the *Herald* of the same day:

Many will deplore the violent attack on the Abbey players last night when they were producing Sean O'Casey's play, *The Plough and the Stars*. However hurtful to a section of the audience the play might be, the protests should have taken a more humane form. The brutal attack on one of the actresses deserves severe censure. Apart from the ugly feature of the protest it would seem that the new play casts aspersions on those who figured in the 1916 trouble. The remarks of last night's audience left no doubt that the author's presentation of the events was an unpleasant spectacle. It was indicated that the play was a slander on the Citizen Army and the men of Easter Week. The scene which caused the protest was one in which a publichouse was depicted in which was a woman of the streets fraternising and drinking with those who were supposed to be attending a meeting outside. The presence of a flag in one of the actor's hands caused excitement amongst the interrupters. A most significant remark was made that the Government were subsidising the theatre.

There is one way to stop a recurrence of those unfortunate protests, and that is to grant powers for a censor of plays as well as films. Those who saw *The Plough and the Stars* say that as a film the censors would not have passed an act of it. From time to time plays which have been censored in London have free scope in Dublin. But by far the worst kind of play is that which shows Irishmen up to the ridicule of foreigners. The scenes in this play are known to be sordid and by no means typical of the Irish. The author seems to have singled out the dregs of the slum dwellings and the slum publichouses to give an impression to Ireland and the world that would bring a blush of shame to a decent-minded man or woman. The cure lies in official censorship.[45]

An official censorship of plays—as opposed to an unofficial censorship by theatrical managers and occasional official pressure—never came about. However, readers of previous volumes of this history will remember the frequent public outcries about the licentiousness of the stage, and realize that there would have been widespread public support for theatrical censorship. That this calamity never occurred was fortuitous, indeed; and, although the stage escaped the Jansenistic censorship that was imposed on books and films, the danger was never greater than after the production of *The Plough and the Stars*. And we might even remark further that, although *The Plough and the Stars* came to be recognised as one of the greatest glories of the modern Irish drama, a partial effect of its production was that it made the Irish theatre a little more timid in the years ahead.

In addition to adding some further details about the row, The *Evening Mail* reported the effect upon the box office and interviewed Yeats:

One result of last night's scene at the Abbey Theatre has been the large demand to-day for seats for Mr. Sean O'Casey's new play, *The Plough and the Stars*, which provoked the disturbance.

The house, however, had been all booked up for to-night, to-morrow's matinee and to-morrow night. Standing room only is available.

There were many applications for tickets for next week.

Asked as to whether the play would be re-staged next week, in consequence of the demand, Senator W. B. Yeats, one of the directors of the theatre, told an *Evening Mail* reporter to-day that nothing had then been decided.

It is understood, however, that the play will not be produced next week, and that the original intention (as announced on the programme at the beginning of the week) to produce *Doctor Knock* (by Jules Romains) will be adhered to.

A determined attempt to stop the play was made last night by a number of women and men. From the beginning of the second act, there were continual interruptions—boohing, hissing and shouting—and for some time the players could not be heard. . . .

When interviewed concerning the disturbance to-day, Senator Yeats said: —

"These people will never have sense. There was a row at *The Playboy of the Western World* and within three months Synge had won European fame. This row over O'Casey's play will probably result in all the players being invited to London. In any case, the play will be taken at theatres where it would never have been thought of. The best thing these people could have done would be to have kept quiet."

"The play," continued Senator Yeats, "is a purely pacifist play. At the end of the first act the Munster Fusiliers march past, and the consumptive girl says 'Is there anyone with a titter of sense?'

"It is a play like Tolstoi's *Sebastopool*, expressing the feelings of a sensitive nature at the spectacle of war. I know O'Casey was fresh from Tolstoi's *Sebastopool* when he wrote it.

"It is not an imitation of *Sebastopool*; it is quite a different kind of play, but it is the same kind of inspiration.

"There is no ridicule of 1916 any more than there is of the Munster Fusiliers.

"It is simply the effect of war upon the lives of people by a man who had lived the same life of these people.

"It is the life of tenements by a man who has lived in tenements."[46]

It was another commentator in The *Dublin Evening Mail* for 12 February who amusingly offered a definition of Yeats' word "apotheosis":

Apotheosis is a sledge hammer, if Ministers only knew it, the sort of word that ought to disarm and pacify the most murderous mob. I am not so sure that Mr. Sean O'Casey will fully understand what the romantic Senator intended to convey. Apotheosis, according to Chambers, is

> the deification, especially the formal attribution of divine honours to a deceased Roman Emperor, or special object of imperial favour—a logical corollary to the worship of ancestors, degenerating naturally by anticipation into the adoration of the living; the glorification of a principle or person; ascension to glory, release from earthly life, resurrection.

I hope that whatever else apotheosis may mean for Mr. O'Casey it will not mean a release from earthly life.

• • •

When I read the account of this riot I began to think that there is a great deal in the statement which appears in the booklet of one of the Irish touring companies, that Geographically Ireland is a peculiar country. It has no backbone, and its mountain ranges mostly follow the coast line.[47]

On 13 February, the *Independent* reported on the reception of the Friday night performance, and then printed various letters about the play:

A couple of additional protests were the only incidents at last night's production of Sean O'Casey's play, *The Plough and the Stars*, at the Abbey Theatre. The house was full.

At the conclusion of Act II., the portion of the play which gave rise to the scenes of the previous night, tricolours are brought into the publichouse. There upon a man shouted "That flag was never in a publichouse." At the end of the act a man who exclaimed "That is a terrible insult to James Connolly and Padraig Pearse," stood up and left.

At the curtain there was mingled applause and hissing. Lady Gregory, who is a director of the theatre, was present.

A gentleman giving the nom-de-plume of "Gregory," writes, expressing astonishment on reading of Thursday night's scenes in the Abbey Theatre in the *Irish Independent*, and says:—"The conduct of the evidently small, but noisy, section indicates that the traditional Irish trait of courtesy and good breeding is being submerged in the welter of modern politics. Even if a section of the audience did not approve of the sentiments in the play there must have been others present who appreciated art for art's sake. The minority should respect the desires of the rest of the audience, and not provide Donnybrook Fair.

"A man is entitled to free speech, and to hold his own opinion, but if our noisy friends had their way we would not be allowed to hold any opinions contrary to those of these agitators. A nation must necessarily be composed of a number of organisations, whose members hold divergent views, as otherwise there would be stagnation and no progress. But if the people who caused the scenes were in power it can only be inferred that no opposition to their views would be tolerated. Mussolini would not be in it with them, and the Saorstat would rapidly be reduced to a condition akin to that of Soviet Russia to-day.

"Is it too much to ask our friends to respect the good name of our country in future, and realise that the Sovereign Saorstat is greater than the minority of its citizens? If their policy is allowed to develop at the expense of the feelings of others, the country is in danger of being reduced to a state which will merit the fate of Sodom and Gomorrah."

"Pettite" also protests against the return of the interrupters, and goes on:—"I saw the play on Wednesday night, and the principal idea I took away from it was a sense of horror at the rottenness, brutality, and futility of war. I saw nothing that an enlightened, intelligent playgoer should object to. Of course I can understand certain elements that thrive on war objecting to the glamour being torn away therefrom.

"Perhaps the ugliest thing in a night of brutality and ignorant behaviour was the hypocrisy of certain persons who applauded Shaw's *John Bull's Other Island* and *Blanco Posnet*, Eugene O'Neill's *Different* and *Anna Christie*, Ibsen's *Ghosts* and *The Wild Duck*, and other such plays, in protesting against *The Plough and the Stars*. It was disgusting. So much so that one begins to suspect the bona-fides of those that took part in it."[48]

Another batch of letters appeared in the *Evening Herald* on 13 February:

A Chara—In the names of those who gave their lives for Ireland in Easter Week, 1916, I protest against the scurrilous insinuations in *The Plough and the Stars*.

Your front page article on the play was indeed welcome last night, if only to show that there are some who are not swept along by the tide of enthusiasm that has heralded O'Casey's latest perpetration.

Senator W. B. Yeats has indeed taken an important role on himself when he dictates, Mussolini-like, to a Dublin audience. Because a "shoneen" claque in the Abbey boost Sean O'Casey, we are all to give him and his works a triumphant reception.

As one who was fortunate enough to take a part in that most glorious episode of

Irish history which laid the foundations of the present State, I give the lie to the suggestions of O'Casey that those who fought had no ideals, were cowards and buffoons. Lastly I might say that our women—wives, sisters, and mothers—were a source of inspiration to our men during the revolt and urged them on—not hindered them.

Sean O'Shea

Sir—In reply to Mr. Whelan's letter, I beg to inform him that I was fighting in North King Street in 1916, so that I had more than a "passing interest" in the Rising.

Perhaps Mr. Whelan would be so good as to inform the public what part he took in that fight.

M. Collins

Sir—I do not profess to be a dramatic critic, and I endeavour to be strictly non-political. On Wednesday night last I visited the Abbey Theatre, and I came away, like Mr. Collins, very disappointed indeed. The play, to my mind, was very mediocre, richly flavoured with vulgarity and profanity, much of which could be dispensed with without detracting from its merits.

For instance, why introduce a prostitute in the second act? I venture to suggest she was thrown in to make good weight; certainly she did not form a connecting link in the "plot," as we saw no more of her in the succeeding acts.

Still, I see no good reason why objection should be taken on political grounds. Offence was not given to any part whatever; in fact, the whole piece could be construed to laud the actions of the brave men of the Citizen Army.

I certainly cannot agree that the work is "the work of a genius," as Professor Yeats has described it, for in the hands of other than the very capable Abbey Players, I believe the whole thing would be an absolute failure.

John McQueen[49]

But not every Republican opposed the play. "Sgáthán," for instance, wrote to the *Evening Mail*:

Sir—I went to the Abbey to see Sean O'Casey's play, expecting to be shocked by the scene in the publichouse, and was surprised to find it all so natural, with an entire absence of any suggestiveness or unpleasantness. It seemed a very natural thing that the Republicans should want a drink at such a time, and have it. The little "woman of the streets" was not in the bar with them; but I must say when she was in the bar I was struck by her refinement and cleanliness, and my mind was taken back to similar people in plays in other cities of th eworld, where they are represented in such a way as to make one wish one had not got a man sitting beside one.

I have heard objections raised to the display of drunkenness in the play. Do the Irish people now wish to become a nation of ostriches and bury their heads in the sand? Doesn't everyone know that drunkenness exists, else why at every corner is there a gay, bright, cheerful-looking "pub"? To abolish an evil, one must first show up the horrors of the real. The play is the highest form of art. It is real, without being coarse or unpleasant, most delightfully witty—there is a laugh in almost every line—and for those who have eyes to see and ears to hear, most instructive. In some respects it is even better than *Juno and the Paycock*, and I hope it will have as successful a run in London as *Juno* has had. The only word that can be applied to the author is "genius"—a very subtle, charming, and powerful genius. At all events, that is the verdict of an ardent Republican Irishwoman re-visiting Dublin.[50]

The *Evening Mail* also noted that Lady Gregory was present at the Friday performance: "She described the play as 'wonderful.' O'Casey's play, she said, was humanity."[51] In her journal, Lady Gregory wrote:

> The papers said Miss Delany had been struck on the face by a young man. But the actors said he came next morning, very indignant at the accusation, said he had thrown something at Seaghan Barlow and it had accidentally hit Miss Craig. Miss Richards says she herself threw a shoe at one of the intruders and it missed its aim and one of them took it up and threw it at Yeats, but it then also missed its aim. . . . An overpowering play. I felt at the end of it as if I should never care to look at another; all others would seem so shadowy to the mind after this.[52]

On Saturday morning, 13 February, O'Casey's play occasioned a real life comedy-cum-melodrama; as the *Irish Times* reported:

> A last desperate attempt to stop the performance of *The Plough and the Stars* at the Abbey Theatre was made last Saturday morning, when three youths, armed with revolvers, tried to kidnap Mr. Barry Fitzgerald, whose part of "Fluther Good" is the backbone of the play.
>
> The "gunboys"—they did not look old enough for the description of "gunmen"—were baulked in their object, and the play was presented to two packed houses on Saturday, and concluded its first run at the Abbey amidst a storm of enthusiastic approval of O'Casey's work.
>
> The raid was made on the house of Mr. Fitzgerald's mother in Seafield road, a quiet corner of Clontarf. Mr. Fitzgerald's name appears in the Directory as the occupant of the house; but, as a matter of fact, he lives elsewhere. Residing with the old lady is her daughter, the wife of Mr. R. J. Mortished, Assistant Secretary of the Irish Labour Party; her husband and children. Another daughter, the wife of Commandant Saurer, of the National Army, was on a visit there on Saturday.
>
> At 9.30 Mrs. Mortished answered a knock at the door, and found three young men. One of them asked was Mr. Fitzgerald in, and got the reply that he did not live there. The trio then produced revolvers, and said that they would have to get him to prevent him from playing in the Abbey that day. The spokesman ordered Mrs. Mortished to put her hands up, and she point blank refused. Her mother and sister then appeared on the scene, and also refused to put their hands up.
>
> The visitors forced their way into some of the rooms, and then Mr. Mortished appeared. He ignored the usual first direction of the gunmen. He was asked: "Aren't you Barry Fitzgerald?" and he replid, giving his name and the address of his office in Abbey street. They assured the old lady that no harm would come to her son, but they had their orders to keep him in a place of safety until it was too late for him to appear on the Abbey stage. All the time the kidnappers were ill at ease, nervous-looking, and evidently in a great hurry to get away.
>
> Mr. Fitzgerald's mother told an *Irish Times* reporter that Mrs. Mortished told them in vigorous sentences, and "without putting a tooth in it," what she thought of them, and those who sent them. She admitted that she knew where her brother lived, but would not tell them.
>
> This added to their hurry to get out, and after a stay of a little over five minutes they left and drove away in a covered motor car, which was waiting on the roadway. The police were communicated with, and twenty minutes later a number of detectives were at the house. The "gunboys," however had made good their escape, and up to last night there were no arrests.

Mr. O'Casey's play was presented to a completely-filled house at the afternoon performance, and was accepted with every demonstration of approval. The numbers of those inside, and of those who could not get in, make a theatre record for an international afternoon in Dublin.

After the matinee it was considered better that the players should remain in the theatre to await the evening performance. The decision brought them a rare experience. Mr. Walter Rummel, the great pianist, at the conclusion of his recital in the Theatre Royal, came straight to the Abbey, and sitting down at Dr. Larchet's piano, played for a full hour. His impromptu programme included the "Moonlight" Sonata, and a varied selection of Chopin pieces. It was a fine—but, for Rummel, characteristic—expression of comradeship from one artist to his fellows. It is hardly necessary to say that it was appreciated by the players and the stage staff.

The final performance of *The Plough and the Stars*, on Saturday, was something to dwell in the memory of those who were there. The greater part of the "house" was booked from early in the week, and for the 150 unreserved seats in the pit, at least four hundred people were in the queue as the afternoon audience was leaving.

The players surpassed themselves at this last performance.

Each of the curtains was followed by applause that could be heard on the street outside. At the end the whole company were called back no fewer than four times. Then came the big scene of the night, started with a demand, which soon became a roar, for "Author; author." Rising above the noise there came from the pit the voice of a full-throated man, repeating over and over again, "Good ould Dublin workingman!"

At last Mr. O'Casey came on, rather was he forced on, to the stage, and the demonstration which followed lasted for a full five minutes.

The Plough and the Stars will come on again in the usual round of the Abbey productions, which means that it will not be due for several weeks yet.

Both the management and the players, collectively and individually, have received many telegrams and cablegrams of congratulation from different parts of the world. That which is most keenly appreciated is a message sent from America by Mr. J. M. Kerrigan, the famous Abbey actor of the past, and now at the top of his profession in the States.[53]

Possibly there were also feeble attempts to kidnap Ria Mooney and Shelah Richards. As Ria Mooney wrote:

Shelah and I kept our doors firmly locked at night. Nevertheless, we were both disturbed by imperative knocking during the early morning hours, and when we compared notes, we found that these knockings were similar: a series of single knocks, so unlike what was customary, that one would almost think it was a kind of warning not to respond. As these efforts to gain admittance did not begin until after midnight, I couldn't help feeling that our would-be kidnappers were more than pleased when we didn't answer.[54]

Shelah Richards did not remember this incident; however, Ria Mooney also interestingly wrote:

After the first performance of this O'Casey play in Dublin, some of the girls I had known at school saw fit to cut me in the street; others noticed me for the first time. I'd had some flattering reviews in the papers, and my photograph appeared almost every day. My father and I received some threatening letters through the post. I remember one postcard on which he was asked if he was going to let his daughter "come to the same end as Honor Bright among the literary gentlemen of the Abbey Theatre?" . . .

It was many years later that I wakened up to the fact that, before the first production of *The Plough and the Stars*, I had appeared on the Abbey Stage as Darling Dora in Shaw's *Fanny's First Play*, and received only a pleasurable reaction from the audience—not a murmur of adverse criticism. Was this because Dora was an *English* prostitute?[55]

On Monday, 15 February, *The Plough* was replaced by Jules Romains' *Doctor Knock*, and also on Monday the *Independent* printed more letters about the play. The most interesting letter was from Mrs. Sheehy-Skeffington, who had been a leader in the protest of Thursday night:

Your editorial misses what was apparent in your report regarding the Abbey Theatre protest. The demonstration was not directed against the individual actor, nor was it directed to the moral aspect of the play. It was on national grounds solely, voicing a passionate indignation against the outrage of a drama staged in a supposedly national theatre, which held up to derision and obloquy the men and women of Easter Week.

The protest was made, not by Republicans alone, and had the sympathy of large numbers in the house. There is a point beyond which toleration becomes merely servility, and realism not art, but morbid perversity. The play, as a play, may be left to the judgment of posterity, which will rank it as artistically far below some of Mr. O'Casey's work. It is the realism that would paint not only the wart on Cromwell's nose, but that would add carbuncles and running sores in a reaction against idealisation. In no country save in Ireland could a State-subsidised theatre presume on popular patience to the extent of making a mockery and a byword of a revolutionary movement on which the present structure claims to stand.

I am one of those who have gone for over 20 years to performances at the Abbey, and I admire the earlier ideals of the place that produced *Kathleen Ni Houlihan*, that sent Sean Connolly out on Easter Week; that was later the subject of a British "Royal" Commission; the Abbey, in short, that helped to make Easter Week, and that now in its subsidised, sleek old age jeers at its former enthusiasms.

The incident will, no doubt, help to fill houses in London with audiences that come to mock at those "foolish dead," "whose names will be remembered for ever."

The only censorship that is justified is the free censorship of popular opinion. The Ireland that remembers with tear-dimmed eye all that Easter Week stands for, will not, and cannot, be silent in face of such a challenge.[56]

Also on 15 February, Lady Gregory had tea with O'Casey and Lyle Donaghy, and wrote:

Casey in good spirits after his reception last night. One of the objections made was the rebel flag having been carried into a public-house, but two old I. R. A. men have since told him that they themselves had brought the flag into pubs. He reminded some of the men who objected to a streetwalker having been put on, how often they had received food and shelter from these women when being hunted by the Black-and-Tans.

He stayed talking till near 8 o'clock, has his mind full of plays, too full perhaps, but his eyes have been very troublesome again. He has a difficulty in typing what he has written. His doctor says he must get a better lodging where he can have his food cooked for him, for he is indolent about doing it himself and is letting down his strength. One of the accusations of the interrupters had been that he did not make the Tommies offensive enough. But he says they were usually quite civil until they were frightened and turned cruel. They could come into the house and say "Mother, give us some tea," or whatever they wanted.[57]

On 16 February, the *Evening Herald* printed a long, thoughtful letter from Stephen J. Fitzgerald, which criticised the inclusion of Rosie Redmind, but otherwise admired the play.[58] On 17 February, J. Finigan somewhat truculently replied, and on 18 February C. P. Conway of Clontarf entered the fray to support Fitzgerald and attack Finigan[59]; but the most significant letter was printed in the *Times* on 19 February and in a slightly longer version in the *Independent* on 20 February. That letter was by O'Casey who finally entered the lists himself and tilted at Mrs. Sheehy-Skeffington:

Sir—A space, please, to breathe a few remarks opposing the screams and the patter antagonistic to the performance of *The Plough and the Stars*. in the Abbey Theatre.

In her long letter to the *Irish Independent* Mrs. Sheehy-Skeffington does not drag before us the parts of the play that spread irritating thoughts over the minds of herself and her allies, but a talk with some of the young Republican women which I had after the disturbance enabled me to discover that the National tocsin of alarm was sounded because some of the tinsel of sham was shaken from the body of truth.

They objected to Volunteers and men of the I. C. A. visiting a public-house. Do they want us to believe that all these men were sworn teetotallers? Are we to know the fighters of Easter Week as "The Army of the Unco' Guid"? Were all Ireland's battles fought by Confraternity men? The Staff of Stonewall Jackson complained bitterly to him of the impiety of one of their number. "A blasphemous scoundrel," said the General, "but a damned fine artillery officer." Some of the men of Easter Week liked a bottle of stout, and I can see nothing derogatory in that.

They objected to the display of the Tricolour, saying that that flag was never in a public-house. I myself have seen it there. I have seen the Green, White and Gold in strange places. I have seen it painted on a lavatory in "The Gloucester Diamond"; it has been flown from some of the worst slums in Dublin; I've see it thrust from the window of a shebeen in "The Digs"; but perhaps the funniest use it was put to was when it was made to function as a State robe for a Southern Mayor.

They murmured against the viewpoint of Nora Clitheroe, saying it did not represent the feeling of Ireland's womanhood. Nora voices not only the feeling of Ireland's women, but the women of the human race. The safety of her brood is the true mark[60] of every woman. A mother does not like her son to be killed—she doesn't like him even to get married.

The Republican women shouted with a loud voice against the representation of fear in the eyes of the fighters. If this be so, what is the use of sounding forth their praises? If they knew no fear, then the fight of Easter Week was an easy thing, and those who participated deserve to be forgotten in a day, rather than to be remembered for ever. And why is the sentiment expressed in *The Plough and the Stars* condemned, while it goes unnoticed (apparently) in other plays?

In *The Old Man* (written by a Republican[61]), during a crisis, the many fall back, only the few press forward. In *Sable and Gold*[62] (played by the Republican Players), a volunteer who is a definite coward, is one of the principal characters, and yet no howl has proclaimed the representation to be false or defaming. And are the men of Easter Week greater than those whose example they are said to have followed? Were they all unhuman in that they were destitute of the first element in the nature of man?

"Upon the earth there is not his like," says Job, "who is made without fear." Even the valiant Hector, mad with fear, was chased around the walls of Troy. And do the Republicans forget the whisper of Emmet to the question of the executioner. "Are you ready, sir?" "Not yet . . . not yet."

I wonder do the Republicans remember how Laoghaire and Conall, two of the champions of the Red Branch, ran, as rabbits would run, from what they believed to be the certainty of death; and how Cuchullain alone remained to face death, with "pale countenance, drooping head, in the heaviness of dark sorrow."

One of the young Republicans whispered to me in admiration the name of Shaw, inferentially to my own shame and confusion. Curious champion to choose, and I can only attribute their choice to ignorance, for if ever a man hated sham, it is Shaw.

Let me give one example that concerns the subject I am writing about. Describing in *Arms and the Man*, a charge of cavalry, Bluntschli says: "It's like slinging a handful of peas against the window-pane: first one comes, then two or three close behind him, then all the rest in a lump." Then Raina answers with dilating eyes (how like a young Republican woman!): "Yes, first One! the bravest of the brave!" followed by the terrible reply: "Hm; you should see the poor devil pulling at his horse!"

As for vanity, I think I remember a long discussion in *The Volunteer* over the adoption of the green and gold, scarlet and blue, black, white and crimson plumed costumes of the Volunteers of "82" for the Volunteers of "13"; and though these were rejected—they had to be—there was still left a good deal of boyish vanity in the distribution of braids, tabs, slung swords and Sam Brown belts. And how rich (to me) was the parade of the stiff and stately uniformed men. "The solemn looking dials of them," as Rosie Redmond says in the play, and they marching to the meeting very serious, very human, but damnably funny.

I am glad that Mrs. Sheehy-Skeffington says that the demonstration was not directed against any individual actor. As Mr. F. J. McCormack [*sic*] told the audience, the author alone is responsible for the play, and he is willing to take it all.

The politicians—Free State and Republican—have the platform to express themselves, and heaven knows they seem to take full advantage of it; the Drama is my place for self-expression, and I claim the liberty in Drama that they enjoy on the platform (and how they do enjoy it!), and am prepared to fight for it.

The heavy-hearted expression by Mrs. Sheehy-Skeffington about "The Ireland that remembers with tear-dimmed eyes all that Easter Week stands for" makes me sick. Some of the men can't get even a job. Mrs. Skeffington is certainly not dumb, but she appears to be both blind and deaf to all the things that are happening around her. Is the Ireland that is pouring to the picture houses, to the dance halls, to the football matches, remembering with tear-dimmed eyes all that Easter Week stands for? Tears may be in the eyes of the navvies working on the Shannon scheme, but they are not for Ireland.

When Mrs. Skeffington roars herself into the position of a dramatic critic, we cannot take her seriously; she is singing here on a high note wildly beyond the range of her political voice, and can be given only the charity of our silence.

In refutation of a story going round, let me say that there never was a question of a refusal to play the part of Rosie Redmond (splendidly acted by Miss Mooney): the part declined by one of the players was the character of "Mrs Gogan."

I have no intention of noticing the poor stupid things written by the Kellys, Burkes, Sheas, and the Finigans.

Sean O Casey[63]

O'Casey, incidentally, was not the only notable playwright in difficulty. Also on 20 February, the *Evening Herald* reported an incident that had occurred a couple of days earlier in Los Angeles:

Los Angeles police have, says the New York correspondent of the *Daily Mail*, arrested the entire cast of *Desire Under the Elms*, Mr. Eugene O'Neill's play, which, after a phenomenal run in New York, is now touring the country.

The actors and actresses were arrested on Thursday 18 February at the close of the night's performance, after it had been viewed by representatives of the Board of Education, the Parents' and Teachers' Associations, several clergymen, and members of the police "vice squad."

The members of the cast are charged with producing an indecent play. They were released on bail of £10 each.[64]

Also on 20 February, J. Finigan contributed his final refutation of Messrs. Fitzgerald and Conway in the letters column of the *Evening Herald*[65]; but there were more prominent and interesting attackers of the play than he. And some were among the ablest Irish writers of O'Casey's generation. For instance, also on 20 February, the *Irish Statesman* publishing the following long letter from Liam O'Flaherty:

Dear Sir,—Permit me to protest in your columns against Mr. Yeats' demonstration in the Abbey Theatre on Thursday last. The protest by those who objected to the play (*The Plough and the Stars*) was undoubtedly in bad taste, but nobody loses anything by it, least of all the author, who gained a good advertisement. But the protest by Mr. Yeats, against the protest of the audience, was an insult to the people of this country. I feel that I am personally justified in protesting against his protest because the manner in which they have received my own work (and in all probability the manner in which they WILL receive my work) defends me from the accusation of appealing to the gallery. Allow me to review the position.

In my opinion *The Plough and the Stars* is a bad play. It would be quite in order for an audience to hiss it as a bad play. It was, however, a boorish thing to hiss it because the opinions expressed by the author injured the feelings of the audience. Every man has a right to his opinions. Mr. O'Casey has a right to his opinions. He has a perfect right to protest himself against this treatment of his work by the audience. But Mr. Yeats had positively no right to strut forward and cry with joy that the people of this country had "been cut to the bone." Our people have their faults. It is a good thing that artists should point out these faults. But it is not a good thing that pompous fools should boast that we have been "cut to the bone."

I say WE, because I too was cut to the bone. I am not a Nationalist in the political sense. But I am an admirer of any man who has the courage to die for an ideal. And I think the most glorious gesture in the history of our country was the gesture of those who died in 1916. No great artist in any country in the world refused to give credit, to glorify men who died likewise. Even Tolstoy, the great pacifist, bowed down before the courage of the Cossacks and of the brigand enemies (even brigands) who died with their death-song on their lips. I bow down before the courage of Pearse and Connolly and their comrades. I did not have the honour to fight with them. But I "am cut to the bone" because an Irish writer did not, unfortunately, do them justice. I do not blame O'Casey. I believe him to be a sincere man. But I am sorry to see him defended by a man who rose to fame on the shoulders of those men who stirred this country to fervent enthusiasm for ideals in the last generation. What does it matter to us whether these ideals were practical? No ideal is practical, but all ideals are the mothers of great poetry, and it is only from the womb of an ideal that a great race, or a great literature, or a great art can spring.

I am not "cut to the bone" because the play was not anti–English. I fervently admire the English race. I envy the English race for their greatness, for their bravery, for the great men they have produced. I envy their Cromwells, their Shakespeares, their Shelleys, their Darwins, their countless heroes who have struggled for the English ideal, whether it be a Wat Tyler or a Frobisher, a Clive or a William Morris. The great poetry of life is the struggle of brave men. And the contemptible thing in life is the strutting of pompous people who spit at the justified anger of enthusiasts. "Let him who is without sin cast the first stone."

Sir, I am of Gaelic stock. My ancestors came into this country sword in hand, as conquerors, as the Danes came and the Normans and the English. To conquer is the right of the strong. We who conquered once have been in turn conquered. I acclaim our conquerors. But now the conquered and the conquerors are one. And out of their seed another race has sprung. We are all brothers. All but those who turn their backs on their people and cry, spitting, that they "have been cut to the bone." It was not so that McCracken cried, or Tone, or Emmet, or even the great Parnell.

Finally, I do not believe in political nationalism. I do not believe in Empires. The human race has advanced considerably since the time of Daithi and even since the time of Napoleon. I believe in the political union of the human race, in the ideal of human brotherhood. But there always will be strife and struggle. Soon perhaps that strife will be intellectual competition. But it is certain that always people born in one place will love that place and try to make it pre-eminent by the achievements of its people. And always brave men will love the weak and struggle with them. And always poets will side with the weak against the strong, and not with the strong against the weak and ignorant. And always great men will not become embittered, even as Synge did not become embittered, but smiled gently like a Christ at those who reviled him. —Yours faithfully,

Liam O'Flaherty[66]

And in the same issue, Austin Clarke wrote from London:

Dear Sir, —May I suggest that in the interests of Irish art the recent ructions at the Abbey Theatre be regarded as merely another "lovers' quarrel"? Many of the old Anglo-Irish school have been inclined to think that only a work of genius can cause disturbance. *The Playboy* was mistaken for a picture of our western people, but, moving in its own rich world of poetry and realistic phantasy, it endures. A bad topical play, run flagrantly in the interests of the party politics of the moment, might give offence, yet remain a bad play. Owing to the strong anti-Irish prejudice in this country, any play that merely belittled our people would be popular, and it is therefore imperative that the question of art should come first. Several writers of the new Irish school believe that Mr. O'Casey's work is a crude exploitation of our poorer people in an Anglo-Irish tradition that is now moribund. Frank discussion can alone bring us the truth. May one hope that your paper, ignoring the recent revival of Anglo-Irish coterie criticism, which is doing so much harm to our art, will open its columns to the discussion of the artistic values in dispute? —Yours faithfully,

Austin Clarke[67]

On Sunday evening, 21 February, May Carey rented the Abbey to stage a very noninflammatory play, Barrie's *Dear Brutus*. Holloway, arriving at the theater, noted:

A big queue was outside the Abbey pit also when I arrived and many waiting outside the vestibule. Sean O'Casey was one of them. He would not shake hands with me; he seems very sore over the opposition to his *Plough and the Stars* evidently. He didn't know Professor Oldham. He never read or saw *Dear Brutus*. In fact, I could see he didn't want to have anything to say to me. I, seeing this, dried up at once. I had a chat with Brinsley MacNamara. He didn't like O'Casey's last play at all, and thought much of its dialogue involved and imitative.[68]

The war of letters to the press went on, and on 23 February there was a letter from Stephen J. Fitzgerald defending O'Casey and one from Sean O'Shea attacking him.[69] On the same day the *Independent* printed Mrs. Sheehy-Skeffington's reply to O'Casey:

In his letter Mr. O'Casey sets himself the task of replying to cetain criticisms of his play. Since receiving Mr. Yeats' police-protected "apotheosis" Mr. O'Casey appears to take himself over-seriously, not sparing those of us who decline to bow the knee before his godhead. His play becomes "the shaking of the tinsel of sham from the body of truth": an over-statement surely, for of the body of truth as portrayed in *The Plough and the Stars* one may only discern a leprous corpse.

As Arthur Griffith wrote nearly twenty years ago, when last police assisted at an Abbey production: "If squalidness, coarseness, and crime are to be found in Ireland, so are cancer, smallpox, and policemen." But because these are to be found it would not be true to claim that nothing but these are present in Ireland. Because Mr. O'Casey has seen the tricolour painted on a lavatory wall he claims the right to parade it in a public-house as typical of the custom of the Citizen Army and the Volunteers. Because indecent and obscene inscriptions are similarly so found one may not exalt them as great literature.

Mr. O'Casey's original version, as is now generally known, was pruned before production. One wonders on what basis certain parts were excluded and others retained. This may, indeed, be the reason for the lopsidedness of some scenes, suffering, as sometimes the picture plays do, from a drastic, ill-concealed cut. Will the original version now appear in London and elsewhere, benefiting by the réclame of a "succès de scandale," a réclame that is usually ephemeral?

As to Mr. O'Casey's ransacking of literature to find soldiers that show fear or vanity, all that is beside the point. Whether the sight of men parading before an action that will lead many of them to their death is "damnably funny," or whether it might be pitiful and heartrending, is also a matter of presentment and point of view. The Greeks, who knew not Mr. O'Casey, used to require of a tragedy that it evoke feelings in the spectator of "pity and terror," and Shakespeare speaks of holding the "mirror up to nature." Submitted to either criteria, *The Plough and the Stars* is assuredly defective. But no doubt Mr. O'Casey would regard such standards as sadly out of date.

A play that deals with Easter Week and what led up to it, that finds in Pearse's words (spoken in almost his very accents) a theme merely for the drunken jibe of "dope," in which every character connected with Citizen Army is a coward, a slacker, or worse, that omits no detail of squalid slumdom, the looting, the squabbling, the disease and degeneracy, yet that omits any revelation of the glory and the inspiration of Easter Week, is a "Hamlet" shown without the Prince of Denmark.

Is it merely a coincidence that the only soldiers whose knees do not knock together with fear and who are indifferent to the glories of their uniform are the Wiltshires? Shakespeare pandered to the prejudices of his time and country by representing Joan of Arc as a ribald, degraded camp-follower. Could one imagine his play being received with enthusiasm in the French theatre of the time, subsidised by the State?

I learn that Mr. O'Casey's personal knowledge of the Citizen Army does not extend beyond 1914–15. To those, however, who remember the men and women of 1916 such presentation in a professedly 'National" theatre seems a gross libel.

Mourning for the men of Easter Week is not incompatible with sympathy for the suffering survivors. The Ireland that is "pouring to the picture houses, the dance halls and the football matches" is the Ireland that forgets—that never knew. It is the Ireland that sits comfortably in the Abbey stalls and applauds Mr. O'Casey's play. It is the Ireland of the garrison, which sung twenty years ago "God Save the King" (while Mr. Yeats then, too, enforced the performance of the *Playboy* with the aid of the police). These do not shed tears for the navvy on the Shannon nor for the men of Easter Week nor for the sorrows of the slums.

Mr. O'Casey accords me as a critic in a shrieking paragraph or two the "charity of his silence." Unfortunately for his play, the professional critics are for the most part on my side, justifying my opinion that his latest play is also his poorest. For (pace Mr. Yeats) the police do not necessarily confer immortality, nor is it invariably a sign of a work of a genius to be hissed by an Irish audience.

Arthur Griffith wrote thus in *Sinn Fein* of a similar episode: —"Mr. Yeats has struck a blow" (by calling in police and arresting certain members of the audience who protested against the *Playboy*) "at the freedom of the theatre in Ireland. It was perhaps the last freedom left to us. Hitherto, as in Paris or in Berlin or in Athens 2,000 years ago, the audience in Ireland was free to express its opposition to a play. Mr. Yeats has denied this right. He has wounded both art and his country."

May I suggest that when Mr. O'Casey proceeds to lecture us on "the true morality of every woman" he is somewhat beyond his depth. Nora Clitheroe is no more "typical of Irish womanhood" than her futile, snivelling husband is of Irish manhood. The women of Easter Week, as we know them, are typified rather in the mother of Padraic Pearse, that valiant woman who gave both her sons for freedom. Such breathe the spirit of Volumnia, of the Mother of the Gracchi.

That Mr. O'Casey is blind to it does not necessarily prove that it is non-existent, but merely that his vision is defective. That the ideals for which these men died have not been achieved does not lessen their glory nor make their sacrifices vain. "For they shall be remembered for ever" by the people if not by the Abbey directorate.[70]

On 26 February, the *Independent* printed O'Casey's second rejoinder to Mrs. Sheehy-Skeffington:

Sir—In a letter on 15th inst. Mrs. Sheehy-Skeffington said that "the demonstration was not directed to the moral aspect of the play. It was on National grounds solely." Yet in her letter of 23rd she viciously affirms what she had before denied, and prancing out, flings her gauntlet in the face of what she calls the "obscenities and indecencies" of the play. She does more: in the righteousness of her indignation, she condemns, by presumption, what she has neither seen nor heard.

This is her interpretation of the Rights of Man. Evidently the children of National light in their generation are as cute as the children of National darkness by placing a puritanical prop under the expression of National dissatisfaction, even though the cuteness requires an action that can be called neither fair nor just.

We know as well as Mrs. Sheehy-Skeffington that obscene and indecent expressions do not make great literature, but we know, too, that great literature may make use of obscene and indecent expressions, without altogether destroying its beauty and its richness. She would hardly question the greatness in literature of Shakespeare (somebody a year or so ago wrote asking if Shakespeare wrote thirty plays without a naughty word, why couldn't O'Casey write them), but in the condemnation of an O'Casey play the green cloak is concealed by the puritanical mantle. Indeed, her little crow over the possible horror of the censored part of the play seems to whisper that the wish is father to the thought, and that, when the play is published, nothing less (or more) will satisfy her than that the united church bells of Dublin, of their own accord, in a piercing peal will clang together— "This is a bad, bad, bad, bad play!"

There is no use of talking now of what Mr. Arthur Griffith thought of or wrote about *The Playboy*. Now the world thinks, and I think so, too, that *The Playboy* is a masterpiece of Irish drama. If these Greeks knew not Mr. O'Casey (how the devil could they), O'Casey knows the Greeks, and hopes that the Republican Players will one of these days produce one of their works dealing with ancient gods and heroes. At present he himself is interested in men and women.

Mrs. Skeffington's statement that "every character connected with the Citizen Army is a coward and a slacker" is, to put it plainly, untrue. There isn't a coward in the play. Clitheroe falls in the fight. Does Mrs. Skeffington want him to do any more? Brennan leaves the burning building when he can do nothing else; is she going to persist in her declaration that no man will try to leap away from a falling building? Will she still try to deny that in a man (even in the bravest) self-preservation is the first law? She may object to this, but, in fairness, she shouldn't blame me.

Langon, wounded in the belly, moans for surgical aid. Does she want me to make him gather a handful of his blood and murmur, "Thank God that this has been shed for Ireland?" I'm sorry, but I can't do this sort of thing.

She complains of the Covey calling sentences of The Voice, dope. Does she not understand that the Covey is a character part, and that he couldn't possibly say anything else without making the character ridiculous? Even the Greeks wouldn't do this. And it doesn't follow that an author agrees with everything his characters say. I happen to agree with this, however; but of these very words Jim Connolly himself said almost the same thing as the Covey.

The Tommies weren't represented without fear; but isn't it natural that they should have been a little steadier than the Irish fighters? Even Mrs. Skeffington will not deny that the odds were terribly in their favour, and that they were comparatively safe. Sixty or more to one would make even a British Tommy feel safe.

The people that go to football matches are just as much a part of Ireland as those who go to Bodenstown, and it would be wise for the Republican Party to recognise this fact, unless they are determined to make of Ireland the terrible place of a land fit only for heroes to live in.

Sean O'Casey[71]

On 27 February, *The Voice of Labour* printed a rather more irascible letter from O'Casey. It was written on 20 February in reply to a review by Tom Irwin which had appeared in the magazine of that date:

> Sir, —Permit me to correct a statement appearing in your paper connecting me with "internal events in the I.C.A. when the late James Connolly was preparing that body for armed revolution."
>
> I had no connection whatever, direct or indirect, with the I.C.A. at that time: I had left, abandoned, deserted, fled from (take your choice of terms) the I.C.A. long before James Connolly had begun to "prepare that body for armed revolution."
>
> Tommy Irwin asks "the author to show us the tenements in Dublin with the three-room flats." He knows of none. The original script has: "The home of the Clitheroes. It consists of the front and back drawing-rooms of a fine old Georgian house." The alteration was made to suit the limitations of the Abbey stage.
>
> May I beg of you for God's sake, and for the reputation of the Irish Labour movement (such as it is) to prevent poor Tommy Irwin from framing his stupidities by trying to write about the Drama? —Sincerely yours,
>
> Sean O'Casey[72]

Cathal O'Shannon, the journal's editor, replied in part:

> That a Dublin man who works and is a son of the tenements should write what he feels about a performance at the Abbey seems to have cut pretty close to the bone of a genius at his apotheosis. It's too bad. Playwrights ought to be protected from working-men in the Press, as they are (sometimes) from hostile demonstrations in the theatre. At all events, Tom Irwin has compelled the admission that at least one "alteration was made to suit the limitations of the Abbey-stage." That isn't a bad achievement for a working-class critic. How many other changes—to suit the spirit of the Abbey directorate—were made the Abbey deities alone know.[73]

One of O'Casey's staunchest defenders was young Lyle Donaghy. In the *Irish Statesman* of 27 February, he wrote:

> Dear Sir,—As one who believes *The Plough and the Stars* to be a great play with technical and artistic defects, may I have a space in your columns to reply to Mr. O'Flaherty?
>
> I, too, am an Irishman and would like to see Ireland great by the achievements of its people (of which achievements I count *The Plough and the Stars* one), but I rejoice to-day with Mr. Yeats that at last in my country a physician has not been afraid to have done with quackery, that the people have been "cut to the bone," that the knife has been put to the gangrene. I am amazed that one who writes, "I believe in the political union of the human race, in the ideal of human brotherhood," should not have seen at once and felt in *The Plough and the Stars* a passion that is national and more than national, a life that is of every country, a battlefield and a desolation that do not belong only to Ireland. I am amazed that the attention of such a one should have been riveted to an earnest standard-bearer in a public-house, while the great ideals about which he is concerned were in vital conflict without, while a serious voice was making its appeal to the national passions. I am amazed that such a one should not have been caught up himself into a great struggle between world forces, and that he should not have felt with the

dramatist, whose part was to suggest the reaction, the futility of the sword, that he should not have sensed throughout the play almost a prophetic undertone, proclaiming "that what was born in blood must die." I am amazed that Liam O'Flaherty should not have felt the time at hand when the pleadings of Christ should be urged upon a slumbering world.

There is a ripeness of time which the reformer must await, but that moment is not always the moment of popular sympathy and acclaim, which at least neither artist nor reformer need attend; and now, it seems to me that the time is ripe for a greater effort, that the dream of all the poets may come into its own, when humanity shall not be divided against itself. The glory of the spirit in man may find expression in many ways. What poet ever scorned that glory, even when it expressed itself through the horrors of a bloody war? Of course Tolstoi did not; nor does Sean O'Casey; but must we, because men err bravely, put aside the truth which has forced itself upon us? The men of 1916 fought for an ideal. Is it to be said that when the streams flowed and horror stalked abroad, when they found themselves men capable of love and hate and fear, they sought to hide the truth from themselves, and that there were none among them like Captain Brennan? Had they lived to pass from ideal to deeper ideal, had they survived to survey the smoking ruins and assess the gains, I do not think that they would have been afraid to face the facts; neither was Sean O'Casey; neither is any artist.

It seems to me that Mr. O'Flaherty is false to the poet in himself; for I do not think that a true artist (such as I believe Mr. O'Flaherty to be) admits the impracticability of ideals. He is constituted to believe in them. Myself, I have worshipped ideals in the past, though rejecting the name, for that I believe true idealism to be in essence a far-sighted realism, and all true ideals practical. I feel that this unbelief in Mr. O'Flaherty has tainted his letter, which appears to hold up great lives as good because they produce great poetry, rather than poetry because it serves life. In fact, I shudder when I hear him speak of the 1916 battle as a gesture, for I feel that he is sinking to the posture more usually, though I think unfairly, attributed to Mr. Yeats, that attitude, adopting which one might wave a thousand to the scaffold for a symbol's sake, when the end of existence, no longer an unknown good, is content to be a temporary pose.

Alas, it is only such a posture that could give way to the tenet that the most exalted strife of the future will be an intellectual competition. Yet such I deduce is Mr. O'Flaherty's belief. Had he used the word "competition," meaning thereby "to seek in company with" or "to content together for an ultimate good in which all may share," then, though it is a post-classic word, I would have taken my hat off to him that used it; but I fear it is not so, and that I must wait until my mind has further developed or my youth has departed, or Mr. O'Flaherty has advanced his standard whether in public house or palace, before I can shake hands with him on the subject. —Yours faithfully.

Lyle Donaghy[74]

In the same issue, Fallon took up his usual noncommittal posture:

Dear Sir—Under *The Plough and the Stars* Mr. O'Flaherty talks of many things and talks of them so breathlessly as to make one believe that it must have been impossible for him, his indignation spent, to know exactly what he, Mr. O'Flaherty, was talking about.

Mr. Yeats' remark that "it appeared that O'Casey had cut to the bone" was made to the players in the Green Room of the Abbey Theatre and was not made in the manner suggested by Mr. O'Flaherty.

It is Mr. O'Flaherty's opinion that *The Plough and the Stars* is a bad play and that O'Casey did not do justice to the men who died in 1916.

That is all that matters in Mr. O'Flaherty's letter.

As for the rest, neither Mr. O'Flaherty's fighting ancestry nor his far-flung beliefs can have any interest for those interested in *The Plough and the Stars*. —Yours Faithfully,

Gabriel J. Fallon[75]

Also in the same issue appeared an essay by Brigid O'Higgins, which discussed not only the theme but also the artistry of the play. One might disagree with some of the writer's particular points, but one must laud the attempt to discuss the artistic issues in a balanced and unemotional way. She wrote:

Sean O'Casey's powerful drama, *The Plough and the Stars*, is in the tradition of the great French and Russian realists, though it is nothing of a slavish imitation, for the dramatist is his own master. In this play he gives a critical, cynical and impassioned picture of existence in the Dublin slums during the historic years of 1915–16. He does not shrink from portraying tenement life as he himself knew it, and if at very rare intervals the tragedy verges on melodrama—for O'Casey still lacks restraint—the man is honestly striving for the truth and is seldom very far from it.

Despite some palpable exaggerations which, when they appear, mar the artistry of the drama, and a certain looseness in construction, there is strength, sincerity and genius behind the work. It does not reach the same heights of dramatic intensity as its predecessor, *Juno and the Paycock*, nor does it touch the emotions so keenly—perhaps it is not so great a play—but there is a more terrible force, a more turbulent passion, a more ghastly Nemesis, which make it more robust than the earlier tragedy.

In his delineation of character, O'Casey is most convincing. He attains less success in the kneading of incident into a dramatic whole. The characters in *The Plough and the Stars* are real men and women, and, while the dramatist is merciless in his depiction of these tenement dwellers, making no excuses for their shiftlessness, their inefficiency, there is nothing condescending in his treatment of them—rather is there a delicacy of touch, for too well O'Casey knows the pride of the poor. Throughout the drama the strength of the blood-tie is there. These people of the slums are his own kith and kin: he understands them, and, while castigating them, he loves them. It is this very love for his kind which causes his terrible cynicism and which gives the passion to his theme . . . .

What the result of this impassioned though cynical analysis of slum conditions in our city is like to be is a debatable point. This at least the dramatist has achieved: by forcing us to face the facts of life as they are, the true, unpleasant things, Sean O'Casey has shaken our smugness; he has ruthlessly dispelled that convenient smoke-screen which would shut out from our comfortable drawing-rooms the awful reality of a side of Dublin life that men and women, our fellow-citizens, are daily up against . . . .

So much for the artist's message! Sometimes an over-emphasis hampers O'Casey in the artistry of its delivery. The lengthy, well-polished speeches do not always sit quite easily on the lips of the men and the women one meets in *The Plough and the Stars*. The form of the drama suffers somewhat from a lack of restraint. With regard to the handling of the matter, it might be remarked that it lacks cohesion, the incidents are isolated and need a linking up. Perhaps O'Casey overcrowds the canvas somewhat? But, realist before artist, he feels that if he is to present any full and faithful picture of the wretched lives of slum dwellers, he must work in incidents which are dramatically unconvincing, but without which no comprehensive account of existence in the tenements would be complete. For this reason he crowds in Rosie Redmond, the street girl, and little Mollser, the consumptive child. These characters are in no wise essential to the dramatic unity of the play—rather do they stand aloof, for neither knits herself into the heart of the tragedy. Ruthless in the presentation of facts, O'Casey philosophically accepts the first as an unpleasant reality and introduces the youthful victim of the white scourge so that her death may lend a deeper tone to the general gloom of the picture . . . .

The introduction of the flag into the public-house in the second act of the play was an unhappy incident. Aesthetically it hurt. It was a crude stroke and hinted at a subconscious pandering to the melodramatic instinct which the author has not yet conquered. Technically, it seems inaccurate. It is possible that what O'Casey stages may have occurred, but it is most improbable . . . But for Sean O'Casey, the champion of the civilians, 1916 only meant war. He rages against all war, because of its terrible reaction on the lives of the people, more especially of the awful tragedies in its wake for women. Influenced by this view, he only sees one side of the 1916 rising, and he is out of sympathy with the higher one . . . He probably viewed it as an ill-planned, ineffective military coup, which brought still more hardships to an already heart-broken people, still more wretchedness into the starkness and horror of life in the slums. To the dramatist who was socialist before nationalist, it was war, and war meant death and madness and terrible futility. But events have disproved this view, and, hopefully and patiently, Ireland awaits her golden-voiced poet to sing the song of glorious'16.

Though one may differ from the results which Mr. O'Casey has drawn from his critical and cynical analysis of the Easter rising, surely that is no excuse for the intolerance displayed at the Abbey Theatre on the first production of the drama. A dramatist is an artist primarily, neither a propagandist nor a politician. It is his ritht and his need to express his individual views on any subject which fires his imagination. Should his verdict wound our sensibilities, when are we, as a people, going to educate ourselves out of our touchiness? . . .

In the meantime, those of us who are not fashioned in heroic mould are deeply indebted to the author of *The Plough and the Stars*, for he is the defender of the rights of the poor, the weak, and the un-heroic. Nay, he is more than champion—he is friend. Good-natured Fluther, good, kindhearted Bessie, and poor little heartbroken Nora will never get beyond slumland, but in Mr. Sean O'Casey they have one who understands them, who thinks for them, and one also who, while he fights with them, loves them—yes, one who in a strange way respects them. To speak of these people and for them, to be the singer of the underworld—that is Mr. O'Casey's mission.[76]

Finally, climactically, there was much less reasoned good sense in evidence on 1 March at the well-attended discussion about the play in the Mills' Hall in Merrion Row. On this occasion the chief attack on the play was by Mrs. Sheehy-Skeffington, and the chief defence by O'Casey. As the *Independent* reported the proceedings:

There was a piquant development last night in the controversy over Mr. Sean O'Casey's play, *The Plough and the Stars*, when the author and the leader of the Abbey opposition, Mrs. Sheehy-Skeffington, debated its merits.

Mrs. Sheehy-Skeffington contended that the play was a travesty of Easter Week, and that it concentrated on pettiness and squalor, unrelieved by a gleam of heroism.

Mr. O'Casey declared that Mrs. Sheehy-Skeffington saw everything through the eyes of a politician, and he through the eyes of a dramatist.

He also said he was not trying, and never would try, to write about heroes. He wrote only about the life he knew and the people he knew.

The dramatist and the leader of the opposition to the play met under the auspices of the Universities' Republican Club in the Mills' Hall, Merrion Row, last night, Prof. A. E. Clery presiding.

Lecturing on the controversy, Mrs. Sheehy-Skeffington said the main point of controversy turned on whether an audience had a right to express disapproval. Most authors and actors agreed that audiences had a right to express approval, and, therefore, the question was, whether an audience had a right to express disapproval by the usual method of hissing and boohing.

She thought that it was necessary that a protest should be made to hit the Abbey directorate in the eye.

There was no other way by which that could be done at present. *The Plough and the Stars* did not strike her as an anti-war play, but as an anti-Easter week play.

Dealing with National Theatres, she personally regretted, not as a Republican, but as a lover of freedom and of the theatre, that the Abbey Theatre had been susbsidised by the Government. It was now a "kept" house, and any theatre lost more than the subsidy it received by giving up its freedom, and should in the natural course of events "kow tow" to the powers that be. Would it be possible in a subsidised theatre in Belfast for the Ulster Players to produce such a travesty as *The Plough and the Stars* of Carson's Volunteers before Sir James Craig and Lord Carson? Would not the theatre be wrecked by the indignant supporters of these two gentlemen?

"With regard to Mr. O'Casey," she continued, "my own impression of him is that he has 'a grouch.' He likes to see rather the meanness, the littleness, the squalor, the slum squabbles, the women barging each other, and the little vanities and jealousies of the Irish Citizen Army. He has rather the art of the photographer rather than the art of the dramatist.

"These scenes are all put together, and the natural conclusion is that this is a typical picture of the men of 1916.

"There is not a single gleam of heroism throughout *The Plough and the Stars*.

"The theme of the play right through is the folly of it. That is why it cut to the bone, because we looked to see some of the heroism that did produce Easter Week."

The present Abbey motto was to see the squalor.

"I am sorry for Mr. O'Casey," she proceeded, "because I do realise that his plays have the mark of genius. He has taken Easter Week for what is, after all, rather a comedy than a tragedy. We do wish that a dramatist will arise who will deal with what is great and fine in 1916." (hear, hear).

Mr. Sean O'Casey, who rose to propose a vote of thanks to the lecturer, only uttered a few sentences when he was overcome by a temporary weakness and had to sit down for a short period.

In the meantime, Mr. Donaghy, a T.C.D. student, carried on the debate.

Mr. O'Casey resumed and said that Mrs. Sheehy Skeffington saw everything through the eyes of a politician, while he saw most things through the eyes of a dramatist. She seemed to pay a great deal of attention to what England or America thought of them. He cared nothing for what these countries thought of Irishmen—even if they thought half of them were pookhas and the other half leprecauns.

Referring to the flag in the play, he said that it was not symbolical or representative of any one country or province, or of the Republicans, but was symbolical of the whole of Ireland, and if it represented the whole of Ireland it would have to take its place amongst the Bessie Burgesses, Judy Gogans, and Fluther Goods—even the Rosie Redmonds, as it did amongst the President of the Dail, the President of the Seanad and President of a Republican convention. One of the golden stars on the tricolour was Easter Week, and in his opinion another was Irish drama. That flag had also to take the spots of disease, of hunger, hardship.

He was not trying, and never would try, to write about heroes. He could write only about the life he knew, and the people he knew.

These people formed the bone and sinew, and ultimately, he believed, they were going to be the brain of the country as well.

Mr. O'Casey then went on to reply in detail to the criticisms, and referring to the publichouse scene said that Mrs. Sheehy-Skeffington evidently wanted to bring everyone out of the publichouse.

Mrs. Sheehy-Skeffington—Hear, hear.

Mr. O'Casey—I am anxious to bring everyone into the publichouses to make them proper places of amusement and refreshment. The play, in my opinion, is the best of the three produced. It has been said I have been writing for England. I am not writing for England. I am writing for England as well as for Ireland, and I don't see why I should not.

The Plough and the Stars was handed in and passed for production long before there was a word of the London production of *Juno and the Paycock*.

All my plays were written for Dublin (applause).

Referring to the critics, he said: "Do not mind the critics. No dependence can be placed on the critics. To my mind, the critics of England and Ireland, and particularly in Ireland, are the Bunsbys of the Dramatic movement" (hear, hear).

Mrs. McCarville seconded the vote of thanks, and said that the play was an anti-Pearse play.

Mr. Gabriel Fallon spoke of the protest against the play as mob censorship.

Mr. E. O'Rahilly, Mr. F. J. O'Donnell, and Madame Gonne MacBride also spoke.[77]

Holloway, of course, attended the debate, and reported that the hall was thronged, and that T. C. Nally, T. C. Murray, Mrs. Despard, Maud Gonne MacBride, John Burke, Shelah Richards, Gabriel Fallon, F. J. McCormick, Arthur Shields, Ria Mooney, Joseph O'Reilly, Mrs. Tom Kettle and many others he knew were present. He also paraphrased Maud Gonne's remarks:

Maud Gonne said she didn't see the play, but from what O'Casey said he had no right to introduce a real hero—Padraic Pearse—into his play, and from O'Casey's own words could clearly see why the protest was made.[78]

There was one religious response to the debate, and this was a letter to the press by a writer who signed himself P. M. J.:

In two daily papers this week there are reports of a lecture on the qualities of a play recently given for the entertainment of the Dublin public. An anomalous situation arose at the lecture, owing to the fact that the author proposed a vote of thanks to the lecturer, who had commented adversely upon his play. The author went on to say that he did not write of heroes, but of the slum population—as he knew it.

Authors are usually assumed to have some super-knowledge of the subject they intend to write about before they do so, or at least to have made some special study of it. One would like to ask the author of *The Plough and the Stars* had he never found heroes in slum life. For there are heroes and heroines to be found in the slums. There died in Dublin less than two years ago a Loreto nun named Sister Mary Bega, and last June a poor labourer named Matt Talbot. Both these were sprung from lowly parents, and both were reared and lived in the lowliest quarters of our city. And we know now that the one was a heroine and the other a hero.

The discovery of the secret lives of these two might be said, humanly speaking, to be almost accidental. Of the thousands who lead good, and even saintly, lives amidst the direst povery, who ever hears a word? Who trots them out as examples to be followed? Would it not be well if some authors sat down to write a drama portraying their beautiful lives lived under cruel circumstances amidst want and misery and temptation?

The author of the life of Matt Talbot has done a real service by giving us the story of this holy man. A welcome would be given to the life of Sister Mary Bega similar in form to the one of Matt Talbot published by the Catholic Truth Society.[79]

The attack most dismissive of the artistic merits of the play was probably by F. R. Higgins, the poet who was to become something of a protege of Yeats and eventually, before his untimely death, the Managing Director of the Abbey. In its number of 6 March, *The Irish Statesman* printed the following letter from Higgins:

Dear Sir, —From the controversy appearing in your columns regarding an interpretation of Mr. Sean O'Casey's recent tragedy, it is quite evident that the main questions at issue are merely based upon a revival of that arrogance of the Gall, recently dormant, towards the Gael. Personally. I consider that arrogance beside the point. Now that some have forgotten the cold logic of *Sixteen Dead Men* and their influence on those

"That converse bone to bone"

and of a time when

"A terrible beauty is born."

let the bone be left to those who first snarled over it.

It is rather interesting to note that none of Mr. O'Casey's defenders have taken up the suggestion made by Mr. Austin Clarke that *The Plough and the Stars* should be considered primarily from an art standard. Mr. Yeats and AE saved poetry and the drama from political rhetoric and it is strange that, notwithstanding the "dedavisiation" of the stage, a new political creed is the only quality, for which Mr. O'Casey is offered applause.

One is eager to have the opinions of our dramatic critics on a technique largely based upon the revue structure, in the quintessence of an all-Abbey burlesque, intensified by "divarsions" and Handy Andy incidents, with the more original settings offered by Sean O'Casey. That aspect of comedy so gushly over-portrayed from Dublin artisan life, as seen only by this playwright, merely affords laborious bowing on one-string fiddle—and "Fluther" Good's is just the successor of Captain Boyle's more lively ragtime.

Mr. Sean O'Casey, in his new play, entirely lacks the sincerity of an artist. One, of course, is frankly suspicious of reputations largely advertised by such a slogan as "docker dramatist" —the artist can only be judged by his work and as an artist he is beside his class—this label is just the condescension of intellectual snobbery. If, as a sincere artist, Mr. O'Casey interpreted the raw life he is supposed to know, the sure strokes of a great dramatist would have painted such a picture of the Dublin underworld that instead of driving some to demolish the theatre, they would be driven out in horror to abolish the slum. Yours truly,

F. R. Higgins[80]

However, by 6 March, the playwright had left Ireland—although, according to Gabriel Fallon, reluctantly. J. B. Fagan, the playwright and producer, had sent him a ticket to England to see Fagan's successful London production of *Juno and the Paycock*; and on 23 March in London he received the Hawthornden Prize for that play. He was much admired in London, even lionized, and what he said was widely reported in the press. He was to lunch with Shaw, he was being painted by John, and *The Plough* was to open in London. By July he had taken a flat in Chelsea and brought his books over from Dublin. As he told a reporter from the *Daily Sketch*:

I am going to write a play about London people, for one thing. Human nature is just the same in a Chelsea environment as in Dublin . . . .

Besides I have to find a place for my feet somewhere, and people don't seem to like me in Ireland anymore. I should not care to write a play about Ireland just now with a possible bitterness in my heart.[81].

Or, as he remarked to a correspondent of the *Independent*:

I like London, and London likes me. That's more than I can say of Ireland. I have a good deal of courage, but not much patience, and it takes both courage and patience to live in Ireland. The Irish have no time for those that don't agree with their ideas, and I have no time for those who don't agree with mine. So we decided to compromise, and I am coming here.[82]

And how was all of this received in Dublin? As Holloway reported:

Again the Abbey was thronged . . . I had a chat with Brinsley MacNamara, who had been ill for some time. He spoke about the snobbery of O'Casey and his stage Irishman publicity stunt. Mac thinks that O'Casey's plays lower the tone of the Abbey, the players, and the audience. Now that Ireland is getting re-Anglicized, O'Casey's plays just suit the new class of audience who come to see them. O'Casey is insincere, and holds no opinions of his own, and also is devoid of gratitude for good turns done him.

Mrs. Frank Fay thinks the same about him now. His was the snobbery of humility. When she asked him to dinner one Sunday, he replied he always stayed in bed on Sunday, and even though his brother was ill he wouldn't get up to enquire for him.

Monty thought this rather callous on his part and said to him, "I am sure if your mother were ill you'd get up to see *her*?"

And he replied, "Not damn likely; why should I?"

Mrs. Fay lost all interest in him after that. Neither Mac nor Dolan has any place for O'Casey as a friend . . . O'Casey as a depicter of the Irish is only a false prophet with an insincere and distorted view of persons and things.[83]

Or, as John Burke remarked: "Last year it was all Sean O'Casey; now it is all shun O'Casey."[84] Yet it should be pointed out that O'Casey and his play had many supporters in Ireland, and that the initial reception was extremely laudatory. It is true that O'Casey might have looked for support from colleagues like O'Flaherty, Clarke, Higgins, MacNamara, and McCormick. But the Irish are the Irish, and O'Casey was O'Casey; so he said his "Inishfallen, Fare Thee Well," and like Shaw and Joyce was almost never to set foot again in the island for the rest of his long life.

It was not that O'Casey did not love Ireland in his way, or not that Ireland ever ceased to fascinate him. He did write a couple of Englishy plays, but they were probably his least popular ones, and he was never really to be anything but an Irish writer. He was to write of Ireland in the years to come with great and individual brilliance, and some of what he wrote was tinged with acrimony and bitterness. And the acrimony and bitterness were amply reciprocated by some of the Irish; and exacerbated by the war of letters over *The Silver Tassie*, by the mild fuss over *The Bishop's Bonfire*, and by the nonsensical nonproduction of *The Drums of Father Ned*.

One is rather reminded of Faulkner's Quentin Compson who said of the American South, "I don't hate it . . . *I don't hate it* . . . I don't. I don't!"

But whatever the relation, love or hate or some inextricable amalgam of both, it was one that could only be stilled by the playwright's death. By the 1990s the Abbey Theatre has produced most of the later O'Casey plays which it never produced in his lifetime. He, like Yeats and Synge and Shaw and Joyce has been assimilated by time into honour. He is now a Great Irish Writer. Bord Failte has erected a plaque on the site in Dorset Street where he was born. Conceivably, some day someone may erect a statue; for, after all, there are statues of Shaw and Yeats and Joyce. And even Jim Larkin.

But for Ireland, the years of O'Casey ended in March of 1926. There were only three years really, but they were three of the most remarkable in the extraordinary history of the modern Irish drama.

Appendix 1: Edward Martyn and F. J. McCormick on Acting

Astorea Redux by Edward Martyn

The greatest difficulty with which a reforming dramatist in Ireland has to contend is the kind of people whom he is forced to employ as actors. Here he is up against a class of people for the most part whose very last thought is reform. Who, indeed, expects to hear of a performer being a reformer? On the contrary, is it not he, or rather she, that has got the drama into that state of decadence as calls for the reforming dramatist, whose first work must be to depress the performer, since it was the performer's too assertive personality and importance that mostly brought about such decadence? Mind I wish it to be understood that I am now speaking of the ordinary commercial actor and actress. If any of their emulous if un-professional brothers or sisters take my remarks as alluding to themselves, it must be for the urgent reason that their consciences, upon examination, convict them, and they are naturally indignant at an exposure of their being found wanting in amiability and lofty concern for the advancement of Art. I may say at once that for some of the unprofessional brotherhood I have much respect and appreciation.

What is it then that makes the performers' influence so fatal in general to the drama of ideas? The answer is very simple. To promote such a drama you must be interested in ideas. This is obvious. But at the same time it is obvious that the performer is, as a rule, only interested in the vanity of his or her own personality. It is impossible for two such interests to be more dissimilar. You cannot reconcile them. One or other must prevail. One must extinguish the other; and as in this world inferiority often prevails, it is not surprising that this ignoble contest has over and over again led to the shameful decadence of the drama.

And how silly it all is when you consider the average performer's attitude towards an average audience, or the attitude of the audience to the performer. One vies with the other in puerility of aim and abnegation of good sense. Now these people in their ordinary vocations are often sensible enough, a good few often even intellectual; but there is something about the atmosphere of the Theatre which induces a mood of silliness that precludes all sufferance of intellectual preoccupation. It is needless to say that in such an atmosphere the work of a reformer with aspirations towards the realization of an Art Theatre is anything but likely to arrive at an approach to usefulness or even to a hope of satisfactory results. And yet, with the few enthusiasts who are undoubtedly to be found, there is hope nevertheless, that we may gather and keep together, a company that will be more interested in Art than in Philistinism and personal vanity. Then we may be sure that none of these will neglect Art in a chase after flys and futility, none of these will scrap rehearsal for some twopenny-halfpenny tea party, nor swagger about to victimise the unhappy playwright by boasting that the first two or three performances must only be considered as rehearsals, nor frighten the manager with vapours into abdicating his authority in the settlement of the cast, nor join in hostile combinations nor in fine practise any of these old bad insubordinations which somehow have been the disconcerting weakness of the acting crowd.

No, I feel in future I may hope from my actors a new era of Art and peace.

Banba 1 (May 1921), p. 57.

(In a letter to the editor of *Banba*, quoted on p. 61 of the May issue, Martyn adds: "I have thrown together in this little article all I have to say about the Drama at present. It is quite futile to talk about our work in the Theatre at present until some change as is here hinted at takes place. Most of the people around me made development impossible, and finally made chaos.")

Mr. Martyn and the Actor by F. J. McCormick

Mr. Edward Martyn is dissatisfied with Actors. In fact, he is very dissatisfied with them. So much so, that in "Astorea Redux" he tells them bluntly that they are the cause of the decadence of the Drama. It is the Actor's "too assertive personality," his puerility of aim," his want of interest in ideas, and unconcern for "the advancement of Art, "that has brought about the decadence of the Drama. This is what Mr. Martyn says, and considering that he is a dramatist of repute, and has had much to do with actors in his own Theatre in Hardwicke Street, it is natural that people who are interested in the Drama will take his charge against actors very seriously. It is also natural that the actors themselves will take his charge very seriously, and far more natural that their seriousness will be the seriousness of indignant denial. So it is important to ask, is Mr. Martyn's charge true?

In the first place, it is not very clear what Mr. Martyn means by "the shameful decadence of the drama." Is it the decadence of the drama considered merely as dramatic literature, or the decadence of its stage-presentation and treatment by actors, or the decadence of the public taste for dramatic fare? Which is it? Obviously not the first. For drama considered merely as dramatic literature (i.e., written drama as distinct from acted drama) can in no way be affected in its decadence or reform by the actor who doesn't act it, or the audience which doesn't see it acted. The dramatist, safe in the privacy of his study from the vain incompetence of the actor and the philistinism of the audience, can give the most unhampered flight to his creative faculty. He can write what sort of play he likes in whatever manner he likes and embodying what ideas he likes. In the creation of dramatic literature, therefore, the dramatist enjoys a peaceful independence of actor and audience. Consequently, when Mr. Martyn blames actor and audience for the decadence of the drama he can only have in mind the drama as acted and "audienced," if I may coin a word.

But the decadence which Mr. Martyn chiefly deplores is the decadence of the actor-medium through which the dramatist desires to bring his play into fulness of life before the public. That the dramatist does desire this public fulness of life for his play is evident. For when he has written it he is not content merely to read it to a select circle of understanding friends, or to give it to the world in ubiquitous volumes. No! His desire is to clothe the dry bones of his written play with the flesh and blood of acted drama—to give it to an audience *via* the stage. When the dramatist yields to his natural desire to give his play a stage-presentation, then, and then only, does he come into "conflict" with the actor.

Now, whether the actor be a good medium or a bad medium, he is most certainly the only medium through which the dramatist is satisfied to reach the public. And considering that the actor is the only satisfying medium at the dramatist's disposal, it is futile for the dramatist to be impatient with the natural limitations of the medium.

There is not much sense in deploring the fact that we cannot fly. There is more sense in being thankful that we can walk, and there is much more sense in trying to correct lameness. But to indulge in impatient protest against its inconvenience and incapacity is not the way to correct it.

Mr. Martyn has, no doubt, a reasonable cause for his dissatisfaction with actors. If he were, for instance, to bewail the fact that all actors are not good actors, or to imagine that bad actors can be transformed into good ones by hearkening to the needs, or the castigation, of a reforming dramatist—then he would be most unreasonable. But even allowing that Mr. Martyn has a reasonable cause for his dissatisfaction, he has not in "Astorea Redux" made that reasonable cause clear.

It is not, for instance, very clear when and where in his article Mr. Martyn shifts his denunciation from the "commercial" actor to his un-professional brother. It may be mental obfuscation on my part, but I certainly cannot segregate his views on the insubordinate amateur, the "enthusiast," and the commercial actor. No commercial actor, for example, would be guilty of the "bad insubordination" of scrapping rehearsal for "a twopenny-halfpenny tea party" or questioning the manager's settlement of the cast. However lacking the commercial actor may be in "a lofty concern for the advancement of Art" he certainly is not lacking in attention to his business. His Manager sees to that. But since Mr. Martyn states that his remarks particularly apply to the commercial actor, it may be well to question his article from the standpoint of the commercial actor alone.

The performer's influence, he says, is fatal to the "Drama of Ideas," because the performer is not, as a rule, interested in ideas but "only interested in the vanity of his or her own personality." Now, I would like to know what Mr. Martyn means by the Drama of Ideas. "Drama" is a vague term, and "ideas" is a vague term, but linked together they are, to me, annoyingly vague. Does the "Drama of Ideas" mean what the philistinic Yanks call "High-Brow" plays, or, worse still, plays that cater for the esoteric few? If is does, then Mr. Martyn is right when he says that the commercial actor has no interest in it. For the average commercial actor (poor, blind Philistine that he is!) is steeped in a native desire to portray full-blooded human emotions. Rightly or wrongly, he has an inborn objection to become an anaemic mouthpiece for dramatic speculation on the shams of civilisation, the subtleties of sex, or, mayhap, a Neo-Dramatic vision of the Mystery of Being. Rightly or wrongly, he plumps for the normal humanity of ordinary drama and turns his back on the "Drama of Ideas" without even a hint of his having committed artistic suicide.

When Mr. Martyn says that the actor is, as a rule, "only interested in the vanity of his own personality" I confess I don't understand him. If, through any congenital defect of character, an actor's vanity should lead him into thinking: "I'm a fine fellow! a specially-favoured Thespian. My stage-presence is irresistible and my voice captivates the multitude. I'm the greatest thing that ever happened. I'm the last word in acting—your Coquelins and Irvings have nothing on me"; if, by any unfortunate chance, an actor should secretly or openly allow his vanity to carry him into such extravagance—alas! he would be a lamentable idiot. If an actor is blind to his faults and limitations; if through lack of a rational self-criticism he regards himself as a "finished" artist; if he thinks he knows more about the play than the author does, and more about acting than the producer does; if he regards rehearsing as an unnecessary bore, and has an unbounded confidence in things being "all right on the night"; if through sheer superabundance of self-satisfaction he imagines that he can act competently by a spontaneous, undirected urge of Nature—then, indeed, he fully merits Mr. Martyn's condemnation. There may be such vain fools in the acting world—professional and unprofessional. But since Mr. Martyn thinks that vanity is a weakness specially peculiar to the commercial actor, I, as a commercial actor, can assure him that he is mistaken. I know many competent commercial actors in whom not vanity, but its opposite, is a weakness. But supposing that it were true that most commercial actors were eaten up with vanity—better their competent vanity than the incompetent vanity of the amateur. Better the vanity of the professional who *must* try to learn his business than the vanity of the amateur who indulges in "bad insubordinations."

There is, however, a sense in which Mr. Martyn's statements about the actor's personal vanity are true. Even the most brilliant actor does not, I imagine, put his best into a part through any disinterested desire for the "advancement of Art." When he is given a part with "possibilities" in it, be does not, I imagine, apostrophise the abstract advancement of Art, and cry: "Oh! Art! I see thy need of advancement. Let me, according to the measure of my gifts, strive, in this part, to be the humble instrument of thy advancement." From what one knows of actors, that is just what they do not do. The actor's concern is, or should be, to interpret his part as well as he can. He cannot, and he should not try to, stifle that natural pride of personal achievement which is the driving force of his effort to play his part "as well as in him lies." Consequently, any advancement the gifted actor brings to Art will be by the way. If he is a great actor, his advancement of the actors' art will be shown in his work and in the standard he has reached, and accordingly his advancement of the darma will be in his perfecting of the medium through which the drama finds its fullest expression. The drama, therefore, will never suffer through the good actor being swayed by the motive force of personal achievement. But the drama can most certainly suffer through want of proper expression—in other words, through *bad* actors.

I cannot see how Mr. Martyn is going to help the advancement of the drama by selecting both actor and audience for a collective "dig" about their vieing with one another in "puerility of aim and abnegation of good sense." Assuming, even, that actor and audience are hopelessly blind to the high aims of Art, or peculiarly incapable of "intellectual preoccupation," yet Mr. Martyn cannot force them through a process of artistic or intellectual transformation. If they ever come to see the attractive merit of the Drama of Ideas it will be only by voluntary self-adjustment. Having a rather deep sense of their right to their own artistic self-disposal, they will not readily submit to an operation for Aesthetic cataract. They will see the merit of high Art because they *want* to see it and not because Mr. Martyn thinks they *ought* to see it, and if Mr. Martyn wants them to see it he will not achieve his purpose by telling them they are stupidly blind.

Again, I would like to know why the average actor is dubbed "commercial." What constitutes his "commercialism"? Is it the fact that he plays in the drama that managers with a box-office sagacity provide for a philistine public? Or is it because he enters into crassly economic agreements for the sale of such artistry as he has? If the term "commercial" connotes either of these undoubted activities of the average actor, then I think it is a pretty needless term. For by some strange design of Providence actors like to live in houses and wear clothes and eat and drink and smoke and amuse themselves just as reforming dramatists do. And since the actor tries to follow out the design of Providence, he is forced to make such economic agreements as are necessary to the following out of the design. He sells his artistry because selling it is a necessity, and if the pressing desire to live in moderate comfort should drive him from the arid stretches of High Art into the ones of commercial melodrama—then the actor is merely human in preferring melodrama and comfort to the Drama of Ideas and the poorhouse.

Finally, it is regrettable, but true, that the majority of dramatists are not great dramatists. It is equally regrettable and equally true that the majority of actors are not great actors. It is still more regrettable and still more true that the majority of audiences are not understanding ones. And the depressing total of the three regrets is the futile regret that Nature should be so strangely unconcerned about the needs of dramatic reform when she persistently refuses to turn out the much-desired tripartite harmony of author, actor, and audience. Still, there is comfort in the reflection that much has been, and can be, done with Nature.

Banba 1 (June 1921), pp. 141–144.

Appendix 2: Cast Lists

This list attempts to give the date of first publication, the date of first production, and the original cast of the most significant plays of the Irish theater during these years. It includes only the most important plays written in the Irish language; it includes notable foreign plays which were performed by such groups as the Abbey Theatre and the Dublin Drama League; and it omits plays which lack any tincture of literary or theatrical or historical merit.

The plays are listed by date of first production. When the plays were not produced or when the production date is uncertain, they are listed by the date of their first publication. The cast lists, whenever possible, are based upon the original programs, rather than upon the sometimes variant cast lists to be found in the books of some published plays. Often, neither program nor published book was available, and in such cases the cast lists have been formed by a comparison of available newspaper accounts.

Actors occasionally used different forms or even different spellings of their names. We have followed the form used on the particular occasion.

As in the previous two volumes, we have footnoted some of the errors of our colleagues or some of our own uncertainties. Our motive is not a desire to denigrate the work of previous writers, for we owe too great a debt to it. Nevertheless, a checklist of this nature offers the possibility for endless error; and we trust that future historians will correct whatever errors have crept into the present work.

1921

GEORGE SHIELS
Bedmates
A Comedy in One Act.
First produced: 6 January 1921, by the Abbey Company, at the Abbey Theatre, Dublin.

CAST

Pius Kelly	Barry Fitzgerald
Andrew Riddle	Tony Quinn
Bertie Smith	Michael J. Dolan
Molly Swan	Maureen Delany

Unpublished.

Ireland in Revolt
A Documentary Film in Five or Six Reels, produced by *The Chicago Tribune*.
Trade showing in the United States: ca. 5 February 1921.
Photographed by Capt. Edwin F. Weigle

HANS WIERS-JENNSEN
The Witch
A Drama in Four Acts, translated from the Norwegian by John Masefield.

First produced by the Dublin Drama League: 23 February 1921, at the Abbey Theatre, Dublin.*

CAST

Anne	Elizabeth Young

Also with Katherine MacCormack, Amy Lloyd Desmond, Ralph Brereton Barry, Miles Dillon, James Dillon, Gerald Norman, and Michael J. Dolan.

Directed by Elizabeth Young

First published: as *Anne Pedersdotter* (Boston: Little, Brown, 1917); as *The Witch* (New York: Brentano's, 1926).

JOHN MacDONAGH
Paying the Rent
A Film produced by the Film Company of Ireland.
First public showing: (?) 2 February 1921, at the Empire Theatre, Dublin.
The cast included Arthur Sinclair and Jack Morrow.

Written and Directed by John MacDonagh
Photographed by Brian MacGowan

TERENCE J. MacSWINEY
The Revolutionist
A Play in Five Acts.
First produced: 24 February 1921, by the Abbey Company, at the Abbey Theatre, Dublin.

CAST

Mrs. Sullivan	Maureen Delany
John Mangan	Barry Fitzgerald
Father O'Connor, C. C.	Michael J. Dolan
Hugh O'Neill	F. J. McCormick
Con Sheehan	Peter Nolan
Doyle	Maurice Esmonde
Nora Mangan	Gertrude Murphy
Fan O'Byrne	Christine Hayden
Dr. Foley	Alan Duncan
Father O'Hanlon	Eric Gorman
Mackay	P. Kirwin
Bennett	J. Lynch
Maher	G. J. Fallon
Kiely	V. Young
Rohan	Hubert McGuire
Keane	Tony Quinn
Lawlor	U. Wright

Servants, followers, etc.: J. Barlow, P. MacDonnèll, J. McCarthy, M. Gogarty.

Directed by Lennox Robinson

First published: Dublin and London: Maunsel, 1914.

After SAMUEL LOVER
Handy Andy
A Film of 5,900 ft., produced by Ideal Film Company.
London trade showing: February 1921.

* Production unremarked by Clarke and Ferrar.

The cast included Kathleen Vaughan, Fred Morgan, Wallace Bosco, Warwick Ward and Peter Coleman.

Directed by Bert Wynne
Scenario by Eliot Stannard

LADY GREGORY
Aristotle's Bellows
A Wonder Play in Three Acts.
First produced: 17 March 1921, by the Abbey Company, at the Abbey Theatre, Dublin.

CAST

The Mother	Maureen Delany
Celia	Gertrude Murphy
Conan	Barry Fitzgerald
Timothy	F. J. McCormick
Neighbours:	
Rock	Peter Nolan
Flannery	Michael J. Dolan
First Cat	Seaghan Barlow
Second Cat	P. Kirwan

Directed by Lennox Robinson

First published: in *Three Wonder Plays* (London: Putnam, 1923); reprinted in *Collected Plays*, vol. 3 (Gerrards Cross, Buckinghamshire: Colin Smythe, 1970).

NIKOLAI EVREINOV
A Merry Death
A Harlequinade in One Act, translated from the Russian by C. E. Bechhofer.
First produced by the Dublin Drama League: 29 June 1921, at the Abbey Theatre, Dublin.*

CAST

Harlequin	Sydney La Velle
Pierrot	Michael J. Dolan
Columbine	Aida Browne
Doctor	Vincent Kelly
Death	Tony Quinn

Directed by Michael J. Dolan

This translation first published: in *Five Russian Plays* (New York: E. P. Dutton, 1916).

ANATOLE FRANCE
The Man Who Married a Dumb Wife
A Farce in Two Acts, translated from the French by Wilfred and Emilie Jackson.
First produced by the Dublin Drama League: 29 June 1921, at the Abbey Theatre, Dublin.*

CAST

Leonard Botal	F. J. McCormick
Catherine Botal	Christine Hayden

Also with Sydney La Velle, Michael J. Dolan, Peter Nolan, Vincent Kelly, Tony Quinn, Christine Hayden, Madeleine Carroll and Aida Browne.†

Directed by Lennox Robinson

---

* Production unremarked by Clarke and Ferrar.

† Gary Phillips in an unpublished list includes Will Shields (Barry Fitzgerald) in the cast.

This translation first published: in R. M. Smith, *Types of Farce-Comedy* (New York: Prentice-Hall, 1928).

MISS A. M. BUCKTON
The Joy of St. Anne
A Play in Four Scenes.
First produced; ca. 1 August 1921, on the terrace of the Lake Hotel, Glendalough.

CAST

St. Anne	Mrs. Kennedy Cahill
Judith	Lydia Sheean
Joachim	Miles Dillon
Hunter-shepherds	Lettice Baker, Emily Sheean
Young Prince	Miles Dillon
Mountain shepherd	J. Richardson
Hannah	Peggy Richardson

Also with Aileen Smith, Miss Forbes of Avondale, a sheep dog and others.
Directed by Miss A. M. Buckton
No record of publication.

after GEORGE A. BIRMINGHAM
General John Regan
A Film of 6,000 ft., produced by Stoll Picture Productions.
London trade showing: October 1921; viewed by the Irish censor during the week of 21 November 1921.

CAST

Lucius O'Grady	Milton Rosmer
Mary Ellen	Madge Stuart
Horace P. Billings	Ward McAllister
Gallagher	Bertie Wright
Timothy Doyle	Edward O'Neill
Constable Moriarity	Teddy Arundell
Kerrigan	Judd Green
Major Kent	Gordon Parker
Sergeant Colgan	Robert Vollis

Also with Edward Arundell, Wyndham Guise and Mabel Archdale.
Directed by Harold Shaw
Scenerio by W. J. Elliott
Photographed by J. J. Cox
Art Direction by Walter Murton

NIKOLAI EVREINOV
A Merry Death
A Harlequinade in One Act, translated from the Russian by C. E. Bechhofer.
First produced by the Abbey Company: 18 October 1921, at the Abbey Theatre, Dublin.

CAST

Harlequin	Ralph Brereton Barry
Pierrot	Michael J. Dolan
Columbine	Cecile Perry
Doctor	P. Kirwan
Death	Tony Quinn

This translation first published in *Five Russian Plays* (New York: E. P. Dutton, 1916).

CHARLES K. AYRE (CHARLES KERR)
Loaves and Fishes
A Comedy in Three Acts.
First produced: 2 November 1921, by the Ulster Theatre, at the Grand Opera House, Belfast.

CAST

Charlie Curran	C. K. Ayre
James Sloan	Walter Kennedy
Nelly Doran	Marian Crimmins
Mr. Doran	Patrick Denley
Sgt. Lenaghan	J. M Owen
Mrs. Bradley	Muriel Woods
Holy Joe	H. R. Hayward
Mrs. Small	Rose M'Quillan
Auctioneer Bob	J. Black
Tommy Chambers	Norman Gray
Arter Fitzpatrick	Gerald MacNamara

Unpublished.

EDWARD McNULTY
The Courting of Mary Doyle
A Comedy in Three Acts.
First produced: 8 November 1921, by the Abbey Company, at the Abbey Theatre, Dublin.

CAST

Mary Doyle	Florence Marks
John William Rattigan	Michael J. Dolan
Jessie Kieran	Eileen Crowe
Herbert Tisdall	Tony Quinn
Mrs. Kieran	Annie Kirby
Terence Kieran	Barry Fitzgerald
Peter Carmody	Peter Nolan
Townspeople	

First published: Dublin: Gill, 1944.

AUGUST STRINDBERG
The Stronger
A Play in One Act.
First produced by the Dublin Drama League: 13 and 14 November 1921, at at the Abbey Theatre, Dublin.

CAST

Madame X	Elizabeth Young
Mademoiselle Y	Dorothy Casey

A translation by F. I. Ziegler published in *Poet Lore* (Boston, 1906).

HENRY JAMES
The Saloon
A Play in One Act.
First produced by the Dublin Drama League: 13 and 14 November 1921, at the Abbey Theatre, Dublin.

CAST

Owen Wingrave	Brereton Barry
Spencer Coyle	James Duncan
Bobby Lechmere*	Alan Duncan
Kate Julian	Nell Stuart
Mrs. Julian	Elspeth Stephens†
Mrs. Coyle	Jessie Hill†

First published: in *The Complete Plays of Henry James* (Philadelphia: J. B. Lippincott, 1949).

EMILE MAZAUD
A Perfect Day
A Comedy in One Act, translated from the French by Esther Sutro.
First produced by the Dublin Drama League: 13 and 14 November 1921, at the Abbey Theatre, Dublin.

CAST

Mr. Pique	G. J. Fallon‡
Mr. Trouchard	Michael J. Dolan
Mr. Mouton	Peter Nolan
Marie	May Craig
Milkman	G. J. Fallon‡

Unpublished but a typewritten prompt script, dated 1921, is noted in the *National Union Catalogue*.

W. B. YEATS
The King's Threshold, revised version[§]
A Play in One Act.
First production of this version: 15 November 1921, by the Abbey Company, at the Abbey Theatre, Dublin.

CAST

King Guaire	Maurice Esmonde
Seanchan	Frank J. Fay
His pupils	P. J. Carolan, J. Hugh Nagle
The Mayor of Kinvara	Barry Fitzgerald
Two Cripples	M. Connolly, G. J. Fallon
Brian	P. Kirwan
The Lord High Chamberlain	Michael J. Dolan
A Soldier	
A Monk	Eric Gorman
Court Ladies	
First Princess	
Second Princess	Kathleen Fogarty

* Incorrectly spelled "Lechemere" by Clarke and Ferrar.
† These characters unremarked by Clarke and Ferrar.
§ This significant production has been ignored by the historians; however, the critic S. B. Bushrui ably discusses the revision in *Yeats's Verse Plays: The Revisions, 1900–1910* (Oxford: Clarendon Press, 1965).

Fedelm	Eileen Crowe

First publication of this version in *Seven Poems and a Fragment* (Dundrum: The Cuala Press, 1922); slightly revised in *Plays in Prose and Verse* (London: Macmillan, 1922); reprinted in The *Variorum Edition of the Plays of W. B. Yeats*, ed. Russell K. Alspach and Catherine C. Alspach (London: Macmillan; New York: Macmillan, 1966).

BERNARD DUFFY
The Piper of Tavran
A Play in One Act.
First produced: 15 November 1921, by the Abbey Company, at the Abbey Theatre, Dublin.

CAST

The Bishop	Peter Nolan
The Abbot	J. A. Hand
Brother Anselm	V. Young
Brother Lucas	Gabriel J. Fallon
A Lay Brother	Matt Connolly
Donogh O'Grady, the Piper of Tavran	P. Kirwan
A Messenger	Tony Quinn

Friars P. J. Carolan, J. H. Nagle, etc.
Directed By Michael J. Dolan
Unpublished.

ANON.
Room 67
A Play in One Act.
First Irish production: 6 December 1921, at the Theatre Royal, Dublin.

CAST

Stella Courtland	Sara Allgood

Also with Fred O'Donovan, Breffni O'Rourke and Moira Breffni.
No record of publication.

EMILE MAZAUD
A Perfect Day
A Comedy in one Act, translated from the French by Esther Sutro.
First produced by the Abbey Company: 6 December 1921, at the Abbey Theatre, Dublin.*

CAST

Mr. Pique	Gabriel J. Fallon
Mr. Mouton	Peter Nolan
Mr. Trouchard	Michael J. Dolan
Marie	May Craig
Milkman	Gabriel J. Fallon

Unpublished but a typewritten prompt script dated 1921 is noted in the *National Union Catalogue*.

HAROLD CHAPIN
The Marriage of Columbine

*MacNamara and Hunt incorrectly cite 18 October 1921.

A Comedy in Four Acts.
First produced by the Dublin Drama League: 11, 12 and 18 December 1921, at the Abbey Theatre, Dublin.

CAST*

Columbine	Eileen Crowe
Scaramouche	P. J. Carolan
Old Circus Eider	Annie Kirby
Geo. Salamandro	Michael J. Dolan
Alfred Scott	Eric Gorman
Landlady	Mrs. Kirkwood Hackett
Servant at the Inn	Shelah Richards
Servant at the Inn	Alan Duncan
Scott's fiancée	Lini Doran
Clown's small child	James Shields†

First published: London: Samuel French, 1924.

JOHN MacDONAGH
The Irish Jew
A Comedy in Four Acts.
First produced: 12 December 1921, at the Empire Theatre, Dublin.

CAST

Abraham Golder	Pol O'Fearghail
Alderman Daniel Barry	Harry O'Donovan
Councillor Woods	James O'Dea
Sir Alfred Peel	Frank J. Fay
Alderman O'Reilly	Dick Smith
Councillor Sarah Quinn	Mrs. Sean Connolly
Mrs. Golder	Fay Sargent
Douglas	Laurence O'Dea
Mrs. Barry	Patricia Beardwood
Professor Marcano	Frank Purcell

Also with Miss Ellis and S. D. Ellis

Directed by John MacDonagh

Unpublished.

GEORGE SHIELS
Insurance Money
A Comedy in Three Acts.
First produced: 13 December 1921, by the Abbey Company, at the Abbey Theatre, Dublin.

CAST

Richard Moone	Peter Nolan
Tam Erwin	Gabriel J. Fallon
Ann Lilly	Eileen O'Kelly
Thomas Hayes	Tony Quinn
Myles O'Donnegan	Michael J. Dolan
Sheila O'Donnegan	Eileen Crowe

Directed by Lennox Robinson

Unpublished.

*Clarke and Ferrar record only Crowe as Columbine and Carolan as Scaramouche.
†In Phillips' list.

1922

T. C. MURRAY
Aftermath
A Play in Three Acts.
First produced: 10 January 1922, by the Abbey Company, at the Abbey Theatre, Dublin.

CAST

Mrs. O'Regan	Florence Marks
Myles O'Regan	P. J. Carolan
Grace Sheridan	Eileen Crowe
Mrs. Dillon	May Craig
Mrs. Hogan	Maire Sweeney
Mary Hogan	Eileen O'Kelly
Dr. Hugh Manning	Gabriel J. Fallon
Hannah Geary	Helena Moloney
Mrs. McCarthy	Annie Kirby

Directed by Lennox Robinson

First published: Dublin: Talbot Press, 1922.

ANTON CHEKHOV
The Bear
A Jest in One Act, translator unknown.
First produced by the Dublin Drama League: 29 and 30 January 1922, at the Abbey Theatre, Dublin.

CAST*

Popova, Yeliena Ivanovna	Katherine McCormack
Smirnov, Gregory Stepanovich	Paul Farrell
Looka	James O'Dea

Directed by Katherine McCormack

OSCAR WILDE
A Florentine Tragedy
Opening Scene by T. Sturge Moore.
First produced by the Dublin Drama League: 29 and 30 January 1922, at the Abbey Theatre, Dublin.

CAST†

Simone	Paul Farrell
Guido Bardi	Ralph Brereton Barry
Bianca	Elizabeth Young
Marie	Cecile Perry

Directed by Dorothy Macardle‡

First published in *Salome, A Florentine Tragedy, Vera* (Boston and London: J. W. Luce, 1908).

---

*Other than O'Dea as "an aged Footman," the cast is not identified by Clarke and Ferrar.

†Clarke and Ferrar incorrectly list ten players in the cast, and so apparently had not looked at the play.

‡Unremarked by Clarke and Ferrar.

ARTHUR SCHNITZLER*
The Festival of Bacchus
A Comedy in One Act, translator unknown.
First produced by the Dublin Drama League: 29 and 30 January 1922, at the Abbey Theatre, Dublin.

CAST†

Felix Staufner	Alan Duncan
Agnes Staufner	Edith Fitzgerald
Dr. Guido Wernig	Gerald Norman
Waitress	Shelah Richards
Railway Porter	Geoffrey Phibbs‡

Directed by Thomas McGreevy§
A translation by Pierre Loving appears in F. Shay, *Twenty-five Short Plays, International* (New York, 1925).

LENNOX ROBINSON
The Round Table
A Comic Tragedy in Three Acts.
First produced: 31 January 1922, by the Abbey Company, at the Abbey Theatre, Dublin.

CAST

Mrs. Drennan	Helena Moloney
Her children:	
De Courcy Drennan	Barry Fitzgerald
Daisy Drennan	Eileen Crowe
Bee Drennan	Eileen O'Kelly
Jonty Drennan	J. Hugh Nagle
Miss Williams-Williams	May Craig
Christopher Pegum	P. J. Carolan
Mrs. Pegum	Esme Ward
Miss Pegum	Annie Kirby
Philip Flahive	Michael J. Dolan
Fran Franks	Dorothy Lynd
A Woman	Beatrice Elvery
Tom Breen	Tony Quinn
Two Men	Peter Nolan, Gabriel J. Fallon
An elderly woman	Maire Sweeney
A Porter	Patrick Kirwan

Directed by Lennox Robinson
First published: London: Putnam, 1924; revised version, London: Macmillan, 1928.

CANON SHEEHAN
My New Curate
A Religious Drama.
First Irish production: January 1922, by the boys of the Artane Industrial School, Artane.

---

*Clarke and Ferrar incorrectly list H. Schnitzler.
†Not listed by Clarke and Ferrar.
‡In Phillips' list.
§Not listed by Clarke and Ferrar.

A dramatization by John Jordan Douglass was published in Louisville, Kentucky, around 1919.

J. BERNARD MacCARTHY
The Rising Generation
A Comedy in Three Acts.
First public production: 20 February 1922, by the Ballykinlar Players, at the Queen's Theatre, Dublin.*

CAST

James Breen	Jimmie Mulkerns
Mrs. Breen	Dick Saunders
Ita	George Hogan
Kevin Kennedy	Paddy Byrne
Captain Roche	Kit Mullen
Cassidy	Miceal O'Leime
Scattered Sam	Peter Mulvey

First published: Dublin: James Duffy, 1922?

GEORGE BERNARD SHAW
Augustus Does His Bit
A Play in One Act.
First produced by the Dublin Drama League: 6 March 1922, at the Abbey Theatre, Dublin.†

Cast Unknown

First published: in *Heartbreak House, Great Catherine, and Playlets of the War* (New York: Brentano's, 1919); reprinted in *The Bodley Head Bernard Shaw*, Vol. 5 (London: Max Reinhardt, 1972).

GEORGE BERNARD SHAW
The Man of Destiny
A Trifle in One Act.
First produced by the Abbey Company: 9 March 1922, at the Abbey Theatre, Dublin.

CAST

General Napoleon Bonaparte	P. J. Carolan
Giuseppe Grandi	Michael J. Dolan
The Lieutenant	Tony Quinn
The Strange Lady	Eileen Crowe

Directed by Lennox Robinson

First published: in *Plays: Pleasant and Unpleasant* (London: Grant Richards, 1898); reprinted in *The Bodley Head Bernard Shaw*, Vol. 1 (London: Max Reinhardt, 1970).

EUGENE O'NEILL
Diff'rent
A Play in Two Acts.
First produced by the Dublin Drama League: 19 and 20 March, at the Abbey Theatre, Dublin.

---

*Possibly there was an earlier public performance by the Ossory Players, at the Empire Theatre, Kilkenny, on 19 June 1920.

†Unremarked by Clarke and Ferrar.

CAST

Capt. Caleb Williams	P. J. Carolan
Emma Crosby	May Craig
Capt. John Crosby	Barry Fitzgerald
Mrs. Crosby	Edith Dodd
Jack Crosby	Tony Quinn
Harriet Williams	Annie Kirby
Alfred Rogers	Hugh Nagle
Benny Rogers	Alan Duncan

Directed by Lennox Robinson

First published: New York: Boni & Liveright, 1921.

HAROLD CHAPIN
Augustus in Search of a Father
A Play in One Act.
First produced by the Dublin Drama League: 19 and 20 March 1922, at the Abbey Theatre, Dublin.

CAST

Watchman	Michael J. Dolan
Policeman	J. McGrath
Augustus	Ralph Brereton Barry

Directed by Kathleen McCormack

First Published: London: Gowans & Gray, 1911.

JOHN MacDONAGH
The Pride of Petravore
A Comedy in One Act.
First produced: 20 March 1922, at the Empire Theatre, Dublin.

CAST

P. J. Mullarkey, J. P.	James O'Dea
Major Darling, R. M.	Charles L. Keogh
Sergeant Shoebottom, R. I. C.	Harry O'Donvan
Samuel Locke, J. P.	Dick Smith
Andrew Stapleton	Ralph Goggin
Padney Flannery	Patrick Hayden
Eileen O'Brien	Fay Sargent

Directed by John MacDonagh

Unpublished.

DOROTHY MACARDLE
Ann Kavanagh
A Play in One Act.
First produced: 6 April 1922, by the Abbey Company, at the Abbey Theatre, Dublin.

CAST

Miles Kavanagh	P. J. Carolan
Ann	May Craig
Stephen	Tony Quinn
Of the Insurgent Army:	
Redmond	M. Connolly
Ryan	Gabriel J. Fallon
Moran	Maurice Esmonde

Directed by Lennox Robinson

First published: New York: Samuel French, [1937].

M. M. BRENNAN
The Young Man from Rathmines
A Play in One Act.
First produced: 6 April 1922, by the Abbey Company, at the Abbey Theatre, Dublin.

CAST

Mr. Dowd	Michael J. Dolan
Mrs. Dowd	Mai Neville
Mary	Crissie Byrne
Mrs. Sullivan	Sheila Murray
Barney Reilly	Tony Quinn
George Jackson	Gabriel J. Fallon

Directed by Lennox Robinson

First published: Dublin: Talbot Press, 1923.

CHRIS SILVESTER
All in the Play
A Comic Sketch in One Act.
First produced: 17 April 1922, by Chris Silvester's Company, in Cork.

CAST

Patsy	Chris Silvester
Miss Hunter	Kathleen Silvester
The Hon. Mr. Fitzherbert	Jack Courtney
Mr. Hamilton	Leo Keogh

Directed by Chris Silvester

Unpublished.

DR. W. M. CROFTON
The Tangle
A Play in Three Acts, dramatized from an unpublished novel by a Mr. Wilson.
First produced: 22 May 1922, by Madame Kirkwood-Hackett's Company, at the Abbey Theatre, Dublin.

CAST

Prof. Serpl-Bruce	Harry O'Donovan
Marjorie Jackson*	Ellen Hare
Dr. James Donovan	Richard Bryan (Bryan Cooper)
Mrs. Serpl-Bruce	Mme. Kirkwood-Hackett
Copley [?]	James O'Dea

Also with Beatrice Elvery, May Burke, Joclyn Foster and F. Richards.

Directed by Madame Kirkwood-Hackett

Unpublished.

FHEIR MAIGHE
The Cure for Nerves
A Farce in One Act.
First produced: 29 May 1922, by the Leeside Players, at the Opera House, Cork.

CAST

Matron	Nan Barry
Nurse Rooney	Hanna MacCarthy
Nurse Banks	Criss Egar

*Frank J. Hugh O'Donnell says "Dawson."

The Porter	D. J. Daly
Mr. McGufferty, Junr	Jack Healy
Mr. McGufferty, Senr	Robert F. Day
Dr. Thomas Brennan	Tim O'Connell

Unpublished.

JOHN MacDONAGH
The Casey Millions
A Film of Four Reels, produced by Irish Photo-Plays, Ltd.
First trade showing: 25 July 1922, at the Grafton Picture House, Dublin.

CAST

Bert Casey	Fred Jeffs
Peg Casey	Nan Fitzgerald
Jerry	Chris Silvester
Luke Casey	James O'Dea
The Widow Casey	Kathleen Drago
Prof. Al Fresco	Barrett McDonnell

Also with Joan Fitzgerald, Christine Hayden and Frank J. Fay
Written and directed by John MacDonagh
Photographed by Alfred H. Moise

R. J. RAY
The Moral Law
A Play in One Act.
First produced: 29 August 1922, by the Abbey Company, at the Abbey Theatre, Dublin.

CAST

John Shannon	Michael J. Dolan
Mrs. Shannon	Helena Moloney
Michael Shannon	P. J. Carolan
Sergeant Bullen	Maurice Esmonde
A Military Captain	Eric Gorman
Two Soldiers	P. J. McDonnell, W. O'Hara

Unpublished.

M. M. BRENNAN
*A Leprechaun in the Tenement**
A Play in One Act.
First produced: 5 September 1922, by the Abbey Company, at the Abbey Theatre, Dublin.

CAST

Mr. Reilly†	Barry Fitzgerald
Mrs. Reilly	Sheila Murray
Alice Kate	Eileen Crowe
Mickey Reilly	Tony Quinn
The Widow Murphy	May Craig
A dog‡	

*MacNamara, Fay and Hunt incorrectly record *The Leprechaun in the Tenement*.
†W. J. Lawrence in *The Stage* lists "Pat Reilly."
‡This actor unremarked by previous historians.

Directed by Lennox Robinson

Unpublished.

GERALD MacNAMARA
Throwbacks
First produced: 8 September 1922, by the Ulster Theatre, at the Playhouse, Liverpool.
Cast unknown

Unpublished.

ANON.
True Irish Hearts
A Play in Six Scenes.
First Irish production: 25 September 1922, at the Queen's Theatre, Dublin.

CAST

Rev. Jim O'Neill	Valentine Vousden
Grizzley Adams	Frank Dalton
Bob O'Neill	William Melvyn
Laddie O'Neill	Charles L. Keogh
Mrs. Donovan	Molly Douglas
May Driscoll	Dallas Yorke
Joan Corrigan	Mabel Spencer
Crowley	Gilbert Elvin
Gad	Babs Dalton

No record of publication.

GEORGE SHIELS
Paul Twyning
A Comedy in Three Acts.
First produced: 3 October 1922, by the Abbey Company, at the Abbey Theatre, Dublin.

CAST

Paul Twyning	Barry Fitzgerald
James Deegan	Gabriel J. Fallon
Dan Deegan	Michael J. Dolan
Patrick Deegan	P. J. Carolan
Mrs. Deegan	May Craig
Jim Deegan	Tony Quinn
Denis M'Gothigan	Eric Gorman
Rose M'Gothigan	Eileen Crowe
Daisy Mullen	Christine Hayden
Mr. O'Hagan	Peter Nolan

Directed by Lennox Robinson

Fisst published in *Professor Tim and Paul Twyning* (London: Macmillan, 1927).

PADRAIC COLUM and E. WASHBURN FREUND*
Grasshopper†

*MacNamara omits Freund.

†In Belasco's original production in New York, the play was also simply called *Grasshopper*. Probably through carelessness, MacNamara, Fay, and Hunt cite *The Grasshopper*. However, Colum himself may not have made up his mind; for instance, on the holograph title page of the manuscript in the library of the State University of New York, Binghamton, he uses the article.

A Play in Four Acts, adapted from the German of Count Keyserling.
First produced by the Abbey Company: 24 October 1922, at the Abbey Theatre, Dublin.

CAST

Role	Actor
Michael Dempsey	Gabriel J. Fallon
Anne Dempsey	Aoife Taafe
Maeve Dempsey	May Craig
Bridget	Christine Hayden
Sheila	Eileen Crowe
Thady	P. J. Carolan
Matt O'Connor	Maurice Esmonde
Judy	Eileen O'Kelly
Jillin	Sheila Murray
Father Myles	Michael J. Dolan
Sara	Kathleen Fortune
Johanna	Irene Murphy
Tracey Nowlan	Tony Quinn
Thomas Bacach	Michael J. Dolan
Bat Croskerry	M. Connolly
Mark Brogan	P. J. Carolan
Eamon Hynes	M. McCarthy
Murty Lynott	Clement Kenny
Mrs. Gilsenin	Sheila Murray
Old Catty	Lini Doran

Directed by Lennox Robinson

Unpublished.

EUGENE BRIEUX
The Three Daughters of M. Dupont
A Play in Four Acts, translated from the French by St. John Hankin.
First produced by the Dublin Drama League: 5 and 6 November 1922, at the Abbey Theatre, Dublin

CAST

Role	Actor
M. Dupont	James O'Dea
Mme. Dupont	Edith Dodd
Courthezon*	Michael J. Dolan
Caroline*	May Craig
Julie†	Margot Brunton
Justine*	
M. Mairaut*	Gabriel J. Fallon
Mme. Mairaut*	Christine Hayden
Antonin Mairaut	Ralph Brereton Barry
Lignol*	P. J. Carolan
M. Pouchelet*	Eric Gorman
Mme. Pouchelet*	Edith Brambell‡
Francoise*	Shelah[§] Richards
Angele*	Cecile Perry

*These characters unremarked by Clarke and Ferrar.
†Merely called Antonin's Wife by Clarke and Ferrar.
‡Incorrectly spelled "Brombell" by Clarke and Ferrar.
§Incorrectly spelled "Shelia" by Clarke and Ferrar.

Directed by Michael J. Dolan

This translation first published in *Three Plays* (London: A. C. Fifield, 1911).

LENNOX ROBINSON

Crabbed Youth and Age

A Little Comedy in One Act.

First produced: 14 November 1922, by the Abbey Company, at the Abbey Theatre, Dublin.

CAST

Mrs. Swan	Helena Moloney
Her daughters:	
Minnie Swan	Christine Hayden
Eileen Swan	May Craig
Dolly Swan	Eileen Crowe
Gerald Booth	Gabriel J. Fallon
Charlie Duncan	P. J. Carolan
Tommy Mims	Tony Quinn

Directed by Lennox Robinson

First published: Dublin and New York: Putnam, 1924.

JOHN MacDONAGH

Wicklow Gold

A Film in Four Reels, produced by Irish Photo-Plays, Ltd.

First trade showing: ca. 20 November 1922, at La Scala Theatre, Dublin.

CAST

Dr. Daniel MacCarthy	Fred Jeffs
Larry O'Toole	Jimmy O'Dea
Kitty O'Byrne	Ria Mooney
Ned O'Toole	Chris Sylvester
Moira Cullen	Nan Fitzgerald
Widow O'Byrne	Kathleen Carr

Also with Barrett MacDonnell, Frank J. Fay, Eileen Hayden, Joan Fitzgerald and Mme. Kirkwood-Hackett.

Directed by John MacDonagh

ROBERT BROWNING

*A Blot on the 'Scutcheon**

A Tragedy in Three Acts, abridged by Lennox Robinson.

First produced by the Dublin Drama League: 3 and 4 December 1922, at the Abbey Theatre, Dublin

CAST

Mildred Tresham	Eileen Crowe
Guendolen Tresham	Jessie Hill†
Thorold, Lord Tresham‡	P. J. Carolan
Henry, Earl Mertoun	Torrance Gardener (Gardener Hill)§

*Clarke and Ferrar incorrectly cite *The Blot in the Scutcheon*.

†This character and actress unremarked by Clarke and Ferrar.

‡This character unremarked by Clarke and Ferrar.

§Phillips lists this actor as Torrance Gardner; Clarke and Ferrar list him as Gardiner Hill; we are not sure what is correct.

Gerard*	Michael J. Dolan
Austin Tresham†	J. A. Hand

Directed by Frank J. Fay
Casting by Lennox Robinson

ANTON CHEKHOV
The Jubilee
A Jest in One Act, translator unknown.
First produced by the Dublin Drama League: 3 and 4 December 1922, at the Abbey Theatre, Dublin.

CAST‡

Andrey Shiputchin	Andrew Dillon
Tatyana Alexeyevna	Angela Coyne
Nastasya Fyodorovna	Katherine MacCormack
Ivan Fyodorovna	James O'Dea

after DION BOUCICAULT
My Wild Irish Rose
A Film of Seven Reels and about 7,650 ft., produced by the Vitagraph Company of America and based on *The Shaughraun*.
New York premiere: 11 June 1922.
Irish trade showing: 8 December 1922, at the Corinthian Theatre, Dublin.

CAST

Conn the Shaughraun	Pat O'Malley
Arte O'Neale	Helen Howard
Claire Ffolliott	Maud Emery
Moya	Pauline Starke
Robert Ffolliott	Edward Cecil
Captain Molineaux	Henry Herbert
Corry Kinchella	James Farley
Harvey Duff	Bobby Mack
Father Dolan	Frank Clark
Barry	Richard Daniels

Directed by David Smith
Scenario by C. Graham Baker
Photographed by Stephen Smith, Jr.

GUZMAN ENNIS
Jack the Giant-Killer
A Pantomime.
First produced: 26 December 1922, at the Everyman Theatre, the Rotunda, Dublin.

CAST

Jack of the Magic Sword	Kathleen Page
Weary Willie	Noel Purcell
Molly Green	Winnie Atkinson
Inn-Keeper	G. Williams

*Incorrectly spelled by Clarke and Ferrar.
†This character and actress unremarked by Clarke and Ferrar.
‡Clarke and Ferrar supply the last names of the actors, but not the names of the characters.

Dame Swanky	Joe Masterson
Waiter	John McKeon
Constable	J. McNamee
Tragedian	Will Andrews
Dandy Dan	G. Gilbert
Gipsy Queen	Norah Drury
Fairy Queen	Pauline Roche
Demon King	Charles Farrell
Giant Blunderbore	Guzman Ennis
Imps	Misses E. and N. Kavanagh Masters M. Conroy and W. Carson

Directed by T. J. Powell
Ballet trained by Aileen Lennox-Magee
Orchestra of ten, conducted by John Clarke

Unpublished.

MARGARET E. DOBBS
Village Plays: Four Plays from the County Antrim
Containing *The Doctor and Mrs. Macauley, She's Going to America,** *A Man and a Brother*, and *Storm in a Tea Cup*.
First published: Dundalk: Tempest, 1922.

P. J. O'CONNOR DUFFY
The Treasure of the Mountain: The Victory of Christ
Two One-Act Plays.
First published: London: Arthur H. Stockwell, 1922.

CONSTANCE POWELL-ANDERSON
The Courting of the Widow Malone
A Comedy in One Act.
First published: London & Glasgow: Gowans and Gray; Boston: L. Phillips, 1922; first published in Irish as *An Suirghle leis an mBaintreach*, translated by Fiachra Eilgeach (Richard Foley) (Ath Cliath: An Comhar, 1927).

1923

J. BERNARD MacCARTHY
The Long Road to Garranbraher
A Play in One Act.
First producted: 9 January 1923, by the Abbey Company, at the Abbey Theatre, Dublin.

CAST

Captain Peter Hanley	Michael J. Dolan
Jude, his wife	Eileen O'Kelly
Dan, their son	F. J. McCormick
Marcus Coyle	Tony Quinn
Seumas Doran	P. J. Carolan
Mrs. O'Brien	Christine Hayden

*This play had previously been separately published: (Dundalk: Dundalgan, 1920).

Maura Mulligan	May Craig

First published: Dublin: Gill, 1928.

after GERTRUDE PAGE
Paddy-the-Next-Best-Thing
A Film of 7,200 ft., produced by the Graham-Wilcox Company, London, and based on the Page novel and the Gayer-Mackay play.
London trade showing: January 1923.
Cast included Mae Marsh as Paddy, Lilian Douglas, Darby Foster, G. K. Arthur, Haidee Wright, Nina Boucicault, Tom Coventry, Simeon Stuart and Mildred Evelyn.

Directed by Graham Cutts
Photographed by Rene Guissart

ST. JOHN HANKIN
The Return of the Prodigal
A Comedy in Four Acts.
First produced by the Dublin Drama League: 11 and 12 February 1923, at the Abbey Theatre, Dublin.

CAST

Samuel Jackson*	Fred Jeffs
Mrs. Jackson†	Mrs. Kirkwood Hackett
Henry Jackson*	Hugh O'Neill
Eustace Jackson	Ralph Brereton Barry
Violet Jackson‡	M. Coghlan[§]
Sir John Faringford*	Walter Bryan
Lady Faringford[//]	C. White[#]
Stella Faringford*	M. Harmon Whyte[#]
Dr. Glaisher	James O'Dea
The Rev. C. Pratt*	Barrett MacDonnell
Mrs. Cyril Pratt*	Freda Fay
Baines*	Jackson Dunne[¶]
Footman*	H. Phillipson

First published: New York: Samuel French, ca. 1907; reprinted in *The Dramatic Works of St. John Hankin*, Vol. 1 (London: Martin Secker, 1912)

CONSTANCE POWELL-ANDERSON
The Passing of Peter
A Comedy in Three Acts.
First produced: 22 February 1923, at a charity matinee at the Gaiety Theatre, Dublin.
Cast included Averil Deverill, Miss L. Bailey, Helga Burgess, Edgar Davidson, Herbert Bailey, and J. P. Hogan.

Directed by Herbert Bailey

---

*This character unremarked by Clarke and Ferrar.
†Called The Mother by Clarke and Ferrar.
‡Called The Sister by Clarke and Ferrar.
§Possibly Margaret Coughlin.
//Misspelled Farrington by Clarke and Ferrar.
#Clarke and Ferrar incorrectly cite Harman White.
♦Clarke and Ferrar spell this actress's name as Harman White.
¶Clarke and Ferrar spell this actor's name as Dunn.

CONSTANCE POWELL-ANDERSON
The Heart of a Clown
A Fantasy in One Act.
First produced: (?) 22 February 1923, at a charity matinee at the Gaiety Theatre, Dublin.

CAST

Columbine	Phyllis Wakely
Gipsy	Lydia Sheehan
Harlequin	Ralph Brereton Barry
Clown	Herbert Bailey

First published: London and Glasgow: Gowans and Gray; Boston: L. Phillips, 1920.

JOHN STEPHENSON
Sally Kavanagh
A Play adapted from the novel by Charles J. Kickham.
First produced: 25 February 1923, by the Father Mathew Dramatic Society, at the Father Mathew Hall, Dublin.

CAST

Sally Kavanagh	Mary Rowe
Coner Shea	John Hill

Also with John Buckley, Joseph Duffy and John Buckley, Jr.
Unpublished.

GEORGE FITZMAURICE
'Twixt the Giltinans and the Carmodys*
A Comedy in One Act.
First produced: 8 March 1923, by the Abbey Company, at the Abbey Theatre, Dublin.

CAST

Bileen Twomey	Arthur Shields
Shuvawn	Eileen O'Kelly
Old Jane	May Craig
Michael Clancy	Michael J. Dolan
Bridie Giltinan	Eileen Crowe
Mrs. Giltinan	Maureen Delany
Simon Giltinan	F. J. McCormick
Madge Carmody	Gertrude Murphy
Mrs. Carmody	Christine Hayden
Jamesie Carmody	Peter Nolan

Directed by Lennox Robinson

First published in *The Dublin Magazine* (Jan.–Mar. 1943); first book publication in *The Plays of George Fitzmaurice: Realistic Plays* (Dublin: Dolmen Press, 1970).

HENRIK IBSEN
A Doll's House
A Play in Three Acts, translated by R. Farquharson Sharp.
First produced by the Abbey Company: 22 March 1923, at the Abbey Theatre, Dublin.

CAST

Torvald Helmer	F. J. McCormick
Nora	Eileen Crowe

*Incorrectly spelled as "Giltenans" by Malone, MacNamara, Kavanagh, and Hunt.

Doctor Rank	Michael J. Dolan
Mrs. Linde	Christine Hayden
Nils Krogstad	Arthur Shields
Helen	May Craig
Children	James Shields, Raymond Fardy
A Porter	P. J. McDonnell

Directed by Lennox Robinson

This translation first published in *A Doll's House, and Two Other Plays* (London: J. M. Dent; New York: E. P. Dutton, [1910].

GERALD MacNAMARA
Fee Faw Fum
An Heroic Farce in One Act.
First produced: in Easter Week, 1923, by the Ulster Theatre, in Derry.

CAST

Conn Lig, an Ulster giant	Rutherford Mavne
Brigid, his wife	Rose M'Quillan
Cliodhna, their daughter	Marian Crimmins
Scrapius	Walter Kennedy
MacNab	J. R. Mageean
Dubh, a Druid	Gerald MacNamara
Olaf	H. Richard Hayward

Unpublished.

OLIVER GOLDSMITH
She Stoops to Conquer
A Comedy in Five Acts.
First produced by the Abbey Company: 2 April 1923, at the Abbey Theatre, Dublin.*

CAST

Sir Charles Marlow	Maurice Esmonde
Young Marlow	Arthur Shields
Hardcastle	Michael J. Dolan
Mrs. Hardcastle	Maureen Delany
Miss Hardcastle	Eileen Crowe
Tony Lumpkin	Barry Fitzgerald
Hastings	F. J. McCormick
Miss Neville	Christine Hayden
Diggory	Gabriel J. Fallon
Pimple	May Craig
Landlord	P. J. Carolan

Servants and Shabby Fellows: G. Lavelle, P. J. McDonnell, Seaghan Barlow, Tony Quinn, J. Finn, J. Bunyan, W. O'Hara, etc.

Directed by Lennox Robinson

First published: London: F. Newbery, 1773

SEAN O'CASEY
The Shadow of a Gunman
A Tragedy in Two Acts.
First produced: 12 April 1923, by the Abbey Company, at the Abbey Theatre, Dublin.†

*Malone, MacNamara, Kavanagh, and Hunt incorrectly list 22 April.
†Malone, MacNamara, Kavanagh, and Hunt incorrectly list 9 April.

Residents in the tenement:	
Donal Davoren	Arthur Shields
Seumas Shields	F. J. McCormick
Tommy Owens	Michael J. Dolan
Adolphus Grigson	P. J. Carolan
Mrs. Grigson	May Craig
Minnie Powell	Gertrude Murphy
Mr. Mulligan	Eric Gorman
Mr. Maguire	G. V. Lavelle
Residents of an adjoining tenement:	
Mrs. Henderson	Christine Hayden
Mr. Gallogher	Gabriel J. Fallon
An Auxiliary	Tony Quinn

Directed by Lennox Robinson

First published: in *Two Plays* (London: Macmillan, 1925); reprinted separately, London and New York: French's Acting Edition, 1932; in *Collected Plays*, vol. 1 (London: Macmillan, 1949).

GEORGE BERNARD SHAW
Misalliance
First produced by the Dublin Drama League: 16, 17, and 18 April 1923, at the Abbey Theatre, Dublin, in a presentation by A. E. Filmer's Company from Birmingham.*

CAST

John Tarleton	Graham Stuart
Bentley Summerhays	Walter McEwen
Hypatia Tarleton	Phyllis Relph
Mrs. Tarleton	Ethel Lodge
Lord Summerhays	John H. Moore
Johnny Tarleton	Ernest Holloway
Joseph Percival	Ronald Sinclair
Lina Sczepanowska	Beatrice Filmer
Julius Baker	Charles Marford

Directed by A. E. Filmer

LUIGI PIRANDELLO
Six Characters in Search of an Author
Translated by Mrs. W. A. Greene.
First produced by the Dublin Drama League: 19, 20, and 21 April 1923, by A. E. Filmer's Company from Birmingham.†

CAST

Father	Orlando Barnet
Mother	Beatrice Filmer
Step Daughter	Phyllis Relph
Son	Graham Stuart
Boy	S. Ellis
Little Girl	Eileen Cullen
Madame Page	Ethel Lodge
Actor	Ernest Holloway

*Not cited by Clarke and Ferrar.
†Not cited by Clarke and Ferrar.

Leading Lady	Erin Creswell
Leading Man	John Moore
Heavy Lady	Freda Fay
Juvenile Lady	Miss Thornton
Juvenile Man	Ronald Sinclair
Stage Manager	Frank J. Fay
Prompter	Charles Marford
Stage Door Keeper	Walter McEwen

Directed by A. E. Filmer

ST. JOHN ERVINE
Mary, Mary, Quite Contrary
A Light Comedy in Four Acts.
First produced: 14 May 1923, by Players from the Abby Theatre, at the Abbey Theatre, Dublin.*

CAST

Mrs. Considine	May Craig
Sheila, her niece	Margot Brunton
Geoffrey, her son	Arthur Shields
Sir Henry Considine	F. J. McCormick
Rev. Canon Peter Considine, M. A.	Barry Fitzgerald
Mary Westlake	Christine Hayden
Mr. Hobbs	Michael J. Dolan
Jenny	Gertrude Murphy
Miss Mimms	Nell Stuart
Mr. Beeby	Peter Nolan

Directed by Eric Gorman
First published: London: George Allen and Unwin, [1923].

ANTON CHEKHOV
An Bear
A Play in One Act, translated into Irish from the Russian by Risteard O Foghludha.
First produced: (?) 24 July 1923, at the Gaiety Theatre, Dublin.
No record of publication.

RISTEARD O FOGHLUDHA
Cambeal na Ceille Meire
A Play in One Act.
First produced: 24 July 1923, at the Gaiety Theatre, Dublin.
No record of publication.

GEAROID O LOCHLAINN
Bean an Milliuna
A Play in One Act.
First produced: (?) 24 July 1923, at the Gaiety Theatre, Dublin.
Cast included Maire Ni hOisin, Padraig O Broite, Tadg O Scanaill, and Gearoid O Lochlainn.
First Published: Baile Atha Cliath: Clodhanna Gaedhealacha, 1923.

*Not, however, an Abbey production.

G. MOLYNEUX PALMER and REV. THOMAS O'KELLY
Sruth na Maoile
An Opera with Music by Palmer and Libretto in Irish by O'Kelly.
First produced: 25 July 1923, at the Gaiety Theatre, Dublin.

CAST

Aebhric	Joseph O'Neill
Caitlin	Nora Hill
Finola	Eileen Gunning
Fiachra	Monica Warner
Conn	Miss Galloway Rigg
Bobh Dearg	J. W. Hobbs
Lir	O'Carroll Reynolds

Also with Miss Doran, Joan Burke, Florence Howley, Miss Hill, Josephine Lyons, W. J. Lemass and Mr. Reynolds.

Directed by Joseph O'Mara
Conducted by Vincent O'Brien
Costumes by P. J. Tuohy and P. J. Bourke
Dances by Miss Murtagh's pupils

No record of publication.

FAND O'GRADY (KATHLEEN CRUISE O'BRIEN)
Apartments
A Comedy in One Act.
First produced: 3 September 1923, by the Abbey Company, at the Abbey Theatre, Dublin.

CAST

Mrs. MacCarthy*	Sara Allgood
Michael MacCarthy	Michael J. Dolan
Her daughters:	
Geraldine MacCarthy	Gertrude Murphy
Maude MacCarthy†	Irene Murphy
Boarders at Mrs. MacCarthy's:	
Mr. Kiernan	Arthur Shields
Mr. O'Flaherty	F. J. McCormick
Miss O'Rourke	Pearl Moore
Mrs. Quinn	Eileen Crowe

Directed by Lennox Robinson

First published in *The Journal of Irish Literature*, vol. 13, no. 3 (September 1984), pp. 54–70.

SEAN O'CASEY
Kathleen Listens In‡

**The Journal of Irish Literature* printing, following Fand O'Grady's typescript, has "McCarthy."

†*The Journal of Irish Literature* printing, following Fand O'Grady's typescript, describes this character as Mrs. McCarthy's sister-in-law, and omits her first name.

‡In the original production, the title was spelled *Cathleen Listens In*, although the character's name in the cast list is spelled "Kathleen. Also in the original program, O'Houlihan's first name is spelled "Meehawl" and Thornton's first name is given as "Thomas." The spellings in this list are based on those of the extant Abbey typescripts of the play, and were used in they play's first book publication.

A Phantasy in One Act.
First produced: 1 October 1923, by the Abbey Company, at the Abbey Theatre, Dublin.

CAST

Miceawl O'Houlihan	F. J. McCormick
Sheela O'Houlihan	Maureen Delany
Kathleen	Eileen Crowe
Tomaus Thornton	Barry Fitzgerald
Jimmy	Michael J. Dolan
The Man in the Kilts	Gabriel J. Fallon
The Free Stater	Arthur Shields
The Republican	Tony Quinn
The Business Man	U. Wright
The Farmer	Maurice Esmonde
The Doctor	Eric Gorman
The Man with the Big Drum	Peter Nolan
Two Men	Walter Dillon, P. J. Carolan

Directed by Lennox Robinson

First published in *Tulane Drama Review* (June 1961); revised version in *Feathers from the Green Crow*, ed., Robert Hogan (Columbia: University of Missouri Press, 1962; London: Macmillan, 1963).

ARCHIE INGLIS
The Inheritance
A Drama in One Act.
First produced: 1 October 1923, by the Queen's Island Operatic and Dramatic Society, at the Ulster Hall, Belfast.

CAST

Quinton Cole	G. L. Clarke
Margaret	Mary Munn
Lucy	Jean Gulston
Simon Cole	Jackson G. Smyth
Mrs. Jane Cole	Nan Bell
Peter Cole	Wilfred Campbell
Fenton Monteith	A. Inglis

No record of publication.

VICTOR O'D. POWER
The Lost Heir
First produced: 15 October, in Dublin.

CAST

Jacky Lee	Harry O'Donovan
Father Jerry	Gerald Rock
Denis McGrath	Brendan O'Sullivan
Flurry Conn	Frank O'Donovan
Nellie	Ada Keogh
Nonie	Kitty MacMahon
Kitty the Hare	Molly Douglas

No record of publication.

GREGORIO MARTINEZ SIERRA
The Kingdom of God
A Play in Three Acts, translated from the Spanish by Helen and Harley Granville-Barker.

First produced by the Dublin Drama League: 21 and 22 October 1923, at the Abbey Theatre, Dublin.

CAST

Old man	Tony Quinn
Gabriel	Michael J. Dolan
Trajano	Barry Fitzgerald
Sister Gracia*	Eileen Crowe
Sister Juliana	Gertrude Murphy
Sister Manuela	Christine Hayden
Don Lorenzo	J. Hand
Maria Isabel	J. Hill Tulloch
Lulu	Edith Campbell†
Liborio	Gabriel Fallon
Candelas	Katherine MacCormack
Cecilia	Beatrice Elvery
The Dumb Girl	Shelah Richards
Sister Cristiana	Esme Ward
Sister Feliciana	Dorothy Lynd
Quica	Lini Doran
Margarita	Margaret Guinness
Enrique	F. J. McCormick
Sister Dionisia	Maureen Delany
Engracia	Joan Sullivan
Lorenza	Pearl Moore
The Innocent	Cecile Perry
Morineto	James Shields
Policarpo	Eric Gorman
Vincente	P. J. Carolan
Paquita	Norma Joyce
Juan de Dios	Ralph Brereton Barry
Felipe	Tony Quinn

Directed by Arthur Shields
Sets by Seaghan Barlow

First publication of this translation in *The Plays of G. Martinez Sierra*, vol. 2 (London: Chatto and Windus, 1923).

HENRIK IBSEN
An Enemy of the People
A Play in Five Acts, translator unknown.
First produced by the Northern Drama League: 8, 9, and 10 November 1923, at the Great Hall of Queen's University, Belfast.

CAST

Dr. Stockmann	Robert H. McCandless
Mrs. Stockmann	Mary Crothers
Peter Stockmann	Charles E. Harwood
Morten Kiil	Archie Inglis
Hovsted	Robert Ervine
Billing	George C. Clarke

*Misspelled Garcia by Clarke and Ferrar.
†Misspelled Cambell by Clarke and Ferrar.

Aslaksen — James Egan
Petra — Irene Boyd
Ejlif and Morten — Robert K. Hobsen and Lucie Young
Captain Horster — John Hagan
Citizens: Doreen Crawford, Florence M'Leish, Alfred Kerr, Wilfred Campfield, Edward N. Crothers and Wm. L. Brattan.

Directed by Robert H. M'Candless
Stage Manager, Archie Inglis

MAIRE NI CHINNEIDE
An Dutchas
A Play in One Act.
Produced: 12 November 1923, by the Gaelic Players, at the Abbey Theatre, Dublin.*
First published: Baile Atha Cliath: Connradh na Gaedhilge, 1908.

J. M. SYNGE
Vaigneas an Ghleanna
A Play in One Act, translated by Fiachra Eilgeach (Richard Foley) from Synge's *In the Shadow of the Glen*.
First produced: (?) 12 November 1923, by the Gaelic Players, at the Abbey Theatre, Dublin.
No record of publication.

PIARAS BEASLAOI
Fear an Sceilin Ghrinn
A Play in One Act.
First produced: 12 November 1923, by the Gaelic Players, at the Abbey Theatre, Dublin.
First published: Ath Cliath: an Comhar Dramuiochta, n.d.

HUBERT BATH and CARLOS LINATE
Bubbles
An Opera in One Act, with Music by Bath and Libretto by Linate, based on *Spreading the News* by Lady Gregory.
First produced: 26 November 1923, by the Carl Rosa Opera Company, at the Grand Opera House, Belfast.

CAST

Mrs. Fallon — Eva Turner
Mrs. Tarpey — Gladys Parr
Mrs. Tully — Olive Gilbert
Bartley Fallon — Appleton Moore
Jack Smith — Ben Williams
The Magistrate — Booth Kitchen
The Policeman — Parkyn Newton
Timothy Casey — Jack Wright
Shaun Early — Martin Quinn

*Assuredly not the first production, but the first we have noticed.

James Ryan	Martin O'Connor

No record of publication.

BRINSLEY MacNAMARA (JOHN WELDON)
The Glorious Uncertainty
A Comedy in Three Acts.
First produced: 27 November 1923, by the Abbey Company, at the Abbey Theatre, Dublin.

CAST

Gabriel Cunneen	P. J. Carolan
Julia Cunneen	Sara Allgood
Susie Cunneen	Eileen Crowe
Sam Price	Barry Fitzgerald
Simon Swords	Michael J. Dolan
Mortimer Clyne	Peter Nolan
Andy Whelehan	F. J. McCormick
Montague Smith-Willoughby*	Arthur Shields
Sylvester Seery	Gabriel J. Fallon

Directed by Lennox Robinson
First published: Dublin: P. J. Bourke, 1959.

RUTHERFORD MAYNE (SAMUEL J. WADDELL)
Phantoms
A Play in One Act.
First produced: 28 November 1923, by the Ulster Theatre, at the Gaiety Theatre, Dublin.

CAST

Gnu	J. R. Mageean
Hag U.	Josephine Mayne
Danon	Richard Hayward
Seeki	Charles K. Ayre
The Gowlan	Rutherford Mayne
Seeva	Jean Woods

First published in *The Dublin Magazine* (December 1923).

M. M. BRENNAN
Napoleon and the Triplets
A Play in One Act.
First produced: 2 December 1923, by the Kincora Players, at the Abbey Theatre, Dublin.
No record of publication.

HENRI LENORMAND
Time Is a Dream
A Play in Six Scenes, translated from the French by Thomas McGreevy.†
First produced by the Dublin Drama League: 9 and 10 December 1923, at the Abbey Theatre, Dublin.

*Robinson incorrectly has "Montague-Smith Willoughby."
†Translator not noted by Clarke and Ferrar.

CAST

Nico Van Eyden	F. J. McCormick*
Saidyah	M. J. Dolan†
Romee Cremers	Eileen Crowe
Riemkie Van Eyden	Edith Dodd
Mrs. Beunke	Lini Saurin

Directed by Arthur Shields

This translation unpublished.

GILBERT CANNAN
Everybody's Husband
A Play in One Act.
First produced by the Dublin Drama League: 9 and 10 December 1923, at the Abbey Theatre, Dublin.

CAST

A Girl	Shelah Richards
Her Mother	Angela Coyne
Her Grandmother	Margaret Guinness
Her Great Grandmother	Katherine MacCormack
A Maid	Judith Wilson
A Domino	Andrew Dillon

Directed by Katherine MacCormack

First published: London: Martin Secker, [1917].

ANTON CHEKHOV
Cursai Cleamhnais
A Play in One Act, translated from *The Proposal* by Muiris O Cathain.
First produced: (?) 17 December 1923, by the Gaelic Dramatic League, at the Abbey Theatre, Dublin.
First published: Baile Atha Cliath: Oifig diolta foillseachain rialtais, 1933.

J. M. SYNGE
An Mhuir
A Play in One Act, translated from *Riders to the Sea* by Sean Toibin.
First produced: (?) 17 December 1923, by the Gaelic Dramatic League, at the Abbey Theatre, Dublin.
No record of publication.

MOLIERE
An Dochtuir Breige
A Three Scene Version of *Le Medecin Malgre Lui*, translated by Fionan O Loingsigh.
First produced: (?) 17 December 1923, by the Gaelic Dramatic League, at the Abbey Theatre, Dublin.
No record of publication.

EURIPIDES
The Trojan Women

*Clarke and Ferrar say Arthur Shields, but Susan L. Mitchell, who was thoroughly familiar with Abbey actors and who reviewed the play, says McCormick. The *Freeman's Journal* agrees with her.

†Clarke and Ferrar say McCormick; Susan L. Mitchell and the *Freeman's Journal* say Dolan.

A Tragedy, translated from the Greek by Gilbert Murray.
First produced by the Northern Drama League: 20, 21, and 22 December 1923, at the Great Hall of Queen's University, Belfast.

CAST

Hecuba	Mrs. Leslie Porter
Andromache	Mrs. C. M. Tedlie
Cassandra	Mrs. Percy Lewis
Helen	Dorothy Cambin
Chorus Leader	Molly Russell
Menelaus	C. E. Kerr
Herald of the Greeks	S. A. Bullock

Chorus: May Turtle, Gladys Leslie, Helen Tinsley, Doreen Crawford, Mrs. A. Glendinning, Mr. H. Hamilton, and Mr. R. Northridge.
Trumpeters in the Army of the Greeks: Drum-Major Ritchie, V. C., Cpl. Dawson, Drummer Norman and Drummer Macfarlane of 1srt. Battalion Seaforth Highlanders.

Directed by S. A. Bullock

First published: London: G. Allen, 1912.

GEORGE SHIELS
First Aid
A Play in One Act.
First produced: 26 December 1923, by the Abbey Company, at the Abbey Theatre, Dublin.

CAST

Nora	Eileen Crowe
Shawn Egan	Arthur Shields
Padraig Harte	Tony Quinn
Eileen Harte	Maureen Delany
Drogheda Moore	F. J. McCormick
Tommy Moody	Michael J. Dolan

Directed by Michael J. Dolan

Unpublished.

LADY GREGORY
The Old Woman Remembers
A Poem
First produced: 31 December 1923, by the Abbey Company, at the Abbey Theatre, Dublin.
Spoken by Sara Allgood.
First published in *The Irish Statesman* (22 March 1924); reprinted in *Collected Plays*, vol. 2 (Gerrards Cross: Colin Smythe, 1970).

1924

G. MARTINEZ SIERRA
The Two Shepherds
A Comedy in Two Acts, translated from the Spanish by Helen and Harley Granville-Barker.
First produced by the Abbey Company: 12 February 1924, at the Abbey Theatre, Dublin.

CAST

Dona Paquita	Sara Allgood
Lucia	Eileen Crowe
Dona Gertrudis	Christine Hayden
The Schoolmistress	May Craig
The Mayoress	Maureen Delany
Rosita	Shelah Richards
Nina	Irene Murphy
A Young Lady	May Kavanagh
Another Young Lady	Eveline Kavanagh
Don Antonio	Michael J. Dolan
Don Francisco	Gabriel J. Fallon
Don Jose Maria	F. J. McCormick
Don Juan de Dios	Eric Gorman
Juanillo	Tony Quinn
Mateo	Arthur Shields
Demetrio	Maurice Esmonde
Niceto	P. J. Carolan
The Mayor	Peter Nolan
The Colonel of the Civil Guard	P. J. Carolan

Directed by Michael J. Dolan

First publication of this translation in *The Plays of G. Martinez Sierra*, vol. 2 (London: Chatto and Windus, 1923).

after DION BOUCICAULT
The Colleen Bawn
A Film produced by Stoll Picture Productions, based on the play by Boucicault.
First trade showing in Dublin: 15 February 1924; first public showing in Ireland: 17 March 1924, at the Theatre De-Luxe, Camden Street, Dublin.

CAST

The Colleen Bawn	Colette Brettel
Hardress Cregan	Henry Victor
Myles na Gopaleen	Stewart Rome
Danny Mann	Clive Currie
Shelah	Marie Ault
Mrs. Cregan	Marguerite Leigh
Sir Patrick Chute	Aubrey Fitzgerald
Anne Chute	Gladys Jennings

And others.

Directed by W. P. Kellino

PAUL CLAUDEL
The Hostage
A Play in Three Acts, translated from the French by Bryan Cooper.
First produced: 17 and 18 February 1924, by the Dublin Drama League, at the Abbey Theatre, Dublin.

CAST

Georges Vicomte de Coufontaine	Arthur Shields
Toussaint Baron Turelure	F. J. McCormick
Sygne de Coufontaine	Eileen Crowe
Pope Pius	Michael J. Dolan
Father Badilon	Barry Fitzgerald

Directed by Arthur Shields

This translation unpublished.

LENNOX ROBINSON
Never the Time and the Place
A Little Comedy in One Act.
First produced: 19 February 1924, by the Abbey Company, at the Abbey Theatre, Dublin.*

CAST

Mrs. Mooney	Maureen Delany
Mrs. Sheep	Sara Allgood
Mrs. Fitzsimons	Eileen Crowe
Roderigo Callanan†	Arthur Shields

Directed by Lennox Robinson
First published in *The Dublin Magazine* (May 1924); first book publication: with *Crabbed Youth and Age* (Belfast: Carter, 1953).

J BERNARD MacCARTHY
The Down Express
A Farcical Comedy in Three Acts.
First produced: 25 February 1924, by the Irish Players, at the Queen's Theatre, Dublin.

CAST

Patricia Maud Tobin	Nora Kane
Donal Oge O'Sullivan	Felix Hughes
Mrs. Tobin	Kathleen Drago
Peter O'Sullivan	Sydney J. Morgan
Thady Brady	J. A. O'Rourke
Henry Kearns	Fred Jeffs
Michael Crowley	Harry Hutchinson

First published: Dublin: Gill, 1928.

SEAN O'CASEY
Juno and the Paycock
A Tragedy in Three Acts.
First produced: 3 March 1924, by the Abbey Company, at the Abbey Theatre, Dublin.

CAST

Residents in the Tenement:	
"Captain" Jack Boyle	Barry Fitzgerald
"Juno" Boyle	Sara Allgood
Johnny Boyle	Arthur Shields
Mary Boyle	Eileen Crowe
"Joxer" Daly	F. J. McCormick
Mrs. Maisie Madigan	Maureen Delany
"Needle" Nugent	Michael J. Dolan
Mrs. Tancred	Christine Hayden
Jerry Devine	P. J. Carolan
Charlie Bentham	Gabriel J. Fallon
First Irregular	Maurice Esmonde
Second Irregular	Michael J. Dolan
First Furniture Remover	Peter Nolan

*MacNamara and Hunt incorrectly cite 8 April 1924.
†Misprinted in Robinson as "Rogerigo Callanan."

Second Furniture Remover	Tony Quinn
Coal-block Vendor	Tony Quinn
Sewing-machine Man	Peter Nolan
Two Neighbours	Eileen O'Kelly, Irene Murphy

Directed by Michael J. Dolan

First published: in *Two Plays* (London: Macmillan, 1925); reprinted in *Collected Plays*, vol. 1 (London: Macmillan, 1949).

W. G. YEATS
*At the Hawk's Well**
A Noh Play in One Act.
First Irish production: 30 & 31 March 1924, by the Dublin Drama League at an At Home in Yeats' residence in Merrion Square.†

CAST

The Hawk Girl	Eileen Magee
The Chorus Leader	Lennox Robinson
The Old Man	Frank J. Fay
Cuchulain	Michael J. Dolan

Costumes, Masks and Music by Edmund Dulac

First published in *The Wild Swans at Coole, Other Verses and a Play in Verse* (Churchtown, Dundrum: Cuala, 1917); in *Four Plays for Dancers* (London: Macmillan, 1921); in *The Collected Plays of W. B. Yeats* (London: Macmillan, 1934); and in *The Variorum Edition of the Plays of W. B. Yeats*, ed. Russell K. Alspach and Catherine C. Alspach (London: Macmillan; New York: Macmillan, 1966).

BERNARD DUFFY
The Spell
A Comedy in One Act.
First produced: 4 April 1924, by the Irish Literary Society, at the Ashburton Club Theatre, London.
Cast included Mrs. A. Freeman, Miss H. O'Callaghan, Miss W. Walshe, Conor Fahy, J. H. Cooke and Frank Brewe.
Incidental music by Dr. Larchet and performed by a piper (H. R. Hough) and a fiddler (Mona Fahy).
First published: Dublin: Talbot, 1922.

LADY GREGORY
The Story Brought by Brigit
A Passion Play in Three Acts.
First produced: 15 April 1924, by the Abbey Company, at the Abbey Theatre, Dublin.‡

CAST

Joel	Arthur Shields
Daniel	Michael J. Dolan
Marcus	Maurice Esmonde
Silas	Barry Fitzgerald

*Clarke and Ferrar omit the apostrophe.
†Liam Miller in *The Noble Drama of W. B. Yeats* gives the date as 23 March 1924.
‡MacNamara and Hunt incorrectly list 14 April 1924 as the premiere.

Pilate	F. J. McCormick
Judas Iscariot	Eric Gorman
St. John	P. J. Carolan
St. Brigit	Christine Hayden
First Woman	Sara Allgood
Second Woman	Maureen Delany
Third Woman	Eilleen O'Kelly
First Man	Peter Nolan
Second Man	Bernard Swan
First Soldier	Gabriel J. Fallon
Second Soldier	F. J. McCormick
Third Soldier	Tony Quinn
A Young Scribe	Gabriel J. Fallon
An Egyptian Nurse	May Craig
The Mother	Eileen Crowe*
The Christ	Lyle Donaghy†

Directed by Michael J. Dolan

First published: London: Putnam, 1924; reprinted in *Collected Plays*, vol. 3 (Gerrards Cross: Colin Smythe, 1970).

JAMES MacNAMEE
A Few Matches
A Farce in One Act.
First produced: 21 April 1924, by the Pierce O'Reilly Players, at Grangegorman.

CAST

Tom Borran	William Murphy
Tom Borran, his son	Bernard Cahill
Bartle Mahon	Frank Hanna
Sarah Brady	Cissie Dalton

Unpublished.

TOM MADDEN and EDWARD McNULTY
Acushla
A Musical Comedy.
First produced: 28 April 1924, at the Queen's Theatre, Dublin.
Cast included George Casey, Lily Wick, Esther Warnock, Terry Lester, Kathleen Fay Markey, George Cooke, Viva Joyce, and Gerald Fitzgerald.
Unpublished.

FRED J. COGLEY
Liz
A Comedy.
First produced: 5 May 1924, at the Queen's Theatre, Dublin.

CAST

Liz	Irene Murphy
Henry Larissey	Sydney J. Morgan
Aunt Julia	May Fitzpatrick

Also with Effie Taaffe, Nicholas Hays, Jack Neville, Thomas Silke, J. Begley, and J. Moran.
Unpublished.

---

*Not recorded by Robinson.
†Not recorded by Robinson.

TADHG O SCANAIL
Eirghe Anairde (Snobbery)
A Play in One Act.
First produced: 5 May 1924, by Na hAisteoiri, at the Abbey Theatre, Dublin.
No record of publication.

GEORGE SHIELS
The Retrievers
A Comedy in Three Acts.
First produced: 12 May 1924, by the Abbey Company, at the Abbey Theatre, Dublin.

CAST

Peter Duat	Michael J. Dolan
Grace Duat	Shelah Richards
Steve Maguire	Arthur Shields
Sally Scullion	Sara Allgood
Mrs. Snider	Ria Mooney
Reub Snider	F. J. McCormick
John Dollas	P. J. Carolan
Mrs. Dollas	Maureen Delany
Maurya Dollas	May Craig
Joe Kiernan	Peter Nolan
Pat Hacket	Tony Quinn
Dan Mulgrew	Gabriel J. Fallon

Directed by Michael J. Dolan

Unpublished

JOHN MacDONAGH
Brains
A Comedy in Four Acts.
First produced: 2 June 1924, at the Olympia Theatre, Dublin.

CAST

Lord Amberdale	Jack Dwan
Lady Amberdale	Mme. Kirkwood-Hackett
Hon. Reginald Wye	Jimmy O'Dea
Rev. Reginald Flagg	Valentine Vousden
Mabel Flagg	Mabel Home
Shaw	Frank J. Fay
Mr. Queue	Pol O'Fearghail
Horatio Best	F. J. McCormick
Bessie Best	Kathleen Drago

Directed by John MacDonagh

Unpublished

LUIGI PIRANDELLO
Henry IV
A Tragedy in Three Acts, translated from the Italian by Edward Storer.
First produced by the Dublin Drama League: 27 and 28 April 1924, and revived on 10 August 1924, at the Abbey Theatre, Dublin.

CAST

Henry IV	Paul Ruttledge (Lennox Robinson)
The Marchioness Matilda Spina	Elizabeth Young
Frida	Ria Mooney
Marquis Charles di Nolli	Arthur Shields
Baron Tito Belcredi	F. J. McCormick

Doctor Dionysius Genoni*	Michael J. Dolan
Harold (Frank)	Edmund Dillon
Landolph (Lolo)	Tony Quinn
Ordulph (Momo)	Gabriel J. Fallon
Berthold (Fino)	Barry Fitzgerald
John, the old waiter†	Eric Gorman
A Valet‡	P. J. Carolan

Directed by Arthur Shields

First publication of this translation: in *Three Plays* (London: J. M. Dent; New York: E. P. Dutton, 1922).

MAJOR A. T. LAWLOR
The Vision Play of Queen Tailte
In Six Narrations and Six Tableaux.
First produced: 12 August 1924, by the Pupils of Madame Rock, at a Matinee at the Theatre Royal, Dublin.

CAST

A seanchidhe	Elizabeth Young
The cantora	M. J. Dolan and F. J. McCormick
Queen Tailte	Nancy Rock
Eochaidh Mac Erc	
Lugh of the Long Hand	
Lugh as a child	Thelma Murphy
Streng	Miss Ho. Rock
Tailte's second husband	Eileen Gray
Druids	Margaret Lawlor and Eugenie Moriarity
Breas	Dodo Maguire
The steward	Clara O'Toole
Cian	Miss A. X. Lawlor
The Banshee	Agnes O'Kelly

Directed by Madame Rock and the Misses Rock, assisted by Miss Gannon of Cavan
Music by Dr. Larchet's augmented orchestra

Unpublished.

HAROLD R. WHITE and R. J. HUGHES
Shaun the Post
A Romantic Opera in Three Acts and Eight Scenes, with music by White and book and lyrics by Hughes, and based on Boucicault's *Arrah na Pogue*.
First produced: 15 August 1924, at the Theatre Royal, Dublin.

CAST

Shaun the Post	Joseph O'Mara
Beamish MacCoul	Joseph O'Neill
The O'Grady	Irvine Lynch
Major Coffin	Richard MacNevin§

*Misspelled "Genomi" by Clarke and Ferrar.
†Merely called the Old Waiter by Clarke and Ferrar.
‡There are two valets in the original script.
§W. J. Lawrence in *The Stage* has "MacNivin."

Chief Secretary for Ireland	T. O'Carroll Reynolds
Oiney Farrell	William Lewis*
Paddy Regan	Leo Brady
Sergeant	T. C. Earls
Fanny Power	Teresa Owens
Arrah Meelish	Winifred Brady

Directed by Herbert Bailey
The Theatre Royal Orchestra conducted by Harold R. White

Unpublished.

FRANK DALTON
Wolfe Tone
An Historical Melodrama.
First produced: 1 September 1924, at the Queen's Theatre, Dublin.

CAST

Wolfe Tone	Noel Dalton
Napper Tandy	P. O'Flanagan
Thomas Russell	Desmond O'Donovan
Magroney	Frank Dalton
Sir George Hill	Valentine Vousden
Napoleon	Valentine Vousden
Madge Nuneil	May Fitzpatrick
Rev. Mr. Fanning	L. P. O'Toole
Lord Cavan	P. J. M'Nevin
Major Sandys	J. Davis
Matilda Witherington	Pearl O'Donnell

And others.
Unpublished.

T. C. MURRAY
Autumn Fire
A Play in Three Acts.
First produced: 8 September 1924, by the Abbey Company, at the Abbey Theatre, Dublin.

CAST

Owen Keegan	Michael J. Dolan
Ellen Keegan	Sara Allgood
Michael Keegan	Arthur Shields
Morgan Keegan	Barry Fitzgerald
Mrs. Desmond	Maureen Delany
Nance Desmond†	Eileen Crowe
Tom Furlong	F. J. McCormick
Molly Hurley	Helen Cullen

Directed by Michael J. Dolan
First published: London: George Allen and Unwin, 1925.

SEAN O'CASEY
Nannie's Night Out
A Comedy in One act.

*W. J. Lawrence in *The Stage* has "Lewin."
†Robinson incorrectly says "Nancy."

First produced: 29 September 1924, by the Abbey Company, at the Abbey Theatre, Dublin.

CAST

Mrs. Polly Pender	Maureen Delany
Sweet on Polly:	
Oul Johnny	Barry Fitzgerald
Oul Jimmy	Michael J. Dolan
Oul Joe	Gabriel J. Fallon
Irish Nannie	Sara Allgood
Robert	Gerald Breen
A Ballad Singer	F. J. McCormick
A Young Man	Arthur Shields
A Young Girl	Eileen Crowe

Crowd: Seaghan Barlow, F. Ellis, W. O'Hara, and M. Judge.

Directed by Michael J. Dolan

First published in *Feathers from the Green Crow*, ed. Robert Hogan (Columbia: University of Missouri Press, 1962; London: Macmillan, 1963).

G. MARTINEZ SIERRA

The Kingdom of God

A Play in Three Acts, translated from the Spanish by Helen and Harley Granville-Barker.

First produced by the Abbey Company: 3 November 1924, at the Abbey Theatre, Dublin.

CAST

Act I

Old Man	Tony Quinn
Gabriel	P. J. Carolan
Tranjano	Michael J. Dolan
Sister Gracia	Eileen Crowe*
Sister Manuela	Eileen O'Kelly
Don Lorenzo	Maire McIntyre
Maria Isabel	Tom Moran†
Lulu	Maeve McMurrough†
Liborio	Gabriel J. Fallon

Act II

Candelas	Maureen Delany
Cecilia	Toni Desmond
The Dumb Girl	Shelah Richards
Sister Christina	May Craig
Sister Feliciana	Ria Mooney
Quica	Lini Doran
Sister Gracia	Eileen Crowe
Margarita	Sara Allgood
Enrique	F. J. McCormick

*Robinson incorrectly has Eileen Crowe playing Sister Juliana and does not list the actress who did play the part.

†It would seem more probable that Moran played Don Lorenzo and McMurrough played Maria Isabel.

Act III

Sister Dionisia	Maureen Delany
Engracia	Joan Sullivan
Lorenza	Ria Mooney
The Innocent	Dolly Lynd
Morineto	U. Wright
Policarpo	Eric Gorman
Vicente	P. J. Carolan
Sister Gracia	Eileen Crowe
Paquita*	Norma Joyce
Juan de Dios	Arthur Shields
Felipe	Tony Quinn
Boys	J. Breen, G. Breen and others.

Directed by Michael J. Dolan

This translation first published in *The Plays of G. Martinez Sierra*, vol. 2 (London: Chatto and Windus, 1923).

JACINTO BENAVENTE
The Passion Flower

A Play in Three Acts, translated from the Spanish probably by John Garrett Underhill.

First produced by the Dublin Drama League: 9 and 10 November 1924, and revived on 7 and 8 December 1924, at the Abbey Theatre, Dublin.

CAST

Raimunda	Sara Allgood
Acacia	Eileen Crowe†
Juliana	Maureen Delany‡
Milagros	Norma Joyce
Dona Isabel	Shelah Richards§
Fidela	Mary McAuliffe
Engracia	Maeve McMurrough
Bernabea	Gladys Monk
Gaspara	May Craig
Esteban//	Sydney J. Morgan
Norberto#	F. J. McCormick
Faustino	P. J. Carolan
Tio Eusebio	Gabriel J. Fallon
Bernarbe	Tony Quinn
Rubio	Michael J. Dolan
Friends:	Mary Hickey, Joan Harold and Kate Knowles

The Underhill translation first published in *Plays by Jacinto Benavente* (New York: Charles Scribner's, 1917).

*Misspelled as "Paguita" by Robinson.

†Clarke and Ferrar cite Shelah Richards in this role, but *The Irish Times*' account would suggest that Eileen Crowe played it.

‡Misspelled "Delancy" by Clarke and Ferrar.

§Clarke and Ferrar cite Gertrude McInery in this role, but a list compiled by Gary Phillips for Shelah Richards cites her in the role.

//Misspelled "Estaban" by Clarke and Ferrar.

#Misspelled "Norbert" by Clarke and Ferrar.

PADRAIC O CONAIRE
A Chead Bhean (His First Wife)
A Play in One Act, adapted by the author from his short story.
First produced: (?) 17 November 1924, by Na hAisteoiri, at the Abbey Theatre, Dublin.
With Tadhg O Scannaill, P. Brophy, and Maire Ni Shiochain.
No record of publication.

UNKNOWN
An Craipi Og (The Croppy Boy)
A Play in One Act.
First produced: 17 November 1924, by Na hAisteoiri, at the Abbey Theatre, Dublin.
With Muiris O Cathain and Gearoid O Lochlainn
No record of publication.

AN SEABHAC (PADRAIG O SIOCHFHRADHA)
The Parliament of Women (Dail na mBan)
A Comedy in One Act.
First produced: 17 November 1924, by Na hAisteoiri, at the Abbey Theatre, Dublin.

CAST

The Woman of the House	Mrs. Fitzgerald
The Man of the House	Tadgh O Scannaill

And others.
No record of publication.

CONSTANCE POWELL-ANDERSON
The Greatest Gift
A Play in One Act.
First produced: 27 November 1924, at a Charity Matinee at the Gaiety Theatre, Dublin.

CAST

Pierrette	Gladys Monks
Pierrot	Gilbert Green
Just Any Girl	Joyce Chancellor
Mrs. Ways and Means	Mrs. Rawkins
A Pedlar	F. H. Williams

First published: London and Glasgow: Gowans and Gray, 1926.

DOROTHEA DONN-BYRNE
The Land of the Stranger
A Comedy in Three Acts and Five Scenes.
First produced by the Ulster Players: 8 December 1924, at the Gaiety Theatre, Dublin.

CAST

Exile Pat McCann	Gerald MacNamara
Dennis McCann	H. Richard Hayward
Maureen O'Brien	Jean Woods
Antonio Chiapetta	J. R. Mageean
Bartley O'Toole	Charles K. Ayre
Mrs. Levinsky	Elma Ward
Martin O'Brien	Charles K. Ayre
Mary O'Brien	Marian Crimmins
Ellen O'Brien	Nora Barnett

Willie John McFee	Walter Kennedy
Dr. John Taylor	Herbert Grant

First published: London: Low, Marston, 192?.

KENNETH SARR (KENNETH REDDIN)
The Passing
A Tragedy in Vignette in One Act.
First produced: 9 December 1924, by the Abbey Company, at the Abbey Theatre, Dublin.*

CAST

Nann	Sara Allgood
Jimmie	Michael J. Dolan

Directed by Michael J. Dolan
First published: Dublin and Cork: Talbot Press, 1924.

ST. JOHN ERVINE
The Ship
A Play in Three Acts.
First produced by the Ulster Players: 10 December 1924, at the Gaiety Theatre, Dublin.

CAST

Old Mrs. Thurlow	Josephine Mayne
John Thurlow	Rutherford Mayne
Janet	Elma Ward
Jack	H. Richard Hayward
Hester	Nora Barnett
Captain Cornelius	J. B. Mageean
George Norwood	C. K. Ayre
A maid	

First published: New York: Macmillan, 1922.

H. RICHARD HAYWARD
Huge Love
A Burlesque in Four Acts.
First produced: 10 December 1924, by the Ulster Players, at the Gaiety Theatre, Dublin.

CAST

Jasper	J. R. Mageean

Also with Rutherford Mayne, Josephine Mayne, Jean Woods, Nora Barnett, H. Grant, and Rose McQuillan.
Unpublished.

SHAN F. BULLOCK
The Stranger
A Comedy in One Act.
First produced 21 December 1924, by the Irish Literary Society, at the Rehearsal Theatre, London.

*MacNamara and Hunt incorrectly list 16 December 1924 as the premiere.

Cast included Aida Freeman, Kathleen White, Lucy Morris, Prof. Keelan, P. J. Dowling, and John Cooke.

Directed by Conor Fahy

No record of publication.

KENNETH SARR (KENNETH REDDIN)

Old Mag

A Christmas Play in One Act.

First produced: 22 December 1924, by the Abbey Company, at the Abbey Theatre, Dublin.

CAST

Old Mag	Maureen Delany
Terry	P. J. Carolan
Women	May Craig, Joan Sullivan, Dolly Lynd, Eileen O'Kelly, Norma Joyce

Sailors:
Gabriel J. Fallon, Tony Quinn, Tom Moran, F. J. McCormick.

Directed by Michael J. Dolan

First published: Dublin and Cork: Talbot Press, 1924.

SAM BOLTON

Miss Clegg's Legacy

A Comedy in One Act.

First produced: 28 December (or possibly November) 1924, by the Northern Drama League, at Rosemary Street Hall, Belfast.

CAST

Sandy Haggis	James Hodgen
John M'Wha	J. Story

Also with W. R. Gordon and Miss Crothers.

No record of publication.

1925

D. M'LOUGHLIN

Andrew M'Ilfatrick, J. P.

A Comedy in Three Acts.

First produced: 2 January 1925, by the Carrickfergus Repertory Players, at the Alexandra Park Avenue Hall, Carrickfergus.

Cast included R. H. MacCandless and others.

Directed by R. H. MacCandless

Unpublished.

SAM R. BOLTON

Going West

A Drama in One Act.

First produced: 2 January 1925, by the Carrickfergus Repertory Players, at Alexandra Park Avenue Hall, Carrickfergus.

Cast included R. H. MacCandless, Tony Mack, and others.

Directed by R. H. MacCandless

No record of publication.

ERNST TOLLER
Masses and Man
A Drama, translated from the German by Vera Mendel.
Firs produced by the Dublin Drama League: 4 and 5 January 1925, at the Abbey Theatre, Dublin.

CAST

Sonia	Dorothy Lynd
Her Husband	Arthur Shields
The Nameless One	Sydney J. Morgan
The Guide	Gabriel Fallon
An Officer	T. Aye
A Priest	Michael J. Dolan
Two Prisoners	Joan Sullivan, Shelah Richards

Working Men and Women: Edith Dodd, J. Tayler, M. Ross, Maeve MacMoragh, Joan Sullivan, Shelah Richards, R. Geary, J. Dillon, R. Murphy, J. Straw, T. Aye.
Directed by Arthur Shields
First publication of this translation: London: Nonesuch Press, 1923.

GEORGE DUNNING GRIBBLE
The Scene That Was to Write Itself
A Tragi-Comedy in One Act.
First produced by the Dublin Drama League: 4 and 5 January 1925, at the Abbey Theatre, Dublin.

CAST

The Wife	Margot Brunton
The Husband	Rutherford Mayne
The Author	Gerald Fitzpatrick

Directed by Lennox Robinson
First published in *Contemporary British Dramatists*, vol. 12 (London: Ernest Benn, 1925).

JOHN MacDONAGH
Cruiskeen Lawn
A Film in Five Reels, produced by Irish Photo-plays, Ltd.
First trade showing: 16 January 1925, at La Scala Theatre, Dublin.
First public showing: 8 June 1925, at the Rotunda, Dublin.*

CAST

Nora Blake	Kathleen Armstrong
Boyle Roche	Tom Moran
Samuel Silke	Jimmy O'Dea
Sheila	Fay Sargent
Darby	Chris Silvester
Dublin Dan	Barrett MacDonnell
Dick Blake	Fred Jeffs
Carleton	Frank J. Fay

Also with Frank Dalton.
Written and directed by John MacDonagh

*Although released in 1925, this film was shot in 1922.

LEO TOLSTOY
Fioraon le Fiaran
A Translation by Fiachra Eilgeach (Risteard O Foghluda) of *Falsely True*.
First produced: 19 January 1925, by An Comhar, at the Abbey Theatre, Dublin.

CAST

The Wanderer	Piaras Beaslai
The Old Woman of the House	Maire Ni Chinneide
Her Son	Muiris O Cathain

Also with Gearoid O Lochlainn
No record of publication.

JACINTO BENAVENTE
*A School of Princesses**
A Comedy in Three Acts, translated from the Spanish by John Garrett Underhill.

CAST

King Gustavus Adolphus of Alfania	W. D. Johnston (Denis Johnston)
Princess Constanza	Shelah Richards
Princess Felicia	Joyce Chancellor
Prince Maximo	Eric Gorman
Princess Eudoxia	Christine Hayden
Prince Silvio	Arthur Ward
Duke Alexander	Arthur Shields
Prince Albert of Suavia	T. Aye
The Duchess of Berlandia	Edith Dodd
The Ambassador of Suavia	G. McClinchie
The Ambassador of Franconia	L. Elyan
The Ambassadress of Franconia	Maureen Delany
The President of the Ministry	Andrew Dillon
An Usher	G. McClinchie

Directed by Lennox Robinson

First publication of this translation in *Plays by Jacinto Benavente, Fourth Series* (New York and London: Charles Scribner's Sons, 1924)

CONSTANCE POWELL-ANDERSON
Ag Suirghe Leis an mBaintreach
A Comedy in One Act, translated from *The Courting of the Widow Malone* by Fiachra Eilgeach.
First produced: 16 February 1925, by An Comhar, at the Abbey Theatre, Dublin.
Cast included Tadhg O Scanaill, Gearoid O'Loughlin, and Maire Ni Oisin.
First published: Ath Cliath: An Comhar, 1927.

LIAM GOGAN
An Saoghal Eile (The Other World)
A Play in One Act.
First produced: 16 February 1925, by An Comhar, at the Abbey Theatre, Dublin.
Unpublished.

---

*Clarke and Ferrar list *A School for Princesses*.

†The printed text also includes these characters: The Ambassadress of Suavia, Princess Alicia, Princess Miranda.

DOROTHY MACARDLE
The Old Man
A Play in Two Acts.
First produced: 24 February 1925, by the Abbey Company, at the Abbey Theatre, Dublin.

CAST

Cornelius Sheridan	Barry Fitzgerald
Pauline Sheridan	Joyce Chancellor
Robert Emmet Sheridan	Tony Quinn
Francis Meagher	F. J. McCormick*
William Scully	Tom Moran†
David	Eric Gorman
Hugh	Peter Nolan
Joe	Desmond Finn
John	Walter Dillon
Michael	M. J. Scott
Tom	Michael J. Dolan
Nick	Arthur Shields
M'Crae	U. Wright
M'Guire	P. J. Carolan

Directed by Michael J. Dolan

Unpublished.

EMILE VERHAEREN
The Cloister
A Drama, translated from the French by Osman Edwards.
First produced by the Dublin Drama League: 15 and 16 March 1925, at the Abbey Theatre, Dublin.

CAST

Dom Balthasar	James Stephenson
Dom Mark	Thomas McGreevy‡
The Prior	Frank J. Fay
Father Thomas	William Dennis (Denis Johnston)
Dom Militien	Gabriel J. Fallon§
Idesbald	Norman Reddin§
Theodule	Dermond Van Starn§

Directed by Frank J. Fay

First publication of this translation in *The New Poetry Series* (London: Constable, 1915).

FRANK J. HUGH O'DONNELL
Anti-Christ
A Commentary in Six Scenes//
First produced: 17 March 1925, by the Abbey Company, at the Abbey Theatre, Dublin.

---

*Robinson omits this character and actor.
†Robinson omits this character and actor.
‡Clarke and Ferrar Say Michael Enright.
§These characters and actors omitted by Clarke and Ferrar.
//Robinson erroneously cites only five scenes.

CAST

John Boles	Michael J. Dolan
Oscar Murphy	Arthur Shields
Frederick Nixon	F. J. McCormick
Pamela Fortescue	Shelah Richards
John Desmond	Walter Dillon
Alfred Sanderson	Tony Quinn
John Drysdale, V. C.	Arthur Shields
Grahame Belton	Barry Fitzgerald
Captain Millar	P. J. Carolan
Other Men	Desmond Finn, W. O'Hara, Tom Moran
Sandwichmen:	
Bill	P. J. Carolan
Tom	Tony Quinn
Mike	Desmond Finn
Alf	Walter Dillon
Pat	Barry Fitzgerald
Joe	W. O'Hara
Arthur	Tom Moran
Policeman	Peter Nolan
Newsboy	John O'Neill
Cecil Graham	Peter Nolan
Mr. Bachup	Eric Gorman
General Dingby	F. J. McCormick
Mr. Burhslip	M. J. Scott
Manservant	Desmond Finn
Maidservant	May Craig
Maude Plumer	Joyce Chancellor
Dolly Drysdale	May Craig
Alf Pollehoff	Barry Fitzgerald
George Drysdale	P. J. Carolan
Joe Giddings	Tony Quinn

Directed by Michael J. Dolan

Unpublished.

REV. THOMAS O'KELLY
An Foghmar
A Tragedy in Three Acts, revised by Gearoid O Lochlainn.
First produced: 9 March 1925, by an Comhar, at the Abbey Theatre, Dublin.
Cast included Maire Ni Chinneide, Brid Ni Eigeartaigh, Muiris O Cathain, Piaras Beaslai, and Tormad O Roideain.
No record of publication.

LENNOX ROBINSON
Portrait
In Two Sittings (Acts).
First produced: 31 March 1925, by the Abbey Company, at the Abbey Theatre, Dublin.

CAST

Maggie Barnado	Sara Allgood
Peter Barnado	Arthur Shields
Mrs. Barnado	Maureen Delany
Mr. Barnado	Barry Fitzgerald

Mrs. Chambers (Mary)	Joan Sullivan
Charlie Brandon	Tony Quinn
Tom Hughes	P. J. Carolan
Mrs. Brandon	May Craig

Directed by Lennox Robinson

First published in *Plays* (London: Macmillan, 1928).

AUGUST STRINDBERG

The Spook Sonata

A Dream Play, translator unknown.

First produced by the Dublin Drama League: 19 & 20 April 1925, at the Abbey Theatre, Dublin.

CAST

Old Hummel	Gabriel Fallon
Arkenholtz	Paul Ruttledge (Lennox Robinson)
The Milkmaid	Annie Fvans
The Housekeeper	May Craig
The Ghost of the Consul	Arthur Shields
The Dark Lady	Joan Sullivan
The Colonel	F. J. McCormick
The Mummy	Maeve McMorrough
The Girl	Shelah Richards
The Aristocrat	Tony Quinn
Johansson	Michael J. Scott
Bengtsson	P. J. Carolan
The Fiancee	Dorothy Lynd
The Cook	Christine Hayden

Directed by Arthur Shields

ARTHUR SCHNITZLER

The Wedding Morn

A Comedy in One Act, translator unknown.

First produced by the Dublin Drama League: 19 and 20 April 1925, at the Abbey Theatre, Dublin.

CAST

Anatol	Arthur Ward
Max	Pablo Quesada
Ilona*	Margot Brunton
Franz	R. H. Colwill

Directed by Arthur Ward

GEORGE BERNARD SHAW

Fanny's First Play

A Play in Three Acts.

First produced by the Abbey Company: 21 April 1925, at the Abbey Theatre, Dublin.

CAST

Mrs. Gilbey	Maureen Delany
Mr. Gilbey	Michael J. Dolan
Juggins	Arthur Shields†

*Clarke and Ferrar incorrectly say "Iona."

†Robinson incorrectly states that Arthur Sinclair played the role.

Miss Dora Delaney	Sara Allgood
Mrs. Knox	Christine Hayden
Mr. Knox	P. J. Carolan
Margaret Knox	Shelah Richards
Monsieur Dunallet	F. J. McCormick
Bobby Gilbey	Michael Scott

Directed by Lennox Robinson

First published in German as *Fannis erstes Stuck* in *Neue Freie Presse* of Vienna (16 July–8 October 1911); in English in *Misalliance, The Dark Lady of the Sonnets*, and *Fanny's First Play* (New York: Brentano's, 1914); reprinted in *The Bodley Head Bernard Shaw*, vol. 4 (London: Max Reinhardt, 1972).

ANTON CHEKHOV
The Proposal
A Play in One Act, translator unknown.
First produced by the Abbey Company: 28 April 1925, at the Abbey Theatre, Dublin.

CAST

Stepan Stepanovitch Tchubukov	Michael J. Dolan
Natalya Stepanovna	Ria Mooney
Ivan Vassilyevitch Lomov	F. J. McCormick

Directed by Michael J. Dolan

EURIPIDES
*Iphigenia in Tauris**
A Tragedy, translated from the Greek by Gilbert Murray†
First produced by the Dublin Drama League: 11 July 1925, at the Abbey Theatre, Dublin.

CAST

Iphigenia	Elizabeth Yough
Orestes	Lennox Robinson
Pylades	Arthur Shields
Thoras	Denis Johnston‡
Herdisme	May Carey‡
Amorspor	William Carey‡
Chorus	Miss Carey, Miss Casey, Edith Orr‡
Soldiers	Cecil Davison, Eric Britton, Bertie Barret, Ronald Lyon‡
Athene	Eileen Crowe‡

Directed by Lennox Robinson§

First publication of this translation: London: G. Allen, 1910.

JOSEPH SWEENEY
The Girl from Rathmines
A Musical Comedy Revue in Eleven Scenes.
First produced: 13 July 1925, at the Olympia Theatre, Dublin.
Cast included Myles Kelly, Lily Moloney, Kathleen Sweeney, Michael Lawlor, Misses Ho and Nancy Rock, Ernest Lovell, E. O'Kelly, Joseph Duffy and May Neville.
Unpublished.

*Clarke and Ferrar say *Iphingenia in Tauris*.
†Unrecorded by Clarke and Ferrar.
‡These characters and actors unrecorded by Clarke and Ferrar.
§Unrecorded by Clarke and Ferrar.

GEORGE SHIELS
Professor Tim
A Comedy in Three Acts.
First produced: 14 September 1925, by the Abbey Company, at the Abbey Theatre, Dublin.

CAST

John Scally	Eric Gorman
Mrs. Scally	Sara Allgood
Peggy Scally	Eileen Crowe
Professor Tim	F. J. McCormick
James Kilroy	Peter Nolan
Mrs. Kilroy	Christine Hayden
Joseph Kilroy	Barry Fitzgerald
Hugh O'Cahan	P. J. Carolan
Paddy Kinney	Arthur Shields
Moll Flannagan	Maureen Delany
Mr. Allison	J. Stephenson

Directed by Michael J. Dolan
First published in *Professor Tim and Paul Twyning* (London: Macmillan, 1927).

HERBERT HALL WINSLOW
Land of Her Fathers
A Film produced by John Hurley.
First trade showing: 1 October 1925, at the Grafton Picture House, Dublin.
Cast included Phyllis O'Hara (sometimes called Phyllis Wakely), Micheal MacLiammoir, Frank J. Hugh O'Donnell, Tom Moran, Michael J. Dolan, Eileen Crowe, F. J. McCormick, Barry Fitzgerald, and Maureen Delany.
Written and directed by Herbert Hall Winslow

PADRAIG O BROITHE (PATRICK BROPHY)
Reidhteach na Ceiste (The Settling of the Question)
A Play in One Act.
First produced: 5 October 1925, by An Comhar, at the Abbey Theatre, Dublin.
Cast included Muiris O Cathain, Maire Ni Oisin, Maire Ni Shiochain, and Caitlin Ni Raghallaigh.
Unpublished.

LENNOX ROBINSON
The White Blackbird
A Play in Three Acts.
First produced: 12 October 1925, by the Abbey Company, at the Abbey Theatre, Dublin.

CAST

Mrs. Naynoe	Lini Doran
Mr. Naynoe	Michael J. Dolan
Molly	Ria Mooney
Violet	Maeve McMurrough
Tinker	Arthur Shields
Bella	Shelah Richards
William	F. J. McCormick
Connie	Eileen Crowe

Directed by Lennox Robinson
First published: Dublin and Cork:
Talbot Press, 1926; reprinted in *Plays*
(London: Macmillan, 1928).

MARBHAN (SEAN O CIARGHUSA)
Na Dibeartaigh O Shean-Shasana (The Exiles from Old England)
A Play in One Act.
First produced: 2 November 1925, by An Comhar, at the Abbey Theatre, Dublin.
Unpublished.

Irish Luck
A Film in Seven Reels and 7,000 ft., produced by Famous Players-Lasky, and distributed by Paramount; exteriors shot in Ireland, interiors on Long Island.
New York premiere: 22 November 1925.

CAST

Tom Donahoe (Lord Fitzhugh)	Thomas Meighan
Lady Gwendolyn	Lois Wilson
Douglas	Cecil Humphreys
Solicitor	Claude King
Earl	Ernest Lawford
Doctor	Charles Hammond
Aunt	Louise Grafton
Uncle	S. B. Carrickson
Denis MacSwiney	Charles McDonald
Kate MacSwiney	Mary Foy

Directed by Victor Heerman
Scenario by Tom J. Geraghty, after Norman Venner's novel *The Perfect Imposter*
Photographed by Alvin Wyckoff

AUGUST STRINDBERG
The Dance of Death, Part I
Translated by Edwin Bjorkman.
First produced by the Dublin Drama League: 29 and 30 November 1925, at the Abbey Theatre, Dublin.

CAST

Edgar	Paul Ruttledge (Lennox Robinson)
Alice	Maeve McMurrough
Curt	Barry Fitzgerald
Jinny	Joan Sullivan
An Old Woman	Christine Hayden

Directed by Arthur Shields
First publication of this translation in *Plays*, 7 vols. (London: Duckworth, 1912–1913).

M. J. MacKEOWN
The Real McCoy
A Comedy.
First produced: 9 December 1925, at the Town Hall, Dundalk.

CAST

Robbie John McCoy	M. J. MacKeown
Rosy McCoy	Minnie McKitterick
Sgt. Brown	Frank Johnston
Amen, the princess	Nan Brennan
The R. M.	Bill M'Court
Maggie	May Brennan

Billy M'Candless	Paddy O'Connell

Directed by M. J. MacKeown

First published as *The Rale McCoy* (Dublin: Duffy, [1930].

T. C. MURRAY
Athbarra
A Translation of *Aftermath* by Michael Sugrue.
First produced: 11 December 1925, by An Comhar, at the Abbey Theatre, Dublin.
First published: [Dublin]: Muinntir C. S. O'Fallamhain, 1930.

CHARLES K. AYRE
Missing Links
A Comedy in Three Acts.
First produced: 15 December 1925, by the Ulster Theatre, at the Gaiety Theatre Dublin.

CAST

Prof. Bryce	J. R. Mageean
William	Charles K. Ayre
Molly	Jean Woods
Henry O'Neill	
Frank O'Hogan	
Rowley Johnson	Gerald MacNamara
Sam Bradley	Walter Kennedy
Mrs. Orr	Rose McQuillan
Lord Springfield	H. R. Hayward
Dora Wallace	Elma Ward

Also with Jack Gavan and Conor MacHugh.
Unpublished.

1926

SEAN O'CASEY
The Plough and the Stars
A Tragedy in Four Acts.
First produced: 8 February 1926, by the Abbey Company, at the Abbey Theatre, Dublin.

CAST

Commandant Jack Clitheroe	F. J. McCormick
Nora Clitheroe	Shelah Richards
Peter Flynn	Eric Gorman
The Young Covey	Michael J. Dolan
Fluther Good	Barry Fitzgerald
Bessie Burgess	Maureen Delany
Mrs. Gogan	May Craig
Mollser	Kitty Curling
Captain Brennan	Gabriel J. Fallon
Lieut. Langon	Authur Shields
Rosie Redmond	Ria Mooney
A Barman	P. J. Carolan
A Woman	Eileen Crowe

The Voice	J. Stephenson
Corporal Stoddard	P. J. Carolan
Sergeant Tinley	J. Stephenson

Directed by Lennox Robinson

First published: London: Macmillan, 1926; acting edition (London and New York: Samuel French, [1932]; in *Collected Plays*, vol. 1 (London: Macmillan, 1949).

Notes

Chapter 1. 1921

1. *Irish Times*, 1 Jan. 1921, p. 7.
2. Letter of Lady Gregory to John Quinn, 2 Jan. 1921, John Quinn Papers, New York Public Library.
3. Letter of Maud Gonne MacBride to John Quinn, 21 Feb. 1921, John Quinn Papers,
4. Letter of St. John Ervine to Dudley Digges, 24 Feb. 1921, Dudley Digges Papers, New York Public Library.
5. *Irish Times*, 1 Apr. 1921, p. 5.
6. *Irish Times*, 11 June 1921, p. 5.
7. Letter of Lady Gregory to John Quinn, 8 July 1921, John Quinn Papers.
8. Letter of Lady Gregory to John Quinn, 7 Dec. 1921, John Quinn Papers.
9. "Panic in City Theatre—Man Shot at and Wounded." *Evening Telegraph*, 13 Jan. 1921, p. 1.
10. "Disastrous Effects of Early Curfew," *Evening Telegraph*, 7 Feb. 1921, p. 1.
11. "Invasion of the Abbey," *Irish Independent*, 23 Feb. 1921, p. 6.
12. "More 'Curfew' in Dublin, Nine O'Clock Rule To-night." *Freeman's Journal*, 4 Mar. 1921, p. 5.
13. Daniel J. Murphy, ed., *Lady Gregory's Journals,* vol.1 (New York: Oxford University Press, 1978), p. 239.
14. Letter of Sara Allgood to W. B. Yeats, 12 Mar. 1921, ms. 10,952, National Library of Ireland.
15. Ibid.
16. St. John Ervine, "At the Play," *Observer*, 3 Apr. 1921, p. 7.
17. "The Whiteheaded Boy," *Evening Telegraph*, 7 Apr. 1921, p. 2.
18. Lennox Robinson, *Ireland's Abbey Theatre* London: Sidgwick & Jackson, 1951); pp. 123–24.
19. Ibid.
20. Murphy, *Journals*, 1:247.
21. Frank J. Hugh O'Donnell, "Work of the Abbey Theatre," *Irish Independent*, 11 Apr. 1921, p. 4.
22. "The Abbey Theatre," *Freeman's Journal*, 23 Apr. 1921, p. 3.
23. "The Abbey Theatre," *Irish Times*, 6 May 1921, p. 5. Yeats also lectured on 11 May at Mrs. Herbert Jackson's house, and brought in £39. Cf. Murphy, *Journals*, 1:252.
24. Murphy, *Journals*, 1:250.
25. Joseph Holloway in his *Impressions of a Dublin Playgoer*, ms. 1861, p. 911, National Library of Ireland, preserved this clipping from a newspaper, which he said was *Freeman's Journal*, 13 May 1921. We can discover no such story in the paper of that date.
26. Ibid.
27. This £39 would seem to be the receipts of Yeats's 11 May lecture, mentioned in footnote 23 above.
28. Murphy, *Journals*, 1:252–53.
29. Letter of Lady Gregory to John Quinn, dated 29 May 1921, in the John Quinn Papers, New York Public Library.
30. "Our London Letter," *Irish Independent*, 20 May 1921, p. 4.
31. "Mr. G. B. Shaw's Impish Wit," *Irish Independent*, 27 May 1921, p. 6.
32. "The Spur of the Moment," *Irish Times*, 27 May 1921, p. 4.
33. Letter of Lady Gregory to John Quinn, 29 May 1921, John Quinn Papers.

34. Letter of Lady Gregory to John Quinn, 8 July 1921, John Quinn Papers.
35. Letter of George Shiels to Lennox Robinson, 8 June 1921, Berg Collection, New York Public Library.
36. "Our London Letter," *Irish Independent*, 11 June 1921, p. 4.
37. Murphy, *Journals*, 1:269
38. Ibid., 1:270.
39. Dorothy Macardle, *The Irish Republic* (London: Corgi Books, 1968), p. 436.
40. "Abbey Optimist," *Evening Telegraph*, 26 July 1921, p. 2.
41. J. A. P[ower], "Some Words to the Abbey," *Evening Telegraph*, 6 Aug. 1921, p. 3.
42. Ibid.
43. J., "Music and Drama Notes," *Evening Herald*, 16 July 1921, p. 5.
44. J. A. P[ower], "Theatrical Topics," *Evening Telegraph*, 23 July 1921, p. 4.
45. Hugh Francis [Frank J. Hugh O'Donnell], "The Play of the Future," *Freeman's Journal*, 11 Aug. 1921, p. 3.
46. Letter of George Russell (AE) to John Quinn, 26 Oct. 1921, John Quinn Papers.
47. The reference to the lighthouse play is apparently to F. J. H. O'Donnell's *The Keeper of the Lights*, which the Abbey did not produce.
48. Trevor Allen, "A Talk with Jack Yeats," *Westminster Gazette*, 21 Dec, 1921, p. 8.
49. Irish writers were sometimes the cause of theatrical rumpuses outside of Ireland. For instance, on 1 Feb., *Irish Times* noted that Bulgarian students tried to break up a performance of *Arms and the Man* at the Schiller Theatre in Berlin, when Mrs. Petkoff remarked that her house contained the only library in the country ("Angry Audiences," p. 4.). On 12 June in Vienna, Bulgarians staged an even stronger protest against a production of the play at the Schloss Theatre:

> When Raina boasted of his [*sic*] library, claiming it to be the only one in Bulgaria, there was an outbreak of shouting and yelling which delayed the performance until the police had ejected several people. At the commencement of the second act there was another outbreak. Major Petkoff was remarking that he could not understand western extravagance with soap and water and comparing it with Bulgarian economy in these matters when the whole Bulgarian crowd was on its feet once more protesting. Bulgarians in the stalls were specially indignant and one said to be a member of the Bulgarian Embassy here shouted that Bulgaria was an ally of Austria during the war and was now insulted from the Austrian stage.
>
> Further forays by the police ended in more demonstrators being ejected. The interruptions continued until at last the audience itself turned upon the Bulgarian cohorts who, finding public opinion against them, gave up the struggle and sat through the remainder in pained silence.

"Bularians Shout Against Shaw Play," *Irish Times*, 13 June 1921, p. 15.
50. Murphy, *Journals*, 1:289. Lady Gregory's annoyance with Robinson reached Dublin's literary circle, and on 9 Sept. Brinsley MacNamara wrote to Frank J. Hugh O'Donnell:

> That is very interesting about Robinson and Lady G. If I were sure that he had quite definitely severd connections I might think of looking for the job for a while, as her ladyship and myself are very good friends. But of course it is the devil's own job and how Robinson has stuck it so long is one of the marvels of the universe. However, it might not be a bad idea to be stuck in there now as the old control is not likely to last forever.

Letter of Brinsley MacNamara to Frank J. Hugh O'Donnell, 9 Sept. 1921, ms. 21,715, National Library of Ireland.
51. Murphy, *Journals*, 1:290.
52. Ibid., 1:298.
53. Letter of T. C. Murray to Joseph Holloway, 5 Oct. 1921, ms. 1865, National Library of Ireland.
54. Letter of Maire Nic Shiubhlaigh to Joseph Holloway, dated 1921 and probably written around 5 Oct., ms. 1865, National Library of Ireland.
55. But if carping criticism is the way of the world of the theater, so also is idealism; and it was hardly two months after the truce that a plea for an Irish language theater appeared in the *Leader*:

> In a recent Tuesday issue of a Dublin daily paper there were two half-columns under the heading, "Round the Dublin Theatres." We suppose it is, more or less, a weekly feature of all the Dublin dailies. Nearly all the space was devoted to imported musical comedy, imported hippodrome turns, imported

music-hall stuff. It was not for the perpetration of such imported stuff that Dublin men died. When are we to see a serious attempt made to create an Irish stage—or, as we had better call it for clearness, an Irish language stage—in all classes—serious plays, high comedy and variety entertainments? The last ten months was, of necessity, practically a dead period; even the curfew hit the imported entertainers badly. But if peace is arranged, or if the Truce lasts out the winter, there ought to be some efforts made to deal with this important side of Irish national life. It is important: the imported stage apart, from any objection on the grounds of morality and good taste, is a live Anglicising agent working persistently every week-night in the year.

The Irish-Ireland movement was never particularly strong on the dramatic side. It always had to be amateur, as its public has yet largely to be created. No one, so far, has come along to subsidise an Irish language theatre. There is practically nothing but a partial fame to be made out of writing Irish plays or acting them. The Aisteori, so far as we know or observed, were the best company of players that appeared in Dublin, but nearly all the members of that company are now members of An Dail, so we may take it that their amateur play-acting days are over, and we must look to other young people for the formantion of new Irish acting companies. . . .

If we had an Irish-speaking population of 100,000 in Dublin our Irish stage would spring up out of economic necessity. At the moment an Irish stage is not, unfortunately, a business proposition, and yet it is in great need. . . .

"Wanted—An Irish Language Theatre," *Leader*, 10 Sept. 1921, pp. 107–8.

There were other such voices—such as an anonymous article in the *Leader* on 15 October, and a plea by O'Donnell for an Irish pantomime in the *Gael* on 28 Nov. Something would be done, but the Irish Language Theatre was still to remain the most feeble off-shoot of the modern Irish drama.

At the same time, voices were raised, as they have continued to be over the years, for the development of an Irish film industry. In the *Evening Telegraph*, Joseph Power contended that certain success awaited worthy Irish films in the United States since the Film Company of Ireland's biggest production, *Knocknagow*, was still drawing large crowds across the Atlantic. In a chat with a Mr. Hartley of the McConnell-Hartley film publicity service about the possibility of future film production in Ireland, Power learned that such a possibility was imminent. Hartley believed that, despite the political conditions, well-produced Irish films would receive a sympathetic reception in England. "Stage and Screen, *Evening Telegraph*, 22 Oct. 1921, p. 6. About the only film of Irish interest produced during the year was *General John Regan*. Based on George A. Birmingham's play, which in its day had occasioned the most violent riot in modern Irish theatrical history, the film was now seen as pleasantly innocuous. As the *Irish Times* reported:

In this instance there will probably be general unanimity about the merit of the film, as undoubtedly the principal artists have done their work exceedingly well. Here and there there may be a few incidents exaggerated, but then the film does not assume to reflect faithfully rural life in Ireland, even in Ballymoy. It is all good, wholesome fun. . . .

Around the part of Mary Ellen, both in the novel and the play, much controversy arose. It is not likely to be renewed in Miss Madge Stewart's study of the part, as she infuses into it a becoming sense of self-importance and personal charm.

"General John Regan Filmed," *Irish Times*, 26 Nov. 1921, p. 9. The principal actors, however, were English, and this is not really an Irish film. Canon Hannay, incidentally, was quite pleased with the film. See "Irish Author's Tribute," *Irish Times*, 5 Nov. 1921, p. 9.

56. Frank J. Hugh O'Donnell, "Theatrical Tattle," *Gael*, 7 Nov. 1921, p. 13.
57. R. Hogan and M. J. O'Neill, *Joseph Holloway's Abbey Theatre* (Carbondale and Edwardsville: Southern Illinois University Press, 1967), p.211
58. "The Abbey Theater," *Irish Times*, 7 Jan. 1921, p. 6.
59. Jacques, "Music and Drama Notes," *Evening Herald*, 8 Jan. 1921, p. 5.
60. Holloway, *Impressions*, ms. 1859, 6 Jan. 1921, p. 55, National Library of Ireland.
61. Letter of George Shiels to Lady Gregory, 14 Dec. 1923, Berg Collection.
62. "A Work of Merit," *Evening Telegraph*, 22 Feb. 1921, p. 2.
63. L. M. probably stands for the Lord Mayor.
64. Sinn-Feiner.
65. Letter of Lennox Robinson to Lady Gregory, 17 Feb. 1921, Berg Collection.
66. Jacques, "The Revolutionist," *Evening Herald*, Feb. 1921, p. 5.
67. Murphy, *Journals*, 1:228.
68. Ibid.

69. Ibid.
70. "The Revolutionist," *Freeman's Journal*, 25 Feb. 1921, p.4.
71. "The Abbey Theater," *Irish Times*, 25 Feb. 1921, p. 5; Jacques, "The Revolutionist," *Evening Herald*, 25 Feb. 1921, p. 5.
72. *Irish Times*, 25 Feb. 1921, p. 5.
73. *Evening Herald*, 25 Feb. 1921, p. 5.
74. Holloway, *Impressions*, ms. 1860, pp. 439–40.
75. "Curfew Hour," *Evening Telegraph*, 9 Mar. 1921, p. 1.
76. Letter of Maud Gonne MacBride to W. B. Yeats, 21 Mar. 1921, Berg Collection.
77. Letter of Lennox Robinson to Lady Gregory, Aug. 1921, Berg Collection.
78. Murphy, *Journals*, 1:222.
79. "New Abbey Play," *Evening Telegraph*, 18 Mar. 1921 p. 2.
80. "The Abbey Theatre," *Irish Times*, 17 Mar. 1921, p. 6.
81. Holloway, *Impressions*, ms. 1860, pp. 564–67.
82. Jacques, "Aristotle's Bellows," *Irish Independent*, 18 Mar. 1921, p. 4.
83. Holloway, *Impressions*, ms. 1860, p. 571.
84. Letter of T. C. Murray to Joseph Holloway, 29 Oct. 1921, ms. 1865, National Library of Ireland.
85. Holloway, *Impressions*, ms. 1865, pp. 683–85.
86. J. A. P[ower], "Stage and Screen," *Evening Telegraph*, 19 Nov. 1921, p. 2.
87. F. J. H. O'D[onnell], "A New Abbey Play," *Irish Independent*, 9 Nov. 1921, p. 4. Brinsley MacNamara wrote to O'Donnell, saying, "very glad to see that you have supplanted 'Jacques' as dramatic critic of *Independent*. Congratulations. I trust that you will become a real dramatic critic—not like the other man whose last state was immeasurably worse than his first." Letter, 15 Nov. 1921, ms. 21,715, National Library of Ireland.
88. Hugh Francis [Frank J. Hugh O'Donnell], "Dramaticwise and Otherwise," *Gael*, 21 Nov. 1921, p. 13.
89. F. J. H. O'D[onnell], "A New Abbey Play," *Irish Independent*, 9 Nov. 1921, p. 4.
90. Mary Frances McHugh, "Delightful Comedy," *Freeman's Journal*, 9 Nov. 1921, p. 3.
91. Murphy, *Journals*, 1:307
92. Holloway, *Impressions*, ms. 1865, pp. 683–85.
93. F. J. H. O'D[onnell], "A New Abbey Play," *Irish Independent*, 16 Nov. 1921, p. 4.
94. J. A. P[ower], "Stage and Screen," *Evening Telegraph*, 19 Nov. 1921, p. 2.
95. Ibid.
96. Holloway, *Impressions*, ms. 1866, p. 910.
97. Hugh Francis [Frank J. Hugh O'Donnell], "Dramaticwise and Otherwise," *Gael*, 28 Nov. 1921, p. 15.
98. "The Abbey Theatre," *Irish Times*, 16 Nov. 1921, p. 4.
99. "Abbey Productions," *Freeman's Journal*, 16 Nov. 1921, p. 4.
100. Hugh Francis [Frank J. Hugh O'Donnell], "Dramaticwise and Otherwise," *Gael*, 28 Nov. 1921, p. 15.
101. "Abbey Productions," *Freeman's Journal* 16 Nov. 1921, p. 4.
102. Hugh Francis [Frank J. Hugh O'Donnell], "Dramaticwise and Otherwise," *Gael*, 28 Nov. 1921, p. 15.
103. Holloway, *Impressions*, ms. 1866.
104. Murphy, *Journals*, 1:306.
105. "New Play at the Abbey," *Freeman's Journal*, 14 Dec. 1921, p. 4.
106. "New Abbey Play," *Evening Herald*, 14 Dec. 1921, p. 2.
107. Hugh Francis [Frank J. Hugh O'Donnell], "Dramaticwise and Otherwise," *Gael*, 26 Dec. 1921, p. 14.
108. Holloway, *Impressions*, ms. 1866, p. 1065.
109. Ibid., p. 1081.
110. "Dublin Amusements," *Freeman's Journal*, 6 Dec. 1921, p. 3.
111. M. R. W., "Sara Allgood at the Royal," *Irish Independent*, 6 Dec. 1921, p. 4.
112. J. A. P[ower], "Sara Allgood," *Evening Telegraph*, 6 Dec. 1921, p. 2.
113. J. A. P[ower], "Theatrical Topics," *Evening Telegraph*, 17 Sept. 1921, p. 4.
114. "Public Amusements, The Gaiety Theatre," *Irish Times*, 6 Sept. 1921, p. 4.
115. "Here as Paddy," *Eveving Telegraph*, 6 Sept. 1921, p. 1.

116. "'The Irish Jew'—A Talk with John Macdonagh," *Weekly Independent*, 11 Dec. 1921. Holloway, ms. 1866, p. 1061.
117. "Theatrical Topics," *Evening Telegraph*, 3 Dec. 1921, p. 3.
118. "This Week in the Dublin Theatres," *Evening Telegraph*, 13 Dec. 1921, p. 4.
119. "A First Night," *Irish Independent*, 13 Dec. 1921, p. 4.
120. "A Look Round," *Evening Herald*, 13 Dec. 1921, p. 2.
121. "The Abbey Theatre," *Irish Times*, 24 Feb. 1921, p. 8.
122. "The Abbey Theatre," *Irish Times*, 30 June 1921, p. 5.
123. Jacques, "Fantasy and Farce," *Evening Herald*, 30 June 1921, p. 2.
124. "The Abbey Theatre," *Irish Times*, 30 June 1921, p. 5.
125. "Dublin Drama League," *Irish Times*, 14 Nov. 1921, p. 5.
126. "Abbey Theatre," *Irish Times*, 12 Dec. 1921, p. 3.
127. "A Pastoral Play at Glendalough," *Irish Times*, 4 Aug. 1921, p. 4.
128. "The Ulster Theatre," *Northern Whig*, 3 Nov. 1921, p. 8.
129. Ibid.
130. "The Ulster Theatre," *Belfast News Letter*, 3 Nov. 1921, p. 10.
131. "Ulster Theatre," *Irish News*, 3 Nov. 1921, p. 6.
132. Ibid.
133. "This Week's Amusements," *Belfast News Letter,* 22 Nov. 1921, p. 8.
134. Letter of J. O. Flynn (Maurice Lee) to Joseph Holloway, 26 July 1921, ms. 1863, National Library of Ireland.
135. "Amusements," *Cork Constitution*, 2 Aug. 1921, p. 4.
136. Letter of Brinsley MacNamara to Joseph Holloway, 23 Dec. 1921, ms. 22,413, National Library of Ireland.
137. Alexander Woolcott, "The Play," *New York Times*, 16 Sept. 1921, p. 20.
138. "Theatrical Topics—Irish Players in Strong Demand," *Evening Telegraph*, 20 Aug. 1921, p. 3.
139. Letter of F. J. McCormick to Joseph Holloway, 9 Nov. 1921, ms. 1866, National Library of Ireland.
140. Letter of F. J. McCormick to Joseph Holloway, 21 Nov. 1921, ms. 1866, National Library of Ireland, contains this letter of Robinson.
141. Ibid.
142. Ibid.
143. Murphy, *Journals*, 1:316.
144. Ibid., 1:316.
145. Digges's letter is contained in Holloway's article, "Irish Actor in U.S.A.," *Evening Telegraph*, 1 Oct. 1921, p. 3.
146. Murphy, *Journals*, 1:307.
147. Ibid., 1:308–9.
148. Ibid., 1:651–52.
149. Ibid., 1:512.
150. "Lord Dunsany," *Evening Telegraph*, 3 Feb. 1921, p. 2.
151. Ibid.
152. "The Gaiety—Miss Horniman's Farewell to Manchester," *Manchester Guardian*, 2 May 1921, p. 3.
153. Letter of A. E. F. Horniman to Joseph Holloway, 31 Nov. 1921, ms. 1858, National Library of Ireland.
154. "Manchester's Threatened Loss," *Manchester Guardian*, 30 Nov. 1920, p. 5.

Chapter 2. 1922

1. Letter of Lady Gregory to John Quinn, 29 Jan. 1922, Berg Colletion, New York Public Library.
2. Alfred Willmore, the artist and former child actor, became the notable Dublin actor, Micheál Mac Liammóir.
3. Joseph Holloway, *Impressions of a Dublin Playgoer*, ms. 1869, National Library of Ireland, 15 May 1922, p. 764.

4. Letter of W. B. Yeats to John Quinn, 5 June 1922, Berg Collection.
5. "Candidate Ill-Used," *Evening Herald*, 13 June 1922, p. 3.
6. "Bombs in Cinemas," *Evening Herald*, 14 June 1922, p. 1
7. "Siege of Four Courts in Progress," *Evening Herald*, 28 June 1922, p. 1.
8. "Music and Drama," *Evening Herald*, 1 July 1922, p. 3.
9. Holloway, *Impressions*, ms. 1870, pp. 1017 *passim*; ms. 1871, pp. 1–9.
10. Letter of Lady Gregory to John Quinn, 2 July 1922, Berg Collection.
11. "Scene of Desolation," *Evening Herald*, 6 July 1922, p. 1.
12. Letter of Lennox Robinson to Lady Gregory, 8 July 1922, Berg Colloction.
13. Holloway, *Impressions*, ms. 1871, 25 July 1922, p. 148.
14. "Music and Drama," *Evening Harald*, 22 July 1922, p. 5.
15. Letter of Lennox Robinson to Lady Gregory, 16 Aug. 1922, Berg Collection.
16. Letter of W. B. Yeats to John Quinn, 19 Oct. 1922, Berg Collection.
17. Letter of St. John Ervine to Dudley Digges, 28 Aug. 1922, Berg Collection.
18. Holloway, *Impressions*, ms. 1873, 26 oct. 1922, pp. 712–13. Earlier, on 23 Sept., Holloway had reported, "Frank Dalton was in an Ambush on Eden Quay and a bullet pierced his hat, and he had to get drunk to soothe his nerves—poor, little, dwarfish Dalton, he is always meeting with adventure." ms. 1872, pp. 543–44.
19. Holloway, *Impressions*, ms. 1873, 13 Nov. 1922, p. 822.
20. Holloway, *Impressions*, ms. 1873, 23 Nov. 1922, pp. 896–97.
21. Fred Harris.
22. Letter of Lady Gregory to John Quinn, 10 Dec. 1922, Berg Collection.
23. Holloway, *Impressions*, ms. 1867, 12 Mar. 1922, p. 436.
24. Holloway, *Impressions*, ms. 1867, 24 Mar. 1922, p. 504.
25. Holloway, *Impressions*. ms. 1867, 17 Apr. 1922, p. 624.
26. Nichevo, "Irishmen of To-Day," *Irish Times*, 3 June 1922, p. 9.
27. Holloway, *Impressions*, ms. 1867, 23 June 1922 p. 990.
28. Holloway, *Impressions*, ms. 1870, 8 Aug. 1922, p. 237.
29. Holloway, *Impressions*, ms. 1870, 10 Aug. 1922, p. 263.
30. Holloway, *Impressions*, ms. 1873, 20 Oct. 1922, p. 690.
31. Holloway, *Impressions*, ms. 1873, 11 Nov. 1922, p. 808.
32. Holloway, *Impressions*, ms. 1873, 7 Dec. 1922, pp. 970–71.
33. Holloway, *Impressions*, ms. 1867, 7 Feb. 1922, p. 228.
34. Holloway, *Impressions*, ms. 1868, 14 Feb. 1922, pp. 277–78.
35. Holloway, *Impressions*, ms. 1868, 16 Feb. 1922, p. 292.
36. Holloway, *Impressions*, ms. 1868, 18 Mar. 1922, p. 465.
37. Holloway, *Impressions*, ms. 1868, 17 Mar. 1922, pp. 469–70.
38. J. A. P. [Joesph A. Power], "Theatrical Topics," *Evening Telegraph*, 6 May 1922, p. 5.
39. Thomas McGreevy, "A Rare Bird in Ireland or—Elsewhere," *Irish Independent*, 13 Sept. 1922, p. 4.
40. Since O'Donnell as playwright and critic figures so often in these years, it seems appropriate to append this sketch of his early life, which appeared in the *Tuam Herald* of 22 July 1922:

> A young gentleman well known in literature and commercial circles in Dublin is Mr. Frank Hugh O'Donnell, only son of the late John O'Donnell, Esq., Merchant, Shop Street. He was a prominent and well known resident in Tuam, where he and his brother, Mr. Patrick O'Donnell, lived, carried on business for many years, and were respected by all classes. Mr. John O'Donnell was for a short time only a member of the Town Board, as he did not interest himself much in public affairs preferring to give his attention, which he did closely and consistently, to the carrying on of his business. He married Miss Delia Carr, daughter of the late Charles Carr of Shop Street, a gentleman who carried on a successful saddlery business in Tuam. . . .
>
> Mr. John O'Donnell having died, his business was given up and his young son, Frank Hugh, went to live at Milltown with his father's people. There he was educated and he owes a good deal of his early training and particularly his great love for and knowledge of English Literature to the skilful and experienced direction of his studies by the late Mr. J. H. Sheridan, Principal of the National School at Milltown and a very clever man and deep and fervent reader of the English classics. Mr. O'Donnell gratefully remembers the early training he got from that capable teacher. . . .
>
> Coming to Dublin some years ago he devoted himself to business and in his spare moments to literature.

41. Letter of T. C. Murray to Frank J. Hugh O'Donnell, 5 Oct. 1921, ms. 21,715, National Library of Ireland.

42. Letter of T. C. Murray to Joseph Holloway, contained in *Impression*, ms. 1867, p. 30 verso.

43. "The Aftermath," *Dublin Evening Mail*, 11 Jan. 1922, p. 5.

44. "New Abbey Play," *Evening Telegraph*, 11 Jan. 1922, p. 2.

45. Jacques, "Aftermath," *Evening Herald*, 11 Jan. 1922, p. 3. Jacques returned to the matter later, remarking:

> *Aftermath* is not a great play. It has not the strength and sweeping onwardness of *Birthright*; but it is a splendid example of untheatrical, progressive development in which realism is so natural, and the results so inevitable that we are left almost stunned at the last. It is free from any suggestion of blather or high-falutin. In its construction it coils us with each succeeding loop of interest which the author fashions around us like an expert lassoer. . . . The mind-presence of the two ladies in the first scene when the big Irish terrier strayed in from the street on to the stage was highly commendable.

Quoted in "Music and Drama," *Evening Herald*, 14 Jan. 1922, p. 5.

46. Hugh Francis [F. J. H. O'Donnell], "Dramaticwise and Otherwise," *Gael*, 16 Jan. 1922, p. 15.

47. Ibid.

48. Letter of T. C. Murray to Frank J. Hugh O'Donnell, 19 Jan. 1922, ms. 21,715, National Library of Ireland.

49. Peter Drewiany's Ph.D. diss. "The Irish Theatrical Criticism of W. J. Lawrence" (University of Delaware, 1981), gathers together Lawrence's fugitive reviews and is worth consulting. Many of these he then published under the title of "The Drama Criticism of W. J. Lawrence" in *The Journal of Irish Literature*, 18 (May and September 1989).

50. Holloway, *Impressions*, ms. 1867, 31 Jan. 1922.

51. "The Round Table," *Evening Telegraph*, 1 Feb. 1922, p. 4.

52. Jacques, "The Round Table," *Evening Herald*, 1 Feb. 1922, p. 3.

53. Holloway, *Impressions*, ms. 1867, 2 Feb. 1922.

54. Hugh Francis [F. J. H. O'Donnell], "Dramaticwise and Otherwise," *Gael*, 13 Feb. 1922, p. 11.

55. Quoted in Holloway, *Impressions*, ms. 1867, p. 228 verso.

56. Holloway, *Impressions*, ms 1868, p. 424.

57. Holloway, *Impressions*, ms. 1868, 9 Mar. 1922, p. 418.

58. Jacques, "Tragedy and Comedy," *Evening Herald*, 7 Apr. 1922, p. 3.

59. Quoted in Hugh Francis [F J. H. O'Donnell], "Dramaticwise and Otherwise," *Gael*, 1 May 1922, p. 6.

60. Ibid.

61. Holloway, *Impressions*, ms. 1869, 6 Apr. 1922, p. 575.

62. Holloway, who is usually right in such matters, remarked that the notice was by Miss McHugh. See *Impressions*, ms. 1872, p. 399 verso.

63. "The Moral Law," *Evening Telegraph*, 30 Aug. 1922, p. 2.

64. Jacques, "New Abbey Play," *Evening Herald*, 30 Aug. 1922, p. 4.

65. "Abbey Theatre," *Evening Mail*, 30 Aug. 1922, p. 4.

66. Hugh Francis [F. J. H. O'Donnell], "Dramaticwise and Otherwise," *Gael*, 11 Sept. 1922, p. 1.

67. Holloway, *Impressions*, ms. 1872, 29 Aug. 1922, p. 389.

68. "A Leprechaun Tale," *Evening Telegraph*, 8 Sept. 1922, p. 2.

69. Jacques, "Rags and Tatters," *Evening Herald*, 6 Sept. 1922, p. 4.

70. Holloway, *Impressions*, ms. 1872, 13 Sept. 1922, p. 491.

71. "The Abbey Theatre," *Evening Telegraph*, 26 Sept. 1922, p. 3.

72. "At the Abbey," *Evening Telegraph*, 4 Oct. 1922, p. 4.

73. Frank J. Hugh O'Donnell, "Comedy or Farce?" *Evening Herald*, 4 Oct. 1922, p. 4.

74. Jacques, "Beware of Lozenges," *Irish Independent*, 4 Oct. 1922, p. 4.

75. Ibid.

76. Holloway, *Impressions*, ms. 1873, 3 Oct. 1922, p. 604.

77. Holloway, *Impressions*, ms. 1873, 3 Oct. 1922, p. 606.

78. Colum and his wife visited Ireland during part of the summer and fall, and on 24 Aug. Holloway met him at the Abbey:

> Between Acts One and Two just as the gong had been struck for the third time who should come into the Vestibule but Padraic Colum, and he seemed delighted to see me again, and so little changed. He arrived

> from America on Sunday and intends staying for some months over here. He is under signed contract with the U.S. to go on to the South Sea Islands and write up the folklore there. He hopes to make sufficient money to take a house in Ireland and settle down. Times are changed in Ireland he finds, and many of the old faces and things vainshed. . . . He saw Sinclair and Maire O'Neill in *The Whiteheaded Boy* in Boston, and they played for the laughs. He liked the quieter comedy playing of the company at the Abbey. . . .

Holloway, *Impressions*, ms. 1872, 24 Aug. 1922, pp. 357–58.

79. M.H.J.B., "The Grasshopper," *Evening Herald*, 25 Oct. 1922, p. 3.
80. "Music and Drama," *Evening Herald*, 28 Oct. 1922, p. 6.
81. "The Grasshopper," *Evening Telegraph*, 25 Oct. 1922, p. 3.
82. Jacques, "Grasshopper," *Irish Independent*, 25 Oct. 1922, p. 4.
83. "New Abbey Play," *Irish Times*, 25 Oct. 1922, p. 6.
84. Holloway, *Impressions*, ms. 1873, 26 Oct. 1922, pp. 713–14.
85. Ibid.
86. Ibid.
87. "New and Old," *Evening Telegraph*, 15 Nov. 1922, p. 6.
88. Bertha Buggy, "Abbey Audiences, A Study in Types," *Sunday Independent*[?], 24 Dec. 1922; see also Holloway, *Impressions*, ms. 1874, October–December 1922, p. 1069.
89. Frankly, "Some of Our Lecturers: II—Lennox Robinson," *Evening Herald*, 25 Mar. 1922, p. 6.
90. Holloway, *Impressions*, ms. 1872, 22 Sept. 1922, p. 537.
91. "Music and Drama," *Evening Herald*, 21 Jan. 1922, p. 5.
92. "Music and Drama," *Evening Herald*, 4 Feb. 1922, p. 5. However, in the same production, Robinson did incorporate a mild novelty in blocking. As the above-cited article also notes:

> The author produced the play and was no doubt responsible for the arrangement of putting the fireplace of Mr. Drennan's sittingroom (in the first two acts) back to the audience so that the people on the stage faced out to us when sitting and chatting around the fire. This fireplace idea was, if I remember aright, first used in the boarding-house play, *The Passing of the Third Floor Back*.

93. Holloway, *Impressions*, ms. 1873, 17 Oct. 1922, pp. 675–76.
94. Holloway, *Impressions*, ms. 1867, 7 Feb. 1922, p. 228.
95. Holloway, *Impressions*, ms. 1868, 16 Feb. 1922, p. 292.
96. Holloway, *Impressions*, ms. 1867, 2 Jan. 1922, p. 12.
97. Holloway, *Impressions*, ms. 1873, 11 Nov. 1922, p. 811.
98. Holloway, *Impressions*, ms. 1874, 17 Dec. 1922, p. 1026.
99. Holloway, *Impressions*, ms. 1871, 10 Aug. 1922, pp. 255–56.
100. Letter of Lennox Robinson to Lady Gregory, Aug. 1922, Berg Collection.
101. "Successful Opening of Abbey Season," *Evening Mail*, 5 Aug. 1922, p. 5.
102. Holloway, *Impressions*, ms. 1871, 7 Aug. 1922, pp. 234–35.
103. Holloway, *Impressions*, ms. 1872, 22 Aug. 1922, p. 349.
104. Holloway, *Impressions*, ms. 1872, 25 Aug. 1922, p. 361.
105. Holloway, *Impressions*, ms. 1872, 26 Aug. 1922, pp. 368-69. Holloway, incidentally, reports "this anecdote on 27 Aug.:

> Miss Allgood narrated her meeting with John MacCormack in London some time ago. They met and she queried, "Do you remember me?" And he said he did. "Well, who am I?" And he couldn't think of her name, and she said, "Miss Allgood!"
> "Oh! You've grown as big as the side of a house," said he. . . .
> "You're not behind the door either," was her retort. (p. 373)

106. "Frank Fay at the Abbey," *Evening Mail*, 15 Oct. 1922, p. 5.
107. Holloway, *Impressions*, ms. 1868, 23 Mar. 1922, pp. 499–500.
108. Ibid., p. 515.
109. Holloway, *Impressions*, ms. 1871, 27 July 1922, p. 164.
110. Holloway, *Impressions*, ms. 1869, Apr. 1922, pp. 571–72.
111. Holloway, *Impressions*, ms. 1873, 15 Nov. 1922, p. 6.
112. Holloway, *Impressions*, ms 1867, 12 Jan. 1922, p. 49.
113. Holloway, *Impressions*, ms. 1871, 7 Aug. 1922, pp. 234–35.
114. Ibid., 10 Aug. 1922, pp. 256-57.

115. Daniel J. Murphy, ed., *Lady Gregory's Journals*, vol. 1 (New York: Oxford University Press, 1978), entry for 11 Jan. 1922, p.319.

116. Letter of Lennox Robinson to W. B. Yeats, 24 Apr. 1922, ms. 13,068, National Library of Ireland.

117. Ibid.

118. Ibid.

119. Murphy, *Journals*, 1:405. Lady Gregory's corrections were incorporated in a later draft. See ms. 20,670, National Library of Ireland.

120. Ms. 13,068, National Library of Ireland.

121. Jacques, "Pride of Petravore," *Evening Herald*, 21 Mar. 1922, p. 5.

122. Hugh Francis [F. J. H. O'Donnell], "Dramaticwise and Otherwise," *Gael*, Apr. 1922, p. 3.

123. "The Star Theatre," *Evening Mail*, 28 Dec. 1922, p. 3.

124. In March, Gertrude Page died in Salisbury, Rhodesia. Her play had initially run for three years at the Savoy in London.

125. John W. Coulter, "The Modern Drama—III, Ireland's Part," *Irish Timas*, 2 May 1922, p. 4.

126. Holloway, *Impressions*, ms. 1872, 23 Aug. 1922, pp. 357-58.

127. "Stage and Gallery," *Evening Mail*, 12 Dec. 1922, p. 5.

128. Holloway, *Impressions*, ms. 1874, 13 Dec. 1922, pp. 1003–4.

129. "The Ulster Players," *The Irish Times*, 15 Dec. 1922, p. 8.

130. "Ulster Players," *Evening Telegraph*, 15 Dec. 1922, p. 5.

131. Holloway, *Impressions*, ms. 1867, 9 Feb. 1922, p. 235.

132. Letter of Fred Allan to Joseph Holloway, 17 Feb. 1922, contained in *Impressions*, ms. 1868, p. 298 verso.

133. However, a letter to the *Herald* by J. Brophy of 4 St. Rioch's St., Kilkenny, says that *The Rising Generation* was first produced by the Ossory Players at the Empire Theatre, Kilkenny, on 19 June 1920, under the auspices of the Gaelic League. See "Editor's Postbag," *Evening Herald*, 25 Feb. 1922, p. 7.

134. Holloway, *Impressions*, ms. 1868, 24 Feb. 1922, p. 336.

135. "The Ballykinlar Players," *Evening Herald*, 21 Feb. 1922, p. 2.

136. "Music and Drama," *Evening Herald*, 9 Sept. 1922, p. 5.

137. Holloway, *Impressions*, ms. 1872, 13 Sept. 1922, pp. 479–80.

138. Ibid., 16 Sept. 1922, p. 497.

139. Ibid., 30 Sept. 1922, p. 585. Vousden was not the son but "only a relative" of the late nineteenth-century entertainer of the same name. In a conversation with R. J. Walshe, the dramatiser of *Knocknagow*, Holloway reported that Walshe

> spoke of old Vousdan and recalled a time when he had over £3000 in the Bank, and afterwards he saw him in his stocking feet with a mirror under his arm on his way to the pawnshop in Blessington Street. He also recalled his coming before the audience in the Rotunda and apologising for his being too drunk to perform and dispersing those in front. Yet he never broke with his patrons; they were faithful to him to the end of his public career. . . . Old Walshe thought him a great artist in his line.

Impressions. ms. 1782, 30 Sept. 1922, p. 582.

140. Holloway, *Impressions*, ms. 1873, 14 Oct. 1922, pp. 655–56.

141. Ibid., 28 Oct. 1922, pp. 729–30.

142. "Music and Drama," *Evening Herald*, 28 Oct. 1922, p. 6.

143. Holloway, *Impressions*, ms. 1873, 28 Oct. 1922, pp. 732–33.

144. Holloway, *Impressions*, ms. 1869, 13 Apr. 1922, pp. 610 and 612.

145. Ira Allen, "The Old Muzzle Loader," *Evening Telegraph*, 30 Sept. 1922, p. 3.

146. "Abbey Theatre," *Evening Mail*, 9 May 1922, p. 5.

147. "Stage and Screen," *Evening Telegraph*, 13 May 1922, p. 5.

148. "At the Abbey," *Evening Mail*, 23 May 1922, p. 4.

149. Holloway, *Impressions*, ms. 1870, 22 Apr. 1922, p. 826.

150. Ibid., p. 837.

151. Ibid., pp. 819–20.

152. J. H. Cox, "Triple Bill at the Abbey," *Evening Herald*, 30 Jan. 1922, p. 2.

153. Holloway, *Impressions*, ms. 1867, 29 Jan. 1922, pp. 168–69.

154. Ibid., pp. 170–72
155. Ibid., pp. 168–69.
156. Hugh Francis [F. J. H. O'Donnell], "Dramaticwise and Otherwise," *Gael*, 13 Mar. 1922, p. 17.
157. Holloway, *Impressions*, ms. 1868, 20 Mar. 1922, p. 474.
158. Ibid.
159. Ibid., p. 477.
160. F.J.H.O'D. [F. J. H. O'Donnell], "Drama League," *Evening Herald*, 6 Nov. 1922, p. 3.
161. Holloway, *Impressions*, ms. 1873, 5 Nov. 1922, p. 773.
162. P.[*sic*]J.H.O'D. [F. J. H. O'Donnell], "Dublin Drama League," *Evening Herald* (4 Dec. 1922), p. 2.
163. Holloway, *Impressions*, ms. 1874, 3 Dec. 1922, p. 948.
164. "Music and Drama," *Evining Herald*, 2 Dec. 1922, p. 5.
165. "Everyman Theatre," *Evening Herald*, 26 Dec. 1922, p. 3.
166. Holloway, *Impressions*, ms. 1873, 11 Nov. 1922, p. 808.
167. "Music and Drama," *Evening Herald*, 30 Dec. 1922, p. 5.
168. F. Jay, "Music and Drama," *Evening Herald*, 25 Mar. 1922, p.5.
169. Arthur Gaynor, "The Irish Dramatic Union," *Evening Herald*, 1 Apr. 1922, p. 5.
170. Frank J. Hugh O'Donnell, "Music and Drama," *Evening Herald*, p. 7.
171. Holloway, *Impressions*, ms. 1870, 3 June 1922, pp. 884–86.
172. "Film Censorship," *Evening Herald*, 6 Nov. 1922, p.3.
173. "The Dublin Cinemas," *Evening Herald*, 2 Jan. 1922, p. 1.
174. "Flickers form Filmland," *Evening Herald*, 7 Jan. 1922, p. 7.
175. "Film Censorship," *Evening Telegraph*, 6 Jan. 1922, p. 2.
176. "Clean Films" *Evening Telegraph*, 6 Feb. 1922, p. 2.
177. "Flickers from Filmland," *Evening Herald*, 21 Jan. 1922, p. 2.
178. "This Week in Dublin Theatres," *Evening Telegraph*, 31 Jan. 1922, p. 2.
179. Jacques, "By the Way," *Evening Herald*, 18 Feb. 1922, p. 7.
180. "This Week in Dublin Theatres," *Evening Telegraph*, 31 Jan. 1922, p. 2.
181. "Ireland a Nation," *Evening Mail*, 26 June 1922, p. 5.
182. "Flickers from Filmland," *Evening Herald*, 10 June 1922, p. 6.
183. J. M., "Flickers from Filmland," *Evening Herald*, 15 July 1922, p. 2.
184. Hugh Francis [F. J. H. O'Donnell], "Dramaticwise and Otherwise," *Gael*, 26 June 1922, p. 14.
185. Holloway, *Impressions*, ms. 1871, 25 July 1922, pp. 141–142.
186. "New Irish Film." *Evening Telegraph*, 25 July 1922, p. 1.
187. "Flickers from Filmland," *Evening Herald*, 29 July 1922, p. 6.
188. "Flickers from Filmland," *Evening Herald*, 5 Aug. 1922, p. 6.
189. "Flickers from Filmland," *Evening Herald*, 16 Sept. 1922, p. 6.
190. "Hear All Sides," *Evening Telegraph*, 28 Sept. 1922, p. 2.
191. Quoted in Holloway, *Impressions*, ms. 1874, pp. 1108.
192. "The Ulster Theatre," *Belfast News-Letter*, 19 Oct. 1922, p. 6.
193. "Opera House, Amusements," *Cork Constitution*, 30 May 1922, p. 8.
194. Advertisement entitled "To Authors and Playwrights," *Cork Examiner*, 17 July 1922, p. 3.
195. Holloway, *Impressions*, ms. 1874, p. 1039.
196. J. Bernard MacCarthy, "How to Write a Film Play, Some Points for Movies," *Irish Independent*, 17 Nov. 1922, p. 4.
197. J. Bernard MacCarthy, "The Literature of Simple Things," *Irish Independent*, 15 Dec. 1922, p. 4.
198. T. C. Murray, "Catholics and the Theatre," *Evening Herald*, 12 Oct. 1922, p. 1.
199. B. M. [Brinsley MacNamara], "Books and Their Writers," *Gael*, 20 Mar. 1922, pp. 22–23.
200. Holloway, *Impressions*, ms. 1867, pp. 111–13.
201. See "Lynchehaun Reappears," *Evening Telegraph*, contained in Holloway, *Impressions*, ms. 1868, p. 212 verso.
202. Holloway, *Impressions*, ms 1871, 18 Aug. 1922, pp. 324–25.
203. Holloway, *Impressions*, ms. 1873, 27 Dec. 1922, pp. 1073–74.

204. Earlier in the year, on 3 Mar., her husband, who was Chairman of the Prisons' Board, was shot dead while grappling with a bank robber in Stephen's Green.
205. Caitlin, "Distinguished Irishwomen," *Gael*, 4 Sept. 1922, p. 8.
206. Alice L. Milligan, "The Clergy and the Drama," *Irish Independent*, 21 cot. 1922, p. 6.
207. Murphy, *Journals*, 1:339.
208. Ibid., 1:655.

Chapter 3. 1923

1. Dorothy Macardle, *The Irish Republic* (London: Corgi Books, 1968), pp. 756–57.
2. "Fire Follows Mine," *Irish Times*, 1 Feb. 1923, p. 9.
3. "Wreck of Kilteragh," *Irish Times*, 1 Feb. 1923, p. 7.
4. "Lord Mayo's Loss," *Irish Times*, 1 Feb. 1923, p. 9.
5. "Another Mine," *Irish Times*, 1 Feb. 1923, p. 7.
6. "Another House Burned," *Irish Times*, 2 Feb. 1923, p. 7.
7. "Moore Hall," *Irish Times*, 6 Feb. 1923, p. 7. Collectors of bizarre facts may be interested to know that the IRA, sometime after gutting Moore Hall, erected a plaque on the shell of the building to commemorate a previous Moore whose politics they found more agreeable.
8. Daniel J. Murphy, ed., *Lady Gregory's Journals*, vol. 1 (New York: Oxford University Press, 1978), p. 425.
9. Ulick O'Connor in his *Oliver St. John Gogarty* erroneously states that the date of this event was 20 Jan. However, Gogarty states that it occurred on 12 Jan., and Lady Gregory read an *Irish Times* account of the matter on 15 Jan.
10. Quoted in Ulick O'Connor's *Oliver St. John Gogarty* London: New English Library, 1967), p. 177.
11. This was Thomas F. Higgins, Kevin O'Higgins's father.
12. All from the *Evening Herald*.
13. Murphy, *Journals*, 1:439.
14. "Cork Theatres," *Irish Times*, 30 Jan. 1923, p. 6.
15. Murphy, *Journals*, 1:443–44. Robinson's remark about his "stormiest moments in the Theatre" was a reference to the brouhaha in 1910 when he did not close the Abbey on the day of Edward VII's death. See vol. 4 of this history.
16. Murphy, *Journals*, 1:447.
17. Macardle, *Irish Republic*, p. 758.
18. Maire and Conor Cruise O'Brien, *A Concise History of Ireland* (London: Thames & Hudson, 1972), p. 152.
19. St. John Ervine, "At the Play, Three Irish Dramatists," *Observer*, 7 Jan. 1923; see also Holloway, *Impressions*, ms. 1875, January–March 1923, p. 36.
20. Claude Ashe, "The Future of the Irish Theatre," *Sunday Independent*, 11 Mar. 1923; see also Holloway, *Impressions*, ms. 1876, January–March 1923, p. 476.
21. Jacques, "At the Abbey," *Evening Herald*, 7 Feb. 1923, p. 4.
22. "No longer a fault in 1927." W. J. Lawrence's note, written in his scrapbooks contained in the National Library of Ireland.
23. W. J. Lawrence, "The Long Road to Garranbraher," *Stage*; see also Lawrence's scrapbooks, ms. 4304, p. 48, National Library of Ireland.
24. "Abbey Theatre," *Irish Times*, 10 Jan. 1923, p. 4.
25. Jacques, "Spray from the Sea," *Irish Independent*, 10 Jan. 1923, p. 4.
26. "New Abbey Play," *Evening Herald*, 10 Jan. 1923, p. 4.
27. Holloway, *Impressions*, ms. 1876, 9 Jan. 1923, pp. 60–69.
28. Prior, "Abbey Theatre," *Irish Times*, 9 Mar. 1923, p. 6.
29. Jacques, "More Matchmaking," *Evening Herald*, 9 Mar. 1923, p. 2.
30. Holloway, *Impressions*, ms. 1876, 8 Mar. 1923, pp. 455, 464.
31. W. J. Lawrence, "'Twixt the Giltinan's and the Carmody's," *Stage*; see also Lawrence's scrapbooks, ms. 4304, p. 54.
32. Holloway, *Impressions*, ms. 1876, 8 Mar. 1923, pp. 455, 464.

33. See. for instance, Fitzmaurice's letters of 1935 and 1939 refusing projected revivals of *The Country Dressmaker*, in *Journal of Irish Literature* 10 (May 1981), pp. 125–27.
34. Holloway, *Impressions*, 10 Mar. 1923, p. 466, Ms. 1876, National Library of Ireland.
35. "Abbey Theatre," *Irish Times*, 23 Mar. 1923, p. 4.
36. Letter of W. B. Yeats to Lady Gregory, 29 Mar. 1923, ms. 18,741, National Library of Ireland.
37. Pierrot, "Of Playwrights and Players," *Dublin Magazine*, 1 Feb. 1924, pp. 577.
38. Pierrot, "Of Playwrights and Players," *Dublin Magazine*, 1 Mar. 1924, pp. 759–60.
39. Letter of W. B. Yeats to Lady Gregory, 8 Apr. 1923, ms. 18,741, National Library of Ireland.
40. R. Hogan and M. J. O'Neill, *Joseph Holloway's Abbey Theatre* (Carbondale and Edwardsville: Southern Illinois University Press, 1967), p. 215.
41. A lost manuscript entitled *The Frost in the Flower*.
42. Murphy, pp. 445–46.
43. Frank J. Hugh O'Donnell, "Treat at the Abbey," *Evening Herald*, 13 Apr. 1923, p. 2.
44. Prior, "Abbey Theatre," *Irish Times*, 13 Apr. 1923, p. 4.
45. P. S. O'Hegarty, "A Drama of Disillusionment," *Irish Statesman*, 7 June 1924, p. 399.
46. "New Play at the Abbey," *Evening Herald*, 4 Sept. 1923, p. 4.
47. Prior, "Abbey Theatre," *Irish Times*, 4 Sept. 1923, p. 4.
48. Ronald Ayling and Michael J. Durkan, *Sean O'Casey, a Bibliography* (Seattle: University of Washington Press, 1978), p. 129.
49. Prior, "Abbey Theatre," *Irish Times*, 4 Oct. 1923, p. 4.
50. Frank J. Hugh O'Donnell, "Cathleen Listens In." *Evening Herald*, 2 Oct. 1923, p. 2.
51. S. L. M. [Susan L. Mitchell], "Dramatic Notes," *Irish Statesman*, 6 Oct. 1923, p. 122.
52. Jacques, "A Dark Horse," *Evening Herald*, 28 Nov. 1923, p. 2.
53. J. B. H., "New Abbey Play," *Freeman's Journal*, 28 Nov. 1923, p. 4.
54. S. L. M. [Susan L. Mitchell], "The Abbey Theatre," *Irish Statesman*, 8 Dec. 1923, pp. 406–8.
55. Robert Hogan, ed., *Dictionary of Irish Literature* (Westport Conn.: Greenwood Press, 1979), p. 418.
56. "The Abbey Theatre," *Irish Times*, 27 Dec. 1923, p. 4.
57. S. L. M. [susan L. Mitchell], "Drama Notes," *Irish Statesman*, 5 Jan. 1924, p. 528.
58. "Comedy and Politics," *Evening Herald*, 27 Dec. 1923, p. 2.
59. "Before the Footlights," *Irish Independent*, 1 Jan. 1924, p. 6.
60. Pierrot, "Of Playwrights and Players," *Dublin Magazine* 1 Feb. 1924, p. 577.
61. Letter of W. B. Yeats to Lady Gregory, 30 Oct. 1923, ms. 18,741, National Library of Ireland.
62. "Changes at the Abbey Theatre," *Irish Times*, 29 Nov. 1923, p. 6.
63. Letter of Michael J. Dolan to Lady Gregory, 30 Nov. 1923, Berg Collection, New York Public Library.
64. Letter of Michael J. Dolan to Joseph Holloway, 30 Nov. 1923, ms. 22,404, National Library of Ireland.
65. Murphy, *Journals*, 1:434.
66. Ibid., 1:435.
67. Ibid., 1:436.
68. Ibid., 1:446–47.
69. Ibid., 1:461.
70. Ibid., 1:466.
71. Robinson in his *Ireland's Abbey Theatre* is often inaccurate about dates. On the same page on which he quotes the 27 June letter, he misdates two of Lady Gregory's journal entries—one of 22 Dec. 1921, he enters as 19 Dec. 1923; and one of 11 Jan. 1922 he enters as 11 Jan. 1924.
72. Lennox Robinson, *Ireland's Abbey Theatre* (London: Sidgwick and Jackson, 1951), pp. 125–126.
73. Letter of Lennox Robinson to Lady Gregory, dated 13 July 1923, Berg Collection.
74. Robinson, *Abbey Theatre*, p. 126.
75. Murphy, *Journals*, 1:469.
76. Ibid., 1:472.

77. Letter of W. B. Yeats to Lady Gregory, 16 Oct. 1923, ms. 18,741, National Library of Ireland. The *Irish Statesman* ran from 15 Sept. 1923 through 12 Apr. 1930, and was not edited by Robinson or by Robert Lynd, but by AE. In August 1923, another distinguished Irish periodical was founded; this was *Dublin Magazine*, edited by Seumas O'Sullivan. Commencing as a monthly, it became after two years a quarterly and continued its long life until the second issue of 1958. Both magazines contain many useful theatrical reviews, and *Dublin Magazine* also published some important plays by George Fitzmaurice and others.

78. "Gaiety Theatre," *Irish Times*, 26 July 1923, p. 8.

79. Endymion's real name was Jimmy Farrell, and Denis Johnston includes him in the cast of his play, *The Scythe and the Sunset*.

80. F.J.H.O'D. [Frank J. Hugh O'Donnell], "St. John Ervine," *Evening Herald*, 15 May 1923, p. 5.

81. "St. John Ervine's Play," *Irish Times*, 15 May 1923, p. 6.

82. John Corbin, "The Play—Mrs. Fiske at the Belasco," *New York Times*, 12 Sept. 1923, p. 14.

83. F.J.H.O'D [Frank J. Hugh O'Donnell], "A Matter of Fact," *Evening Herald*, 6 June 1923, p. 2.

84. On 25 March, the Dublin Jewish Dramatic Society played Masefield's version of Racine's *Esther* at the Abbey, on a double bill with Leon Kobrin's Yiddish play *Der Zeitgeist*.

85. Grizelda Hervey was said to have been the great-great-great-grandaughter of Lord Edward.

86. See Jacques, "The Rivals," *Evening Herald*, 24 July 1923, p. 4.

87. "The Dramatic Art," *Evening Herald*, 23 Apr. 1923, p. 2. In the course of an article mainly on the acting of Charlie Chaplin, Robinson made a few remarks which have considerable application to his own directing and writing:

> I remember seeing Lady Gregory's *Jackdaw* long ago and dismissing it with the arrogance of a twenty-year old as "only a farce." I know better now and envy her every line of it. If people only knew how easy it is to end a play with a pistol-shot, an "Oh my God," a weeping parent, and to get curtain after curtain as a reward, and how supremely difficult to write a page of real comedy to get a laugh—as Charlie gets it—by a turn of the head, an expression of the hands or face. ("Literature and life, The Comic Muse," *Irish Statesman*, 27 Oct. 1923, pp. 205–6).

In another article, mainly about modern fiction, Robinson made some similar points:

> I think I learnt in the Abbey Theatre the value of economy of movement and gesture. Twenty years ago on the English stage (and you can see it still in third rate companies and ignorant amateurs) at the end of almost every sentence the speaker crossed the stage or moved up or down, certain gestures were automatically used—they survive still in great opera. The result, of course, was that the movement and gesture ceased to have meaning at all. By using movement sparingly, and using it always for some definite purpose, the Irish Theatre gave it back its old value, it used gesture boldly and with meaning or not at all. To me Mr. [D. H.] Lawrence and his school, seem to cross the stage at the end of every paragraph, semaphoring as they go. To be frank, they rant. ("Life and Literature, The Use of Trumpets," *Irish Statesman*, 1 Dec. 1923, p. 368).

88. "Dublin Drama League," *Irish Times*, 12 Feb. 1923, p. 4.

89. Jacques, "Some Shavian Slush," *Irish Independent*, 17 Apr. 1923, p. 4.

90. F.J.H.O'D. [Frank J. Hugh O'Donnell], "Kingdom of God," *Evening Herald*, 22 Oct. 1923, p. 2.

91. L. Elyan, "Dublin Drama League," *Evening Herald*, 24 Oct. 1923, p. 3.

92. Undoubtedly Harold R. White.

93. James Murray, "Our Dramatic Critics," *Evening Herald*, 27 Oct. 1923, p. 8.

94. F.J.H.O'D. [Frank J. Hugh O'Donnell], "Is Life Life?" *Evening Herald*, 10 Dec. 1923, p. 2.

95. Pierrot, "Of Playwrights and Players," *Dublin Magazine* 1 (January 1924), pp. 543–44.

96. S. L. M. [Susan L. Mitchell], "The Dublin Drama League," *Irish Statesman*, 15 Dec. 1923, p. 434.

97. Murphy *Journals*, 1:489.

98. "Theatre Inspection," *Evening Herald*, 12 Feb. 1923, p. 2.

99. Kevin Rockett, *Film & Ireland: A Chronicle* (London: A Sense of Ireland, 1980), p. 5. See also "Film Censorship," *Evening Herald*, 9 May 1923, p. 2.

100. See "Big City Explosion," *Evening Herald*, 27 Apr. 1923, p. 1.
101. See "Man Shot Dead in Dublin Theatre," *Irish Times*, 28 Mar. 1923, p. 5; and "Theatre Shooting," *Irish Times*, 19 Apr. 1923, p. 9. The only other theatrical murder we have noted in the year occurred in Spain early in March: "The well-known journalist and author, Senor Luis Anton del Olmet was shot dead in the Eslava Theatre, during an altercation, by a friend, Senor Vidal Planas, whose literary work he had criticised." ("Theatre Tragedy," *Evening Herald*, 3 Mar. 1923, p. 1). The heated critical discussion occurred during a rehearsal of Olmet's *Le Capitain Sans Ame*.
102. "Dull Days for Dublin," *Evening Herald*, 16 June 1923, p. 1.
103. Edward McNulty, "The Irish Stage," *Evening Herald*, 5 May 1923, p. 8.
104. Harry O'Donovan, "Local Talent," *Evening Herald*, 8 May 1923, p. 5.
105. "The Ulster Theatre," *Belfast News-Letter*, 20 Apr. 1923, p. 11.
106. "Ulster Players at the Gaiety Theatre," *Irish Times*, 28 Nov. 1923, p. 4.
107. J. G. S., "Drama in Dublin," *Irish Statesman*, 8 Dec. 1923, p. 406.
108. "Ulster Players," *Irish Times*, 29 Nov. 1923, p. 6.
109. Jacques, "Phantoms," *Irish Independent*, 29 Nov. 1923, p. 6.
110. Holloway, *Impressions*, ms. 1882, 28 Nov. 1923, p. 1004, National Library of Ireland.
111. "The Ulster Theatre," *Belfast News-Letter*, 14 Dec. 1923, p. 10.
112. "Belfast Playwright," *Irish News*, 27 Nov. 1923, p. 7.
113. "This Week's Amusements," *Belfast News-Letter*, 27 Nov. 1923, p. 11.
114. F.J.H.O'D. [Frank J. Hugh O'Donnell], "Bubbles Produced," *Evening Herald*, 1 Dec. 1923, p. 2.
115. "The Players Dramatic Club," *Belfast News-Letter*, 30 Oct. 1923, p. 10.
116. "Amateur Opera in Belfast," *Belfast News-Letter*, 2 Oct. 1923, p. 12.
117. "Northern Drama League," *Belfast News-Letter*, 9 Nov. 1923, p. 10.
118. F. R., "Ibsen in Belfast," *Irish Statesman*, 17 Nov. 1923, p. 306.
119. Letter of Dudley Digges to Padraic Colum, 13 July 1923, Berg Collection.
120. "Mr. Yeats and the Abbey," *Irish Times*, 17 Nov. 1923, p. 9. Incidentally, a few days earlier, on 8 Nov., at a meeting of the Dublin University Philosophical Society in Trinity, Yeats made an interesting response to a paper on "The Modern Novel":

> Mr. W. Beare, B.A., President of the Society, read the inaugural address, his subject being "The Modern Novel." . . .
>
> Mr. W. B. Yeats proposed that the thanks of the society were due to the President for his address. He said that the address of the Auditor had been full of knowledge, full of accurate description, and in it there had been some acute criticism. He thought in its selection of authors it was an achievement of catholicity. His (Mr. Yeats's) only complaint was that in his measure of time the Auditor was not catholic enough; he confined himself chiefly in his discussion of the modern novel to the last twenty years; in fact, he could see that the time when he was young was not really modern in the Auditor's eye, and that when his father was a young man was to the Auditor ancient time.
>
> He (Mr. Yeats) was a reader of poetry. He occasionally read a novel, and it was natural, therefore, that he should demand in an author the same powerful intelligence that he found in the poet. He did not expect great intelligence from the English novel, and he certainly did not find it; but the one thing he did find in the English novel that he cared for supremely was something that had nothing whatever to do with intellect.
>
> Somewhere in the middle of the eighteenth century there came into the faces of women, as painted by the great painters, an exquisite subtlety which they called a mark of high breeding. They got it in Gainsborough and one or two painters before him, and they got it in the first volume of *Sir Charles Grandison*. Then he found the same thing in the novels of Jane Austen. These novels were simply a description, an elaboration, of the pursuit of good breeding—that was to say, a quality which only a few happily nurtured people ever found. Then he did not find that pursuit again until they got to the writings of Henry James.
>
> He discovered, about five years ago, the particular devil that spoiled that celebrated quality in literature. "Pickwick was the [word illegible, but apparently something like "culprit" or "villain" was intended.]" In *Pickwick* the qualities celebrated were qualities any man could possess: good humour, a certain amout of openness of heart, kindness—qualities which every man might hope to possess; they were democratic qualities. It gave them the kind of sculpture they saw in Dublin, like Tom Moore and the statue in Leinster Lawn. That smile of vacuous benevolence came out of *Pickwick*.
>
> One writer the Auditor had mentioned—James Joyce—was certainly as voluminous as Johnson's dictionary and as foul as Rabelais; but he was the only Irishman who had the intensity of the great novelist. The novel was not his (Mr. Yeats's) *forte*. All he could say was that there was the intensity of the great writer in Joyce. The miracle was possible there; that was all he felt he had a right to say, and, perhaps, the intensity was there for the same reason as the intensity of Tolstoi and Balzac.
>
> When James Joyce began to write in Ireland they had not come to their recent peril of the robbery and the

murder and the things that came with it, but he thought that the shadow of peril was over everyone when men were driven to intensity. The book *Ulysses* was a description of a single day in Dublin twenty years ago. He thought it was possible that Ireland had had that intensity out of which great literature might arise, and it was possible that James Joyce was merely the first drop of a shower. ("The Modern Novel," *Irish Times*, 9 Nov. 1923, p. 9.

121. Hogan and O'Neill, *Abbey Theatre*, p. 222.
122. Letter of W. J. Lawrence to Joseph Holloway, 26 Nov. 1923, Ms. 13,267, National Library of Ireland.
123. Letter of Lady Gregory to John Quinn, 28 Nov. 1923, Quinn Papers, Berg Collection.
124. From "Notes of the Week" in *Irish Statesman*, 13 Jan. 1923, reprinted in *Selections from the Contributions to The Irish Homestead*, vol. 2, edited by Henry Summerfield (Gerrards Cross, Bucks.: Colin Smythe; Atlantic Highlands, N. J.: Humanities Press, 1978), pp. 992–93.
125. Letter of Lady Gregory to John Quinn, Oct. 1923, Berg Collection.
126. Hogan and O'Neill, *Abbey Theatre*, p. 214.
127. Murphy, *Journals*, 1:494–95.
128. "Lowly Resting Place," *Evening Herald*, 20 Dec. 1923, p. 2.
129. Hogan, *Dictionary*, p. 440.
130. John MacDonagh, "Edward Martyn," *Dublin Magazine* 1 (January 1924), pp. 465–67.
131. Hogan and O'Neill, *Abbey Theatre*, pp. 216–21.

Chapter 4. 1924

1. Oliver Gogarty won the poetry competition for his book, *An Offering of Swans*. The title of this volume refers to an event that took place on 26 April (not in March as Ulick O'Connor states in his *Oliver St. John Gogarty*); as the *Evening Herald* reported:

> In the midst of soft April rain a distinguished and happy party assembled on the banks of the Liffey at Islandbridge this afternoon, to be reminded in a very vivid way of a tragic night sixteen months ago, when Senator Oliver St. John Gogarty, M.D., was kidnapped from his home in Dublin, and only made his escape by swimming the swollen river.
>
> The meeting took place at the Dublin University Boat Club premises, and the party, which included President Cosgrave and his Aide-de-Camp. Col. O'Reilly, Senator Dr. Yeats, Mr. and Mrs. Lennox Robinson, Mrs. Dorman, Mr. T. S. C. Dagg, and Mr. George O'Brien, were entertained to luncheon by Senator and Mrs. Gogarty, who were accompanied by their three children, to mark the occasion of a novel presentation to the river, which took the shape of a pair of beautiful swans.
>
> The best of good humour prevailed and after the point where the Senator took the cold wintry plunge in the darkness of the night had been viewed and the birds were brought to the ship and released from two boxes by the Senator, assisted by Dr. Yeats.
>
> The ceremony did not take long to perform, but had an interest peculiarly fascinating associated with it.
>
> The two beautiful birds, which had been cooped up for some days left their boxes with all the majesty of their kind, and were evidently delighted at entering the water. They stretched their wings and took to a refreshing little flight before they settled down a few hundred yards away.
>
> As explained by Senator Gogarty, the novel ceremony had a significance all its own attached to it. It appears that on the trying night of January 12, 1923, whilst he was battling with the torrent in an endeavour to reach the opposite bank, he vowed that if he reached it he would present two swans to the river. . . .
>
> It had no political significance the Senator explained, beyond the fact that he hoped that he being able to stand on the bank once again from which he took the plunge into the icy water indicated that better times had since dawned on the country.

"A Vow Fulfilled," *Evening Herald*, 26 Apr. 1924, p. 1.

Gogarty's kidnapping had occurred because he was a Free State Senator. Another political incident involving him was the burning of his home in the West in February 1923. On 10 Apr. 1924, the *Evening Herald* reported a dispiriting sequel to that burning:

> Mary Anne Ruddy, aged over 70 years, and her son, John Thomas Ruddy, of Tully, Renvyle, Connemara, were charged at Galway Quarter Sessions to-day . . . with unlawful possession of antique furniture, consisting of a number of livingroom chairs, chests of drawers, books, etc., looted from Renvyle House, the residence of Senator Gogarty, when it was maliciously burned in February last year. . . .
>
> The jury found both accused guilty, recommending them to mercy. . . .

> John Walters, a carter on the roads, charged with having a Queen Anne stool, the property of Mrs. Gogarty, was found not guilty and discharged.
>
> Addressing the jury, the judge said: "That is your verdict not mine. It is a regrettable thing that you should disregard your oath in the face of the clearest possible evidence. . . ."
>
> At Clifden Sessions Judge Bayle granted an award of £23,873 for the malicious burning of Renvyle House, the residence of Senator Gogarty.

"Antiques," *Evening Herald*, 10 Apr. 1924, p. 1.

2. James Bernard Fagan and Lennox Robinson, "Preface," *The Passing*, by Kenneth Sarr (Dublin & Cork: The Talbot Press, 1924), pp. 4–5.

3. R. Brereton-Barry, "The Need for a State Theatre," *Irish Statesman*, 25 Oct. 1924, pp. 210, 212.

4. Ibid.

5. Ibid.

6. Ibid.

7. Mac, "Too Much Laughter at the Abbey—A Cure Wanted," *Irish Statesman*, 20 Sept. 1924, p. 46.

8. George Jean Nathan, "Erin Go Blah," *Newsweek* 10 (27 Dec. 1937), p. 24.

9. C, "Mr. Lennox Robinson in Oxford," *Irish Statesman* (1 Mar. 1924), p. 786.

10. R. J. P. Mortished, "What Is Wrong with the Abbey Theatre?" *Irish Statesman*, 15 Mar. 1924, p. 13.

11. "The Abbey Theatre," *T. C. D.: A College Miscellany*, 14 Feb. 1924, p. 106.

12. In an Abbey press release, Yeats also paid a fine tribute to Sara Allgood during the year:

> Miss Sara Allgood is a great folk-actress. As so often happens with a great actor or actress, she rose into fame with a school of drama. She was born to play the old woman in *The Well of the Saints*, and to give their first vogue to Lady Gregory's little comedies. It is impossible for those of us who are connected with the Abbey management to forget that night in December, 1904, when for the first time she rushed among the stage crowd in *The Spreading of the News*, calling out, "Give me back my man!" We never know until that moment that we had, not only a great actress, but that rarest of all things, a woman comedian; for stage humour is almost a male prerogative.
>
> It has been more difficult in recent years to supply her with adequate parts, for Dublin is a little tired of its admirable folk-arts, political events having turned our minds elsewhere. Perhaps the Spaniard, Sierra, who in his plays expounds a psychological and modern purpose through sharply defined characters, themselves as little psychological and modern as Mrs. Broderick herself, may give her the opportunity she needs. I am looking forward with great curiosity to seeing her in his *Two Shepherds*, which is now just going into rehearsal, and one of our Irish dramatists, Mr. Casey, has, in his new play, *Juno and the Paycock*, given her an excellent part.
>
> Miss Allgood is no end of a problem, and the sooner our dramatists get that into their heads and write for her the better for them and us. If we knew how to appreciate our geniuses, they would not have wasted her so scandalously.

W. B. Yeats, "Miss Sara Allgood," *Irish Times*, 19 Jan. 1924, p. 9.

13. Pierrot (Seumas O'Sullivan), "Of Playwrights and Players," *Dublin Magazine*, April 1924, pp. 803–4.

14. F.J.H.O'D. (Frank J. Hugh O'Donnell), "The Two Shepherds," *Evening Herald*, 13 Feb. 1924, p. 2.

15. "Abbey Theatre," *Irish Times*, 20 Feb. 1924, p. 6.

16. F. O'D. (Frank J. Hugh O'Donnell), "Fortune-telling at the Abbey," *Evening Herald*, 20 Feb. 1924, p. 4.

17. Jacques, "Truth and Tragedy," *Evening Herald*, 4 Mar. 1924, p. 2.

18. "Abbey Theatre," *Irish Times*, 4 Mar. 1924, p. 8.

19. R. Hogan and M. J. O'Neill, *Joseph Holloway's Abbey Theatre* (Carbondale and Edwardsville: Southern Illinois University Press, 1967), p. 226.

20. Ibid.

21. Ibid., p. 227.

22. Letter of James Stephens to Michael J. Dolan, 12 Mar. 1924, ms. 22,555, National Library of Ireland.

23. W. J. Lawrence, "*Juno and the Paycock* at the Abbey," *Irish Statesman*, 15 Mar. 1924, p. 16.

24. Gabriel Fallon, *Sean O'Casey, the Man I Knew* (London: Routledge & Kegan Paul, 1965), pp. 21–22.

25. See Daniel J. Murphy, ed., *Lady Gregory's Journals*, vol. 1 (New York: Oxford University Press, 1978), p. 441.

26. This is probably a reference to an early rejected piece called *The Harvest Festival* (Gerrards Cross, Buckinghamshire: Colin Smythe, 1980).

27. Lennox Robinson, ed., *Lady Gregory's Journals, 1916–1930* (New York: Macmillan, 1947), pp. 74–75.

28. The Irish artist Sean Keating, who, however, did not play the part.

29. Letter of Lennox Robinson to Lady Gregory, 25 Mar. 1924, the Berg Collection, the New York Public Library.

30. Murphy, *Journals*, 1:520.

31. Ibid., 1:521.

32. Ibid., 1:522.

33. Ibid., 1:523.

34. "The Story Brought by Brigit," *Irish Times*, 16 Apr. 1924, p. 6.

35. "Remarkable Drama," *Irish Independent*, 16 Apr. 1924, p. 6.

36. F.J.H.O'D. (Frank J. Hugh O'Donnell), "The Greatest Tragedy," *Evening Herald*, 16 Apr. 1924, p. 4.

37. J. D., "A New Play by Lady Gregory," *Manchester Guardian Weekly*, 21 Nov. 1924; see also Holloway, *Impressions*, ms. 1890, October–December 1924, p. 1103.

38. Y. O. (AE), "The Story Brought by Brigit," *Irish Statesman*, 26 Apr. 1924, p. 207.

39. Holloway, *Impressions*, ms. 1885, 15 Apr. 1924, pp. 669–70. Nevertheless, the comments of two of O'Casey's prominent colleagues might also be mentioned. On 13 May 1924, T. C. Murray wrote to Lady Gregory:

> My very cordial congratulations on your passion play. It was moving and beautiful, and its construction was supremely well done. I should like to see it again on a larger stage and with bigger crowds. I trust you will soon have the play published? I have memories of many beautiful speeches which I should like to keep fresh in my mind.

Letter of T. C. Murray to Lady Gregory, dated 13 May 1924, the Berg Collection. Murray's letter to Lady Gregory might, however, be modified by his first-night reaction, as reported by Holloway: "Had a chat with T. C. Murray who was impressed by the Passion Play, but did not like its Kiltartan flavour." Holloway, *Impressions*, ms. 1885, 15 Apr. 1924, p. 688, National Library of Ireland.

On 5 May George Shiels wrote to Lady Gregory:

> As I have not been inside a church door for over fifteen years, reading *Brigit* yesterday (Sunday) was a religious event—a one man revival. If you could imagine a forgotten geranium on some old lobby window getting a good dash of cold water—I was like that.
>
> I read the play twice over and it went to the marrow of my bones. I think you have treated the great subject worthily and struck a variety of new chords. The peasant Christ makes strong appeal to my peasant mind. Everytime He speaks, the drama mounts to the sky. Of the other characters I warm most to "Brigit." Something deep down—perhaps some old Gaelic peasant—stirred in me when she showed up at the Gate of Jerusalem. When she spoke, the icy chills ran among the roots of my hair. And this is the more remarkable since I know little or nothing about our national saint. But I am going to make her acquaintance soon. Again I wish I could have seen it on the stage. But disappointment and I are old bedfellows. I don't think I shall ever see the inside of the Abbey.

Letter of George Shiels to Lady Gregory, dated 5 May 1924, the Berg Collection.

40. The book is undoubtedly *Dramatic Technique*, and George Pierce Baker (1866–1935), through his courses in playwriting at Harvard and then at Yale, trained Eugene O'Neill and many other American playwrights who were to make their mark in the 1920s.

41. Letter of George Shiels to Lady Gregory, 8 Feb. 1924, the Berg Collection.

42. F.J.H.O'D. (Frank J. Hugh O'Donnell), "A Look Round, the Retrievers," *Evening Herald*, 13 May 1924, p. 2.

43. "The Retrievers," *Irish Times*, 13 May 1924, p. 6.

44. S. L. M. (Susan L. Mitchell), "Drama Notes," *Irish Statesman*, 17 May 1924, p. 303.

45. Holloway, *Impressions*, ms. 1885, 12 May 1924, pp. 900–1, National Library of Ireland.

46. Murphy, *Journals*, 1:606.

47. P. S. O'H. (P. S. O'Hegarty), "A Drama of Disillusionment," *Irish Statesman*, 7 June 1924, p. 399.

48. Letter of T. C. Murray to Frank J. Hugh O'Donnell, 10 Feb. 1924, ms. 21,715, National Library of Ireland.

49. Letter of T. C. Murray to John Burke, 7 Sept. 1924, in Holloway, *Impressions*, ms. 1888, pp. 495–96, National Library of Ireland.

50. Holloway, *Impressions*, ms. 1888, pp. 380–81, National Library of Ireland.

51. Ibid., pp. 501–6.

52. S. L. M. (Susan L. Mitchell), "Drama Notes," *Irish Statesman*, 13 Sept. 1924, p. 20.

53. Jacques, "New Play Redeemed by Artists," *Irish Independent*, 9 Sept. 1924, p. 4.

54. Ibid.

55. Holloway, *Impressions*, ms. 1888, 8 Sept. 1924, pp. 501–6, National Library of Ireland.

56. Ibid., p. 510.

57. Letter of T. C. Murray to Frank J. Hugh O'Donnell, 10 Sept. 1924, ms. 21,715, National Library of Ireland.

58. An Lonndubh, "The Worker at the 'Abbey,'" *Voice of Labour*, 13 Sept. 1924, p. 7.

59. Dolan remarked to Holloway about Murray and his play that "the text got mixed up in his trying to be poetical. He seems to have Synge in his eye most of the time in his later plays—his *Birthright* and *Maurice Harte* were more natural and direct in speech." Holloway, *Impressions*, ms. 1888, p. 507, National Library of Ireland.

What Dolan probably had in mind is a speech like Nance's late in the last act:

> Say all the bitter things you like against me. I'll—I'll listen and no word o' complaint you'll hear from my lips. To live is to suffer, and I'm satisfied.

T. C. Murray, *Autumn Fire* (Dublin: James Duffy, 1964), p. 86.

In content here is an obvious reminiscence of Maurya's last speech in *Riders to the Sea* (which Murray occasionally quoted in letters or conversation); but the reminiscence is only in content and never in richness of style.

60. Murray, *Autumn Fire*, p. 2.

61. Ibid., p. 86.

62. Ibid., pp. 87–88.

63. Ibid., pp. 84–85.

64. Murphy, *Journals*, 1:546.

65. David Krause, ed., *The Letter of Sean O'Casey, 1910–41*, vol. 1 (New York: Macmillan, 1975), p. 116.

66. Murphy *Journals*, 1:586.

67. The play was once revived by the Abbey, and O'Casey apparently withdrew it then from production. So far as we know, there have been only two subsequent productions, one in March 1961, in Lafayette, Indiana, and one in the winter of 1967–68 at University College, Dublin. Both of these productions were directed by Robert Hogan, and both made use of the two endings. The play was first concluded with the ending of Nannie being hauled off to Mountjoy, and then after a brief blackout the actors played the ending of Nannie's death.

68. Hogan and O'Neill, *Abbey Theatre*, p. 238.

69. "New Comedy at the Abbey," *Irish Times*, 30 Sept. 1924, p. 4.

70. W. J. Lawrence, "Irish Production," *Stage*, 2 Oct. 1924; see also Lawrence's scrapbook, ms. 4305, National Library of Ireland, and the reprinting of the article in the *Journal of Irish Literature* 18, no. 3 (September 1989), p. 33.

71. Y. O. (AE), "Nannie's Night Out," *Irish Statesman*, 11 Oct. 1924, p. 144.

72. Sean O'Casey, *Inishfallen Fare Thee Well* (New York: Macmillan, 1956), p. 234. O'Casey was to cross swords rather acrimoniously with AE in the pages of the *Irish Statesman*; and, although AE pretty well preserved his tolerance and benevolence, O'Casey remained one of the few Dublin writers who had little good to say of AE. Indeed, even in his last years, he dismissed AE to one of the present writers as "an oul' cod."

73. Quoted in *Feathers from the Green Crow, Sean O'Casey, 1905–1925*, edited by Robert Hogan (Columbia: University of Missouri Press, 1962), pp. 300–1.

74. Krause, 1:119.

75. Hogan and O'Neill, *Abbey Theatre*, pp. 238–39.

76. It may be of some interest to recount the publishing history of *Nannie*. In 1960, one of the present writers was engaged in collecting the early fugitive material of O'Casey and made the acquaintance of Gabriel Fallon, the one-time actor, one-time friend of O'Casey and but recently a director of the Abbey Theatre. In addition to many letters (subsequently sold to the University of Texas), and a great fund of reminiscence (subsequently embodied in his book *Sean O'Casey,*

the Man I Knew), Fallon possessed versions of the texts of *Kathleen Listens In* and *Nannie's Night Out*. The text of *Kathleen Listens In* was a carbon of O'Casey's original type script, lacking only the first page, which was subsequently supplied by the author. The text of *Nannie's Night Out* was composed of fragments of various versions, all in Abbey typescripts. The entire play seemed to be there, even in its two endings and one subending, and with various versions of speeches, but it existed as a jigsaw puzzle to be assembled. O'Casey gave only a grudging imprimatur to this collection, as he was not really keen to have all of this early and apprentice work disinterred, and indeed probably allowed the collection to be made partly out of kindness to the editor. In any event, he would have nothing to do with the reassemblage of *Nannie*; and so the printed version is a recension which attempts to approximate what the author's intentions would have been had he printed it shortly after it was produced. Needless to say, the editorial job was one of considerable fascination; and, as the editor was in this case something of an editorial midwife, it is possible that his judgment is biased in favor of the play. He does not, however, think so.

The manuscripts of the plays were, on O'Casey's suggestion, then given to the man who was at that time chancellor of the University of California in Los Angeles.

In his book on O'Casey, Gabriel Fallon gives some account of the various ill-natured public squabbling that surrounded this matter. From the vantage point of twenty-five years on, that insignificant footnote to literary history would have interest only as an example of the bad manners to which critics are too often prone, and its principals ultimately had the good sense to bury their shillelaghs.

77. Hogan, *Feathers*, pp. 301–2.

78. Murphy, *Journals*, 1:594.

79. "New Play at the Abbey," *Irish Independent*, 10 Dec. 1924, p. 4.

80. "Abbey Theatre," *Irish Times*, 10 Dec. 1924, p. 5.

81. Holloway, *Impressions*, ms. 1890, 13 Dec. 1924, p. 1186, National Library of Ireland.

82. Ibid., p. 1158. According to Holloway, the play had been written some five and a half years earlier, and Seumas O'Sullivan was satirically amused by Robinson having rejected the play at that time. See Holloway's *Impressions*, ms. 1888, pp. 353–54.

83. S. L. M. (Susan L. Mitchell), "Drama Notes," *Irish Statesman*, 20 Dec. 1924, pp. 470, 472.

84. "Abbey Theatre," *Irish Times*, 23 Dec. 1924, p. 6.

85. "Before the Footlights," *Irish Independent*, 23 Dec. 1924, p. 6.

86. Holloway, *Impressions*, ms. 1890, 30 Dec. 1924, p. 1272, National Library of Ireland.

87. W. J. Lawrence, "Irish Production," *Stage*, 1 Jan. 1925, p. 48.

88. Holloway, *Impressions*, ms. 1890, 22 Dec. 1924, p. 1238, National Library of Ireland.

89. P. S. O'Hegarty. "A Drama of Disillusionment," *Irish Statesman*, 7 June 1924, p. 399.

90. There is disagreement about precisely when in March the play was staged. Liam Miller in *The Noble Drama of W. B. Yeats* (Dublin: Dolmen Press, 1977) cites 23 March; Brenna Katz Clarke and Harold Ferrar in *The Dublin Drama League, 1919–1941* cite 30 and 31 March.

91. "Dublin Drama League," *Irish Times*, 18 Feb. 1924, p. 4.

92. Paul Ruttledge is the leading character in Yeats's play *Where There Is Nothing*.

93. "Drama League," *Irish Independent*, 29 Apr. 1924, p. 8.

94. M. F. McH. (Mary Frances McHugh), "The Power of Luigi Pirandello," *Irish Independent*, 3 May 1924, p. 6.

95. Holloway, *Impressions*, ms. 1885, 27 Apr. 1924, p. 763, National Library of Ireland.

96. M, "Perfect Madam" [evidently a typo for "Madman"], *Evening Herald*, 28 Apr. 1924, p. 3.

97. Hogan and O'Neill, *Abbey Theatre*, p. 227.

98. Lennox Robinson, "The Art of Gagging," *Observer*, 16 Mar. 1924, and "At the Play," *Observer*, 24 Aug. 1924. Holloway, *Impressions*, ms. 1884, January–March 1924, p. 510, and ms. 1888, July–September 1924, p.385, National Library of Ireland.

99. "The Passion Flower," *Irish Times*, 10 Nov. 1924, p. 4.

100. Hogan and O'Neill, *Abbey Theatre*, p. 229.

101. O'Casey, *Inishfallen, Fare Thee Well*, pp. 373–74. An irreverent pastiche of this performance appears in the play *What Is the Stars?* by Robert James:

> [*The people cluster to one side as the gong sounds again. Then from the wings enters a very tall, very thin man wearing a duck mask and a simple white tunic that comes halfway down his scrawny, hairy legs. He is followed by a short, tubby man wearing a mouse mask and a simple yellow tunic that flows almost to his ankles. The fat mouse carries a folded up Hopi Indian blanket. They turn and face each other.*]
>
> DUCK: Quock.

MOUSE: Eek.

[*They tiptoe to each other and unfold the blanket which they lay on the floor. Then each proceeds to an upstage corner of the blanket, in slow and ponderous fashion.*]

MOUSE: Eek.

DUCK: Quock.

JACK: Uh, what are they?

WOMAN: They're the Dancers. Shh.

SLATE: Enter First Musician.

[*A short figure enters covered from the top of his head to his knees in a Hopi Indian blanket. Only his arms protrude. He carries a tin whistle.*]

SLATE: Enter Second Musician.

[*A second but very tall figure enters with a blanket over his head. He carries a triangle and spoon.*]

SLATE: Ah, I should explain that this musician was to have accompanied the action on his zither, but due to unforeseen circumstances, we have had to improvise. And that, after all, is the Art of the Theatre. Andiamo!

[*The first musician walks into the crowd, bumping into people. The second musician walks off.*]

SLATE: Where are they going? Bring that musician back. Oh, God, what are they doing?

MUSICIAN 1: Somewan forgot ta cut th' eyeholes in th' blankets, Misther Slate.

SLATE: Oh, for heaven's sake! [*To his audience.*] This will take just a minute. [*He goes to collect his musicians.*

JACK: Uh, could ya tell me what's happening a-tall?

WOMAN: Certainly. Mr. Slate is attempting to combine the ritual of the Hopi Indian rain dance with our own Celtic mythology. Fascinating, isn't it?

JACK: Oh, er, yeh.

[*Slate guides his musicians back onto the rug and sits one at the lower left and one at the lower right corner.*]

SLATE: Sit there! And you there, drat you! Now, I believe our mimes are ready. Andiamo! Andiamo! Start!!

[*The second musician hits his triangle with his spoon.*]

TRIANGLE: Ping!

[*The first musician puts, after a little difficulty, his whistle into a small mouth hole in his blanket.*]

WHISTLE: Peep!

[*Silence. Then Slate steps forward, into the center of the blanket and bows. Applause.*]

JACK: Uh, is it over?

WOMAN: That was Act One. Shh!

WHISTLE: Peep!

[*The duck begins to roll up his part of the blanket.*]

TRIANGLE: Ping!

[*The mouse begins to roll up his side of the blanket.*]

WHISTLE: [*Sotto voce*]: That was my turn!

DUCK: Quock!

TRIANGLE: Ping!

WHISTLE: It's my bloody turn, I'm tellin' ya!

MOUSE: Eek! Not so fast, Seamus, yer goin' too fast.

TRIANGLE: Ping!

DUCK: Eek! I mean, quock!

TRIANGLE: Ping!

WHISTLE: I'm gonna flatten him!

MOUSE: Jaysus, Seamus, yer afther gettin' th' shaggin' thing all twisted!

TRIANGLE: Ping!

WHISTLE: Peep! Peep! Peep! Peep! Peep!

[*Jack walks out of the scene, halts and shakes his head.*]

Journal of Irish Literature 10 (May 1981), pp. 108–110.

102. "Gaelic Drama," *Irish Times*, 12 Feb. 1924, p. 4. In *Daniel Corkery* (Cranbury, N.J.: Bucknell University Press, 1973), George Brandon Saul tells us that *O Failbhe Mor* was earlier produced by the author in Cork on, 4 Apr. 1919, with Sean O'Faolain in the leading role—a fact not noted in volume 5 of this history.

103. "Gaelic Plays at the Abbey," *Irish Times*, 11 Mar. 1924, p. 7.

104. "Gaelic Plays at the Abbey," *Irish Times*, 6 May 1924, p. 4.

105. "Abbey Gaelic Plays," *Irish Times*, 18 Nov. 1924, p. 7.

106. "Dublin To-Night." *Evening Herald*, 5 Feb. 1924, p. 2.

107. Jacques, "Dublin To-Night," *Evening Herald*, 12 Feb. 1924, p. 2. It might be appropriate to append here John MacDonagh's not entirely facetious article, "How to Write a Revue."

I am asked occasionally how I manage to write revues so plentifully, and for the benefit of those interested,

I shall endeavour to set down how the trick is done. I fear my explanation will resemble "Conjuring Tricks Explained," for what looks so difficult is so simple, that it becomes really difficult.

A revue has come to mean a collection of scenes of the one family, but not on speaking terms, so to speak, with dialogue, songs and dances, therefore, all you have to do is to map out your scenes something in this fashion.

Scene 1. Exterior of the Mansion House. the citizens are summoned by the Town Crier (with song) to hearken to a pronouncement by the Mayor. They pass the time merrily, sining and dancing, the joyous lay of a coloured gentleman to his sweetie who has gone sour on him, one "Chili Bom Bom," until the orchestra announces the arrival of the city parent. This quaintly dressed gentleman (principal comedian) explains with quip and jest, that he has decided to resign the Mayoralty in deference to the popular clamour of "one man, one job." In future he intends to devote his talents to picking winners, and throws among the populace handfuls of bank notes, his official salary for years.

The crowd acclaim him, and he responds with the latest terrific comedy vocal two-step "Summer comes one day each year" (patented).

Above all be topical, that is, up to the minute. A good plan to acquire topicality is a serious and constant study of the telephone city directories; thus you will learn who's who, where and how they live.

Having mastered these simple, but useful "editions de luxe," you next apply yourself to the newspapers, selecting one or more daily, in consonance with your political ambitions. The result of this course works out ususlly as follow:—

You read that X was fined for motor speeding. In the Telephone Directory you find his address; the Street Directory tells you that X is a Bookmaker; then you set to work and, after days, evolve something like this for your comedians:—

"I see X was stopped by a policeman yesterday."

"What did he stop him for—speeding?"

"No, he wanted to put a bob on (here insert popular race-horse)."

This is sure to create long, sustained and persistent laughter among the "Sports" and the mere audience will join in as they hate to be left out of a joke.

Another sure-fire applause getter is the Dodder, which I understand is a romantic river resort for very young couples, whose constitutions are equal to the particularly virulent effects of the moonlight in that sector. Personally I consider the Dodder a mascot, having used it in every Revue to the delighted approbation of any devotees who are having night's rest in the theatre.

Everyone can see how easy it is to turn out a Revue. All that is required is time, not perseverence, as is popularly supposed; a fair supply of ordinary rule paper, any shade but blue; an Austrian lead pencil, twenty years theatre experience, and a regular job in the daytime:

From *Sunday Independent*, 20 Sept. 1924.

108. "Queen's Theatre," *Irish Times*, 26 Feb. 1924, p. 3.

109. F. O'D. (Frank J. Hugh O'Donnell), "A Look Round," *Evening Herald*, 26 Feb. 1924, p. 2.

110. Holloway, *Impressions*, ms. 1884, 25 February 1924, p. 356, National Library of Ireland.

111. "A Look Round, Acushla," *Evening Herald*, 29 Apr. 1924, p. 2.

112. Incidentally, on 4 Feb., McNulty wrote to Maire Nic Shiubhlaigh, who was involved in a revival of *Mrs. Mulligan's Millions*, a few lines worth quoting about that play and also about *The Lord Mayor:*

> It was Miss O'Sullivan who essayed "Mrs. Mulligan" with Fred O'Donovan. She was the original Mrs. Murphy, the charwoman in *The Lord Mayor*. Fred Jeffs is quite capable of playing it or playing anything, but thank heaven I never saw him in the part. There are few things I dislike—one is to see a man play a woman's role or vice versa. I don't think so experienced and accomplished an actress as you requires outside elucidation of a character: and I fear I can add nothing more illuminative than the text of the play. . . . You will note, of course, that Mrs. Mulligan has the strain of tenderness inherent in every woman (?) obscurely secreted somewhere in her heart: and that in her young days, she buried a husband and child. Otherwise she is a rough, old savage with some sense of humour.

Letter of Edward McNulty to Maire Nic Shiubhlaigh, 4 Feb. 1924, ms. 22,563, National Library of Ireland.

113. "A Look Round, New Irish Comedy," *Evening Herald*, 6 May 1924, p. 2.

114. "Abbey Theatre," *Irish Times*, 16 Sept. 1924, p. 3.

115. "Music and Drama, What Do They Want?" *Evening Herald*, 31 May 1924, p. 7.

116. "Brains," *Irish Independent*, 3 June 1924, p. 6.

117. Holloway, *Impressions*, ms. 1886, 4 June 1924, pp. 1038–43, National Library of Ireland.

118. Holloway, *Impressions*, ms. 1886, 16 June 1924, pp. 1127–28, National Library of Ireland.

119. Holloway, *Impressions*, ms. 1886, 4 June 1924, p. 1046, National Library of Ireland. In the same entry, Holloway reported some facts about Fay's recent career:

> I met Eileen at Eason's and, as we spoke, Frank Fay came up, and I walked home with him. He seems very happy over his appointment of dramatic director of Father Mathew Hall Co. He always longed to have a capable lot of players to form into a stock company. He hopes to play *Hamlet* and *The Merchant of Venice* and revive some of the old standard plays. . . . He will rehearse some of the earlier Abbey plays to bring back the Abbey tradition which is lost at the Abbey and will welcome dramatists turned down by the Abbey if their work deserves production. He will always welcome dramatists at rehearsal.

Fay played in and staged a couple of amateur Shakespearean productions at the Father Mathew Hall, but the venture never came to much.

120. The Sherlock Holmes figure had recently been utilised in a number of British films, and *The Return of Sherlock Holmes* featured Eille Norwood, the actor who played Holmes in at least forty-eight of these films. On his appearance at the Gaiety, he was interviewed by an *Evening Herald* reporter, and as a contribution to the Inanities of Yesteryear we cannot resist appending the following excerpt:

> "Personally (though my powers of observation were always rather strong) I have learnt a great deal from the study of Holmes."
>
> Mr. Norwood paused for awhile and looked around the room. Then at length: "You see that man over there."
>
> I looked in the direction indicated. "Yes," I said, "The man that is laughing just now?"
>
> "Exactly. Well, I could take a large bet that that man is a pipe-smoker."
>
> "But how do you know?" I asked in surprise.
>
> "It is very simple," Mr. Norwood replied. "You may observe that an upper tooth in the left-hand corner of his mouth is sunk well into the gum—more so than any of the others."
>
> "That's quite right," I said.
>
> "Well, that little 'clue' tells me the man is a pipe-smoker. The continual presence of the stem of the pipe on that tooth has driven it deep into the gum. If he were a cigar or a cigarette smoker the tooth would be just as the others."

Desmond Murphy, "Sherlock Homes," *Evening Herald*, 3 Apr. 1924, p. 5.

121. "Irish Opera," *Irish Times*, 12 Aug. 1924, p. 4.

122. "Queen Tailte," *Irish Times*, 13 Aug. 1924, p. 9.

123. "Shaun the Post," *Irish Times*, 16 Aug. 1924, p. 8.

124. Frank J. Hugh O'Donnell, "The Immortality of the Stage Irishman," an unpublished article rejected by AE for the *Irish Statesman* in December 1924. Ms. 21,715, National Library of Ireland.

O'Donnell, incidentally, continued to write plays prolifically and to bombard people with them. Much of his work was submitted to the Abbey, and he regularly received notes of rejection from Robinson. Eventually, however, Robinson wrote the following kind note:

> I know you don't like a written criticism but I am not sure when I shall see you. Both Lady Gregory and I have read your play, and we are practically in agreement about it: it is, I think, the best play you have done but it is not a good play. I do not think it would continue to interest an audience, and for this reason—the situation through the three acts is virtually the same—Paul's endeavour to escape. . . . But there are things in the play that one dwells on in one's mind; it is not easily forgotten; you have something in you somewhere. Have you tried writing other things besides plays? Perhaps the concentration and reshortening necessary in a play cramps you—you might do better in a long story or a novel. I don't want unnecessarily to discourage you, but I know it's bloody for you to keep writing plays and for me to keep turning them down (and I'd rather you got a success with a play than most people I know)—but I suggest that as you *can* write, it may be that you've chosen the wrong medium.

This letter (ms. 21,715, National Library of Ireland) is dated only 18 March, but obviously written before the acceptance of *Anti-Christ*. In *Anti-Christ*, O'Donnell finally wrote a play that was interesting in both technique and theme, and on 22 April 1924 Robinson wrote to him:

> You must forgive me for keeping your play so long. . . . I've just read it. I like it very much indeed. I like the little scenes best of all—and the last scene. Scenes like the first and third I feel to be a little "thick"—I mean I'd have compressed them a little more and tried to get every ounce of intensity into them. But different men, different methods. I feel Mr. Bachup and the secretary unnecessary or should have been more faintly indicated—but these are all small criticisms—You've attempted a difficult thing—I don't know that

you've quite succeeded, but it's a very interesting and gallant attempt. (ms. 21,715, National Library of Ireland)

Eventually the Abbey was to accept *Anti-Christ* and to produce it in 1925. Among the various writers from whom O'Donnell solicited opinions about it was Padraic Colum, who wrote to him on 20 October 1924, very justly:

Thank you very much for letting me see *Anti-Christ*. I like the idea well, but I think that there is not enough human interest in the play. It seems to me that in a play that's broken up into a great many scenes every scene has to be concentrated drama. In your play the interest is logical, not human. You have got to make your man an exciting personality; you have got to make every scene vibrant with him. I think you are too much concerned with arguing about your idea. (ms. 21,715, National Library of Ireland)

125. "The Films Censorship," *Evening Herald*, 16 Jan. 1924, p. 2.
126. "Big Motion Picture Project," *Evening Herald*, 19 Jan. 1924, p. 6.
127. "Can We Do It?" *Evening Herald*, 30 Jan. 1924, p. 1.
128. Untitled story, *Evening Herald*, 16 Feb. 1924, p. 2.
129. "Other People's Views, Rowdyism in Dublin Theatre," *Evening Herald*, 6 Feb. 1924, p. 2.
130. "Behaviour in the Theatre," *Irish Times*, 13 Mar. 1924, p. 5.
131. "Broadcast from Belfast," *Irish Times*, 24 Oct. 1924, p. 5.
132. Tyrone Guthrie, *A Life in the Theatre* (London: Hamish Hamilton, 1960), pp. 31–33.
133. Jacques, "Ulster Players at the Gaiety," *Irish Independent*, 9 Dec. 1924, p. 6.
134. S. L. M. (Susan L. Mitchell), "Drama Notes," *Irish Statesman*, 13 Dec. 1924, p. 436.
135. W. J. Lawrence, "Irish Production," *Stage*, 11 Dec. 1924; see also Lawrence's scrapbooks, ms. 4305, Naitonal Library of Ireland, p. 32.
136. Holloway, *Impressions*, ms. 1890, 8 Dec. 1924, pp. 1163–66, National Library of Ireland.
137. H. Richard Hayward, "St. John Greer Ervine," *Ulster Review*, Sept. 1924, p. 85.
138. T. C. M. (probably T. C. Murray), "Playwright, Critic and Novelist," *Irish Independent*, 10 Dec. 1924, p. 6.
139. "The Ulster Players," *Irish Times*, 11 Dec. 1924, p. 8.
140. H. R. W. (probably Harold R. White), "The Ulster Players," *Irish Independent*, 11 Dec. 1924, p. 6.
141. S. L. M. (Susan L. Mitchell), "Drama Notes," *Irish Statesman*, 20 Dec. 1924, p. 472.
142. Holloway, *Impressions*, ms. 1890, pp. 1181–83, National Library of Ireland.
143. H. R. W., "The Ulster Players," *Irish Independent*, 11 Dec. 1924, p. 6.
144. S. L. M. (Susan L. Mitchell), "Drama Notes," *Irish Statesman*, 20 Dec. 1924, p. 472.
145. Holloway, *Impressions*, ms. 1890, pp. 1181–83, National Library of Ireland.
146. In a conversation with the present authors a few years ago, Mr. Hayward's widow remarked that she did not think highly of her husband's efforts for the Ulster Players.
147. F. R., "The Northern Drama League," *Irish Statesman*, 6 Dec. 1924, p. 404.
148. Ibid., p. 406.
149. A. S. M. (probably Alf. S. Moore), "Plays for Thinkers," *Ulster Review*, Dec. 1924, pp. 153–54.
150. "Literary Life of Belfast," *T. P. and Cassell's Weekly*, 29 Mar. 1924, p. 822.
151. The world premiere had occurred at the end of 1923, on 28 Dec., in New York, when the Theatre Guild produced it at the Garrick Theatre with Winifred Lenihan.
152. "Mr. Duffy's New Comedy," *Irish Independent*, 5 Apr. 1924, p. 6.
153. "Irish Plays," *Irish Independent*, 22 Dec. 1924, p. 4.
154. Holloway, *Impressions*, ms. 1886, 30 June 1924, p. 1233, National Library of Ireland.
155. "Well-Known Entertainer," *Evening Herald*, 8 July 1924, p. 2..
156. Hogan and O'Neill, *Abbey Theatre*, pp. 224–40, includes the conversations with O'Casey.

Chapter 5. 1925

1. "Hollywood and Ireland," *Irish Times*, 5 Sept. 1925, pp. 6, 9.
2. *Evening Herald*, 15 June 1925, p. 6.
3. "'I Love Them,'" *Evening Herald*, 27 July 1925, p. 2.

4. "Cruiskeen Lawn," *Evening Herald*, 17 Jan. 1925, p. 5. A couple of authorities say that Irish Photoplays, Ltd., shot its three films in 1922. See *Cinema Ireland 1895–1976* (Dublin: Dublin Arts Festival, 1976), p. 22; and also Kevin Rockett, *Film and Ireland: A Chronicle* (London: A Sense of Ireland, 1980), p. 47. However, *Cruiskeen Lawn* and *Wicklow Gold* were really only released in 1925.

5. "A Film of the Week," *Irish Times*, 15 Dec. 1925, p. 6.

6. Both *Cinema Ireland* and *Film and Ireland* give the producer as John Hurley: however, the *Evening Herald* in its contemporary review gives the producer as "Mr. Winslow." This was apparently Herbert Hall Winslow, an American playwright and producer who had spoken of his plans for an Irish film to the Dublin Rotary Club in July.

7. Both *Cinema Ireland* and *Film and Ireland* give this actress's name as Phyllis Wakely.

8. F. S. [probably Fay Sargent], "Land of Her Fathers," *Evening Herald*, 3 Oct. 1925, p. 6.

9. "Film Star Welcomed," *Saturday Herald*, 8 Aug. 1925, p. 6.

10. "Years Behind," *Evening Herald*," 7 Nov. 1925, p. 7.

11. On 20 July, for instance, Herbert Hall Winslow spoke enthuslastically to the Dublin Rotary Club about "Ireland as a prospective film producing centre." Bryan Cooper dryly remarked that "an Irish film-producing company would have to do three-quarters of its work in the studio." See "Wonderful Opportunity," *Evening Herald*, 20 July 1925, p. 1. Also on 18 July, Eppels Films announced its plans; see "Flickers from Filmland," *Evening Herald*, 18 July 1925, p. 6. On 21 July Denis F. McSweeney announced that Wingfield Sheehan, an American theater owner, was planning to shoot a series of educational films in Ireland; see "An Irish Film," *Evening Herald*, 21 July 1925, p. 2. One unnamed syndicate, possibly the Eppels group, announced the formation of an Irish College of Film Acting at the Antient Concert Rooms, as well as a film beauty competition; see "Film Beauty Competition," *Evening Herald*, 1 July 1925, p. 4. On 4 November, the following account appeared in the press:

> Miss Phyllis Wakely, of Elmhurst, Temple Garden, Rathmines, was this afternoon, in the Southern District Court, fined £1 1/—costs for unlawfully leaving a carriage of the Great Southern Railway Co., while a train was in motion . . . .
>
> It was stated that Miss Wakely was acting for a film when she jumped out of a first class carriage between Stillorgan and Dundrum, on September 15. . . .
>
> Mr. Cussen said this was a bad example to set the boys and girls of Dublin, and he was sure Miss Wakely would be sorry if her example led to loss of life.

"A Mad Act," *Evening Herald*, 4 Nov. 1925, p. 5. Phyllis Wakely under the name of Phyllis O'Hara was the heroine of *Land of her Fathers*.

12. On 20 November, the press reported:

> About 7 o'clock this morning the Masterpiece Cinema, in which the war film, *Ypres*, was being shown this week, was badly damaged by a mine.
>
> Subsequently two Guards, who were in plain clothes encountered two suspicious looking persons, who opened fire on them with revolvers.
>
> Guard Joseph Murphy, 185C, was shot through the stomach and seriously wounded, and Guard Willam Timmins, 83C, was shot through the left forearm. . . .
>
> The vestibule of the cinema was completely wrecked, the ceiling being badly broken and torn.

"Dublin's Rude Awakening—Cinema Theatre Blown Up," *Evening Herald*, 20 Nov. 1925, p. 1. On 30 November, the press reported:

> The war film, *Zeebrugge*, has been seized and burned by armed men near Galway, in pursuance of the campaign which is being directed against certain pictures.
>
> When seizing the reels, the leader of the band told the manager of the cinema that he had instructions to take away propaganda films.
>
> The affair took place at midnight on a lonely road when the manager was bringing the picture back from Athenry.

"Another Film Destroyed," *Evening Herald*, 30 Nov. 1924, p. 1.

13. In a page one story, "Movie 'Ads'" The *Evening Herald* of 1 May 1925 reported:

> Mr. O'Higgins, Minister for Justice, moved the second reading of the Censorship of Films (Amendment) Bill, 1925, which was intended, he said, to supplement the Act passed in 1923. Pictures shown within the

Saorstat, the Minister pointed out, were required to pass the official censor; but there was nothing to prevent persons advertising these by means of posters which, in themselves, were suggestive and improper, and which often conveyed an entirely false impression of the sort of entertainment given. . . . The present Bill proposed to extend the censorship to these posters and advertisements in connection with the film trade.

Mr. Figgis said that the Bill was intended to bring pressure upon people who were exhibiting advertisements that were false and not in accordance with the facts. . . .

Major Bryan Cooper considered that they might have to pass legislation for the suppression of election speakers (laughter). He regarded the proposal in the Bill as merely a logical sequence to the creation of a film censorship.

14. Jack Broadcaster, "Wireless Notes," *Evening Herald*, 10 Feb. 1925, p. 5.
15. "Seen and Heard," *Evening Herald*, 6 Feb. 1925, p. 4.
16. Cathal MacGarvey, "Broadcasting," *Evening Herald*, 27 Jan. 1925, p. 7.
17. "Dublin Calling!" *Evening Herald*, 14 Dec. 1925, p. 1.
18. "2RN Calling," *Evening Herald*, 16 Dec. 1925, p. 6.
19. "Cats-whisker," "Other People's Views, Dublin Broadcasting," *Evening Herald*, 17 Dec. 1925, p. 5.
20. "Gaelic Plays at the Abbey Theatre," *Irish Times*, 29 Jan. 1925, p. 4.
21. "Abbey Theatre," *Irish Times*, 17 Feb. 1925, p. 4.
22. "Gaelic Plays at the Abbey Theatre," *Irish Times*, 9 Mar. 1925, p. 4.
23. "Gaelic Plays at the Abbey Theatre," *Irish Times*, 19 May 1925, p. 9.
24. "Gaelic Plays at the Abbey," *Irish Times*, 6 Oct. 1925, p. 8.
25. "Gaelic Plays at the Abbey Theatre," *Irish Times*, 3 Nov. 1925, p. 8.
26. "Gaelic Dramatic League," *Irish Times*, 17 Nov. 1925, p. 11.
27. W. E. Godfrey, "Drama at the Abbey," *Evening Herald*, 21 Sept. 1925, p. 2.
28. Actually O'Gorman's troupe had not been in Ireland since September 1915, when they played at the Coliseum in Henry Street. O'Gorman was a Dublin man who went on the stage at the age of fifteen and worked for twenty years on the English variety circuit with a partner, as Tennyson and O'Gorman. He was a singer and comedian, and led his troupe all over the world.
29. "A Look Round," *Evening Herald*, 14 July 1925, p. 6.
30. "A Look Round," *Evening Herald*, 8 Dec. 1925, p. 6.
31. C. K. Ayre, "Ulster Players' Visit," *Evening Herald*, 12 Dec. 1925, p. 5. Although unsigned, this facetious piece is obviously a self-interview of the kind that Bernard Shaw often wrote for the press on the occasion of a new production. The quality of its wit may be fairly suggested by the following exchange:

"By the way, Mr. Ayre," I asked, "you invariably chose a seaside town as the scene of your comedies. Is there any significance?"

"Assuredly," said he. "It's the C. Ayre that does it."

32. F.J.H.O'D [undoubtedly Frank J. Hugh O'Donnell], "Missing Links," *Evening Herald*, 16 Dec. 1925, p. 6.
33. In the *Irish Statesman*, F. R. remarked that *Everyman* "was, on the whole, very successful" (31 Jan. 1925, p. 662), that *Uncle Vanya* "was interesting rather than convincing" (4 Apr. 1925, p. 114), and that *The Knight of the Burning Pestle* was "good fun" (21 Nov. 1925, p. 338). In the *Ulster Review*, Richmond Noble wrote that the players in *The Knight of the Burning Pestle* "electrified a delighted audience with a performance that has every right to be termed memorable" (December 1925, p. 331). Equally admiring of *The Younger Generation* was A. S. M. in the *Ulster Review* who wrote of "the captivating freshness of the production, both in acting and mounting. The lighting throughout was beautiful. You could not have guessed that this was entirely an amateur cast, and no professional could have much surpassed them" (March 1925, p. 223). A. S. M., however, sounds suspiciously gushy.
34. From the League's annual report, as quoted by A. S. M. in "Northern Drama League," the *Ulster Review*, January 1925, p. 176.
35. Ibid.
36. G. H. P. Buchanan, "What is a Highbrow?" *Ulster Review*, March 1925, pp. 232–3.
37. John Boyd took the role of Doctor Grimthorne in *Magic*, and, according to K. T. Little, should have appeared more elderly. See "Queen's Dramatic Society," *Ulster Review*, March 1925, p. 224.
38. Ibid.
39. A. S. M., "Carrickfergus Players," *Ulster Review*, January 1925, p. 2. A. S. M. interestingly remarks "anent the originality of the orchestra—a flute and grand piano—which,

while admirable at times, would have earned my plaudits by a still more careful selection of items. It is a revelation of what talent and individuality can achieve."

40. "Irish Theatrical Experiment," *Irish Times*, 15 June 1925, p. 5.

Two other names to be associated with the Gate Theatre made early appearances on the boards during the year. For the week of 9 Feb., the Dublin University Dramatic Society played at the Gaiety in Shaw's *Captain Brassbound's Conversion* and Milne's *Belinda*. According to the *Evening Herald*, Shaw's Lady Cecily "as played by Miss Meriel Moore was particularly fascinating. Word perfect, she spoke her lines with fluency and acted with refreshing ease." See "A Look Round," *Evening Herald*, 10 Feb., p. 2. The account also adds, "Among the smaller parts players was Mr. W. D. Johnston." Later in the year, Denis Johnston and Shelagh Richards both appeared prominently, as Cusins and Barbara, in Madame Kirkwood Hackett's production of Shaw's *Major Barbara*. This first production in Ireland of Shaw's masterpiece was done at the Abbey in the week of 7 Dec. Frank J. Hugh O'Donnell called the entire production "excellent—or, if not excellent, adequate." See "A Look Round," *Evening Herald*, 8 Dec. 1925, p. 6.

41. Roisin Walsh, "The Tawin Players," *Irish Statesman*, 19 Dec. 1925, pp. 464–65.

42. Ibid.

43. "Saw Through It," *Evening Herald*, 27 Aug. 1925, p. 1.

44. Nevertheless, despite cinema bombings, fires, and the hurling of ink bottles (see "Ink on Screen" the *Evening Herald*, 28 Aug. p. 7), beer bottles (see "Scene in City Theatre," *Evening Herald*, 29 May, p. 1), and cushions (see "Theatre Rowdyism," *Evening Herald*, 29 Aug. p. 7), nothing quite so dramatic happened in Ireland in 1925 as the following incident, which occurred in Vienna on 9 May:

> An extraordinary dramatic murder took place in the Vienna Municipal Theatre last night, during the performance of Ibsen's tragedy, *Peer Gynt*.
>
> At the very moment that Peer Gynt was stimulating [*sic*] death on the stage, a beautiful young Macedonian woman, Mencia Karniciu, rose from her chair in a private box, where she was sitting with a party, drew an automatic pistol and fired six shots into the dress circle a few feet below.
>
> When the lights were turned up, Todor Dimitoroff, a Macedonian secret agent, was found shot dead, his wife mortally wounded, and another person badly hurt.
>
> The audience stampeded for the exits, and the police rushed to the woman's box and arrested her.
>
> She declared that she had avenged treason against her countrymen by the act. . . .
>
> Mencia Karniciu presented a striking figure when she appeared before the Vienna Chief of Police to-day to be examined. She is 26 years old, and is the daughter of one of the richest families in Macedonia. She is a young woman of extraordinary beauty, tall and with jet black hair and blazing dark eyes. She was utterly defiant in face of the murder charge.

"Shot Dead in a Theatre," *The Evening Herald* (11 May 1925), p. 7.

45. L. Fallon, "Other People's Views, Theatre Misconduct," *Evening Herald*, 11 Dec. 1925, p. 6.

46. Although not hugely germane to our purpose, the death of Figgis and the unfortunate preliminary circumstances seem worth recounting, for he was occasionally a dramatist and he also wrote a still lively and interesting book on Shakespeare. Late in 1924, Figgis's wife one night ordered a cab, drove out to Rathfarnham, and shot herself. The reason given in the press was despondency. On 23 Oct. 1925, the following account appeared in the *Evening Herald*:

> At Hendon (Middlesex) yesterday, Dr. Cohen held an inquiry into the death of Rita North, aged 21, a dancing mistress, which occurred in Hendon Cottage Hospital, and, after a prolonged hearing, adjourned the proceedings until November 5, when he stated that medical evidence would be given by three witnesses.
>
> Mr. Francis North, of 52 Thomas street, Dublin, said that he last saw his daughter alive three weeks ago. She had previously complained of pains, but he had no diea that she was pregnant. She went for a motor tour in Devonshire in April last.
>
> Mr. Darrell Figgis, of 17 Fitzwilliam street, Dublin, journalist, said that he had known the deceased for two years, and first knew she was pregnant on October 5. Deceased declined to allow witness to inform her parents of her condition, but later consented to her sisters' being acquainted with the state of her health. She consulted Dr. Smerke Zarchi, of Shaftesbury avenue, W., whose name had been mentioned to him by a fellow-member of the R. A. C., and in a letter deceased informed him that she was going to a nursing home, but would return to her hotel, the Astoria.
>
> When he asked the doctor for the address of the nursing home, he replied that, if he gave it to him he was sure to visit deceased, and that she ought not to be disturbed. Later he was informed that an operation would be necessary. This was performed at the Hendon Central Hospital. Deceased had told the hospital Authorities that he was her husband.

When witness again suggested that her uncle should be informed, she urged him to do nothing of the kind, saying that she would be well in two or three days, and they could get married, and her friends and relations need know nothing of the condition in which she had been. "It would be kinder for them, and better for both of us," she added. The doctor described her as a brave little soul, a great fighter, and said that her great chance was that she was sure she was going to get through. Owing to her condition, another operation was performed, but she died on Monday.

Questioned by the Coroner, witness said that he gave his name to the hospital as that of Souths, and deceased had registered in that name; but to Dr. Lake, the surgeon there, he gave his correct name. He told the doctor that he had never sailed under false colours in his life.

"Death of Miss North," *Evening Herald*, 23 Oct. 1925, p. 2. On 27 October, the following account appeared in the *Evening Herald*:

Darrell Figgis, member of Dail Eireann, and well-known writer, was found dead under tragic circumstances in London this morning. . . .

The Press Association states that Darrell Figgis was found dead about 8 o'clock in a room he occupied at No. 4 Grenville Street, Bloomsbury. . . .

The landlady of No. 4 Grenville Street told a Press Association representative this morning that Mr. Figgis went there yesterday and took a bed-sittingroom. He paid a deposit for the room, and she said he appeared to be a thorough gentleman in every respect.

She did not see any signs of agitation about him, and he gave her the impression that he was staying in London for some days on business. There was nothing about him to suggest that anything untoward might happen.

Mr. Figgis, she added, went out in the evening for about an hour, and she assumed that he had gone to get supper. Before going out he called her attention to the gas stove, in which some of the asbestos had been smashed. She promised to replace the broken pieces, and when he returned at 10 o'clock he expressed himself as being satisfied with what she had done.

When a maid took hot water up to his room this morning, she found that something was wrong, and called the landlady. Mr. Figgis was lying on the bed, and there was a strong smell of gas in the room.

They opened the window and resorted to artificial respiration, but without success, and when a doctor was summoned he stated that death had taken place some time earlier.

The Press Association understands that a number of letters addressed in Mr. Figgis's handwriting to personal friends were found in the room.

"Darrell Figgis Meets Tragic End," *Evening Herald*, 27 Oct. 1925, p. 1.

At the inquest, some further details emerged:

Frank J. Maurice, an engineer, of Belsize Park Gardens, Hampstead, said he had known Mr. Figgis for 15 years, and for almost a year he had seemed depressed.

The cause, witness thought, was the death of his wife. During the last week of his life he was very sad and depressed. . . .

Harry Gordon Watney, a distiller, of Thurlow Hotel, Cromwell Place, Kensington, said that he had known Figgis as a fellow-member of the Royal Automobile Club.

"On Monday night," said witness, "Figgis was extremely unhappy. He called me out of the chess room, and he was about as unhappy as a man could be. I tried to find out the cause of his unhappiness, but he would not tell me. It was not financial."

"Attacks of Depression," *Evening Herald*, 28 Oct. 1925, p. 1.

The inquest was concluded on 3 Nov., and at that time the press reported:

Referring briefly to the letters which had been found, the Coroner said that in one of them were these words: "It is really the only way." . . .

In another letter there was this: "This, really, is the only way. God bless you all."

Then there was a postscript: "Give the dear soul who runs this place—(mentioning the sum) for the trouble to which I am putting her."

The jury returned a verdict of "suicide while of unsound mind."

"The Figgis Tragedy—Story of Resumed Inquest," *Evening Herald*, 3 Nov. 1925, p. 1.

Figgis was buried on 30 Oct. in Bloomsbury. Probably because the circumstances of his last year were both sad and scandalous, his literary work has been, since his death, almost totally ignored. Perhaps now, more than half a century later, the merit of his best work may be reappraised. In the opinion of the present writers, that merit is sometimes astonishing.

47. "Little Theatre," *Times*, 14 Mar. 1925, p. 10.
48. "Q Theatre," *Times*, 17 Mar. 1925, p. 12.
49. "Wyndham's Theatre," *Times*, 12 May 1925, p. 14.

50. "Lady Gregory's Adaptation," *Evening Herald*, 19 Aug. 1925, p. 5.
51. "Synge Revival at the Royalty," *Times*, 13 Oct. 1925, p. 14.
52. "Royalty Theatre," *Times*, 18 Nov. 1925, p. 12.
53. Letter of W. B. Yeats to Lady Gregory, 26 Mar. 1925, ms. 18,743, National Library of Ireland.
54. Letter of Lennox Robinson to Lady Gregory, 6 Jan. 1925, Berg Collection, the New York Public Library.
55. Joseph Holloway, *Impressions of a Dublin Playgoer*, ms. 1892, 24 Feb. 1925, pp. 341–42, National Library of Ireland.
56. S. L. M. [Susan L. Mitchell], "Drama Notes," *Irish Statesman*, 7 Mar. 1925, p. 822.
57. "The Old Man," *Irish Times*, 25 Feb. 1925, p. 5.
58. Andrew E. Malone, "From the Stalls," *Dublin Magazine*, May 1925, p. 633.
59. "New Play at Abbey," *Evening Herald*, 18 Mar. 1925, p. 2.
60. "Anti-Christ," *Irish Times*, 8 Mar. 1925, p. 6.
61. S. L. M. [Susan Mitchell], "Drama Notes," *Irish Statesman*, 28 Mar. 1925, p. 84.
62. Letter of T. C. Murray to Frank J. Hugh O' Donnell, 18 Mar. 1925, ms. 21,715, National Library of Ireland.
63. Andrew E. Malone, "From the Stalls," *Dublin Magazine*, May 1925, pp. 633–34.
64. Letter of T. C. Murray to Frank J. Hugh O'Donnell, 13 May 1925, ms. 21,715, National Library of Ireland.
65. Maurice Donne, "Correspondence, Irish Drama," *Irish Statesman*, 11 Apr. 1925, p. 141.
66. J. J. Hayes, Ibid.
67. Holloway, *Impressions*, ms. 1892, 17 Aug. 1925, pp. 504–7.
68. See Hogan's "O'Casey, Influence and Impact," *Irish University Review*, Spring 1980, pp. 146–158.
69. S. L. M. [Susan L. Mitchell], "'Portrait' at the Abbey Theatre," *Irish Statesman*, 4 Apr. 1925, pp. 114–15.
70. "New Play at the Abbey Theatre," *Irish Times*, 1 Apr. 1925, p. 9.
71. F.J.H.O'D. [Frank J. Hugh O'Donnell], "Portrait," *Evening Herald*, 1 Apr. 1925, p. 4.
72. Andrew E. Malone, "From the Stalls," *Dublin Magazine*, May 1925, pp. 631–32.
73. Ibid, pp. 632–33.
74. Holloway, *Impressions*, ms. 1892, pp. 601–2.
75. In letters to Lady Gregory during the year, Robinson gave his opinions of both Sara Allgood and Shelah Richards. On 6 January he wrote:

> I had Sally in with me yesterday begging for the £10. . . . I think Sally is still extraordinarily good in certain parts—in Juno and others, but she finds it almost physically impossible to memorise words, and that is a bad handicap in a theatre like ours where plays have to be got together very swiftly. I was very disappointed with her Pegeen: I think that even you would have thought it bad. She's a strength to us in many ways but not a great public draw, and I feel that we shouldn't give her a fancy salary while others are so underpaid, but I also feel that we must consider her old association with the theatre and not be ungenerous. (Berg Collection)

And on 28 November he wrote:

> Yeats and I had to come to a sudden decision last week; Miss Richards who—after Miss Crowe—is our most promising actress and one whom Yeats thinks very highly of went for a week to London and got an offer to play Peg for six months at £8 a week. She wrote to me and asked me to advise her, said she'd rather stay in Dublin and work at the Abbey but of course the money was tempting. She had to give a definite decision the next day and I had to wire my reply. I showed the letter to Yeats and he felt very strongly and I agree with him that she is valuable to the theatre and suppose that Miss Crowe doesn't renew her contract next May we would be very badly off for a young girl. (Miss Richards has a great deal of youthful charm). He thought that she should be offered a twelve months contract at the Abbey for £4 a week, so I wired this to her and she was delighted to accept it. It was a very difficult matter to decide but I think we were wise. She is a real actress but wants to be worked hard. She played Margaret in *Fanny's First Play*, the young girl in my last play (a very good performance) and is to be Major Barbara in a fortnight when Mrs. Hackett puts on that play—this is to show you that she plays large parts and isn't just the third girl in *Playboy*, etc. (Berg Collection)

76. Letter of T. C. Murray to Joseph Holloway, dated 13 [?] July 1925, ms. 13,267, National Library of Ireland.
77. H. N. K., "A New Play by Mr. Lennox Robinson," *Manchester Guardian Weekly*, 10 Apr. 1925; see also Holloway, *Impressions*, ms. 1893, Apr. 1925, p. 661.

78. Letter of W. B. Yeats to Lady Gregory, 27 Apr. 1925, ms. 18,743, National Library of Ireland.

79. Letter of George Shiels to Lady Gregory, 29 May 1925, Berg Collection.

80. Letter of George Shiels to Lady Gregory, 15 June 1925, Berg Collection.

81. S. L. M. (Susan L. Mitchell), "Drama Notes," *Irish Statesman*, 19 Sept. 1925, p. 50.

82. "The Abbey Theatre," *Manchester Guardian*, 17 Sept. 1925; see also Holloway, *Impressions* ms. 1896, September 1925, p. 714.

83. F. J. McCormick was much admired in the title role, even though his drunkenness was considered by some a bit too emphasized. McCormick, however, was always a thoroughly professional player and would never stoop to make a point by comic exaggeration. Sara Allgood, Barry Fitzgerald, and Maureen Delany, brilliant actors as they were, all needed a firm directorial hand, particularly in comedy. The director on this occasion was Michael J. Dolan, who obviously did not give it. However, Robinson was also in the theater, and could certainly have controlled the production had he wanted. Robinson's own feelings at this time about direction were summed up in a speech he made in Manchester:

> Mr. Lennox Robinson addressed members of the Manchester Playgoers' Club last Sunday on the art of the theatre. . . . Mr. Robinson emphasised the necessity for fusion of the parts of the playwright, the producer, and the actors in the production of a work of art in the theatre, and he had something also to say of the reaction of the audience upon the actors.
>
> We heard much, he said, of the poor playwright who had his plays so badly interpreted by the players, but little about the poor producer who, standing between them, was perfectly neutral, and whose task, he sometimes thought, was the hardest of all.
>
> He did not see why, if you had a really sincere and conscientious producer, who was thinking of the play as a whole, as a work of art, he should not be allowed to shape it a little to suit the company; and, if you liked, the audience. When he was told, as at Sheffield, that the players were allowed to give *Back to Methuselah*, by Mr. Shaw, on condition that they did not cut a word, he thought the condition was monstrous.
>
> He could not see why at the theatre they should be at the tyranny of the written word. We should only get real art in the theatre by a closer and closer combination between the playwright, the producer, and the player, and that was only to be got by more and more intelligent production. This, he thought, we could only get by acknowledgement of the fact that the playwright had to bow his head, as the player had to bow his. There were players doing things that no player 25 years go would have thought any producer would require. The obedience from the player added enormously to the development of the art of the theatre, but there had not been the slightest bowing of the head from the playwright. This, he thought, would have to come, and in certain ways it was going to help the playwright.

"Real Art in the Theatre," *Manchester Weekly Guardian*, 22 Jan. 1925; see also Holloway, *Impressions*, ms. 1891, Jan. 1925, p. 195.

This strikes the present authors as an extraordinary attitude for a serious playwright, and one that was to bode only ill for both Robinson's future career and for theater in general.

84. Holloway, *Impressions*, ms. 1896, 16 Sep. 1925, pp. 692–93.

85. Letter of George Shiels to Lady Gregory, 17 Sept. 1925, Berg Collection.

86. Lennox Robinson, ed., *Lady Gregory's Journals*, 1916–1930 (New York: Macmillan, 1947), p. 92.

87. Holloway, *Impressions*, ms. 1897, 13 Oct. 1925, pp. 840–42. Robinson's "blasphemous story" was an innocuous little piece called "The Madonna of Slieve Dun," which was printed in 1924 in the very short-lived journal, *Tomorrow*. The story caused a much publicized brouhaha when members of the Advisory Committee of the Carnegie Library Trust, of which Robinson was secretary, strongly objected to the story. In this instance, Robinson was hotly defended by Lady Gregory, who was a member of the committee, but the upshot was that the committee was disbanded and Robinson was dismissed. Robinson's story is reprinted in the *Journal of Irish Literature*. 9, no. 1. The whole business, which also involved a rather mischievous Yeats, is now merely a footnote in Irish literary history, but it is certainly symptomatic of the rigorous moral milieu of the times.

88. J. B., "A Look Round, The White Blackbird," *Evening Herald*, 13 Oct. 1925, p. 2.

89. "Abbey Theatre," *Irish Times*, 13 Oct. 1925, p. 3.

90. Robinson's *The Round Table* also offers a provocative antithesis to *The Whiteheaded Boy*.

91. Letter of W. B. Yeats to Lady Gregory, 27 April 1925, ms. 18,743, National Library of Ireland.

92. Daniel J. Murphy, ed., *Lady Gregory's Journals*, vol. 1 (New York: Oxford University Press, 1978), p. 622.

93. "State-Endowed Theatre," *Daily Mail*, 10 Aug. 1925; see also Holloway, *Impressions*, ms. 1895, July-September 1925, p. 315.

94. Holloway, *Impressions*, ms. 1895, 8 Aug. 1925, pp. 283–84.

95. The figure of 216 does not include the twenty-one plays presented by the National Theatre Society and its predecessors before the opening of the Abbey Theatre. These plays, however, are also listed in the anniversary program.

95. The Abbey symbol of Queen Maeve and the wolfhound is the work of Elinor Monsell.

97. The reference is, of course, to Fred O'Donovan.

98. "Abbey Theatre," *Irish Times*, 28 Dec. 1925, pp. 5–6.

Chapter 6. Early 1926

1. This is the most usually quoted version of the speech. Some slight variants of it are to be found in the *Irish Times, the Irish Independent*, and the *Evening Mail* for 12 Feb. 1926.

2. Carbon copy of a letter from Michael J. Dolan to Lady Gregory, dated 1 Sept. 1924, ms. 22,557, National Library of Ireland. Also quoted in *Lady Gregory's Journals, 1916–1930* Lennox Robinson, ed. (New York: Macmillan, 1947), p. 88.

3. Letter of George O'Brien to W. B. Yeats, 5 Sept. 1925, ms. 13,068, National Library of Ireland. In Robinson's edition of *Lady Gregory's Journals*, the beginning of the letter is misquoted: "Mr. Yeats and I have read O'Casey's new play and are convinced that it would be quite as successful as any of his others if produced." Whether this is Lady Gregory's or Robinson's error in transcription, we have no way of determining.

4. Letter of W. B. Yeats to George O'Brien, 10 September 1925, ms. 13,068, National Library of Ireland.

5. Letter of George O'Brien to W. B. Yeats and Lennox Robinson, 13 Sept. 1925, ms. 13,068, National Library of Ireland.

6. Robinson, ed., *Lady Gregory's Journals*, pp. 87–88.

7. Ibid., pp. 91–92.

8. Ria Mooney, *Players and Painted Stage*, Val Mulkerns, ed., in *George Spelvin's Theatre Book* 1 (Summer 1978), p. 49.

9. Fallon here neglects to mention that the obvious casting of Fluther was Barry Fitzerald.

10. Gabriel Fallon, *Sean O'Casey, The Man I Knew* (London: Routledge & kegan Paul, 1965), pp. 87–88.

11. *The Letters of Sean O'Casey, 1910–41*, vol. I, David Krause, ed. (New York: Macmillan, 1975), pp. 165–66.

12. "The Plough and the Starts," *Irish Times*, 12 Jan. 1926, p. 9.

13. *The Oxford English Dictionary* (1971) does not agree with Yeats, but cites these etymological predecessors: Middle Dutch "snottich," Northern Frisian "snotting," Older Danish "snøttig" and the obsolete German "schnutzig."

14. Letter of W. B. Yeats to Lady Gregory, 15 Jan. 1926, ms. 18,744, National Library of Ireland.

15. "New Sean O'Casey Play at the Abbey," *Dublin Evening Mail*, 9 Feb. 1926, p. 3.

16. R. Hogan & M. J. O'Neill, eds. *Joseph Holloway's Abbey Theatre* (Carbondale & Edwardsville: Southern Illinois University Press, 1967), p. 251.

17. James Montgomery, the Irish film censor.

18. It is impossible to say which Reddin brother Holloway means, but it is interesting if it was Kenneth Reddin, who as "Kenneth Sarr" had written one of the best plays before *The Plough* about a slum prostitute. This was, of course, his *The Passing* of 1924.

19. Hogan and O'Neill, *Abbey Theatre*, pp. 251–52.

20. Fallon, *O'Casey*, p. 80.

21. Mooney, *Players*, pp. 44–45.

22. "The Plough and the Stars," *Irish Times*, 9 Feb. 1926, p. 7.

23. "Plough and the Stars," *Evening Herald*, 9 Feb. 1926, p. 2.

24. J. W. G., "Sean O'Casey's New Play," *Irish Independent*, 9 Feb. 1926, p. 9.

25. "New Sean O'Casey Play at the Abbey," *Dublin Evening Mail*, 9 Feb. 1926, p. 3.

26. Shelah Richards, with Robert Hogan, *Let's Play Ghosts*, an unpublished memoir.

27. Fallon, *O'Casey*, p. 90.

28. Ibid., p. 88.

29. Letter of Lennox Robinson to Lady Gregory, 1 Feb. 1926, Berg Collection. New York Public Library.

30. Letter of Lennox Robinson to Lady Gregory, 9 Feb. 1926, Berg Collection.

31. Hogan and O'Neill *Abbey Theatre*, pp. 252–53.

32. Ibid., p. 253.

33. In vol. 1 of O'Casey's *Letters*, David Krause incorrectly states Wednesday night.

34. Not according to Shelah Richards's account below.

35. "Abbey Theatre Scene," *Irish Times*, 12 Feb. 1926, pp. 7–8.

36. This wandering shoe seems to have hit quite a number of people. See, for instance, Shelah Richards's account below.

37. Mooney, *Players*, pp. 45–46.

38. Shelah Richards's unpublished memoir.

39. Hogan and O'Neill, *Abbey Theatre*, pp. 253–55. "Honor Bright" was a recently murdered prostitute.

40. Ibid., p. 255.

41. Robinson, ed., *Lady Gregory's Journals*, p. 99.

42. "Riotous Scenes," *Irish Independent*, 12 Feb. 1926, p. 7.

43. One response was from William Whelan, who wrote:

> Sir—In reply to Mr. Collins's letter in last night's *Herald*, I may say I have been a regular attendant at the Abbey Theatre since the Molesworth Hall days, and I was present on Monday night at a packed house, when enthusiasm prevailed and not a jarring note was heard.
>
> Speaking for myself, I feel proud of the work of a fellow Dublin man, who knows his Dublin folk. It must be remarked the play centres around a tragic incident in the life of our country which took place in Dublin, and must appeal in a special way to Dubliners who were mainly concerned in it and who lived through it, and this may explain some poeople's disappointment who had no more than a passing interest in the episode I mention.

The same issue saw a letter from J. Finnegan, who was appreciative of the play's merits but sorrowful about its gloom:

> Sir—I was present at the performance on Wednesday night, and I did not hear any hissing. There was a slight disturbance when a girl became hysterical and cried out on two occasions during the performance.
>
> I consider *The Plough and the Stars* a very powerful piece of work—a play that perhaps no one but its author could write. Its realism is almost unnerving (it was when a "scrap" between two viragos on the stage was in progress that the girl in the audience broke down), and as one who lived in Dublin through the events portrayed I think Mr. O'Casey has caught the atmosphere of those days with amazing success.
>
> Having said so much, I would ask: Is any useful purpose served by the production of a play of the kind at this time? I feel we are still rather too near the actual happenings to have them served up as "entertainments." The play deals with a period of grave national crisis, with days of dread and fear, and its theme is destruction and death! The memories of those days are too poignant as yet, too fresh in the minds of our people to allow of their portrayal on a stage being generally acceptable. That I am not alone in that belief is, I think, borne out by the brief and very restrained applause with which the acts, and even the final falling of the curtain, were received.
>
> I submit, too, that a sense of loyalty to the poorer classes should prevent a too realistic presentation of their failings and weaknesses as a commercial enterprise.
>
> The author's work of characterisation is so good, and the acting so natural, as to make it seem almost an offence against taste to put the squalor, the grime, and the coarse dialect of our slums, as a delectation for an audience mostly, we may assume, more fortunately placed in life than the pitiable victims of circumstances whose peculiarities are the outstanding characteristics of Mr. O'Casey's works.
>
> I look forward to future work by Mr. O'Casey in the hope that he may direct his natural insight and his sense of humour towards the brighter side of life. He has taken us into the shadows so often that I long to sit a while with him on the sunny side of the hill.

Both letters appeared in "Other People's Views," *Evening Herald*, 12 Feb. 1926, p. 2.

44. "New Play Resented," *Evening Herald*, 12 Feb. 1926, p. 1.

45. "The Abbey Melee," *Evening Herald*, 12 Feb. 1926, p. 4.

46. "These People Will Never Learn Sense," *Evening Mail*, 12 Feb. 1926, p. 5.

47. "Listening-In, A Daily Dublin Survey of Men and Things," *Evening Mail*, 12 Feb. 1926, p. 2.

48. "Abbey Protests," *Irish Independent*, 13 Feb. 1926, p. 5.

49. "Plough and the Stars," *Evening Herald*, 13 Feb. 1926, p. 3.

50. "Sgáthán," "The Plough and the Stars," *Evening Mail*, 13 Feb. 1926, p. 5.
51. "The Abbey Theatre," *Evening Mail*, 13 Feb. 1926, p. 5.
52. Robinson, ed., *Lady Gregory's Journals*, pp. 96–98.
53. "Abbey Kidnapping Plot Fails," *Irish Times*, 15 Feb. 1926, p. 5.
54. Mooney, *Players*, pp. 46–47.
55. Ibid., pp. 49–50.
56. "No Opposition," *Irish Independent*, 15 Feb. 1926, p. 8.
57. Robinson, ed., *Lady Gregory's Journal*, pp. 99–100.
58. Sir—Having witnessed *The Plough and the Stars*, I fail to

realise where it has given offence that would call for such a protest as that which took place on Thursday evening. Admittedly the presence of a certain character in Act II needs some explanation. G. B. Shaw portrays such a character in some of his works, notably in *Blanco Posnet*, *Mrs. Warren's Profession*, and *Fanny's First Play*, but in each of these cases the "Rose Redmond" type is interwoven in the plot, and is essential to the denouement, whereas in Mr. O'Casey's play she appears but once, and is nonessential and an incongruity. Surely the dramatist is not under the impression that the average city "pub" harbours such shawl-clad specimens of the sad sisterhood? When your correspondents state she "fraternised" with those who attended the "meeting" they are incorrect. The only character she "fraternised" with was "Fluther Good," who was portrayed as a flag-waving buffoon. The other "unconscious comedian," Peter Flynn, comes within the same category. The presence of "Rosie Redmond," coupled with the brawl between the two females in the same act, was, I submit, introduced as "padding," and tends to show a lack of good taste on the author's part rather than a considered insult or deliberate offence against the memory of those whom he intended to eulogise.

Notwithstanding the assertion of "Sean O'Shea," the display of hysterical emotion and maddened terror on the part of Mrs. Clitheroe in her efforts to restrain her husband from again entering the fight is again a portrayal of truth and a "holding of the mirror to Nature." No mother or woman worthy of the name has ever willingly sent her husband, lover, or son as a sacrifice to war. To say, as "Sean O'Shea" does, that "the women urged them on," is a libel on Irish womanhood and a denial of facts self-evident to everyone.

"J. Finnegan" objects to the portrayal of slum life, and states "a sense of loyalty should prevent the portrayal of these poor people's failings and weaknesses." I'm afraid this correspondent is unaware of the object of Dramatic Art. The Abbey Theatre was instituted to portray Irish life in all its phases. Does he imagine that sordidness and misery can be abolished by simply drawing a veil over them instead of flooding them with the light of publicity? Assuredly a strange viewpoint in the second quarter of the twentieth century. A real sense of loyalty calls for an effort to awaken public opinion to these horrors, then some effort may be made to abolish them. This is the playwright's idea. If this correspondent wishes to view the lighter side of life, there are other theatres where he will see life as he wished it to be.

Your front page correspondent of Friday who asks for a censorship should visit local music halls. There he will find a greater need for the blue pencil than at the Abbey. He will witness filth masquerading as cleverness, and trash as talent.

Mr. O'Casey is to be congratulated on his work. Let "Rose Redmond" be withdrawn from Act II. This is the only fault in the production, which otherwise is a worthy addition to the repertoire of—not only the Abbey—but any theatre that specialises in real Dramatic Art as distinguished from the stupid gyrations of gilded noodles.

"Other People's Views, The Plough and the Stars," *Evening Herald*, 16 Feb. 1926, p. 7.

59. Finigan, or Finnegan—whose name is variously spelled in the press—wrote:

Sir—Kindly allow me to reply to that portion of a letter appearing in to-night's *Herald* from Mr. Stephen J. Fitzgerald in which he refers to a letter of mine under the above heading in an earlier issue. That the spirit of my letter was appreciated, I have had evidence quite sufficient to compensate me for the fact that Mr. Fitzgerald decries it.

I would first suggest that before he sets out to criticise a letter he should read it properly, and try to understand it. Secondly, his attitude of a hectoring highbrow is uncalled for and quite unnecessary. He adopts the method of that undesirable type of controversialist who quotes mutilated sentences for the purpose of putting up something that may be easily knocked down—a trick that has only its antiquity to recommend it.

Mr. Fitzgerald says I object to the portrayal of slum life. That is not correct. What I do object to is the holding up, for the amusement of play-goers, and for their heartless laughter, of the weaknesses and shortcomings of the unfortunate people who are compelled to live in slums. He asks do I imagine that "sordidness and misery can be abolished by simply drawing a veil over them"? Certainly not, any more than I believe they can be removed or ameliorated, by being staged as "entertainment," or dished up as a marketable commodity in the amusement market.

The Plough and the Stars was not staged as a piece of propaganda directed towards the abolition of slums and slum life, and I am certain it did not send a single individual on a philanthropic mission to the putrid purlieus to be found not a hundred miles from the Abbey Theatre.

> This correspondent is afraid I am "unaware of the object of dramatic art." Now grand! Here we have once again the old parrot-cry that is repeated of every form of dramatic muckraking! Mr. Fitzgerald may cast out his fear, but even though he may regard it as another "strange view-point in the second quarter of the twentieth century," I assure him I have no use for that school of befogged mentality that throws a bucketful of slops on a stage and calls it "art for art's sake"!

This letter was printed in "Other People's Views, The Plough and the Stars," *Evening Herald*, 17 Feb. 1926, p. 6. C. P. Conway's letter added little new to the discussion except perhaps this comment:

> The Victorian delicacy of Mr. Finnegan is not all-embracing, evidently, as he forgets to denounce the demoralising and vulgar environments of some of our other resorts of amusement. If we had a few more places like the Abbey to give us a mental clean up, instead of so many retailing centres of unhealthy entanglements that pander to the baser side of human nature, we would be better enabled to rectify, or at least relieve, our national ailments.

This letter was printed in "Other People's Views, The Plough and the Stars," *Evening Herald*, 18 Feb. 1926, p. 6.

60. David Krause in vol. 1 of his edition of O'Casey's Letters has noted, "In the *Irish Times* this word appears as 'morality.'"

61. By Dorothy Macardle.

62. By Maurice Dalton.

63. Sean O'Casey, "Plough and the Stars," *Irish Independent*, 20 Feb. 1926, p. 3; reprinted in O'Casey's *Letters*, vol. 1, pp. 168–71.

64. "Objectionable Play," *Evening Herald*, 20 Feb. 1926, p. 1.

65. "Other People's Views, The Plough and the Stars," *Evening Herald*, 20 Feb. 1926, p. 6.

66. Liam O'Flaherty, "Correspondence, The Plough and the Stars," *Irish Statesman*, 20 Feb. 1926, pp. 739–40.

67. Ibid., p. 740.

68. Hogan and O'Neill, *Abbey Theatre*, p. 260. Up to this time, O'Casey had been on good terms with Holloway, and we might plausibly assume that his gruffness here was a result of Donaghy having related to him the dialogue he had with Holloway on the night of the riot. As we have noted above, Donaghy told the story to Lady Gregory on 15 Mar., when he also had tea with O'Casey and Lady Gregory. In later years, O'Casey spoke well of Donaghy as a promising poet, but was quite critical of Holloway's ability as anything but a gossip.

69. Fitzgerald wrote:

> Sir—Mr. Finegan's description of *The Plough and the Stars* as a callous exploitation of the "unhappy dwellers in the slums" is, I submit, unfair, and a misreading of the facts. The playwright set out to reproduce on the stage a reflection of certain events that took place a decade ago, the principal characters being Irish Volunteers and the Citizen Army. To do justice to his subject and remain true to his art Mr. O'Casey could no more eliminate "the unhappy dwellers in the slums" than Shakespeare could abstain from introducing Goneril, Cordelia, and Regan into *King Lear*. Would your correspondent condemn G. B. Shaw for the presence of Mat Haffigan and Barney Doran in *John Bull's Other Island*? Did he object to Joxer and Captain Boyle in Mr. O'Casey's other play? He might explain how "a very powerful piece of work"—as he described the play in his first letter—deteriorated within a week to "low buffoonery."

And Sean O'Shea wrote:

> A Chara—I was surprised on reading the concluding paragraph of Mr. O'Casey's letter, inasmuch as what went before was obviously an effort to demolish all his critics at once. . . . This type of shut-your-mouth argument is, however, pretty well known and hardly worthy of Mr. O'Casey. He must realise that the Kellys, Burkes, Sheas, and Finnegans are his public, and if they see things from a different angle to him it does not follow they are wrong and he is right. His characters he makes representative of classes, not individuals acting individual parts.

Both of these letters appeared in "Other People's Views, The Plough and the Stars," *Evening Herald*, 23 Feb. 1926, p. 6.

70. Mrs. H. Sheehy-Skeffington, "The Plough and the Stars," *Irish Independent*, 23 Feb. 1926, p. 9; reprinted in O'Casey's *Letters*, vol. 1, pp. 171–73.

71. Sean O'Casey, "Mr. O'Casey's Play," *Irish Independent*, 26 Feb. 1926, p. 8; reprinted in O'Casey's *Letters*, vol. 1, pp. 174–75.

72. Reprinted in O'Casey's *Letters*, vol. 1, p. 176.

73. Ibid., p. 177.

74. Lyle Donaghy, "Correspondence, The Plough and the Stars," *Irish Statesman*, 27 Feb. 1926, pp. 767–68.

75. Ibid., p. 768.

76. Ibid., pp. 770–71.

77. "The Plough and the Stars," *Irish Independent*, 2 Mar. 1926, p. 7. The proceedings were also fully reported by the *Times*, and that account may clarify and amplify certain details:

> Mr. Sean O'Casey's play, *The Plough and the Stars*, the production of which recently, at the Abbey Theatre provoked "scenes in the body of the house," was the subject of a lectrue last night by Mrs. Sheehy Skeffington in the Mills' Hall, Dublin, under the auspices of the University Republican Club.
>
> The lecturer claimed that audiences had the right to express their disapproval of a play by hissing or booing, and said that *The Plough and the Stars* was not a typical picture of the men of 1916. There was not a gleam of heroism in it; its theme was the folly of the rising, and that was why it cut to the bone.
>
> Mr. O'Casey, the author, who replied to the lecturer, said that he did not try, and never would try, to write about heroes. He only wrote about the people that he knew—the bone and sinew of the country, the people who would ultimately be the brain of the country as well.
>
> The main point of the controversy, said Mrs. Sheehy Skeffington, turned on whether an audience had a right to express its disapproval of a play. Most authors and actors agreed that audiences had a right to express approval of a play, and, therefore, the question was whether an audience had a right to express disapproval by the usual method of hissing and boohing. She thought it was necessary that a protest should be made to hit the Abbey directorate in the eye. There was no other way by which that could be done at the present time. *The Plough and the Stars* did not strike her as an anti-war play, but as an anti–Easter week play. She understood that the play had been censored to a certain extent by some private person, and she did not know why he had stopped where he did; but her view was that the only censor necessary in drama, art and literature was the censorship of the public.
>
> Dealing with National Theatres, she said that she, personally, regretted, not as a Republican, but as a lover of freedom and of the theatre, that the Abbey Theatre had been subsidised by the Government. It was now a "kept" house, and any theatre lost more than the subsidy that it received by giving up its freedom, and it would, in the natural course of events, "kow tow" to the powers that be. Would it, for instance, be possible in a subsidised theatre in Belfast for the Ulster Players to produce such a travesty as *The Plough and the Stars* of Carson's Volunteers before Sir James Craig or Lord Carson? Would not the theatre be wrecked by the indignant supporters of these two gentlemen?
>
> Referring to Mr. O'Casey, the author of the play, she said that her own impression was that he had a "grouch," as the Americans say. He liked to use rather the meanness, the littleness, the squalor, the slum squabbles, the women barging each other, and the little vanities and jealousies of the Irish Citizen Army. He had rather the art of the photographer than the art of the dramatist. These scenes were all put together, and the material conclusion was that this was a typical picture of the men of 1916. There was not a single gleam of heroism throughout the play, and its theme was the folly of it. That was why it cut to the bone, because they looked to see some of the heroism that produced Easter Week.
>
> The present Abbey motto was to see the squalor. Mr. O'Casey had taken Easter Week for a comedy, and they wished that a dramatist would arise who would deal with what was great and fine in 1916.
>
> Mr. O'Casey, who proposed a vote of thanks to the lecturer, had only been on his feet for a second or two when he became weak and had to return to his seat for a short time.
>
> When he resumed he said that Mrs. Sheehy-Skeffington saw everything through the eyes of a politician, while he saw most things through the eyes of a dramatist. She seemed to pay a great deal of attention to what England or America thought of them. He cared nothing for what these countries thought of Irishmen.
>
> Referring to the flag in the play, he said that it was not symbolical, typical or representative of any one county or province, or of the Republicans, but it was representative of the whole of Ireland, and if that was true it would have to take its place amongst the "Bessie Burgess's," the "Judy Gogans" and the "Fluther Goods"—even the "Rosie Redmonds," as it did amongst the President of the Dail, the President of the Senate, or the president of a Republican convention. One of the golden stars in the Tricolour was Easter Week, and, in his opinion, another was the Irish drama. That flag had also to take the spots of disease, of hunger and hardship, as well as the golden stars.
>
> While Mr. O'Casey was referring to the part of "Rosie Redmond" and the lesson that it was intended to convey, one of the audience interrupted, saying: "Get away from your favourite subject."
>
> Mr. O'Casey—If that is so, I will not say anything further.
>
> Asked by the audience to proceed, he said that he was not trying, and never would try, to write about heroes. He could write only about the life and the people that he knew. These people formed the bone and sinew, and ultimately he believed they would be the brain of the country as well.
>
> Replying to the criticisms of the play, he said, with regard to the public-house scene, that the lecturer evidently wanted to bring everyone out of the public-house, but he was anxious to bring everyone into the public-houses and make them proper places for amusement and refreshment.
>
> "The play," he continued, "is, in my opinion, the best of the three produced. It has been said that I have been writing for England. I am not writing for England. I am writing for England as well as for Ireland, and I

do not see why I should not. *The Plough and the Stars* was handed in and passed for production long before there was a word of the London production of *Juno and the Paycock*. All my plays have been written for Dublin." (Applause.)

Concluding, he said that no dependence could be placed on the critics of England or Ireland, particularly of Ireland. (Applause.)

Mrs. McCarville, M.A., in seconding the vote of thanks, said that the play was an anti-Pearse play.

Mr. Gabriel Fallon described the protest against the play as mob censorship.

Professor A. E. Clery presided and conveyed the thanks of the audience to the lecturer.

This account was published under the title "The Plough and the Stars" in *Irish Times,* 2 Mar. 1926, p. 5.

78. Hogan and O'Neill, *Abbey Theatre*, p. 266.

79. P. M. J., "Other People's Views, The Plough and the Stars," *Evening Herald*, 6 Mar. 1926, p. 6.

80. F. R. Higgins, "The Plough and the Stars," *Irish Statesman*, 6 Mar. 1926, pp. 797–98.

81. Hogan and O'Neill, *Abbey Theatre*, p. 269.

82. Ibid., p. 270.

83. Ibid., pp. 270–71.

84. Ibid., p. 271.

Index